John Dewey

The Later Works, 1925–1953

Volume 5: 1929–1930

EDITED BY JO ANN BOYDSTON

TEXTUAL EDITOR, KATHLEEN E. POULOS

With an Introduction by Paul Kurtz

Southern Illinois University Press

Carbondale and Edwardsville

Copyright © 1984 by the Board of Trustees,
Southern Illinois University
All rights reserved
Manufactured in the United States of America
Designed by Richard Hendel

CENTER FOR
SCHOLARLY EDITIONS
AN APPROVED TEXT
MODERN LANGUAGE
ASSOCIATION OF AMERICA

®

Editorial expenses for this edition have been met in part by grants from the
Editions Program of the National Endowment for the Humanities, an independent Federal agency, and from the John Dewey Foundation. Publishing expenses
have been met in part by a grant from the John Dewey Foundation.

Library of Congress Cataloging in Publication Data

Dewey, John, 1859–1952.
  The later works, 1925–1953.

  Vol. 5 has introd. by Paul Kurtz.
  Continues The middle works, 1899–1924.
  Includes bibliographies and indexes.
  CONTENTS: v. 1. 1925—   —v. 5. 1929–1930.
  1. Philosophy—Collected works.   I. Boydston, Jo Ann, 1924–.
B945.D41 1981   191   80-27285
ISBN 0-8093-1163-1 (v. 5)

Contents

Introduction

By Paul Kurtz

John Dewey's writings for the years covered in this volume, 1929 and 1930, are for the most part practical in content. Dewey's philosophy has had a profound normative impact, and this volume illustrates throughout the basic continuity of his philosophical thought with normative interests, for Dewey's philosophical ideas cannot be fully understood or evaluated independently of the social context in which they are written. We should note that 1929 was the year in which both *The Quest for Certainty* and the revised edition of *Experience and Nature* appeared. Dewey was at the height of his powers and influence. In retrospect, 1929 also marked the end of an era, the age of prosperity, and the beginning of the Great Depression of the 1930s that overtook America and the world. Dewey's papers in this volume should be read as they were written—against the background of both the 1929 financial collapse and the sense that a new liberal tide was beginning to emerge in America.

The year 1929 was also a time when Dewey was being heralded as America's greatest philosopher: for example, the first of three Festschrifts was published in his honor and many influential leaders of American thought—Jane Addams, James Angell, George Herbert Mead, Ralph Barton Perry, and William Heard Kilpatrick—participated in a seventieth birthday celebration.

This volume, like the others in this series, illustrates anew the prodigious output and wide range of Dewey's works. Since the volume includes more than fifty selections, I will focus the following discussion on three main areas: (1) Education, including the short book *The Sources of a Science of Education*; (2) Political and Social Philosophy, including the book *Individualism, Old and New*; and (3) Philosophical Controversies, in which a number of issues basic to Dewey's central concepts are discussed and in which he replies to criticisms by other philosophers.

I. Education

In *The Sources of a Science of Education* Dewey raises questions about the nature of a science of education. He asks, "Can there be a science of education?" and if so, "How does it proceed and what is its function?" Dewey makes clear that by "science" he is referring to the use of objective *methods* in dealing with the subject matter of education. The methods of scientific inquiry are brought to bear on a range of facts, enabling educators to understand and control those facts more intelligently. Thus by the question "What are the sources of a science of education?" Dewey means "What are the ways by means of which the function of education . . . can be conducted with systematic increase of intelligent control and understanding?"

Education, like engineering, he says, is an art. There is, however, no sharp distinction between science and art; both engineering and education are related to the general sciences and draw upon them in dealing with concrete experience and practical operations. Many people look to the science of education for simple recipes or guides for educational practice, but these they find difficult to deduce. First, educational science is still in a backward state: no genuine science can be founded on isolated conclusions; rather these conclusions need to be linked together to form a "coherent system" in which they confirm and illustrate each other. Second, educational science cannot be developed simply by borrowing the techniques of the physical sciences. Even could we arrive at general laws and facts, they might not yield simple rules of practice and they would be of only indirect value for their effect on educators attempting to deal with concrete problems of educational practice. The function of the science of education, Dewey maintains, is to provide "intellectual instrumentalities" for educators. The results of science thus provide rules for "the conduct of observations and inquiries," not rules for overt action. Here Dewey is referring to the use of scientific findings by administrators and researchers. His conclusion is that "the final reality of educational science is . . . in the minds of those engaged in directing educational activities." Dewey stresses that "we must distinguish between the *sources of educational science* and scientific content." We must not forget, he says, that the results of science are only sources to be used "through the medium of the minds of educators, to make educational functions more intelligent."

This statement by Dewey may come as a surprise, for it may suggest a subjectivistic character to inquiry, especially insofar as it focuses on the minds of educators. Dewey goes on to relate scientific inquiry, however, to educational practices. He says that "educational practices" provide the data and subject matter that form the problems of inquiry and also the final test of the value of the conclusions of such research. Thus the starting point and nexus of educational science refer to actual educational behavior in the schools and these precede scientific investigation. Science thus is an intermediary tool of education and not the reverse. He does not wish an independent science to dictate the educational process; rather science should serve the educational process and is meaningful only in relation to it. Dewey reiterates that these educational practices furnish the materials and problems of educational science. However, he also says that there is no independent science of education per se. Following the analogy with engineering, he points out that the materials derived from the other sciences provide the content of educational science and these must be related to educational practices.

A vital give and take occurs, of course, between practitioners of education and scientific researchers. The educational practitioner or field worker needs to draw upon a variety of sciences in solving educational problems. These include the philosophy of science (which may help in discovering and introducing creative hypotheses), psychology, and sociology, among other sciences. Dewey makes clear that "concrete educational experience is the primary source of all inquiry and reflection because it sets the problems, and tests, modifies, confirms or refutes the conclusions of intellectual investigation."

Dewey also raises the question of how educational values and objectives are derived, denying that philosophy provides the ends for the educator and science the means. Rather, he argues, "education is autonomous." Hence, it "should be free to determine its own ends, its own objectives." To go outside education to an external source is to surrender the educational cause. Dewey is thus encouraging educators to have the independence and courage to insist that educational aims must be developed within the educative process. Educators do not create these aims, however, although they do play a role in the process; education itself is a process of discovering worthwhile values and objectives. Dewey insists that there is no fixed and final set of unchanging objectives, but a process in which means and ends are interrelated in the context of educational inquiry and practice. "The sources of educational science are any portions of ascertained knowledge that enter into the heart, head and hands of educators, and which, by entering in, render the performance of the educational function more enlightened, more humane, more truly educational than it was before."

Dewey thus places education at the very center of social change. The educator is not subservient to external scientists or to society. The vital function of the educator is to contribute to social transformation by using science and by developing values within the educational process. Education is an ongoing activity that should include science within its process.

It is interesting to read Dewey's educational writings today when schools, especially public schools, are under heavy criticism. When Dewey wrote *The Sources of a Science of Education* the public schools were accomplishing a heroic task in teaching the large number of immigrant children the ethics and practice of democracy and the open society. It seemed appropriate to argue that education had a vital role in this process of social change—a positive attitude that was applicable for at least another generation. In recent years, however, Dewey's influence in education has come under sustained attack, not only from right wing foes but from partisans of the left. Conservatives have strongly rejected Dewey's recommendation that educators should examine and clarify values, seek to fashion new habits in the young, and contribute to social change. Any questioning of traditional values and beliefs, particularly those with a religious foundation, has been anathema to many parents, preachers, and politicians. In the post-Sputnik era of the late fifties, Dewey was accused of loosening standards and was held responsible for the schools' failure to educate students in science—a paradoxical charge in view of Dewey's great emphasis on understanding science as an essential part of the curriculum.

In the seventies and eighties Dewey has been accused of fathering "secular humanism" and thus eroding religious values. The critics are no doubt correct in identifying the schools as agents of social change and in attributing to Dewey the view that such a function is appropriate for the schools. It is a pity that educators have sometimes retreated in the face of militant vigilantes who oppose the schools' efforts to engage in moral education or to clarify and transform values, for this examination is a vital part of any education relevant to contemporary problems. Dewey argues that values are not absolute or fixed but need to be reappraised and evaluated in the context of contemporary society through the use of critical intelligence. In these days of budget-cutting and scalp-hunting, the teacher has often become the sacrificial lamb who is blamed for all the evils of the modern world and transformations of the old moral verities. But Dewey's outline of a program of educational reform still has merit and can be read with profit today.

Of considerable interest also for the light that they shed on later debates are several other writings on education, particularly those in which Dewey criticizes so-called progressive educators. His discussions are noteworthy in view of the radical educational reform movements of the late sixties and early seventies, when higher education became embroiled in intense controversy. The war cry was for "relevance" and the loosening of curriculum standards. Dewey, often thought to be the progenitor of the protests, was blamed by Admirals Radford and Rickover and others for these anti-intellectual excesses. Yet, interestingly, Dewey writing in 1930 denies that he defends unlimited or anarchic student freedom, and he makes clear that he opposed de-emphasizing the intellectual content of education.

In the essay "How Much Freedom in New Schools?" Dewey observes that many parents send their children to progressive schools because they are reacting against the formalism and regimentation of traditional education. These "child-centered schools," in which children are not taught dead subject matter, emphasize freedom, esthetic enjoyment and artistic development, and learning through activity. Dewey believes that this revolt produced a one-sided emphasis. Rebellion against the conventional schoolroom was needed, he says, but it overlooked the need to develop a new subject matter organized as well as or better than the old. Education should center on the pupil, but that pupil does not live in isolation and must learn to "reach out into a world of objects and persons" under proper "guidance and direction." The child's impulses and desires should be encouraged to mature by development of thought. Dewey deplores the indulgence of some schools in unrestrained action, speech, and manners by students, nearly to the point of license and anarchy; he believes that subject matter must be taught and that, above all, the discipline of intellectual control, objective knowledge, and understanding should be cultivated. He says, that "it is the absence of intellectual control through significant subject matter which stimulates the deplorable egotism, cockiness, impertinence and disregard for the rights of others apparently considered by some persons to be the inevitable accompaniment, if not the essence, of freedom." He recommends in its place not subjective but rational freedom. He criticizes the tendency of progressive schools to emphasize the things that make schooling immediately enjoyable rather than the things that give understanding and capacity relevant to contemporary life. Dewey wants education to have more depth and rigor and, in particular, to instill an understanding of the relation of science to industrial society.

How pertinent his analysis still is today, not only to public schools but to schools of higher learning. For example, in his essay "Philosophy and Education" Dewey maintains that the "ultimate aim of education" is "the creation of human beings in the fulness of their capacities. . . . generous in aspiration, liberal in thought, cultivated in taste, and equipped with knowledge and competent method." Through the development of such human beings, society is "constantly remade." Speaking of the universities, he says, "After a long period in which education was treated as a matter of routine experience, tradition, and mere apprenticeship, we are engaged once more in regarding education as a pursuit having intellectual foundations, and needing systematic intellectual guidance."

II. Political and Social Philosophy

In the late 1920s and in the 1930s, Dewey authored a number of important books on politics, including *The Public and Its Problems* (1927), *Liberalism and Social Action* (1935), and *Freedom and Culture* (1939), in which he sought to work out a new definition of liberalism, emphasizing that liberalism should not be identified with a particular party platform or program but rather with a method of intelligence to be used in a democracy to solve social problems. Dewey was attempting to break away from the traditional nineteenth-century conception of classical liberalism.

Dewey's role in the growth of a liberal movement in the United States is important, illustrating anew his deep involvement in public affairs. For example, in September 1929, Dewey was elected Chairman of the League for Independent Political Action, which comprised liberals, socialists, and pacifists, including Paul H. Douglas, Oswald Garrison Villard, Reinhold Niebuhr, Stuart Chase, and Norman Thomas. In his essay "What Do Liberals Want?" Dewey deplores the fact that liberals are so hard to organize. He notes a body of progressive sentiment in the United States and an immense sympathy for the underdog, as well as dissatisfaction with the existing alignment of political parties. The purpose of the League, he says, is to work out a body of political principles adapted to economic and social conditions. The *New York Times* reported that Dewey, as chairman of the League, urged Senator George W. Norris to lead a new third party (see Miscellany, "Dewey Asks Norris to Lead New Party"); Senator Norris later rejected this call (see Appendix 6, "Insurgents Back Norris in Refusing to Quit Republicans").

Individualism, Old and New, in the present volume, is a part of Dewey's effort to develop this new conception of liberalism. It is especially interesting that the chapters of this book began appearing in the *New Republic* on 24 April 1929, during a period of relatively high prosperity, and continued after the great stock market crash of October 1929. These articles reflect the intense dissatisfaction that Dewey and others felt with the classical liberal defense of laissez-faire economics and the capitalist system. Marxist ideas were spreading and one can see their influence on Dewey. Nevertheless, *Individualism, Old and New* is prophetic in anticipating the kind of welfare liberalism that would emerge shortly with the New Deal.

The central question of *Individualism, Old and New* is how to create a new form of individualism appropriate to the kind of society in which we actually live. Dewey begins his discussion by examining the contradictions he finds in American culture, particularly "between our institutions and practice on one hand,

and our creeds and theories on the other." In the late twenties, the philosophy of rugged individualism dominated the thinking of a large sector of society. How does such a philosophy square with the traditional religion and morality we have inherited? We are unprepared, he suggests, for the industrialization of our civilization. Although we claim to believe in the ideals of individualism, equality of opportunity, and freedom for all, these are perverted by a dominant "pecuniary culture" that justifies inequality and oppression in the name of an economic struggle for survival of the fittest.

Dewey discusses the widespread European criticism of American cultural traits that were allegedly conquering the globe: quantification, mechanization, standardization, material success, and technique—all being condemned for submerging individuality. Dewey defends the use of technology as a means of emancipating individuality; the most serious defect of our civilization and the major threat to individualism, he finds, comes from the control of technology primarily for "private profit." The deepest problem of our time is "constructing a new individuality consonant with the objective conditions under which we live." Dewey maintains that the United States had entered a "collective age," moving from an earlier "pioneer individualism" of the small entrepreneur to a society in which large-scale business corporations and trusts dominate economic activities. Indeed, Dewey bemoans the increased concentration of economic power by corporations. The realities of a mass production economy are mass education, advertising, and consumerism, which further contribute to the repression of the individual.

Dewey analyzes the plight of the lost individual in corporate society. The salient traits of a person's life are insecurity, fear of unemployment, and the oncoming of old age. Dewey deplores that individualism had been equated with private economic gain in our business-oriented civilization. The paradox is that while our material culture is corporate, our moral culture and ideology are saturated with values of an individualism derived from a pre-technological age and rooted in medieval religion and the feudal period. The Protestant emphasis on abstract rights that are uniquely individual and on economic enterprise has been overshadowed by the later developments of the industrial age and is no longer viable. For Dewey, economic individualism based on private gain is often a parasite on the great productive forces of society that are scientific and technical. The key questions are, "How shall the individual find himself in an unprecedentedly new situation?" and "What qualities will the new individualism exhibit?"

Dewey suggests that a new individualism can be achieved only through the controlled use of all our social resources. The call for national planning became especially prominent in the 1930s. Although Dewey was a critic of Bolshevik Russia, he nevertheless says that "the future historian of our times will [admire] those who had the imagination first to see that the resources of technology might be directed by organized planning to serve chosen ends." This course would, he indicated, embark us "constructively and voluntarily" upon the road that Soviet Russia was travelling with so much "destruction and coercion." Dewey later became an even more vigorous critic of Russia and headed a special commission in the late thirties to investigate the charges against Leon Trotsky, charges he found largely to have been fabricated by Stalinists. In retrospect, liberal opinion today has lost much of its confidence that national plans can fulfill high expectations and there is greater reluctance to undermine the operation of the free market with overall programs of governmental planning.

Dewey does not always indicate the exact form that the new individualism will take. In criticizing modern Luddites who reject machine technology and science, which they consider the enemy, he suggests that an emergent individualism must refashion the role of the individual in the corporate world and use science and technology for social purposes. Maintaining that we need to introduce social responsibilities into the business system, he recommends the establishment of "a coordinating and directive council in which captains of industry and finance would meet with representatives of labor and public officials." They would cooperatively "plan the regulation of industrial activity," somewhat as in Germany and other mixed economies in the world today. Dewey incidentally criticized Marx for not sufficiently appreciating the dynamic role of technology and the capacities for expanding industry by developing new inventions. Nor did Marx recognize, he says, that employers would rush to sustain consumption by granting high wages and not seek to bring workers down to a subsistence level.

In *Individualism, Old and New* Dewey criticizes the prevailing economic system with its large scale maldistribution of income, disproportionate income tax, quiescent labor movement, unregulated industry, and no social security or unemployment insurance. All these problems were later addressed by the New Deal, the Fair Deal, the Great Society, and the labor-liberal coalition that emerged.

"We are in for some kind of socialism," says Dewey, "call it by whatever name we please." The difference, he says, is between a socialism that is public and democratic and one that is capitalistic in character.

Dewey diagnoses the crisis in our culture. In one aspect of this crisis, those engaged in production and distribution have no imaginative, intellectual, or emotional share in directing their activities. To bring about a new individualism, he suggests some form of participatory democracy and a system of cooperative control of industry. If so developed, industry could become a primary educative and cultural force for those involved in it. The focus of industry would be on social utility, not simply pecuniary profit—which is responsible, Dewey says, for our distorted cultural development. In this new individualism, industry would be conducted from the standpoint of the user and enjoyer of goods and services, not the captains of industry or finance. Intellectuals now disenchanted with mass culture or seeking to escape from it would have a role: they can contribute to inquiry and thus help "humanize industrial civilization" and make it and technology "a servant of human life."

In a sense, says Dewey, the suppression of individuality is the individual's own responsibility; the first move to recover individuality therefore rests "with the individual himself." One cannot hope to develop integrated individuality by an all-embracing social program alone. We must cultivate our own garden, but that garden has no sharp fence about it. Our garden is the world—including the corporate and industrial world in which we live and function. Dewey recommended the adoption of the scientific method in human affairs and its application to morals, religion, politics, and industry. If so used, it can lead not only to social improvement but also to an appreciation of the free working of mind as a source of creativity and joy.

At the time Dewey wrote these views, socialist ideas were everywhere present, serving as a promise of a better tomorrow. The infamous tyrannies of Marxist dictatorships were not clearly seen by intellectuals; moreover, capitalism began to undergo a serious economic crisis. Today, more than a half century later, the kind of libertarian individualism that Dewey condemned has had a resurgence: economic libertarians and neo-conservatives deplore the growth of government regulations and the increase in taxation and welfare policies in democratic societies. Since Dewey wrote, old age security, unemployment insurance, and other governmental programs of regulation have been enacted to mitigate some of the insecurities that concerned him. Capitalist societies are now "mixed economies" with a large public sector. Although they still face serious problems of unemployment, inflation, and economic cycles, and the trend toward mergers and conglomerates continues unabated, many would not wish to weaken the free market. Moreover, the individual is often as alienated and estranged in welfare societies as he was in free enterprise economies, though the threats to his existence assume other forms. The continued growth of the mass media further exacerbates the problem of submerged individuality. And mass society raises anew the question of the appropriate role of government in society. Some of Dewey's followers today are social democrats or democratic socialists who still wish to use the state as an instrument of social welfare. Others have reevaluated capitalism and wish to democratize and humanize, not abandon, it. They place far greater trust in the marketplace than did Dewey, and they are now convinced that political and social liberty cannot be guaranteed without a wide measure of economic freedom. Perhaps one conclusion to be drawn is that economics is still an art rather than a science and that economists differ as much as philosophers. They divide into schools which are often contradictory in their analyses of economic problems and in their recommendations for dealing with them. Dewey's *Individualism, Old and New* was a product of the period in which he wrote, on the eve of the Great Depression; nevertheless, the submerging of the individual that concerned Dewey is as serious a problem in our present post-industrial age as it was in the thirties. His work helps us identify that problem, although what course society should take in rescuing and restoring individuality is still largely an unanswered question.

III. Philosophical Controversies

This volume includes more than a dozen of Dewey's strictly philosophical essays; my comments are therefore highly selective.

In "From Absolutism to Experimentalism" Dewey gives a personal account of his own philosophical development, beginning as an undergraduate at the University of Vermont, where he studied with H. A. P. Torrey. Dewey tells how, under the tutelage of George Sylvester Morris and W. T. Harris, Hegel's philosophy had a strong early appeal because "it supplied a demand for unification that was doubtless an intense emotional craving." Hegel's synthesis of subject and object, matter and spirit, the divine and the human had a particular attraction for Dewey. He recounts how he drifted away from Hegel's thought over the next several years, though it left a "permanent deposit" upon his philosophy.

Four points stand out in Dewey's intellectual development: first is the importance for him of the theory and practice of education, especially the education of the young. Second, Dewey became increasingly troubled by the dualism in logical standpoint and method between science and morals, which led to his development of instrumentalism. Third is the influence of William James's *Psychology*, especially his biological conception of experience and thought and its impact on philosophy. Fourth is his perception of the importance of social categories, especially of communication and participation, which led to an appreciation for the influence of the social sciences on philosophy, education, morals, and religion.

This fourth theme is reiterated by Dewey in his essay "Philosophy," where he argues that philosophy is one of the social studies, and both philosophy and the social sciences have suffered because they have been isolated from each other. Dewey believes that the history of philosophic thought offers a field for social research and that philosophy cannot be fully understood apart from its social environment. The business of philosophy is to criticize the dominant beliefs of a culture. These beliefs, however, need to be examined as social products and forces. This applies from the earliest Greek philosophers to the present, including the relationship of logical studies, often considered in abstraction from a social context, to practical social questions. Dewey further observes that the subjectivistic controversies between empiricists and rationalists were abstract and that philosophers should instead deal with and consider the "phenomenon of social interactions, as real in their own right." From this point of view the basic source of philosophical fallacies is the conversion of a temporary abstraction for purposes of analysis to a permanent one. Dewey complains that the divorce of philosophy from the social sciences has led to the "over-technicality of philosophical systems" and to an "undue emphasis upon intellectual gymnastics and dialectic" at the expense of their bearing upon life. This evaluation might well apply to the kind of linguistic and analytical philosophy that dominated Anglo-American philosophy in the post-Deweyan period, making it seem too often trivial, formal, and dead. Excessive focus on analytic distinctions quite independent of their social context and the failure to examine psychological premises in the light of social science research have only intensified this problem. Many analytic philosophers have insisted that epistemological or logical issues can be pursued independently of psycho-genetic inquiries, but such issues often only mask unexamined psycho-logistic assumptions.

This volume contains a number of spirited discussions between Dewey and his critics. Among these is an exchange with Ernest Nagel and another replying to F. J. E. Woodbridge, William Ernest Hocking, and C. I. Lewis, who critically analyzed the adequacy of Dewey's instrumentalism in a special American Philosophical Association symposium on 30 December 1929. These commentators discuss Dewey's theory of logic and reflective inquiry in the light of alternative metaphysical positions, whether realism or idealism, and their criticisms are extremely useful in clarifying the ontological ground of Dewey's philosophy. Many writers have been puzzled by Dewey's basic categories; some have found them "idealistic" in character. "Interactions" and "transactions" seem to be ultimately "real," which raises questions about their relationship to the world of nature. Does nature exist independently of reflective inquiry? What role do the principles of logic have in the executive order of nature? What is the relationship between "primary" and "secondary" experience, i.e., are antecedent objects, as directly or immediately experienced or had, "real," and in what sense; or are only those objects "real" that are defined and explained in the course of reflective thinking and inquiry? Some critics have thought that Dewey was equivocating on these issues, or that he was himself uncertain about their precise status. His critics, all influential philosophers, pose probing questions about aspects of Dewey's philosophy that even his most sympathetic readers find troubling. Thus Dewey's responses to his critics are valuable and contribute significantly to an understanding of his philosophical assumptions.

Dewey's debate with Ernest Nagel, his former student at Columbia who later became Professor of Philosophy there, is especially instructive. First, Dewey raises a question about "the kind of subject-matter to which the formal principles of logic are legitimately applicable." In "The Sphere of Application of the Excluded Middle" Dewey says that the formal principles of logic "are applicable only to formal or non-existential subject-matter." Logical principles, such as the excluded middle, identity, and contradiction, are universal propositions. They do not denote anything about the real world as such, nor do they have existential import. To be applicable to existence, independent assertions of a matter-of-fact kind must be made in the form of a particular proposition. To say that "A is either B or non-B is . . . indifferent to the question whether anything exists having the properties designated by A and B." It would be fallacious, says Dewey, to move from a universal property to a material or existential one. The Aristotelian conception, he thinks, confuses the relationship between the formal and material, the "essential" and the existential, and begs the question of the relationship between the logical and the ontological or existent. Does the principle of the excluded middle apply to nature? Dewey is impressed by the contingency or particularity of existence and events, and by the fact that existence undergoes change and transition. Does the principle of the excluded middle apply to propositions about the future? Although Dewey otherwise agrees with Nagel, he challenges Nagel's statement in "Intuition, Consistency, and the Excluded Middle" (see *Journal of Philosophy*, volume 26) that it is possible "to enumerate exhaustive (though very general) properties about the future if that future is not altogether independent of the past." Dewey considers the term "exhaustive" unfortunate, since it would remove all contingency from the future and make it so determinate that the principle of the excluded middle would apply. On the contrary, Dewey finds the future to be conditional and to have a temporal quality that makes it indeterminate. The principle of the excluded middle not only does not apply to the future, it does not apply to the past or present either. Dewey concludes his article by raising questions of the status of the principle of the excluded middle in the broader question of the relationship of the logical and the ontological, the formal and the existential.

Nagel responds to Dewey in "Can Logic Be Divorced from Ontology?" (see Appendix 1) protesting the diremption between a method of inquiry and "the irreducible traits" of subject matter explored. He says that Dewey's writings provide both a metaphysics that describes the "generic traits of existence" and a logic of the method of inquiry. Nagel says that one can infer on the basis of Dewey's work that there are generic factors which are the traits of every subject of scientific investigation. These ontological characteristics become objects of knowledge as conclusions of a process of inquiry; they do not exist fully antecedent to inquiry. Nagel believes that Dewey himself seems to ask whether these "ontological traits can be identified, at least in part, with the logical traits."

According to Nagel, if logical traits are cut off from ontological traits, then Dewey's belief, as expressed in *The Quest for Certainty*, for example, that the "precarious" and the "stable" are not only features of human experience but of nature, would be untenable. Dewey's chief argument for the view that both nature and experience contain generic characteristics is the continuity between them. Nagel quotes approvingly Dewey's statement that "one who believes in continuity may argue that, since human experience exhibits such traits, nature *must* contain their prototypes." And Nagel concludes that although there may be other ontological traits besides the logical to which our common-day experience certifies, nature must at least reflect and contain the logical as well, and this is revealed in the course of reflective history.

Nagel finds the laws of logic unique, in that they turn up in every conceivable inquiry; therefore they represent factors invariant in every subject matter. A whole-hearted naturalist, Nagel insists, cannot break the continuity between logic and metaphysics. Although it is true, he says, that logical principles are concerned with the mutual relations of propositions, not with the mutual relations of things, nevertheless the ground of the principles of contradiction and the excluded middle is not to be found in the propositions but in the nature of things which the propositions state.

Dewey's response to Nagel came quickly in "The Applicability of Logic to Existence." A reader sympathetic to Dewey may find his reply rather curious. At first he seems to concede Nagel's point and to have been convinced by him. He states at once that he does not think "that logic can be divorced from ontology," and that the "ground" of the logical "must be found in the ontological," and that there is a "continuity between logic and metaphysics." But he asks, in what sense, and what kind of continuity is there? He doubts Nagel's answer to these questions, maintaining that logical character can be employed practically upon existences, though they do not inherently characterize other existences or afford premises in which existential inferences may be directly based. He denies that formal logical principles can be directly assigned to actual existences, even though they are applicable in dealing with such existential premises. Dewey regrets that his earlier discussion was so narrow and is willing to deal with the larger issues named by Nagel. He agrees with Nagel that "logical principles are concerned with the mutual relations of propositions, not with the mutual relations of things." But, says Dewey, he would not dream of denying that valid objects of thought are conditioned by prior existences or are indirectly applicable to them by means of existential operations. Moreover, he agrees that he would not deny that contingent existence has elements of definite characteristics, so that logical principles would apply to them as well. He adds that reflective inquiry *itself* exists and is in turn conditioned by existential objects. To clarify his point further, Dewey introduces here the distinction between the potential and actual. "Existence apart from that of reflection is logi*cible*, but not logi*cized*," until the actual operations of human organisms supervene. These operations produce additive consequences, so that qualities and relations that were previously only potential "become actualized." Dewey is dealing with issues implied in one form or another in *Experience and Nature* and *The Quest for Certainty* that have puzzled other philosophers. Only later, in *Logic: The Theory of Inquiry*, published in 1938, does he eventually attempt to develop a broader theory of the nature and function of logical principles.

F. J. E. Woodbridge, Dewey's colleague at Columbia and editor of the *Journal of Philosophy*, contributed his share to the critical analysis of Dewey's thought with the important article "Experience and Dialectic." Woodbridge, who had a powerful influence on many of Dewey's students, expressed a kind of Aristotelian realism; his main criticisms of Dewey's instrumentalism are two-fold: first he questions Dewey's distinction between "antecedent objects" and "known objects," as he believes that objects exist independently of and prior to being known. He questions Dewey's statement in *The Quest for Certainty* that "only the conclusion of reflective inquiry is known." This, complains Woodbridge, could throw him into the arms of the idealists. He wishes to distinguish clearly between knowledge and its object. "If any objects whatever are known," he says, then it is "irrelevant whether they exist prior or subsequent to the act of knowing."

In his "In Reply to Some Criticisms" Dewey responds that he does not understand why anyone should think he was "denying the existence of antecedent things." On the contrary, he insists that "things had in direct experience exist prior to being known." Dewey denies, however, that he is identifying the "things had in direct experience with the object of knowledge." He and Woodbridge, he says, differ only about the character of the antecedent existence with respect to knowledge while it is known. Dewey claims that "*the* object is the eventual product of reflection," whereas "antecedent existences" are the "subject-matter *for* knowledge."

Woodbridge's second criticism is that since Dewey does not attempt to demonstrate his theory empirically but rather uses a dialectical argument, this implies that nature is at root dialectical and that the dialectic is implemented by the practical procedure of intelligence. Dewey again denies that his method is purely dialectical and insists that he depended upon empirical evidence drawn from the experimental sciences. Dialectic is used, but only to invite others to experience the empirical consequences of experimental inquiry.

Harvard philosopher William Ernest Hocking also criticizes Dewey, but from the standpoint of objective idealism (see Appendix 2, "Action and Certainty"). He defends *a priori* truth, the idea of an eternal aspect to total reality, and certainty. Hocking nonetheless finds some sympathy with Dewey insofar as he reads him as an "experimental idealist." Hocking denies, however, the basic premise of instrumentalism, according to which we must judge the validity of propositions by seeing how they function. He rejects the notion that there is a correspondence between meaning and working. "If we only know a thing when we see what comes of it, then indeed, we never know anything; for we never have in hand what is yet to eventuate." The meaning of an idea is not exhausted in our interest in it. There is "fact-meaning" independent of "active-meaning." Hocking believes that even partial truths not worked out have some "consistency of meaning."

In response, Dewey maintains that Hocking's objection is implicit in his own theory that "truth is conceived of as an inherent property of some meanings, ideas, or propositions." But he says that "any idea or proposition is relevant to its *own* problematic situation in which it arises and which it intends to resolve." It is validated as "true" insofar as it does resolve it. And this may produce still another situation that needs resolution, and so on. Even partial truths are meanings in process of development; thus meanings have indeterminate aspects.

Dewey also denies that meanings apart from their application are more than claims to truth. The so-called "immediacies of truth" of the rationalist apply to meanings, nothing more. Although he objects to Hocking's use of the term "eternal," he grants that the "stability of truth" like "reality" represents an ideal limit, but this does not enable us to convert this limit into an inherent or antecedent property of meanings. He fears that Hocking's reference to "absolute" can easily convert into a fixed dogma.

Dewey also maintains that he has never doubted that there are *a priori* meanings in an empirical sense; these are, however, "prospective postulates," and one must guard against converting their meaning-as-postulates into truths. Hocking asserts that we can deduce "necessary consequences" from their postulates. But Dewey finds this ambiguous, depending on whether it signifies "logical implications" or "existential outcomes." The fallacy arises in supposing the latter should be identical with the former, which Dewey thinks can lead to "dogmatism in thought" and "fanaticism in action."

Harvard pragmatist C. I. Lewis agrees basically with Dewey's position (see Appendix 3, "Pragmatism and Current Thought"). He shares William James's conviction that pragmatism is not a doctrine but a method. Viewed logically, it involves a single principle of procedure; i.e., the pragmatic test of significance is to examine ideas by their practical bearings or consequences in experience. Dewey agrees when he says that "ideas are plans of action" and that "concepts are prescriptions of certain operations whose empirical consequences determine their significance."

Lewis believes that Dewey's "functional theory of the concept" also has important implications for logical theory, to which, incidentally, Lewis directed a good deal of his philosophical attention in his most important work, *An Analysis of Knowledge and Valuation*. Lewis agrees with Dewey that the concepts of physics and mathematics have been abstracted from the context of inquiry, but they nonetheless play an important and vital role in the intermediate stage of knowledge. For Lewis, although meanings as connotation refer to abstract configurations of relations, meanings as descriptions or empirical applications refer to a process which begins and ends with something done "in the operation which translates a presented datum into an instrument of prediction and control." This interpretation he shares with Dewey's instrumentalism.

Dewey responds in "In Reply to Some Criticisms" that he finds himself in sympathy with Lewis. He does not mean to deny the vital role of abstractions in science and thought. The use of abstractions lies at "the heart of thought." The only way we can effectively control concrete experience is by means of an intermediate use of conceptual thought. "What I regret," he concludes, "is the effort to erect the abstractions into complete and self-subsistent things, or into a kind of superior Being," or the tendency of many inquirers in the social sciences to be overawed by the abstract concepts of the physical sciences and their failure to develop abstractions appropriate to their own subject matter. Thus Dewey reaffirms his instrumentalist theory, seeking to ground it in his broader theory of experience that leaves room for both immediate and reflective inquiry.

Two essays in this volume deserve special comment. They not only anticipate many of the ideas later to emerge in *A Common Faith* (1934) but also help define what Dewey means by humanism. Dewey has in recent years been bitterly attacked for signing *A Humanist Manifesto*, a document issued in 1933 and endorsed by thirty-four liberal philosophers, writers, and Unitarian ministers. Many of Dewey's foes blame the growth of secular humanism in later years on his influence. Dewey is clearly a humanist, but in what sense?

In the first essay, "What Humanism Means to Me," Dewey points out that the term "humanism" has a great number of different meanings attributed to it. He wants especially to distinguish his conception from a view then prominently advocated by a number of American literary critics, notably Paul Elmer More and Irving Babbitt. Dewey finds their humanism too negative, "anti-romantic," and "anti-naturalistic." It sets man off from nature; it condemns and rejects science. He criticizes its "transcendental imagination" and, implicit in its Kantian ethics, its divorce of man from nature. It has more in common with romanticism than it is aware of.

Humanism, says Dewey, originally referred to the revival of learning in the fifteenth and sixteenth centuries and to the keen interest men of letters felt in the literature of ancient Greece and Rome. Renaissance humanism was in violent rebellion against authority. The humanities thus were held in opposition to theology. Another form of humanism emphasized the values of human life, past and present, as the center of our concern. Walter Pater expressed the belief that nothing that ever interested men and women can lose its vitality. Another phase of humanism was that espoused by Francis Bacon, Condorcet, and Comte, who wished to apply the sciences to the improvement of the human condition. The Oxford pragmatist F. C. S. Schiller also defended humanism; like Protagoras, he said that "man is the measure of all things," and especially the measure of value.

Dewey's own humanism is like Bacon's, for it attempts to integrate science and to use it in the service of mankind. Dewey concludes with a statement of what humanism means to him: "Humanism . . . is an expansion, not a contraction, of human life, an expansion in which nature and the science of nature are made the willing servants of human good." Dewey's definition is especially interesting in view of the recent development of the ecological movement. This new romanticism, in the name of humanism, often condemns science and technology, seeks to preserve nature and to return to it as the idyllic womb and standard of all value. In one sense it is not unlike the literary humanism of More and Babbitt that Dewey was objecting to.

In "What I Believe" Dewey further defines a humanistic conception of religion, rejecting the classical notion of a transcendent or supernaturalistic faith in which the meaning of nature and human life has its source "above and beyond experience." Christianity, he says, offers "a fixed revelation of absolute, unchanging Being and truth," which was elaborated into a "system of definite rules and ends" used for the direction of life. But this system led to "fixed dogma and rigid institutionalism." Dewey denies that Christianity as such has any ready-made remedies for present ills and social problems. Instead, he offers a naturalistic conception of faith. It is not a faith based upon a creed accepted from on high; it is rather a faith that provides an inspiration for action and endeavor, one that is rooted in human experience as "the sole ultimate authority" of knowledge and conduct. Central to this philosophy of experience is the principle derived from the natural sciences that to exist is to be in process and change. This means that we must be willing to modify social institutions and traditional moral attitudes. The chief danger to religion, thinks Dewey, is that it has become so respectable that it sanctions what exists in society and has therefore become an obstacle to moral change. For Dewey "the future of religion is connected with . . . faith in the possibilities of human experience and human relationships that will create a vital sense of the solidarity of human interests and inspire action to make that sense a reality." Dewey wishes to use the resources of science and technology to improve human life and in particular to reconstruct economic forces. Dewey rails against excessive Cassandrian gloom. Man has lost confidence in reason. Faith in progress has been shaken. Skepticism has become rampant, not only against the older creeds but also against any kind of far-reaching ideas that may help us to direct human affairs intelligently.

In such a context, says Dewey, "a thoroughgoing philosophy of experience, framed in the light of science and technique, has its significance." Such a philosophy, he urges, can be "brought unitedly to bear upon industry, politics, religion, domestic life, and human relations in general." Dewey expresses a deep faith in human potentialities and intelligence that is the hallmark of his humanism and permeates his thought and action. "A philosophic faith, being a tendency to action," he concludes, "can be tried and tested only in action. I know of no viable alternative in the present day to such a philosophy. . . ."

The Sources of a Science of Education

I

Education as a Science

The title may suggest to some minds that it begs a prior question: *Is* there a science of education? And still more fundamentally, Can there be a science of education? Are the procedures and aims of education such that it is possible to reduce them to anything properly called a science? Similar questions exist in other fields. The issue is not unknown in history; it is raised in medicine and law. As far as education is concerned, I may confess at once that I have put the question in its apparently question-begging form in order to avoid discussion of questions that are important but that are also full of thorns and attended with controversial divisions.

It is enough for our purposes to note that the word "science" has a wide range.

There are those who would restrict the term to mathematics or to disciplines in which exact results can be determined by rigorous methods of demonstration. Such a conception limits even the claims of physics and chemistry to be sciences, for according to it the only scientific portion of these subjects is the strictly mathematical. The position of what are ordinarily termed the biological sciences is even more dubious, while social subjects and psychology would hardly rank as sciences at all, when measured by this definition. Clearly we must take the idea of science with some latitude. We must take it with sufficient looseness to include all the subjects that are usually regarded as sciences. The important thing is to discover those traits in virtue of which various fields are called scientific. When we raise the question in this way, we are led to put emphasis upon *methods* of dealing with subject-matter rather than to look for uniform objective traits in subject-matter. From this point of view, science signifies, I take it, the existence of systematic methods of inquiry, which, when they are brought to bear on a range of facts, enable us to understand them better and to control them more intelligently, less haphazardly and with less routine.

No one would doubt that our practices in hygiene and medicine are less casual, less results of a mixture of guess work and tradition, than they used to be, nor that this difference has been made by development of methods of investigating and testing. There is an intellectual technique by which discovery and organization of material go on cumulatively, and by means of which one inquirer can repeat the researches of another, confirm or discredit them, and add still more to the capital stock of knowledge. Moreover, the methods when they are used tend to perfect themselves, to suggest new problems, new investigations, which refine old procedures and create new and better ones.

The question as to the sources of a science of education is, then, to be taken in this sense. What are the ways by means of which the function of education in all its branches and phases— selection of material for the curriculum, methods of instruction and discipline, organization and administration of schools—can be conducted with systematic increase of intelligent control and understanding? What are the materials upon which we may —and should—draw in order that educational activities may become in a less degree products of routine, tradition, accident and transitory accidental influences? From what sources shall we draw so that there shall be steady and cumulative growth of intelligent, communicable insight and power of direction?

Here is the answer to those who decry pedagogical study on the ground that success in teaching and in moral direction of pupils is often not in any direct ratio to knowledge of educational principles. Here is "A" who is much more successful than "B" in teaching, awakening the enthusiasm of his students for learning, inspiring them morally by personal example and contact, and yet relatively ignorant of educational history, psychology, approved methods, etc., which "B" possesses in abundant measure. The facts are admitted. But what is overlooked by the objector is that the successes of such individuals tend to be born and to die with them: beneficial consequences extend only to those pupils who have personal contact with such gifted teachers. No one can measure the waste and loss that have come from the fact that the contributions of such men and women in the past have been thus confined, and the only way by which we can prevent such waste in the future is by methods which enable us to make an *analysis* of what the gifted teacher does intuitively, so that something accruing from his work can be communicated to others. Even in the things conventionally recognized as sciences, the insights of unusual persons remain important and there is no levelling down to a uniform procedure. But the existence of science gives common efficacy to the experiences of the genius; it makes it possible for the results of special power to become part of the working equipment of other inquirers, instead of perishing as they arose.

The individual capacities of the Newtons, Boyles, Joules, Darwins, Lyells, Helmholtzes, are not destroyed because of the existence of science; their differences from others and the impossibility of predicting on the basis of past science what discoveries they would make—that is, the impossibility of regulating their activities by antecedent sciences—persist. But science makes it possible for others to benefit systematically by what they achieved.

The existence of scientific method protects us also from a danger that attends the operations of men of unusual power; dangers of slavish imitation partisanship, and such jealous devotion to them and their work as to get in the way of further progress. Anybody can notice to-day that the effect of an original and powerful teacher is not all to the good. Those influenced by him often show a one-sided interest; they tend to form schools, and to become impervious to other problems and truths; they incline to swear by the words of their master and to go on repeating his thoughts after him, and often without the spirit and insight that originally made them significant. Observation also shows that these results happen oftenest in those subjects in which scientific method is least developed. Where these methods are of longer standing students adopt methods rather than merely results, and employ them with flexibility rather than in literal reproduction.

This digression seems to be justified not merely because those who object to the idea of a science put personality and its unique gifts in opposition to science, but also because those who recommend science sometimes urge that uniformity of procedure will be its consequence. So it seems worth while to dwell on the fact that in the subjects best developed from the scientific point of view, the opposite is the case. Command of scientific methods and systematized subject-matter liberates individuals; it enables them to see new problems, devise new procedures, and, in general, makes for diversification rather than for set uniformity. But at the same time these diversifications have a cumulative effect in an advance shared by all workers in the field.

Education as an Art

This theme is, I think, closely connected with another point which is often urged, namely, that education is an art rather than a science. That, in concrete operation, education is an art, either a mechanical art or a fine art, is unquestionable. If there were an opposition between science and art, I should be compelled to side with those who assert that education is an art. But there is no opposition, although there is a distinction. We must not be misled by words. Engineering is, in actual practice, an art. But it is an art that progressively incorporates more and more of science into itself, more of mathematics, physics and chemistry. It is the kind of art it is precisely because of a content of scientific subject-matter which guides it as a practical operation. There is room for the original and daring projects of exceptional individuals. But their distinction lies not in the fact that they turn their backs upon science, but in the fact that they make new integrations of scientific material and turn it to new and previously unfamiliar and unforeseen uses. When, in education, the psychologist or observer and experimentalist in any field reduces his findings to a rule which is to be uniformly adopted, then, only, is there a result which is objectionable and destructive of the free play of education as an art.

But this happens not because of scientific method but because of departure from it. It is not the capable engineer who treats scientific findings as imposing upon him a certain course which is to be rigidly adhered to: it is the third- or fourth-rate man who adopts this course. Even more, it is the unskilled day laborer who follows it. For even if the practice adopted is one that follows from science and could not have been discovered or employed except for science, when it is converted into a uniform rule of procedure it becomes an empirical rule-of-thumb procedure—just as a person may use a table of logarithms mechanically without knowing anything about mathematics.

The danger is great in the degree in which the attempt to develop scientific method is recent. Nobody would deny that education is still in a condition of transition from an empirical to a scientific status. In its empirical form the chief factors determining education are tradition, imitative reproduction, response to various external pressures wherein the strongest force wins out, and the gifts, native and acquired, of individual teachers. In this situation there is a strong tendency to identify teaching ability with the use of procedures that yield immediately successful results, success being measured by such things as order in the class-room, correct recitations by pupils in assigned lessons, passing of examinations, promotion of pupils to a higher grade, etc.

For the most part, these are the standards by which a community judges the worth of a teacher. Prospective teachers come to training schools, whether in normal schools or colleges, with such ideas implicit in their minds. They want very largely to find out *how to do* things with the maximum prospect of success. Put baldly, they want recipes. Now, to such persons science is of value because it puts a stamp of final approval upon this and that specific procedure. It is very easy for science to be regarded as a guarantee that goes with the sale of goods rather than as a light to the eyes and a lamp to the feet. It is prized for its prestige value rather than as an organ of personal illumination and liberation. It is prized because it is thought to give unquestionable authenticity and authority to a specific procedure to be carried out in the school room. So conceived, science *is* antagonistic to education as an art.

EXPERIENCE AND ABSTRACTION

The history of the more mature sciences shows two characteristics. Their original problems were set by difficulties that offered themselves in the ordinary region of practical affairs. Men obtained fire by rubbing sticks together and noted how things grew warm when they pressed on each other, long before they had any theory of heat. Such everyday experiences in their seeming inconsistency with the phenomena of flame and fire finally led to the conception of heat as a mode of molecular motion. But it led to this conception only when the ordinary phenomena were reflected upon in detachment from the conditions and uses under which they exhibit themselves in practices. There is no science without abstraction, and abstraction means fundamentally that certain occurrences are removed from the dimension of familiar practical experience into that of reflective or theoretical inquiry.

To be able to get away for the time being from entanglement in the urgencies and needs of immediate practical concerns is a condition of the origin of scientific treatment in any field. Preoccupation with attaining some direct end or practical utility, always limits scientific inquiry. For it restricts the field of attention and thought, since we note only those things that are immediately connected with what we want to do or get at the moment. Science signifies that we carry our observations and thinking further afield and become interested in what happens on its own account. Theory is in the end, as has been well said, the most practical of all things, because this widening of the range of attention beyond nearby purpose and desire eventually results in the creation of wider and farther-reaching purposes and enables us to use a much wider and deeper range of conditions and means than were expressed in the observation of primitive practical purposes. For the time being, however, the formation of theories demands a resolute turning aside from the needs of practical operations previously performed.

This detachment is peculiarly hard to secure in the case of those persons who are concerned with building up the scientific content of educational practices and arts. There is a pressure for immediate results, for demonstration of a quick, short-time span of usefulness in school. There is a tendency to convert the results of statistical inquiries and laboratory experiments into directions and rules for the conduct of school administration and instruction. Results tend to be directly grabbed, as it were, and put into operation by teachers. Then there is not the leisure for that slow and gradual independent growth of theories that is a necessary condition of the formation of a true science. This danger is peculiarly imminent in a science of education because its very recentness and novelty arouse skepticism as to its possibility and its value. The human desire to prove that the scientific mode of attack is really of value brings pressure to convert scientific conclusions into rules and standards of school-room practice.

It would perhaps be invidious to select examples too near to current situations. Some illustration, however, is needed to give definiteness to what has been said. I select an instance which is remote in time and crude in itself. An investigator found that girls between the ages of eleven and fourteen mature more rapidly than boys of the same age. From this fact, or presumed fact, he drew the inference that during these years boys and girls should be separated for purposes of instruction. He converted an intellectual finding into an immediate rule of school practice.

That the conversion was rash, few would deny. The reason is obvious. School administration and instruction is a much more complex operation than was the one factor contained in the scientific result. The significance of one factor for educational practice can be determined only as it is balanced with many other factors. Taken by itself, this illustration is so crude that to generalize from it might seem to furnish only a caricature. But the principle involved is of universal application. No conclusion of scientific research can be converted into an immediate rule of educational art. For there is no educational practice whatever which is not highly complex; that is to say, which does not contain many other conditions and factors than are included in the scientific finding.

Nevertheless, scientific findings are of practical utility, and the situation is wrongly interpreted when it is used to disparage the value of science in the art of education. What it militates against is the transformation of scientific findings into *rules* of action. Suppose for the moment that the finding about the different rates of maturing in boys and girls of a certain age is confirmed by continued investigation, and is to be accepted as fact. While it does not translate into a specific rule of fixed procedure, it is of some worth. The teacher who really knows this fact will have his personal attitude changed. He will be on the alert to make certain observations which would otherwise escape him; he will be enabled to interpret some facts which would otherwise be confused and misunderstood. This knowledge and understanding render his practice more intelligent, more flexible and better adapted to deal effectively with concrete phenomena of practice.

Nor does this tell the whole story. Continued investigation reveals other relevant facts. Each investigation and conclusion is special, but the tendency of an increasing number and variety of specialized results is to create new points of view and a wider field of observation. Various special findings have a cumulative effect; they reenforce and extend one another, and in time lead to the detection of principles that bind together a number of facts that are diverse and even isolated in their *prima facie* occurrence. These connecting principles which link different phenomena together we call laws.

Facts which are so interrelated form a system, a science. The practitioner who knows the system and its laws is evidently in possession of a powerful instrument for observing and interpreting what goes on before him. This intellectual tool affects his attitudes and modes of response in what he does. Because the range of understanding is deepened and widened he can take into account remote consequences which were originally hidden from view and hence were ignored in his actions. Greater continuity is introduced; he does not isolate situations and deal with them in separation as he was compelled to do when ignorant of connecting principles. At the same time, his practical dealings become more flexible. Seeing more relations he sees more possibilities, more opportunities. He is emancipated from the need of following tradition and special precedents. His ability to judge being enriched, he has a wider range of alternatives to select from in dealing with individual situations.

WHAT SCIENCE MEANS

If we gather up these conclusions in a summary we reach the following results. In the first place, no genuine science is formed by isolated conclusions, no matter how scientifically correct the technique by which these isolated results are reached, and no matter how exact they are. Science does not emerge until these various findings are linked up together to form a relatively coherent system—that is, until they reciprocally confirm and illuminate one another, or until each gives the others added meaning. Now this development requires time, and it requires more time in the degree in which the transition from an empirical condition to a scientific one is recent and hence imperfect.

ILLUSTRATIONS FROM THE PHYSICAL SCIENCES

The physical sciences have a much longer past behind them than psychological and social inquiries. In addition, they deal with subjects that are intrinsically less complex, involving fewer variables. This difference in the degree of maturity is at the bottom of what was said regarding the danger of premature transfer of special scientific findings into educational practice. It explains why scientific investigations regarding educational problems must go on, for a considerable time, in comparative remoteness and detachment from direct application, and why the pressure to demonstrate *immediate* utility in school administration and instruction is dangerous.

The way in which physical science was put upon its present foundations proves the scientific necessity of knowledge of relationships forming a system; it proves also the dependence of this knowledge upon a scheme of *general thought*, if experiments and measurements are to have scientific value. The history of physics proves conclusively that measurements and correlations, no matter how quantitatively exact, cannot yield a science except in connection with general principles which indicate *what* measurements to conduct and *how* they are to be interpreted. Galileo's experiments and measurements form the basis of modern science; they were made in connection with rolling of balls on an inclined plane, movements of pendulums and the dropping of balls from the Leaning Tower of Pisa.

Galileo had, however, first performed an experiment in thought, leading him to the hypothesis that the time of falling bodies is proportional to the square of the space traversed. It was this general idea, arrived at by thinking, that gave point to his experiment in Pisa, and that gave meaning to his measurement of the elapsed time of falling of bodies of various textures and volumes. His conception of what was measured, namely a generalization about relations of space, time and motion as the true objects of physical measurement, gave his measurements scientific status. Without these ideas he would not have known what to measure; he would have measured at random. Nor would he have known the meaning of his measurements after they were made; they would have remained mere intellectual curiosities.

It was also his preliminary hypotheses framed by thought which gave revolutionary import to his measurements of rolling balls. His experiments here and with pendulums went to confirm his theory that bodies in motion continue to move with the same velocity and direction unless externally acted upon. The result in connection with that at Pisa enabled acceleration to be measured and a general formula to be framed. In consequence, there was opened to subsequent experimenters the road of indirect measurement. Indirect measurements through calculation are much more important in science than are direct measurements, the latter merely supplying data and checks. The experimenters knew at the same time *what* they were measuring, namely, relations of mass, space, time, and motion. These general conceptions bound together their specific observations into a system.

II

Borrowed Techniques Insufficient

These considerations bring us to our second point, which is the negative side of our first. Educational science cannot be constructed simply by borrowing the techniques of experiment and measurement found in physical science. This could happen only if some way had been found by which mental or psychological phenomena are capable of statement in terms of units of space, time, motion, and mass. It is unnecessary to state that this condition has not been fulfilled. Nor have we as yet any *other* general hypotheses in the light of which to know *what* we are measuring and by which we can interpret results, place them in a system and lead on to fruitful indirect measurements. This principle is practically important at the present time. There is a tendency to assume that we are getting the material of a science of education merely because the techniques of older, better established sciences are borrowed and used.

It is no reproach to a would-be science that in early stages it makes experiments and measurements the results of which lack generalized significance. A period of groping is inevitable. But the lack of an intellectually coherent and inclusive system is a positive warning against attributing scientific value to results merely because they are reached by means of recognized techniques borrowed from sciences already established and are capable of being stated in quantitative formulae. Quantity is not even the fundamental idea of mathematics.

III

Laws vs. Rules

The third point is that laws and facts, even when they are arrived at in genuinely scientific shape, do not yield *rules of practice*. Their value for educational practice—and *all* education is a mode of practice, intelligent or accidental and routine—is indirect; it consists in provision of *intellectual instrumentalities* to be used by the educator. The meaning of this statement, in the contrast it draws between rules and intellectual instrumentalities, may be suggested by an illustrative instance told me by a friend. A manufacturer of paints utilizes results gained in the chemical laboratory. But the results in the factory vary from those obtained in the laboratory by from twenty to two hundred per cent. The first reaction might seem to be that the scientifically obtained conclusions are of no practical use, at least in the case of the larger divergence.

But the manufacturer does not draw this inference. What he is interested in is *improvement* of his factory practices, so that its operations give an increased yield in relation to the amount of labor and materials consumed. He is aware that factory conditions involve more variables, and variables harder to control, than are found in the conditions of laboratory experiment. The divergence of actual results from strictly scientific results is, therefore, a direction to him to observe more exactly and, upon a larger scale, all the conditions which affect his result. He notes variations in the time and temperature of different processes, the effect of surrounding heat and moistures, the reaction of gases incidentally generated, and so on. As he discovers that and how they affect his results he modifies his practical procedures. Thus he hopes to better his practice, each step calling attention to the influence of subtler and more obscure conditions which affect results, so that improvement is reasonably progressive.

If, in such a case, the manufacturer took the scientific data as a fixed rule, he would either follow it inflexibly with no improvement in the elimination of waste and loss; or, more likely, he would become disgusted with the discrepancies between laboratory and factory output, and would decide that science was not good for his purpose and fall back upon empirical procedures. Actually, he employs the scientific results as intellectual tools *in* his empirical procedures. That is, they *direct his attention*, in both observation and reflection, to conditions and relationships which would otherwise escape him. If we retain the word "rule" at all, we must say that scientific results furnish a rule for the conduct of *observations and inquiries*, not a rule for overt action. They function not directly with respect to practice and its results, but indirectly, through the medium of an altered mental attitude. The manufacturer becomes more efficient practically because he is more intelligent and complete in his observations, knowing what to look for, and is guided in his interpretation of what he sees because he now sees it in the light of a larger set of relationships.

SCIENTIFICALLY DEVELOPED ATTITUDES

If we turn from the scientific investigator to the administrator and teacher in the school and ask what is the bearing of these considerations upon the use to be practically made of scientific findings, the answer to be given is fairly clear. I knew a teacher in a training school for teachers who used to tell his students, "If you find that what I am telling you, or what another teacher here tells you, gets in the way of your common sense, of your use of your own judgment in an actual school situation, forget what you have learned and rely upon what your own judgment tells you is the best thing to do under the circumstances."

I never understood this saying to mean that the teacher thought that personal common-sense judgments and intuitions were the sole and sufficient guides of the teacher, or that he regarded the principles and facts which were taught to those in training of no practical value. I imagine that what he said was a negative way of stating that the value of the science, the history and philosophy of education acquired in the training school, resides in the enlightenment and guidance it supplies to observation and judgment of actual situations as they arise. If, in any particular case, the students saw no connection between what they had learned and the school situation, instead of trying to derive a rule from what they had learned they should depend upon their judgment as that had been developed by theoretical learnings and as these might operate unconsciously. In short, it was a way of saying that the value of definite instruction with respect to educational matters consists in its effect upon the formation of personal attitudes of observing and judging.

Sources vs. Content

The net conclusion of our discussion is that the final reality of educational science is not found in books, nor in experimental laboratories, nor in the class-rooms where it is taught, but in the minds of those engaged in directing educational activities. Results may be scientific, short of their operative presence in the attitudes and habits of observation, judgment and planning of those engaged in the educative act. But they are not *educational* science short of this point. They are psychology, sociology, statistics, or whatever.

This is the point upon which my whole discussion turns. We must distinguish between the *sources of educational science* and scientific content. We are in constant danger of confusing the two; we tend to suppose that certain results, because they are scientific, are already educational science. Enlightenment, clarity and progress can come about only as we remember that such results are *sources* to be used, through the medium of the minds of educators, to make educational functions more intelligent.

EDUCATIVE PROCESSES AS A SOURCE

The first question which comes before us is what is the place and role of educative processes and results in the school, family, etc., when they are viewed as a *source*? The answer is (1) that educational *practices* provide the data, the subject-matter, which form the *problems* of inquiry. They are the sole source of the ultimate problems to be investigated. These educational practices are also (2) the final *test of value* of the conclusion of all researches. To suppose that scientific findings decide the value of educational undertakings is to reverse the real case. Actual activities in *educating* test the worth of scientific results. They may be scientific in some other field, but not in education until they serve educational purposes, and whether they really serve or not can be found out only in practice. The latter comes first and last; it is the beginning and the close: the beginning, because it sets the problems which alone give to investigations educational point and quality; the close, because practice alone can test, verify, modify and develop the conclusions of these investigations. The position of scientific conclusions is intermediate and auxiliary.

ILLUSTRATION FROM ENGINEERING

The development of engineering science affords a pertinent illustration and confirmation. Men built bridges before there was any science of mathematics and physics. But with the latter development, with formulae of mechanics, statics, thrusts, stresses and strains, there arose the possibility of building bridges more efficiently, and ability to build them under conditions which previous methods were incompetent to cope with. *Bridge building* sets problems to be dealt with theoretically. Mathematics and mechanics are the sciences which handle the question. But their results are tried out, confirmed or the contrary, in new practical enterprises of bridge building, and thus new material is acquired which sets new problems to those who use mathematics and physics as tools, and so on indefinitely.

There is a science of bridge building in the sense that there is a certain body of *independent* scientific material, say mathematics and mechanics, from which selections may be made and the selections organized to bring about more effective solution in practice of the difficulties and obstructions that present themselves in actual building of bridges. It is the way the material is handled and organized with reference to a purpose that gives us a right to speak of a science of bridge building, although the building itself is an art, not a science. The sciences of mechanics and mathematics are, in themselves, the sciences which they are, not sciences of bridge building. They *become* the latter when selected portions of them are focused upon the problems presented in the art of bridge building.

Science of Education not Independent

Two conclusions as to the sources of educational science are now before us.

First, educational practices furnish the material that sets the problems of such a science, while sciences already developed to a fair state of maturity are the sources from which material is derived to deal intellectually with these problems. There is no more a special independent science of education than there is of bridge making. But material drawn from *other* sciences furnishes the content of educational science when it is focused on the problems that arise in education.

ILLUSTRATIONS FROM MEASUREMENTS

Illustrations may be given of the use of measurements to guide the intelligence of teachers instead of as dictating rules of action. Thus it is reported that teachers in a high school were puzzled by discrepancies between achievements and intelligence quotients. So one of the teachers was relieved of some of her classes to visit parents and homes and interview students. Within two years this had become a full time position, contacts with clinics and other public agencies established, and there was an extension of the concept "problem student" to include other types of maladjustment than the intellectual. Again it is reported that psychological ratings were used as tentative guides to shift children about till the place was found where they could do their best work. In other schools that have taken over more or less of the work of the juvenile court, truant officers, medical inspectors and visiting nurses, the I.Q. reports are correlated with factors ascertained in these other lines before there is direct use of them.[1] A homogeneous grouping without intervening inquiries approximates dangerously to transforming a theoretical finding into a rule of action.

It is empirically noted that one teacher has upon pupils an effect that is qualitatively termed inspiring, awakening, and that the personality of another teacher is relatively deadening, dull-

---

1. The illustrations are taken from Thomas, W. and D. S., *The Child in America.*

ing. Now here is a problem set for inquiry, whether the sciences which have to be drawn upon are sufficiently advanced to provide material for its solution or not. In this case, the science upon which a draft must be made is presumably that of social psychology, dealing with the interactions of persons. The original facts are raw material, crude data. They are not part of the science save as they set the problem and give direction to inquiry: in so doing they may lead to developments within social psychology itself. But it is the latter which is the direct source of the content of educational science in this case.

If it is empirically noticed that the stimulating effect of some teachers is followed later on by a blasé indifference, or in emotional over-excitability, on the part of some students, a further problem is set, new discriminations have to be made, and so on.

It is noted that children in some rooms, or at certain times of day are languid and dull and work inefficiently. This condition, even on an empirical basis, raises the question of ventilation, heating, etc. There is a problem set for scientific inquiry. Not education but physiology and chemistry are the sources drawn upon. Some statement of the detailed correlation between conditions of air, temperature and moisture and the state of organic efficiency of pupils may be reached; a solution in terms of a definite mechanism, of *how* things are linked together.

Difficulties arising in temperament and deep-seated habits may be so great that the scientific result in the first case will not seriously affect the teacher whose influence on pupils is undesirable. But it *may* be of aid in correction of attitudes; and, in any case, it gives useful information to administrators in dealing with such persons. In the other instance, teachers have an intellectual ground for alertness in observing physical conditions in their class-rooms and organic symptoms in their children that they did not have before. There is then a case of educational science in operation. What is done consists of acts, not of science. But science takes effect in rendering these activities more intelligent. If teachers are sufficiently alert and intelligent, they go on to notice conditions of the same general nature, but more subtle, and set a problem for further more refined inquiry. In any case, there will be a distinct difference in attitude between the teacher who merely puts into effect certain rules about opening windows, reducing temperature, etc., and the one who performed similar acts because of personal observation and understanding.

A further conclusion follows regarding the sciences that are the source of effective means for dealing with them. We may fairly enough call educational practice a kind of social engineering. Giving it that name at once provokes notice that as an art it is much more backward than branches of physical engineering, like land surveying, bridge-building and construction of railways. The reason is obvious. After all allowance is made for less systematic training for persons who engage in the art of education, the outstanding fact is that the sciences which must be drawn upon to supply scientific content to the work of the practitioner in education are themselves less mature than those which furnish the intellectual content of engineering. The human sciences that are sources of the scientific content of education—biology, psychology and sociology—for example, are relatively backward compared with mathematics and mechanics.

This statement is not an innocuous truism, for important consequences flow from taking it to heart. In the first place, just as the problems arising on the practical side in modern industry, for example, have been an important factor in stimulating researches in heat, electricity and light, so the problems that show themselves in educational practice should furnish agencies to direct the humane sciences into intellectually fruitful channels. It is not practice alone that has suffered from isolation of thinkers in the social and psychological disciplines from the occurrences taking place in schools. Indifference to the latter, a hardly veiled intellectual contempt for them, has undoubtedly strengthened the rule of convention, routine and accidental opinion in the schools. But it has also deprived the sciences in question of problems that would have stimulated significant inquiry and reflection. Much of the barrenness and loose speculation in the humane sciences is directly due to remoteness from the material that would stimulate, direct and test thought. Nothing in our recent situation is more promising for scientific development than the fact that the intellectual distance between university and elementary school, for example, is lessening.

In the second place, frank recognition of the relative backwardness of the sciences that must form the main content of educational science is a protection as well as a stimulus. Recognition that genuine growth in educational science is dependent upon prior advance in other subjects prevents us from entertaining premature and exaggerated expectations. It would, if fully recognized, deter workers in the field from efforts at premature introduction into school practice of materials whose real value lies only in the contribution they may make to the further building up of scientific content; it would militate against exploitation of results that are as yet only half-baked. And it would impress upon workers in the field of educational science the need for thorough equipment in the sciences upon which the science of education must draw.

At this point, the fact that educational practices are a source of the *problems* of educational science rather than of its definite material is especially significant. Adequate recognition that the source of the really scientific content is found in other sciences would compel attempt at mastery of what they have to offer. With respect to statistical theory this lesson has been pretty well learned. Whether it has been with respect to other disciplines, or even with respect to the separate and exclusive application of statistics to the solution of educational problems, is open to doubt.

Finally, recognition of this obvious fact would be a protection against attempting to extract from psychology and sociology definite solutions which it is beyond their present power to give. Such attempts, even when made unconsciously and with laudable intent to render education more scientific, defeat their own purpose and create reactions against the very concept of educational science. Learning to wait is one of the important things that scientific method teaches, and the extent in which this lesson has been learned is one fair measure of the claim to a hearing on the part of workers in the field of education.

Arm-chair Science

There is a second and more positive connection between educational practices which set problems and the sciences that are sources of material for dealing with them. The objection to arm-chair science is not that thinking is done in arm-chairs. A certain amount of downright thinking going on quietly in the head is as necessary to the development of any science as is the activity of the senses and the hands in the laboratory. The arm-chair may be a good place in which to do this thinking. The objection is to the remoteness of the thinking which is done from the original source of intellectual supplies. This remoteness may exist in work done in laboratories as well as in the arm-chair of the study. It is found whenever there is lack of vital connection between the field-work practice and the research work.

The practical obstacles here are numerous. The research persons connected with school systems may be too close to the practical problems and the university professor too far away from them, to secure the best results. The former may get too entangled in immediate detailed problems for the best work. Minor problems for immediate solution may be put up to him and not leave him time for investigations having a longer time-span. The latter may not have enough first-hand contact to discriminate the important problems from the secondary and the conditions which render them problems. He is then likely, also, to occupy himself with isolated and relatively trivial problems, a kind of scientific "busy-work," and yet may expect his results to be taken seriously by workers in the field.

Physical contact in any case is not so important as intellectual contact of a sympathetic sort. The indispensable necessity is that there be some kind of vital current flowing between the field worker and the research worker. Without this flow, the latter is not able to judge the real scope of the problem to which he addresses himself. He will not know enough of the conditions under which the particular problem presents itself in school to control his inquiry, nor be able to judge whether the resources of other sciences at his command enable him to deal with it effectively. Nor will he understand enough of the concrete situations under which his finally preferred solution is to be applied to know whether it is a real or an artificial and arbitrary solution. If it is the latter, it may succeed in dealing with the more obvious difficulties of a situation, the external symptoms, but fail to hit basic causes, and may even set up more difficult because more obscure and subtle complications when it is applied.

ILLUSTRATIONS FROM SCHOOL REPORTS

The problem here is not, however, a one-sided one. It concerns the teacher and administrator, the field worker, as well as the researcher. Special conditions are required if the material of school practices is to be presented to others in such shape as to form the data of a problem. It perhaps suffices to refer, in illustration of this point, to the great improvement already brought in the handling of school reports, both administrative and instructional. Since the value of any piece of research is definitely conditioned by the data at command, it is almost impossible to put too much emphasis upon the importance of records and reports, and of the manner in which they are kept, qualitative as well as quantitative.

The value of this material to the investigator in education is almost like that of systematic and cumulative clinical records for medical science. There is an evident circle in this matter. The kind of reports that are asked for and secured depend upon the existing state of the science, upon the scientific interests that dominate at a particular time. They also furnish data for further inquiries and conclusions. Hence the need that they should not be too rapidly mechanized into a standard fixed form. There must be flexible room for change or else scientific arrest will come from a too rigid fixation of the molds in which data are cast.

THE TEACHER AS INVESTIGATOR

This factor of reports and records does not exhaust, by any means, the role of practitioners in building up a scientific content in educational activity. A constant flow of less formal reports on special school affairs and results is needed. Of the various possibilities here I select one for discussion. It seems to me that the contributions that might come from *class-room* teachers are a comparatively neglected field; or, to change the metaphor, an almost unworked mine. It is unnecessary to point out the large extent to which superintendents and principals have been drawn into the work of studying special problems and contributing material relative to them. It is to be hoped that the movement will not cease until all active class-room teachers, of whatever grade, are also drawn in.

There are undoubted obstacles in the way. It is often assumed, in effect if not in words, that class-room teachers have not themselves the training which will enable them to give effective intelligent cooperation. The objection proves too much, so much so that it is almost fatal to the idea of a workable scientific content in education. For these teachers are the ones in direct contact with pupils and hence the ones through whom the results of scientific findings finally reach students. They are the channels through which the consequences of educational theory come into the lives of those at school. I suspect that if these teachers are mainly channels of reception and transmission, the conclusions of science will be badly deflected and distorted before they get into the minds of pupils. I am inclined to believe that this state of affairs is a chief cause for the tendency, earlier alluded to, to convert scientific findings into recipes to be followed. The human desire to be an "authority" and to control the activities of others does not, alas, disappear when a man becomes a scientist.

A statistical study of, say the reports of the N.E.A., would show the actual percentage of contributions to educational discussion made by class-room teachers on that level. It would perhaps raise the query whether some of the incapacity, real or alleged, of this part of the corps of educators, the large mass of teachers, is not attributable to lack of opportunity and stimulus, rather than to inherent disqualifications. As far as schools are concerned, it is certain that the problems which require scientific treatment arise in actual relationships with students. Consequently, it is impossible to see how there can be an adequate flow of subject-matter to set and control the problems investigators deal with, unless there is active participation on the part of those directly engaged in teaching.

No Intrinsic Educational Science Content

If we now turn to the subjects from which are drawn the materials that are to be brought to bear upon educational problems, we are forced to recognize a fact already incidentally noted. There is no subject-matter intrinsically marked off, earmarked so to say, as the content of educational science. Any methods and any facts and principles from any subject whatsoever that enable the problems of administration and instruction to be dealt with in a bettered way are pertinent. Thus, in all that concerns the bearing of physical conditions upon the success of school work

—as in the case of ventilation, temperature, etc., already mentioned—physiology and related sciences are sources of scientific content. In other problems, such as making budgets, cost-accountings, etc., economic theory is drawn upon. It may be doubted whether with reference to some aspect or other of education there is any organized body of knowledge that may not need to be drawn upon to become a source of educational science.

This consideration explains many phenomena in the present situation. It accounts for the rapid growth of interest in the development of scientific content for educational practices in so many different lines of activity. We have become only recently alive to the complexity of the educative process and aware of the number and variety of disciplines that must contribute if the process is to go on in an intelligently directed way. In accounting for the manifestation of enthusiastic activity on the part of some, the situation also explains the skeptical indifference of many about the whole matter. Not merely inert conservatives in the general public but many professors in other lines in universities have not been awakened to the complexity of the educational undertaking. Hence, such persons regard the activities of those in departments of education as futile and void of serious meaning.

Failure to perceive that educational science has no content of its own leads, on the other hand, to a segregation of research which tends to render it futile. The assumption, if only tacit, that educational science has its own peculiar subject-matter results in an isolation which makes the latter a "mystery" in the sense in which the higher crafts were once mysteries. A superficial token of this isolation is found in the development of that peculiar terminology that has been called "pedagese." Segregation also accounts for the tendency, already mentioned, to go at educational affairs without a sufficient grounding in the non-educational disciplines that must be drawn upon, and hence to exaggerate minor points in an absurdly one-sided way, and to grasp at some special scientific technique as if its use were a magical guarantee of a scientific product.

Recognition of the variety of sciences that must be focused when solving any educational problem tends to breadth of view and to more serious and prolonged effort at balance of the variety of factors which enter into even the simplest problems of teaching and administration. The uncontrolled succession of waves of one-sided temporarily dominating interests and slogans that have affected educational practice and theory could thus be reduced.

Special Sources

In spite of the wide and indeterminate field of sciences that are sources of scientific content in education, there are certain subjects that occupy a privileged position. By common consent, I suppose, psychology and sociology hold such positions. The philosophy of education is a source of the science of education, but one less often recognized as such. We are, I think, habituated to thinking of the sciences as feeders of philosophy rather than of philosophy as a source of science. Philosophy is looked at by those who dignify it as a subject which analyzes critically the premises that are uncritically assumed in the special sciences, or else as a complete intellectual organization of their results. Others take a less respectful and perhaps more popular view of it, and regard it as a constantly vanishing quantity, dealing by way of opinion and speculation with matters that sciences have not got around to dealing with in a positive way. Personally, I think there is truth in both of these views, but that neither one touches the heart of the relationship of philosophy and science. There is in every subject at every time a serial progression from the more specific to the more general. The only distinction we can profitably draw is to say that science lies toward the specific pole and philosophy toward the general, while there is no definite line where one leaves off and the other begins.

It is because of this fact that there is a reciprocal relation between them, each feeding the other as a source. Were this the time and place, it could be shown from the history of the sciences, mathematical, physical and biological, that ideas originating at the philosophic end (general, often vague and speculative, if you please) have been indispensable factors in the generation of science. An examination of history would also show that there is no steady one-way movement; the movement from general to special is not one that has a definite conclusion that stays put. Specialized results recurrently get too set and rigid because of isolation due to the very specialization by which they are obtained. Fermentation and fructification then come in from the pole of general ideas and points of view. Specific results are shaken up, loosened and placed in new contexts.

ILLUSTRATIONS

The revolution in astronomical and physical science effected by Galileo, Descartes and Newton is a case in point. The controlling hypotheses were derived from philosophic ideas that seemed to their early contemporaries highly speculative. The idea of "evolution" was developed in philosophy before it made its appearance in biology. Metaphysical speculations regarding the relation of mind and body conditioned the creation and growth of physiological psychology.

These illustrations do not prove that the influence of philosophy as a source of science has been wholly to the good. On the contrary, there have been in every instance hang-overs from earlier philosophies which have been detrimental, and which have had to be eliminated from science with toil and pain. But aside from the fact that new general ideas have always played a part in finally getting rid of these hang-overs, it is an undeniable fact that the human mind works in this way, and that whether desirable or undesirable, it cannot be eliminated.

HYPOTHESES

If we ask why this should be so, we are at once confronted with the role of *hypotheses* in every scientific undertaking, because of the necessary place they occupy in every intellectual operation. Hypotheses form a scale from more general to more specific, and at every point the more general ones affect the more specific. This fact of dependence is overlooked only because the more general one is so incorporated in the special and detailed ones that it is forgotten. Then some crisis in scientific development leads to its detection and revision. Physical science is at present undergoing precisely such a reconstruction.

Philosophy of education is, accordingly, a source of the science of education in the degree in which it provides working hypotheses of comprehensive application. Both "working" and "hypotheses" are important. It is hypotheses, not fixed and final principles or truths that are provided; they have to be tested and modified as they are used in suggesting and directing the detailed work of observation and understanding. They are *working* ideas; special investigations become barren and one-sided in the degree in which they are conducted without reference to a wider, more general view. This statement is particularly applicable in the early stages of formation of a new science. Physics, chemistry, biology, all have behind them a history that has put them in possession of relatively tested and solid general principles. Just because educational science has no such achievement of laws to fall back upon, it is in a tentative and inchoate state which renders it especially in need of direction by large and fruitful hypotheses. No matter how these are obtained, they are intrinsically philosophical in nature, good or bad philosophy as the case may be. To treat them as scientific rather than as philosophic is to conceal from view their hypothetical character and to freeze them into rigid dogmas that hamper instead of assisting actual inquiry.

THE PURPOSE OF THE PHILOSOPHY OF EDUCATION

It is sometimes said that philosophy is concerned with determining the ends of education while the science of education determines the means to be used. As one who is a philosopher rather than a scientist I might be inclined to welcome a statement that confers upon philosophy such an honorable position. Without a good deal of interpretation, it is, however, likely to give rise to more false than true conceptions. In this interpretation there are two important considerations.

In the first place, the notion easily gives rise to, even if it does not logically imply, a misapprehension of the relation of a philosophy of education to educational practices and direct experience in the field. In any vital sense it is these practices which determine educational ends. Concrete educational experience is the primary source of all inquiry and reflection because it sets the problems, and tests, modifies, confirms or refutes the conclusions of intellectual investigation. The philosophy of education neither originates nor settles ends. It occupies an intermediate and instrumental or regulative place. Ends actually reached, consequences that actually accrue, are surveyed, and their values estimated in the light of a general scheme of values.

But if a philosophy starts to reason out its conclusions without definite and constant regard to the concrete experiences that define the problem for thought, it becomes speculative in a way that justifies contempt. As far as ends and values are concerned, the empirical material that is necessary to keep philosophy from being fantastic in content and dogmatic in form is supplied by the ends and values which are produced in educational processes as these are actually executed. What a philosophy of education can contribute is range, freedom and constructive or creative invention. The worker in any field gets preoccupied with more immediate urgencies and results. When one begins to extend the range, the scope, of thought, to consider obscure collateral consequences that show themselves in a more extensive time-span, or in reference to an enduring development, that one begins to philosophize whether the process is given that name or not. What is *termed* philosophy is only a more systematic and persistent performance of this office.

What I have termed the contribution of "freedom," of liberation, is a necessary accompaniment of this breadth of survey of actual ends or consequences. The professional practitioner in any field, from a factory to a church and schoolhouse, is in danger of getting tied down, of getting habit-bound, compensating for this rigidity by impulsive excursions, undertaken according to temperament and circumstance, when routine becomes intolerable. I do not say that philosophers see life steadily and see it whole; complete achievement in this respect is humanly impossible. But *any one* is philosophical in the degree in which he makes a consistent effort in this direction. The result is emancipation. When this liberation is confined within the mind, the inner consciousness, of any one, it affords intense personal gratification, but it effects nothing and becomes specious. Its effect is found only in operation. For a philosophy of education this operation is found in enabling practitioners to carry on their work in a more liberal spirit, with escape from tradition and routine and one-sided personal interests and whims.

This contribution is made by way of the third function mentioned; namely, constructive imagination and invention. It is not enough to criticize the narrow limitations of accepted ends and values. This needful task is but the negative side of the function of suggesting new ends, new methods, new materials. In performing this office, provision of scope of estimate and liberation of mind comes to a head. As far as the philosophy of education effects anything important, this is what it accomplishes for those who study it. Ideas are ideas, that is, suggestions for activities to be undertaken, for experiments to be tried. The proof of the pudding is in the eating. The philosophy of education not only draws its original material as to ends and value from actual experience in education, but it goes back to these experiences for testing, confirmation, modification, and the provision of further materials. This is what is meant when it is said that its work is intermediate and instrumental, not original nor final.

Our other point concerns the relations of science and philosophy with respect to means and ends. The statement as often made gives rise to misapprehension. It leads to the notion that means and ends are separate from each other, each having its own fixed province. In reality, ends that are incapable of realization are ends only in name. Ends must be framed in the light of available means. It may even be asserted that ends are only means brought to full interaction and integration. The other side of this truth is that means are fractional parts of ends. When means and ends are viewed as if they were separate, and to be dealt with by different persons who are concerned with independent provinces, there is imminent danger of two bad results.

Ends, values, become empty, verbal; too remote and isolated to have more than an emotional content. Means are taken to signify means already at hand, means accepted because they are already in common use. As far as this view prevails, the work of a science of education is reduced to the task of refining and perfecting the existing mechanism of school operations. Lack of efficiency, unnecessary waste, in the teaching of reading, writing, numbers, history, geography are detected so that they may be eliminated. More efficient methods of accomplishing the ends that already obtain are devised. This is good as far as it goes. But it overlooks a fundamental issue. How far do the existing ends, the actual consequences of current practices go, even when perfected? The important problem is devising *new* means in contradistinction to improved use of means already given. For "new means" does not signify merely new ways of accomplishing more efficiently ends already current, but means that will yield consequences, ends, that are qualitatively different. We can assign means to science and ends to philosophy only under the condition that there be persistent and unremitting interaction between the two.

PSYCHOLOGY

Little space remains in which to consider psychology and sociology as sources of educational science. However, the considerations already adduced supply, I think, suggestions by which many of the most important issues in these fields may be dealt with. For example, there is general agreement that psychology lies nearer to the question of means and the social sciences nearer to that of ends, or that the first is more closely connected with *how* pupils learn, whether knowledge or skill, and the latter with *what* they are to learn. But such a statement only brings us to the threshold of the problem of the relation between the "how" and the "what," means and ends. If the how and the what, the psychological and the social, method and subject-matter, must interact cooperatively in order to secure good results, a hard and fast distinction between them is fraught with danger. We want a method that will select subject-matter that aids psychological development, and we want a subject-matter that will secure the use of methods psychologically correct. We cannot begin by dividing the field between the psychology of individual activity and growth and studies or subject-matters that are socially desirable, and then expect that at the end in practical operation the two things will balance each other.

An unbiased survey of the situation will, I think, show that the danger is not merely theoretical. When we make a sharp distinction between *what* is learned and *how* we learn it, and assign the determination of the process of learning to psychology and of subject-matter to social science, the inevitable outcome is that the reaction of what is studied and learned upon the development of the person learning, upon the tastes, interests, and habits that control his future mental attitudes and responses is overlooked. In that degree the psychological account of the process of personal learning and growth is deficient and distorted. It then deals with a short segment of the learning process instead of with its continuities.

Social needs and conditions are said to dictate, for example, the necessity of instruction in reading, writing and number at a fairly early age. It is also recognized that these are useful factors in later personal growth, being the means of opening up learning in a variety of subjects. So far the two aspects seem to be in harmony. But suppose the question of how children learn most effectively to master these skills then be taken up in isolation, and methods are devised to promote the ready acquisition of the skills in question. The larger question is what other habits, including tastes and desires, are being collaterally formed.

That a person can learn efficiently to read and yet not form a taste for reading good literature, or without having curiosities aroused that will lead him to apply his ability to read to explore fields outside of what is conventionally termed good reading matter, are sad facts of experience. Learning to read may develop book-worms, children who read omnivorously, but at the expense of development of social and executive abilities and skills. The question of *what* one learns to read is thus inextricably bound up with the question of *how* one learns to read. Unfortunately, experience shows that the methods which most readily and efficiently bring about skill to read (or write, or figure) in its narrower sense of ability to recognize, pronounce and put together words, do not at the same time take care of the formation of attitudes that decide the uses to which the ability is to be put. This is the more important issue.

It will not do for the psychologist to content himself with saying in effect: "These other things are none of my business; I have shown how the child may most readily and efficiently form the skill. The rest is up to somebody else." It will not do because one skill is acquired, other abilities, preferences and disabilities are also learned, and these fall within the province of the psychological inquirer. This conclusion does not mean that the demonstration of how a particular skill is most readily formed is of no value. But it does mean that educationally speaking the problems of attendant radiations, expansions and contractions, are in the end more important, and that it is dangerous to take the part for the whole. Nor is it satisfactory to say that the part must be mastered before the whole can be attacked. For, by the nature of the case, the whole enters into the part, that is, it is a determining factor in the *way* in which one learns to read. Thus the consideration of how one learns to read in its connection with its effect upon future personal development and interests demands attention to desirable subject-matter. The social question is intertwined with the psychological.

QUALITATIVE VS. QUANTITATIVE VALUES

Interdependence determines the limits of quantitative measurements for educational science. That which can be measured is the specific, and that which is specific is that which can be isolated. The prestige of measurements in physical science should not be permitted to blind us to a fundamental educational issue: How far is education a matter of forming specific skills and acquiring special bodies of information which are capable of isolated treatment? It is no answer to say that a human being is always occupied in acquiring a special skill or a special body of facts, if he is learning anything at all. This is true. But the *educational* issue is what *other* things in the way of desires, tastes, aversions, abilities and disabilities he is learning along with his specific acquisitions.

The control of conditions demanded by laboratory work leads to a maximum of isolation of a few factors from other conditions. The scientific result is rigidly limited to what is established with these other conditions excluded. In educating individualities, no such exclusion can be had. The number of variables that enter in is enormous. The intelligence of the teacher is dependent upon the extent in which he takes into account the variables that are not obviously involved in his immediate special task. Judgment in such matter is of qualitative situations and must itself be qualitative.

The parent and educator deal with situations that never repeat one another. Exact quantitative determinations are far from meeting the demands of such situations, for they presuppose repetitions and exact uniformities. Exaggeration of their importance tends to cramp judgment, to substitute uniform rules for the free play of thought, and to emphasize the mechanical factors that also exist in schools. They contribute at most to the more efficient working of present practices in some subjects. They have already been fruitful in securing eliminations, especially in the more routine skills, such as the three R's. But they do not give any help in larger questions of reconstruction of curriculum and methods. What is worse, they divert attention and energy from the need of reconstructions due to change of social conditions and to the inertia of traditions of the school system.

More important psychological contributions may be expected from the psychology of individual growth. The greatest aid at this point is to be derived from biological psychology, social psychology and psychiatry. Biology is not at present in any large measure a quantitative science, and only harm can result from the attempt to build up a scientific content of education that skips over the biological sciences and allies itself with the physical and mathematical, those furthest remote from the needs, problems and activities of human beings. In the biological field, general considerations regarding processes of development are more fundamental than is the anatomy of the nervous system. The latter is important, but it is dangerous to build educational theory upon details selected from what is known and current at a particular time.

ILLUSTRATION FROM S-R PSYCHOLOGY

The stimulus-response psychology in the form in which it prevails at the present time, is an illustration. There is no doubt that the stimulus-response idea presents a truth of great value. But just now it tends to be interpreted in a way that isolates a particular narrow part of it, based on the mechanisms of reflex actions, from the general course of biological development. Then the idea of the bond that connects stimulus and response is taken to be of a hard and fast performed character, instead of a flexible and functional one. In addition, the place of any particular S-R bond in the entire system of behavior is overlooked, or else the whole system is reduced to an algebraic summation of original fixed, isolated units. The important activities of the sympathetic nervous system, and the fact that even the reflexes function in the service of needs of the whole system is overlooked. Moreover, particular S-R connections interpreted on the basis of isolated reflexes, are viewed as static cross-sections, and the factor most important in education, namely, the longitudinal, the temporal span of growth and change is neglected.

ILLUSTRATION FROM PSYCHIATRY

In many respects the findings of social psychology and psychiatry reenforce each other. For the latter has clearly brought out that most arrests of development, fixations and morbid human attitudes, are due to the reaction of association with others back upon the formation of attitudes and their subsequent career. The most harmful and undesirable emotional attitudes of children, so fundamental in development, especially fears, inferiorities, etc., have been shown to be due mainly to social conditioning. It has been practically demonstrated that no amount of repetition really fixes a habit apart from attendant emotional responses, and that these are influenced by association with others. Opportunities for constant success and positive achievement have been shown to be indispensable conditions for preventing the growth of inferiority complexes. The unconscious character of the major part of human motivation reveals the unwisdom of determining the selection of the activities of children on the basis of what they say when asked what they want to do—indeed of being very sparing in asking the question. It also forces greater attention to the attitudes that control, unconsciously, the dealings of adults with the young. Most positively of all, it compels constant attention to what children actually do in order that there may be ability to understand the forces that actually move them in their behavior.

No apology is made for emphasis upon the psychiatric side. The increasing number of insane and neurotics is itself evidence of great failure and evil in our educational processes, parental and scholastic. Even more significant is the discovery in psychiatry itself of the number of morbid displacements, injurious to both happiness and social usefulness, found in persons called normal. Conventional and traditional methods, in instruction and discipline, are continuously engaged in manufacturing morbid fixations and dislocations. But when the latter reveal themselves they are usually attributed to some inherent psychological cause, some element of defect or perversity, inherent in the human nature of those taught, while in fact by far the greater part of them are induced growths, having their cause in the relations set up in some social contact. A knowledge of social psychology in connection with psychiatry, both being used to interpret the processes of normal physiological activity, are indispensable to any rounded out scientific content for educational activity.

SOCIOLOGY

I come now to the contribution of sociology—by which for present purposes I mean all the social disciplines—to the scientific content of education. Fortunately, it is not necessary to insist at this day and date upon the importance of this factor. Like the word "social," the words "socialized education" are in the air. The questions that call for discussion concern how the idea is to be interpreted. Time permits of mention of only two points. One relates to the position of *social tools*. The most obvious example of such tools is skill in language (reading, spelling and writing) and number. But these are only instances. Manners also form a social tool and so do morals in one of its aspects. A considerable portion of geography and history do so, and also elementary science, as well as some traits of the fine arts. In fact, it would be hard to draw a line at any point in the educational scheme; consider, for example, the necessities of the professional students in medicine and law to master certain skills and bodies of fact as social tools. The only difference among subjects of the curriculum as to social tools seems to be a matter of degree.

In view of this fact, the current habit of speaking only of some skills as social tools suggests the need for thought. The cause for their being selected as *the* social tools becomes evident, I think, when we notice that the things usually called social tools are the most *formal* parts of the curriculum. These subjects and skill in employing them are formal because they are separated from social content; they are social tools prospectively rather than at the time they are learned. Emphasis upon repetition, making their acquisition a frequency function, is proof of this isolation from direct social subject-matter and value.

I am not going to discuss this point. I use it as an illustration of the current division, found in many subjects, between social tools and social consequences. The net effect of this division upon the contribution social subject-matter makes to educational science is serious. The tools that are recognized to be social are not treated socially but are relegated to the mechanics of psychology. In so far as they are not socially controlled, the social use to which they are finally put is accidental. School practices are in this respect, in many modern schools, ahead of theory. Those engaged in the act of teaching know that the social tools are best acquired in a social context and for the sake of some social application falling within a nearby phase of life.

When skill in and with tools is not socially formed, that is, generated for social ends, the latter are separated from the means by which they should be controlled. To take just one instance: The kind of reading-matter that now most abounds socially, as may be gathered from a glance at newsstands, is largely of a socially *undesirable* character. Yet it can be sold only to readers, to those in possession of the so-called social tools. Pages of exposition would not speak more eloquently of what is bound to happen when educational theory separates, in the name of science, the psychological processes that regulate the mere mechanism of acquiring a skill from the social conditions and needs which have to do with the application of that skill.

The other point about the contribution of sociology to educational science concerns the determination of values, of objectives. The shortest cut to get something that looks scientific is to make a statistical study of existing practices and desires, with the supposition that their accurate determination will settle the subject-matter to be taught, thus taking curriculum-forming out of the air, putting it on a solid factual basis. This signifies, in effect and in logic, that the kind of education which the social environment gives unconsciously and in connection with all its defects, perversions and distortions, is the kind of education the schools should give consciously. Such an idea is almost enough to cause one to turn back to the theories of classicists who would confine the important subject-matter of instruction to the best of the products of the past, in disregard of present and prospective social conditions. It is hard to see any cause for such a procedure except a desire to demonstrate the value of "educational science" by showing that it has something immediate and direct to furnish in the guidance of schools.

Educational Values

This matter opens up the field of educational values and objectives. How are they to be determined? From what are they derived? The assumption that gives rise to the procedures just criticized is the belief that social conditions determine educational objectives. This is a fallacy. Education is autonomous and should be free to determine its own ends, its own objectives. To go outside the educational function and to borrow objectives from an external source is to surrender the educational cause. Until educators get the independence and courage to insist that educational aims are to be formed as well as executed within the educative process, they will not come to consciousness of their own function. Others will then have no great respect for educators because educators do not respect their own social place and work.

Such a statement will seem to many persons both absurd and presumptuous. It would be presumptuous if it had been said that *educators* should determine objectives. But the statement was that the *educative process* in its integrity and continuity should determine them. Educators have a place in this process, but they are not it, far from it. The notion that it is absurd springs from failure to view the function in its entirety. For education is itself a process of discovering what values are worth while and are to be pursued as objectives. To see what is going on and to observe the results of what goes on so as to see their further consequences in the process of growth, and so on indefinitely, is the only way in which the value of what takes place can be judged. To look to some outside source to provide aims is to fail to know what education is as an ongoing process. What a society is, it is, by and large, as a product of education, as far as its animating spirit and purpose are concerned. Hence it does not furnish a standard to which education is to conform. It supplies material by which to judge more clearly what education as it has been carried on has done to those who have been subjected to it. Another conclusion follows. There is no such thing as a fixed and final set of objectives, even for the time being or temporarily. Each day of teaching ought to enable a teacher to revise and better in some respect the objectives aimed at in previous work.

In saying these things, I am only recurring in another form to the idea with which I set out. The scientific content of education consists of whatever subject-matter, selected from other fields, enables the educator, whether administrator or teacher, to see and to think more clearly and deeply about whatever he is doing. Its value is not to supply objectives to him, any more than it is to supply him with ready-made rules. Education is a mode of life, of action. As an act it is wider than science. The latter, however, renders those who engage in the act more intelligent, more thoughtful, more aware of what they are about, and thus able to rectify and enrich in the future what they have been doing in the past. Knowledge of the objectives which society actually strives for and the consequences actually attained may be had in some measure through a study of the social sciences. This knowledge may render educators more circumspect, more critical, as to what they are doing. It may inspire better insight into what is going on here and now in the home or school; it may enable teachers and parents to look further ahead and judge on the basis of consequences in a longer course of developments. But it must operate through their own ideas, plannings, observations, judgments. Otherwise it is not *educational* science at all, but merely so much sociological information.

General Conclusion

The sources of educational science are any portions of ascertained knowledge that enter into the heart, head and hands of educators, and which, by entering in, render the performance of the educational function more enlightened, more humane, more truly educational than it was before. But there is no way to discover what *is* "more truly educational" except by the continuation of the educational act itself. The discovery is never made; it is always making. It may conduce to immediate ease or momentary efficiency to seek an answer for questions outside of education, in some material which already has scientific prestige. But such a seeking is an abdication, a surrender. In the end, it only lessens the chances that education in actual operation will provide the materials for an improved science. It arrests growth; it prevents the thinking that is the final source of all progress. Education is by its nature an endless circle or spiral. It is an activity which *includes* science within itself. In its very process it sets more problems to be further studied, which then react into the educative process to change it still further, and thus demand more thought, more science, and so on, in everlasting sequence.

Individualism, Old and New

Prefatory Note

I am obliged to the courtesy of the editors of the *New Republic* for permission to use material that originally appeared in the columns of that journal and which is now incorporated in connection with considerable new matter, in this volume. It is a pleasure to acknowledge my particular indebtedness to Mr. Daniel Mebane, the treasurer of the *New Republic*, for valuable suggestions and assistance.

1. The House Divided against Itself

It is becoming a commonplace to say that in thought and feeling, or at least in the language in which they are expressed, we are living in some bygone century, anywhere from the thirteenth to the eighteenth, although physically and externally we belong to the twentieth century. In such a contradictory condition, it is not surprising that a report of American life, such as is contained, for example, in *Middletown*, should frequently refer to a "bewildered" or "confused" state of mind as characteristic of us.

Anthropologically speaking, we are living in a money culture. Its cult and rites dominate. "The money medium of exchange and the cluster of activities associated with its acquisition drastically condition the other activities of the people." This, of course, is as it should be; people have to make a living, do they not? And for what should they work if not for money, and how should they get goods and enjoyments if not by buying them with money—thus enabling someone else to make more money, and in the end to start shops and factories to give employment to still others, so that they can make more money to enable other people to make more money by selling goods—and so on indefinitely. So far, all is for the best in the best of all possible cultures: our rugged—or is it ragged?—individualism.

And if the culture pattern works out so that society is divided into two classes, the working group and the business (including professional) group, with two and a half times as many in the former as in the latter, and with the chief ambition of parents in the former class that their children should climb into the latter, that is doubtless because American life offers such unparalleled

[First published as "The House Divided against Itself," in *New Republic* 58 (24 April 1929): 270–71.]

opportunities for each individual to prosper according to his virtues. If few workers know what they are making or the meaning of what they do, and still fewer know what becomes of the work of their hands—in the largest industry of Middletown perhaps one-tenth of one percent of the product is consumed locally—this is doubtless because we have so perfected our system of distribution that the whole country is one. And if the mass of workers live in constant fear of loss of their jobs, this is doubtless because our spirit of progress, manifest in change of fashions, invention of new machines and power of overproduction, keeps everything on the move. Our reward of industry and thrift is so accurately adjusted to individual ability that it is natural and proper that the workers should look forward with dread to the age of fifty or fifty-five, when they will be laid on the shelf.

All this we take for granted; it is treated as an inevitable part of our social system. To dwell on the dark side of it is to blaspheme against our religion of prosperity. But it is a system that calls for a hard and strenuous philosophy. If one looks at what we do and what happens, and then expects to find a theory of life that harmonizes with the actual situation, he will be shocked by the contradiction he comes upon. For the situation calls for assertion of complete economic determinism. We live as if economic forces determined the growth and decay of institutions and settled the fate of individuals. Liberty becomes a well-nigh obsolete term; we start, go, and stop at the signal of a vast industrial machine. Again, the actual system would seem to imply a pretty definitely materialistic scheme of value. Worth is measured by ability to hold one's own or to get ahead in a competitive pecuniary race. "Within the privacy of shabby or ambitious houses, marriage, birth, child-rearing, death, and the personal immensities of family life go forward. However, it is not so much these functional urgencies of life that determine how favorable this physical necessity shall be, but the extraneous detail of how much money the father earns." The philosophy appropriate to such a situation is that of struggle for existence and survival of the economically fit. One would expect the current theory of life, if it reflects the actual situation, to be the most drastic Darwinism. And, finally, one would anticipate that the personal traits most prized would be clear-sighted vision of personal advantage and resolute ambition to secure it at any human cost. Sentiment and sympathy would be at the lowest discount.

It is unnecessary to say that the current view of life in Middletown, in Anytown, is nothing of this sort. Nothing gives us Americans the horrors more than to hear that some misguided creature in some low part of the earth preaches what we practise—and practise much more efficiently than anyone else— namely, economic determinism. Our whole theory is that man plans and uses machines for his own humane and moral purposes, instead of being borne wherever the machine carries him. Instead of materialism, our idealism is probably the loudest and most frequently professed philosophy the world has ever heard. We praise even our most successful men, not for their ruthless and self-centered energy in getting ahead, but because of their love of flowers, children, and dogs, or their kindness to aged relatives. Anyone who frankly urges a selfish creed of life is everywhere frowned upon. Along with the disappearance of the home, and the multiplication of divorce in one generation by 600 percent, there is the most abundant and most sentimental glorification of the sacredness of home and the beauties of constant love that history can record. We are surcharged with altruism and bursting with desire to "serve" others.

These are only a few of the obvious contradictions between our institutions and practice on one hand, and our creeds and theories on the other, contradictions which a survey of any of our Middletowns reveals. It is not surprising that the inhabitants of these towns are bewildered, uneasy, restless, always seeking something new and different, only to find, as a rule, the same old thing in a new dress. It may all be summed up, perhaps, by saying that nowhere in the world at any time has religion been so thoroughly respectable as with us, and so nearly totally disconnected from life. I hesitate to dwell on the revelation that this book gives of "religious" life in Middletown. The glorification of religion as setting the final seal of approval on pecuniary success, and supplying the active motive to more energetic struggle for such success, and the adoption by the churches of the latest devices of the movies and the advertiser, approach too close to the obscene. Schooling is developed to the point where more pupils reach the high school than in other lands; and one-half of the pupils in the last years of the high school think that the first chapters of the Hebrew Scriptures give a more accurate account of the origin and early history of man than does science, and only one-fifth actively dissent. If the investigation had been made when a certain questionnaire was distributed among our school children, it is likely that the usual percentage of youth would have recorded their belief that Harding was the greatest man in the world. In another way, the whole story is told in brief when one contrasts what is actually happening to family life and the complete secularization of daily activities with a statement from the pulpit that "the three notable words in the English language are mother, home and heaven," a remark that would certainly pass unquestioned in any representative American audience.

It makes little difference whether one selects important or trivial aspects of the contradiction between our life as we outwardly live it and our thoughts and feelings—or what we at least say are our beliefs and sentiments. The significant question is: What is the cause of this split and contradiction? There are those, of course, who attribute it to the fact that people being, generally speaking, morons and boobs, they must be expected to act out the parts to which they are assigned. The "explanation" does not take us very far, even if one accepts it. The particular forms that the alleged boobery takes are left quite unaccounted for. And the more one knows of history, the more one comes to believe that traditions and institutions count more than native capacity or incapacity in explaining things. It is evident enough that the rapid industrialization of our civilization took us unawares. Being mentally and morally unprepared, our older creeds have become ingrowing; the more we depart from them in fact, the more loudly we proclaim them. In effect we treat them as magic formulae. By repeating them often enough we hope to ward off the evils of the new situation, or at least to prevent ourselves from seeing them—and this latter function is ably performed by our nominal beliefs.

With an enormous command of instrumentalities, with possession of a secure technology, we glorify the past, and legalize and idealize the *status quo*, instead of seriously asking how we are to employ the means at our disposal so as to form an equitable and stable society. This is our great abdication. It explains how and why we are a house divided against itself. Our tradition, our heritage, is itself double. It contains in itself the ideal of equality of opportunity and of freedom for all, without regard to birth and status, as a condition for the effective realization of that equality. This ideal and endeavor in its behalf once constituted our essential Americanism; that which was prized as the note of a new world. It is the genuinely spiritual element of our tradition. No one can truthfully say that it has entirely disappeared. But its promise of a new moral and religious outlook has not been attained. It has not become the well-spring of a new intellectual consensus; it is not (even unconsciously) the vital source of any distinctive and shared philosophy. It directs our politics only spasmodically, and while it has generously provided schools it does not control their aims or their methods.

Meanwhile our institutions embody another and older tradition. Industry and business conducted for money profit are nothing new; they are not the product of our own age and culture; they come to us from a long past. But the invention of the machine has given them a power and scope they never had in the past from which they derive. Our law and politics and the incidents of human association depend upon a novel combination of the machine and money, and the result is the pecuniary culture characteristic of our civilization. The spiritual factor of our tradition, equal opportunity and free association and intercommunication, is obscured and crowded out. Instead of the development of individualities which it prophetically set forth, there is a perversion of the whole ideal of individualism to conform to the practices of a pecuniary culture. It has become the source and justification of inequalities and oppressions. Hence our compromises, and the conflicts in which aims and standards are confused beyond recognition.

2. "America"—By Formula

We have heard a good deal of late years of class-consciousness. The phrase "nation-conscious" does not happen to be current, but present-day nationalism is an exacerbated expression of it in fact. A still more recent manifestation might be called "culture-consciousness" or "civilization-consciousness." Like class-consciousness and nationalism, it assumes an invidious form; it is an exponent—and a coefficient—of conflict between groups. The war and its consequences may not have produced in our own country a consciousness of "Americanism" as a distinctive mode of civilization but they have definitely had that effect among the intellectual elite of Europe.

Americanism as a form of culture did not exist, before the war, for Europeans. Now it does exist and as a menace. In reaction and as a protest, there is developing, at least among literary folk, the consciousness of a culture which is distinctively European, something which is precious and whose very existence is threatened by an invasion of a new form of barbarism issuing from the United States. Acute hostility to a powerful alien influence is taking the place of complacent ignoring of what was felt to be negligible. It would take a wider knowledge than mine to list even the titles of books and articles coming yearly from the presses of Europe whose burden is the threat of "America" to the traditional culture of Europe.

I am not concerned here with the European side of the matter. Most social unifications come about in response to external pressure. The same is likely to be true of a United States of Europe. If the ideal is approximated in reality, it will probably be as a protective reaction to the economic and financial hegemony of the United States of America. The result would probably be a good

[First published as "'America'—By Formula," in *New Republic* 60 (18 September 1929): 117–19.]

thing for Europe, and thus unwittingly we should serve one good purpose, internationally speaking. But it is, in the end, no great consolation to know that in losing our own soul we have been a means of helping save the soul of some one else. Just what is the America whose picture is forming in the minds of European critics?

Some of the writers are ignorant as well as bitter. These may be neglected. Others are intelligent, as well-informed as any foreigner can be about a foreign country, and not devoid of sympathy. Moreover their judgments agree not only with one another but with the protests of native-born dissenters. For convenience and because of the straightforward intelligence of its author, I take as a point of departure, the description of the American type of mind and character presented by Mueller Freienfels.[1] His treatment is the fairer because he understands by "American" a type of mind that is developing, from like causes, all over the world, and which would have emerged in time in Europe, even if there were no geographical America, although its development in the rest of the world has been accelerated and intensified by the influence of this country.

As far as any actual American is true to the type that is proclaimed to be *the* American, he should be thrilled by the picture that is drawn of him. For we are told that the type is a genuine mutation in the history of culture; that it is new, the product of the last century, and that it is stamped with success. It is transforming the external conditions of life and thereby reacting on the psychical content of life; it is assimilating other types of itself and re-coining them. No world-conquest, whether that of Rome or Christendom, compares with that of "Americanism" in extent or effectiveness. If success and quantity are in fact the standards of the "American," here are admissions that will content his soul. From the standpoint of the type depicted, he is approved; and what do adverse criticisms matter?

But either the type is not yet so definitely fixed as is represented, or else there are individual Americans who deviate from type. For there are many who will have reserves in their admira-

---

1. *Mysteries of the Soul*, translated from the German by Bernard Miall; New York, Knopf, 1929. It may be well to add, in view of the title, that there is nothing occult nor obscurantist about the book. By "soul" is meant "the manifold living reciprocal reactions between the self and the universe."

tion of the picture that is presented. Of course the dissenters may be, as the European critics say, impotent sports, fish out of water and affected with nostalgia for the European tradition. Nevertheless, it is worth while to raise the question as to whether the American type, supposing there is to be one, has as yet taken on definitive form. First, however, what are alleged to be the characteristics of the type?

Fundamentally, they spring from impersonality. The roots of the intellect are unconscious and vital, in instincts and emotions. In America, we are told, this subconsciousness is disregarded; it is suppressed or is subordinated to conscious rationality, which means that it is adapted to the needs and conditions of the external world. We have "intellect," but distinctly in the Bergsonian sense; mind attuned to the conditions of action upon matter, upon the world. Our emotional life is quick, excitable, undiscriminating, lacking in individuality and in direction by intellectual life. Hence the "externality and superficiality of the American soul"; it has no ultimate inner unity and uniqueness—no true personality.

The marks and signs of this "impersonalization" of the human soul are quantification of life, with its attendant disregard of quality; its mechanization and the almost universal habit of esteeming technique as an end, not as a means, so that organic and intellectual life is also "rationalized"; and, finally, standardization. Differences and distinctions are ignored and overridden; agreement, similarity, is the ideal. There is not only absence of social discrimination but of intellectual; critical thinking is conspicuous by its absence. Our pronounced trait is mass suggestibility. The adaptability and flexibility that we display in our practical intelligence when dealing with external conditions have found their way into our souls. Homogeneity of thought and emotion has become an ideal.

Quantification, mechanization and standardization: these are then the marks of the Americanization that is conquering the world. They have their good side; external conditions and the standard of living are undoubtedly improved. But their effects are not limited to these matters; they have invaded mind and character, and subdued the soul to their own dye. The criticism is familiar; it is so much the burden of our own critics that one is never quite sure how much of the picture of foreign critics is drawn from direct observation and how much from native novels and essays that are not complacent with the American scene. This fact does not detract from the force of the indictment; it rather adds to it, and raises the more insistently the question of what our life means.

I shall not deny the existence of these characteristics, nor of the manifold evils of superficialism and externalism that result in the production of intellectual and moral mediocrity. In the main these traits exist and they characterize American life and are already beginning to dominate that of other countries. But their import is another thing than their existence. Mueller Freienfels is intelligent enough to acknowledge that they are transitional rather than final. He recognizes that the forces are so intrinsic that it is foolish to rebel against them and lament the past. "The question is how we are to pass through them and transcend them." It is this note which distinguishes his appraisal from so many others.

In reply to the question, one may at least say that we are still in an early stage of the transition. Anything that is at most but a hundred years old has hardly had time to disclose its meaning in the slow secular processes of human history. And it may be questioned whether even our author has not sometimes succumbed to the weakness of lesser critics in treating the passing symptoms as inherent characters. I do not have in mind here an "optimistic" appeal to future time and its possibilities. I rather wish to raise the question as to how many of the defects and evils that are supposed to belong to the present order are in fact projections into it of a departing past order.

Strength, power, is always relative, not absolute. Conquest is an exhibition of weakness in the conquered as well as of strength in the conqueror. Transitions are out of something as well as into something; they reveal a past as well as project a future. There must have been something profoundly awry in the quality, spirituality and individualized variety of the past, or they would not have succumbed as readily as we are told they are doing to the quantification, mechanization and standardization of the present. And the defective and perverse elements have certainly not been displaced. They survive in the present. Present conditions give these factors an opportunity to disclose themselves. They are not now kept under and out of sight. Their overt manifestation is not a cheering spectacle. But as long as they did not show themselves on a scale large enough to attract notice, they could not be dealt with. I wonder very much whether many of the things that are objected to in the present scene—and justly so—are not in fact revelations of what the older type of culture covered up, and whether their perceptible presence is not to be credited rather than debited to the forces that are now active.

It is possible of course to argue—as Keyserling for example seems to do—that the new or American order signifies simply that the animal instincts of man have been released, while the older European tradition kept them in disciplined subjection to something higher, called with pleasing vagueness "spirituality." The suspicion that suppression is not solution is not confined to America. Undue and indiscriminate greediness in the presence of accessible food may be a symptom of previous starvation rather than an inevitable exhibition of the old Adam. A culture whose tradition rests on depreciation of the flesh and on making a sharp difference between body and mind, instinct and reason, practice and theory, may have wrought corruption of flesh and degeneration of spirit. It would take a degree of wisdom no one possesses to tell just what, in the undesirable features of the present, is a reflection of an old but not as yet transformed system of life and thought, and how much is a genuine product of the new forces.

One thing seems to be reasonably certain. The prized and vaunted "individuality" of European culture that is threatened by the leveling standardization and uniformity of the American type was a very limited affair. If one were to retort in kind, one could ask how much share in it was had by the peasant and proletarian. And it is much more than a retort to say that a peasantry and proletariat which has been released from intellectual bondage will for a time have its revenge. Because there is no magic in democracy to confer immediately the power of critical discrimination upon the masses who have been outside any intellectual movement, and who have taken their morals and their religion from an external authority above them—an authority which science is destroying—it does not follow that the ineptitude of the many is the creation of democracy.

Take one instance—the present interest in technique, and the domination of the "American type" by technique. It will hardly be argued I suppose that the mere absence of technique—intelligent means and methods for securing results—is itself a mark of an intrinsically desirable civilization. Nor is it surprising that the discovery of the actuality and potentiality of technique in all branches of human life should have an immediately intoxicating effect. What is called the American mentality is characterized by this discovery, and by the exaggerations that come with the abruptness of the discovery. There is much to be said against quantification and standardization. But the discovery of competent technique stands on a different level. The world has not suffered from absence of ideals and spiritual aims anywhere nearly as much as it has suffered from absence of means for realizing the ends which it has prized in a literary and sentimental way. Technique is still a novelty in most matters, and like most novelties is played with for a while on its own account. But it will be used for ends beyond itself sometime; and I think that interest in technique is precisely the thing which is most promising in our civilization, the thing which in the end will break down devotion to external standardization and the mass-quantity ideal. For its application has not gone far as yet; and interest in it is still largely vicarious, being that, so to say, of the spectator rather than of naturalization in use. In the end, technique can only signify emancipation of individuality, and emancipation on a broader scale than has obtained in the past.

In his most hopeful anticipation of a future to which we may be moving, Freienfels calls attention to the fact that the impoverishment of the individual is accompanied, even now, by an enrichment of community resources. Collectively, present society, he says, is marked by a power over nature and by intellectual resource and power exceeding that of the classic Athenian and the man of the Renaissance. Why is it that this collective enrichment does not operate to elevate correspondingly the life of individuals? This question he does not ask. Failure to consider it constitutes to my mind the chief failure of critics whether foreign or native. Our materialism, our devotion to money making and to having a good time are not things by themselves. They are the product of the fact that we live in a money culture; of the fact that our technique and technology are controlled by interest in private profit. There lies the serious and fundamental defect of our civilization, the source of the secondary and induced evils to which so much attention is given. Critics are dealing with symptoms and effects. The evasion of fundamental economic causes by critics both foreign and native seems to me to be an indication of the prevalence of the old European tradition, with its disregard for the body, material things and practical concerns. The development of the American type, in the sense of the critics, is an expression of the fact that we have retained this tradition and the economic system of private gain on which it is based, while at the same time we have made an independent development of industry and technology that is nothing short of revolutionary. When our critics deal with this issue instead of avoiding it there will be something really doing.

Until the issue is met, the confusion of a civilization divided against itself will persist. The mass development, which our European critics tell us has submerged individuality, *is* the product of a machine age; in some form it will follow in all countries from the extension of a machine technology. Its immediate effect has been, without doubt, a subjection of certain types of individuality. As far as individuality is associated with aristocracy of the historic type, the extension of the machine age will presumably be hostile to individuality in its traditional sense all over the world. But the strictures of our European critics only define the issue touched upon in the previous chapter. The problem of constructing a new individuality consonant with the objective conditions under which we live is the deepest problem of our times.

There are two "solutions" that fail to solve. One of these is the method of avoidance. This course is taken as far as it is assumed that the only valid type of individuality is that which holds over from the ages that anteceded machine technology and the democratic society it creates. The course that is complementary to the method of escape springs from assumption that the present situation is final; that it presents something inherently ultimate and fixed. Only as it is treated as transitive and moving, as material to be dealt with in shaping a later outcome, only, that is, as it is treated as a *problem*, is the idea of any solution genuine and relevant. We may well take the formula advanced by European critics as a means of developing our consciousness of some of the conditions of the problem. So regarded, the problem is seen to be essentially that of creation of a new individualism as significant for modern conditions as the old individualism at its best was for its day and place. The first step in further definition of this problem is realization of the collective age which we have already entered. When that is apprehended, the issue will define itself as utilization of the realities of a corporate civilization to validate and embody the distinctive moral element in the American version of individualism: Equality and freedom expressed not merely externally and politically but through personal participation in the development of a shared culture.

3.   The United States, Incorporated

It was not long ago that it was fashionable for both American and foreign observers of our national scene to sum up the phenomena of our social life under the title of "individualism." Some treated this alleged individualism as our distinctive achievement; some critics held that it was the source of our backwardness, the mark of a relatively uncivilized estate. To-day both interpretations seem equally inept and outmoded. Individualism is still carried on our banners and attempts are made to use it as a war-cry, especially when it is desired to defeat governmental regulation of any form of industry previously exempt from legal control. Even in high quarters, rugged individualism is praised as the glory of American life. But such words have little relation to the moving facts of that life.

There is no word which adequately expresses what is taking place. "Socialism" has too specific political and economic associations to be appropriate. "Collectivism" is more neutral, but it, too, is a party-word rather than a descriptive term. Perhaps the constantly increasing role of corporations in our economic life gives a clue to a fitting name. The word may be used in a wider sense than is conveyed by its technical legal meaning. We may then say that the United States has steadily moved from an earlier pioneer individualism to a condition of dominant corporateness. The influence business corporations exercise in determining present industrial and economic activities is both a cause and a symbol of the tendency to combination in all phases of life. Associations tightly or loosely organized more and more define the opportunities, the choices and the actions of individuals.

I have said that the growth of legal corporations in manufac-

[First published as "Individualism, Old and New. I: The United States, Incorporated," in *New Republic* 61 (22 January 1930): 239–41.]

turing, transportation, distribution and finance is symbolic of the development of corporateness in all phases of life. The era of trust-busting is an almost forgotten age. Not only are big mergers the order of the day, but popular sentiment now looks upon them with pride rather than with fear. Size is our current measure of greatness in this as in other matters. It is not necessary to ask whether the opportunity for speculative manipulation for the sake of private gain, or increased public service at a lower cost, is the dominant motive. Personal motives hardly count as productive causes in comparison with impersonal forces. Mass production and mass distribution inevitably follow in the wake of an epoch of steam and electricity. These have created a common market, the parts of which are held together by intercommunication and interdependence; distance is eliminated and the tempo of action enormously accelerated. Aggregated capital and concentrated control are the contemporary responses.

Political control is needed, but the movement cannot be arrested by legislation. Witness the condition of nearly innocuous desuetude of the Sherman Anti-Trust Act. Newspapers, manufacturing plants, utilities supplying light, power and local transportation, banks, retail stores, theaters and the movies, have all joined in the movement toward integration. General Motors, the American Telegraph and Telephone Company, United States Steel, the rapid growth of chain-store systems, combinations of radio companies with companies controlling theaters all over the country, are familiar facts. Railway consolidations have been slowed up by politics and internal difficulties, but few persons doubt that they, too, are coming. The political control of the future to be effective must take a positive instead of negative form.

For the forces at work in this movement are too vast and complex to cease operation at the behest of legislation. Aside from direct evasions of laws, there are many legal methods of carrying the movement forward. Interlocking directorates, interpurchase of stocks by individuals and corporations, grouping into holding companies, investing companies with enough holdings to sway policies, effect the same end as do direct mergers. It was stated at a recent convention of bankers that eighty per cent of the capitalization of all the banks of the country is now in the hands of twelve financial concerns. It is evident that virtual control of the other twenty per cent, except for negligible institutions having only local importance, automatically ensues.

An economist could multiply instances and give them a more precise form. But I am not an economist, and the facts in any case are too well known to need detailed rehearsal. For my purpose is only to indicate the bearing of the development of these corporations upon the change of social life from an individual to a corporate affair. Reactions to the change are psychological, professional, political; they affect the working ideas, beliefs and conduct of all of us.

The sad decline of the farmer cannot be understood except in the light of the industrialization of the country which is coincident with its "corporization." The government is now going to try to do for the collectivizing of the agriculturists the sort of thing that business acumen has already done—temporarily against the desire of the government—for manufactures and transportation. The plight of the uncombined and unintegrated is proof of the extent to which the country is controlled by the corporate idea. Sociologists who concern themselves with rural life are now chiefly occupied with pointing out the influence of urban districts—that is, of those where industrial organization predominates—upon the determination of conditions in country districts.

There are other decays which tell the same story. The old-type artisan, trained by individual apprenticeship for skilled individual work, is disappearing. Mass production by men massed together to operate machines with their minute divisions of labor, is putting him out of business. In many cases, a few weeks at a machine give about all the education—or rather training— that is needed. Mass production causes a kind of mass education in which individual capacity and skill are submerged. While the artisan becomes more of a mechanic and less of an artist, those who are still called artists either put themselves, as writers and designers, at the disposal of organized business, or are pushed out to the edge as eccentric bohemians. The artist remains, one may say, as a surviving individual force, but the esteem in which the calling is socially held in this country measures the degree of his force. The status of the artist in any form of social life affords a fair measure of the state of its culture. The inorganic position of the artist in American life to-day is convincing evidence of what happens to the isolated individual who lives in a society growing corporate.

Attention has recently been called to a new phenomenon in human culture:—the business mind, having its own conversation and language, its own interests, its own intimate groupings in which men of this mind, in their collective capacity, determine the tone of society at large as well as the government of industrial society, and have more political influence than the government itself. I am not concerned here with their political power. The fact significant for present discussion, is that we now have, although without formal or legal status, a mental and moral corporateness for which history affords no parallel. Our indigenous heroes are the Fords and Edisons who typify this mind to the public. Critics may find amusement in ridiculing Rotarians, Kiwanians and Lions, but the latter can well afford to disregard the ridicule because they are representatives of the dominant corporate mentality.

Nowhere is the decline of the old-fashioned individual and individualism more marked than in leisure life, in amusements and sports. Our colleges only follow the movement of the day when they make athletics an organized business, aroused and conducted under paid directors in the spirit of pure collectivism. The formation of theater chains is at once the cause and the effect of the destruction of the older independent life of leisure carried on in separate homes. The radio, the movies, the motor car, all make for a common and aggregate mental and emotional life. With technical exceptions, to be found in special publications and in some portion of all newspapers, the press is the organ of amusement for a hurried leisure time, and it reflects and carries further the formation of mental collectivism by massed methods. Crime, too, is assuming a new form; it is organized and corporate.

Our apartments and our subways are signs of the invasion and decline of privacy. Private "rights" have almost ceased to have a definable meaning. We live exposed to the greatest flood of mass suggestion that any people has ever experienced. The need for united action, and the supposed need of integrated opinion and sentiment, are met by organized propaganda and advertising. The publicity agent is perhaps the most significant symbol of our present social life. There are individuals who resist; but for a time at least, sentiment can be manufactured by mass methods for almost any person or any cause.

These things are not said to be deplored, nor even in order to weigh their merits and demerits. They are merely reported as indications of the nature of our social scene, of the extent to which it is formed and directed by corporate and collective factors toward collective ends. Coincident with these changes in mentality and prestige are basic, if hardly acknowledged, changes in the ideas by which life is interpreted. Industry, again, provides the striking symbols.

What has become of the old-fashioned ideal of thrift? Societies for the promotion of savings among the young were much hurt in their feelings when Henry Ford urged a free scale of expenditures instead of a close scale of personal savings. But his recommendation was in line with all the economic tendencies of the day. Speeded-up mass production demands increased buying. It is promoted by advertising on a vast scale, by instalment selling, by agents skilled in breaking down sales resistance. Hence buying becomes an economic "duty" which is as consonant with the present epoch as thrift was with the period of individualism. For the industrial mechanism depends upon maintaining some kind of an equilibrium between production and consumption. If the equilibrium is disturbed, the whole social structure is affected and prosperity ceases to have a meaning. Replacement and extension of capital are indeed more required than they ever were. But the savings of individuals, as such, are petty and inadequate to the task. New capital is chiefly supplied by the surplus earnings of big corporate organizations, and it becomes meaningless to tell individual buyers that industry can be kept going only by their abstinence from the enjoyments of consumption. The old plea for "sacrifice" loses its force. In effect, the individual is told that by indulging in the enjoyment of free purchasing he performs his economic duty, transferring his surplus income to the corporate store where it can be most effectively used. Virtue departs from mere thrift.

The corresponding change in the ruling conceptions of the older economic theory is, of course, the obligation upon employers to pay high wages. Growing consumption through increased expenditure that effects a still greater amount of production cannot be maintained unless consumers have the wherewithal. The consumption demand of the well-to-do is limited; and their number is limited. Purchase of luxuries by this class has, indeed, become a necessity rather than a vice, since it helps to keep moving the wheels of industry and commerce. Luxury may still be condemned as a vice, just as old habits still show themselves in approving thrift as a virtue. But the condemnation is almost an idle beating of the air, because it goes contrary to the movement of industry and trade. In any case, however, there is a definite limit to the consumption of luxuries, as well as of what used to be called necessary commodities, on the part of the wealthy. The demands that make production and distribution "going concerns" must come from the mass of the people, that is, from workers and those in subordinate salaried positions. Hence the "new economy" based on the idea of the identity of high wages with industrial prosperity.

It is difficult, perhaps impossible, to measure the full import of this revaluation of those concepts of saving and low wages which were basic in the older doctrine. If it merely expressed a change in abstract economic theory, its significance would not be great. But the change in theory is itself a reflex of a social change, which is hardly less than revolutionary. I do not mean that I think that the "new economy" is firmly established as a fact, or that the endless chain of speeding up mass consumption in order to speed up production is either endless or entirely logical. But certain changes do not go backward. Those who have enjoyed high wages and a higher standard of consumption will not be content to return to a lower level. A new condition has been created with which we shall have to reckon constantly in the future. Depressions and slumps will come, but they can never be treated in the future in the casual and fatalistic way in which they have been accepted in the past. They will appear abnormal instead of normal, and society, including the industrial captains, will have to assume a responsibility from which it and they were previously exempt. The gospel of general prosperity in this life will have to meet tests to which that of salvation in the next world, as a compensation for the miseries of this one, was not subjected. "Prosperity" is not such an assured fact in 1930 as it seemed to many to be in the earlier part of 1929. The slump or the depression makes the problem caused by the growth of corporate industry and finance the more acute. An excess income of eight billions a year will only aggravate the economic situation unless it can find outlet in productive channels. It cannot do this unless consumption is sustained. This cannot happen unless organization and control extend from production and distribution to consumption. The alternatives seem to be either a definite expansion of social corporateness to include the average consumer or else economic suffering on a vast scale.

I have said that the instances cited of the reaction of the growing corporateness of society upon social mind and habit were not given in order to be either deplored or approved. They are set forth only to call out the picture of the decline of an individualistic philosophy of life, and the formation of a collectivistic scheme of interdependence, which finds its way into every cranny of life, personal, intellectual, emotional, affecting leisure as well as work, morals as well as economics. But because the purpose was to indicate the decay of the older conceptions, although they are still those that are most loudly and vocally professed, the illustrations given inevitably emphasize those features of growing standardization and mass uniformity which critics justly deplore. It would be unfair, accordingly, to leave the impression that these traits are the whole of the story of the "corporization" of American life.

The things which are criticized are the outward signs of an inner movement toward integration on a scale never known before. "Socialization" is not wholly a eulogistic term nor a desirable process. It involves danger to some precious values; it involves a threat of danger to some things which we should not readily lose. But in spite of much cant which is talked about "service" and "social responsibility," it marks the beginning of a new era of integration. What its ultimate possibilities are, and to what extent these possibilities will be realized, is for the future to tell. The need of the present is to apprehend the fact that, for better or worse, we are living in a corporate age.

It is of the nature of society as of life to contain a balance of opposed forces. Actions and reactions are ultimately equal and counterpart. At present the "socialization" is largely mechanical and quantitative. The system is kept in a kind of precarious balance by the movement toward lawless and reckless overstimulation among individuals. If the chaos and the mechanism are to generate a mind and soul, an integrated personality, it will have to be an intelligence, a sentiment and an individuality of a new type.

Meanwhile, the lawlessness and irregularity (and I have in mind not so much outward criminality as emotional instability and intellectual confusion) and the uniform standardization are two sides of the same emerging corporate society. Hence only in an external sense does society maintain a balance. When the corporateness becomes internal, when, that is, it is realized in thought and purpose, it will become qualitative. In this change, law will be realized not as a rule arbitrarily imposed from without but as the relations which hold individuals together. The balance of the individual and the social will be organic. The emotions will be aroused and satisfied in the course of normal living, not in abrupt deviations to secure the fulfillment which is denied them in a situation which is so incomplete that it cannot be admitted into the affections and yet is so pervasive that it cannot be escaped: a situation which defines an individual divided within himself.

4.   The Lost Individual

The development of a civilization that is outwardly corporate—or rapidly becoming so—has been accompanied by a submergence of the individual. Just how far this is true of the individual's opportunities in action, how far initiative and choice in what an individual does are restricted by the economic forces that make for consolidation, I shall not attempt to say. It is arguable that there has been a diminution of the range of decision and activity for the many along with exaggeration of opportunity of personal expression for the few. It may be contended that no one class in the past has the power now possessed by an industrial oligarchy. On the other hand, it may be held that this power of the few is, with respect to genuine individuality, specious; that those outwardly in control are in reality as much carried by forces external to themselves as are the many; that in fact these forces impel them into a common mold to such an extent that individuality is suppressed.

What is here meant by "the lost individual" is, however, so irrelevant to this question that it is not necessary to decide between the two views. For by it is meant a moral and intellectual fact which is independent of any manifestation of power in action. The significant thing is that the loyalties which once held individuals, which gave them support, direction and unity of outlook on life, have well-nigh disappeared. In consequence, individuals are confused and bewildered. It would be difficult to find in history an epoch as lacking in solid and assured objects of belief and approved ends of action as is the present. Stability of individuality is dependent upon stable objects to which allegiance firmly attaches itself. There are, of course, those who are

[First published as "Individualism, Old and New. II. The Lost Individual," in *New Republic* 61 (5 February 1930): 294–96.]

still militantly fundamentalist in religious and social creed. But their very clamor is evidence that the tide is set against them. For the others, traditional objects of loyalty have become hollow or are openly repudiated, and they drift without sure anchorage. Individuals vibrate between a past that is intellectually too empty to give stability and a present that is too diversely crowded and chaotic to afford balance or direction to ideas and emotion.

Assured and integrated individuality is the product of definite social relationships and publicly acknowledged functions. Judged by this standard, even those who seem to be in control, and to carry the expression of their special individual abilities to a high pitch, are submerged. They may be captains of finance and industry, but until there is some consensus of belief as to the meaning of finance and industry in civilization as a whole, they cannot be captains of their own souls—their beliefs and aims. They exercise leadership surreptitiously and, as it were, absent-mindedly. They lead, but it is under cover of impersonal and socially undirected economic forces. Their reward is found not in what they do, in their social office and function, but in a deflection of social consequences to private gain. They receive the acclaim and command the envy and admiration of the crowd, but the crowd is also composed of private individuals who are equally lost to a sense of social bearings and uses.

The explanation is found in the fact that while the actions promote corporate and collective results, these results are outside their intent and irrelevant to that reward of satisfaction which comes from a sense of social fulfillment. To themselves and to others, their business is private and its outcome is private profit. No complete satisfaction is possible where such a split exists. Hence the absence of a sense of social value is made up for by an exacerbated acceleration of the activities that increase private advantage and power. One cannot look into the inner consciousness of his fellows, but if there is any general degree of inner contentment on the part of those who form our pecuniary oligarchy, the evidence is sadly lacking. As for the many, they are impelled hither and yon by forces beyond their control.

The most marked trait of present life, economically speaking, is insecurity. It is tragic that millions of men desirous of working should be recurrently out of employment; aside from cyclical depressions there is a standing army at all times who have no regular work. We have not any adequate information as to the number of these persons. But the ignorance even as to numbers is slight compared with our inability to grasp the psychological and moral consequences of the precarious condition in which vast multitudes live. Insecurity cuts deeper and extends more widely than bare unemployment. Fear of loss of work, dread of the oncoming of old age, create anxiety and eat into self-respect in a way that impairs personal dignity. Where fears abound, courageous and robust individuality is undermined. The vast development of technological resources that might bring security in its train has actually brought a new mode of insecurity, as mechanization displaces labor. The mergers and consolidations that mark a corporate age are beginning to bring uncertainty into the economic lives of the higher salaried class, and that tendency is only just in its early stage. Realization that honest and industrious pursuit of a calling or business will not guarantee any stable level of life lessens respect for work and stirs large numbers to take a chance of some adventitious way of getting the wealth that will make security possible: witness the orgies of the stock-market in recent days.

The unrest, impatience, irritation and hurry that are so marked in American life are inevitable accompaniments of a situation in which individuals do not find support and contentment in the fact that they are sustaining and sustained members of a social whole. They are evidence, psychologically, of abnormality, and it is as idle to seek for their explanation within the deliberate intent of individuals as it is futile to think that they can be got rid of by hortatory moral appeal. Only an acute maladjustment between individuals and the social conditions under which they live can account for such widespread pathological phenomena. Feverish love of anything as long as it is a change which is distracting, impatience, unsettlement, nervous discontentment, and desire for excitement, are not native to human nature. They are so abnormal as to demand explanation in some deep-seated cause.

I should explain a seeming hypocrisy on the same ground. We are not consciously insincere in our professions of devotion to ideals of "service"; they mean something. Neither the Rotarian nor the big business enterprise uses the term merely as a cloak for "putting something over" which makes for pecuniary gain. But the lady doth protest too much. The wide currency of such professions testifies to a sense of a social function of business which is expressed in words because it is so lacking in fact, and yet which is felt to be rightfully there. If our external combinations in industrial activity were reflected in organic integrations of the desires, purposes and satisfactions of individuals, the verbal protestations would disappear, because social utility would be a matter of course.

Some persons hold that a genuine mental counterpart of the outward social scheme is actually forming. Our prevailing mentality, our "ideology," is said to be that of the "business mind" which has become so deplorably pervasive. Are not the prevailing standards of value those derived from pecuniary success and economic prosperity? Were the answer unqualifiedly in the affirmative, we should have to admit that our outer civilization is attaining an inner culture which corresponds to it, however much we might disesteem the quality of that culture. The objection that such a condition is impossible, since man cannot live by bread, by material prosperity alone, is tempting, but it may be said to beg the question. The conclusive answer is that the business mind is not itself unified. It is divided within itself and must remain so as long as the results of industry as the determining force in life are corporate and collective while its animating motives and compensations are so unmitigatedly private. A unified mind, even of the business type, can come into being only when conscious intent and consummation are in harmony with consequences actually effected. This statement expresses conditions so psychologically assured that it may be termed a law of mental integrity. Proof of the existence of the split is found in the fact that while there is much planning of future development with a view to dividends within large business corporations, there is no corresponding coordinated planning of social development.

The growth of corporateness is arbitrarily restricted. Hence it operates to limit individuality, to put burdens on it, to confuse and submerge it. It crowds more out than it incorporates in an ordered and secure life. It has made rural districts stagnant while bringing excess and restless movement to the city. The restriction of corporateness lies in the fact that it remains on the cash level. Men are brought together on the one side by investment in the same joint stock company, and on the other hand by the fact that the machine compels mass production in order that investors may get their profits. The results affect all society in all its phases. But they are as inorganic as the ultimate human motives that operate are private and egoistic. An economic individualism of motives and aims underlies our present corporate mechanisms, and undoes the individual.

The loss of individuality is conspicuous in the economic region because our civilization is so predominantly a business civilization. But the fact is even more obvious when we turn to the political scene. It would be a waste of words to expatiate on the meaninglessness of present political platforms, parties and issues. The old-time slogans are still reiterated, and to a few these words still seem to have a real meaning. But it is too evident to need argument that on the whole our politics, as far as they are not covertly manipulated in behalf of the pecuniary advantage of groups, are in a state of confusion; issues are improvised from week to week with a constant shift of allegiance. It is impossible for individuals to find themselves politically with surety and efficiency under such conditions. Political apathy broken by recurrent sensations and spasms is the natural outcome.

The lack of secure objects of allegiance, without which individuals are lost, is especially striking in the case of the liberal. The liberalism of the past was characterized by the possession of a definite intellectual creed and program; that was its distinction from conservative parties which needed no formulated outlook beyond defense of things as they were. In contrast, liberals operated on the basis of a thought-out social philosophy, a theory of politics sufficiently definite and coherent to be easily translated into a program of policies to be pursued. Liberalism today is hardly more than a temper of mind, vaguely called forward-looking, but quite uncertain as to where to look and what to look forward to. For many individuals, as well as in its social results, this fact is hardly less than a tragedy. The tragedy may be unconscious for the mass, but they show its reality in their aimless drift, while the more thoughtful are consciously disturbed. For human nature is self-possessed only as it has objects to which it can attach itself.

I do not think it is fantastic to connect our excited and rapacious nationalism with the situation in which corporateness has gone so far as to detach individuals from their old local ties and allegiances but not far enough to give them a new centre and order of life. The most militaristic of nations secures the loyalty of its subjects not by physical force but through the power of ideas and emotions. It cultivates ideals of loyalty, of solidarity, and common devotion to a common cause. Modern industry, technology and commerce have created modern nations in their external form. Armies and navies exist to protect commerce, to make secure the control of raw materials, and to command markets. Men would not sacrifice their lives for the purpose of securing economic gain for a few if the conditions presented themselves to their minds in this bald fashion. But the balked demand for genuine cooperativeness and reciprocal solidarity in daily life finds an outlet in nationalistic sentiment. Men have a pathetic instinct toward the adventure of living and struggling together; if the daily community does not feed this impulse, the romantic imagination pictures a grandiose nation in which all are one. If the simple duties of peace do not establish a common life, the emotions are mobilized in the service of a war that will supply its temporary simulation.

I have thus far made no reference to what many persons would consider the most serious and the most overtly evident of all the modes of loss of secure objects of loyalty—religion. It is probably easy to exaggerate the extent of the decadence of religion in an outward sense, church membership, church-going and so on. But it is hardly possible to overstate its decline as a vitally integrative and directive force in men's thought and sentiments. Whether even in the ages of the past that are called religious, religion was itself the actively central force that it is sometimes said to have been may be doubted. But it cannot be doubted that it was the symbol of the existence of conditions and forces that gave unity and a centre to men's views of life. It at least gathered together in weighty and shared symbols a sense of the objects to which men were so attached as to have support and stay in their outlook on life.

Religion does not now effect this result. The divorce of church and state has been followed by that of religion and society. Wherever religion has not become a merely private indulgence, it has become at best a matter of sects and denominations divided from one another by doctrinal differences, and united internally by tenets that have a merely historical origin, and a purely metaphysical or else ritualistic meaning. There is no such bond of social unity as once united Greeks, Romans, Hebrews, and Catholic medieval Europe. There are those who realize what is portended by the loss of religion as an integrating bond. Many of them despair of its recovery through the development of social values to which the imagination and sentiments of individuals can attach themselves with intensity. They wish to reverse the operation and to form the social bond of unity and of allegiance by regeneration of the isolated individual soul.

Aside from the fact that there is no consensus as to what a new religious attitude is to centre itself about, the injunction puts the cart before the horse. Religion is not so much a root of unity as it is its flower or fruit. The very attempt to secure integration for the individual, and through him for society, by means of a deliberate and conscious cultivation of religion, is itself proof of how far the individual has become lost through detachment from acknowledged social values. It is no wonder that when the appeal does not take the form of dogmatic fundamentalism, it tends to terminate in either some form of esoteric occultism or private estheticism. The sense of wholeness which is urged as the essence of religion can be built up and sustained only through membership in a society which has attained a degree of unity. The attempt to cultivate it first in individuals and then extend it to form an organically unified society is fantasy. Indulgence in this fantasy infects such interpretations of American life as are found, to take one signal example, in Waldo Frank's *The Rediscovery of America*.[1] It marks a manner of yearning and not a principle of construction.

For the idea that the outward scene is chaotic because of the machine, which is a principle of chaos, and that it will remain so until individuals reinstitute wholeness within themselves, simply reverses the true state of things. The outward scene, if not fully organized, is relatively so in the corporateness which the machine and its technology have produced; the inner man is the jungle which can be subdued to order only as the forces of organization

---

1. After a brilliant exposition of the dissolution of the European synthesis, he goes on to say "man's need of order and his making of order are his science, his art, his religion; and these are all to be referred to the initial sense of order called the self," quite oblivious of the fact that this doctrine of the primacy of the self is precisely a reaction of the romantic and subjective age to the dissolution he has depicted, having its meaning only in that dissolution.

at work in externals are reflected in corresponding patterns of thought, imagination and emotion. The sick cannot heal themselves by means of their disease, and disintegrated individuals can achieve unity only as the dominant energies of community life are incorporated to form their minds. If these energies were, in reality, mere strivings for private pecuniary gain, the case would indeed be hopeless. But they are constituted by a collective art of technology, which individuals merely deflect to their private ends. There are the beginnings of an objective order through which individuals may get their bearings.

Conspicuous signs of the disintegration of individuality due to failure to reconstruct the self so as to meet the realities of present social life have not been mentioned. In a census that was taken among leaders of opinion concerning the urgency of present social problems, the state of law, the courts, lawlessness and criminality stood at the head of the list, and by a considerable distance. We are even more emphatically than when Kipling wrote the words, the people that make "the laws they flout, and flout the laws they make." We combine an ardor unparalleled in history for "passing" laws with a casual and deliberate disregard for them when they are on the statute books. We believe—to judge by our legislative actions—that we can create morals by law (witness the prohibition amendment for an instance on a large scale) and neglect the fact that all laws except those which regulate technical procedures are registrations of existing social customs and their attendant moral habits and purposes. I can, however, only think of this phenomenon as a symptom, not as a cause. It is a natural expression of a period in which changes in the structure of society have dissolved old bonds and allegiances. We attempt to make good this social relaxation and dissolution by legal enactments, while the actual disintegration discloses itself in the lawlessness which reveals the artificial character of this method of securing social integrity.

Volumes could be formed by collecting articles and editorials written about relaxation of traditional moral codes. A movement has caught public attention, which, having for some obscure reason assumed the name "humanism," proposes restraint and moderation, exercised in and by the higher volition of individuals, as the solution of our ills. It finds that naturalism as practiced by artists and mechanism as taught by philosophers who take their clew from natural science, have broken down the inner laws and imperatives which can alone bring order and loyalty. I should be glad to be able to believe that artists and intellectuals have any such power in their hands; if they had, after using it to bring evil to society, they might change face and bring healing to it. But a sense of fact, together with a sense of humor, forbids the acceptance of any such belief. Literary persons and academic thinkers are now, more than ever, effects, not causes. They reflect and voice the disintegration which new modes of living, produced by new forms of industry and commerce, have introduced. They give witness to the unreality that has overtaken traditional codes in the face of the impact of new forces; indirectly, they proclaim the need of some new synthesis. But this synthesis can be humanistic only as the new conditions are themselves taken into account and are converted into the instrumentalities of a free and humane life. I see no way to "restrain" or turn back the industrial revolution and its consequences. In the absence of such a restraint (which would be efficacious if only it could occur), the urging of some inner restraint through the exercise of the higher personal will, whatever that may be, is itself only a futile echo of just the old individualism that has so completely broken down.

There are many phases of life which illustrate to anyone who chooses to think in terms of realities instead of words the utter irrelevance of the proposed remedy to actual conditions. One might take the present estate of amusements, of the movies, the radio, and organized vicarious sport, and ask just how this powerful eruption in which the resources of technology are employed for economic profit is to be met by the application of the inner *frein* or brake. Perhaps the most striking instance is found in the disintegration due to changes in family life and sex morale. It was not deliberate human intention that undermined the traditional household as the centre of industry and education and as the focus of moral training; that sapped the older institution of enduring marriage. To ask the individuals who suffer the consequences of the general undermining and sapping to put an end to the consequences by acts of personal volition is merely to profess faith in moral magic. Recovery of individuals capable of stable and effective self-control can be had only as there is first a humbler exercise of will to observe existing social realities and to direct them according to their own potentialities.

Instances of the flux in which individuals are loosened from the ties that once gave order and support to their lives are glaring. They are indeed so glaring that they blind our eyes to the causes which produce them. Individuals are groping their way through situations which they do not direct and which do not give them direction. The beliefs and ideals that are uppermost in their consciousness are not relevant to the society in which they outwardly act and which constantly reacts upon them. Their conscious ideas and standards are inherited from an age that has passed away; their minds, as far as consciously entertained principles and methods of interpretation are concerned, are at odds with actual conditions. This profound split is the cause of distraction and bewilderment.

Individuals will refind themselves only as their ideas and ideals are brought into harmony with the realities of the age in which they act. The task of attaining this harmony is not an easy one. But it is more negative than it seems. If we could inhibit the principles and standards that are merely traditional, if we could slough off the opinions that have no living relationship to the situations in which we live, the unavowed forces that now work upon us unconsciously but unremittingly would have a chance to build minds after their own pattern, and individuals might, in consequence, find themselves in possession of objects to which imagination and emotion would stably attach themselves.

I do not mean, however, that the process of rebuilding can go on automatically. Discrimination is required in order to detect the beliefs and institutions that dominate merely because of custom and inertia, and in order to discover the moving realities of the present. Intelligence must distinguish, for example, the tendencies of the technology which produce the new corporateness from those inheritances proceeding out of the individualism of an earlier epoch which arrest and divide the operation of the new dynamics. It is difficult for us to conceive of individualism except in terms of stereotypes derived from former centuries. Individualism has been identified with ideas of initiative and invention that are bound up with private and exclusive economic gain. As long as this conception possesses our minds, the ideal of harmonizing our thought and desire with the realities of present social conditions will be interpreted to mean accommodation and surrender. It will even be understood to signify rationalization of the evils of existing society. A stable recovery of individuality waits upon an elimination of the older economic and political individualism, an elimination which will liberate imagination and endeavor for the task of making corporate society contribute to the free culture of its members. Only by economic revision can the sound element in the older individualism—equality of opportunity—be made a reality.

It is the part of wisdom to note the double meaning of such ideas as "acceptance." There is an acceptance that is of the intellect; it signifies facing facts for what they are. There is another acceptance that is of the emotions and will; that involves commitment of desire and effort. So far are the two from being identical that acceptance in the first sense is the precondition of all intelligent refusal of acceptance in the second sense. There is a prophetic aspect to all observation; we can perceive the meaning of what exists only as we forecast the consequences it entails. When a situation is as confused and divided within itself as is the present social estate, choice is implicated in observation. As one perceives different tendencies and different possible consequences, preference inevitably goes out to one or the other. Because acknowledgment in thought brings with it intelligent discrimination and choice, it is the first step out of confusion, the first step in forming those objects of significant allegiance out of which stable and efficacious individuality may grow. It might even perform the miracle of rendering conservatism relevant and thoughtful. It certainly is the prerequisite of an anchored liberalism.

5. Toward a New Individualism

Our material culture, as anthropologists would call it, is verging upon the collective and corporate. Our moral culture, along with our ideology, is, on the other hand, still saturated with ideals and values of an individualism derived from the pre-scientific, pre-technological age. Its spiritual roots are found in medieval religion, which asserted the ultimate nature of the individual soul and centered the drama of life about the destiny of that soul. Its institutional and legal concepts were framed in the feudal period.

This moral and philosophical individualism anteceded the rise of modern industry and the era of the machine. It was the context in which the latter operated. The apparent subordination of the individual to established institutions often conceals from recognition the vital existence of a deep-seated individualism. But the fact that the controlling institution was the Church should remind us that in ultimate intent it existed to secure the salvation of the individual. That this individual was conceived as a soul, and that the end served by the institution was deferred to another and everlasting life conceal from contemporary realization the underlying individualism. In its own time, its substance consisted in just this eternal spiritual character of the personal soul; the power of the established institutions proceeded from their being the necessary means of accomplishing the supreme end of the individual.

The early phase of the industrial revolution wrought a great transformation. It gave a secular and worldly turn to the career of the individual, and it liquefied the static property concepts of feudalism by the shift of emphasis from agriculture to manufac-

[First published as "Toward a New Individualism. The Third Article in Professor Dewey's Series, 'Individualism, Old and New,'" in *New Republic* 62 (19 February 1930): 13–16.]

turing. Still, the idea persisted that property and reward were intrinsically individual. There were, it is true, incompatible elements in the earlier and later versions of individualism. But a fusion of individual capitalism, of natural rights, and of morals founded in strictly individual traits and values remained, under the influence of Protestantism, the dominant intellectual synthesis.

The basis of this synthesis was destroyed, however, by the later development of the industrial system, which brought about the merging of personal capacity, effort and work into collective wholes. Meanwhile, the control of natural energies eliminated time and distance, so that action once adapted to local conditions was swallowed up in complex undertakings of indefinite extent. Yet the older mental equipment remained after its causes and foundations had disappeared. This, fundamentally, is the inner division out of which spring our present confusion and insincerities.

The earlier economic individualism had a definite creed and function. It sought to release from legal restrictions man's wants and his efforts to satisfy those wants. It believed that such emancipation would stimulate latent energy into action, would automatically assign individual ability to the work for which it was suited, would cause it to perform that work under stimulus of the advantage to be gained, and would secure for capacity and enterprise the reward and position to which they were entitled. At the same time, individual energy and savings would be serving the needs of others, and thus promoting the general welfare and effecting a general harmony of interests.

We have gone a long way since this philosophy was formulated. Today, the most stalwart defenders of this type of individualism do not venture to repeat its optimistic assertions. At most, they are content to proclaim its consistency with unchanging human nature—which is said to be moved to effort only by the hope of personal gain—and to paint dire pictures of the inevitable consequences of change to any other regime. They ascribe all the material benefits of our present civilization to this individualism—as if machines were made by the desire for money profit, not by impersonal science; and as if they were driven by money alone, and not by electricity and steam under the direction of a collective technology.

In America, the older individualism assumed a romantic form. It was hardly necessary to elaborate a theory which equated personal gain with social advance. The demands of the practical situation called for the initiative, enterprise and vigor of individuals in all immediate work that urgently asked for doing, and their operation furthered the national life. The spirit of the time is expressed by Dr. Crothers, whose words Mr. Sims has appropriately taken for part of the text of his "Adventurous America":

> If you would understand the driving power of America, you must understand "the divers discontented and impatient young men" who in each generation have found an outlet for their energy. . . . The noises which disturb you are not the cries of an angry proletariat, but are the shouts of eager young people who are finding new opportunities. . . . They represent today the enthusiasm of a new generation. They represent the Oregons and Californias toward which sturdy pioneers are moving undisturbed by obstacles. This is what the social unrest means in America.

If that is not an echo of the echo of a voice of long ago, I do not know what it is. I do not, indeed, hear the noises of an angry proletariat; but I should suppose the sounds heard are the murmurs of lost opportunities, along with the din of machinery, motor cars and speakeasies, by which the murmurs of discontent are drowned, rather than shouts of eagerness for adventurous opportunity.

The European version of the older individualism had its value and temporal justification because the new technology needed liberation from vexatious legal restrictions. Machine industry was itself in a pioneer condition, and those who carried it forward against obstacles of lethargy, skepticism and political obstruction were deserving of special reward. Moreover, accumulation of capital was thought of in terms of enterprises that today would be petty; there was no dream of the time when it would reach such a mass that it would determine the legal and political order. Poverty had previously been accepted as a dispensation of nature that was inevitable. The new industry promised a way out, at least to those possessed of energy and will to save and accumulate. But there was no anticipation of a time when the development of machine technology would afford the material basis for reasonable ease and comfort and of extensive leisure for all.

The shift that makes the older individualism a dying echo is more marked as well as more rapid in this country. Where is the wilderness which now beckons creative energy and affords untold opportunity to initiative and vigor? Where is the pioneer who goes forth rejoicing, even in the midst of privation, to its conquest? The wilderness exists in the movie and the novel, and the children of the pioneers, who live in the midst of surroundings artificially made over by the machine, enjoy pioneer life idly in the vicarious film. I see little social unrest which is the straining of energy for outlet in action; I find rather the protest against a weakening of vigor and a sapping of energy that emanate from the absence of constructive opportunity; and I see a confusion that is an expression of the inability to find a secure and morally rewarding place in a troubled and tangled economic scene.

Because of the bankruptcy of the older individualism, those who are aware of the break-down often speak and argue as if individualism were itself done and over with. I do not suppose that those who regard socialism and individualism as antithetical really mean that individuality is going to die out or that it is not something intrinsically precious. But in speaking as if the only individualism were the local episode of the last two centuries, they play into the hands of those who would keep it alive in order to serve their own ends, and they slur over the chief problem—that of remaking society to serve the growth of a new type of individual. There are many who believe that socialism of some form is needed to realize individual initiative and security on a wide scale. They are concerned about the restriction of power and freedom to a few in the present regime, and they think that collective social control is necessary, at least for a time, in order to achieve its advantages for all. But they too often seem to assume that the result will be merely an extension of the earlier individualism to the many.

Such thinking treats individualism as if it were something static, having a uniform content. It ignores the fact that the mental and moral structure of individuals, the pattern of their desires and purposes, change with every great change in social constitution. Individuals who are not bound together in associations, whether domestic, economic, religious, political, artistic or educational, are monstrosities. It is absurd to suppose that the ties which hold them together are merely external and do not react into mentality and character, producing the framework of personal disposition.

The tragedy of the "lost individual" is due to the fact that while individuals are now caught up into a vast complex of associations, there is no harmonious and coherent reflection of the import of these connections into the imaginative and emotional outlook on life. This fact is of course due in turn to the absence of harmony within the state of society. There is an undoubted circle. But it is a vicious circle only as far as men decline to accept—in the intellectual, observing and inquiring spirit defined in the previous chapter—the realities of the social estate, and because of this refusal either surrender to the division or seek to save their individuality by escape or sheer emotional revolt. The habit of opposing the corporate and collective to the individual tends to the persistent continuation of the confusion and uncertainty. It distracts attention from the crucial issue: How shall the individual refind himself in an unprecedentedly new social situation, and what qualities will the new individualism exhibit?

That the problem is not merely one of extending to all individuals the traits of economic initiative, opportunity and enterprise; that it is one of forming a new psychological and moral type, is suggested by the great pressure now brought to bear to effect conformity and standardization of American opinion. Why should regimentation, the erection of an average struck from the opinions of large masses into regulative norms, and in general the domination of quantity over quality, be so characteristic of present American life? I see but one fundamental explanation. The individual cannot remain intellectually a vacuum. If his ideas and beliefs are not the spontaneous function of a communal life in which he shares, a seeming consensus will be secured as a substitute by artificial and mechanical means. In the absence of mentality that is congruous with the new social corporateness that is coming into being, there is a desperate effort to fill the void by external agencies which obtain a factitious agreement.

In consequence, our uniformity of thought is much more superficial than it seems to be. The standardization is deplorable, but one might almost say that one of the reasons it is deplorable is because it does not go deep. It goes far enough to effect suppression of original quality of thought, but not far enough to achieve enduring unity. Its superficial character is evident in its instability. All agreement of thought obtained by external means, by repression and intimidation, however subtle, and by calculated propaganda and publicity, is of necessity superficial; and whatever is superficial is in continual flux. The methods employed produce mass credulity, and this jumps from one thing to another according to the dominant suggestions of the day. We think and feel alike—but only for a month or a season. Then comes some other sensational event or personage to exercise a hypnotizing uniformity of response. At a given time, taken in cross-section, conformity is the rule. In a time span, taken longitudinally, instability and flux dominate. . . . I suppose there are others who have a feeling of irritation at such terms as "radio-conscious" and "air-minded," now so frequently forced upon us. I do not think the irritation is wholly due to linguistic causes. It testifies to a half-conscious sense of the external ways in which our minds are formed and swayed and of the superficiality and inconsistency of the result.

There are, I suppose, those who fancy that the emphasis which I put upon the corporateness of existing society in the United States is in effect, even if not in the writer's conscious intent, a plea for greater conformity than now exists. Nothing could be further from the truth. Identification of society with a level, whatever it be, high as well as low, of uniformity is just another evidence of that distraction because of which the individual is lost. Society is of course but the relations of individuals to one another in this form and that. And all relations are interactions, not fixed molds. The particular interactions that compose a human society include the give and take of participation, of a sharing that increases, that expands and deepens, the capacity and significance of the interacting factors. Conformity is a name for the absence of vital interplay; the arrest and benumbing of communication. As I have been trying to say, it is the artificial substitute used to hold men together in lack of associations that are incorporated into inner dispositions of thought and desire. I often wonder what meaning is given to the term "society" by those who oppose it to the intimacies of personal intercourse, such as those of friendship. Presumably they have in their minds a picture of rigid institutions or some set and external organization. But an institution that is other than the structure of human contact and intercourse is a fossil of some past society; organization, as in any living organism, is the cooperative consensus of multitudes of cells, each living in exchange with others.

I should suppose that the more intelligent of those who wield the publicity agencies which produce conformity would be disturbed at beholding their own success. I can easily understand that they should have a cynical sense of their ability to obtain the results they want at a given time; but I should think they would fear that like-mindedness might, at a critical juncture, veer in an unexpected direction and turn with equal unanimity against the things and interests it has been manipulated to support. Crowd psychology is dangerous in its instability. To rely upon it for permanent support is playing with a fire that may get out of control. Conformity is enduringly effective when it is a spontaneous and largely unconscious manifestation of the agreements that spring from genuine communal life. An artificially induced uniformity of thought and sentiment is a symptom of an inner void. Not all of it that now exists is intentionally produced; it is not the result of deliberate manipulation. But it is, on the other hand, the result of causes so external as to be accidental and precarious.

The "joining" habit of the average American, and his excessive sociability, may well have an explanation like that of conformity. They, too, testify to nature's abhorrence of that vacuum which the passing of the older individualism has produced. We should not be so averse to solitude if we had, when we were alone, the companionship of communal thought built into our mental habits. In the absence of this communion, there is the need for reinforcement by external contact. Our sociability is largely an effort to find substitutes for that normal consciousness of connection and union that proceeds from being a sustained and sustaining member of a social whole.

Just as the new individualism cannot be achieved by extending the benefits of the older economic individualism to more persons, so it cannot be obtained by a further development of generosity, good will and altruism. Such traits are desirable, but they are also more or less constant expressions of human nature. There is much in the present situation that stimulates them to active operation. They are probably more marked features of American life than of that of any other civilization at any time.

Our charity and philanthropy are partly the manifestation of an uneasy conscience. As such a manifestation, they testify to a realization that a régime of industry carried on for private gain does not satisfy the full human nature of even those who profit by it. The impulse and need which the existing economic régime chokes, through preventing its articulated expression, find outlet in actions that acknowledge a social responsibility which the system as a system denies. Hence the development of philanthropic measures is not only compensatory to a stifling of human nature undergone in business, but it is in a way prophetic. Construction is better than relief; prevention than cure. Activities by way of relief of poverty and its attendant mental strains and physical ills—and our philanthropic activities including even the endowment of educational institutions have their ultimate causes in the existence of economic insecurity and distress—suggest, in dim forecast, a society in which daily occupations and relationships will give independence and substantial living to all normal individuals who share in its ongoings, reserving relief for extraordinary emergencies. One does not need to reflect upon the personal motives of great philanthropists to see in what they do an emphatic record of the breakdown of our existing economic organization.

For the chief obstacle to the creation of a type of individual whose pattern of thought and desire is enduringly marked by consensus with others, and in whom sociability is one with co-operation in all regular human associations, is the persistence of that feature of the earlier individualism which defines industry and commerce by ideas of private pecuniary profit. Why, once more, is there such zeal for standardized likeness? It is not, I imagine, because conformity for its own sake appears to be a great boon. It is rather because a certain kind of conformity gives defense and protection to the pecuniary features of our present regime. The foreground may be filled with depiction of the horror of change, and with clamor for law and order and the support of the Constitution. But behind there is desire for perpetuation of that regime which defines individual initiative and ability by success in conducting business so as to make money.

It is not too much to say that the whole significance of the older individualism has now shrunk to a pecuniary scale and measure. The virtues that are supposed to attend rugged individualism may be vocally proclaimed, but it takes no great insight to see that what is cherished is measured by its connection with those activities that make for success in business conducted for personal gain. Hence, the irony of the gospel of "individualism" in business conjoined with suppression of individuality in thought and speech. One cannot imagine a bitterer comment on any professed individualism than that it subordinates the only creative individuality—that of mind—to the maintenance of a regime which gives the few an opportunity for being shrewd in the management of monetary business.

It is claimed, of course, that the individualism of economic self-seeking, even if it has not produced the adjustment of ability and reward and the harmony of interests earlier predicted, has given us the advantage of material prosperity. It is not needful to raise here the question of how far that material prosperity extends. For it is not true that its moving cause is pecuniary individualism. That has been the cause of some great fortunes, but not of national wealth; it counts in the process of distribution, but not in ultimate creation. Scientific insight taking effect in machine technology has been the great productive force. For the most part, economic individualism interpreted as energy and enterprise devoted to private profit, has been an adjunct, often a parasitical one, to the movement of technical and scientific forces.

The scene in which individuality is created has been transformed. The pioneer, such as is depicted in the quotation from Crothers, had no great need for any ideas beyond those that sprang up in the immediate tasks in which he was engaged. His intellectual problems grew out of struggle with the forces of physical nature. The wilderness was a reality and it had to be subdued. The type of character that evolved was strong and hardy, often picturesque, and sometimes heroic. Individuality was a reality because it corresponded to conditions. Irrelevant traditional ideas in religion and morals were carried along, but they were reduced to a size where they did no harm; indeed, they could easily be interpreted in such a way as to be a reinforcement to the sturdy and a consolation to the weak and failing.

But it is no longer a physical wilderness that has to be wrestled with. Our problems grow out of social conditions: they concern human relations rather than man's direct relationship to physical nature. The adventure of the individual, if there is to be any venturing of individuality and not a relapse into the deadness of complacency or of despairing discontent, is an unsubdued social frontier. The issues cannot be met with ideas improvised for the occasion. The problems to be solved are general, not local. They concern complex forces that are at work throughout the whole country, not those limited to an immediate and almost face-to-face environment. Traditional ideas are more than irrelevant. They are an encumbrance; they are the chief obstacle to the formation of a new individuality integrated within itself and with a liberated function in the society wherein it exists. A new individualism can be achieved only through the controlled use of all the resources of the science and technology that have mastered the physical forces of nature.

They are not controlled now in any fundamental sense. Rather do they control us. They are indeed physically controlled. Every factory, power-house and railway system testifies to the fact that we have attained this measure of control. But control of power through the machine is not control of the machine itself. Control of the energies of nature by science is not controlled use of science. We are not even approaching a climax of control; we are hardly at its feeble beginnings. For control is relative to consequences, ends, values; and we do not manage, we hardly have commenced to dream of managing, physical power for the sake of projected purposes and prospective goods. The machine took us unawares and unprepared. Instead of forming new purposes commensurate with its potentialities, we accordingly tried to make it the servant of aims that were the expression of an age when mastery of natural energies on any large scale was the fantasy of magic. As Clarence Ayres has said: "Our industrial revolution began, as some historians say, with half a dozen technical improvements in the textile industry; and it took us a century to realize that anything of moment had happened to us beyond the obvious improvement of spinning and weaving."

I do not say that the aims and values of the earlier day were petty in themselves. But they are almost inconceivably petty in comparison with the means now at our command—if we had an imagination large enough to encompass their potential uses. They are worse than petty; they are confusing and distracting when men are confronted with the physical instrumentalities and agencies which, in the lack of comprehensive purpose and concerted planning, work blindly and carry us drifting hither and yon. I cannot obtain intellectual, moral or esthetic satisfaction from the professed philosophy which animates Bolshevik Russia. But I am sure that the future historian of our times will combine admiration of those who had the imagination first to see that the resources of technology might be directed by organized planning to serve chosen ends with astonishment at the intellectual and moral hebetude of other peoples who were technically so much further advanced.

There is no greater sign of the paralysis of the imagination which custom and involvement in immediate detail can induce than the belief, sedulously propagated by some who pride themselves on superior taste, that the machine is itself the source of our troubles. Of course immense potential resources impose responsibility, and it has yet to be demonstrated whether human capacity can rise to utilization of the opportunities which the machine and technology have opened to us. But it is hard to think of anything more childish than the animism that puts the blame on machinery. For machinery means an undreamed-of reservoir of power. If we have harnessed this power to the dollar rather than to the liberation and enrichment of human life, it is because we have been content to stay within the bounds of traditional aims and values although we are in possession of a revolutionary transforming instrument. Repetition of the older credo of individualism is but the evidence of contentment within these bonds. I for one think it is incredible that this particular form of confession of inferiority will endure very much longer. When we begin to ask what can be done with the machine for the creation and fulfillment of values corresponding to its potency and begin organized planning to effect these goods, a new individual correlative to the realities of the age in which we live will also begin to take form.

Revolt against the machine as the author of social evils usually has an esthetic origin. A more intellectual and quasi-philosophic reaction finds natural science to be their source; or if not science itself (which is allowed to be all very well if it keeps its appropriate humble place) then the attitude of those who depend upon science as an organ of vision and light. Contempt for nature is understandable, at least historically; even though it seems both intellectually petty and morally ungracious to feel contempt for the matrix of our being and the inescapable condition of our lives. But that men should fear and dislike the method of approach to nature I do not find understandable. The eye sees many foul things and the arm and hand do many cruel things. Yet the fanatic who would pluck out the eye and cut off the arm is recognized for what he is. Science, one may say, is but the extension of our natural organs of approach to nature. And I do not mean merely an extension in quantitative range and penetration, as a microscope multiplies the capacity of the unaided eye, but an extension of insight and understanding through bringing relationships and interactions into view. Since we must in any case approach nature in some fashion and by some path—if only that of death—I confess my total inability to understand those who object to an intelligently controlled approach—for that is what science is.

The only way in which I can obtain any sympathetic realization of their attitude is by recalling that there have been those who have professed adoration of science—writing it with a capital S—; those who have thought of it not as a method of approach but as a kind of self-enclosed entity and end in itself, a new theology of self-sufficient authoritatively revealed inherent and absolute Truth. It would, however, seem simpler to correct their misapprehension than first to share it and then to reverse their worship into condemnation. The opposite of intelligent method is no method at all or blind and stupid method. It is a curious state of mind which finds pleasure in setting forth the "limits of science." For the intrinsic limit of knowledge is simply ignorance; and the point in extolling ignorance is not clear except when expressed by those who profit by keeping others in ignorance. There is of course an extrinsic limit of science. But that limitation lies in the ineptitude of those who put it to use; its removal lies in rectification of its use, not in abuse of the thing used.

This reference to science and technology is relevant because they are the forces of present life which are finally significant. It is through employing them with understanding of their possible import that a new individualism, consonant with the realities of the present age, may be brought into operative being. There are many levels and many elements in both the individual and his relations. Neither can be comprehended nor dealt with in mass. Discriminative sensitivity, selection, is imperative. Art is the fruit of such selection when it is given objective effect. The art which our times needs in order to create a new type of individuality is the art which, being sensitive to the technology and science that are the moving forces of our time, will envisage the expansive, the social, culture which they may be made to serve. I am not anxious to depict the form which this emergent individualism will assume. Indeed, I do not see how it can be described until more progress has been made in its production. But such progress will not be initiated until we cease opposing the socially corporate to the individual, and until we develop a constructively imaginative observation of the role of science and technology in actual society. The greatest obstacle to that vision is, I repeat, the perpetuation of the older individualism now reduced, as I have said, to the utilization of science and technology for ends of private pecuniary gain. I sometimes wonder if those who are conscious of present ills but who direct their blows of criticism at everything except this obstacle are not stirred by motives which they unconsciously prefer to keep below consciousness.

6.   Capitalistic or Public Socialism?

I once heard a distinguished lawyer say that the earlier American ideas about individual initiative and enterprise could be recovered by an amendment of a few lines to the federal Constitution. The amendment would prohibit all joint stock enterprises and permit only individual liability to have a legal status. He was, I think, the only unadulterated Jeffersonian Democrat I have ever met. He was also logical. He did not delude himself into supposing that the pioneer gospel of personal initiative, enterprise, energy and reward could be maintained in an era of aggregated corporate capital, of mass production and distribution, of impersonal ownership and of ownership divorced from management. Our political life, however, continues to ignore the change that has taken place except as circumstances force it to take account of it in sporadic matters.

The myth is still current that socialism desires to use political means in order to divide wealth equally among all individuals, and that it is consequently opposed to the development of trusts, mergers and consolidated business in general. It is regarded, in other words, as a kind of arithmetically fractionized individualism. This notion of socialism is of the sort that would naturally be entertained by those who cannot get away from the inherent conception of the individual as an isolated and independent unit. In reality, Karl Marx was the prophet of just this period of economic consolidation. If his ghost hovers above the American scene, it must find legitimate satisfaction in our fulfilment of his predictions.

In these predictions, however, Marx reasoned too much from psychological economic premises and depended too little upon

[First published as "Capitalistic or Public Socialism? The Fourth Article in Professor Dewey's Series, 'Individualism, Old and New,'" in *New Republic* 62 (5 March 1930): 64–67.]

technological causes—the application of science to steam, electricity and chemical processes. That is to say, he argued to an undue extent from an alleged constant appropriation by capitalists of all surplus values created by the workers—surplus being defined as anything above the minimum needed for their continued subsistence. He had no conception, moreover, of the capacity of expanding industry to develop new inventions so as to develop new wants, new forms of wealth, new occupations; nor did he imagine that the intellectual ability of the employing class would be equal to seeing the need for sustaining consuming power by high wages in order to keep up production and its profits. This explains why his prediction of a revolution in political control, caused by the general misery of the masses and resulting in the establishment of a socialistic society, has not been realized in this country. Nevertheless, the issue which he raised—the relation of the economic structure to political operations—is one that actively persists.

Indeed, it forms the only basis of present political questions. An intelligent and experienced observer of affairs at Washington has said that all political questions which he has heard discussed in Washington come back ultimately to problems connected with the distribution of income. Wealth, property and the processes of manufacturing and distribution—down to retail trade through the chain system—can hardly be socialized in outward effect without a political repercussion. It constitutes an ultimate issue which must be faced by new or existing political parties. There is still enough vitality in the older individualism to offer a very serious handicap to any party or program which calls itself by the name of Socialism. But in the long run, the realities of the situation will exercise control over the connotations which, for historical reasons, cling to a word. In view of this fact, the fortunes of a party called by a given name are insignificant.

In one important sense, the fundamental character of the economic question is not ignored in present politics. The dominant party has officially constituted itself the guardian of prosperity; it has gone further and offered itself as the author of prosperity. It has insinuated itself in that guise into the imagination of a sufficient number of citizens and voters so that it owes its continuing domination to its identification with prosperity. Our presidential elections are upon the whole determined by fear. Hundreds of thousands of citizens who vote independently or for Democratic candidates at local elections and in off-year congressional elections regularly vote the Republican ticket every four years. They do so because of a vague but influential dread lest a monkey-wrench be thrown into the economic and financial machine. The dread is as general among the workers as among small traders and storekeepers. It is basically the asset that keeps the dominant party in office. Our whole industrial scheme is so complex, so delicately interdependent in its varied parts, so responsive to a multitude of subtle influences, that it seems definitely better to the mass of voters to endure the ills they may already suffer rather than take the chance of disturbing industry. Even in the election of 1928, in spite of both the liquor and the Catholic issue, this was, I believe, the determining factor.

Moreover, the fact that Hoover offered himself to the popular imagination as a man possessed of the engineer's rather than the politician's mind was a great force. Engineering has accomplished great things; its triumphs are everywhere in evidence. The miracles that it has wrought have given it the prestige of magical wonder-working. A people sick of politicians felt in some half-conscious way that the mind, experience and gifts of an engineer would bring healing and order into our political life. It is impossible to present statistics as to the exact force of the factors mentioned. Judgment on the two points, especially the latter, must remain a matter of opinion. But the identification of the Republican party with the maintenance of prosperity cannot be denied, and the desire for the engineer in politics is general enough to be at least symptomatic.

Prosperity is largely a state of mind, and belief in it is even more so. It follows that skepticism about its extent is of little importance when the mental tide runs with the idea. Although figures can be quoted to show how spotty it is, and how inequitably its economic conditions are distributed, they are all to no avail. What difference does it make that eleven thousand people, having each an annual income of over $100,000, appropriated in 1927 about one twenty-fifth of the net national income? What good does it do to cite official figures showing that only 20 percent of the income of the favored eleven thousand came from salaries and from profits of the businesses they were personally engaged in, while the remaining 80 percent was derived from investments, speculative profits, rent, etc.? That the total earnings of eight million wage workers should be only four times the amount of what the income-tax returns frankly call the "unearned" income of the eleven thousand millionaires goes almost without notice. Moreover, income from investments in corporate aggregations increases at the expense of that coming from enterprises personally managed. For anyone to call attention to this discrepancy is considered an aspersion on our rugged individualism and an attempt to stir up class feeling. Meanwhile, the income-tax returns for 1928 show that in seven years the number of persons having an annual income of more than $1,000,000 has increased from sixty-seven to almost five hundred, twenty-four of whom had incomes of over $10,000,000 each.

Nevertheless, the assumption of guardianship of prosperity by a political party means the assumption of responsibility, and in the long run the ruling economic-political combination will be held to account. The over-lords will have to do something to make good. This fact seems to me to be the centre of the future political situation. Discussion of the prospective political development in connection with corporate industry may at least start from the fact that the industries which used to be regarded as staple, as the foundations of sound economy, are depressed. The plight of agriculture, of the coal and textile industries, is well known. The era of great railway expansion has come to a close; the building trades have a fluctuating career. The counterpart of this fact is that the now flourishing industries are those connected with and derived from new technical developments. Without the rapid growth in the manufacture and sale of automobiles, radios, airplanes, etc.; without the rapid development of new uses for electricity and super-power, prosperity in the last few years would hardly have been even a state of mind. Economic stimulus has come largely from these new uses for capital and labor; surplus funds drawn from them have kept the stock market and other forms of business actively going. At the same time, these newer developments have accelerated the accumulation and concentration of super-fortunes.

These facts seem to suggest the issue of future politics. The fact of depression has already influenced political action in legislation and administration. What will happen when industries now new become in turn overcapitalized and consumption does not keep up in proportion to investment in them; when they, too, have an excess capacity of production? There are now, it is estimated, eight billions of surplus savings a year, and the amount is increasing. Where is this capital to find its outlet? Diversion into the stock market gives temporary relief, but the resulting inflation is a "cure" which creates a new disease. If it goes into the expansion of industrial plants, how long will it be before they, too, "overproduce"? The future seems to hold in store an extension of political control in the social interest. We already have the Interstate Commerce Commission, the Federal Reserve Board, and now the Farm Relief Board—a socialistic undertaking on a large scale sponsored by the party of individualism. The probabilities seem to favor the creation of more such boards in the future, in spite of all concomitant denunciations of bureaucracy and proclamations that individualism is the source of our national prosperity.

The tariff question, too, is undergoing a change. Now, it is the older industries which, being depressed, clamor for relief. The "infant" industries are those which are indifferent, and which, with their growing interest in export trade, are likely to become increasingly indifferent or hostile. The alignment of political parties has not indeed been affected so far by economic changes— beyond the formation of insurgent blocs within the old parties. But this fact only conceals from view the greater fact that, under cover of the old parties, legislation and administration have taken on new functions due to the impact of trade and finance. The most striking example, of course, is the effort to use governmental agencies and large public funds to put agriculture on a parity with other forms of industry. The case is the more significant because the farmers form the part of the population that has remained most faithful to the old individualistic philosophy, and because the movement is definitely directed to bringing them within the scope of collective and corporate action. The policy of using public works to alleviate unemployment in times of depression is another, if lesser, sign of the direction which political action is taking.

The question of whether and how far the newer industries will follow the cycle of the older and now depressed ones, becoming overcapitalized, overproductive in capacity and overcharged with carrying costs, is, of course, a speculative one. The negative

side of the argument demands, however, considerable optimism. It is at least reasonably certain that if depression sets in with them, the process of public intervention and public control will be repeated. And in any case, nothing can permanently exclude political action with reference to old age and unemployment. The scandalous absence even of public inquiry and statistics is emphasized at present by the displacement of workers through technical developments, and by the lowering, because of speeded-up processes, of the age-limit at which workers can be profitably employed. Unemployment, on the scale at which it now "normally" exists—to say nothing of its extent during cyclic periods of depression—is a confession of the breakdown of unregulated individualistic industry conducted for private profit. Coal miners and even farmers may go unheeded, but not so the industrial city workers. One of the first signs of the reawakening of an aggressive labor movement will be the raising of the unemployment problem to a political issue. The outcome of this will be a further extension of public control.

Political prophecy is a risky affair and I would not venture into details. But large and basic economic currents cannot be ignored for any great length of time, and they are working in one direction. There are many indications that the reactionary tendencies which have controlled American politics are coming to a term. The inequitable distribution of income will bring to the fore the use of taxing power to effect redistribution by means of larger taxation of swollen income and by heavier death duties on large fortunes. The scandal of private appropriation of socially produced values in unused land cannot forever remain unconcealed. The situation in world production and commerce is giving "protection and free trade" totally new meanings. The connection of municipal mismanagement and corruption with special favors to big economic interests, and the connection of the alliance thus formed with crime, are becoming more generally recognized. Local labor bodies are getting more and more discontented with the policy of political abstention and with the farce of working through parties controlled by adverse interests. The movement is cumulative and includes convergence to a common head of many now isolated factors. When a focus is reached, economic issues will be openly and not merely covertly political. The problem of social control of industry and the use of governmental agencies for constructive social ends will become the avowed centre of political struggle.

A chapter is devoted to the political phase of the situation not because it is supposed the place of definitely political action in the resolution of the present split in life is fundamental. But it is accessory. A certain amount of specific change in legislation and administration is required in order to supply the conditions under which other changes may take place in non-political ways. Moreover, the psychological effect of law and political discussion is enormous. Political action provides large-scale models that react into the formation of ideas and ideals about all social matters. One sure way in which the individual who is politically lost, because of the loss of objects to which his loyalties can attach themselves, could recover a composed mind, would be by apprehension of the realities of industry and finance as they function in public and political life. Political apathy such as has marked our thought for many years past is due fundamentally to mental confusion arising from lack of consciousness of any vital connection between politics and daily affairs. The parties have been eager accomplices in maintaining the confusion and unreality. To know where things are going and why they are is to have the material out of which stable objects of purpose and loyalty may be formed. To perceive clearly the actual movement of events is to be on the road to intellectual clarity and order.

The chief value of political reference is that politics so well exemplify the existing social confusion and its causes. The various expressions of public control to which reference has been made have taken place sporadically and in response to the pressure of distressed groups so large that their voting power demanded attention. They have been improvised to meet special occasions. They have not been adopted as parts of any general social policy. Consequently their real import has not been considered; they have been treated as episodic exceptions. We live politically from hand to mouth. Corporate forces are strong enough to secure attention and action now and then, when some emergency forces them upon us, but acknowledgment of them does not inspire consecutive policy. On the other hand, the older individualism is still sufficiently ingrained to obtain allegiance in confused sentiment and in vocal utterance. It persists to such an extent that we can maintain the illusion that it regulates our political thought and behavior. In actuality, appeal to it serves to perpetuate the current disorganization in which financial and industrial power, corporately organized, can deflect economic consequences away from the advantage of the many to serve the privilege of the few.

I know of no recent event so politically interesting as President Hoover's calling of industrial conferences after the stock-market crash of 1929. It is indicative of many things, some of them actual, some of them dimly and ambiguously possible. It testifies to the disturbance created when the prospect of an industrial depression faces a party and administration that have assumed responsibility for prosperity through having claimed credit for it. It testifies to the import of the crowd psychology of suggestion and credulity in American life. Christian Science rules American thought in business affairs; if we can be led to think that certain things do not exist, they perforce have not happened. These conferences also give evidence of our national habit of planlessness in social affairs, of locking the barn-door after the horse has been stolen. For nothing was done until after a crash which every economist—except those hopelessly committed to the doctrine of a "new economic era"—knew was certain to happen, however uncertain they may have been as to its time.

The more ambiguous meaning of these conferences is connected with future developments. It is clear that one of their functions was to add up columns of figures to imposing totals, with a view to their effect on the public imagination. Will there be more than a psychological and arithmetical outcome? A hopeful soul may take it as the beginning of a real application of the engineering mind to social life in its economic phase. He may persuade himself that it is the commencement of the acceptance of social responsibility on a large scale by American industrialists, financiers and politicians. He may envisage a permanent Economic Council finally growing out of the holding of a series of conferences, a council which shall take upon itself a planned coordination of industrial development. He may be optimistic enough to anticipate a time when representatives of labor will meet on equal terms, not for the sake of obtaining a pledge to abstain from efforts to obtain a rise of wages and from strikes, but as an integral factor in maintaining a planned regulation of the bases of national welfare.

The issue is still in the future and uncertain. What is not uncertain is that any such move would, if carried through, mark the acknowledged end of the old social and political epoch and its dominant philosophy. It would be in accord with the spirit of American life if the movement were undertaken by voluntary agreement and endeavor rather than by governmental coercion. There is that much enduring truth in our individualism. But the outcome would surely involve the introduction of social responsibility into our business system to such an extent that the doom of an exclusively pecuniary-profit industry would follow. A coordinating and directive council in which captains of industry and finance would meet with representatives of labor and public officials to plan the regulation of industrial activity would signify that we had entered constructively and voluntarily upon the road which Soviet Russia is traveling with so much attendant destruction and coercion. While, as I have already said, political action is not basic, concentration of attention upon real and vital issues such as attend the public control of industry and finance for the sake of social values would have vast intellectual and emotional reverberations. No phase of our culture would remain unaffected. Politics is a means, not an end. But thought of it as a means will lead to thought of the ends it should serve. It will induce consideration of the ways in which a worthy and rich life for all may be achieved. In so doing, it will restore directive aims and be a significant step forward in the recovery of a unified individuality.

I have tried to make a brief survey of the possibilities of the political situation in general, and not to make either a plea or a prophecy of special political alignments. But any kind of political regeneration within or without the present parties demands first of all a frank intellectual recognition of present tendencies. In a society so rapidly becoming corporate, there is need of associated thought to take account of the realities of the situation and to frame policies in the social interest. Only then can organized action in behalf of the social interest be made a reality. We are in for some kind of socialism, call it by whatever name we please, and no matter what it will be called when it is realized. Economic determinism is now a fact, not a theory. But there is a difference and a choice between a blind, chaotic and unplanned determinism, issuing from business conducted for pecuniary profit, and the determination of a socially planned and ordered development. It is the difference and the choice between a socialism that is public and one that is capitalistic.

7. The Crisis in Culture

Discussion of the state and prospects of American culture abounds. But "culture" is an ambiguous word. With respect to one of its meanings I see no ground for pessimism. Interest in art, science and philosophy is not on the wane; the contrary is the case. There may have been individuals superior in achievement in the past, but I do not know of any time in our history when so many persons were actively concerned, both as producers and as appreciators, with these culminating aspects of civilization. There is a more lively and more widespread interest in ideas, in critical discussion, in all that forms an intellectual life, than ever before. Anyone who can look back over a span of thirty or forty years must be conscious of the difference that a generation has produced. And the movement is going forward, not backward.

About culture in the sense of cultivation of a number of persons, a number on the increase rather than the decrease, I find no ground for any great solicitude. But "culture" has another meaning. It denotes the type of emotion and thought that is characteristic of a people and epoch as a whole, an organic intellectual and moral quality. Without raising the ambiguous question of aristocracy, one can say without fear of denial that a high degree of personal cultivation at the top of society can coexist with a low and unworthy state of culture as a pervasive manifestation of social life. The marvelous achievement of the novel, music and the drama in the Russia of the Tsar's day sufficiently illustrates what is meant. Nor is preoccupation with commerce and wealth an insuperable bar to a flourishing culture. One may cite the fact that the highest phase of Dutch painting came in a time of just

[First published as "The Crisis in Culture. The Fifth Article in Professor Dewey's Series, 'Individualism, Old and New,'" in *New Republic* 62 (19 March 1930): 123–26.]

such expansion. And so it was with the Periclean, Augustan and Elizabethan ages. Excellence of personal cultivation has often, and perhaps usually, been coincident with the political and economic dominance of a few and with periods of material expansion.

I see no reason why we in the United States should not also have golden ages of literature and science. But we are given to looking at this and that "age" marked with great names and great productivity, while forgetting to ask about the roots of the efflorescence. Might it not be argued that the very transitoriness of the glory of these ages proves that its causes were sporadic and accidental? And in any case, a question must be raised as to the growth of native culture in our own country. The idea of democracy is doubtless as ambiguous as is that of aristocracy. But we cannot evade a basic issue. Unless an avowedly democratic people and an undeniably industrial time can achieve something more than an "age" of high personal cultivation, there is something deeply defective in its culture. Such an age would be American in a topographical sense, not in a spiritual one.

This fact gives significance to the question so often raised as to whether the material and mechanistic forces of the machine age are to crush the higher life. In one sense I find, as I have already said, no special danger. Poets, painters, novelists, dramatists, philosophers, scientists, are sure to appear and to find an appreciative audience. But the unique fact about our own civilization is that if it is to achieve and manifest a characteristic culture, it must develop, not on top of an industrial and political substructure, but out of our material civilization itself. It will come by turning a machine age into a significantly new habit of mind and sentiment, or it will not come at all. A cultivation of a class that externally adorns a material civilization will at most merely repeat the sort of thing that has transiently happened many times before.

The question, then, is not merely a quantitative one. It is not a matter of an increased number of persons who will take part in the creation and enjoyment of art and science. It is a qualitative question. Can a material, industrial civilization be converted into a distinctive agency for liberating the minds and refining the emotions of all who take part in it? The cultural question is a political and economic one before it is a definitely cultural one.

It is a commonplace that the problem of the relation of mechanistic and industrial civilization to culture is the deepest and most urgent problem of our day. If interpreters are correct in saying that "Americanization" is becoming universal, it is a problem of the world and not just of our own country—although it is first acutely experienced here. It raises issues of the widest philosophic import. The question of the relation of man and nature, of mind and matter, assumes its vital significance in this context. A "humanism" that separates man from nature will envisage a radically different solution of the industrial and economic perplexities of the age than the humanism entertained by those who find no uncrossable gulf or fixed gap. The former will inevitably look backward for direction; it will strive for a cultivated élite supported on the backs of toiling masses. The latter will have to face the question of whether work itself can become an instrument of culture and of how the masses can share freely in a life enriched in imagination and esthetic enjoyment. This task is set not because of sentimental "humanitarianism," but as the necessary conclusion of the intellectual conviction that while man belongs in nature and mind is connected with matter, humanity and its collective intelligence are the means by which nature is guided to new possibilities.

Many European critics openly judge American life from the standpoint of a dualism of the spiritual and material, and deplore the primacy of the physical as fatal to any culture. They fail to see the depth and range of our problem, which is that of making the material an active instrument in the creation of the life of ideas and art. Many American critics of the present scene are engaged in devising modes of escape. Some flee to Paris or Florence; others take flight in their imagination to India, Athens, the Middle Ages or the American age of Emerson, Thoreau and Melville. Flight is solution by evasion. Return to a dualism consisting of a massive substratum of the material upon which are erected spiritually ornamented façades, is flatly impossible, except upon the penalty of the spiritual disenfranchisement of those permanently condemned to toil mechanically at the machine.

That the cultural problem must be reached through economic roads is testified to by our educational system. No nation has ever been so actively committed to universal schooling as are the people of the United States. But what is our system for? What ends does it serve? That it gives opportunity to many who would otherwise lack it is undeniable. It is also the agency of important welding and fusing processes. These are conditions of creation of a mind that will constitute a distinctive type of culture. But they are conditions only. If our public-school system merely turns out efficient industrial fodder and citizenship fodder in a state controlled by pecuniary industry, as other schools in other nations have turned out efficient cannon fodder, it is not helping to solve the problem of building up a distinctive American culture; it is only aggravating the problem. That which prevents the schools from doing their educational work freely is precisely the pressure—for the most part indirect, to be sure—of domination by the money-motif of our economic regime. The subject is too large to deal with here. But the distinguishing trait of the American student body in our higher schools is a kind of intellectual immaturity. This immaturity is mainly due to their enforced mental seclusion; there is, in their schooling, little free and disinterested concern with the underlying social problems of our civilization. Other typical evidence is found in the training of engineers. Thorstein Veblen—and many others have since repeated his idea—pointed out the strategic position occupied by the engineer in our industrial and technological activity. Engineering schools give excellent technical training. Where is the school that pays systematic attention to the potential social function of the engineering profession?

I refer to the schools in connection with this problem of American culture because they are the formal agencies for producing those mental attitudes, those modes of feeling and thinking, which are the essence of a distinctive culture. But they are not the ultimate formative force. Social institutions, the trend of occupations, the pattern of social arrangements, are the finally controlling influences in shaping minds. The immaturity nurtured in schools is carried over into life. If we Americans manifest, as compared with those of other countries who have had the benefits of higher schooling, a kind of infantilism, it is because our own schooling so largely evades serious consideration of the deeper issues of social life; for it is only through induction into realities that mind can be matured. Consequently the effective education, that which really leaves a stamp on character and thought, is obtained when graduates come to take their part in the activities of an adult society which put exaggerated emphasis upon business and the results of business success. Such an education is at best extremely one-sided; it operates to create the specialized "business mind," and this, in turn, is manifested in leisure as well as in business itself. The one-sidedness is accentuated because of the tragic irrelevancy of prior schooling to the controlling realities of social life. There is little preparation to induce either hardy resistance, discriminating criticism, or the vision and desire to direct economic forces in new channels.

If, then, I select education for special notice, it is because education—in the broad sense of formation of fundamental attitudes of imagination, desire and thinking—is strictly correlative with culture in its inclusive social sense. It is because the educative influence of economic and political institutions is, in the last analysis, even more important than their immediate economic consequences. The mental poverty that comes from one-sided distortion of mind is ultimately more significant than poverty in material goods. To make this assertion is not to gloss over the material harshness that exists. It is rather to point out that under present conditions these material results cannot be separated from development of mind and character. Destitution on the one side and wealth on the other are factors in the determination of that psychological and moral constitution which is the source and the measure of attained culture. I can think of nothing more childishly futile, for example, than the attempt to bring "art" and esthetic enjoyment externally to the multitudes who work in the ugliest surroundings and who leave their ugly factories only to go through depressing streets to eat, sleep and carry on their domestic occupations in grimy, sordid homes. The interest of the younger generation in art and esthetic matters is a hopeful sign of the growth of culture in its narrower sense. But it will readily turn into an escape mechanism unless it develops into an alert interest in the conditions which determine the esthetic environment of the vast multitudes who now live, work and play in surroundings that perforce degrade their tastes and that unconsciously educate them into desire for any kind of enjoyment as long as it is cheap and "exciting."

It is the work of sociologists, psychologists, novelists, dramatists and poets to exhibit the consequences of our present economic regime upon taste, desire, satisfaction and standards of value. An article like this cannot do a work which requires many volumes. But a paragraph suffices to call attention to one central fact. Most of those who are engaged in the outward work of production and distribution of economic commodities have no share—imaginative, intellectual, emotional—in directing the activities in which they physically participate.

It was remarked in an earlier chapter that there is definite restriction placed upon existing corporateness. It is found in the fact that economic associations are fixed in ways which exclude most of the workers in them from taking part in their management. The subordination of the enterprises to pecuniary profit reacts to make the workers "hands" only. Their hearts and brains are not engaged. They execute plans which they do not form, and of whose meaning and intent they are ignorant—beyond the fact that these plans make a profit for others and secure a wage for themselves. To set forth the consequences of this fact upon the experience and the minds of uncounted multitudes would again require volumes. But there is an undeniable limitation of opportunities, and minds are warped, frustrated, unnourished by their activities—the ultimate source of all constant nurture of the spirit. The philosopher's idea of a complete separation of mind and body is realized in thousands of industrial workers, and the result is a depressed body and an empty and distorted mind.

There are instances, here and there, of the intellectual and moral effects which accrue when workers can employ their feelings and imaginations as well as their muscles in what they do. But it is still impossible to foresee in detail what would happen if a system of cooperative control of industry were generally substituted for the present system of exclusion. There would be an enormous liberation of mind, and the mind thus set free would have constant direction and nourishment. Desire for related knowledge, physical and social, would be created and rewarded; initiative and responsibility would be demanded and achieved. One may not, perhaps, be entitled to predict that an efflorescence of a distinctive social culture would immediately result. But one can say without hesitation that we shall attain only the personal cultivation of a class, and not a characteristic American culture, unless this condition is fulfilled. It is impossible for a highly industrialized society to attain a widespread high excellence of mind when multitudes are excluded from occasion for the use of thought and emotion in their daily occupations. The contradiction is so great and so pervasive that a favorable issue is hopeless. We must wrest our general culture from an industrialized civilization; and this fact signifies that industry must itself become a primary educative and cultural force for those engaged in it. The conception that natural science somehow sets a limit to freedom, subjecting men to fixed necessities, is not an intrinsic product of science. Just as with the popular notion that art is a luxury, whose proper abode is the museum and gallery, the notion of literary persons (including some philosophers) that science is an oppression due to the material structure of nature, is ultimately a reflex of the social conditions under which science is applied so as to reach only a pecuniary fruition. Knowledge takes effect in machinery and in the minds of technical directors, but not in the thoughts of those who tend the machines. The alleged fatalism of science is in reality the fatalism of the pecuniary order in which science is employed.

If I have emphasized the effect upon the wage workers, it is not because the consequences are not equally marked with respect to the few who now enjoy the material emoluments of the system and monopolize its management and control. There will doubtless always be leaders, those who will have the more active and leading share in the intellectual direction of great industrial undertakings. But as long as the direction is more concerned with pecuniary profit than with social utility, the resulting intellectual and moral development will be one-sided and warped. An inevitable result of a cooperatively shared control of industry would be the recognition of final use or consumption as the criterion of valuation, decision and direction. When the point of view of consumption is supreme in industry, the latter will be socialized, and I see no way of securing its genuine socialization save as industry is viewed and conducted from the standpoint of the user and enjoyer of services and commodities. For then human values will control economic values. Moreover, as long as means are kept separate from human ends (the consequences produced in human living), "values in use" will be so dominated by exchange or sale values that the former will be interpreted by means of the latter. In other words, there is now no inherent criterion for consumption-values. "Wealth," as Ruskin so vehemently pointed out, includes as much *illth* as well-being. When values in use are the ends of industry they will receive a scrutiny and criticism for which there is no foundation at present, save external moralizing and exhortation. Production for private profit signifies that any kind of consumption will be stimulated that leads to private gain.

There can be no stable and balanced development of mind and character apart from the assumption of responsibility. In an industrialized society, that responsibility must for the most part be associated with industry, since it will grow indirectly out of industry even for those not engaged in it. The wider and fuller the sense of social consequences—that is, of the effect on the life-experience of the consumer—the deeper and surer, the more stable, is the intelligence of those who have the foremost place in the direction of industry. A society saturated with industrialism may evolve a class of highly cultivated persons in the traditional sense of cultivation. But there will be something thin and meagre about even this meed of cultivation if it evolves in isolation from the main currents of action in which thought and desire are engaged. As long as imagination is concerned primarily with obtaining pecuniary success and enjoying its material results, the type of culture will conform to these standards.

Everywhere and at all times the development of mind and its cultural products have been connate with the channels in which mind is exercised and applied. This fact defines the problem of creating a culture that will be characteristically our own. Escape from industrialism on the ground that it is unesthetic and brutal can win only a superficial and restricted success of esteem. It is a silly caricature to interpret such statements as meaning that science should devote itself directly to solving industrial problems, or that poetry and painting should find their material in machines and in machine processes. The question is not one of idealizing present conditions in esthetic treatment, but of discovering and trying to realize the conditions under which vital esthetic production and esthetic appreciation may take place on a generous social scale.

And similarly for science; it is not in the least a matter of considering this and that particular practical application to be squeezed out of science; we have a great deal of that sort of thing already. It is a question of acknowledgment on the part of scientific inquirers of intellectual responsibility; of admitting into their consciousness a perception of what science has actually done, through its counterpart technologies, in making the world and life what they are. This perception would bear fruit by raising the question of what science can do in making a different sort of world and society. Such a science would be at the opposite pole to science conceived as merely a means to special industrial ends. It would, indeed, include in its scope all the technological aspects of the latter, but it would also be concerned with control of their social effects. A humane society would use scientific method, and intelligence with its best equipment, to bring about human consequences. Such a society would meet the demand for a science that is humanistic, and not just physical and technical. "Solutions" of the problem of the relation of the material and the spiritual, of the ideal and the actual, are merely conceptual and at best prophetic unless material conditions are idealized by contributing to cultural consequences. Science is a potential tool of such a liberating spiritualization; the arts, including that of social control, are its fruition.

I do not hold, I think, an exaggerated opinion of the influence that is wielded by so-called "intellectuals"—philosophers, professional and otherwise, critics, writers and professional persons in general having interests beyond their immediate callings. But their present position is not a measure of their possibilities. For they are now intellectually dispersed and divided; this fact is one aspect of what I have called "the lost individual." This internal dissolution is necessarily accompanied by a weak social efficacy. The chaos is due, more than to anything else, to mental withdrawal, to the failure to face the realities of industrialized society. Whether the ultimate influence of the distinctively intellectual or reflective groups is to be great or small, an initial move is theirs. A consciously directed critical consideration of the state of present society in its causes and consequences is a pre-condition of projection of constructive ideas. To be effective, the movement must be organized. But this requirement does not demand the creation of a formal organization; it does demand that a sense of the need and opportunity should possess a sufficiently large number of minds. If it does, the results of their inquiries will converge to a common issue.

This point of view is sometimes represented as a virtual appeal to those primarily engaged in inquiry and reflection to desert their studies, libraries and laboratories and engage in works of social reform. That representation is a caricature. It is not the abandonment of thinking and inquiry that is asked for, but more thinking and more significant inquiry. This "more" is equivalent to a conscious direction of thought and inquiry, and direction can be had only by a realization of problems in the rank of their urgency. The "clerk" and secretary once occupied, if we may trust history, places of great influence if not of honor. In a society of military and political leaders who were illiterate, they must have done much of the thinking and negotiating for which the names of the great now receive credit. The intellectuals of the present are their descendants. Outwardly they have been emancipated and have an independent position formerly lacking. Whether their actual efficacy has been correspondingly increased may be doubted. In some degree, they have attained their liberty in direct ratio to their distance from the scenes of action. A more intimate connection would not signify, I repeat, a surrender of the business of thought, even speculative thought, for the sake of getting busy at some so-called practical matter. Rather would it signify a focussing of thought and intensifying of its quality by bringing it into relation with issues of stupendous meaning.

I am suspicious of all attempts to erect a hierarchy of values: their results generally prove to be inapplicable and abstract. But there is at every time a hierarchy of problems, for there are some issues which underlie and condition others. No one person is going to evolve a constructive solution for the problem of humanizing industrial civilization, of making it and its technology a servant of human life—a problem which is once more equivalent, for us, to that of creating a genuine culture. But general guidance of serious intellectual endeavor by a consciousness of the problem would enable at least one group of individuals to recover a social function and so refind themselves. And recovery by those with special intellectual gifts and equipment from their enforced social defection is at least a first step in a more general reconstruction that will bring integration out of disorder.

Accordingly, I do not wish my remarks about escape and withdrawal to be interpreted as if they were directed at any special group of persons. The flight of particular individuals is symptomatic of the seclusion of existing science, intelligence and art.

The personal gap which, generally speaking, isolates the intellectual worker from the wage earner is symbolic and typical of a deep division of functions. This division is the split between theory and practice in actual operation. The effects of the split are as fatal to culture on the one side as on the other. It signifies that what we call our culture will continue to be, and in increased measure, a survival of inherited European traditions, and that it will not be indigenous. And if it is true, as some hold, that with the extension of machine technology and industrialism the whole world is becoming "Americanized," then the creation of an indigenous culture is no disservice to the traditional European springs of our spiritual life. It will signify, not ingratitude, but the effort to repay a debt.

The solution of the crisis in culture is identical with the recovery of composed, effective and creative individuality. The harmony of individual mind with the realities of a civilization made outwardly corporate by an industry based on technology does not signify that individual minds will be passively molded by existing social conditions as if the latter were fixed and static. When the patterns that form individuality of thought and desire are in line with actuating social forces, that individuality will be released for creative effort. Originality and uniqueness are not opposed to social nurture; they are saved by it from eccentricity and escape. The positive and constructive energy of individuals, as manifested in the remaking and redirection of social forces and conditions, is itself a social necessity. A new culture expressing the possibilities immanent in a machine and material civilization will release whatever is distinctive and potentially creative in individuals, and individuals thus freed will be the constant makers of a continuously new society.

It was said in an earlier chapter that "acceptance" of conditions has two very different meanings. To this statement may now be added the consideration that "conditions" are always moving; they are always in transition to something else. The important question is whether intelligence, whether observation and reflection, intervenes and becomes a directive factor in the transition. The moment it does intervene, conditions become conditions of forecasting consequences; when these consequences present themselves in thought, preference and volition, planning and determination, come into play. To foresee consequences of existing conditions is to surrender neutrality and drift; it is to take sides in behalf of the consequences that are preferred. The cultural consequences that our industrial system now produces have no finality about them. When they are observed and are related discriminatingly to their causes, they become conditions for planning, desiring, choosing. Discriminating inquiry will disclose what part of present results is the outcome of the technological factors at work and what part is due to a legal and economic system which it is within the power of man to modify and transform. It is indeed foolish to assume that an industrial civilization will somehow automatically, from its own inner impetus, produce a new culture. But it is a lazy abdication of responsibility which assumes that a genuine culture can be achieved except first by an active and alert intellectual recognition of the realities of an industrial age, and then by planning to use them in behalf of a significantly human life. To charge that those who urge intellectual acknowledgment or acceptance as the first necessary step stop at this point, and thus end with an optimistic rationalization of the present as if it were final, is a misconstruction that indicates a desire to shirk responsibility for undertaking the task of reconstruction and direction. Or else it waits upon a miracle to beget the culture which is desired by all serious minds.

8. Individuality in Our Day

In the foregoing chapters, I have attempted to portray the split between the idea of the individual inherited from the past and the realities of a situation that is becoming increasingly corporate. Some of the effects produced on living individuality by this division have been indicated. I have urged that individuality will again become integral and vital when it creates a frame for itself by attention to the scene in which it must perforce exist and develop. It is likely that many persons will regard my statement of the problem as a commonplace. Others will deplore my failure to offer a detailed solution and a definite picture of just what an individual would be if he were in harmony with the realities of American civilization. Still others will think that a disease has been described as a remedy; that the articles are an indiscriminate praise of technological science and of a corporate industrial civilization; that they are an effort to boost upon the bandwagon those reluctant to climb.

I have indeed attempted analysis, rather than either a condemnation of the evils of present society or a recommendation of fixed ends and ideals for their cure. For I think that serious minds are pretty well agreed as to both evils and ideals—as long as both are taken in general terms. Condemnation is too often only a way of displaying superiority; it speaks from outside the scene; it discloses symptoms but not causes. It is impotent to produce; it can only reproduce its own kind. As for ideals, all agree that we want the good life, and that the good life involves freedom and a taste that is trained to appreciate the honorable, the true and the beautiful. But as long as we limit ourselves to generalities, the phrases that express ideals may be transferred

[First published as "Individuality in Our Day. The Sixth and Final Article in Professor Dewey's Series, 'Individualism, Old and New,'" in *New Republic* 62 (2 April 1930): 184–88.]

from conservative to radical or vice versa, and nobody will be the wiser. For, without analysis, they do not descend into the actual scene nor concern themselves with the generative conditions of realization of ideals.

There is danger in the reiteration of eternal verities and ultimate spiritualities. Our sense of the actual is dulled, and we are led to think that in dwelling upon ideal goals we have somehow transcended existing evils. Ideals express possibilities; but they are genuine ideals only in so far as they are possibilities of what is now moving. Imagination can set them free from their encumbrances and project them as a guide in attention to what now exists. But, save as they are related to actualities, they are pictures in a dream.

I have, then, ventured to suppose that analysis of present conditions is of primary importance. Analysis of even a casual kind discloses that these conditions are not fixed. To accept them intellectually is to perceive that they are in flux. Their movement is not destined to a single end. Many outcomes may be projected, and the movement may be directed by many courses to many chosen goals, once conditions have been recognized for what they are. By becoming conscious of their movements and by active participation in their currents, we may guide them to some preferred possibility. In this interaction, individuals attain an integrated being. The individual who intelligently and actively partakes in a perception that is a first step in conscious choice is never so isolated as to be lost nor so quiescent as to be suppressed.

One of the main difficulties in understanding the present and apprehending its human possibilities is the persistence of stereotypes of spiritual life which were formed in old and alien cultures. In static societies—those which the industrial revolution has doomed—acquiescence had a meaning, and so had the projection of fixed ideals. Things were so relatively settled that there was something to acquiesce in, and goals and ideals could be imagined that were as fixed in their way as existing conditions in theirs. The medieval legal system could define "just" prices and wages, for the definition was a formulation of what was customary in the local community; it operated merely to prevent exorbitant deviations. It could prescribe a system of definite duties for all relations, for there was a hierarchical order, and occasions for the exercise of duty fell within an established and hence known order. Communities were local; they did not merge, overlap and interact in all kinds of subtle and hidden ways. A common church was the guardian and administrator of spiritual and ideal truth, and its theoretical authority had direct channels for making itself felt in the practical details of life. Spiritual realities might have their locus in the next world, but this after-world was intimately tied into all the affairs of this world by an institution existing here and now.

To-day there are no patterns sufficiently enduring to provide anything stable in which to acquiesce, and there is no material out of which to frame final and all-inclusive ends. There is, on the other hand, such constant change that acquiescence is but a series of interrupted spasms, and the outcome is mere drifting. In such a situation, fixed and comprehensive goals are but irrelevant dreams, while acquiescence is not a policy but its abnegation.

Again, the machine is condemned wholesale because it is seen through the eyes of a spirituality that belonged to another state of culture. Present evil consequences are treated as if they were eternally necessary, because they cannot be made consistent with the ideals of another age. In reality, a machine age is a challenge to generate new conceptions of the ideal and the spiritual. Ferrero has said that machines "are the barbarians of modern times, which have destroyed the fairest works of ancient civilisations." But even the barbarians were not immutably barbarous; they, too, were bearers of directive movement, and in time they wrought out a civilization that had its own measure of fairness and beauty.

Most attacks on the mechanistic character of science are caused by the survival of philosophies and religions formed when nature was the grim foe of man. The possibility of the present, and therefore its problem, is that through and by science, nature may become the friend and ally of man. I have rarely seen an attack on science as hostile to humanism which did not rest upon a conception of nature formed long before there was any science. That there is much at any time in environing nature which is indifferent and hostile to human values is obvious to any serious mind. When natural knowledge was hardly existent, control of nature was impossible. Without power of control, there was no recourse save to build places of refuge in which man could live in imagination, although not in fact. There is no need to deny the grace and beauty of some of these constructions. But when their imaginary character is once made apparent, it is futile to suppose that men can go on living and sustaining life by them. When they are appealed to for support, the possibilities of the present are not perceived, and its constructive potentialities remain unutilized.

In reading many of the literary appreciations of science, one would gather that until the rise of modern science, men had not been aware that living in nature entails death and renders fortune precarious and uncertain; "science" is even treated as if it were responsible for the revelation of the fact that nature is often a foe of human interests and goods. But the very nature of the creeds that men have entertained in the past and of the rites they have practiced is proof that men were overwhelmingly conscious of this fact. If they had not been, they would not have resorted to magic, miracles, myth and the consolations and compensations of another world and life. As long as these things were sincerely believed in, dualism, anti-naturalism, had a meaning, for the "other world" was then a reality. To surrender the belief and retain the dualism is temporarily possible for bewildered minds. It is a condition which it is impossible to maintain permanently. The alternative is to accept what science tells us of the world in which we live and to resolve to use the agencies it puts within our power to render nature more amenable to human desire and more contributory to human good. "Naturalism" is a word with all kinds of meanings. But a naturalism which perceives that man with his habits, institutions, desires, thoughts, aspirations, ideals and struggles, is within nature, an integral part of it, has the philosophical foundation and the practical inspiration for effort to employ nature as an ally of human ideals and goods such as no dualism can possibly provide.

There are those who welcome science provided it remain "pure"; they see that as a pursuit and contemplated object it is an addition to the enjoyed meaning of life. But they feel that its applications in mechanical inventions are the cause of many of the troubles of modern society. Undoubtedly these applications have brought new modes of unloveliness and suffering. I shall not attempt the impossible task of trying to strike a net balance of ills and enjoyments between the days before and after the practical use of science. The significant point is that application is still restricted. It touches our dealings with things but not with one another. We use scientific method in directing physical but not human energies. Consideration of the full application of science must accordingly be prophetic rather than a record of what has already taken place. Such prophecy is not however without foundation. Even as things are there is a movement in science which foreshadows, if its inherent promise be carried out, a more humane age. For it looks forward to a time when all individuals may share in the discoveries and thoughts of others, to the liberation and enrichment of their own experience.

No scientific inquirer can keep what he finds to himself or turn it to merely private account without losing his scientific standing. Everything discovered belongs to the community of workers. Every new idea and theory has to be submitted to this community for confirmation and test. There is an expanding community of cooperative effort and of truth. It is true enough that these traits are now limited to small groups having a somewhat technical activity. But the existence of such groups reveals a possibility of the present—one of the many possibilities that are a challenge to expansion, and not a ground for retreat and contraction.

Suppose that what now happens in limited circles were extended and generalized. Would the outcome be oppression or emancipation? Inquiry is a challenge, not a passive conformity; application is a means of growth, not of repression. The general adoption of the scientific attitude in human affairs would mean nothing less than a revolutionary change in morals, religion, politics and industry. The fact that we have limited its use so largely to technical matters is not a reproach to science, but to the human beings who use it for private ends and who strive to defeat its social application for fear of destructive effects upon their power and profit. A vision of a day in which the natural sciences and the technologies that flow from them are used as servants of a humane life constitutes the imagination that is relevant to our own time. A humanism that flees from science as an enemy denies the means by which a liberal humanism might become a reality.

The scientific attitude is experimental as well as intrinsically communicative. If it were generally applied, it would liberate us from the heavy burden imposed by dogmas and external standards. Experimental method is something other than the use of blow-pipes, retorts and reagents. It is the foe of every belief that permits habit and wont to dominate invention and discovery, and ready-made system to override verifiable fact. Constant revision is the work of experimental inquiry. By revision of knowledge and ideas, power to effect transformation is given us. This attitude, once incarnated in the individual mind, would find an operative outlet. If dogmas and institutions tremble when a new idea appears, this shiver is nothing to what would happen if the idea were armed with the means for the continuous discovery of new truth and the criticism of old belief. To "acquiesce" in science is dangerous only for those who would maintain affairs in the existing social order unchanged because of lazy habit or self-interest. For the scientific attitude demands faithfulness to whatever is discovered and steadfastness in adhering to new truth.

The "given" which science calls upon us to accept is not fixed; it is in process. A chemist does not study the elements in order to bow down before them; ability to produce transformations is the outcome. It is said, and truly, that we are now oppressed by the weight of science. But why? Some allowance has to be made, of course, for the time it takes to learn the uses of new means and to appropriate their potentialities. When these means are as radically new as is experimental science, the time required is correspondingly long. But aside from this fact, the multiplication of means and materials is an increase of opportunities and purposes. It marks a release of individuality for affections and deeds more congenial to its own nature. Even the derided bathtub has its individual uses; an individual is not perforce degraded because he has the chance to keep himself clean. The radio will make for standardization and regimentation only as long as individuals refuse to exercise the selective reaction that is theirs. The enemy is not material commodities, but the lack of the will to use them as instruments for achieving preferred possibilities. Imagine a society free from pecuniary domination, and it becomes self-evident that material commodities are invitations to individual taste and choice, and occasions for individual growth. If human beings are not strong and steadfast enough to accept the invitation and take advantage of the proffered occasion, let us put the blame where it belongs.

There is at least this much truth in economic determinism. Industry is not outside of human life, but within it. The genteel tradition shuts its eyes to this fact; emotionally and intellectually it pushes industry and its material phase out into a region remote from human values. To stop with mere emotional rejection and moral condemnation of industry and trade as materialistic is to leave them in this inhuman region where they operate as the instruments of those who employ them for private ends. Exclusion of this sort is an accomplice of the forces that keep things in the saddle. There is a subterranean partnership between those who employ the existing economic order for selfish pecuniary gain and those who turn their backs upon it in the interest of personal complacency, private dignity, and irresponsibility.

Every occupation leaves its impress on individual character and modifies the outlook on life of those who carry it on. No one questions this fact as respects wage-earners tied to the machine, or business men who devote themselves to pecuniary manipulations. Callings may have their roots in innate impulses of human nature but their pursuit does not merely "express" these impulses, leaving them unaltered; their pursuit determines intellectual horizons, precipitates knowledge and ideas, shapes desire and interest. This influence operates in the case of those who set up fine art, science, or religion as ends in themselves, isolated from radiation and expansion into other concerns (such radiation being what "application" signifies) as much as in the case of those who engage in industry. The alternatives are lack of application with consequent narrowing and overspecialization, and application with enlargement and increase of liberality. The narrowing in the case of industry pursued apart from social ends is evident to all thoughtful persons. Intellectual and literary folks who conceive themselves devoted to pursuit of pure truth and uncontaminated beauty too readily overlook the fact that a similar narrowing and hardening takes place in them. Their goods are more refined, but they are also engaged in acquisition; unless they are concerned with use, with expansive interactions, they too become monopolists of capital. And the monopolization of spiritual capital may in the end be more harmful than that of material capital.

The destructive effect of science upon beliefs long cherished and values once prized is, and quite naturally so, a great cause of dread of science and its applications in life. The law of inertia holds of the imagination and its loyalties as truly as of physical things. I do not suppose that it is possible to turn suddenly from these negative effects to possible positive and constructive ones.

But as long as we refuse to make an effort to change the direction in which imagination looks at the world, as long as we remain unwilling to reexamine old standards and values, science will continue to wear its negative aspect. Take science (including its application to the machine) for what it is, and we shall begin to envisage it as a potential creator of new values and ends. We shall have an intimation, on a wide and generous scale, of the release, the increased initiative, independence and inventiveness, which science now brings in its own specialized fields to the individual scientist. It will be seen as a means of originality and individual variation. Even to those sciences which delight in calling themselves "pure," there is a significant lesson in the instinct that leads us to speak of Newton's and Einstein's law.

Because the free working of mind is one of the greatest joys open to man, the scientific attitude, incorporated in individual mind, is something which adds enormously to one's enjoyment of existence. The delights of thinking, of inquiry, are not widely enjoyed at the present time. But the few who experience them would hardly exchange them for other pleasures. Yet they are now as restricted in quality as they are in the number of those who share them. That is to say, as long as "scientific" thinking confines itself to technical fields, it lacks full scope and varied material. Its subject-matter is technical in the degree in which application in human life is shut out. The mind that is hampered by fear lest something old and precious be destroyed is the mind that experiences fear of science. He who has this fear cannot find reward and peace in the discovery of new truths and the projection of new ideals. He does not walk the earth freely, because he is obsessed by the need of protecting some private possession of belief and taste. For the love of private possessions is not confined to material goods.

It is a property of science to find its opportunities in problems, in questions. Since knowing is inquiring, perplexities and difficulties are the meat on which it thrives. The disparities and conflicts that give rise to problems are not something to be dreaded, something to be endured with whatever hardihood one can command; they are things to be grappled with. Each of us experiences these difficulties in the sphere of his personal relations, whether in his more immediate contacts or in the wider associations conventionally called "society." At present, personal frictions are one of the chief causes of suffering. I do not say all suffering would disappear with the incorporation of scientific method into individual disposition; but I do say that it is now immensely increased by our disinclination to treat these frictions as problems to be dealt with intellectually. The distress that comes from being driven in upon ourselves would be largely relieved; it would in part be converted into the enjoyment that attends the free working of mind, if we took them as occasions for the exercise of thought, as problems having an objective direction and outlet.

We all experience, as I have said, the perplexities that arise in the intimacies of personal intercourse. The more remote relations of society also present their troubles. There is much talk of "social problems." But we rarely treat them as problems in the intellectual sense of that word. They are thought of as "evils" needing correction; as naughty or diabolic things to be "reformed." Our preoccupation with these ideas is proof of how far we are from taking the scientific attitude. I do not say that the attitude of the physician who regards his patient as a "beautiful case" is wholly ideal. But it is more wholesome and more promising than the persistence of the pre-scientific habit of anxious concerns with evils and their reform. The current way of treating criminality and criminals is, for example, reminiscent of the way in which diseases were once thought of and dealt with. Their origin was once believed to be moral and personal; some enemy, diabolic or human, was thought to have injected some alien substance or force into the person who was ailing. The possibility of effective treatment began when diseases were regarded as having an intrinsic origin in interactions of the organism and its natural environment. We are only just beginning to think of criminality as an equally intrinsic manifestation of interactions between an individual and the social environment. With respect to it, and with respect to so many other evils, we persist in thinking and acting in prescientific "moral" terms. This pre-scientific conception of "evil" is probably the greatest barrier that exists to that real reform which is identical with constructive remaking.

Because science starts with questions and inquiries it is fatal to all social system-making and programs of fixed ends. In spite of the bankruptcy of past systems of belief, it is hard to surrender our faith in system and in some wholesale belief. We continually reason as if the difficulty were in the particular system that has failed and as if we were on the point of now finally hitting upon one that is true as all the others were false. The real trouble is with the attitude of dependence upon any of them. Scientific method would teach us to break up, to inquire definitely and with particularity, to seek solutions in the terms of concrete problems as they arise. It is not easy to imagine the difference which would follow from the shift of thought to discrimination and analysis. Wholesale creeds and all-inclusive ideals are impotent in the face of actual situations; for doing always means the doing of something in particular. They are worse than impotent. They conduce to blind and vague emotional states in which credulity is at home, and where action, following the lead of overpowering emotion, is easily manipulated by the self-seekers who have kept their heads and wits. Nothing would conduce more, for example, to the elimination of war than the substitution of specific analysis of its causes for the wholesale love of "liberty, humanity, justice and civilization."

All of these considerations would lead to the conclusion that depression of the individual is the individual's own liability, were it not for the time it takes for a new principle to make its way deeply into individual mind on a large scale. But as time goes on, the responsibility becomes an individual one. For individuality is inexpugnable and it is of its nature to assert itself. The first move in recovery of an integrated individual is accordingly with the individual himself. In whatever occupation he finds himself and whatever interest concerns him, he is himself and no other, and he lives in situations that are in some respect flexible and plastic.

We are given to thinking of society in large and vague ways. We should forget "society" and think of law, industry, religion, medicine, politics, art, education, philosophy—and think of them in the plural. For points of contact are not the same for any two persons, and hence the questions which the interests and occupations pose are never twice the same. There is no contact so immutable that it will not yield at some point. All these callings and concerns are the avenues through which the world acts upon us and we upon the world. There is no society at large, no business in general. Harmony with conditions is not a single and monotonous uniformity, but a diversified affair requiring individual attack.

Individuality is inexpugnable because it is a manner of distinctive sensitivity, selection, choice, response and utilization of conditions. For this reason, if for no other, it is impossible to develop integrated individuality by any all-embracing system or program. No individual can make the determination for anyone else; nor can he make it for himself all at once and forever. A native manner of selection gives direction and continuity, but definite expression is found in changing occasions and varied forms. The selective choice and use of conditions have to be continually made and remade. Since we live in a moving world and change with our interactions in it, every act produces a new perspective that demands a new exercise of preference. If, in the long run, an individual remains lost, it is because he has chosen irresponsibility; and if he remains wholly depressed it is because he has chosen the course of easy parasitism.

Acquiescence, in the sense of drifting, is not something to be achieved; it is something to be overcome, something that is "natural" in the sense of being easy. But it assumes a multitude of forms, and Rotarian applause for present conditions is only one of these forms. A different form of submission consists in abandoning the values of a new civilization for those of the past. To assume the uniform of some dead culture is only another means of regimentation. True integration is to be found in relevancy to the present, in active response to conditions as they present themselves, in the effort to make them over according to some consciously chosen possibility.

Individuality is at first spontaneous and unshaped; it is a potentiality, a capacity of development. Even so, it is a unique manner of acting in and with a world of objects and persons. It is not something complete in itself, like a closet in a house or a secret drawer in a desk, filled with treasures that are waiting to be bestowed on the world. Since individuality is a distinctive way of feeling the impacts of the world and of showing a preferential bias in response to these impacts, it develops into shape and form only through interaction with actual conditions; it is no more complete in itself than is a painter's tube of paint without relation to a canvas. The work of art is the truly individual thing; and it is the result of the interaction of paint and canvas through the medium of the artist's distinctive vision and power. In its determination, the potential individuality of the artist takes on visible and enduring form. The imposition of individuality as something made in advance always gives evidence of a mannerism, not of a manner. For the latter is something original and creative; something formed in the very process of creation of other things.

The future is always unpredictable. Ideals, including that of a new and effective individuality, must themselves be framed out of the possibilities of existing conditions, even if these be the conditions that constitute a corporate and industrial age. The ideals take shape and gain a content as they operate in remaking conditions. We may, in order to have continuity of direction, plan a program of action in anticipation of occasions as they emerge. But a program of ends and ideals if kept apart from sensitive and flexible method becomes an encumbrance. For its hard and rigid character assumes a fixed world and a static individual; and neither of these things exists. It implies that we can prophesy the future—an attempt which terminates, as someone has said, in prophesying the past or in its reduplication.

The same Emerson who said that "society is everywhere in conspiracy against its members" also said, and in the same essay, "accept the place the divine providence has found for you, the society of your contemporaries, the connection of events." Now, when events are taken in disconnection and considered apart from the interactions due to the selecting individual, they conspire against individuality. So does society when it is accepted as something already fixed in institutions. But "the connection of events," and "the society of your contemporaries" as formed of moving and multiple associations, are the only means by which the possibilities of individuality can be realized.

Psychiatrists have shown how many disruptions and dissipations of the individual are due to his withdrawal from reality into a merely inner world. There are, however, many subtle forms of retreat, some of which are erected into systems of philosophy and are glorified in current literature. "It is in vain," said Emerson, "that we look for genius to reiterate its miracles in the old arts; it is its instinct to find beauty and holiness in new and necessary facts, in the field and road-side, in the shop and mill." To gain an integrated individuality, each of us needs to cultivate his own garden. But there is no fence about this garden: it is no sharply marked-off enclosure. Our garden is the world, in the angle at which it touches our own manner of being. By accepting the corporate and industrial world in which we live, and by thus fulfilling the pre-condition for interaction with it, we, who are also parts of the moving present, create ourselves as we create an unknown future.

Construction and Criticism

Construction and Criticism

My subject this evening sounds rather high-brow, and I fear my treatment of it will not get down to concrete matters as much as is desirable. I have used the word construction rather than creation because it seems less pretentious. But what I mean by it is the creative mind, the mind that is genuinely productive in its operations. We are given to associating creative mind with persons regarded as rare and unique, like geniuses. But every individual is in his own way unique. Each one experiences life from a different angle than anybody else, and consequently has something distinctive to give others if he can turn his experiences into ideas and pass them on to others. Each individual that comes into the world is a new beginning; the universe itself is, as it were, taking a fresh start in him and trying to do something, even if on a small scale, that it has never done before. I have always been struck by the interest taken in small children, in their doings and sayings. Discount as much as we will the doting fondness of relatives, yet there is something left over. This something is, I believe, the recognition of originality; a response to the fact that these children who appeal so much to their family and friends bring something fresh into the world, a new way of looking at it, a new way of feeling it. And the interest in this freshness is also a sign of something else. It indicates that adults are looking precisely for something distinctive of individuality. They are sick of constant repetition and duplication, of opinions that are stereotyped and emotions that are pale stencils of something that someone else has once experienced.

When I think of this fresh reaction of little children to the world, I am led to ask why it so soon gets dimmed; why it gets so soon covered up and a kind of mental rubber stamp or phonograph record takes its place. It may be thought absurd to demand originality of everyone. But I think this idea of absurdity is due to having a wrong measure by which to judge originality. It is not to be measured by its outer product; it is rather an individual way of approaching a world that is common to us all. An individual is not original merely when he gives to the world some discovery that has never been made before. Every time he really makes a discovery, even if thousands of persons have made similar ones before, he is original. The value of a discovery in the mental life of an individual is the contribution it makes to a creatively active mind; it does not depend upon no one's ever having thought of the same idea before. If it is sincere and straightforward, if it is new and fresh to me or to you, it is original in quality, even if others have already made the same discovery. The point is that it be first-hand, not taken second-hand from another.

Mr. Crothers has told in his delightful way of a man in a Massachusetts village who climbed a tree to get a new view and who came down and announced that he had seen the Pacific Ocean. He had observed as a matter of fact a pond in a neighboring town. But what of that? Mr. Crothers went on to say. He had the will of discovery, and if only the Pacific Ocean had been accommodating enough to be there, he would have seen it.

The anecdote suggests something else. This New Englander was evidently what other New Englanders call a "character." Such men were more often found in our pioneer days than they are now. Our forefathers were constantly moving on. Many of them moved on physically. Their migrations and new settlements created a constantly expanding frontier and horizon. But even those who stayed in one place always found, as long as pioneer days existed, something new to do. There was some forest to cut down to make way for grain fields; there were houses and fences to put up, and with their own hands; there were all the household articles and clothing to be made at home; skins to be tanned, soap to be manufactured, candles to be dipped, and so on in almost endless variety. They did not live in a ready-made world, but in a world they were themselves making. They had no Woolworth and chain stores to draw upon. If they wanted schools and churches they had to produce them. Versatility and inventiveness, ready adaptation to new conditions, minds of courage and fertility in facing obstacles, were the result. Original work was once done in politics and government in this country because there were so many minds trained to dealing with unprecedented conditions in daily life. Men were not then afraid to experiment and improvise; they had to do these things in order not to be overwhelmed by alien forces.

I doubt if any social change has taken place in any country at any time as great as that marked by the disappearance of the pioneer in the last fifty years. Perhaps the most striking idea evolved in the interpretation of the history of the United States is the importance of the frontier. But the frontier has virtually disappeared, and with it has disappeared the pioneer. We still move about a great deal, but we do it in ready-made motor and Pullman cars, and we go to places that are similar in habits of mind and feeling to the places which we have left; where people get the same news in their papers, read the same best sellers, and listen to the same music and talks, including advertisements of the same ready-made goods, over the radio.

I am old enough to have known and talked with some of these pioneers. I recall one who went from New York when a boy with his family who were looking for new territory to conquer. He went to Michigan, then a wilderness, and became a fur trader in the north, lived with Chippewa Indians and was adopted as a member of their tribe, later becoming a millwright and farmer, and as civilization closed in around him went west in advance of the railway and shot buffaloes; after he was seventy he went gold hunting in Colorado and lived in a mining camp ten thousand feet above the sea. His life was a true American Odyssey, and there were thousands like him.

In the last few months I have read a diary of my great-grandfather, who only a little more than a hundred years ago moved when a boy with his family to a portion of Vermont which was then a virtual wilderness; there they founded a school and a church, built a gristmill and sawmill, and started a store. While still hardly more than a boy he drove cattle on foot to Boston. I do not refer to these incidents because there is anything especially unusual about them, but rather because they are typical of what was going on a hundred years ago, and because it goes beyond the limits of imagination to appreciate the tremendous change in habits of thought and emotion that has taken place in this same short time along with the changes in outer conditions. We have passed in less than a hundred years from a pioneer civilization to the most highly industrialized civilization on earth, where the ready-made and the readily accessible without individual creative effort abound more than anywhere else in the world. Where on earth and in what period of time can you find such a change?

We realize, albeit somewhat dimly, the outward change that has taken place; dimly, because we are so completely surrounded with what now exists and so absorbed in it that it is about as hard to form a realistic picture of what has vanished as it is upon a cold day in winter to form a vivid sense of the heat of summer. But when we pride ourselves upon the extent of this physical change and our subduing of the wilderness, and succeed in forming a picture of it, we are still likely to forget the significance and scope of the psychological change, the change in mental and moral attitudes, that has taken place. So I repeat we have come from a civilization where everything was still to do, and men's minds were everywhere provoked and incited by the imperious need to create and produce, into a world where things are made for us; where energy is spent in making things that some unknown person is going to use in some remote part of the country, and then in buying and using things that some other unknown person has produced by mechanical means in some far-away and unknown corner. We have passed, so to speak, from a face-to-face contact with nature to a contact with the results of machines and artifice; from a world, social and physical, that was in process of making to one that is for most of us made; and hence from a world that was a constant stimulus to some kind of originality and inventiveness to one that puts a premium upon receptivity and reduplication.

I am not, I hope, referring to this difference in order to adopt the too easy habit of old age and sing the praise of a bygone age, lamenting the good old days of yore. There was too much that was harsh and crude in the old conditions to indulge in immoderate idealization; we have thousands of advantages unknown to our forbears. But the tremendous change raises a question. How shall we today under our conditions develop the same independence and initiative of mind with respect to our problems that they were forced to evolve in the face of their problems?

I shall not take a long time in which to speak of the particular difficulties we experience. A large scale machine production and distribution tends to produce homogeneity just as it tends to produce the urbanization of population out of once scattered rural villages. As Bertrand Russell has recently pointed out in an article called "Homogeneous America," even the farmer who lives in comparative physical isolation produces with machines and for a distant market, and these facts tend to assimilate his mental habits to those of others. The mechanics of news gathering and circulation generate a common mental diet. The leveling of classes has resulted in a definite uniformity of garb very different from the distinctive attire of localities and classes found in the less industrialized portions of Europe. This similarity is the outward counterpart and symbol of the forces that make for mental uniformity and that tend to stifle mental independence. I do not suggest that these conditions are at all fatal to the creative mind. But they render it a deliberate aim, something to be sedulously cultivated, instead of its being a kind of by-product of social conditions as it once was.

As I have referred to the young as evidence that a certain originality of mental attitude is a spontaneous trait of human individuals, so I must now refer to education as one great force that may either preserve and propagate this attitude or that may slowly and surely choke it. Education is one of the great opportunities for present day pioneering. It is also one of the fields which is hedged about with greatest difficulties. Our forefathers, to return to them for the moment, could afford to be traditionalists in their schools; they almost had to be in order not to lose contact with the older heritage of culture because of their physical remoteness from its sources. And they got education of another sort in their daily lives and their practical contacts. To a considerable extent, notwithstanding changes in schools that seem revolutionary when we take them en masse, we have retained much of their traditionalism, in spite of the losses in other directions of opportunities for manifesting inventiveness and initiative.

The bare fact that a child goes to school in order to learn tends to make learning a synonym for taking in and reproducing what other persons have already found out. Ready-made materials in material things have their oppressive counterpart in ready-made intellectual information and ideas, and education is supposed to consist in a transfer of these goods into the mind. Schools tend to be pipe-lines and delivery wagons. The increase, the rapid and extensive increase, of knowledge enlarges the stock that flows from the storehouses and tanks of learning into the minds of pupils. Packaged goods are as much in vogue intellectually as they are commercially. The formation of the course of study is largely a matter of doing up bundles of knowledge in sizes appropriate to age and arranging for their serial distribution, each in its proper year, month, and day. In school as in business we pay more attention than used to be done to having the packages look neat and pasting attractive labels upon them. But one like the other comes pre-prepared, with a view to putting the least possible tax on individual powers of digestion.

Our laudable effort at universal education adds to the premium upon the ready-made article and its mechanical transfer. Big buildings and large classes to each teacher mechanize administration and teaching; time seems to be lacking in which students, young or old, may engage in independent and productive intellectual activity. With so much material to deliver in geography, history, literature, the sciences and arts, and so many potential consumers to reach, the outcome is a chain-belt system of systematized mass manufacture. It is not, perhaps, surprising that the efforts of those engaged in what is euphemistically called a science of education aim at setting so-called norms which are only averages of large numbers, or that their ideal is to introduce better order and economy into the distribution and delivery system. A large part of the business of the teachers as of the sellers of commercial products is to break down sales resistance; for the individual mind of the student retains, save in cases of extreme docility, enough of its individuality to wish to play hookey and to escape loading up with the goods offered. Physical truancy is probably diminishing, but the mental truancy known as not paying attention is still carried on with great success, in spite of the greater attractiveness of the packaged goods.

It is not difficult to list the main traits of a genuinely creative or productive mental activity. They are such things as independence, initiative, and the exercise of discriminating judgment. Unfortunately, it is easier to understand and interpret these in a physical sense than in an intellectual one. Doing as one pleases signifies a release from truly *intellectual* initiative and independence, unless taste has been well developed as to *what* one pleases. Perhaps you have heard the story of the child who in a school that prided itself on its freedom inquired of the teacher, "Do we *have* to do what we want to do today?" The story if not true is at least "well found." It requires a cultivated mind to have significant conscious desires, to know what one really wants. It is easy to take what is suggested in any chance way or by what others are seen to do as what one wants to do, when in reality the so-called want is only a desperate effort to escape from a mental void. In order to obtain genuine independence and initiative of thought a good deal more is required than the label of "progressive," and unless it is *thinking* which is independent and initiating, there is merely undirected bodily activity—which is a long way off from that mental freedom which is a condition of creation. Release of the body, of hand, eye, and ear, from physical conditions that cramp and mechanize is a precondition of more independent thought, but it is only a condition, not the thing itself.

In spite of appearances I am not, however, engaged in giving a lecture on pedagogy. I am only trying to illustrate through the familiar example of the schools a dilemma we all face, adults out of school as well as children in it. Adults also alternate between mental subjection to routine and unordered physical activity. They also strive to compensate for subjection to tasks of absorption and reproduction by excess aimless mobility. The standardized factory and the automobile racing from nowhere in particular to nowhere else in particular with no special purpose except to get there and back as fast as possible are the Siamese twins of our civilization. The chief difficulty with adults is very much like that from which children suffer in schools. We do not know what we really want and we make no great effort to find out. We, too, allow our purposes and desires to be foisted upon us from without. We, too, are bored by doing what we want to do, because the want has no deep roots in our own judgment of values. There is a vicious circle. We yield to one kind of external pressure in doing what we like just as we yield to another kind in having to do what we don't like. The only difference is that pressure in the latter case is obvious and direct; in the former case it is subtle and indirect.

It is at this point that the part of my title of which I have so far said nothing comes in: Criticism. Criticism, I hardly need point out to this audience, is not fault finding. It is not pointing out evils to be reformed. It is judgment engaged in discriminating among values. It is taking thought as to what is better and worse in any field at any time, with some consciousness of *why* the better is better and *why* the worse is worse. Critical judgment is therefore not the enemy of creative production but its friend and ally. I have heard intelligent persons say that their college education overdeveloped their critical faculties at the expense of their productive capacities. I have heard them envy colleagues who had escaped the blight of constant exercise of their critical powers, on the ground that the latter were much surer of themselves and possessed of greater confidence in projecting and executing new courses of action.

We can easily understand what these persons mean. We have all seen cases of partial paralysis of powers of action, due apparently to excessive development of powers of thought. Consciousness if not conscience seems to make cowards of us all. Thought makes us aware of many alternative possibilities, and in widening the range of possible choices makes energetic choice difficult. It leads to doubt and hesitation. In becoming critical of values we become uncertain as to whether any value is really worth the effort required to realize it; in thinking of whether there may not be something else more valuable we avoid committing ourselves in action to any chosen good. I cannot agree, however, that the result is due to cultivation of critical ability. It is rather the product of students being swamped with criticisms emanating from other minds. We forget that criticisms exist ready-made as much as anything else, and that absorption of ready-made criticisms is a very different thing from exercise of critical power. I have referred to the case of college students, but the principle applies everywhere.

The primary requisite of critical ability is courage; its great enemy is cowardice, even though it take that mitigated form called intellectual laziness. The easy course is always to accept what is handed out. It not only saves effort but it places responsibility on someone else. I have recently been reading an account of a contact of Gandhi with a Plymouth Brother in South Africa. The latter urged the acceptance of Christianity upon Gandhi on the ground that it was impossible to live sinless in this world and that consequently unless one accepted the redemptive act performed by another, "life was restless and uncertain in this world of sin." To which Gandhi replied that he was not interested in redemption from the consequences of sin but from sin itself. I do not suppose the statement of the particular missionary in question would be received as authoritative by all Christians. But the incident is worth referring to as evidence of the fact that the transfer of responsibility from self to someone else has found its way into the imagination of multitudes through the gateway of popular religious beliefs.

The same thing has happened in all other fields of belief and action. There are many persons who are busy telling us that democracy is a political failure. In as far as it is a failure, it is because the idea of democracy involves individual responsibility for judgment and choice, while large numbers of men and women refuse to take upon themselves the burden of this responsibility. The account with democratic ideals is still far from being settled. But if it turns out in the end a failure, it will not be because it is too low a doctrine but because it is too high morally for human nature, at least as that human nature is now educated. It is a strenuous doctrine that demands courage of thought and belief for realization.

There is also much condemnation of democracy for its unwillingness to admit experts and expert advice and leadership. Anyone who has followed the history of even New York City politics knows facts that bear out the accusation. But the facts as they first appear only raise a question as to the source of this opposition to experts. And this question if followed up will lead to the conclusion that the real cause of the objection is not any objection to experts as such, but knowledge of the fact that taking their counsel and directions would involve disturbance of vested corrupt influences. Too many people, as it is, are willing to "let George do it," and would willingly, too willingly, follow in the wake of expert leadership if they were not afraid it would interfere with some private purpose.

Indeed, I should be willing to go so far as to say that we in this country are too submissive to what are termed authorities in different fields, and too little given to questioning their right to speak with authority. It is a common complaint that we are too credulous a people and are only too ready to swallow any bunk if it is offered with the prestige of apparent authority. Advertising pages teem with recommendations of everything from medicines to beds and foods, which are to influence the buying public because they come from someone prominent on the stage, in baseball, or in "society." I heard recently of an instance in which the business manager of an explorer wrote to firms dealing in such articles as the explorer might need to take with him, proposing financial arrangements for future testimonials. We let ourselves off too easily when we attribute this state of affairs to the advertisers. The matter goes back to the uncritical state of popular opinion which makes this kind of publicity effective. We are in a passive and submissive state toward whatever passes as "authority."

I hope the citation of instances does not distract the mind from the main point. They are cited only because of their force as types and illustrations of a general condition of mind: the failure of individuals to exercise personal discrimination—to be critical. This failure has its roots in many cases in lack of the kind of education which prepares for the exercise of independent judgment and choice. But there are many persons intellectually prepared for their exercise who fail from a moral cause—lack of courage first to think and then to think out loud. Surrender of the mind to the clamor of strident publicity would not be particularly important if it were not the symptom of a deeper disease.

If causes were excuses it would be easy to find justification for the prevalence of the submissive, unresisting, because uncritical, mind. We are born infants, dependent upon others. The habit of leaning on others is formed while we are so unconscious that we are not aware of its existence. Few parents and few teachers rejoice in the growing independence of those who are in their charge. There is something flattering to our self-love in having others dependent upon us; unregenerate love of power urges us on to perpetuate that which we think of as authority. Even our altruistic desires, our love of doing things for others, conspire with our wish for prestige and recognition. We forget that the best thing we can do for another is to assist him to stand on his own feet so that he can get along without our assistance. We forget that the companionship, the give and take, of equals is immensely more rewarding than that of inferiors. Power in the shape of command over the thoughts and beliefs of others is a cheap substitute for the power that comes from command of ourselves.

This force, working for the stifling of independent judgment, is constant. It is with us always in the continuous relation of the generations of the young and of the adult. Those who have been forced into mental and moral subjection when young compensate by the use of extraneous authority when they in turn become the trainers of youth. But there are forces that are especially characteristic of our own age. We are committed to universal schooling. In ensuring the ability to read, we multiply indefinitely the number of external influences that can play upon an individual mind. He who has learned as we call it to read without having learned to judge, discriminate, and choose has given hostages of dependence to powers beyond his control. He has prepared for himself a readiness to undergo new modes of intellectual servitude. Add to this fact the other fact that three-quarters of our school population leave school at the age of fourteen and that their schooling has consisted up to that time mainly in absorption of information and acquisition of modes of skill acquired mainly by mechanical imitation and repetition, and it is not surprising that we have a people given to credulity, apt to be stirred by whatever is urged loudly and repeatedly upon their attention.

The educative or formative force that follows upon that of the school is that of one's occupation and vocation. A relatively small number are privileged to select callings that demand the exercise of personal reflection and understanding. The mass go into shops and factories in which mental submission to conditions and aims in which they do not mentally share is the rule. They may be rebellious to conditions, but they are forced to be obedient to the orders and directions that issue from the machinery they tend. They are servants, employees, not only of other persons but even more of impersonal agencies whose continual mechanical motions they must follow and to which they must accommodate themselves. Personal judgment and initiative have no organic place; their exercise would seem to be evidence of overt rebellion. Economic conditions reinforce the work of formal schooling and of much parental guidance in developing the uncritical and passive mind.

Yet human nature was not made for servility. If one looks at law and lawlessness, at order and disorder, in our contemporary scene, nothing would seem more absurd than the assertion that a marked trait of our life is the submissive mind. Complaints of the disappearance of the spirit of obedience, of loyalty to constituted authority and law, are as well based as they are rife. Laws on every conceivable subject are multiplied only to be recklessly broken. Yet there is no contradiction between this phenomenon and the existence of uncritical and uncreative mind. Rather they complement and demand each other. No one can be constantly under the surveillance of a dictator of his thought; an individual released from the period of submission in which he has experienced no cultivation of his own judgment is, at the moment of his release, at the mercy of untrained appetite and impulse, as the pupils subject to the most severe external discipline during school hours are usually the most boisterous and unruly when they escape from the eye and hand of the supervising disciplinarian. Desire may be covered up but it cannot be suppressed, for it is one vital energy. If it is not unified with ideas and directed by judgment it will find a chance outlet.

Creation and criticism are companions. Genuine discrimination is creative because it expresses an original response to what is presented; it is an exercise of personal taste. A good deal of fun has been made of the saying so often uttered in the presence of paintings: "I don't know anything about art, but I know what I like." Nevertheless, the saying expresses the starting point of all critical appreciation. It is only the start, however. For as a rule it is not true. The person saying it does not as a rule *know* what he likes. Knowledge is something more serious than a casual and incidental affection of favor. A passing response of liking is something quite different from an intelligent judgment. The chief trouble with those who say that they know what they like is that it usually implies a certain finality. It too often signifies that this thing which I like is not only good enough for me, but that it will remain so. I do not propose to learn to see anything different or to like in any new way.

Nevertheless, liking itself and a certain trust in one's liking are a good beginning. If the liking proceeds from one's own true nature there is an independent and original activity. I fear, however, that in many cases the liking itself is not primitive and spontaneous. It is a product of earlier conventional education which has given a set to the mind that stifles independent reaction. The preservation of original spontaneity of emotional response is very difficult, and to discover and trust to its subconscious stirrings is even more difficult. I have noticed, for instance, that children not yet influenced by current example and precept have no such difficulty in perceiving and liking many pictures of the so-called modern style as is experienced by adults. What the latter suppose they like is not in fact what *they* like; they have learned through the years what *others* say they like until their own liking has been overlaid with a borrowed standard. To strip away these accretions, to get down to some deeper and more primitive reaction of emotion and give it a free opportunity to operate, is with most persons the beginning of a genuine liking and appreciation of paintings.

I have referred to painting not so much for its own sake as because the case of pictures seems to exemplify a general principle of fundamental importance. As Emerson says in his essay on "Self-Reliance": "A man should learn to detect and watch that gleam of light which flashes across his mind from within," and "Great works of art have no more affecting lesson for us than this. They teach us to abide by our spontaneous impression with good-humored inflexibility then most when the whole cry of voices is on the other side. Else to-morrow a stranger will say with masterly good sense precisely what we have thought and felt all the time, and we shall be forced to take with shame our own opinion from another."

But it is not easy to detect and watch the gleams of light that flash from within. Education and social surroundings are in a conspiracy to dim these flashes and to attract our watching to other things. Language does not help us at this point; rather the habits of our vocabulary betray us. For the only words we have to designate these original gleams are impression and intuition, and these words have themselves got overlaid with all kinds of conventions and acquired secondary doctrines. To know what the words mean we have to forget the words and become aware of the occasions when some idea truly our own is stirring within us and striving to come to birth. The beginning of all development of individuality with adults usually comes when one learns to throw off an outer slavery to second-hand and ready-made opinions and begins to detect, watch, and trust one's own intuitions, that is, one's own spontaneous, unforced reactions. And the statement holds good whether originality finds expression in some endeavor at a new construction or in criticism of some scene, whether of nature or of social institutions.

Creation and criticism cannot be separated because they are the rhythm of output and intake, of expiration and inspiration, in our mental breath and spirit. To produce and then to see and judge what we and others have done in order that we may create again is the law of all natural activity. As it is the same bodily mechanism that regulates both the intaking of air and the breathing of it out, so it is the same mind which by its own identity of structure expresses itself in productive action and in critical discrimination. Production that is not followed by criticism becomes a mere gush of impulse; criticism that is not a step to further creation deadens impulse and ends in sterility. As breathing in and breathing out are cooperative manifestations by which life is sustained and carried on, so criticism and creation are connected manifestations of the same psychical life. The more normally one expels air from the lungs, the more, that is, one breathes out in accord with the structure of lungs and diaphragm, the more deeply will one inhale, and the more completely in turn will he exhale. Receptivity and assimilation are as much forms of vital action as are the overt actions that are visible.

Our mental irregularities and troubles come from failure to observe the law of rhythm in creation and criticism. We are not too receptive of impressions, but we are indiscriminate and unselective in our receptions. Passivity is necessary to receptivity, but we allow the passivity of reception to become converted into passivity of reaction. Hence we are flooded by impressions forced upon us from without, and the outcome is a stagnant pool that permits all kinds of alien things to be thrown in. When we act, we act spasmodically or violently as if in an effort to throw off the very things that should have nourished us but that are only choking us. What should in the normal course of mental life have been a constructive utterance in word or deed becomes a somnolent snore or an aimless splutter, or a plaintive sigh that expresses our inability to cope constructively with what oppresses us. We have neither the wit to permit selected impressions to sink in until they have become truly our own capital to work with, nor the courage to give out with assertive energy—or else the assertion from lack of depth in prior thought becomes hard and dogmatic.

Education is so fundamental in establishing a balance that I have felt some difficulty in preventing this talk from becoming a pedagogical sermon. Partly as an aid in resisting the temptation,

I shall conclude with some remarks about the relation of philosophy to criticism and creative action. There are those who look upon philosophy as a revelation of something foreign to everyday experience, or as a key that opens a door to realms otherwise inaccessible which have a supreme and final value. There are those who have once believed they found this ultimate revelation and this powerful key in religion, and who, having been disillusioned there, search in philosophy for what they have missed. When they do not find what they are after, they turn away disappointed or invent a system of fantasy according to their wishes and label it philosophy.

But philosophy is not a special road to something alien to ordinary beliefs, knowledge, action, enjoyment, and suffering. It is rather a criticism, a critical viewing, of just these familiar things. It differs from other criticism only in trying to carry it further and to pursue it methodically. If it has disclosures to offer it is not by way of revelation of some ultimate reality, but as disclosures follow in the way of pushing any investigation of familiar objects beyond the point of previous acquaintance. Men thought before there was logic, and they judged right and wrong, good and evil, before there was ethics. Before there was ever anything termed metaphysics men were familiar with distinctions of the real and the unreal in experience, with the fact that processes whether of physical or human nature have results, and that expected and desired results often do not happen because some process has its path crossed by some other course of events. But there is confusion and conflict, ambiguity and inconsistency, in our experience of familiar objects and in our beliefs and aspirations relating to them. As soon as anyone strives to introduce definiteness, clarity, and order on any broad scale, he enters the road that leads to philosophy. He begins to criticize and to develop criteria of criticism, that is, logic, ethics, esthetics, metaphysics.

I am not concerned at the tail of this evening's talk to elaborate this idea about philosophy. Rather I shall assume it, and ask what is the value of this generalized form of criticism for the release of creative productivity. More definitely, what is the value of criticism as philosophy in our American civilization? The theme is not so remote from what has already been said as might appear. There is a great disparity between a large body of inherited ideas and ideals and those which grow out of present activities. Almost every discussion of religion and politics going on about us testifies to the reality of this conflict. One can hardly go to an art gallery without seeing a struggle between the old on one hand and modernism and futurism on the other. The conflict reaches into the details of our daily lives. One of the results of the confusion is a common scepticism, cynicism, and disillusionment as to any principles and any aims that look beyond getting personal pleasure and profit out of a tangled scene.

We live, someone has said, in a haphazard mixture of a museum and a laboratory. Now it is certain that we cannot get rid of the laboratory and its consequences, and we cannot by a gesture of dismissal relegate the museum and its specimens to the void. There is the problem of selection, of choice, of discrimination. What are the things in the past that are relevant to our own lives and how shall they be reshaped to be of use? Does anyone suppose that our education, our legal system, and our politics would not take on new life if we could answer this question and apply our answer in practice? Formal philosophy should at least provide a method which may be used in this questioning of what has come to us from the past. But I am more concerned to suggest that there is here indicated a service for criticism that is universal. There is no one among us who is not called upon to face honestly and courageously the equipment of beliefs, religious, political, artistic, economic, that has come to him in all sorts of indirect and uncriticized ways, and to inquire how much of it is validated and verified in present need, opportunity, and application. Each one finds when he makes this search that much is idle lumber and much is an oppressive burden. Yet we give storeroom to the lumber and we assume the restriction of carrying the burden.

If I do not try to point out just the ways in which creative energy would be freed to operate if we got rid of the lumber and the burden, it is because there is a weightier reason than even the fact that my time is drawing to a close. It is because every individual is in some way original and creative in his very make-up; that is the meaning of individuality. What is most needed is to get rid of what stifles and chokes its manifestation. When the oppressive and artificial load is removed, each will find his own opportunity for positive constructive work in some field. And it is not the extent, the area, of this work that is important as much as its quality and intensity, and the cumulative effect of a multitude of individual creations, no matter how quantitatively limited each is by itself. Creative activity is our great need; but criticism, self-criticism, is the road to its release.

Essays

From Absolutism to Experimentalism

In the late 'seventies, when I was an undergraduate, "electives" were still unknown in the smaller New England colleges. But in the one I attended, the University of Vermont, the tradition of a "senior-year course" still subsisted. This course was regarded as a kind of intellectual coping to the structure erected in earlier years, or, at least, as an insertion of the keystone of the arch. It included courses in political economy, international law, history of civilization (Guizot), psychology, ethics, philosophy of religion (Butler's *Analogy*), logic, etc., not history of philosophy, save incidentally. The enumeration of these titles may not serve the purpose for which it is made; but the idea was that after three years of somewhat specialized study in languages and sciences, the last year was reserved for an introduction into serious intellectual topics of wide and deep significance—an introduction into the world of ideas. I doubt if in many cases it served its alleged end; however, it fell in with my own inclinations, and I have always been grateful for that year of my schooling. There was, however, one course in the previous year that had excited a taste that in retrospect may be called philosophical. That was a rather short course, without laboratory work, in Physiology, a book of Huxley's being the text. It is difficult to speak with exactitude about what happened to me intellectually so many years ago, but I have an impression that there was derived from that study a sense of interdependence and interrelated unity that gave form to intellectual stirrings that had been previously inchoate, and created a kind of type or model of a view of things to which material in any field ought to conform. Subcon-

[First published in *Contemporary American Philosophy: Personal Statements*, ed. George Plimpton Adams and William Pepperell Montague (London: George Allen and Unwin; New York: Macmillan Co., 1930), 2:13–27.]

sciously, at least, I was led to desire a world and a life that would have the same properties as had the human organism in the picture of it derived from study of Huxley's treatment. At all events, I got great stimulation from the study, more than from anything I had had contact with before; and as no desire was awakened in me to continue that particular branch of learning, I date from this time the awakening of a distinctive philosophic interest.

The University of Vermont rather prided itself upon its tradition in philosophy. One of its earlier teachers, Dr. Marsh, was almost the first person in the United States to venture upon the speculative and dubiously orthodox seas of German thinking—that of Kant, Schelling, and Hegel. The venture, to be sure, was made largely by way of Coleridge; Marsh edited an American edition of Coleridge's *Aids to Reflection*. Even this degree of speculative generalization, in its somewhat obvious tendency to rationalize the body of Christian theological doctrines, created a flutter in ecclesiastical dovecots. In particular, a controversy was carried on between the Germanizing rationalizers and the orthodox representatives of the Scottish school of thought through the representatives of the latter at Princeton. I imagine—although it is a very long time since I have had any contact with this material—that the controversy still provides data for a section, if not a chapter, in the history of thought in this country.

Although the University retained pride in its pioneer work, and its atmosphere was for those days theologically "liberal"—of the Congregational type—the teaching of philosophy had become more restrained in tone, more influenced by the still dominant Scotch school. Its professor, Mr. H. A. P. Torrey, was a man of genuinely sensitive and cultivated mind, with marked esthetic interest and taste, which, in a more congenial atmosphere than that of northern New England in those days, would have achieved something significant. He was, however, constitutionally timid, and never really let his mind go. I recall that, in a conversation I had with him a few years after graduation, he said: "Undoubtedly pantheism is the most satisfactory form of metaphysics intellectually, but it goes counter to religious faith." I fancy that remark told of an inner conflict that prevented his native capacity from coming to full fruition. His interest in philosophy, however, was genuine, not perfunctory; he was an excellent teacher, and I owe to him a double debt, that of turning my thoughts definitely to the study of philosophy as a life-pursuit, and of a generous gift of time to me during a year devoted privately under his direction to a reading of classics in the history of philosophy and learning to read philosophic German. In our walks and talks during this year, after three years on my part of high-school teaching, he let his mind go much more freely than in the classroom, and revealed potentialities that might have placed him among the leaders in the development of a freer American philosophy—but the time for the latter had not yet come.

Teachers of philosophy were at that time, almost to a man, clergymen; the supposed requirements of religion, or theology, dominated the teaching of philosophy in most colleges. Just how and why Scotch philosophy lent itself so well to the exigencies of religion I cannot say; probably the causes were more extrinsic than intrinsic; but at all events there was a firm alliance established between religion and the cause of "intuition." It is probably impossible to recover at this date the almost sacrosanct air that enveloped the idea of intuitions; but somehow the cause of all holy and valuable things was supposed to stand or fall with the validity of intuitionalism; the only vital issue was that between intuitionalism and a sensational empiricism that explained away the reality of all higher objects. The story of this almost forgotten debate, once so urgent, is probably a factor in developing in me a certain scepticism about the depth and range of purely contemporary issues; it is likely that many of those which seem highly important to-day will also in a generation have receded to the status of the local and provincial. It also aided in generating a sense of the value of the history of philosophy; some of the claims made for this as a sole avenue of approach to the study of philosophic problems seem to me misdirected and injurious. But its value in giving perspective and a sense of proportion in relation to immediate contemporary issues can hardly be overestimated.

I do not mention this theological and intuitional phase because it had any lasting influence upon my own development, except negatively. I learned the terminology of an intuitional philosophy, but it did not go deep, and in no way did it satisfy what I was dimly reaching for. I was brought up in a conventionally evangelical atmosphere of the more "liberal" sort; and the struggles that later arose between acceptance of that faith and the discarding of traditional and institutional creeds came from personal experiences and not from the effects of philosophical teaching. It was not, in other words, in this respect that philosophy either appealed to me or influenced me—though I am not sure that Butler's *Analogy*, with its cold logic and acute analysis, was not, in a reversed way, a factor in developing "scepticism."

During the year of private study, of which mention has been made, I decided to make philosophy my life-study, and accordingly went to Johns Hopkins the next year (1884) to enter upon that new thing, "graduate work." It was something of a risk; the work offered there was almost the only indication that there were likely to be any self-supporting jobs in the field of philosophy for others than clergymen. Aside from the effect of my study with Professor Torrey, another influence moved me to undertake the risk. During the years after graduation I had kept up philosophical readings and I had even written a few articles which I sent to Dr. W. T. Harris, the well-known Hegelian, and the editor of the *Journal of Speculative Philosophy*, the only philosophic journal in the country at that time, as he and his group formed almost the only group of laymen devoted to philosophy for non-theological reasons. In sending an article I asked Dr. Harris for advice as to the possibility of my successfully prosecuting philosophic studies. His reply was so encouraging that it was a distinct factor in deciding me to try philosophy as a professional career.

The articles sent were, as I recall them, highly schematic and formal; they were couched in the language of intuitionalism; of Hegel I was then ignorant. My deeper interests had not as yet been met, and in the absence of subject-matter that would correspond to them, the only topics at my command were such as were capable of a merely formal treatment. I imagine that my development has been controlled largely by a struggle between a native inclination toward the schematic and formally logical, and those incidents of personal experience that compelled me to take account of actual material. Probably there is in the consciously articulated ideas of every thinker an over-weighting of just those things that are contrary to his natural tendencies, an emphasis upon those things that are contrary to his intrinsic bent, and which, therefore, he has to struggle to bring to expression, while the native bent, on the other hand, can take care of itself. Anyway, a case might be made out for the proposition that the emphasis upon the concrete, empirical, and "practical" in my later writings is partly due to considerations of this nature. It was a reaction against what was more natural, and it served as a protest and protection against something in myself which, in the pressure of the weight of actual experiences, I knew to be a weakness. It is, I suppose, becoming a commonplace that when anyone is unduly concerned with controversy, the remarks that seem to be directed against others are really concerned with a struggle that is going on inside himself. The marks, the stigmata, of the struggle to weld together the characteristics of a formal, theoretic interest and the material of a maturing experience of contacts with realities also showed themselves, naturally, in style of writing and manner of presentation. During the time when the schematic interest predominated, writing was comparatively easy; there were even compliments upon the clearness of my style. Since then thinking and writing have been hard work. It is easy to give way to the dialectic development of a theme; the pressure of concrete experiences was, however, sufficiently heavy, so that a sense of intellectual honesty prevented a surrender to that course. But, on the other hand, the formal interest persisted, so that there was an inner demand for an intellectual technique that would be consistent and yet capable of flexible adaptation to the concrete diversity of experienced things. It is hardly necessary to say that I have not been among those to whom the union of abilities to satisfy these two opposed requirements, the formal and the material, came easily. For that very reason I have been acutely aware, too much so, doubtless, of a tendency of other thinkers and writers to achieve a specious lucidity and simplicity by the mere process of ignoring considerations which a greater respect for concrete materials of experience would have forced upon them.

It is a commonplace of educational history that the opening of Johns Hopkins University marked a new epoch in higher education in the United States. We are probably not in a condition as yet to estimate the extent to which its foundation and the development of graduate schools in other universities, following its example, mark a turn in our American culture. The 'eighties and 'nineties seem to mark the definitive close of our pioneer period, and the turn from the civil war era into the new industrialized and commercial age. In philosophy, at least, the influence of Johns Hopkins was not due to the size of the provision that was made. There was a half-year of lecturing and seminar work given by Professor George Sylvester Morris, of the University of Michigan; belief in the "demonstrated" (a favorite word of his) truth of the substance of German idealism, and of belief in its competency to give direction to a life of aspiring thought, emotion, and action. I have never known a more single-hearted and whole-souled man—a man of a single piece all the way through; while I long since deviated from his philosophic faith, I should be happy to believe that the influence of the spirit of his teaching has been an enduring influence.

While it was impossible that a young and impressionable student, unacquainted with any system of thought that satisfied his head and heart, should not have been deeply affected, to the point of at least a temporary conversion, by the enthusiastic and scholarly devotion of Mr. Morris, this effect was far from being the only source of my own "Hegelianism." The 'eighties and 'nineties were a time of new ferment in English thought; the reaction against atomic individualism and sensationalistic empiricism was in full swing. It was the time of Thomas Hill Green, of the two Cairds, of Wallace, of the appearance of the *Essays in Philosophical Criticism*, cooperatively produced by a younger group under the leadership of the late Lord Haldane. This movement was at the time the vital and constructive one in philosophy. Naturally its influence fell in with and reinforced that of Professor Morris. There was but one marked difference, and that, I think, was in favor of Mr. Morris. He came to Kant through Hegel instead of to Hegel by way of Kant, so that his attitude toward Kant was the critical one expressed by Hegel himself. Moreover, he retained something of his early Scotch philosophical training in a common-sense belief in the existence of the external world. He used to make merry over those who thought the *existence* of this world and of matter were things to be proved by philosophy. To him the only philosophical question was as to the *meaning* of this existence; his idealism was wholly of the objective type. Like his contemporary, Professor John Watson, of Kingston, he combined a logical and idealistic metaphysics with a realistic epistemology. Through his teacher at Berlin, Trendelenburg, he had acquired a great reverence for Aristotle, and he had no difficulty in uniting Aristoteleanism with Hegelianism.

There were, however, also "subjective" reasons for the appeal that Hegel's thought made to me; it supplied a demand for unification that was doubtless an intense emotional craving, and yet was a hunger that only an intellectualized subject-matter could satisfy. It is more than difficult, it is impossible, to recover that early mood. But the sense of divisions and separations that were, I suppose, borne in upon me as a consequence of a heritage of New England culture, divisions by way of isolation of self from the world, of soul from body, of nature from God, brought a painful oppression—or, rather, they were an inward laceration. My earlier philosophic study had been an intellectual gymnastic. Hegel's synthesis of subject and object, matter and spirit, the divine and the human, was, however, no mere intellectual formula; it operated as an immense release, a liberation. Hegel's treatment of human culture, of institutions and the arts, involved the same dissolution of hard-and-fast dividing walls, and had a special attraction for me.

As I have already intimated, while the conflict of traditional religious beliefs with opinions that I could myself honestly entertain was the source of a trying personal crisis, it did not at any time constitute a leading philosophical problem. This might look as if the two things were kept apart; in reality it was due to a feeling that any genuinely sound religious experience could and should adapt itself to whatever beliefs one found oneself intellectually entitled to hold—a half unconscious sense at first, but one which ensuing years have deepened into a fundamental conviction. In consequence, while I have, I hope, a due degree of personal sympathy with individuals who are undergoing the throes of a personal change of attitude, I have not been able to attach much importance to religion as a philosophic problem; for the effect of that attachment seems to be in the end a subornation of candid philosophic thinking to the alleged but factitious needs of some special set of convictions. I have enough faith in the depth of the religious tendencies of men to believe that they will adapt themselves to any required intellectual change, and that it is futile (and likely to be dishonest) to forecast prematurely just what forms the religious interest will take as a final consequence of the great intellectual transformation that is going on. As I have been frequently criticized for undue reticence about the problems of religion, I insert this explanation: it seems to me that the great solicitude of many persons, professing belief in the universality of the need for religion, about the present and future of religion proves that in fact they are moved more by partisan interest in a particular religion than by interest in religious experience.

The chief reason, however, for inserting these remarks at this point is to bring out a contrast effect. Social interests and problems from an early period had to me the intellectual appeal and provided the intellectual sustenance that many seem to have found primarily in religious questions. In undergraduate days I had run across, in the college library, Harriet Martineau's exposition of Comte. I cannot remember that his law of "the three stages" affected me particularly; but his idea of the disorganized character of Western modern culture, due to a disintegrative "individualism," and his idea of a synthesis of science that should be a regulative method of an organized social life, impressed me deeply. I found, as I thought, the same criticisms combined with a deeper and more far-reaching integration in Hegel. I did not, in those days when I read Francis Bacon, detect the origin of the Comtean idea in him, and I had not made acquaintance with Condorcet, the connecting link.

I drifted away from Hegelianism in the next fifteen years; the word "drifting" expresses the slow and, for a long time, imperceptible character of the movement, though it does not convey the impression that there was an adequate cause for the change. Nevertheless I should never think of ignoring, much less denying, what an astute critic occasionally refers to as a novel discovery—that acquaintance with Hegel has left a permanent deposit in my thinking. The form, the schematism, of his system now seems to me artificial to the last degree. But in the content of his ideas there is often an extraordinary depth; in many of his analyses, taken out of their mechanical dialectical setting, an extraordinary acuteness. Were it possible for me to be a devotee of any system, I still should believe that there is greater richness and greater variety of insight in Hegel than in any other single systematic philosopher—though when I say this I exclude Plato, who still provides my favorite philosophic reading. For I am unable to find in him that all-comprehensive and overriding system which later interpretation has, as it seems to me, conferred upon him as a dubious boon. The ancient sceptics overworked another aspect of Plato's thought when they treated him as their spiritual father, but they were nearer the truth, I think, than those who force him into the frame of a rigidly systematized doctrine. Although I have not the aversion to system as such that is sometimes attributed to me, I am dubious of my own ability to reach inclusive systematic unity, and in consequence, perhaps, of that fact also dubious about my contemporaries. Nothing could be more helpful to present philosophizing than a "Back to Plato" movement; but it would have to be back to the dramatic, restless, cooperatively inquiring Plato of the *Dialogues*, trying one mode of attack after another to see what it might yield; back to the Plato whose highest flight of metaphysics always terminated with a social and practical turn, and not to the artificial Plato constructed by unimaginative commentators who treat him as the original university professor.

The rest of the story of my intellectual development I am unable to record without more faking than I care to indulge in. What I have so far related is so far removed in time that I can talk about myself as another person; and much has faded, so that a few points stand out without my having to force them into the foreground. The philosopher, if I may apply that word to myself, that I became as I moved away from German idealism, is too much the self that I still am and is still too much in process of change to lend itself to record. I envy, up to a certain point, those who can write their intellectual biography in a unified pattern, woven out of a few distinctly discernible strands of interest and influence. By contrast, I seem to be unstable, chameleon-like, yielding one after another to many diverse and even incompatible influences; struggling to assimilate something from each and yet striving to carry it forward in a way that is logically consistent with what has been learned from its predecessors. Upon the whole, the forces that have influenced me have come from persons and from situations more than from books—not that I have not, I hope, learned a great deal from philosophical writings, but that what I have learned from them has been technical in comparison with what I have been forced to think upon and about because of some experience in which I found myself entangled. It is for this reason that I cannot say with candor that I envy completely, or envy beyond a certain point, those to whom I have referred. I like to think, though it may be a defense reaction, that with all the inconveniences of the road I have been forced to travel, it has the compensatory advantage of not inducing an immunity of thought to experiences—which perhaps, after all, should not be treated even by a philosopher as the germ of a disease to which he needs to develop resistance.

While I cannot write an account of intellectual development without giving it the semblance of a continuity that it does not in fact own, there are four special points that seem to stand out. One is the importance that the practice and theory of education have had for me: especially the education of the young, for I have never been able to feel much optimism regarding the possibilities of "higher" education when it is built upon warped and weak foundations. This interest fused with and brought together what might otherwise have been separate interests—that in psychology and that in social institutions and social life. I can recall but one critic who has suggested that my thinking has been too much permeated by interest in education. Although a book called *Democracy and Education* was for many years that in which my philosophy, such as it is, was most fully expounded, I do not know that philosophic critics, as distinct from teachers, have ever had recourse to it. I have wondered whether such facts signified that philosophers in general, although they are themselves usually teachers, have not taken education with sufficient seriousness for it to occur to them that any rational person could actually think it possible that philosophizing should focus about education as the supreme human interest in which, moreover, other problems, cosmological, moral, logical, come to a head. At all events, this handle is offered to any subsequent critic who may wish to lay hold of it.

A second point is that as my study and thinking progressed, I became more and more troubled by the intellectual scandal that seemed to me involved in the current (and traditional) dualism in logical standpoint and method between something called "science" on the one hand and something called "morals" on the other. I have long felt that the construction of a logic, that is, a method of effective inquiry, which would apply without abrupt breach of continuity to the fields designated by both of these words, is at once our needed theoretical solvent and the supply of our greatest practical want. This belief has had much more to do with the development of what I termed, for lack of a better word, "instrumentalism," than have most of the reasons that have been assigned.

The third point forms the great exception to what was said about no very fundamental vital influence issuing from books; it concerns the influence of William James. As far as I can discover one specifiable philosophic factor which entered into my thinking so as to give it a new direction and quality, it is this one. To say that it proceeded from his *Psychology* rather than from the essays collected in the volume called *Will to Believe*, his *Pluralistic Universe*, or *Pragmatism*, is to say something that needs explanation. For there are, I think, two unreconciled strains in the *Psychology*. One is found in the adoption of the subjective tenor of prior psychological tradition; even when the special tenets of that tradition are radically criticized, an underlying subjectivism is retained, at least in vocabulary—and the difficulty in finding a vocabulary which will intelligibly convey a genuinely new idea is perhaps the obstacle that most retards the easy progress of philosophy. I may cite as an illustration the substitution of the "stream of consciousness" for discrete elementary states: the advance made was enormous. Nevertheless the point of view remained that of a realm of consciousness set off by itself. The other strain is objective, having its roots in a return to the earlier biological conception of the *psyche*, but a return possessed of a new force and value due to the immense progress made by biology since the time of Aristotle. I doubt if we have as yet begun to realize all that is due to William James for the introduction and use of this idea; as I have already intimated, I do not think that he fully and consistently realized it himself. Anyway, it worked its way more and more into all my ideas and acted as a ferment to transform old beliefs.

If this biological conception and mode of approach had been prematurely hardened by James, its effect might have been merely to substitute one schematism for another. But it is not tautology to say that James's sense of life was itself vital. He had a profound sense, in origin artistic and moral, perhaps, rather than "scientific," of the difference between the categories of the living and of the mechanical; some time, I think, someone may write an essay that will show how the most distinctive factors in his general philosophic view, pluralism, novelty, freedom, individuality, are all connected with his feeling for the qualities and traits of that which lives. Many philosophers have had much to say about the idea of organism; but they have taken it structurally and hence statically. It was reserved for James to think of life in terms of life in action. This point, and that about the objective biological factor in James's conception of thought (discrimination, abstraction, conception, generalization), is fundamental when the role of psychology in philosophy comes under consideration. It is true that the effect of its introduction into philosophy has often, usually, been to dilute and distort the latter. But that is because the psychology was bad psychology.

I do not mean that I think that in the end the connection of psychology with philosophy is, in the abstract, closer than is that of other branches of science. Logically it stands on the same plane with them. But historically and at the present juncture the revolution introduced by James had, and still has, a peculiar significance. On the negative side it is important, for it is indispensable as a purge of the heavy charge of bad psychology that is so embedded in the philosophical tradition that it is not generally recognized to be psychology at all. As an example, I would say that the problem of "sense data," which occupies such a great bulk in recent British thinking, has to my mind no significance other than as a survival of an old and outworn psychological doctrine—although those who deal with the problem are for the most part among those who stoutly assert the complete irrelevance of psychology to philosophy. On the positive side we have the obverse of this situation. The newer objective psychology supplies the easiest way, pedagogically if not in the abstract, by which to reach a fruitful conception of thought and its work, and thus to better our logical theories—provided thought and logic have anything to do with one another. And in the present state of men's minds the linking of philosophy to the significant issues of actual experience is facilitated by constant interaction with the methods and conclusions of psychology. The more abstract sciences, mathematics and physics, for example, have left their impress deep upon traditional philosophy. The former, in connection with an exaggerated anxiety about formal certainty, has more than once operated to divorce philosophic thinking from connection with questions that have a source in existence. The remoteness of psychology from such abstractions, its nearness to what is distinctively human, gives it an emphatic claim for a sympathetic hearing at the present time.

In connection with an increasing recognition of this human aspect, there developed the influence which forms the fourth heading of this recital. The objective biological approach of the Jamesian psychology led straight to the perception of the importance of distinctive social categories, especially communication and participation. It is my conviction that a great deal of our philosophizing needs to be done over again from this point of view, and that there will ultimately result an integrated synthesis in a philosophy congruous with modern science and related to actual needs in education, morals, and religion. One has to take a broad survey in detachment from immediate prepossessions to realize the extent to which the characteristic traits of the science of to-day are connected with the development of social subjects —anthropology, history, politics, economics, language and literature, social and abnormal psychology, and so on. The movement is both so new, in an intellectual sense, and we are so much of it and it so much of us, that it escapes definite notice. Technically the influence of mathematics upon philosophy is more obvious; the great change that has taken place in recent years in the ruling ideas and methods of the physical sciences attracts attention much more easily than does the growth of the social subjects, just because it is farther away from impact upon us. Intellectual prophecy is dangerous; but if I read the cultural signs of the times aright, the next synthetic movement in philosophy will emerge when the significance of the social sciences and arts has become an object of reflective attention in the same way that mathematical and physical sciences have been made the objects of thought in the past, and when their full import is grasped. If I read these signs wrongly, nevertheless the statement may stand as a token of a factor significant in my own intellectual development.

In any case, I think it shows a deplorable deadness of imagination to suppose that philosophy will indefinitely revolve within the scope of the problems and systems that two thousand years of European history have bequeathed to us. Seen in the long perspective of the future, the whole of western European history is a provincial episode. I do not expect to see in my day a genuine, as distinct from a forced and artificial, integration of thought. But a mind that is not too egotistically impatient can have faith that this unification will issue in its season. Meantime a chief task of those who call themselves philosophers is to help get rid of the useless lumber that blocks our highways of thought, and strive to make straight and open the paths that lead to the future. Forty years spent in wandering in a wilderness like that of the present is not a sad fate—unless one attempts to make himself believe that the wilderness is after all itself the promised land.

Philosophy

My theme is the claims and opportunities of philosophy as a subject of scientific study from the social point of view. It is not usual to regard philosophy as one of the social studies, and I can hardly do otherwise than express my appreciation of the intellectual generosity that inspired its inclusion in this series, and my sense of the wisdom of the policy. For it seems to me that philosophy has suffered, and possibly the social sciences as well, from the tradition that has isolated them from each other. The former has lost vitality and *actualité*, and it is conceivable that the latter might have gained outlook and perspective from a closer connection. I alluded to isolation as a tradition, and yet there was a time when both met in what was termed "Morals"— which was far from signifying moralistic ethics, for it covered the entire humanistic realm. It is, in any event, from the standpoint of integration suggested by the inclusion of philosophy within the scope of social studies that I shall approach the subject.

The inclusion while generous presents for consideration an embarrassing variety of problems and issues. The topic that obviously offers itself is that of social and political philosophy. For at this point the social sciences and philosophy obviously interpenetrate. The moment we pass from description of social phenomena to an attempt at an evaluation of them, so as on the basis of reasoned conclusions to venture to state ends and ideals, that moment we pass from the strict area of science into problems of philosophy—such as the relation of facts and ideals, the nature of value, of criteria for judging it and so on. But perhaps just because this phase of the discussion is the more obvious, it may prove more helpful to try an indirect mode of approach,

[First published in *Research in the Social Sciences: Its Fundamental Methods and Objectives*, ed. Wilson Gee (New York: Macmillan Co., 1929), pp. 241–65.]

starting from considerations that on their face are remote from social phenomena. In approaching the theme in this more circuitous fashion, I shall deal with three affairs, namely, the history of philosophic thought; logic; and that more general phase of philosophy sometimes called metaphysics.

I

Perhaps the advantage of starting the discussion from the side of the history of philosophy is found in a seeming paradox. From one point of view, it can hardly be denied that philosophy viewed historically is a branch of human history, and as such furnishes material for the historian of human development in its most general sense. It affords from this point of view no isolated subject matter, but, like the phenomenon of religion, art or political institutions, is part of the general history of culture. Philosophy, even in its narrower and technical sense, gradually emerged from a background that no one can deny is the appropriate field of the anthropologist, while its whole course exhibits interaction with religious, scientific and political movements that fall within the view of the general historian. On the other hand, existing histories of philosophy have not been written to an appreciable degree from this point of view. They have rather dealt with the history of thought as a self-enclosed field, within which the origin and evolution of special problems and conclusions may be traced independently of any contact with other phases of culture. Such a view is practically necessary as part of the preparation of the student of philosophy, especially when the student is expected to be himself a teacher of the subject. Nevertheless, the point of view, while legitimate, is partial; it needs to be supplemented by placing the material in its wider context of the movement of culture. The picture of philosophers that is drawn when they are thought of as dwelling in cells remote from the current of affairs is so one-sided as to be false. For the philosopher, even in his cell or study, still derives his material and his issues from the currents of life about him. It is of course true that there has been a continuous accumulation of philosophical literature, and that this literary tradition provides the philosophic student with material he must master to come into possession of the tools of his work. But this material did not originate in reflection upon philosophy but in reflection upon experience, and upon experience saturated with the colors of the social life in which it originated. Otherwise, it ceased to be philosophy and became academic scholarship, almost a branch of philology.

Consequently, my first proposition is that the history of philosophic thought, taken in its connection with other movements and modes of human culture, religious, scientific, political, economic, artistic, offers a field of social research. The historian of philosophy must needs first of all be a historian and not just a historian of philosophy. In the degree in which he isolates his material, he loses the key to the significance of that which he studies. Any mode of thought, no matter how abstract in appearance, must have found an audience if it endured sufficiently to become part of the history of thought, and unless the historian knows something of the character of that audience and can judge of the nature of the appeal it made, he is without the clew to the meaning of that way of thinking. And to say that a thinker must find a response in his contemporary audience is to say that he must somehow respond to important needs of his time. Even in considering the nature of a philosophy we cannot get away from the biological idea of human activity as a response to an environment, in this case a reflective response to a social environment. We cannot understand an act, whether overt or reflective, unless we understand the medium in which it occurs and to which it is a response.

These general remarks raise a question. Just what is the distinctive material to which philosophy specifically responds? It does not seem to me that we have to go far in seeking an answer. The immediate subject matter of philosophic thought is the *beliefs* he finds current, especially traditional beliefs, those that are interwoven with institutional life in its diverse forms. It is not of course possible to draw any sharp line between philosophy and science. But one may say that in as far as a thinker occupies himself with phenomena *directly*, he is a scientist, and in as far as he concerns himself with intellectual attitudes and ideas, of a fundamental sort, that have grown up about these phenomena, he is a philosopher. The scientist, that is, concerns himself directly with stars or with political institutions, as the case may be, while the interest of the philosopher is in the beliefs that have developed about the stars, the heavens and earth, as they enter into and operate in the whole scheme of human life, or in the beliefs that sustain institutions and give them their hold on human loyalty and purpose. The line of demarcation is not a sharp one because the scientist, in reaching his results from what seems to him to be a direct study of the phenomena themselves, cannot escape the influence of traditional beliefs and outlooks that have shaped his own mind and interests, and hence his modes of attention and interpretation; while the philosopher needs some direct observations of his own, some direct experience, with which and against which to check the body of current beliefs. But the direction and emphasis of thought in the two matters is so different as to enable us to distinguish two modes of thinking. Thus we may say that the business of philosophy is *criticism of belief*; that is, of beliefs that are so widely current socially as to be dominant factors in culture. Methods of critical inquiry into beliefs mark him off as a philosopher, but the subject matter with which he deals is not his own. The beliefs themselves are social products, social facts and social forces.

It is this basic fact which renders the history of philosophy a problem for social research; a fruitful and important problem at the present time precisely because so little has as yet been done with it. It is hardly too much to say that the writing of the history of thought is still in its infancy. Accounts of this history as forming a special set of problems, set apart as falling within a technical field, are numerous and often excellent. But of the history of thought as an intellectual response to beliefs influential in various epochs and phases of human culture there is little. The causes of this situation are such that the blame cannot justly be put exclusively upon the historian of thought. Till very recently the material necessary for the use of this method has been lacking; in the important field of the history of science, it is still all too scanty. The history of thought as an object of social study depends upon materials that have to be supplied by the historian of other social fields, and until lately that material was not at hand. But I believe that this situation has now so changed that it is possible to make at least a beginning. This possibility determines the character of my primary suggestion—the history of philosophy is a genuine objective of scientific research in the social sciences.

The objective I have suggested is stated in vague and general terms. To be intelligible it ought to be translated into terms of more definite and limited objectives. Here again we have an embarrassment of riches. Every foot, yes, every inch of the way cries out for treatment from the social point of view. Anthropologists, archeologists and historians have, for example, brought to light in the past generation a vast wealth of material regarding early Grecian life and its connection with barbaric and even savage strata of culture. There is in such writers as Cornford, Murray, Jane Harrison and others utilization of this material in the understanding of Greek thought; they have generously prepared the material in forms that call for philosophic appropriation and use. But the older tradition of isolation is far from having given way. There are still, I fear, many philosophers who regard it as an adulteration of the purity of philosophy to admit that there is an intimate connection between Greek philosophic literature and anthropological material.

While it is not especially to the point to pick out one period rather than another of the history of thought as an illustration of the need for social study, the Hellenistic and scholastic epochs suggest themselves almost irresistibly. For both of them present a development of philosophy when the latter was conspicuously a way of life bound up with the dominant tendencies of their eras. Histories of philosophy have always tended to fight shy of dealing with the religious movements that were contemporary with a philosophical development, in spite of the undeniably close connection of the two. Thus in the Greco-Roman period, our treatises give such separate treatments of Neo-Platonic, Stoic and Patristic theories that the student fails to realize the common atmosphere that enveloped them all. In consequence, Gilbert Murray's chapter on the Failure of Nerve in his *Four Stages of Greek Religion* gives more enlightenment as to the actual character of the intellectual movements of that time than do the standard works on philosophy. The history of the philosophy of this period cannot be truly written until all the movements are tied together; the possibility of effecting this union depends upon connecting all of them with such social tendencies as are manifested in the revival of mystery cults, the origins of Christian Churches, the growth of the Roman Empire as an administrative and legal system, the relation of the Church to it, the development of literary studies and methods of exegesis at Athens and Alexandria, and so on.

After a period of long neglect, outside of Catholic circles, there are many signs of a revival of interest in scholasticism. Much excellent work has been done and much remains to be done in the narrower field of study of its literature. But hardly a beginning has been made in the larger field of the relations of this literature to the religious, political, artistic and economic phenomena of the period between the ninth and thirteenth centuries. In the later era of the disintegration of scholasticism and the sporadic revival of Pre-Aristotelian science (the preparation for the movement popularly known as the Renaissance) literary and historical students in other lines have done something, but historians of thought very little. And yet in this period of transition the foundations for that whole point of view we call "modern" were laid.

II

From these scattering superficial illustrations, I pass on to the second main topic, logical theory as a subject falling within the domain of social inquiry. The theme of history just mentioned furnishes a bridge. The dominant Aristotelian tradition in logic, a tradition which led Kant as late as the latter part of the eighteenth century to regard the Aristotelian logic as a closed, complete system, is probably largely responsible for the neglect of study of the history of logical theories. In the nineteenth century the tendency to swallow up logic in epistemology, whether psychological or non-psychological, perpetuated this neglect, and diverted such attention as was given to the history of logic into alien and obscuring considerations. As a matter of fact, in spite of the dominance of Aristotelian orthodoxy, there was as much change and variety in the territory of logical thought as in those of ethical and metaphysical theory, and this history is practically an unwritten chapter—or rather an unwritten series of volumes. I can only say in passing, without any attempt at proof, that it is quite possible to disentangle the development of logic as an account of methods of inquiry and proof from the motivations and problems that have controlled the writing of the history of epistemology.

The logic of Aristotle was no formal logic in the modern sense; it was a reflection of his metaphysics and even more directly of his cosmology. It was a logic appropriate to the view of the world as a system of fixed qualitative kinds, like the species of animals and plants, of a closed physical or astronomical world formulated in terms of an arbitrary application of Euclidean geometry, and of a variety of qualitative movements that corresponded to the qualitative divisions of the cosmos. There are numerous problems of historical research in the career of the Aristotelian logic. One phase of the study concerns the transformation of the Aristotelian logic from an organon of material truths concerning nature and man into a formal dialectic of dispute and controversy. The social connections of this problem are found of course in the history of the Church in its struggles to formulate religious and ecclesiastic doctrine to render them proof against heresies, and so as to afford an instrument of theological education.

Another phase of the problem is the discovery of what actually happened when the old conceptions of the cosmos disintegrated, and the supposed physical and astronomical basis of the Aristotelian system of syllogisms, classifications and definitions in demonstrative reasoning faded away. There is a genuine realm of logical development involved in this inquiry; for the new ideas in astronomy and physics could not have been developed except by the growth and use of new methods of investigation and testing. The extent to which this new logic was implicit in scientific investigations is scattered in the writings of the new scientific investigators, rather than formulated explicitly in logical treatises. But this fact is but another evidence of the futility of separating the history of philosophy from the history of other social changes. It signifies that the materials for the history of logic are to be found primarily in the records of scientific observations, experiments and calculations rather than in the books conventionally labelled philosophical.

A typically significant illustration of the importance of the theme may be drawn from Descartes. The hearer of philosophical lectures and the reader of philosophical books learns the Cartesian rules for method, all about the *Cogito sum* and the ontological argument for the existence of God, and is perhaps instructed in the influence of such ideas upon the later idealistic movement. Incidentally he may learn that Descartes also developed analytic geometry. He is, however, unusually fortunate if he gets an idea of the central place of this mathematical conception in the whole system of Descartes, to say nothing of the connection of the new mathematical movement with the scientific problems of the day, and its influence upon subsequent science and philosophizing. Yet this connection is an indispensable factor in the development of working, as distinct from conventional, logic.

This reference to the history of logic is made, however, incidentally, and by way of connecting this topic with the one previously taken up. While consideration of logical theory as such cannot be severed from the history of the actual developments of scientific inquiry, I am especially concerned with logic itself in its relation to social phenomena. To put the idea that is uppermost in my mind in a summary form I will say that the confusions and uncertainties of inquiry, discussion and controversy in all the social sciences are reflected in the present state of logic as a philosophical discipline. It would be altogether too much to say that the confusions and uncertainties in the methods of the social sciences have their *source* in the confusions and uncertainties of logic itself; such a statement would reverse the way in which logic depends upon actual intellectual undertakings for its facts and ideas. But it is not too much to say that a clarified development of logical theory would give a much needed help to the intellectual tools of the social studies: politics, economics, history, sociology and so on.

In entering upon a discussion of the relations of logic to social studies, as it is involved in the methods of social sciences, certain misconceptions may be avoided by stating in what sense "logic" is here employed. For present purposes, then, "logic" signifies a systematic intellectual statement of the operations of inquiry, test and formulation that enter into the discovery of conclusions having a valid claim to acceptance, to belief. The investigator in the recognized social sciences is certainly interested in the intellectual instruments he uses in investigation, interpretation and statement. While, upon the whole, he must forge these tools in the operations of inquiry, he cannot be indifferent to any contribution to this field which the logician may make. It will be recalled, for example, that it was interest in social inquiry and discussion that underlay the work of John Stuart Mill in composing his classic treatise on Logic. He was not himself an inquirer in the physical field, nor was he by first intention nor of pure blood a logician. Beginning with an interest in practical social reforms, he was compelled to take up political, ethical and economic theories, and was then forced back upon the question of the nature of the methods appropriate to dealing with social phenomena. Naturally, in the relatively undeveloped state of the social studies as compared with the physical and mathematical, he turned to the principles that seemed to him to be involved in the latter to procure instruction and enlightenment. Naturally then he became interested in problems of physical methods of inquiry. Naturally, also, he was concerned to carry into his analysis and exposition the general philosophy of sensationalistic and associational psychology he had learned from his father—almost literally at his father's knee. But while these two considerations are highly important for his whole system, it is significantly true that the Sixth Book of his Treatise, on the Logic of the Moral Sciences, not merely presents the culmination of his entire system, but also contains the reasons for the sake of which his entire logical inquiry was undertaken.

I cite this as an illustration of the interest which social students have in logical theory in connection with the foundation and framework of their own investigations. Mill's writings in politics, economics and ethics do not have the authority they possessed for an earlier generation, but this fact does not impair the illustrative value of reference to him. Any social student of social phenomena who goes far or deep is obliged to do something of the same kind that Mill did, though he usually does it piece-meal and implicitly rather than in the thoroughgoing and explicit way in which Mill undertook the task. If the social student is perforce concerned with logic as soon as he has to reflect upon the adequacy of his methods of inquiry and interpretation, it is equally true that the logician as such must include in his survey of logical problems, data and hypotheses, the conclusions of the social as well as of the physical sciences. Indeed, were it relevant to our purpose, it could be shown that one of the stimulating—and irritating—problems of much recent logical theory has been precisely the seeming discrepancy between the sciences that deal with physical material and those that deal with social and historical material.

The problem is far from being settled. If I mistake not it is still a moot point among some of the social sciences whether their subject matter can be treated in abstraction from history or whether historical concepts intrinsically inhere in it. It is impossible to conceive of a more fundamental question being raised about the very nature of such subjects as economics and politics. For there are some who are convinced that the essential fallacy of the older or classic economic and political theory is precisely that they viewed their subject matter as reducible to abstract universal laws, holding that such "laws" ought to have been treated as inferences regarding tendencies characteristic of particular eras of history, and hence possessed only of a relationship and temporal significance.

We find another illustration of the cooperative reciprocal interest of logicians and social scientists in a phenomenon accompanying the rise of sociology and anthropology. In the period in which they began to take form, it was a commonplace of the prevailing logic of the physical sciences that "laws" are statements of uniform and unconditional uniformities in the succession of phenomena. This notion cut two ways. On the one hand, it eliminated the older notion of explanation in terms of an active force, agency or faculty lying behind the phenomena, and was thus part of the scientific purification that began in the seventeenth century. On the other side, it represented the endeavor to give a positive formulation to the most general conclusions of all physical researches and discoveries. It was inevitable, humanly speaking, that men like Comte or Spencer, when they set out to reduce sociological phenomena to scientific form, should conform to the model set by current conceptions in physical science. They conceived, as a matter of course, that their task was to discover a uniform, unvarying, order of sequence among social phenomena. The result, with Comte, was the law of the three stages: everywhere in all matters, social phenomena begin in a theological stage, pass through a metaphysical stage and terminate in a positivistic—the latter being identical with the possibility of social science itself. With Spencer, the idea took the form of a generalized formula of "evolution," stating forms of unvarying succession through which each sort of social phenomena *must* pass.

Students who do not have a technical acquaintance with the literature of anthropology are sometimes disturbed by finding that there is an influential and growing group that rejects "evolution" as applied to their data. The real meaning of the repudiation and criticism is contained in what has just been said. The distinguished anthropologist Morgan put forth the idea of a uniform succession of stages of culture passed through by all races and social groups all over the globe: this single and uniform succession of stages constituted "evolution." Some peoples have got further than others, but none omits any one of the stages of evolution. Anthropology was thereby committed to studying all its material so as to place it in some compartment of the recognized order of stages. Comparative linguistics, comparative religion, institutional politics and law, while they did not originate wholly in this conception, lent themselves readily to its influence. Comparison leading to scientific results was thought to be possible only because definite and uniform stages could be laid out.

It is an interesting problem for logical research to discover just the underlying conceptions of intellectual method which those anthropologists who have rejected this scheme of reasoning put in its place. But beyond indicating the existence of this logical problem, we are concerned only to point out the source of that "evolutionary" idea now so generally questioned—the implicit supposition that the very existence of science was bound up with discovery of uniformities of succession universally present among social phenomena, comparable to alleged uniformities in physical phenomena. To have denied, at one period, the existence of such uniform stages of succession would have seemed to be the denial of the possibility of any social science whatever. In spite of the acute criticism directed against the idea by some anthropologists, it still runs implicitly through the most widely known writers on mythology, cults and political and legal institutions.

I hope that even these few illustrations may indicate the extent to which the student of logic may find problems, data and hypotheses ready to hand in the social sciences, so that he may reasonably entertain a hope that the results of his own logical inquiries may be of some fruitful service to the workers in those fields. It is here more than anywhere else, I think, that the role of social and political philosophy—the point passed over at the outset—should be most significant. The work of philosophy in these fields, any more than in the physical or biological, cannot rival that of the specialized investigator. If a philosopher attempts to deliver scientific conclusions in the strict sense of the word, that is, apart from direct study of factual data, his results are only too likely to be pseudo-science. But determination of intellectual foundation-concepts, and of the encompassing intellectual framework is another matter; it is an affair with which he is concerned, and in which he may render useful assistance. Social phenomena are after all *the* distinctively human phenomena and therefore those of the greatest import to man. While the statement may, accordingly, mark only a personal prejudice on my part, I cannot refrain from saying that it seems to me that the beliefs most appropriate to receive the attention of philosophic students, and the most rewarding of study, are those of the social sciences, in spite of the vogue of physical and mathematical sciences, which just now exercise such a hypnotic influence in philosophy.

III

Thus far we have been considering connections, cross-fertilizations they might be called, between logic and the social sciences. Leading ideas, controlling concepts, principles, theories, play such a role in all organized method that it is impossible, however, to make a sharp separation between logic and general philosophy. For these large ideas, within the scope of which social theorizing has been carried on, have as a rule been derived, consciously or tacitly, from some comprehensive view of the universe and of man. Here is an enormously rich field of research. There are but few works known to me that trace the philosophical origin of the ideas which have in the past so largely governed special social studies by means of studying the intellectual framework within which the latter are carried on. The philosopher has not as a rule traced the ramifications of his ideas in economics, politics, the writing of history, jurisprudence, or the development of educational theories; workers in the latter fields have often taken current ideas ready-made, and omitted to ask for their source in prior philosophic speculation, and to consider the degree in which they are affected—or infected—by that origin.[1]

---

1. I have in mind as an exception such a work as Bonar's *Philosophy and Political Economy in Some of Their Historical Relations*. London, George Allen & Unwin, Ltd. New York, The Macmillan Co.

Problems for research that fall within the field of the diffusion of philosophic concepts through the social sciences are indefinitely numerous. There are almost innumerable topics in one realm alone, one that is closely allied with logic. Under the influence of the Aristotelian tradition and the older interpretation of the method of Euclidean geometry, subjects were regarded as scientific only when they rested upon ultimate axiomatic, or indemonstrable, first truths, eternally and universally true and carrying their truth in their immediate rational self-evidence. The effect of this conception was to lead social thinkers to strive for deductive and quasi-mathematical systemization. Here is an important theme for investigation. Even more important is the way in which leading ideas, having a temporary value in stimulation and direction of reformatory effort to remedy immediate evils or promote immediate social causes and policies, were erected into eternal and unqualified truths, good at all times and places. It is only comparatively recently that it has been perceived that all such general ideas and principles are in logical import but *hypotheses* and are to be treated as hypotheses are used and tested in other fields of inquiry.[2]

Merely to trace the conversion of working hypotheses into absolute and immutable truths, and to follow out the effect of this conversion in the fields of law, politics, economics, etc., would in the abstract prove rather barren. But if it were employed as a clew to discovery of the particular desires and interests which have dominated movements at various times, it would develop into a series of significant inquiries. We are, for example, only just beginning to recognize the extent in which the whole British empiristic philosophy was developed as a method of criticism of institutions, political and ecclesiastical. It became the working creed of the "liberal" school, because it was originated by Locke in order to provide an analytic method of attack upon beliefs connected with institutions he desired either to abolish or to reform. Then there is the use made by the utilitarian school of an

2. Delaisi's *Political Myths and Economic Realities* contains a wealth of material for the curious student of philosophy. The use of the word "myths" is of course deliberately pejoristic. But such words as we have been employing, "general ideas, principles, first truths," may be readily substituted. The consequences of the failure to recognize that they rightly function only as hypotheses are expressed in the following words: "If the myth's existence were only justified by its *utility*, to change it would be a relatively simple matter. But once it is rooted among the 'immutable verities' it becomes sacrosanct." P. 43.

individualistic and introspective psychology to establish a "scientific" basis for economics and politics. Another phase of the same general movement is the concept of "nature," as developed first in connection with the idea of laws in morals and government, then transferred to the treatment of rights, and afterwards retained by the utilitarians, in spite of their criticism of the natural rights theory, in the form of a native, original structure of wants inhering in every individual, upon which structure as a basis was built their whole science of economic activity. It would not be far-fetched to say that a reminiscent echo of the same idea is found in contemporary efforts to develop social theory from the basis of pure instincts. An important sideline of exploration are the religious connections of this concept of nature, its affiliation with deism and the notion of natural as distinct from revealed religion.

To elaborate this mode of research would, however, encroach unduly upon mention of the theoretic phase of philosophy, often termed metaphysics, in its connection with social studies.

Unfortunately for my purpose, the field in question is most difficult to present in such an address as this. But the underlying idea may be suggested by reminding ourselves that at all times one of the most perplexing problems of general philosophy, including logic, has been the relation of individual and universal; the discrete and the continuous; the immediate and the relational. The student of contemporary philosophy is aware of the extent to which, after a period in which the problem was ignored or even contemptuously dismissed, it looms as the central and dividing issue. That the same question, in the form of the relation of individuality to collectivity, freedom to law, liberty to authority, is and has always been a central issue in social and political thinking, goes without saying. Just here is assuredly a problem in which the interests of the most formal and seemingly abstract branch of philosophy and those of social studies converge to a common focus.

I do not propose to discuss the problem itself, but I wish to call attention to an issue regarding the ultimate basis and nature of philosophic method that is involved in it. Shall philosophy set out from and with the macroscopic or with the microscopic; with the gross and complex or with the minute and elemental? The issue stated in this bald form does not mean much. But social phenomena constitute what I mean by the macroscopic. They are the large, the largest, most inclusive and most complex of all the phenomena with which mind has to deal. They also present the problems with which thought occupies itself in their most direct, urgent and practical form. Is philosophy to start with and from such objects, or with the results of special analyses, mathematical, physical and biological? The problem crucial for philosophy itself is not without fundamental import for the special social sciences. One type of answer to it indicates that social phenomena involve certain categories that are distinctive and unique, and hence not to be resolved into the physical, biological or psychological. The primary problem of method is then to discover just what are these distinctive social marks and categories.[3] An answer in the other sense commits the social student to an effort to reduce all social phenomena to the terms of physical, biological or psychological science. I do not see how any problem can be more far-reaching in its implications.

The bearing of the issue upon philosophical method is equally important. The whole issue of the place and value of empirical method in philosophic thinking is involved in it. It is not too much to say that the heart of the procedure usually termed "rationalistic" is found in the notion that entities or objects of a simple and ultimate nature, discovered by thought, are the "reals" in terms of which philosophy must understand and explain all complex and macroscopic phenomena. In this connection we must not limit the content of "rationalism" to the movements of the seventeenth and eighteenth century that commonly go by that name. It includes also the contemporary movements that finally fall back upon mathematical subsistences; that base themselves upon essences, or that build upon ultimate "sense-data." The issue also concerns the value of the traditional British empirical school. For that school defined experience not in terms of direct and macroscopic phenomena of a social order but in terms of ulterior simple unitary elements, sensations, feelings, ideas. So complete is the identification of "empiricism" with this point of view, that the mere suggestion of the possibility of empirical philosophy of a different type is hard to grasp. But apart from

3. See an article by the writer in the *Monist*, April, 1928, "Social as a Category." [*The Later Works of John Dewey, 1925–1953*, ed. Jo Ann Boydston (Carbondale and Edwardsville: Southern Illinois University Press, 1984), 3:41–54.]

words, there is the possibility of a kind of philosophic enterprise that accepts phenomena in gross; namely, the phenomena of social interactions, as real in their own right, and as the fullest manifestation of the nature of things accessible to the human mind; and that finds in these gross phenomena the clues to the formulation and solution of the other problems with which philosophy is concerned.

From this point of view all intellectual distinctions and classifications proceed from experience in its direct and large social mode; they are instituted for the sake of the control or direction of these common and pervasive phenomena, and they ultimately pass for test and verification back into the direct complex of phenomena from which they were derived. From this point of view, the ultimate source of all philosophic fallacies and errors is conversion of a temporary abstraction from the complex gross scene into a permanent and fixed isolation. It is impossible to follow the idea further on this occasion. But, it may be repeated that the worth and validity of the empirical method as over against the rationalistic (and these are the two forms into which in some way all philosophic divisions resolve themselves and from which all philosophic conflicts arise) stand or fall with the decision of this issue. Moreover, to adopt the macroscopic or social standpoint as a working philosophic hypothesis is to be committed to a standpoint from which all philosophic problems demand revision and restatement.

I may perhaps best conclude by saying that the inclusion of philosophy among the social studies as a theme for research not only evinces liberality of mind, but contains, at least by way of implication, intellectual consequences with which I am in most profound agreement. Indeed, all that I have said, under the captions of the history of thought, logical theory and general philosophy, is but an indication of some of these consequences. I believe that at times philosophy has had direct and immediate social connections; that the failures of philosophy have been largely due to failure to perceive and state these connections, and that the over-technicality of philosophical systems, with the remoteness from common understanding thereby induced, the undue emphasis upon intellectual gymnastics and dialectic at the expense of bearing upon life, have the same source. The divorce of philosophy during the last few centuries from the sciences is now much deplored, and it *is* deplorable. But I believe that the road of alliance of philosophy with the physical and biological sciences is not direct but by the way of the social sciences. I look for a genuine renascence of philosophic interest and service in the degree in which this primary affiliation is held in mind.

Large and general hypotheses have always preceded fruitful special inquiries into detailed matters of fact. At a later period, the original hypotheses are so revised and discarded on one hand, and so incorporated into the systematic body of scientific facts on the other, that they are readily ignored or even spoken of with contempt as mere metaphysical vagaries. But none the less, the specialized and finally verified scientific system found its origin in precisely such general ideas. Our present scientific outlook and achievements has its source in the philosophical speculations of the seventeenth century. The scientific revolution now so far along had to wait upon the birth of new intellectual points of view, new conceptions of the structure and operations of nature. Accumulation of specialized and detailed facts within the old intellectual framework, subjected to the theoretical conditions it imposed, signified merely the building up of a more firm structure of error that had to be battered down. The new and revolutionary ideas had inevitably first to be presented in a highly general and speculative form. Until the ideas were used, there could not possibly be in existence that body of facts that would purify and test the ideas and reduce them from speculative to factual form. It is a favorite idea of mine that we are now in the presence of an intellectual crisis similar to that of the seventeenth century. Then the crisis concerned the free creation of new ideas regarding physical nature, ideas that formed the points of departure for new ways of observing and interpreting physical phenomena. Now the crisis concerns the initiation of new hypotheses regarding man, regarding the nature and significance of those human associations that form the various modes of social phenomena. What philosophy did three centuries ago for physical inquiry, it now has the opportunity of doing for social life.

James Marsh and American Philosophy

In the years 1829, 1831 and 1832 an event of considerable intellectual importance took place in Burlington, Vt. For in these years Chauncey Goodrich published there editions of three of the more important writings of Samuel Taylor Coleridge, namely, *Aids to Reflection*, *The Friend* and *The Statesman's Manual*. The first of these contains the well known Introduction by James Marsh.

In associating the name of Romantic philosophy with the work of James Marsh, it is important that we should appreciate the sense in which the word "romantic" is employed. Words change their meaning, and to-day such a title may seem to imply a certain disparagement, since realism in some form is the now prevailing mode. In the sense in which the word was earlier used, a somewhat technical one, the opposite of romantic was not realistic, but rather classic. The word was used to denote what was taken to be the modern spirit in distinction from that of antiquity, and more particularly the spirit of the Teutonic and Protestant North in distinction from the Latin and Catholic South.

Fortunately an essay written during Dr. Marsh's last year in Andover Seminary and published in the *North American Review* for July, 1822, enables us to seize, independently of labels, what Marsh himself thought the difference in question to consist of. "The modern mind," he says, "removes the centre of its thoughts and feelings from the 'world without' to the 'world within'." More in detail he says in speaking of the Greeks that "they had no conception of a boundless and invisible world in the bosom of which all that is visible sinks into the littleness of a micro-

[First published in *Journal of the History of Ideas* 2 (April 1941): 131–50, from a lecture delivered at the University of Vermont, 26 November 1929, in commemoration of the centenary of the publication of James Marsh's introduction to Coleridge's *Aids to Reflection*.]

cosm."[1] In contrast with this attitude he says: "In the mind of a modern all this is changed. His more serious thoughts are withdrawn from the world around him and turned in upon himself. All the phenomena of external nature, with all the materials, which history and science have treasured up for the use of the poet, are but the mere instruments to shadow forth the fervors of a restless spirit at last conscious of its own powers and expanding with conceptions of the boundless and the infinite." The change is definitely connected with the influence of Christianity in general and of the Protestant and earlier barbarian North in particular.

I am concerned with the ideas and principles of the philosophical work of Marsh rather than with its historical origin, development and influence.[2] But it would be unfitting to pass the occasion by without noting the broad and deep scholarship of Marsh as it is made evident even in this the earliest of his published writings. He had mastered Italian, Spanish and German, as well as Latin, Greek and Hebrew at that early date. This was no mean attainment since he had never been abroad, and since there were few facilities for study at the time. His writings show that he not only knew the languages but had an extensive and familiar acquaintance with their literatures. I may not go into detail, but it is not too much to say that he was probably the first American scholar to have an intimate first-hand acquaintance with the writings of Immanuel Kant, including not only the *Critiques of Pure* and *Practical Reason*, but his *Anthropology* and especially his writings on the philosophic basis of natural science. In the latter connection it is worthy of note that Marsh's readings in the scientific literature of his day were wide and influenced his speculations; Oersted with his principle of polarity influenced him chiefly along with Kant. His interpretation of Kant was affected of course by his admiration of Coleridge but also by his reading of Fries.

While his indebtedness to Coleridge was great, it was somewhat less than his distrust of his own powers would intimate. He came to Coleridge with a preparation both in reading and in his

1. *North American Review*, Vol. XV, p. 107.
2. A careful and thoroughly trustworthy account of the latter has already been given by Professor Marjorie Nicolson. See the article entitled "James Marsh and the Vermont Transcendentalists," in the *Philosophical Review* for Jan. 1925.

thinking which fitted him to appreciate the latter, but which also absolves him from any charge of being a mere disciple. The interest that Marsh had in Coleridge sprang primarily from a common interest in religion and a common desire to arouse among believers in Christianity a vital realization of its spiritual truth. There is much in Coleridge's *Aids to Reflection* that is far outside the main currents of present-day thought even in religious circles. Aside from penetrating flashes of insight a reader to-day is likely to be left indifferent to its substance and repelled by its form. He may easily find it of only antiquarian interest. To employ a juster statement, it is mainly of historical interest. To say this is to say that to grasp its meaning and its influence in its own time we must place it in its own context in the intellectual and moral atmosphere of the early nineteenth century. We must recall that it was a period before Darwin and the evolutionists; before, indeed, modern science had itself left any great impress on the popular mind; a period when the peculiar problems forced upon modern society by the industrial revolution were only beginning faintly to show themselves. It was a time when outside of a few radicals, there was nominal acceptance of established institutions and doctrines but little concern for their inner meaning. It was on the whole a period of intellectual apathy and indifference.

The two essays of John Stuart Mill upon Bentham and Coleridge respectively give a clear picture of the general temper of the day. Among other things Mill says, "The existing institutions in Church and State were to be preserved inviolate, in outward semblance at least, but were required to be, practically, as much of a nullity as possible." More specifically in speaking of the Church he says, "On condition of not making too much noise about religion, or taking it too much in earnest, the Church was supported, even by philosophers, as a 'bulwark against fanaticism,' a sedative to the religious spirit, to prevent it from disturbing the harmony of society or the tranquillity of states." He sums it up by saying that "on the whole, England had neither the benefits, such as they were, of the new ideas nor of the old. We had a Government which we respected too much to attempt to change it, but not enough to trust it with any power, or look to it for any services that were not compelled. We had a Church, which had ceased to fulfil the honest purposes of a church, but which we made a great point of keeping up as the pretence or simulacrum of one. We had a highly spiritual religion (which we were instructed to obey from selfish motives) and the most mechanical and worldly notions on every other subject." As he says "an age like this, an age without earnestness, was the natural era of compromises and half-convictions."

In this situation, Bentham was the innovator, the critic and destroyer of the old. Coleridge was the unusual type of conservative, the thinker who demanded that the *meaning* of the old be comprehended and acted upon. As Mill says "Bentham asked of every custom and institution 'Is it true?' while Coleridge asked 'What is its meaning?'" The latter question, in the existing state of things, was as disturbing as the other; its import was as radical, for it was a challenge to the existing state of belief and action. The more obvious phase of the radicalism of Coleridge in religion is found in his attack on what he called its Bibliolatry. He condemned the doctrine of literal inspiration as a superstition; he urged the acceptance of the teachings of Scripture on the ground that they "find" one in the deepest and most spiritual part of one's nature. Faith was a state of the will and the affections, not a merely intellectual assent to doctrinal and historical propositions. As Mill says he was more truly liberal than many liberals.

But while he disconnected faith from the understanding he connected it with a higher faculty, the Reason, which is one with the true Will of man. Coleridge said: "He who begins by loving Christianity better than Truth, will proceed by loving his own Sect or Church better than Christianity, and end in loving himself better than all." But he held with equal firmness that Christianity is itself a system of truth which, when rightly appropriated in the rational will and affection of men, is identical with the truth of philosophy itself. This assertion of the inherent rationality of Christian truth was the animating purpose of his *Aids to Reflection* and it was this which appealed to James Marsh; and it is in this sense that he may be described as a disciple of Coleridge. It was in a combination of the teaching of the great English divines of the seventeenth century, themselves under the spell of Plato, and the German transcendental philosophy of the late eighteenth and early nineteenth century that Coleridge found the especial philosophical framework by which to support his contention of the intrinsic philosophical truth of the Christian faith.

Since Marsh himself was already a student of the same sources, all the circumstances conspired to attach his exposition to that of Coleridge.

If I dwell upon the inherent liberalism of Coleridge's teaching under the circumstances of his own day, as described by Mill, a member of the opposite school, it is because without allusion to that fact, we are without the historic key to the work of Marsh also. In our own idea, and under present conditions, the philosophy of Marsh seems conservative. There is comparatively little interest, even in theological circles, in the doctrines to whose clarification, in the light of reason, he devoted himself. One sees his thought in its proper perspective only as one places it against the background of the prevailing interests of his own day. By temperament, Marsh shrank from controversy; he deprecated becoming involved in it. But the most casual reader of the introduction prefaced to the republication of Coleridge's *Aids to Reflection* will see that its undercurrent is the feeling that what Coleridge says and what he himself says goes contrary to the doctrines that possess the mind of contemporary religious circles, while conjoined with this is the sense that he is under a religious as well as a philosophical obligation to combat the tendency of these beliefs. It was not just the fate or the spread of a particular philosophical system that he was concerned with, but the re-awakening of a truly spiritual religion which had been obscured and depressed under the influence of the prevalent philosophies of John Locke and the Scottish school. It was as an ally of spiritual and personal religion that he turned to the German philosophy, actuated by the conviction that the same evils which Coleridge found in England were found also in his own country.

It is worth while to quote from the Introduction at some length what he has to say upon this subject. "It is our peculiar misfortune in this country that, while the philosophy of Locke and the Scottish writers has been received in full faith, as the only rational system, and its leading principles especially passed off as unquestionable, the strong attachment to religion and the fondness for speculation, by both of which we are strongly characterized, have led us to combine and associate these principles, such as they are, with our religious interests and opinions, so variously and so intimately, that by most persons they are considered as necessary parts of the same system." He himself held that the philosophical principles thus popularly read into the Christian faith were in fact profoundly discordant with the latter. As he says "a system of philosophy which excludes the very idea of all spiritual power and agency" cannot possibly coexist with a "religion essentially spiritual." Like Coleridge he anticipates being regarded as a heretic in religion because he is desirous of searching out a philosophy that is consistent instead of inconsistent with the spiritual truths of Christianity which are to him its essence.

In the attempt to which I now turn to expound the positive philosophy of Marsh, one may appropriately return to the essay of 1822 to which allusion has already been made. Christianity presented itself to him not only as the great cause of the intellectual and emotional change from the world of classic to that of modern mind, as expressed in literature, politics and social life as well as in religion, but as inherently a revelation of philosophic truth. Revelation from without was required because of the fallen state of man. But the revelation was not external, much less arbitrary, in *content*. It was rather a recovery of the essential ultimate truths about nature, man and ultimate reality. It is for that reason that I said that Christianity was to him a truly philosophic revelation. Were I to attempt to select a single passage that might serve as an illuminating text of what he thought and taught, it would be, I think, the following: A thinking man "has, and can have but one system in which his philosophy becomes religious and his religion philosophical."

As I have already indicated, the full meaning of this position can hardly be recovered at the present time. It must be considered in relation to the time in which Dr. Marsh lived. It had nothing in common with the views upon philosophy which prevailed in the academic audiences and popular thought of the time. These as we have also noted were based upon Locke as modified by the ruling Scotch school, and upon Paley. The orthodox conceived of Christianity as a merely external revelation; the dissenters from orthodoxy relied upon proof from design in nature of the existence of God, and upon what Marsh, following Kant and Coleridge called "Understanding" in distinction from "Reason." There is much evidence that Dr. Marsh felt himself between two dangers. One was that he should be thought to reduce Christianity to a mere body of doctrines, a speculative intellectual scheme. The other was that he should be thought faithless to the living power of Christianity in re-making life, and thus be classed with unbelieving critics. The situation in which he thus found himself accounts, I think, for the air of apologetic timidity which surrounds the expression of his deepest thoughts. In part it was due undoubtedly to his modest distrust of himself, but in larger part, to the situation with which his period confronted him. He was quite right, no one who reads him can doubt that fact, in thinking of himself as a deeply devoted man in his own personality. Indeed, for inner and humble piety and spirituality he had few peers among his contemporaries. But he had in addition the distinctively philosophic instinct. He wanted to see the universe and all phases of life as a whole. When he gave rein to his instinct in this direction, he found himself at once conscious that he was coming into conflict with the ideas which dominated not only American society but the churches themselves. He neither mitigated his own Christian sense nor ceased to philosophize. But his activity in the latter field was, it seems to me, restricted. He never developed the independence in thought which matched his philosophic powers. It is probable, as Dr. Nicolson has made clear, that he was the means of directing Emerson to Coleridge, and indirectly at least made a profound impress upon the American "transcendental" movement. But he never had the detached position which marked Emerson, for example, and accordingly did not reach an unimpeded development of his own powers.

It is, however, time to turn more directly to his basic thought in which for him the religious truth of Christianity was found to be one with the truth of philosophy as a theory of God, the universe and man. Formulae are somewhat dangerous. But for the sake of brevity, if for no other reason, a formula or label seems necessary. I shall, accordingly, venture to say that his philosophy is an Aristotelian version of Kant, made under the influence of a profound conviction of the inherent *moral* truths of the teachings of Christianity. The formula involves unfortunately considerable technical reference to historic systems. The external evidence shows that he was more of a student of Plato and of the great divines of the seventeenth century who are influenced by Plato than of Aristotle. But we know also by external testimony that the *Metaphysics* and the *De Anima* of Aristotle were always by him. And it seems fairly evident that his objective interpretation of Kant, his disregard for the phenomenalism and subjective view of nature found in Kant, came to him ultimately, whether directly or through Coleridge, from Aristotle.

To explain what meaning this statement has in connection with Marsh's own metaphysical system, it is necessary to digress into a technical field which I would otherwise gladly avoid. In Kant, as all students know of him, there is a definite separation made between sense, understanding and reason. In consequence, the affections of the mind called sensations are regarded by him as mental in character, and as organized by forms of space and time which are themselves ultimately mental in character. The categories of the understanding while they provide universality and constancy for these sense impressions do not therefore get beyond knowledge of phenomena. While reason furnishes ideals of unity and complete totality which go beyond the scope of the understanding, they are for us unrealizable ideals. When we suppose that reason gives us knowledge of the real nature of things we are led into illusions. Knowledge must remain within the bounds of phenomena, that is of the logical organization of the materials of sense.

Now it is a striking fact that while Dr. Marsh freely employs the Kantian terminology, and while he uses constantly not only the general distinctions of sense, understanding and reason but also special conclusions reached by Kant in treating them, he never even refers to the Kantian limitation of knowledge to phenomena—what is usually termed the "subjectivism" of Kant.

For example, while he treats, like Kant, mathematics as a science of space and time as necessary and hence a priori forms of perceptual experience, he also has in mind the absolute space and time of Newtonian physics, and not just mental forms. They are forms of actual and external things of nature, not merely forms of mind. Thus our geometry and other mathematics is a rational science of the conditions under which all physical things exist, not merely a science of our conditions of experiencing them. In and of themselves as conditions of the possibility of physical things and their changes, they "constitute" in his own words, "the sphere of possibility and of those possible determinations of quantity and form which are the objects of pure mathematical science." The free development of these possibilities, independent of the restrictions imposed by actual existence, is the work of the productive imagination. But they are also necessary principles of the existence of all physical things and events, since the latter are and occur in space and time. Thus mathematics forms the basis of physical science.

He was probably influenced by Fries in this objective interpretation. But there is the deeper influence which I have called Aristotelian. This influence appears in his treatment of the relations of sense to understanding and of both to reason, and also in his entire philosophy of nature in its relation to mind. Instead of making a separation between sense, understanding and reason they present themselves in Marsh's account as three successive stages in a progressive realization of the nature of ultimate reality. Each of the two earlier, namely, sense and understanding, forms the conditions under which the third manifests itself, and leads up to it. For each contains in itself principles which point beyond itself and which create the necessity of a fuller and deeper apprehension of the nature of the real.

What I have called the Aristotelianism of his position is seen in the fact that he did not isolate this ascending series of sense, understanding and rational will from the natural universe as did Kant, but rather saw in it a progressive realization of the conditions and potentialities found in nature itself. I have not run across in him any allusion to Hegel although he seems to have known Fichte. But like Hegel instead of putting the subject in opposition to the object or the world he regarded the subject, who comes most completely to himself in the rational will, as the culmination, the consummation, of the energies constituting the sensible and physical world. While not a scientist, in any technical sense, Marsh was widely read in the science of his day and thought he found in it the evidence for the truth of the conception that nature presents to us an ascending scale of energies in which the lower are both the conditions and the premonitions of the higher until we arrive at self-conscious mind itself.

His conception of sense is, in the epistemological language of to-day realistic. He holds that in sense we can distinguish the received material, the seen, heard and touched qualities from the acts of mind that form seeing, hearing, touching, and that we refer the material of sensed qualities to a ground of reality outside ourselves, just as we refer the acts of sensing to the self as the abiding ground of their reality. We perceive qualities of sense as qualities of an object existing outwardly and independently. Sense however does not give knowledge, even of the physical world, but only material for knowledge. The understanding is necessary to judge the sensory material and to know *what* is presented in them. We have to interpret the material of sense. The understanding operates by acts of distinguishing, comparing, and thus brings out the relations implicit in sensuous material. Without these connective and organizing relations we do not know an object, but merely have a number of qualities before us. We have the power to become self-conscious of the relating activities of the mind. We note that they proceed by certain necessary laws in as far as they result in knowledge. The understanding is not free to judge in any arbitrary sense of freedom. To attain knowledge we must judge or understand in necessary ways or else we do not attain knowledge of objects but only personal fancies. This law of understanding or knowing objects proceeds from the mind itself and it when we recognize it and take note of it forms what is termed reason. In the understanding, that is in scientific knowledge of nature, this agency operates spontaneously; but when it notes its own operation and becomes self-conscious, we recognize it as rational will which is the animating principle one and the same in character or universal in all knowing minds—and hence identical with the divine intellect which is the light that lighteth every man that cometh into the world. It is reason because it operates by necessary principles; it is will when it is viewed as an agency complete and self-sufficient in itself.

This technical excursion into what Marsh calls rational psychology may help express the sense of what has been called the Aristotelian element in him. He insists that the powers of the mind or self are called forth only by objects correlative to them. The sensibility remains a mere potentiality until it is called into action by nature. We cannot hear or see or touch except as the mind is affected by things having color, sound and solidity. There is no difference between this and the action and reaction of iron and a magnet upon each other. In the same way the powers of the understanding remain mere possibilities until they are called into action by the actual relations which subsist among objects. The orderly logical structure is both the condition that calls the powers into action, and realizes their potentialities, and the object upon which they expend themselves, just as much as the qualities of things are both the actualizing conditions and the objects upon which the capacities of the mind terminate in exercise of sensibility. Similarly the objective of self-conscious rational will is both the condition and the object of the exercise of our reason.

The essentially Aristotelian nature of this conception of each lower stage forming the conditions of the actualizing of some potentiality of mind and then supplying the material upon which a higher expression of the same mind exercises itself will be obvious I think to every philosophic student. It is through the use of this conception that Marsh escapes from the charmed circle of limitation within the self that holds the Kantian philosophy spell-bound. The world in its status as a manifold of qualities, as a logically interconnected whole and as summed up in universal self-conscious will has to be there independently of our minds in order that the capacities of our minds may be stimulated into real existence and have material upon which to work.

It was said, however, that this Aristotelian interpretation of Kant is made under the influence of ideas derived from Christian faith. Marsh separates himself from Greek thought, whether that of Plato or Aristotle, in two ways. First he conceives of mind as identical with the self, the "I" or personality, an identification that is like nothing found in ancient thought and one which he associates with the influence of Christianity. It is another way of saying the same thing to point out that he introduces into the classic conception of reason an element foreign to it in its original statement—namely, the conception of reason as *will*—that is of a power to institute and seek to realize ends that are universal and necessary, that are supplied by nature but which flow from its own nature as a personal rational self. It is the very nature of these ends that they cannot be realized by themselves or by any merely intellectual process. Their nature demands that they be embodied in the material of sense and of the natural world as an object of knowledge, or that all the material of appetite connected with the senses or of desire directed upon natural objects be subdued and transformed into agencies of expressing the true ultimate nature of the rational will. To put it a little more concretely, Aristotle held that reason could be actualized in contemplative knowledge apart from any effort to change the world of nature and social institutions into its own likeness and embodiment. Following the spirit of Christian teaching, Marsh denied any such possibility. He held that reason can realize itself and be truly aware or conscious of its own intrinsic nature only as it operates to make over the world, whether physical or social, into an embodiment of its own principles. Marsh constantly condemns what he calls speculation and the speculative tendency, by which he means a separation of knowledge and the intellect from action and the will. By its own nature, reason terminates in action and that action is the transformation of the spiritual potentialities found in the natural world, physical and institutional, into spiritual realities.

The other point of connection of Marsh's philosophy with the Christian faith is more specific, less general. Accepting the idea that man is a fallen creature, he accepted also the idea of Coleridge that original sin is not a mere historic fact, going back to a historic progenitor, but is the act of the will itself by which it takes as the principle and moving spring of its own action something derived not from its own inherent nature but from some source outside itself—the appetites of sense, or the desires that are aroused by the thought of ends derived from the world about us. I shall not extend my excursion into technicalities to trouble you with his philosophic rendering of the theological doctrines of sin, conscience and freedom of the will. But no exposition of his basic idea of the equation of philosophy with religion would be complete, without reference to the particular way in which he applies his conception of the necessity of a correlative object in order to awaken the potentialities of the self into reality. The correlative object of the conscience and will through which they, as they exist in man, can be aroused into actuality of operation and being, is no abstract law. As will and conscience are personal, belonging to a self, so their correlative object must also be personal. At this point, the religious character of his philosophy most clearly reveals and expresses itself. This correlative personal object is the manifestation of the divine in Christ. In his own words: "The true end of our being presented by the spiritual law, is the realization, practically, in our own being, of that perfect idea which the law itself presupposes, and of which Christ is the glorious manifestation." And again "the spiritual principle may be said to have only a potential reality, or, as it enters into the life of nature, a false and delusive show of reality, until, awakened from above by its own spiritual correlatives, it receives the engrafted word, and is empowered to rise above the thraldom of nature."

The discussion will now turn to a consideration of somewhat more concrete matters (although not according to the view of Marsh more genuinely human interests and concerns)—to what Marsh has to say upon society in general and education in particular. Unfortunately what is left to us in the published record is all too scanty. But there are suggestions adequate to a reconstruction of his fundamental philosophy. Here too we may fittingly begin by recourse to Coleridge in spite of the fact that there is less direct evidence of his connection with Coleridge in this matter than in that of the identification of the Christian religion with true philosophy. Coleridge in common with the German school which he represented conceived social institutions as essentially educative in nature and function. They were the outward manifestation of law and reason by means of which the intelligence and conscience of individuals are awakened and by which they are nourished till they become capable of independent activity, and then express themselves in loyalty to social institutions and devotion to improving them until these institutions are still better fitted to perform their educative task for humanity.

Coleridge with considerable courage applied this conception to the church as an institution in distinction from the inward and spiritual communion of the faithful—an application that took its point of course from the fact that there was an established church allied with the political order in England. With rather surprising daring, he proclaimed that the church, in this institutional sense, is not inherently a religious corporation. In his own words "Religion may be an indispensable ally but is not the essential constitutive end, of that national institute, which is unfortunately, at least improperly, styled the Church; a name which in its best sense is exclusively appropriate to the Church of Christ." Then with an obvious etymological reference to the original meaning of clergy as connected with clerks or writers, he goes on to say "the Clerisy of the nation, or national Church in its primary acceptation and original intention, comprehended the learned of all denominations, the sages and professors of law and jurisprudence, of medicine and physiology, of music, and civil and military architecture, with the mathematical as their common organ; in short, all the arts and sciences, the possession and application of which constitute the civilization of a nation, as well as the theological." The latter, he goes on to say, rightfully claimed the precedence, but only because "theology was the root and trunk of the knowledge of civilized man; because it gave unity and the circulating sap of life to all other sciences, by virtue of which alone they could be contemplated as forming the living tree of knowledge." It is primarily as educators that those especially called clergy of the established church are to be regarded and it was even well according to Coleridge that they should serve an apprenticeship as village schoolmasters before becoming pastors.

It is evident that owing to the non-existence of an established Church in the United States this portion of Coleridge's teaching could not directly influence the thought of Marsh. Indeed, he naturally thought that the condition in which the institutional church was but the outward expression or body of the inner and spiritual church represented a higher principle than could be expressed by any politically established church. But indirectly Marsh's ideas move in a like direction, although with such differences as the difference between the political organization of Great Britain and of our country would naturally suggest.

It is interesting to note that Marsh makes, in a sermon at the dedication of the chapel of the University, a distinction between civilization and culture similar to that drawn by Kant and other German thinkers. Civilization, he says, in effect is concerned with the adaptation of the acts and services of the individual to the needs and conditions of existing society. It is a discipline of the faculties with reference to the occupations of civil society. Culture is the development of the powers of individuals with reference to the ends that make them truly human; it transcends any existing social order and regime because it elevates them into the possession of the spiritual law of reason, of universal will and the end of humanity as such. It aims at control by this inner law of rational will instead of by the ordinances and customs of a given society. From the obligations imposed by the interests of higher and common humanity no state policy can absolve us. The peoples of the East, he says, are perhaps more civilized than those of the West for their institutions and the discipline they provide fit the individual to some definite place and work in the social order. But we, he says, are not destined to be the working instruments for attaining the lower ends imposed by the state of civilization. And he adds these very significant words: "We can hardly, indeed, be said to be subjects of any state, considered in its ordinary sense, as body politic with a fixed constitution and a determinate organization of its several powers. But we are constituent members of a community, in which the highest worth and perfection and happiness of the individual free persons composing it, constitutes the highest aim and the perfection of the community as a whole. With us there is nothing so fixed by the forms of political and civil organization, as to obstruct our efforts for promoting the full and free development of all our powers, both individual and social. Indeed where the principle of self-government is admitted to such an extent as it is in this state, there is in fact nothing fixed or permanent, but as it is made so by that which is permanent and abiding in the intelligence and fixed rational principles of action in the self-governed. The self-preserving principle of our government is to be found only in the continuing determination and unchanging aims of its subjects." From this Dr. Marsh draws the inevitable conclusion that the function of an educational institution is a cultivation of the community, which is identical with the full development of all the powers of its individual persons.

It is to be regretted that Dr. Marsh never achieved a complete exposition of his social and political philosophy. While changes in vocabulary might be needed to adapt the principles he here expresses to present conditions, he has stated it seems to me a principle which is fundamental to the distinctive American social system if we have any such system, and one which stands in need of enforcement at the present time. When Dr. Marsh wrote, the idea of nationalism, in its modern sense, had hardly made its appearance in this country. There was little if any worship of the State as a political organization. Individuals were still conscious of their power organized as a free community to make and unmake states—that is, special forms of political organization. There was indeed great admiration for the American form of government and much patriotism in loyalty to it. But it was devotion to its underlying principle as an expression of a free and self-governing community, not to its form. It was regarded as a symbol and as a means, not as an end fixed in itself to which the will and conscience of individuals must be subordinated.

In my judgment, this subordination of the state to the community is the great contribution of American life to the world's history, and it is clearly expressed in the utterances of Dr. Marsh. But recent events have tended to obscure it. Forces have been at work to assimilate the original idea of the State and its organization to older European notions and traditions. The State is now held up as an end in itself; self-styled patriotic organizations make it their business to proclaim the identity of the loyalty and patriotism of individuals with devotion to the State as a fixed institution. The constitution of the state is treated not as a means and instrument to the well-being of the community of free self-governing individuals but as something having value and sanctity in and of itself. We have, unconsciously in large measure but yet pervadingly, come to doubt the validity of our original American ideal. We tend to submit individuality to the state instead of acting upon the belief that the state in its constitution, laws and administration, can be made the means of furthering the ends of a community of free individuals.

Dr. Marsh wrote in the full if insensible consciousness of the pioneer period of American life. The true individualism of that era has been eclipsed because it has been misunderstood. It is now often treated as if it were an exaltation of individuals free from social relations and responsibilities. Marsh expresses its genuine spirit when he refers, as he does constantly, to the *community* of individuals. The essence of our earlier pioneer individualism was not non-social, much less anti-social; it involved no indifference to the claims of society. Its working ideal was neighborliness and mutual service. It did not deny the claims of government and law, but it held them in subordination to the needs of a changing and developing society of individuals. Community relationships were to enable an individual to reach a fuller manifestation of his own powers, and this development was in turn to be a factor in modifying the organized and stated civil and political order so that more individuals would be capable of genuine participation in the self-government and self-movement of society—so that, in short, more individuals might come into the possession of that freedom which was their birth-right. Depreciation of the value of our earlier pioneer individualism is but the negative sense of our surrender of the native idea of the subordination of state and government to the social community and our approximation to the older European idea of the state as an end in itself. If I may be allowed a personal word, I would say that I shall never cease to be grateful that I was born at a time and a place where the earlier ideal of liberty and the self-governing community of citizens still sufficiently prevailed so that I unconsciously imbibed a sense of its meaning. In Vermont, perhaps even more than elsewhere, there was embodied in the spirit of the people the conviction that governments were like the houses we live in, made to contribute to human welfare, and that those who lived in them were as free to change and extend the one as they were the other when developing needs of the human family called for such alterations and modifications. So deeply bred in Vermonters was this conviction that I still think that one is more loyally patriotic to the ideal of America when one maintains this view than when one conceives of patriotism as rigid attachment to a form of the state alleged to be fixed forever, and recognizes the claims of a common human society as superior to those of any particular political form.

Dr. Marsh's views of education were a reflection of his general social philosophy. It goes without saying that he conceived of education in a deeply religious spirit and that to him religion was in words reminiscent of a passage already quoted from Coleridge "the sap of life to the growing tree of knowledge." But we have also in interpreting his words to recall that to him religious truth was one with rational truth about the universe itself and about man's nature in relation to it. In his own words again, religious truth "is not so much a distinct and separate part of what should be taught in a system of instruction, to be learned and stored up in the mind for future use, as a pervading and life-giving principle and power that should act upon the mind in every stage and process of its developement, and bring all the powers of the soul, as they are unfolded, under its holy and humanizing influence." The conception of what religion and religious truth are may change; they have undergone change since Marsh taught and wrote. But some organizing pervading and life-giving principle to bind together all the specialisms and details which so abound is still as greatly needed in education to-day as it was when Marsh spoke.

The ideas of Dr. Marsh upon more specific matters of the organization and conduct of university education reflect his fundamental conceptions. In stating them I depend chiefly upon the record of his successor in the chair of philosophy, Professor Joseph Torrey in the Memoir he prefixed to the collection of Marsh's writings. It was the latter's opinion "that the rules for the admission of students are too limited and inflexible." There is no reason why those unfortunately prevented from taking advantage of the whole of the course should not have the privilege of taking the part that lies within their means. "He was also for allowing more latitude to the native inclinations and tendencies of different minds. It was absurd to expect every young mind to develope in just the same way; and equally absurd to confine each one to the same kind and quantity of study." Again, "he thought the methods of instruction in use too formal and inefficient. There was not enough of actual teaching, and too much importance was attached to text-books. He wanted to see more constant and familiar intercourse between the mind of teacher and learner." It was more important to invigorate and sharpen the student's powers of independent thought and judgment than to bend them to apprehending the ideas of others. As to college discipline and morals, he also distrusted the system of minute external regulation and conformity. He was also opposed to the then prevailing methods of classification and promotion of students. Merely formal examinations he thought of little value.

These points sound strangely like the criticisms and proposals of educational reformers from his day to this. They were not however with him concessions to practical expediency. They were reflections of his fundamental faith in individuality and in the spirit as opposed to the letter and mechanical form. But this emphasis upon the value of individuality was accompanied in his views on education as elsewhere with an equal sense that the ultimate end was a community of cultivated individuals. The ultimate purpose of education is "to elevate the condition and character of the great body of the people." Nowhere as much as in the United States were schools "made as they are here, an important and leading object in the policy of government" and nowhere else was the experiment given a fair trial of "placing all classes and all individuals upon the same level providing for all the same system of free, public instruction."[3]

I have chosen to try to get some idea of the relation of Dr. Marsh's thought to that of his own time rather than to engage in

3. These words were spoken, be it noted, before the great public school revival of the eighteen forties occurred in this country.

general eulogy of him. But the record discloses a mind at once deeply sensitive and deeply rational. The period was not favorable to far-reaching thought which always demands a certain audacity lacking both to the period and to Dr. Marsh's temperament. He did not carry his questionings beyond the received order of beliefs in religion. He depended upon others, notably Coleridge and the German idealists, for the language in which to clothe his philosophic speculations. But none the less because of his sensitivity one feels that even when he speaks of things that do not make the appeal now that they did in a time when men were more engrossed in theology, there is nothing secondhand in his thought. There were realities of which he had an intimate personal sense behind his most transcendental speculations. It is characteristic of him that he holds that knowledge of spiritual truth is always more than theoretical and intellectual. It was the product of activity as well as its cause. It had to be lived in order to be known. The low rating which he gave sense as compared with understanding was not for example a merely cognitive matter. The "thraldom of sense" was a moral and personal affair. And so his depreciation of understanding in comparison with reason was not technical. In what he called understanding he saw the root of the skills and the conventions which enable men to make a shrewd adjustment of means to ends, in dealing with nature and with fellow-men. It was the key to what is termed success. But the ends which it prescribed were just those of worldly success, and so reason was to him the symbol of the ability of man to live on a higher and more inclusive plane, which he called that of spirit and in which he found the distinctive dignity of man. Religion was to him the supreme worth, and yet his conception of what constitutes religion was a virtual condemnation of a large part of that which passed in his time and still passes for religion, as being merely an attempt to include God and the next world in a scheme of personal advancement and success. Underneath the somewhat outmoded form of his philosophy one feels a rare personality, gifted in scholarship, ever eager for more knowledge, who wished to use scholarship and philosophy, to awaken his fellowmen to a sense of the possibilities that were theirs by right as men, and to quicken them to realize these possibilities in themselves. His transcendentalism is the outer form congenial in his day to that purpose. The underlying substance is a wistful aspiration for full and ordered living.

The Sphere of Application of the Excluded Middle

I wish to raise the question of the kind of subject-matter to which the formal principles of logic are legitimately applicable, centering the discussion for the most part about the principle of excluded middle. Naturally I should not raise the question unless I had in mind a certain idea about the matter. If—as I believe—the principles, since they are purely formal, are applicable only to formal or non-existential subject-matter, confusion is bound to result when they are directly applied as criteria or rules in a philosophy of physical or existential affairs.

I take it there is general acknowledgment that a radical difference is found between universal and particular propositions. The latter alone are existential in import, the former being hypothetical or of the "if-then" type. To secure their existential application, there must be an independent particular proposition asserting the existence of something having the properties denoted by the "if" clause. The principle of excluded middle is assuredly, along with those of identity and contradiction, the content of a universal proposition; indeed, those who set most store by them insist that they are the most universal of all propositions. It would then follow without argument that they are hypothetical or of the "if-then" type, and in themselves imply nothing about applicability to existences. To be applicable to existence there must be independent propositions of a matter-of-fact kind, supported by empirical or matter-of-fact evidence, that things as they exist have the properties which meet the conditions set forth in the universal propositions.

The proposition, that A is either B or non-B, is in itself completely indifferent to the question whether anything exists having the properties designated by A and B. It is a complete fallacy

[First published in *Journal of Philosophy* 26 (19 December 1929): 701–5. For reply by Ernest Nagel, see this volume, Appendix 1. For Dewey's rejoinder, see pp. 203–9.]

to argue from the "*A*" of a formal and universal proposition to an "*A*" which stands for something existent. The two are as unlike as the formal and the material, the "essential" and the existential. But the universals of Aristotle were taken to be existential wholes inclusive of particulars. In spite, then, of the general present recognition of the difference in kind between universal and particular propositions, the Aristotelian conception that the principle of excluded middle applies directly to all existences is retained. Formal characters are thus given material meaning and the troublesome question of the relation of the logical to the ontological or existent is begged wholesale at the outset.

So much for the source of an ambiguity and confusion and the consequent need of raising the question of the legitimate application of the principle of excluded middle. The significant question is whether there are material or matter-of-fact grounds for assigning to actual existences the properties which are designated in the formal propositions. This is a question as to the nature of actual existences. This is obviously too large a question to go into here. But that things have the formal properties that characterize ideas that are employed in reasoning about them and that are necessary for consistent reasoning is in any event an unjustified assumption, and the steady trend of our knowledge of actual existence is one that renders the assumption increasingly incredible.[1]

I shall confine further discussion to two points bearing on this incredibility. One concerns the contingency connected with particularity of existences and events, and the other the fact that existences change and are in transition. The first point may be conveniently introduced by a reference to a sentence in a recent article by Mr. Nagel—with most of which I am in hearty sympathy.[2] "It must be admitted," he says, "that propositions about the future are not categorically true or false"—in other words, that the principle of excluded middle does not apply. But he seemingly qualifies the force of this admission, for he goes on to say that it is possible "to enumerate exhaustive (though very general) properties about the future if that future is not altogether inde-

1. Those who object to the use of the term "ideas" may substitute the terms "essences" or "universals" without its making any difference in the argument.
2. "Intuition, Consistency, and Excluded Middle," *Journal of Philosophy*, Vol. XXVI, the quotation being from p. 488.

pendent of the past." I wonder if Mr. Nagel would not admit that the word "exhaustive" is unfortunate in this context. It may hold in some sense which Mr. Nagel had in mind. But, taken literally, an exhaustive enumeration would remove all contingency from the future and would make, in theory at least, the future in question so determinate as to be of the fixed nature required for the application of the principle of excluded middle. This interpretation, however, would seem to be excluded by the phrase in parenthesis, namely, "very general." For it can hardly be meant that any number of general propositions could exhaustively determine a particular event.

They could not do so even if we had infinite time in which to make the enumeration. For the properties enumerated would still be conditional, and the uniqueness of the occurrence of the event would still escape statement. There are only two theories as far as I can see upon which this conclusion would not follow. One is logical atomism, or the notion that each genuine ultimate existence is wholly simple. In this case, a single proposition would exhaust each ultimate existence. The other alternative is that every particular existence represents in fact an intersection of universals. Both of these theories, however, seem to be dialectic products of the assumption that logical and formal principles have a direct material and ontological application, rather than conclusions from empirical evidence.

The supposition that the uniqueness of an existence can be propositionally and symbolically conveyed by adding a statement of date and place to the enumeration of general properties affords no way out. This device is effectively used in physical science. But the "space" and "time" of physics denote properties in respect to which existences are most generally *comparable* with one another—or are *not* unique. To the wise this fact is a warning that physics is not concerned with the individuality of existences.

The admission that the principle of excluded middle does not directly apply to future existences carries with it the admission that it does not apply to present and past existences. This statement will be challenged, at least as far as the past is concerned; for it may be contended that the past is over and its subject-matter all in and hence determinately fixed. The rejoinder that the past was once a future of something else may seem to be a mere dialectic evasion, since it is *now* past. But, as Mr. Nagel says, the assertion that the future is wholly independent of the present is fatal to all intelligent discourse about existences having temporal quality. The belief that the past is merely past, that it is all ended and over with, rests upon precisely such an assumption of independence of present and future. The past, if taken to be complete in itself, is arbitrarily sheared off from *its* future, which extends to our present and its future. The fixation of a past for purposes of inquiry and reasoning is legitimate, and to this fixation in an idea (or "essence") formal principles apply. But to assume that the actual event has the same properties as has the subject-matter by means of which we reason about it, is to make precisely the same conversion of the logical into the existential, the formal into the material, which is at issue.

Up to this point, the argument has nominally turned about an admission regarding propositions about the future. Many persons will refuse to allow that admission and hence will deny the validity of the argument that has been made. It may be well, then, to point out that the force of the argument does not depend upon the special issue regarding propositions about the future. It depends upon the fact that no number of propositions can exhaustively determine any concrete existence—except upon the assumption of one or other of the two theories previously referred to. The "A" and "B" of the law of excluded middle are always conceptual (or subsistential) in character and the "A" and "B" of an existential proposition are identical only in outward symbolization. The gap between conception (or essence) and existence remains.

Mathematical reasoning, by use of the principle of contradiction, justifiably reaches the conclusion that the value of *Pi* can not be stated in any finite enumeration. But the conclusion has no existential applicability until it is shown, by empirical evidence, that there are existences which have the exact properties of the mathematical circle, diameter and circumference. And I suppose it would be generally admitted that there is no existent circle in the mathematical sense—although existent figures have characteristics that make mathematical conclusions methodologically valuable in our intellectual dealings with them. But this is a very different matter from direct carrying over of logical forms to them.

The implication of the argument is not that things "contradict" one another. It is that contradiction is a purely logical category and is not false but nonsensical or meaningless when applied to things. The counterpart of this fact is that "identity" in the sense in which it figures in formal logic is also irrelevant to existence. Things and events *conflict* with one another and with themselves although our thinking about them must be self-consistent. There is a device often employed for reducing the fact of conflicting qualities—properties that are *physically* opposed —to logical consistency. It is said that all that is necessary in order to make the law of excluded middle directly applicable to things is to discriminate relations. Water may be both cold and not-cold at the same time, but not in the same relation. Specify the nexus and all difficulty disappears, and so with an object which is blue in one aspect and not in another, etc. But this argument points in the direction of our conclusion. For the abstracted relation is purely conceptual—or subsistential and universal—in character. It does not exist by itself in *rerum natura*. It is a way of thinking the existence for the purpose of thinking. The more we discriminate different relations, the more it follows that the existence in question actually possesses opposed—although not *logically* contradictory—properties and the law of excluded middle is not directly applicable to it. Otherwise a relation or universal is hypostatized into an independent existence.

These considerations lead insensibly to the other point. Existences have temporal quality. They are in change or in transition, in movement from one state characterized by certain traits to another. The door, it is said, must be either open or not-open, where "the door" is taken to denote an actual existence. But the statement overlooks two facts. In the first place the door may be opening or shutting, that is, in process from one state to another. The other fact is that there is no existent door which is one hundred per cent. shut. It is shut *enough* for certain practical purposes, but it is also open—there are cracks. The difficulties encountered in a laboratory experiment in securing, say, airtightness are significantly illustrative. They indicate the ideational and ideal character of "open" and "not-open." The ideal is applicable to existence *indirectly* as setting a limit to which to work, but this is a radically different matter from direct application of the principle of excluded middle. "Heat" as a concept or essence is not "cold" or non-heat. As concepts each should have self-identical and mutually exclusive meaning. But an *existence* may be changing from hot to cold or *vice versa*. It is not so much false as meaningless—nonsensical—to assert that it *is* either hot or not-hot, for what it *is* is a *change* from hot to cold.

This property may in turn be fixed in an idea and put in exclusive formal opposition to a state of non-change. But again in this operation we have passed from the sphere of existences to that of ideas about existence. We have passed from conditions of existence to conditions of effective inquiry about existence. The formal properties of the latter operation are important, but their importance is no justification for equating the formal and material, the logical and the ontological. We can not combine in a coherent scheme the metaphysics underlying the Aristotelian logic with the metaphysics implied in our present scientific knowledge of natural existences.

In spite of the positive character of many assertions that have been made, my prime intent is to raise a question. The question of the status of contradiction and excluded middle is a phase of a larger question. The basic issue concerns the relation of the logical and the ontological, the formal and the material or existential, and it can not be intelligibly discussed apart from that issue. Meantime to argue from mathematics to existence is simply to beg this fundamental issue.

The Applicability of Logic to Existence

Toward the close of an article in the *Journal of Philosophy*, I remarked that "in spite of the positive character of many assertions that have been made, my prime intent is to raise a question. . . . The basic issue concerns the relation of the logical and the ontological, the formal and the material or existential."[1] The article by Mr. Nagel "Can Logic Be Divorced from Ontology?"[2] is welcome for two reasons. In the first place, I am convinced that differences of view on this question are fundamental to many other differences among philosophers, and to such an extent that the nature of these differences can be adequately understood only as the underlying difference from which they proceed is made explicit. Next to actual agreement nothing is more clarifying in philosophic discussion than the location of the source of disagreement. So I hope the article of Mr. Nagel will be the first of a number dealing with this issue.

In the second place, Mr. Nagel's contribution has made me aware that there was considerable ambiguity of statement in my previous article, so that I did not make my conception of the issue clear, and gave occasion to stumbling on the part of intelligent readers. So I am glad of the opportunity to restate my view of the nature of the problem—which I was more concerned to raise than, in that article, to try to solve. So let me first say that the question of the *relation* of the logical and the existential was intended to be taken in a positive, not a negative, sense. That is, I should answer the question put in the title of Mr. Nagel's article in the negative; I do not think that logic can be divorced from ontology. I agree that logical characters can not be "cut off"

1. Vol. XXVI, p. 705. [See this volume, p. 202.]
2. Vol. XXVI, pp. 705–712. [See this volume, Appendix 1.]

[First published in *Journal of Philosophy* 27 (27 March 1930): 174–79. For Ernest Nagel's article to which this is a rejoinder, see this volume, Appendix 1. For initial article by Dewey, see pp. 197–202.]

from existential (p. 707 [455])*; that the "ground" of the logical must be found in the ontological (p. 710 [458]); that "method must in some sense reflect or refract orders of things that are knowable orders"; that "the continuity between logic and metaphysics can not be broken" (p. 708 [456]); and, generally, that "there must be a connection between logic and metaphysics" (p. 709 [457]). But these agreements only raise the questions: In what sense? What kind of a continuity is there? What sort of connection holds? There are other relations besides the literal identity or "equating" which I denied. And about Mr. Nagel's answers to these questions I am still in some doubt.

There seem to be two reasons for failure to get the meaning of my previous article. For one of them I am directly responsible. The usual meaning of "apply" is "to bring to bear practically," to use or administer. I employed expressions which contradicted my actual meaning, since my positive point is that logical characters can be employed or brought to bear practically upon other existences, while my negative point is that they do not inherently characterize other existences in such a way as to afford premises on which existential inferences may be directly based. My actual meaning is perhaps expressed in the following sentence: "The significant question is whether there are material or matter-of-fact grounds for *assigning* to actual existences the properties which are designated in the formal propositions" of identity, excluded middle, and contradiction.[3] The principle of contradiction is directly assignable to Pi as a logical or mathematical (symbolic) object, so that, as I pointed out, it justifies a direct conclusion—namely, the non-finite character of enumeration of its value. What I was denying was that it had *that* kind of applicability to physical existence, though I had no intention to deny that the mathematical object could be used, or be applicable, in *dealings* with such existence. Rather, the opposite.

The other ground of misapprehension is perhaps that while my discussion was limited to the three formal "laws," identity, contradiction, and excluded middle (with the emphasis on the latter), Mr. Nagel discusses for the most part the general question. It is true that I said that "the question of the status of con-

---

* Bracketed numbers refer to this volume.

3. P. 702 [198]; italics not in text.

tradiction and excluded middle is a phase of a larger question" (p. 705 [202]), but confusion may arise when what was said of an included phase is carried over too directly to the larger issue which I refrained from discussing. However, as I have already said, it is the larger issue in which I am most interested, and so I welcome Mr. Nagel's discussion.

I

He makes some statements that are in line with what I had in mind, however ambiguously I may have expressed my meaning. Thus he says (p. 709 [457]) that "logical principles are concerned with the mutual relations of propositions, not with the mutual relations of things," and that "only thinking can be said to be self-consistent, however much that consistency is conditioned by things" (p. 711 [459]), and that logic is concerned primarily with "our second intentions of things, with things as objects of reflective thought" (p. 709 [457]). Such statements are in strict harmony with my thought. On the other hand, I should not dream of denying either that valid objects of thought are *conditioned* by prior existence or that they are *indirectly* applicable to them by means of operations, themselves existential, which are integral elements in the *complete* object of thought. Without assuming either agreement or disagreement, I shall now proceed to a discussion of issues in the light of some specific points raised by Mr. Nagel.

I begin with the point that lies nearest to the specific content of my original article—the discussion of excluded middle. In reference to the application of the principle of excluded middle to a door as shut or not-shut, he says, "Fix one context, make explicit by pointing to a set of operations or conditions what it is to be shut, and the moving door does or does not meet those conditions" (p. 710 [459]). Precisely. Fixing context, defining a set of operations, is just the work of thought. Upon *its* product, then, the excluded middle can be directly brought to bear. This was my point. And as I explicitly pointed out, the resulting definition—the reflectively defined object—is of use or avail in *dealing* with actual existence. What was denied was that *apart* from this work of reflection in fixing context and defining meaning, the properties designated by the excluded middle characterize existence. Mr. Nagel has given a valuable explicit statement of what I called "the ideational and ideal character of 'open' and 'shut'" (p. 705 [201]). Instead of the difficulty being due to "failure to define operationally" the ideas used, the reverse is true. This operational definition is precisely what constitutes the object of thought, and its *absence* from *prior* existence is just why the properties of excluded middle do not characterize, and may not be assigned to, the strictly existential door. Exactly the same point may be made about "low pressure" (p. 711 [460]). Mr. Nagel says "while there may not *actually be* low pressure, low pressure is *intelligible*[4] in terms of the operations between existing things." Precisely. I should not desire a better illustration of my meaning.

In the same connection belongs Mr. Nagel's reference to the determinateness of existence. Here he has, unless I err, unwittingly taken advantage of an ambiguity in the term "determinate." When he says "existence is determinately what it is" (p. 710 [458]), he is referring to existence as it is apart from connection with the reflectively determined object. The statement, of course, is true, but it has no bearing upon the relation of contingency to excluded middle. For a contingent or indeterminate thing is "determinately what it is," namely, indeterminate. There is no denying that determination in this sense is existential. But such determinateness is a different sort of thing from the determinateness of objects of thought due to fixing a context and defining operations. What I was objecting to—and Mr. Nagel appears to be committed to the same objection—is the direct carrying over of *such* determination to prior existence.

The same considerations apply to the bearing of the excluded middle upon future events. I did not dream of denying that the contingent has elements of definite characteristics, nor that predictions rest upon elements of continuity of existence between present, past, and future. When Mr. Nagel says (p. 712 [460]): "A sea-fight must either take place to-morrow or not, but it is not necessary that it should take place, neither is it necessary that it should not take place, yet it is necessary that it either should or should not take place," he is pointing out the differ-

4. Italics not in text.

ence that holds between necessity as directly characterizing existence and necessity characterizing the object of thought. It is the disjunction, the "either-or," that is necessary. Does Mr. Nagel hold that this disjunction inherently characterizes existence, or does he hold that an object of thought which is disjunctively defined may then be brought to bear, through operations, upon existence?

II

I turn now to the more general consideration. Mr. Nagel points out quite correctly that I have a metaphysics in the sense of attributing certain generic characters to Nature as existent. He points out with equal correctness that as *objects of knowledge* these properties are reflectively arrived at. He then raises the question of the ground or criterion for distinguishing between logical and ontological characters, since both are the results of reflective inquiry involving inference[5] (p. 706 [453–54]).

In general the answer is simple. The distinction is made on the grounds of experience. Reflective inquiries themselves exist and are *had* in direct experience as other things are had. They are then capable of being made the objects of reflective inquiry. When so inquired into, their distinctive properties are ascertained. Thus the criterion does not differ from that used in distinguishing the properties of a cat from those of a dog. If reflective inquiry were not primarily itself an existence, its distinguishing properties could not be empirically determined. If it is such an existence, we can investigate it. Whether its properties are distinctively different from those found in other things is, of course, itself a matter to be decided by comparing the results of the various inquiries. But the present question concerns simply the criterion of distinction, so that it is not necessary to go into that matter here. It may be pertinent, however, to note that in each case the existential assignment of properties, whether to the existence of

5. I am not sure of the exact implications of Mr. Nagel's own discussion of this point, so I confine myself to the question of the criterion. The source of my inability to understand is his seeming implication (on pp. 706–07 [454–55]) that it follows from what I said that objects of reflection should have *only* logical traits.

inquiry or to other existence, is dependent upon the actual performance or execution of indicated operations, the conclusion remaining propositional, or symbolic, short of such application —short of being brought "practically to bear." Does Mr. Nagel hold, for example, that implicatory relations as such characterize existences apart from reflection just as spatial and temporal qualities so characterize them? Discussion of this question would help define the issue.

III

The previous remarks suggest the answer to the question as to the "ontological status" of logical or intellectual properties, though they do not directly define it. If one takes into account the existence of reflection, then, of course, there is no argument. It is truistic that with respect to this existence, its characteristic properties are ontological—they exist. But this does not settle the question whether they exist apart from reflection, which would be the case were reflection merely a psychological or (better put) pedagogical process leading to the direct apprehension of things as antecedently possessed of logical properties. It does not settle the question as to whether they are ontological in the sense of being generic metaphysical characters similar to those of contingency, perspectives, heres and nows to which Mr. Nagel refers.

While I deny that they are such generic antecedent properties, I do not deny that existence, apart from reflection, *conditions* reflection as an existence, nor that the latter has a temporal continuity with prior existences. The union of stability and precariousness is, as I have tried to show elsewhere, a condition of the occurrence of thought, whose ulterior function is, accordingly, to give to other existences a stability or determination they would not possess without it. My position may perhaps be made clearer by a distinction between the potential and the actual. To use a barbarous locution, I hold that existence apart from that of reflection is logi*cible*, but not logi*cized*. Similarly, certain stuffs in nature are ed*ible* but not eat*en* until certain operations of organisms supervene. These operations produce distinctive additive consequences. Through them, qualities and relations previously potential become actualized.

I am at a loss to see why my reference to the formal properties of machines (p. 712 [460]) should have seemed incompatible with the position taken in my article. Machines are machines, works of art brought into existence by operations that effect a re-disposition of prior existences. The redisposition that constitutes the machines renders new functions and uses possible; the traits that form the structure on which these functions and uses depend provide characteristic formal properties. But the fallacy of transferring these properties to the material on which machines operate is just the fallacy I was engaged in pointing out.

A loom as a reflectively constructed machine is applied, that is, "practically brought to bear," upon yarn—itself, by the way, a manufactured product. In this operation yarn becomes cloth marked by a pattern. This product has an ontological, that is, existential status. But it does not follow from this fact that the formal properties of the machine characterize inherently either the yarn or the cloth. The analogy to my mind with identity, excluded middle, contradiction, as general characters of the objects that are products of the art of reflection is complete and reasonably obvious. These characters are then applicable, useful, in dealing with other existences through operations they symbolically or intellectually define.

In Reply to Some Criticisms[1]

It is inevitable, on an occasion like this, that the adverse criticisms be selected for discussion and reply. This fact gives an unduly controversial character to this article. So I wish to begin by expressing my grateful appreciation of not only the attention given by critics to my thought, but especially of their considerate tone, and their words of generous recognition of some value in my thinking.

I

There are, I take it, two main points and one that is subsidiary, in the article by Professor Woodbridge. Of the main points, one concerns the attitude taken by me toward the antecedents and the consequents of reflection with respect to objects of knowledge; the other concerns the method by which my position is reached—Mr. Woodbridge conceiving it to be purely dialectical and not, as I have maintained and believe, empirical. The point that seems to me subsidiary, deals with the place of the permanent and the changing in existence. With regard to this problem also, Professor Woodbridge believes that I reach my position by dialectic rather than derive it from experience.

1. See the articles read at the meeting of the American Philosophical Association, New York, December, 1929, by Prof. W. E. Hocking ("Action and Certainty"), and Prof. C. I. Lewis ("Pragmatism and Current Thought"), both printed in the *Journal of Philosophy* in the preceding issue, No. 9, and the article by Prof. F. J. E. Woodbridge, which appears in this issue. [See this volume, Appendixes 2, 3, and 4.]

[First published in *Journal of Philosophy* 27 (8 May 1930): 271–77, from an address read at the meeting of the American Philosophical Association, New York City, December 1929. For articles to which this is a reply, see this volume, Appendixes 2, 3, and 4.]

Although Mr. Woodbridge's two main points are related to each other, it will be better to consider the question of the nature of the antecedents and consequents of reflection first and independently of the question of method, because I find attributed to me a somewhat different view from that which I hold. Perhaps the difference in view may be most directly approached through the instance of the patient and the physician (employed by me) to which Mr. Woodbridge refers. I began the discussion of this illustration with the statement, "it is evident that the presence of a man who is ill is the 'given.'" Then I went on to say that *this* "given" is not as such a case of knowledge at all; the particular point I was making being that the given in the sense of data of *knowledge* is the product of reflective analysis of that which is given or had in direct perceptual experience, and which, as such, is not a case of knowledge. Moreover, data for knowledge when once arrived at, define the problem, and hence are not identical with the *object* of knowledge. As I said, in the context referred to, "The original perception furnishes the *problem* for knowing; it is something *to be* known not an object of knowing." But, as I also tried to show, the original experience does not furnish the problem in the sense of constituting it in a defined way; the resolution of the experience into those particulars called data accomplishes this task. The patient having something the matter with him is antecedent; but being ill (*having* the experience of illness) is not the same as being an *object of knowledge*; it is identical, when the further experience had by the physician supervenes, with having a subject-matter *to be* known, to be investigated. If the distinctions (upon which I have insisted at considerable length) between something *had* in experience and the object *known*, between this something and data of knowledge, and between the data and the final object of knowledge, be noted, I do not understand why any one should think I was denying the existence of antecedent things or should suppose that the object of knowledge as I conceive it does away with antecedent existences. On the contrary, the object of knowledge is, according to my theory, a re-disposition *of* the antecedent existences. After quoting a statement of mine that "only the conclusion of reflective inquiry is known" Mr. Woodbridge goes on to say, "I conceive the object to exist prior to its being known." I, too, conceive that things had in direct experience exist prior to being known. But I deny the identity of things had in direct experience with the object of knowledge *qua* object of knowledge. Things that are *had* in experience exist prior to reflection and its eventuation in an *object* of knowledge; but the latter, as such, is a deliberately effected re-arrangement or re-disposition, by means of overt operations, of such antecedent existences. The difference between Mr. Woodbridge and myself, as I see it, is not that he believes in the existence of things antecedent to knowledge and I do not; we differ in our beliefs as to what the character of the antecedent existences with respect to knowledge is. While Mr. Woodbridge says "the object exists prior to *its* being known," I say that "*the* object" is the eventual product of reflection, the prior or antecedent existences being subject-matter *for* knowledge, not *the objects* of knowledge at all.

The foregoing remarks are not intended, of course, to prove that my position is correct, they are meant to show what the position is. The question of correctness brings up the question of the method by which is reached the conclusion that the object consequent on reflective inquiry differs from the antecedently experienced existences, since it is their re-disposition. Mr. Woodbridge thinks that the method is purely dialectical, not empirical. Now, of course, I employ dialectic. I do not suppose that any one could write on philosophy without using it. If I could take the reader by the hand and lead him to see the same things I think I see and have the same experience I have, I would do it. Short of that possibility, I use dialectic. But this is so obvious, it can not be what Mr. Woodbridge objects to. As far as I can make out, the objectionable dialectic consists in laying it down as a premiss that knowledge must have practical efficacy, and then arguing from this premiss to the conclusion that the object of knowledge must differ from what exists antecedent to knowing. If I had been guilty of this practice I should agree with Mr. Woodbridge's criticisms.

As matter of fact, however, I have depended upon empirical evidence. The evidence which I have cited at considerable length, running, in fact, through several chapters, is drawn from the experimental sciences. The argument may be stated in a simple way. The sciences of natural existence are not content to regard anything as an object of knowledge—in its emphatic differential sense—except when the object in question is reached by experimental methods. These experimental methods involve overt operations which re-dispose the existences antecedently had in experience. Q.E.D. Dialectic is used, of course, but it is used in order to invite the reader to experience the empirical procedure of experimental inquiry and then draw his own conclusion. If I am wrong, it is because my empirical analysis is wrong. I regret that none of my critics offered his own interpretation of experimental knowledge and its object. In any case, the practical efficacy of reflective thought (rather than of knowledge) is the conclusion of my empirical analysis, not the premiss of a dialectic.

I have called the criticism regarding my preference for the changing over the immutably fixed, subsidiary. This is because it does not seem to be so important in the criticism nor so well established as that just dealt with. In one respect, my argument on this point is frankly dialectical. The history of thought seems to me to disclose that the belief in immutable existence is an emotional preference dialectically supported. Dialectic is obviously in place in dealing with a position as far as that is itself dialectical. In any case, I have not meant to deny the theory of immutable substances because it is "bad," although it is pertinent to the dialectic to point out that bad consequences have resulted in morals and natural science from its assumption. In addition to this negative reason, derived from dialectic, I find a positive reason in the history of science for my hypothesis that the difference between the apparently permanently permanent and the obviously changing is one of tempo or rate of change. For science seems to have moved constantly away from acceptance of everlasting unchangeable elements. Its continually increasing emphasis upon interaction seems to be compatible empirically only with the fact that things are modified in their interactions. While, then, I would not call the hypothesis in question proved, it appears to me more reasonable than the contrary doctrine.

II

To reply adequately to the points raised by Professor Hocking would involve a substantial statement of my theory of meaning and truth. Consequently, I am compelled to engage in a series of rather summary remarks.

1. In arguing for the non-correspondence of meaning and working, Mr. Hocking says "if we only know a thing when we see what comes of it, then indeed we can never know anything; for we never have in hand what is yet to eventuate." For, as he points out, when ideas are taken as plans of action, they develop later into other plans not even contemplated, much less in process of execution, when the idea was originally conceived. This is an objection which is natural when truth is conceived of as an inherent property of some meanings, ideas, or propositions. By converting my position in terms of his own, Mr. Hocking naturally finds my position unsatisfactory. But if it is taken in its own terms, it is seen that any idea or proposition is relevant to its *own* problematic situation in which it arises and which it intends to resolve. As far as it does resolve it, it is validated or is "true." This resolved situation may produce *another* situation that then requires to be resolved, a further meaning and further truth, and so on. There is continuity between these different situations, in so far as the *subject-matter* is continuous. Looking *back*, it is easy to suppose that there was a single idea or meaning (like that of freedom in Mr. Hocking's illustrations) which has remained identical through a series of partial realizations. But this retrospective survey and the meaning it yields is always in fact—according to my conception—a new meaning arrived at in dealing with a new empirical situation.[2] Without going into detail, I would say that much of Professor Hocking's argument and illustrations (the case of the lover, radio-activity, etc.) seems to me to rest on an identification of truth with meaning which is necessary from his point of view, but which is denied from mine. What he calls "half-truths," "partial truths," are from my point of view *meanings* in process of development; the question of truth arises only when the question of experimental verification enters in. Part of the meaning may be verified, but such verification is not a half-truth; it is the whole truth of that part of the meaning.

2. The same line of argument applies to the question of the immediacy of truth. There is a sense in which truth, as the solution of problems, is immediate; it is the same sense in which a

2. In connection with this point I would call especial attention to the argument *against* the agnostic inference that Mr. Hocking draws from my theory which is found on pp. 192–194 and elsewhere in *The Quest for Certainty* [*Later Works* 4:153–55].

solution *when it is arrived at* is immediate; it immediately exists. But it is arrived at through mediation or reflection involving operations; it is, in good Hegelian language, a mediated immediacy. What is denied is that meanings, apart from their application through operations, are more than *claims* to truth. More specifically, what is denied is that immediate properties, such as clearness, so-called self-evidence, etc. (the properties insisted upon by the rationalistic schools as marks of truth) are more than properties of *meanings*.

3. It is an old story that "eternal" is an ambiguous word. It means both irrelevancy to time and enduring through all time. Taking the word in the latter sense as Professor Hocking's argument seems to require, I should say that stability of truth, like "reality" as defined by C. S. Peirce, represents a *limit*. Of course we want truths to be as stable as they can be. That is to say, we want meanings which have been confirmed in a comprehensive variety of empirical situations and that accordingly offer us the promise of further applications. What is objected to is the conversion of this ideal limit into an inherent and antecedent property of meanings. Such conversion appears to me the essence of dogmatism. And some of Mr. Hocking's illustrations in exemplifying such dogmatisms, also exemplify, to my mind, the objectionableness of the conversion of an ideal limit into an eternal truth. These fixed dogmas work, of course, but I can not share—taking the light of history as a guide that reveals the way in which they have worked—Mr. Hocking's enthusiasm for the "absolute as a battle axe." The fixed truths of paranoiacs also work—but rather disastrously.

4. That there are *a priori meanings* in an empirical sense, I have never denied or doubted. It is the nature of a genuine meaning to be prospective and thus *temporally a priori*. When the nature and function of these meanings are clarified they form what may be called postulates. The value of postulates in science is undoubted. The conversion of meanings-as-postulates into truths, already alluded to, is, once more, natural in the philosophy of Mr. Hocking, but from my point of view it is fallacious. I would have postulates recognized for what they are and not frozen into dogmatic truths. The assertion that "necessary consequences can be perceived and evaluated in advance" rests, to my mind, on an ambiguity in the term "necessary consequences." It may signify

either logical implications or existential outcomes. The fallacy of such ethics as the Kantian, consists, as I see it, in supposing that the former is identical with the latter, or that the latter *ought* to be identical with the former. It therefore leads to a rigidity which is favorable not only to dogmatism in thought, but to fanaticism in action: since the consequences follow logically from the principle they *must* be right and *must* be fought for at all costs. Experience seems to me to testify to the need of an ethics more humble toward existential consequences. Such humility is quite consistent with firm attachment to hypotheses that have had a wide confirmation in the history of the race and of the individual, provided pains are taken to examine the relation between the hypothesis and its consequences so as to give assurance that the latter are genuine confirmations. "The value of trying to realize value" is such a hypothesis—provided one join with it (or interpret it as) a constantly renewed endeavor at "*discovering* the possibilities of the actual."

I recognize the quite summary character of these comments. But as I said at the outset, Mr. Hocking's points raise a large number of fundamental issues in logic and morals, and to do justice to them would require not a few paragraphs, but a treatise.

III

I find myself in such sympathy with the article of Mr. Lewis that I shall confine my comment upon it to one minor point. He says "Professor Dewey seems to view such abstractionism in science as a sort of defect—sometimes necessary, but always regrettable; an inadequacy of it to the fullness of experience." I fear that on occasion I may so have written as to give this impression. I am glad, therefore, to have the opportunity of saying that this is not my actual position. Abstraction is the heart of thought; there is no way—other than accident—to control and enrich concrete experience except through an intermediate flight of thought with conceptions, relations, abstracta. What I regret is the tendency to erect the abstractions into complete and self-subsistent things, or into a kind of superior Being. I wish to agree also with Mr. Lewis that the need of the social sciences at present is precisely such abstractions as will get their unwieldy elephants into box-cars that will move on rails arrived at by other abstractions. What is to be regretted is, to my mind, the tendency of many inquirers in the field of human affairs to be over-awed by the abstractions of the physical sciences and hence to fail to develop the conceptions or abstractions appropriate to their own subject-matter.

In conclusion I wish again to thank the participators in the discussion for their sympathetic treatment of my intellectual efforts. If I have omitted reference to the paper of Mr. Ratner, it is because in his case a sympathetic understanding is manifest which calls for no reply—indeed, his paper seems to me to answer by way of anticipation some of the criticisms upon which I have commented, especially the one concerning the nature of antecedent existences.

Conduct and Experience

"Conduct," as it appears in the title, obviously links itself with the position taken by behaviorists; "experience," with that of the introspectionists. If the result of the analysis herein undertaken turns out to involve a revision of the meaning of both concepts, it will probably signify that my conclusions will not be satisfactory to either school; they may be regarded by members of both as a sterile hybrid rather than a useful mediation. However, there are many subdivisions in each school, and there are competent psychologists who decline to enroll in either, while the very existence of controversy is an invitation to reconsideration of fundamental terms, even if the outcome is not wholly satisfactory.

Before we enter upon the theme, an introductory remark should be made. That is that the subject is so highly complex and has so many ramifications that it is impossible to deal with it adequately. The difficulty is increased by the fact that these ramifications extend to a historical, intellectual background in which large issues of philosophy and epistemology are involved, a background so pervasive that even those who have no interest in, or use for, philosophy would find, if they took the trouble to investigate, that the words they use—the words we all must use—are deeply saturated with the results of these earlier discussions. These have escaped from philosophy and made their way into common thought and speech.

The problem for psychology is connected with the controversy, so active about thirty years ago, between structuralists and functionalists. The introspectionists are more lineal descendants of the structuralists than are the behaviorists of the functional-

[First published in *Psychologies of 1930*, ed. Carl Murchison (Worcester, Mass.: Clark University Press, 1930), pp. 409–22.]

ists, and I do not mean to equate the terms. The basic error of the structuralists was, it seems to me, the assumption that the phenomena they dealt with had a structure which direct inspection could disclose. Admitting, for the moment, that there are such things as conscious processes which constitute "experience" and which are capable of direct inspection, it still involves an immense leap of logic to infer that direct inspection can disclose their structures. One might go so far as to say that, supposing that there are such things, they are just the sort of things that are, in their immediate occurrence, structureless. Or, to put it in a more exact way, if they have any structure, this is not carried in their immediate presence but in facts that are external to them and which cannot be disclosed by the method of direct inspection.

Take, for example, the classification of some immediate qualities as sensations, others as perceptions, and the sub-classification of sensations into auditory, visual, tactile, etc. As a classification, it involves an interpretation, and every interpretation goes outside of what is directly observed. I can attach no meaning to the statement that any immediately present quality announces, "I am sensory, and of the visual mode." It is called visual because it is referred to the optical apparatus, and this reference depends upon facts that are wholly external to the quality's own presence: upon observation of the eyes and anatomical dissection of bodily organs. The distinction between qualities to which the names "sensation" and "perception" are given involves a still more extensive operation of analytic interpretation, depending upon further considerations extraneous to what is immediately present and inspected.

The difficulty cannot be met by saying that a "sensory" quality is immediately given as simple, while a perceptual one is a complex of simples, for this distinction is itself precisely the result of an analytic interpretation and not an immediately given datum. Many "percepts" present themselves originally as total and undifferentiated, or immediately simple, and the least discriminable simple quality termed a sensation is itself arrived at as the end-term of a prolonged research, and is known as an end-term and as simple only because of extraneous reference to bodily organs, which is itself made possible by physical apparatus.

A simple example is found in the fact that sensorimotor schematism of some sort is now a commonplace in most psychological literature. If it could be detected by direct inspection of immediate qualities, it would always have been a commonplace. In fact, it is a product of an independent investigation of the morphology and physiology of the nervous system. If we generalize from such an instance, we shall be led to say that the structure of so-called mental process or conscious process, namely, of those immediate qualities to which the name "experience" was given, is furnished by the human organism, especially its nervous system. This object is known just as any other natural object is known, and not by any immediate act called introspection.

We cannot stop at this point, however. No organism is so isolated that it can be understood apart from the environment in which it lives. Sensory receptors and muscular effectors, the eye and the hand, have their existence as well as their meaning because of connections with an outer environment. The moment the acts made possible by organic structure cease to have relevancy to the milieu, the organism no longer exists; it perishes. The organisms that manifest a minimum of structure within themselves must have enough structure to enable them to prehend and assimilate food from their surroundings. The *structure* of the immediate qualities that have sometimes been called "consciousness," or "experience" as a synonym for consciousness, is so external to them that it must be ascertained by non-introspective methods.

If the implication of the last two paragraphs were made explicit, it would read: The structure of whatever is had by way of immediate qualitative presences is found in the recurrent modes of interaction taking place between what we term organism, on one side, and environment, on the other. This interaction is the primary fact, and it constitutes a *trans-action*. Only by analysis and selective abstraction can we differentiate the actual occurrence into two factors, one called organism and the other, environment. This fact militates strongly against any form of behaviorism that defines behavior in terms of the nervous system or body alone. For present purposes, we are concerned with the fact as indicating that the structure of consciousness lies in a highly complex field outside of "consciousness" itself, one that requires the help of objective science and apparatus to determine.

We have not finished with the topic of the extent of this objective structure. It includes within itself a temporal spread. The interactions of which we have just spoken are not isolated but form a temporal continuity. One kind of behaviorism is simply a generalized inference from what takes place in laboratory experimentation plus a virtual denial of the fact that laboratory data have meaning only with reference to behavior having a before and after—a from which and an into which. In the laboratory a situation is arranged. Instructions being given to the subject, he reacts to them and to some, say, visual stimulus. He accompanies this response with a language response or record of some sort. This is all which is immediately relevant to the laboratory procedure. Why, then, speak of sensations and perceptions as conscious processes? Why not stick to what actually happens, and speak of behavioristic response to stimuli? It is no derogation to the originality of those who began the behaviorist movement to say that a behavioristic theory was bound, logically, to emerge from laboratory procedure. Conscious processes drop out as irrelevant accretions.

There is something in the *context* of the experiment which goes beyond the stimuli and responses directly found within it. There is, for example, the *problem* which the experimenter has set and his *deliberate* arrangement of apparatus and selection of conditions with a view to disclosure of facts that bear upon it. There is also an *intent* on the part of the subject. Now I am not making this reference to "problem," "selective arrangement," and "intent" or purpose in order to drag in by the heels something mental over and beyond the behavior. The object is rather to call attention to a definite characteristic of behavior, namely, that it is not exhausted in the immediate stimuli-response features of the experimentation. From the standpoint of behavior itself, the traits in question take us beyond the isolated act of the subject into a content that has a temporal spread. The acts in question came out of something and move into something else. Their whole scientific point is lost unless they are placed as one phase of this contextual behavior.

It is hardly possible, I think, to exaggerate the significance of this fact for the concept of behavior. Behavior is serial, not mere succession. It can be resolved—it must be—into discrete acts, but no act can be understood apart from the series to which it belongs. Although the word "behavior" implies com-portment, as well as de-portment, the word "conduct" brings out the aspect of seriality better than does "behavior," for it clearly involves the facts both of direction (or a vector property) and of conveying or conducing. It includes the fact of passing through and passing along.

I do not mean to suggest that behaviorists of the type that treats behavior as a succession rather than as serial exclude the influence of temporal factors. The contrary is the case.[1] But I am concerned to point out the difference made in the concept of behavior according as one merely appeals to the *effects* of prior acts in order to account for some trait of a present act, or as one realizes that *behavior* itself is serial in nature. The first position is consistent regarding behavior as consisting of acts which merely succeed one another so that each can be understood in terms of what is actually found in every one act taken by itself, provided one includes the *effects* of prior acts as part of the conditions involved in it. The second position, while, of course, it recognizes this factor, goes further. In introducing into behavior the concept of series, the idea of ordinal position connected with a principle which binds the successive acts together is emphasized.[2]

The import of the formulation just made may be more definitely gathered from a consideration of the stimulus-response concept. That every portion of behavior may be stated as an instance of stimulus-response, I do not doubt, any more than that any physical occurrence may be stated as an instance of the cause-effect relation. I am very sceptical about the value of the result reached, until that which serves as stimulus and as response in a given case has been carefully analyzed. It may be that, when the concept of cause-effect first dawned, some persons got satisfaction by stringing gross phenomena together as causes and effects. But, as physical science advanced, the general relation

1. For example, Hunter says: "Has not the behaviorist always appealed to the results of heredity and previous training as factors which cooperate with present stimuli in determining behavior? Was there ever a behaviorist who explained maze training without calling upon the retained effects of previous training for a part of his explanation, or a behaviorist who ignored childhood peculiarities in accounting for adult behavior?" (2, p. 103 [Dewey's numbers throughout this article refer to numbered references at end of article.]).

2. It is not meant, of course, to carry over in a rigid way the mathematical concept of series, but the idea underlying this concept, namely, that of sequential continuity, is employed. It is meant that even the instances in which abrupt succession is most marked, i.e., jumping at a noise when engaged in deep study, have to be treated as limiting cases of the serial principle and not as typical cases from which to derive the standard notion of behavior-acts.

was forgotten by being absorbed into a definite analytic statement of the particular conditions to which the terms "cause" and "effect" are assigned. It seems to me that there is considerable behavioristic and semi-behavioristic theory in psychology at present that is content merely to subsume the phenomena in question under the rubric of *S-R* as if they were ready-made and self-evident things.

When we turn to the consideration of *what* is a stimulus, we obtain a result which is fatal to the idea that isolated acts, typified by a reflex, can be used to determine the meaning of stimulus. That which is, or operates as, a stimulus turns out to be a function, in a mathematical sense, of behavior in its serial character. Something, not yet a stimulus, breaks in upon an activity already going on and *becomes* a stimulus in virtue of the relations it sustains to what is going on in this continuing activity. As Woodworth has said: "Very seldom does a stimulus find the organism in a completely resting, neutral and unpreoccupied status" (4, p. 124). The remark has to be developed, moreover, by making two additions. The first repeats what has just been said. No external change is a stimulus in and of itself. It *becomes* the stimulus in virtue of what the organism is already preoccupied with. To call it, to think of it, as a stimulus without taking into account the behavior that is already going on is so arbitrary as to be nonsensical. Even in the case of abrupt changes, such as a clap of thunder when one is engrossed in reading, the *particular* force of that noise, its property as stimulus, is determined by what the organism is already doing in interaction with a particular environment. One and the same environmental change becomes, under different conditions of ongoing or serial behavior, a thousand different actual stimuli—a consideration which is fatal to the supposition that we can analyze behavior into a succession of independent stimuli and responses.

The difficulty cannot be overcome by merely referring to the operation of a *prior* response in determining what functions as stimulus, for exactly the same thing holds of that situation. Nor can it be overcome by vague reference to the "organism as a whole." While this reference is pertinent and necessary, the *state* of the whole organism is one of *action* which is continuous, so that reference to the organism as a whole merely puts before us the situation just described: that environmental change *becomes* a stimulus in virtue of a continuous course of behavior. These considerations lead us to the second remark. A stimulus is always a *change* in the environment which is connected with a *change* in activity. No stimulus is a stimulus to action as such but only to a change in the *direction* or intensity of action. A response is not action or behavior but marks a change in behavior. It is the new ordinal position in a series, and the series is the behavior. The ordinary *S-R* statement is seductive merely because it takes for granted this fact, while if it were explicitly stated it would transform the meaning of the *S-R* formula.

The discussion thus far has been so general that it may seem to have evaded the concrete questions that alone are important. What has all this to do with the familiar rubrics of analytic psychology, sensation, perception, memory, thinking, etc., or, more generally speaking, with psychology itself? Taking the last question, our conclusion as to the serial character of behavior and the necessity of placing and determining actual stimuli and responses within its course seems to point to a definite subject-matter characteristic of psychology. This subject-matter is the behavior of the organism so far as that is characterized by changes taking place in an activity that is serial and continuous in reference to changes in an environment that persists although changing in detail.

So far, the position taken gives the primacy to conduct and relates psychology to a study of conduct rather than to "experience." It is, however, definitely in opposition to theories of behavior that begin by taking anything like a reflex as the type and standard of a behavior-act, and that suppose it is possible to isolate and describe stimulus and response as ultimates that constitute behavior, since they themselves must be discovered and discriminated as specifiable determinations within the course of behavior. More definitely the position taken points, as it seems to me, to the conception of psychology recently advanced by Dr. Percy Hughes (1), namely, that psychology is concerned with the life-career of individualized activities.[3] Here we have some-

---

3. It is not germane to my subject to go into detail, but I cannot refrain from calling attention to what Dr. Hughes points out, that behaviorism in one of its narrower senses,—the behavior of the nervous system,—takes its place as a necessary included factor, namely, a study of *conditions* involved in a study of life-careers, while whatever is verifiable in the findings of psychoanalysts, etc., also takes its place in the study of individual life-careers.

thing which marks off a definite field of subject-matter and so calls for a distinctive intellectual method and treatment and thus defines a possible science.

The burning questions, however, remain. What meaning, if any, can be attached to sensation, memory, conceiving, etc., on the basis of conduct or behavior as a developing temporal continuum marked off into specific act-situations? In general, the mode of answer is clear, whatever the difficulties in carrying it out into detail. They designate modes of behavior having their own discernible qualities, meaning by "qualities" traits that enable one to discriminate and identify them as special modes of behavior.

Two considerations are pertinent in this connection, of which the second can best be discussed later along with a discussion of what has been so far passed over: psychology as an account of "experience." The first consideration may be introduced by pointing out that hearing, seeing, perceiving in general, remembering, imagining, thinking, judging, reasoning, are not inventions of the psychologist. Taken as designations of acts performed by every normal human being, they are everyday common-sense distinctions. What some psychologists have done is to shove a soul or consciousness under these acts as their author or locus. It seems to me fair to say that the Wundtian tradition, while it developed in the direction of denying or ignoring the soul and, in many cases, of denying "consciousness" as a unitary power or locus, in its conception of least-discriminable qualities as identical with ultimate simple "conscious processes" took a position which did not come from the facts but from an older tradition.

What we are here concerned with is, however, the fact that the ordinary man, apart from any philosophic or scientific interpretation, takes for granted the existence of acts of this type, which are different from acts of locomotion and digestion. Such acts, in a purely denotative way apart from conceptual connotation, constitute the meaning of the word "mental" in distinction from the physical and purely physiological. Is the use of "mental" as a designative term of specifiable modes of behavior found in every human life-career tabu to one who starts from the standpoint of behavior in the sense mentioned above?

The issue turns, of course, about the introduction of the idea of distinctive and discernible qualities that mark off some kinds of behavior and that supply a ground for calling them mental. To many strict behaviorists any reference to qualities seems a reversion to the slough of old introspectionism and an attempt to smuggle its methods in a covert way into behaviorism. Let us see, then, what happens when the position is analyzed. We can hardly do better than to start from the fact that the physicist observes, recalls, thinks. We must note the fact that the things with which he ends, protons-electrons in their complex interrelations of space-time and motions, are things with which he *ends*, conclusions. He reaches them as results of thinking about observed things when his inferences and calculations are confirmed by further observations. What he starts with are things having *qualities*, things qualitatively discriminated from one another and recurrently identifiable in virtue of their qualitative distinctions.

Dr. Hunter, in justifying the use of ordinary objects, whether of the environment or the organism in connection with *S-R* behavior, instead of trying to formulate everything in terms of protons-electrons, remarks: "Even in physics it is still permissible to speak of steel and carbon and to make studies upon these substances without directly involving the question of the nature of the atom" (2, p. 91; cf. p. 104). To this may be added that it is not only permissible but necessary. The physicist must refer to such things to get any point of departure and any point of application for his special findings. That water is H_2O would reduce to the meaningless tautology H_2O is H_2O unless it were identified by means of the thing known to perception and use as water. Now these common-sense things from which science starts and in which it terminates are qualitative things, qualitatively differential from one another.

There can be no more objection, then, to the psychologist's recognizing objects qualitatively marked out than there is for the physicist and chemist. It is simply a question of fact, not of theory, whether there are modes of behavior qualitatively so characterized that they can be discriminated as acts of sensation, perception, recollection, etc., and just what their qualitative traits are. Like other matters of fact, it is to be decided by observation. I share, however, the feeling against the use of the word "introspection." For that reason, I employed earlier the word "inspection." "Introspection" is too heavily charged with meanings derived from the animistic tradition. Otherwise, it might be fitly used to designate the ordinary act of observation when it is directed toward a special kind of subject-matter, that of the behavior of organisms where behavior is what it is because it is a phase of a particular life-career of serial activity.

Of course, these general conceptions remain empty until the acts of sensation, perception, recalling, thinking, etc., with those of fear, love, admiration, etc., are definitely determined as occurring in specified and distinctive junctures or crises of a life-career. Such a task is undoubtedly difficult; but so is any other scientific inquiry. The chief objection, it seems to me, to the narrower forms of behaviorism is that their obsession against the mental, because of previous false theories about it, shuts the door to even entering upon the inquiry. It should even be possible to give the more general term "awareness" or "consciousness" a meaning on this basis, though it would not be that of an underlying substance, cause, or source. It would be discerned as a specifiable quality of some forms of behavior. There is a difference between "consciousness" as a noun, and "conscious" as an adjective of some acts.

Behaviorists have, some of them at least, implicitly admitted the principle for which I have been arguing. They have said that the psychologist uses perception, thought, consciousness, just as any other scientist does. To admit this and then not go on to say (and act upon the saying) that, while they form no part of the subject-matter of physicist and physiologist, they do form a large part of the subject-matter that sets the problems of the psychologist seems strange to me—so strange as to suggest an emotional complex.

Personally I have no doubt that language in its general sense, or symbols, is connected with all mental operations that are intellectual in import and with the emotions associated with them. But to substitute linguistic behavior for the quality of acts that renders them "mental" is an evasion. A man says, "I feel hot." We are told that the whole affair can be resolved into a sensory process as stimulus and linguistic response. But what *is* the *sensory* process? Is it something *exclusively* capable of visual detection in the nervous system under favorable conditions, or is it something having an immediate quality which is noted without knowing about the sensory physiological process? When a man sees and reports the latter, is there no immediately experienced quality by which he recognizes that he is looking at neuronic structures and not, say, at a balloon? Is it all a matter of another physiological process and linguistic response?

The exposition has brought us to the threshold of the "experience" psychology. Indeed, it will probably seem to some readers that we have crossed the threshold and entered a domain foreign to any legitimate behavioristic psychology. Let me begin, then, by saying that the logic of the above account does not imply that *all* experience is the psychologist's province, to say nothing of its not implying that all experience is psychic in character. "Experience" as James pointed out long ago is a double-barrelled word. The psychologist is concerned exclusively with experienc*ing*, with detection, analysis, and description of its different modes. Experienc*ing* has no existence apart from subject-matter experienced; we perceive objects, veridical or illusory, not percepts; we remember events and not memories; we think topics and subjects, not thoughts; we love persons, not loves; and so on, although the person loved may by metonymy be called a "love." Experiencing is not itself an immediate subject-matter; it is not experienced as a complete and self-sufficient event. But everything experienced is in part made what it is because there enters into it a way of experiencing something; not a way of experiencing *it*, which would be self-contradictory, but a way of experiencing something other than itself. No complete account of what is experienced, then, can be given until we know *how* it is experienced or the mode of experiencing that enters into its formation.

Need of understanding and controlling the things experienced must have called attention very early in the history of man to the way an object is made what it is by the manner in which it is experienced. I heard it, saw it, touched it, are among the first, as they are among the most familiar of these discriminations. "I remember seeing it" would, in most cases at least, be regarded as better evidence for belief than "I remember dreaming it." Such discriminations are not themselves psychology, but, as already stated, they form its raw material just as common-sense determinations of the difference between oil and water, iron and tin, form the original subject-matter of physics and chemistry. There is no more reason for denying the reality of one than of the other, while to deny the reality of either leaves the science in question without any concrete subject-matter.

The discrimination of various modes of experiencing is enormously increased by the need of human beings for instruction and for direction of conduct. It is possible, for example, that a person would never differentiate the fact of getting angry from an experienced obnoxious subject-matter, if others did not call his attention to the role of his own attitude in the creation of the particular hateful situation. Control of the conduct of others is a constant function of life, and it can be secured only by singling out various modes of experiencing. Thus, when I say that such selected experiencings or modes of individual behavior supply primary raw material but are not psychological in themselves, I mean that they are primarily treated as having *moral* significance as matters of a character to be formed or corrected. They are selected and designated not for any scientific reason but in the exigencies, real or supposed, of social intercourse and in the process of social control termed education. The word "moral" hardly conveys in its usual sense the full idea. A child is told to look where he is going and to listen to what he is told, to attend to instructions given him. Indeed, it is rather foolish to cite instances, so much of our contact with others consists in having attention called to attitudes, dispositions, and acts that are referred to selves.

Hence, the statement only raises the question of what takes place when these acts and attitudes, abstracted from the total experience, become definitely psychological subject-matter. The answer is, in general, that they set problems for investigation, just as other qualitative objects, fire, air, water, stars, set problems to other investigations. What is seeing, hearing, touching, recalling, dreaming, thinking? Now inspection of these acts to determine their qualities is as necessary as is observation of physical objects and behaviors to determine their qualities. But just as no amount of direct observation of water could ever yield a scientific account of water, so no amount of direct inspection of these individual attitudes and ways of experiencing could yield a science of psychology. Observation helps determine the nature of the subject-matter to be studied and accounted for; it does not carry us beyond suggestions of possible hypotheses when it comes to dealing scientifically with the subject-matter.

It is at this point that the significance of objective material and methods comes in, that derived from physiology, biology, and the other sciences. Identifying modes of individual experiencing with modes of behavior identified objectively and objectively analyzable makes a science of psychology possible. Such a statement cuts two ways. It gives due recognition, or so it seems to me, to the importance of methods that have nothing to do with the immediate quality of the ways of experiencing, as these are revealed in direct inspection, or, if you please, introspection. But it also indicates that the subject-matter which sets the *problems* is found in material exposed to direct observation. This is no different from what happens in the physical sciences, although *what* is observed is different, and the observation is conducted from a different, because personal and social, standpoint.

At a certain period, for example, religionists and moralists were deeply concerned about the nature and fate of human characters. They made many shrewd and penetrating observations on human dispositions and acts, on ways of experiencing the world. Or, if this illustration does not appeal, substitute modern novelists and dramatists. But aside from an earlier tendency to interpret and classify such observations in terms of the animistic tradition, and later by a logical misconception of Aristotle's potentialities (transformed into "faculties"), these observations did not form a psychology. They do not become truly psychological until they can be attacked by methods and materials drawn from objective sciences. Yet apart from such observations, psychology has no subject-matter with which to deal in any distinctive way in contrast to the physiologist and physicist, on the one hand, and the social student, on the other.

The position here taken differs, then, in two important respects from that of the introspectionist school. The latter assumes that something called "consciousness" is an originally separate and directly given subject-matter and that it is also the organ of its own immediate disclosure of all its own secrets. If the term "experience" be used instead of consciousness, it is assumed that the latter, as it concerns the psychologist, is open to direct inspection, provided the proper precautions are taken and proper measures used. A philosopher by profession who does not know much psychology knows the historic origin of these ideas in Descartes, Locke, and their successors in dealing with epistemological problems. He has even better ground than the professed psychologist for suspecting that they are not indigenous to psychological subject-matter but have been foisted upon psychology from without.

The special matter in point here, however, is not historical origin, but is the doctrine that direct observation, under the title of introspection, can provide principles of analysis, interpretation, and explanation, revealing laws that bind the observed phenomena together. Without repeating what was said at the outset to the effect that the structure of immediately observed phenomena can be discovered only by going outside of the subject-matter inspected, I refer to it here as indicating one difference between the position here taken and that of the introspectionist. It is a difference between subject-matter that constitutes a *problem* and subject-matter that is supposed to resolve the problem. To discriminate and recognize cases of audition, vision, perception, generally, merely exposes a problem. No persistence in the method which yields them can throw any scientific light upon them.

The other difference is even more fundamental. Psychologists of the school in question have assumed that they are dealing with "experience" instead of with a selected phase of it, here termed experiencing. I do not, for example, see anything psychological at all in the determination of all the least-discriminable qualities of "experience." The result may yield something more or less curious and interesting about the world in which we live; the conclusions may be of some use in aesthetics or in morals for aught I know. But all that is strictly psychological in the endeavor consists in whatever it may incidentally teach about the *act* of sensing and the *act* of discrimination. These are modes of experiencing things or ways of behaving toward things, and as such have psychological relevancy. It may be doubted whether more would have not been found out if they had been approached directly as acts and not under the guise of finding out all the qualities which can enter into experience. It is not, in short, the qualities of things experienced but the qualities that differentiate certain acts of the individual that concern the psychologist. They concern him not as ultimates and as solutions but, as has been said, as supplying him with data for investigation by objective methods.

The fallacy contained in the doctrine that psychology is concerned with experience instead of with experiencing may be brought out by considering a style of vocabulary dear to the heart of the introspectionist. When he speaks of sensation, he does not mean an act but a peculiar content.[4] A color or a sound is to him a sensation; an orange, stone, or table is a percept. Now, from the point of view here taken, a color or sound may be an object of an act termed sensing, and a tree or orange may be an object of the act of perceiving, but *they* are not sensations or perceptions, except by a figure of speech. The act of shooting is sometimes called fowling, because fowl are shot at. Speech even reverses the figure of speech and speaks of the birds killed as so many good shots. But, in the latter case, no one dreams of taking the figure literally, ascribing to the dead birds the properties characterizing the shooting. To call a tree a percept is merely a short way of saying a tree is perceived. It tells us nothing about the tree but something about a new relation into which the tree has entered. Instead of cancelling or submerging the tree, it tells of an additive property now taken on by the tree, as much so as if we had said the tree was watered by rain or fertilized.

I hope the aptness of the illustration to the matter of confusion of experiencing with experience is reasonably clear. The tree, when it is perceived, is experienced in one way; when remembered, reflected upon, or admired for its beauty, it is experienced in other ways. By a certain figure of speech we may call it an experience, meaning that it is experienced, but we cannot by any figure of speech call it an experiencing. Nevertheless, the tree *as* experienced lends itself to a different type of analysis than that which is appropriate to the tree as a botanical object. We can first discriminate various ways of experiencing it, namely, perceptually, reflectively, emotionally, practically—as a lumberman might look at it—and then we can attempt to analyze scientifically the structure and mechanism of the various acts involved. No other discipline does this. Some study must deal with the problem. Whether the study is called psychology or by some other name is of slight importance compared with that fact that the problem needs scientific study by methods adapted to its solution.

The results of the analysis, if successful, undoubtedly tell us

---

4. I have alluded to Locke as a part author of the introspectionist tradition. He always, however, refers to sensation as an act. Even his "idea" is an *object* of mind in knowledge, not a state or constituent of mind taking the place of the scholastic species as true object of knowing.

more about the tree as an experienced object. We may be better able to distinguish a veridical tree from an illusory one when we know the conditions of vision. We may be better able to appreciate its aesthetic qualities when we know more about the conditions of an emotional attitude towards it. These are consequences, however, of psychological knowledge rather than a part of psychology. They give no ground for supposing that psychology is a doctrine regarding experience in the sense of things experienced. They are on all fours with the use of the fact of personal equations by an astronomer. The discovery and measurement of personal equation in respect to the time assigned to a perceived event is a psychological matter, because it relates to a way of seeing happenings, but the use of it by an astronomer to correct his time-reading is not a matter of psychology. Much less does it make the star a psychological fact. It concerns not the star but the way the star enters into experience as far as that is connected with the behavior of an experiencing organism.

Returning to the question raised earlier—it now appears that, if the acts of sensing, perceiving, loving, admiring, etc., are termed mental, it is not because they are intrinsically psychic processes but because of something characteristic which they *effect*, something different from that produced by acts of locomotion or digestion. The question whether they do have distinctive consequences is a question of fact, not of theory. An a priori theoretical objection to such terms as conscious, mental, etc., should not stand in the way of a fair examination of facts. No amount of careful examination of the nervous system can decide the issue. It is possible that the nervous system and its behavior are *conditions* of acts that have such characteristic effects that we need a name to differentiate them from the behavior of other things, even of the nervous system *taken by itself*.

The above is written schematically with omission of many important points, as well as somewhat over-positively, in order to save time and space. The account may be reviewed by reference to the historical background to which allusion has been made. Modern psychology developed and formed its terminology—always a very important matter because of the role of symbols in directing thought—under the influence of certain discussions regarding the possibility and extent of knowledge. In this particular context, *acts* were either ignored or were converted into contents. That is, the function, the peculiar consequences of certain acts, that renders them fit to be called mental was made into a peculiar form of existence called mental or psychic. Then these contents were inserted, under the influence of the theory of knowledge, as intermediaries between the mind and things. Sensations, percepts, treated as mental contents, intervened between the mind and objects and formed the means of knowing the latter. Physics dealt with the things as they were in themselves; psychology, with the things as they were experienced or represented in mental states and processes. In this way, the doctrine arose that psychology is the science of all experience *qua* experience; a view later modified, under the influence of physiological discovery, to the position that it is the science of all experience as far as it is dependent upon the nervous system.

The tendency was reinforced by another historical fact. The special formulations of physics were made in disregard, as far as their own content was concerned, of qualities. Qualities ejected from physics found a home in mind, or consciousness. There was supposed to be the authority of physics for taking them to be mental and psychic in nature. The convergence of these two historic streams created the intellectual background of the beginnings of modern psychology and impregnated its terminology. Behaviorism is a reaction against the confusion created by this mixture. In its reaction it has, in some of its forms, failed to note that some modes of behavior have distinctive qualities which, in virtue of the distinctive properties of the consequences of these acts, are to be termed mental and conscious. Consequently, it assumed that a study of the organic conditions of these acts constitutes all there is to behavior, overlooking in the operation two fundamental considerations. One of these is that the distinctive functions of the nervous system cannot be determined except in reference to directly observable qualities of the acts of sensing, perceiving, remembering, imagining, etc., they serve. The other is precisely the fact that their behavior is the behavior of *organs* of a larger macroscopic behavior and not at all the whole of behavior. If it were not for knowledge of behavior gained by observation of something else than the nervous system, our knowledge of the latter would consist merely of heaping up of details highly curious and intricate but of no significance for any account of behavior.

Since this discussion intends to be for the most part a logical analysis, I can hardly do better than close by citing a recent statement from a distinguished logician. Speaking of the reflective and analytic method of philosophy, Mr. C. I. Lewis says: "If, for example, the extreme behaviorists in psychology deny the existence of consciousness on the ground that analysis of the 'mental' must always eventually be in terms of bodily behavior, then it is the business of philosophy to correct their error, because it consists simply in a fallacy of logical analysis. The analysis of any immediately presented X must always interpret this X in terms of its relations to other things—to Y and Z. Such end-terms of analysis— Y and Z—will not in general be temporal or spatial constituents of X but may be anything which bears a constant correlation with it. . . . In general terms, if such analysis concludes by stating X is a certain kind of Y-Z complex, hence X does not exist as a distinct 'reality,' the error consists in overlooking a general characteristic of logical analysis—that it does not discover the 'substance' or cosmic constituents of the phenomenon whose nature is analyzed but only the constant context of experience in which it will be found" (3, p. 5).

References

1. Hughes, P. An introduction to psychology: from the standpoint of life-career. Bethlehem, Pa.: Lehigh Univ. Supply Bureau, 1928.
2. Hunter, W. S. Psychology and anthroponomy. Chap. 4 in Psychologies of 1925. Worcester, Mass.: Clark Univ. Press, 1926. Pp. 83–107.
3. Lewis, C. I. Mind and the world-order. New York: Scribner's, 1929. Pp. 446.
4. Woodworth, R. S. Dynamic psychology. Chap. 5 in Psychologies of 1925. Worcester, Mass.: Clark Univ. Press, 1926. Pp. 111–126.

Psychology and Work

I don't know exactly on what grounds I agreed to speak on my announced subject of "Psychology and Work," and still less do I know on what grounds I was asked to speak on it, for I am not a psychologist; and as for work I have always had great sympathy with a colleague who, when a department of social work was introduced into the University, said he thought it was a very bad precedent to associate the title "Work" with a university department.

However, it occurred to me that the title "Psychology and Work" had two poles, and that the subject might be approached from either one, with the emphasis upon either of the terms, psychology or work. I thought first of speaking about the problem presented to us by work, but I have always been perplexed and challenged by the very wide range, the great scale of different activities to which the name "work" can be given. It means everything,—the voluntary, joyful expenditure of energy, using the whole heart and mind of people like artists, scientific investigators and many professional men; and it means also what we call labor, where the element of pain, sacrifice, what the economist calls "cost," is marked, and yet, on the whole, the activity seems worth while. Then it also means those monotonous, mechanical, perfunctory activities that we call toil, drudgery, which people engage in not at all because they want to, but simply because of some external pressure. So I say it has always seemed to me that there is an extremely interesting problem involved in this very wide range that goes, all of it, by the name of work with different adjectives prefixed. But as I thought about that angle of the subject, I realized that that topic led very far into all kinds of social,

[First published in *Personnel Journal* 8 (February 1930): 337–41, from an address to the Personnel Research Federation, New York City, 15 November 1929.]

economic and even political problems. It was not suitable for an occasion like this, nor a topic on which I was at all competent to speak.

Before, however, approaching it from the other side, there did occur to me a certain consideration associated with a visit to Russia. Although I had no adequate experience and can not speak at all as an expert, anyone who came in contact with what we would call the laboring-class there, could hardly avoid being impressed by the pride and satisfaction with which workers referred to "our" factory. I can not but think that there is a very interesting problem here for psychological investigation regarding the incentives that lead people to engage effectively in labor. I do not mean by that merely the participation of the workers in the management of shops and factories. I am of the opinion that there are places in other countries where shop-committees function quite as well and perhaps better than in Russia. But there is another phase of the situation there which psychologically I think is unique. That is, there is the state Industrial Plan which covers or attempts to cover a general plan for the development of industry for periods of five years ahead. Those plans are made of course, by economists and technologists, engineers and industrialists working together; but the interesting part of the situation is that managers of factories and laborers in factories are taken into some intellectual partnership. They know what the plans and purposes and the system of the Central Planning Committee of the State are; and they get a sense of being partners and fellow-workers in the development of these large plans that coordinate the growth of industry over the whole country.

I have wondered whether there were not in that fact certain suggestions which are quite independent of any general social scheme of communism or capitalism. Is there not a psychological factor involved, that of modifying the attitudes of workers by making them feel that they have some participating share in a large scheme of development?

However, it is to the other pole of the subject that I am turning. Psychology in those days long ago when I might have made some claim to being a psychologist, was almost entirely a study of certain intellectual functions, of powers of knowing. In consequence it was concerned almost exclusively with those functions where the mind, consciousness, or whatever we may call it, had contact and relation with objects, with things, rather than with other persons, very largely to the subordination of all the emotional and active factors that come in when individuals are in relation to each other,—relations of personal contact, intercourse, intercommunication, association, and so on.

When experimental psychology began, it at first took over that same interest. It was very largely an analysis, under more careful conditions, of the reactions of sensation, perception, memory and so on, a coordination of movements connected with these more definitely intellectual functions.

Naturally, when industrial psychology began to be of interest, I take it that it also largely started from the same standpoint for very good reasons. In the first place, because the psychologist had the best training and the greatest expertness in that field, and secondly, because the more obvious interests of employers and managers had to do, or seemed to have to do, with the relation of workers to things,—adjustments to the machines, tools, or products of work that they made, through their sense organs and their muscular coordinations. So it became chiefly a study of what, I suppose, one might call technical efficiency, that is, efficiency as judged from the standpoint of the material output, rather than a study of that larger human efficiency to which we give the somewhat vague name, morale.

However, there was going on independently a consideration of the psychology of human relationships, social psychology, as over against this psychology of the relation of mind to things and objects. In a somewhat striking and unexpected way the development of psychiatry reinforced this tendency because it showed how many of the abnormal idiosyncrasies and disabilities that affect human nature had their origin in social maladjustments, going back sometimes to early family life, or, perhaps, to present marital relations. I take it that contemporaneously with this development in academic psychology and in psychiatry there has come the tendency in industrial psychology to attach greater importance to those phases of the workings of mind and personality that have to do with human adjustments, with the relationships which individuals sustain, in their life and in their work, to one another.

I was very kindly shown by Dr. Bingham some of the recent reports in manuscript, and I was especially struck by the Hawthorne investigation, about which many of you here know much more than I do, to see how much importance was attached as the result of that investigation to the establishing of better human relationships, and how, according to some of the findings at least, such relationships seemed to be more important factors in controlling even the efficiency of material and technical production than did the more specialized technical factors themselves. I was also impressed by what I think can fairly be interpreted,—although, perhaps, these exact words were not used,—as a recognition of the desire of every individual for some acknowledgment of himself, of his personality, on the part of others. It often seems to me that that is the deepest urge of every human being, to feel that he does count for something with other human beings and receives a recognition from them as counting for something. I take it that our sense of our own personality is largely a looking-glass phenomenon. It is a reflex thing. We form our ideas, our estimates of ourselves and of our self-respect in terms of what others think of us, in terms of the way in which they treat us. At all events, this was an angle of that investigation which appealed especially to me: the changed response, the changed attitude even toward technical problems of production, that came about when individuals found that their opinions were regarded as being worth asking for, that they were really worth consulting in the conduct and management of the affairs of the factory.

That is only one illustration, but it seems to me a very fundamental one, of what I mean by the shift from mere technical efficiency to that larger human efficiency of the whole self, the whole personality, involving these factors of social adjustment.

There is just one other factor of this larger human efficiency that cannot escape, at least, mention, and that is the role of thought or understanding, a recognition of the meaning and the significance of the activities that constitute work and labor. I take it that the difference between the activity of the machine and the human robots, of which Mr. Stuart Chase spoke, and a really intelligent being is that the latter has some sense of the meaning of what he is doing. When he enjoys his work, it is partly because of his recognition of its significance. That again is a problem on which, as you all know, considerable work has been done. The problem is evidently most difficult in connection with industries where the mere assembling of parts that are ready made,—nothing to do but go through certain motions of assemblage,—is most prominent. This problem is obviously to a considerable extent a technological one, that of extending still further these inventions of which Mr. Chase also spoke, so that work will more and more be done by real machines instead of by human ones. But it seems to me that there is a problem, at least of degree, in all of these cases; that there is at least a possibility of increasing on the part of every worker his sense of the meaning of the activities that he is carrying on, so that more of his own ideas, thinking, will go into it.

This phase of the matter of course, is not identical with the problem of human and social relationships, and yet it is not wholly independent of it. It might be an agreeable change if I read part of a letter that I received during the past week from a working-man in a Connecticut factory, a man who told me that he had had simply a grammar school education. He is a worker at a machine in a factory who has, on his own account, apparently with no special encouragement from above, taken to reading psychology in order himself to put more of meaning into his own work. He says:

> When I have a thought on a subject I am so constituted that I have got to tell that idea to someone.
>
> For instance I am at work on a machine and an idea comes to me of an improvement on the method of doing the work. I cannot keep it to myself and I have no satisfaction or rest until I tell it to the boss in hopes that he will see the idea the same as I do and do away with the old method. If he cannot see it as I do and does not explain why he does not, I am disappointed but it does not last long for just as soon as a new problem arises it is the same thing over again. When an idea is accepted and used I have great satisfaction even if I do not get a raise in pay although that would also be very satisfactory but the last is not the greatest.
>
> Other men say why do you tell him, he will only use it for his own benefit and I know what they say is true but still I feel the idea is dead if I do not speak and perhaps it may be of great value so I keep on, perhaps with the selfish thought, that someday I will meet a man who will say, there is the kind of a man I am looking for, and from time to time, I

have returns for ideas but only when I was able to go to the head of the concern. Now in most shops, the ordinary workman cannot get in touch with the head of the concern, as he, the head's time is taken up with problems requiring thought that cannot be interfered with by minor details of the business still these details are vital to the whole.

Concerns say we know of such things and that is why we have under officials to look after these details, yes, but do these officials always handle these problems, with an unselfish end in view, do they never advance an idea as being original when it really came from someone else who gets no credit, and from one who works with the thought that the concern is his as much as it is yours for through it he gains his living and through that is able to educate himself to meet new problems as they come and they will always arise for they the new problems cause others to arise so we should endeavor to make the present as near perfect as we can in order to make the future which in time will become the present, perfect. By this time you are saying I know all about that stuff, but I am a business man and have got to produce, I can't see every sweeper in the factory and listen to his idea of what he thinks is the best way to run the concern.

Very true, but you could have a real working Personnel Dept. that the men could go to, in order to express their thoughts and just as freely as they do to one another, whatever ideas given would be taken by the Personnel Dept. with the understanding that the great desire of the company is coöperation, it being especially understood that the official in charge shall receive no personal benefit from suggestions but shall use his best endeavors to see that the ideas be given a hearing. For through that method the Mental attitude of the men will be changed from passive resistance to the feeling that the company has at all times the interest of the men at heart and our mental attitude control our actions.

This Dept. cannot be run by a person with the mentality of a $10.00 a week clerk as it is the most vital in the whole organization.

And then he ends by saying:

It can only be run by an honest man, and a man is never honest until he thinks.

That's a very much better speech than I could have made on my own account. It came to me quite unsolicited from this worker with, as I say, simply an ordinary grammar-school education, but who has evidently got a mind,—I do not need to certify to that,—and who wants to give his mind play and outlet on the work that he is doing. Of course, he is an unusually superior type; but I don't think until these investigations along the lines already started are carried further, that we shall know just how many real minds there are. In all events, these two sentences, about his urge to communicate his ideas, and his concluding sentence that nobody can be really honest unless he thinks, seemed to me to indicate in a concrete way what is meant by saying that there is a real connection between social adjustments and relations and the intellectual powers and qualities that enter into work.

Qualitative Thought

The world in which we immediately live, that in which we strive, succeed, and are defeated is preeminently a qualitative world. What we act for, suffer, and enjoy are things in their qualitative determinations. This world forms the field of characteristic modes of thinking, characteristic in that thought is definitely regulated by qualitative considerations. Were it not for the double and hence ambiguous sense of the term "common-sense," it might be said that common-sense thinking, that concerned with action and its consequences, whether undergone in enjoyment or suffering, is qualitative. But since "common-sense" is also used to designate accepted traditions and is appealed to in support of them, it is safe at the outset to refer simply to that thought which has to do with objects involved in the concerns and issues of living.

The problem of qualitative objects has influenced metaphysics and epistemology but has not received corresponding attention in logical theory. The propositions significant in physical science are oblivious of qualitative considerations as such; they deal with "primary qualities" in distinction from secondary and tertiary; in actual treatment, moreover, these primary qualities are not qualities but relations. Consider the difference between movement as qualitative alteration, and motion as $F=ma$; between stress as involving effort and tension, and as force per unit surface; between the red of the blood issuing from a wound, and red as signifying 400 trillion vibrations per time unit. Metaphysics has been concerned with the existential status of qualitative objects as contrasted with those of physical science, while epistemology, having frequently decided that qualities are subjective and psychical, has been concerned with their relation in knowing

[First published in *Symposium* 1 (January 1930): 5–32.]

to the properties of "external" objects defined in non-qualitative terms.

But a logical problem remains. What is the relation or lack of relations between the two types of propositions, one which refers to objects of physical science and the other to qualitative objects? What, if any, are the distinguishing logical marks of each kind? If it were true that things as things, apart from interaction with an organism, are qualityless, the logical problem would remain. For the truth would concern the mode of production and existence of qualitative things. It is irrelevant to their logical status. Logic can hardly admit that it is concerned only with objects having one special mode of production and existence, and yet claim universality. And it would be fatal to the claims of logic to say that because qualities are psychical—supposing for the moment that they are—therefore logical theory has nothing to do with forms of thought characteristic of qualitative objects. It is even possible that some of the difficulties of metaphysical and epistemological theory about scientific and ordinary objects spring from neglect of a basic logical treatment.

A preliminary introduction to the topic may be found in the fact that Aristotelian logic, which still passes current nominally, is a logic based upon the idea that qualitative objects are existential in the fullest sense. To retain logical principles based on this conception along with the acceptance of theories of existence and knowledge based on an opposite conception is not, to say the least, conducive to clearness—a consideration that has a good deal to do with the existing dualism between traditional and the newer relational logics. A more obviously pertinent consideration is the fact that the interpretation of classic logic treats qualitative determinations as fixed properties of objects, and thus is committed to either an attributive or a classificatory doctrine of the import of propositions. Take the proposition: "The red Indian is stoical." This is interpreted either as signifying that the Indian in question is characterized by the property of stoicism in addition to that of redness, or that he belongs to the class of stoical objects. The ordinary direct sense of the proposition escapes recognition in either case. For this sense expresses the fact that the indigenous American was permeated throughout by a certain quality, instead of being an object possessing a certain quality along with others. He lived, acted, endured stoically.

If one thinks that the difference between the two meanings has no logical import, let him reflect that the whole current subject-predication theory of propositions is affected by the "property" notion, whether the theory speaks in the language of attribution or classification. A subject is "given"—ultimately apart from thinking—and then thought adds to what is given a further determination or else assigns it to a ready-made class of things. Neither theory can have any place for the integral development and reconstruction of subject-matter effected by the thought expressed in propositions. In effect it excludes thought from any share in the determination of the subject-matter of knowledge, confining it to setting forth the results (whether conceived as attributive or classificatory) of knowledge already attained in isolation from the method by which it is attained.

Perhaps, however, the consideration that will appeal to most people is the fact that the neglect of qualitative objects and considerations leaves thought in certain subjects without any logical status and control. In esthetic matters, in morals and politics, the effect of this neglect is either to deny (implicitly at least) that they have logical foundation or else, in order to bring them under received logical categories, to evacuate them of their distinctive meaning—a procedure which produces the myth of the "economic man" and the reduction of esthetics and morals, as far as they can receive any intellectual treatment at all, to quasi-mathematical subjects.

Consider for example a picture that is a work of art and not just a chromo or other mode of mechanical product. Its quality is not a property which it possesses in addition to its other properties. It is something which externally demarcates it from other paintings, and which internally pervades, colors, tones, and weights every detail and every relation of the work of art. The same thing is true of the "quality" of a person or of historic events. We follow, with apparently complete understanding, a tale in which a certain quality or character is ascribed to a certain man. But something said causes us to interject, "Oh, you are speaking of Thomas Jones, I supposed you meant John Jones." Every detail related, every distinction set forth remains just what it was before. Yet the significance, the color and weight, of every detail is altered. For the quality that runs through them all, that gives meaning to each and binds them together, is transformed.

Now my point is that unless such underlying and pervasive qualitative determinations are acknowledged in a distinct logical formulation, one or other of two results is bound to follow. Either thought is denied to the subject-matter in question, and the phenomena are attributed to "intuition" or "genius" or "impulse" or "personality" as ultimate and unanalyzable entities; or, worse yet, intellectual analysis is reduced to a mechanical enumeration of isolated items or "properties." As a matter of fact, such intellectual definiteness and coherence as the objects and criticisms of esthetic and moral subjects possess is due to their being controlled by the quality of subject-matter as a whole. Consideration of the meaning of regulation by an underlying and pervasive quality is the theme of this article.

What is intended may be indicated by drawing a distinction between something called a "situation" and something termed an "object." By the term situation in this connection is signified the fact that the subject-matter ultimately referred to in existential propositions is a complex existence that is held together in spite of its internal complexity by the fact that it is dominated and characterized throughout by a single quality. By "object" is meant some element in the complex whole that is defined in abstraction from the whole of which it is a distinction. The special point made is that the selective determination and relation of objects in thought is controlled by reference to a situation—to that which is constituted by a pervasive and internally integrating quality, so that failure to acknowledge the situation leaves, in the end, the logical force of objects and their relations inexplicable.

Now in current logical formulations, the beginning is always made with "objects." If we take the proposition "the stone is shaly," the logical import of the proposition is treated as if something called "stone" had complete intellectual import in and of itself and then some property, having equally a fixed content in isolation, "shaly" is attributed to it. No such self-sufficient and self-enclosed entity can possibly lead anywhere nor be led to; connection among such entities is mechanical and arbitrary, not intellectual. Any proposition about "stone" or "shaly" would have to be analytic in the Kantian sense, merely stating part of the content already known to be contained in the meaning of the terms. That a tautological proposition is a proposition only in name is well recognized. In fact, "stone," "shaly" (or whatever are subject and predicate) are determinations or distinctions instituted within the total subject-matter to which thought refers. When such propositions figure in logical textbooks, the actual subject-matter referred to is some branch of logical theory which is exemplified in the proposition.

This larger and inclusive subject-matter is what is meant by the term "situation." Two further points follow. The situation as such is not and cannot be stated or made explicit. It is taken for granted, "understood," or implicit in all propositional symbolization. It forms the universe of discourse of whatever is expressly stated or of what appears as a term in a proposition. The situation cannot present itself as an element in a proposition any more than a universe of discourse can appear as a member of discourse within that universe. To call it "implicit" does not signify that it is implied. It is present throughout as that of which whatever is explicitly stated or propounded is a distinction. A quart bowl cannot be held within itself or in any of its contents. It may, however, be contained in another bowl, and similarly what is the "situation" in one proposition may appear as a term in *another* proposition—that is, in connection with some *other* situation to which thought now refers.

Secondly, the situation controls the terms of thought, for they are *its* distinctions, and applicability to it is the ultimate test of their validity. It is this phase of the matter which is suggested by the earlier use of the idea of a pervasive and underlying quality. If the quart container affected the import of everything held within it, there would be a physical analogy, a consideration that may be awkwardly hinted at by the case of a person protesting to a salesman that he has not received a full quart; the deficiency affects everything that he has purchased. A work of art provides an apter illustration. In it, as we have already noted, the quality of the whole permeates, affects, and controls every detail. There are paintings, buildings, novels, arguments, in which an observer notes an inability of the author to sustain a unified attention throughout. The details fall to pieces; they are not distinctions of one subject-matter, because there is no qualitative unity underlying them. Confusion and incoherence are always marks of lack of control by a single pervasive quality. The latter alone enables a person to keep track of what he is doing, saying, hearing, reading, in whatever explicitly appears. The underlying unity of qualitativeness regulates pertinence or relevancy and force of every distinction and relation; it guides selection and rejection and the manner of utilization of all explicit terms. This quality enables us to keep thinking about one problem without our having constantly to stop to ask ourselves what it is after all that we are thinking about. We are aware of it not by itself but as the background, the thread, and the directive clue in what we do expressly think of. For the latter things are *its* distinctions and relations.[1]

If we designate this permeating qualitative unity in psychological language, we say it is felt rather than thought. Then, if we hypostatize it, we call it *a* feeling. But to term it a feeling is to reverse the actual state of affairs. The existence of unifying qualitativeness in the subject-matter defines the meaning of "feeling." The notion that "a feeling" designates a ready-made independent psychical entity is a product of a reflection which presupposes the direct presence of quality as such. "Feeling" and "felt" are names for a *relation* of quality. When, for example, anger exists, it is the pervading tone, color, and quality of persons, things, and circumstances, or of a situation. When angry we are not aware of anger but of these objects in their immediate and unique qualities. In another situation, anger may appear as a distinct term, and analysis may then call it a feeling or emotion. But we have now shifted the universe of discourse, and the validity of the terms of the later one depends upon the existence of the direct quality of the whole in a former one. That is, in saying that something was *felt* not thought of, we are analyzing in a new situation, having its own immediate quality, the subject-matter of a prior situation; we are making anger an object of analytic examination, not being angry.

When it is said that I have a feeling, or impression, or "hunch," that things are thus and so, what is actually designated is primarily the presence of a dominating quality in a situation as a whole, not just the existence of a feeling as a psychical or psychological fact. To say I have a feeling or impression that so and so is the case is to note that the quality in question is not yet resolved into determinate terms and relations; it marks a conclu-

1. The "fringe" of James seems to me to be a somewhat unfortunate way of expressing the role of the underlying qualitative character that constitutes a situation—unfortunate because the metaphor tends to treat it as an additional element instead of an all-pervasive influence in determining other contents.

sion without statement of the reasons for it, the grounds upon which it rests. It is the first stage in the development of explicit distinctions. All thought in every subject begins with just such an unanalyzed whole. When the subject-matter is reasonably familiar, relevant distinctions speedily offer themselves, and sheer qualitativeness may not remain long enough to be readily recalled. But it often persists and forms a haunting and engrossing problem. It is a commonplace that a problem *stated* is well on its way to solution, for statement of the nature of a problem signifies that the underlying quality is being transformed into determinate distinctions of terms and relations or has become an object of articulate thought. But something presents itself as problematic before there is recognition of *what* the problem is. The problem is had or experienced before it can be stated or set forth; but it is had as an immediate quality of the whole situation. The sense of something problematic, of something perplexing and to be resolved, marks the presence of something pervading all elements and considerations. Thought is the operation by which it is converted into pertinent and coherent terms.

The word "intuition" has many meanings. But in its popular, as distinct from refined philosophic, usage it is closely connected with the single qualitativeness underlying all the details of explicit reasoning. It may be relatively dumb and inarticulate and yet penetrating; unexpressed in definite ideas which form reasons and justifications and yet profoundly right. To my mind, Bergson's contention that intuition precedes conception and goes deeper is correct. Reflection and rational elaboration spring from and make explicit a prior intuition. But there is nothing mystical about this fact, and it does not signify that there are two modes of knowledge, one of which is appropriate to one kind of subject-matter, and the other mode to the other kind. Thinking and theorizing about physical matters set out from an intuition, and reflection about affairs of life and mind consists in an ideational and conceptual transformation of what begins as an intuition. Intuition, in short, signifies the realization of a pervasive quality such that it regulates the determination of relevant distinctions or of whatever, whether in the way of terms or relations, becomes the accepted object of thought.

While some ejaculations and interjections are merely organic responses, there are those which have an intellectual import, though only context and the total situation can decide to which class a particular ejaculation belongs. "Alas," "Yes," "No," "Oh" may each of them be the symbol of an integrated attitude toward the quality of a situation as a whole; that it is thoroughly pitiful, acceptable, to be rejected, or is a matter of complete surprise. In this case, they characterize the existent situation and as such have a cognitive import. The exclamation "Good!" may mark a deep apprehension of the quality of a piece of acting on the stage, of a deed performed, or of a picture in its wealth of content. The actual judgment may find better expression in these symbols than in a long-winded disquisition. To many persons there is something artificial and repellent in discoursing about any consummatory event or object. It speaks so completely for itself that words are poor substitutes—not that thought fails, but that thought so completely grasps the dominant quality that translation into explicit terms gives a partial and inadequate result.

Such ejaculatory judgments supply perhaps the simplest example of qualitative thought in its purity. While they are primitive, it does not follow that they are always superficial and immature. Sometimes, indeed, they express an infantile mode of intellectual response. But they may also sum up and integrate prolonged previous experience and training, and bring to a unified head the results of severe and consecutive reflection. Only the situation symbolized and not the formal and propositional symbol can decide which is the case. The full content of meaning is best apprehended in case of the judgment of the esthetic expert in the presence of a work of art. But they come at the beginning and at the close of every scientific investigation. These open with the "Oh" of wonder and terminate with the "Good" of a rounded-out and organized situation. Neither the "Oh" nor the "Good" expresses a mere state of personal feeling. Each characterizes a subject-matter. "How beautiful" symbolizes neither a state of feeling nor the supervening of an external essence upon a state of existence but marks the realized appreciation of a pervading quality that is now translated into a system of definite and coherent terms. Language fails not because thought fails, but because no verbal symbols can do justice to the fullness and richness of thought. If we are to continue talking about "data" in any other sense than as reflective distinctions, the original datum is always such a qualitative whole.

The logic of artistic construction is worth more than a passing notice, whether its product be a painting, a symphony, a statue, a building, a drama, or a novel. So far as it is not evidence of conceit on the part of a specialized class, refusal to admit thought and logic on the part of those who make these constructions is evidence of the breakdown of traditional logic. There are (as we previously noted) alleged works of art in which parts do not hang together and in which the quality of one part does not reinforce and expand the quality of every other part. But this fact is itself a manifestation of the defective character of the thought involved in their production. It illustrates by contrast the nature of such works as are genuine intellectual and logical wholes. In the latter, the underlying quality that defines the work, that circumscribes it externally and integrates it internally, controls the thinking of the artist; his logic is the logic of what I have called qualitative thinking.

Upon subsequent analysis, we term the properties of a work of art by such names as symmetry, harmony, rhythm, measure, and proportion. These may, in some cases at least, be formulated mathematically. But the apprehension of these formal relationships is not primary for either the artist or the appreciative spectator. The subject-matter formulated by these terms is primarily qualitative, and is apprehended qualitatively. Without an independent qualitative apprehension, the characteristics of a work of art can be translated into explicit harmonies, symmetries, etc., only in a way which substitutes mechanical formulae for esthetic quality. The value of any such translation in esthetic criticism is measured, moreover, by the extent to which the propositional statements return to effect a heightening and deepening of a qualitative apprehension. Otherwise, esthetic appreciation is replaced by judgment of isolated technique.

The logic of artistic construction and esthetic appreciation is peculiarly significant because they exemplify in accentuated and purified form the control of selection of detail and of mode of relation, or integration, by a qualitative whole. The underlying quality demands certain distinctions, and the degree in which the demand is met confers upon the work of art that necessary or inevitable character which is its mark. Formal necessities, such as can be made explicit, depend upon the material necessity imposed by the pervasive and underlying quality. Artistic thought is not however unique in this respect but only shows an intensification of a characteristic of all thought. In a looser way, it is a characteristic of all non-technical, non-"scientific" thought. Scientific thought is, in its turn, a specialized form of art, with its own qualitative control. The more formal and mathematical science becomes, the more it is controlled by sensitiveness to a special kind of qualitative considerations. Failure to realize the qualitative and artistic nature of formal scientific construction is due to two causes. One is conventional, the habit of associating art and esthetic appreciation with a few popularly recognized forms. The other cause is the fact that a student is so concerned with the mastery of symbolic or propositional forms that he fails to recognize and to repeat the creative operations involved in their construction. Or, when they are mastered, he is more concerned with their further application than with realization of their intrinsic intellectual meaning.

The foregoing remarks are intended to suggest the significance to be attached to the term "qualitative thought." But as statements they are propositions and hence symbolic. Their meaning can be apprehended only by going beyond them, by using them as clues to call up qualitative situations. When an experience of the latter is had and they are re-lived, the realities corresponding to the propositions laid down may be had. Assuming that such a realization has been experienced, we proceed to consider some further questions upon which qualitative thought throws light.

First as to the nature of the predication. The difficulties connected with the problem of predication are of long standing. They were recognized in Greek thought, and the scepticism they induced was a factor in developing the Platonic theory of the same-and-the-other and the Aristotelian conception of potentiality-and-actuality. The sceptical difficulty may be summed up in the statement that predication is either tautological and so meaningless, or else falsifying or at least arbitrary. Take the proposition "that thing is sweet." If "sweet" already qualifies the meaning of "that thing," the predication is analytic in the Kantian sense, or forms a trivial proposition in the sense of Locke. But if "sweet" does not already qualify "that thing" what ground is there for tacking it on? The most that can be said is that some one who did not know before that it was sweet has now learned it. But such a statement refers only to an episode in the some one's intellectual biography. It has no logical force; it does not touch the question of predication that has objective reference and possible validity.

When, however, it is recognized that predication—any proposition having subject-predicate form—marks an attempt to make a qualitative whole which is directly and non-reflectively experienced into an object of thought for the sake of its own development, the case stands otherwise. What is "given" is not an object by itself nor a term having a meaning of its own. The "given," that is to say the existent, is precisely an undetermined and dominant complex quality. "Subject" and "predicate" are correlative determinations of this quality. The "copula" stands for the fact that one term is predicated of the other, and is thus a sign of the development of the qualitative whole by means of their distinction. It is, so to speak, the assertion of the fact that the distinctions designated in subject and predicate are correlative and work together in a common function of determination.

A certain quality is experienced. When it is inquired into or thought (judged), it differentiates into "that thing" on the one hand, and "sweet" on the other. Both "that thing" and "sweet" are analytic of the quality, but are additive, synthetic, ampliative, with respect to each other. The copula "is" marks just the effect of this distinction upon the correlative terms. They mark something like a division of labor, and the copula marks the function or work done by the structures that exhibit the division of labor. To say that "that thing is sweet" means "that thing" will *sweeten* some other object, say coffee, or a batter of milk and eggs. The intent of sweetening something formed the ground for converting a dumb quality into an articulate object of thought.

The logical force of the copula is always that of an active verb. It is merely a linguistic peculiarity, not a logical fact, that we say "that is red" instead of "that reddens," either in the sense of growing, becoming red, or in the sense of making something else red. Even linguistically our "is" is a weakened form of an active verb signifying "stays" or "stands." But the nature of any act (designated by the true verbal form) is best apprehended in its effect and issue; we say "is sweet" rather than "sweetens," "is red" rather than "reddens" because we define the active change by its anticipated or attained outcome. To say "the dog is ugly" is a way of setting forth what he is likely to *do*, namely to snarl and bite. "Man is mortal" indicates what man does or what actively is done to him, calling attention to a consequence. If we convert its verbal form into "men die," we realize the transitive and additive force of predication and escape the self-made difficulties of the attributive theory.

The underlying pervasive quality in the last instance, when it is put in words, involves care or concern for human destiny. But we must remember that this exists as a dumb quality until it is symbolized in an intellectual and propositional form. Out of this quality there emerges the idea of man and of mortality and of their existential connection with each other. No one of them has any meaning apart from the others, neither the distinctions, the terms, nor their relation, the predication. All the difficulties that attend the problem of predication spring from supposing that we can take the terms and their connection as having meaning by themselves. The sole alternative to this supposition is the recognition that the object of thought, designated propositionally, is a quality that is first directly and unreflectively experienced or had.

One source of the difficulty and the error in the classic theory lies in a radical misconception of the treacherous idea of the "given." The only thing that is unqualifiedly given is the total pervasive quality; and the objection to calling it "given" is that the word suggests something *to* which it is given, mind or thought or consciousness or whatever, as well possibly as something that gives. In truth "given" in this connection signifies only that the quality immediately exists, or is brutely there. In this capacity, it forms that to which all objects of thought refer, although, as we have noticed, it is never part of the manifest subject-matter of thought. In itself, it is the big, buzzing, blooming confusion of which James wrote. This expresses not only the state of a baby's experience but the first stage and background of all thinking on any subject. There is, however, no inarticulate quality which is merely buzzing and blooming. It buzzes to some effect; it blooms toward some fruitage. That is, the quality, although dumb, has as a part of its complex quality a movement or transition in some direction. It can, therefore, be intellectually symbolized and converted into an object of thought. This is done by statement of limits and of direction of transition between them. "That" and "sweet" define the limits of the moving quality, the copula "tastes" (the real force of "is") defines the direction of movement between these limits. Putting the nature of the two limits briefly and without any attempt to justify the statement here, the subject represents the pervasive quality as means or condition and the predicate represents it as outcome or end.

These considerations define not only the subject-predicate structure of categorical propositions but they explain why the selective character of all such propositions with respect to the fullness of existence is not falsifying in character. Idealistic logicians, in calling attention to the partial or selective character of particular judgments, have used the fact to cast logical aspersion upon them, and to infer their need of correction first by transformation into conditional propositions and then finally into a judgment coextensive with the whole universe, arguing that only the latter can be truly true. But enough is always enough, and the underlying quality is itself the test of the "enough" for any particular case. All that is needed is to determine this quality by indicating the limits between which it moves and the direction or tendency of its movement. Sometimes the situation is simple and the most meagre indications serve, like the "safe" or "out" of a baseball umpire. At other times, a quality is complex and prolonged, and a multitude of distinctions and subordinate relations are required for its determinate statement. It would have been logically vicious on one occasion to propound more than "my kingdom for a horse," while under other circumstances it may need a volume to set forth the quality of the situation so as to make it comprehensible. Any proposition that serves the purpose for which it is made is logically adequate; the idea that it is inadequate until the whole universe has been included is a consequence of giving judgment a wrong office—an error that has its source in failure to see the domination of every instance of thought by a qualitative whole needing statement in order that it may function.

At this point a reference to what is termed association of ideas is in place. For while the subject is usually treated as psychological in nature, thinking as an existential process takes place through association; existentially, thinking *is* association as far as the latter is controlled. And the mechanics of thinking can hardly be totally irrelevant to its *logical* structure and function. I shall assume without much argument that "ideas" here signify objects, not psychical entities; objects, that is to say, as meanings to which reference may be made. When one, seeing smoke, thinks of fire he is associating objects, not just states in his own mind. And so when thinking of a hand, one thinks of grasping or of an organism. Thus, when association takes the form of thought, or is controlled and not loose day-dreaming, association is a name for a connection of objects or their elements in the total situation having a qualitative unity. This statement signifies something different than does a statement that associated objects are physical parts of a physical whole. It happens to hold in the case of "hand-organism" and with some qualifications in the case of "smoke-fire." But a philosophical student might be led by the thought of hand to the thought of Aristotle on the ground of a remark made by Aristotle.

In any case an original contiguity (or similarity) is not the *cause* of an association. We do not associate *by* contiguity, for recognition of a whole in which elements are juxtaposed in space or in temporal sequence is the *result* of suggestion. The absurdity of the preposition "by" when applied to similarity is still more obvious. It is the reason why some writers reduce similarity to identity in differences, a position that will be examined later. That by which association is effected, by which suggestion and evocation of a distinct object of thought is brought about, is some acquired modification of the organism, usually designated habit. The conditioning mechanism may not be known at present in detail, but it cannot be an original contiguity because that contiguity is apprehended only in consequence of association. It may well be an organic attitude formed in consequence of a responsive act to things once coexistent or sequential. But this act was unitary; reference to it only accentuates the fact that the quality attending it was spread over and inclusive of the two things in question. That is, it was a response to a *situation* within which objects were related in space or time.

Given the conditions, the real problem is to say why objects once conjoined in a whole are now distinguished as two objects, one that which suggests, and the other that which is suggested. If I think of a chiffonier, the thought does not call up that of drawers as a distinct idea. For the drawers are a part of the object thought of. So when I originally saw, say a bird-in-a-nest, I saw a single total object. Why then does the sight or thought of a bird now call up that of a nest as a distinct idea? In general, the reason is that I have so often seen birds without seeing a nest and nests without birds. Moreover, it must be remembered that a person often sees a bird or nest, and instead of thinking of any other object, he reacts to it directly, as a man does when shooting at a bird or a boy climbing a tree to get the nest. While there is no association without habit, the natural tendency of habit is to produce an immediate reaction, not to evoke another distinct object of thought or idea. As the *dis*association of birds and nests in experience shows, this additional factor is some resistance to the attitude formed by the sight of nest-with-a-bird-in-it. Otherwise we should have the case over again of chiffonier and its drawers, or any object and its constitutive parts. Without the resistant or negative factor, there would be no tension to effect the change from a direct response, an immediate act, to an indirect one, a distinct object of thought.

Not only then is there no association *by* contiguity, but association is not *of* two objects separated yet contiguous in a prior experience. Its characteristic nature is that it presents as distinct but connected objects what originally were either two parts of one situational object, or (in the case that a man had previously always seen birds and nests separately from each other) that it presents in coexistence or sequence with one another objects previously separated in space and time. This consideration is fatal to the notion that the associated objects account by themselves or in their own isolated nature for association. It indicates that coexistence or sequence as a physical existential fact is not the ground of association. What alternative remains save that the quality of a situation as a whole operates to produce a functional connection? Acceptance of this alternative implies that association is an *intellectual* connection, thus aligning association with thought, as we shall now see.

There is nothing intellectual or logical in contiguity, in mere juxtaposition in space and time. If association were, then, either *of* or *by* contiguity, association would not have any logical force, any connection with thought.[2] But in fact association of bare contiguities is a myth. There is an indefinite number of particulars contiguous to one another in space and time. When I think

2. The assumption that in the case of contiguity association is of a merely *de facto* or existential nature is the root of Lotze's (and others') theory that *a priori* logical forms are necessary in order to change juxtaposition of things into coherence of meaning.

of a nest why does a bird come into my mind? As a matter of contiguity, there are multitudinous leaves and twigs which are more frequently and more obviously juxtaposed than is a bird. When I think of a hammer, why is the idea of nail so likely to follow? Such questions suggest, I hope, that even in seemingly casual cases of association, there is an underlying quality which operates to control the connection of objects thought of. It takes something else than contiguity to effect association; there must be relevancy of both ideas to a situation defined by unity of quality. There is coherence of some sort because of mutual pertinency of both ideas (or of all ideas in train) to a basis beyond any of them and beyond mere juxtaposition of objects in space and time.

The usual notion that association is merely *de facto* receives a still more obvious shock in the case of similarity. When I associate bird with nest, there may have been at least some previous conjunction in experience of the two objects, even though that conjunction is not by itself a sufficient condition of the later association. But when troublesome thought suggests the sting of an insect, or when change of fortune suggests the ebb and flow of the sea, there is *no* physical conjunction in the past to which appeal can be made. To try to explain the matter by saying that two objects are associated *because* they are similar is either to offer the problem as a solution or to attribute causal efficacy to "similarity"—which is to utter meaningless words. So-called association "by" similarity is a striking example of the influence of an underlying pervasive quality in determining the connection essential in thought.

There is, as far as I am aware, but one serious attempt to explain such association on some other basis. This is found in the view that there is in what is called similarity an actual existential identity among differences and that this identity works and then reinstates differences by contiguity. I fail to see how the explanation applies in many cases—such as that of the troublesome thought and the sting of an insect, or Socrates and a gadfly. "Identity" seems to be the result rather than the antecedent of the association. But I shall confine the discussion to instances in which it is claimed to work. Bradley has stated the theory in question most clearly and I shall use his illustration.[3]

3. *Logic*, Vol. I, Book II, Part 2, Ch. I, Sec. 30.

Walking on the shore of England, one sees a promontory and remarks how like it is to one in Wales. Bradley's explanation is that there is an actual identity of form in both and that this identical form suggests by contiguity in space certain elements which cannot be referred to the promontory now seen (size, color, etc., being incompatible) and thus constitutes in connection with identical form the content of the idea of the promontory in Wales. The seeming plausibility of this explanation is shattered by the fact that form is not one isolated element among others, but is an arrangement or pattern of elements. Identity of pattern, arrangement of form is something that can be apprehended only *after* the other promontory has been suggested, by comparison of the two objects.

The only way that form or pattern can operate as an immediate link is by the mode of a directly experienced *quality*, something present and prior to and independent of all reflective analysis, something of the same nature which controls artistic construction. In psychological language, it is felt, and the feeling is made explicit or a term of thought in the idea of another promontory. What operates is not an external existential identity between two things, but a present immediate quality—an explanation which is the only one applicable to some cases already cited, and to being reminded of blotting paper by a certain voice. The priority of regulative quality of the situation as a whole is especially obvious in the case of esthetic judgments. A man sees a picture and says at first sight that it is by Goya or by some one influenced by him. He passes the judgment long before he has made any analysis or any explicit identification of elements. It is the quality of the picture as a whole that operates. With a trained observer such a judgment based on pervasive quality may lead later to definite analysis of elements and details; the result of the analysis may confirm or may lead to rejection of the original ascription. But the basic appreciation of quality as a whole is a more dependable basis of such point by point analysis and its conclusion than is an external analysis performed by a critic who knows history and mechanical points of brushwork but who is lacking in sensitiveness to pervasive quality.

Another instance of Bradley's refers to Mill's denial that the suggestion of another triangle by a given triangle can be reduced to contiguity. For, Mill says, "the form of a triangle is not one single feature among others." Bradley thinks such a view absurd;

he cannot, he says, even tell what is meant. The use of the term "feature" may be unfortunate. For when we speak of a nose as a feature of a face, we have in mind one element or part among others. Now triangularity is not such an isolable element. It is a characteristic of the disposition, arrangement, or pattern of all elements, and it must be capable of immediate realization. Even a nose as a feature of a man's face is not completely isolable. For it is characterized by the whole face as well as characterizing that face. A better instance is found, however, when we speak of a man's *expression*. That assuredly is a total effect of all elements in their relation to one another, not a "single feature among others." And so is triangularity. Family resemblances are often detected, and yet one is totally unable to specify the points of resemblance. Unanalyzed quality of the whole accounts for the identification as a *result*, and it is a radically different thing from identification of a man by finger prints.

The outcome of this brief discussion, in revealing the significance of dominant qualitativeness in suggestion and connection of ideas, shows why thinking as an existential process is all one with controlled association.[4] For the latter is not explained by any merely external conjunction or any external identity in things. If it were, association would itself be merely another case of existential sequence, coexistence, or identity and would be lacking in intellectual and logical import. But selection and coherence determined by an immediate quality that constitutes and delimits a situation are characteristics of "association." These traits are different in kind from existential conjunction and physical sameness, and identical with those of thought. The case of similarity or resemblance is almost uniquely significant. The problem of its nature is a crux of philosophies. The difficulty of dealing with it leads one on the one hand to thinking of it as purely psychical in nature, and, on the other hand, to the idealistic identification of the ontological and the logical *via* the principle of identity in difference. The recognition of pervasive quality enables us to

---

4. Were I to venture into speculative territory, I might apply this conception to the problem of "thinking" in animals, and what the *Gestalt* psychologists call "insight." That total quality operates with animals and sometimes secures, as with monkeys, results like those which we obtain by reflective analysis cannot, it seems to me, be doubted. But that this operation of quality in effecting results then goes out into symbolization and analysis is quite another matter.

avoid both extremes. By its means a voice is assimilated to blotting paper, and in more serious intellectual matters analogy becomes a guiding principle of scientific thought. On the basis of *assimilation* a further explicit recognition of similarity takes place. For assimilation is not itself the perception or judgment of similarity; the latter requires a further act made possible by symbols. It involves a proposition. The saying that there is a "tide in the affairs of men, etc." does not of itself involve any direct comparison of human affairs with the ocean and an explicit judgment of likeness. A pervasive quality has resulted in an assimilation. If symbols are at hand, this assimilation may lead to a further act—the judgment of similarity. But *de facto* assimilation comes first and need not eventuate in the express conception of resemblance.[5]

"Assimilation" denotes the efficacious operation of pervasive quality; "similarity" denotes a *relation*. *Sheer* assimilation results in the presence of a single object of apprehension. To identify a seen thing *as* a promontory is a case of assimilation. By some physiological process, not exactly understood at present but to which the name "habit" is given, the net outcome of prior experiences gives a dominant quality, designated "promontory" to a perceived existence. Passage from this object to some other implies resistance to mere assimilation and results in making distinctions. The pervasive quality is differentiated while at the same time these differentiations are connected. The result is an explicit statement or proposition.

I have touched, as I am well aware, only upon the fringes of a complex subject. But in view of the general neglect of the subject, I shall be satisfied if I have turned the attention of those interested in thought and its workings to an overlooked field. Omitting reference to ramifications, the gist of the matter is that the immediate existence of quality, and of dominant and pervasive quality, is the background, the point of departure, and the regulative principle of all thinking. Thought which denies the existential reality of qualitative things is therefore bound to end in self-contradiction and in denying itself. "Scientific" thinking, that expressed in physical science, never gets away from qualita-

5. Thus, to recur to Bradley's example, one may pass directly from the promontory in England to one in Wales and become absorbed in the latter without any judgment of the likeness of the two.

tive existence. Directly, it always has its own qualitative background; indirectly, it has that of the world in which the ordinary experience of the common man is lived. Failure to recognize this fact is the source of a large part of the artificial problems and fallacies that infect our theory of knowledge and our metaphysics, or theories of existence. With this general conclusion goes another that has been emphasized in the preceding discussion. Construction that is artistic is as much a case of genuine thought as that expressed in scientific and philosophical matters, and so is all genuine esthetic appreciation of art, since the latter must in some way, to be vital, retrace the course of the creative process. But the development of this point in its bearing upon esthetic judgment and theory is another story.

What Humanism Means to Me

Humanism is a portmanteau word. A great many incongruous meanings have been packed in it. Words mean what they are made to signify by those who use them. Otherwise, it might be said that the proper use of the word is its historical one.

At least it designated originally a phase of the revival of learning which occurred in the latter part of the Fifteenth and the early part of the Sixteenth Centuries. Applied to this movement, Humanism signifies the activity of a group of men of letters who were intensely interested in the literature of Greece and Rome. They strove to use Latin and Greek as living languages; they had an immense zeal for the propagation of ancient literature; their contempt for the vernaculars of Europe was such that, while they did a great amount of translating, it was from Greek into Latin.

In view of the peculiar meaning assigned the word Humanism by a group of contemporary American literary critics, it is worthy of note that no less an authority than Saintsbury says that the Humanists of that earlier day were in violent rebellion against all authority.

The scope of Humanism widened. It passed from interest in classic literature to concern for all that related to human action and feeling. It made human life in the present and in the past the centre and source of all that is most important, as the Middle Ages had fastened itself upon the supernatural.

Humanitas was the opposite of *divinitas*. The humanities were put in opposition to theology and theological interest. A beautiful if somewhat idealized picture of this phase of Humanism is given by Walter Pater. He said:

> The essence of humanism is the belief that nothing which
> has ever interested living men and women can wholly lose its

[First published in *Thinker* 2 (June 1930): 9–12, as part of a series.]

vitality—no language they have spoken, nor oracle beside which they have hushed their voices, no dreams which have once been entertained by actual human minds, nothing about which they have ever been passionate, or expended time and zeal.

This Humanism is also far removed from the doctrine of restraint and negation that Paul Elmer More and Irving Babbitt have baptized by the same name.

The next phase of Humanism is that initiated by Francis Bacon and his successors, especially the great Frenchmen of the Eighteenth Century, notably Condorcet. Its essence was the conviction that all knowledge and all scientific inquiry should be organized about an ideal of human well-being for the "amelioration of the human estate."

Bacon did not deny the reality of the divine and supernatural, but relegated it wholly to a realm of faith sharply marked off from that of knowledge. With his successors, the human element came more and more to the front. Auguste Comte, with his conception of a religion of humanity and the unification of all the sciences about humanity as its central theme, was greatly influenced by Condorcet.

In contemporary thought, there is an echo of this meaning in the new religious movement that calls itself Humanism. However, it does not propose to worship humanity, much less set up a system of rites which are to do for this worship what the sacraments did for mediaeval Christianity. It finds its conceptions of God and of other religious ideas of the past in the realm of human ideals and aspirations, and would yoke the religious emotions of mankind to the promotion of the ideal phases of human life.

Then there is also a philosophical development of pragmatism to which Schiller, the Oxford thinker, has given the name Humanism. He has taken for his motto the saying of Protagoras: "Man is the measure of all things." He has applied this conception to the rejuvenation of logic, ethics and metaphysics, making the conception of value central in philosophy, and finding the source of value in human desire, purpose and satisfaction.

Even this brief survey shows the variety of meanings conveyed by the term "Humanism." None of them has any close resemblance to the movement signalized in the recent book *Humanism and America*.

Many persons attached to the older and better established meanings will regret that some other name could not have been found for the gospel according to More and Babbitt. Its chief claim to the title of Humanism is negative. It is not only anti-romantic, but also anti-naturalistic. The significance it gives to the "human" can be understood only in antithesis to the view it holds of nature. In philosophical terms, its philosophy is thoroughly dualistic. It holds to a complete gulf between nature and man in his true being, and finds in the irruptions of nature into human life the source of all the evils and all the woes that beset mankind.

This fact accounts for its distinctly negative temper. It attacks a philosopher[1] who, to most readers, is a type of genuine Humanist merely because he has tried to include man and nature in a way which sends the mechanistic aspect of it to the rear. This negative character would seem to doom the new movement to sterility.

Its creed enables it to attack many things in contemporary life which others also find undesirable. But in an age like our own, any philosophy which sets off man from nature, and which condemns science as a foe to higher human interests cannot, it is safe to predict, become productive.

It has much more in common with the romanticism it condemns than it is aware of. Its ethics are essentially those of Kant; its idea of a reason and rule that are divorced from all natural basis and natural positive use is the expression of a "transcendental imagination." If it follows its own logic to its conclusion, it will terminate, like the earlier romanticism, in the bosom of the church.

There remains intact another Humanism. The problem of integrating science in its bearings upon life, and of rendering it the servant instead of the master of human destiny, has grown only the more pressing since the days of Francis Bacon. It was then a possibility; it is now a necessity, if the dignity of human life is not to be submerged.

1. Alfred North Whitehead, English scientist, metaphysicist and mathematician, author of *Science and the Modern World*, etc.—Editor.

Social life itself demands this integration, and science invites to the task. A Humanism of this type will endure long after the much advertised "Humanism" of a present group has found its way into a paragraph in a chapter on early Twentieth Century American letters.

At all events, what Humanism means to me is *an expansion, not a contraction, of human life, an expansion in which nature and the science of nature are made the willing servants of human good.*

What I Believe
Living Philosophies—VII

I

Faith was once almost universally thought to be acceptance of a definite body of intellectual propositions, acceptance being based upon authority—preferably that of revelation from on high. It meant adherence to a creed consisting of set articles. Such creeds are recited daily in our churches. Of late there has developed another conception of faith. This is suggested by the words of an American thinker: "Faith is tendency toward action." According to such a view, faith is the matrix of formulated creeds and the inspiration of endeavor. Change from the one conception of faith to the other is indicative of a profound alteration. Adherence to any body of doctrines and dogmas based upon a specific authority signifies distrust in the power of experience to provide, in its own ongoing movement, the needed principles of belief and action. Faith in its newer sense signifies that experience itself is the sole ultimate authority.

Such a faith has in it all the elements of a philosophy. For it implies that the course and material of experience give support and stay to life, and that its possibilities provide all the ends and ideals that are to regulate conduct. When these implications are made explicit, there emerges a definite philosophy. I have no intention here of trying to unfold such a philosophy, but rather to indicate what a philosophy based on experience as the ultimate authority in knowledge and conduct means in the present state of civilization, what its reactions are upon what is thought and done. For such a faith is not at present either articulate or widely held. If it were, it would be not so much a philosophy as a part of common sense.

[First published in *Forum* 83 (March 1930): 176–82, as part of a series.]

In fact, it goes contrary to the whole trend of the traditions by which mankind is educated. On the whole it has been denied that experience and life can regulate themselves and provide their own means of direction and inspiration. Except for an occasional protest, historic philosophies have been "transcendental." And this trait of philosophies is a reflex of the fact that dominant moral codes and religious beliefs have appealed for support to something above and beyond experience. Experience has been systematically disparaged in contrast with something taken to be more fundamental and superior in worth.

Life as it is actually lived has been treated as a preparation for something outside of it and after it. It has been thought lawless, without meaning and value, except as it was taken to testify to a reality beyond itself. The creeds that have prevailed have been founded upon the supposed necessity of escape from the confusion and uncertainties of experience. Life has been thought to be evil and hopeless unless it could be shown to bear within itself the assured promise of a higher reality. Philosophies of escape have also been philosophies of compensation for the ills and sufferings of the experienced world.

Mankind has hardly inquired what would happen if the possibilities of experience were seriously explored and exploited. There has been much systematic exploration in science and much frantic exploitation in politics, business, and amusement. But this attention has been, so to say, incidental and in contravention to the professedly ruling scheme of belief. It has not been the product of belief in the power of experience to furnish organizing principles and directive ends. Religions have been saturated with the supernatural—and the supernatural signifies precisely that which lies beyond experience. Moral codes have been allied to this religious supernaturalism and have sought their foundation and sanction in it. Contrast with such ideas, deeply embedded in all Western culture, gives the philosophy of faith in experience a definite and profound meaning.

II

Why have men in the past resorted to philosophies of that which is above and beyond experience? And why should it be now thought possible to desist from such recourse? The answer to the first question is, undoubtedly, that the experience which men had, as well as any which they could reasonably anticipate, gave no signs of ability to furnish the means of its own regulation. It offered promises it refused to fulfill; it awakened desires only to frustrate them; it created hopes and blasted them; it evoked ideals and was indifferent and hostile to their realization. Men who were incompetent to cope with the troubles and evils that experience brought with it, naturally distrusted the capacity of experience to give authoritative guidance. Since experience did not contain the arts by which its own course could be directed, philosophies and religions of escape and consolatory compensation naturally ensued.

What are the grounds for supposing that this state of affairs has changed and that it is now possible to put trust in the possibilities of experience itself? The answer to this question supplies the content of a philosophy of experience. There are traits of present experience which were unknown and unpossessed when the ruling beliefs of the past were developed. Experience now owns as a part of itself scientific methods of discovery and test; it is marked by ability to create techniques and technologies—that is, arts which arrange and utilize all sorts of conditions and energies, physical and human. These new possessions give experience and its potentialities a radically new meaning. It is a commonplace that since the seventeenth century science has revolutionized our beliefs about outer nature, and it is also beginning to revolutionize those about man.

When our minds dwell on this extraordinary change, they are likely to think of the transformation that has taken place in the subject matter of astronomy, physics, chemistry, biology, psychology, anthropology, and so on. But great as is this change, it shrinks in comparison with the change that has occurred in method. The latter is the author of the revolution in the content of beliefs. The new methods have, moreover, brought with them a radical change in our intellectual attitude and its attendant morale. The method we term "scientific" forms for the modern man (and a man is not modern merely because he lives in 1930) the sole dependable means of disclosing the realities of existence. It is the sole authentic mode of revelation. This possession of a new method, to the use of which no limits can be put, signifies a new idea of the nature and possibilities of experience. It imports a new morale of confidence, control, and security.

The change in knowledge has its overt and practical counterpart in what we term the Industrial Revolution, with its creation of arts for directing and using the energies of nature. Technology includes, of course, the engineering arts that have produced the railway, steamship, automobile, and airplane, the telegraph, telephone, and radio, and the printing press. But it also includes new procedures in medicine and hygiene, the function of insurance in all its branches, and, in its potentiality if not actualization, radically new methods in education and other modes of human relationship. "Technology" signifies all the intelligent techniques by which the energies of nature and man are directed and used in satisfaction of human needs; it cannot be limited to a few outer and comparatively mechanical forms. In the face of its possibilities, the traditional conception of experience is obsolete.

Different theories have expressed with more or less success this and that phase of the newer movements. But there is no integration of them into the standing habits and the controlling outlook of men and women. There are two great signs and tests of this fact. In science and in industry the fact of constant change is generally accepted. Moral, religious, and articulate philosophic creeds are based upon the idea of fixity. In the history of the race, change has been feared. It has been looked upon as the source of decay and degeneration. It has been opposed as the cause of disorder, chaos, and anarchy. One chief reason for the appeal to something beyond experience was the fact that experience is always in such flux that men had to seek stability and peace outside of it. Until the seventeenth century, the natural sciences shared in the belief in the superiority of the immutable to the moving, and took for their ideal the discovery of the permanent and changeless. Ruling philosophies, whether materialistic or spiritual, accepted the same notion as their foundation.

In this attachment to the fixed and immutable, both science and philosophy reflected the universal and pervasive conviction of religion and morals. Impermanence meant insecurity; the permanent was the sole ground of assurance and support amid the vicissitudes of existence. Christianity proffered a fixed revelation of absolute, unchanging Being and truth; and the revelation was elaborated into a system of definite rules and ends for the direction of life. Hence "morals" were conceived as a code of laws, the same everywhere and at all times. The good life was one lived in fixed adherence to fixed principles.

III

In contrast with all such beliefs, the outstanding fact in all branches of natural science is that to exist is to be in process, in change. Nevertheless, although the idea of movement and change has made itself at home in the physical sciences, it has had comparatively little influence on the popular mind as the latter looks at religion, morals, economics, and politics. In these fields it is still supposed that our choice is between confusion, anarchy, and something fixed and immutable. It is assumed that Christianity is the final religion; Jesus the complete and unchanging embodiment of the divine and the human. It is assumed that our present economic régime, at least in principle, expresses something final, something to endure—with, it is incidentally hoped, some improvements in detail. It is assumed, in spite of evident flux in the actual situation, that the institutions of marriage and family that developed in medieval Europe are the last and unchanging word.

These examples hint at the extent to which ideals of fixity persist in a moving world. A philosophy of experience will accept at its full value the fact that social and moral existences are, like physical existences, in a state of continuous if obscure change. It will not try to cover up the fact of inevitable modification, and will make no attempt to set fixed limits to the extent of changes that are to occur. For the futile effort to achieve security and anchorage in something fixed, it will substitute the effort to determine the character of changes that are going on and to give them in the affairs that concern us most some measure of intelligent direction. It is not called upon to cherish Utopian notions about the imminence of such intelligent direction of social changes. But it is committed to faith in the possibility of its slow effectuation in the degree in which men realize the full import of the revolution that has already been effected in physical and technical regions.

Wherever the thought of fixity rules, that of all-inclusive unity rules also. The popular philosophy of life is filled with desire to attain such an all-embracing unity, and formal philosophies have been devoted to an intellectual fulfillment of the desire. Consider the place occupied in popular thought by search for *the* meaning of life and *the* purpose of the universe. Men who look for a single purport and a single end either frame an idea of them according to their private desires and tradition, or else, not finding any such single unity, give up in despair and conclude that there is no genuine meaning and value in any of life's episodes.

The alternatives are not exhaustive, however. There is no need of deciding between no meaning at all and one single, all-embracing meaning. There are many meanings and many purposes in the situations with which we are confronted—one, so to say, for each situation. Each offers its own challenge to thought and endeavor, and presents its own potential value.

It is impossible, I think, even to begin to imagine the changes that would come into life—personal and collective—if the idea of a plurality of interconnected meanings and purposes replaced that of *the* meaning and purpose. Search for a single, inclusive good is doomed to failure. Such happiness as life is capable of comes from the full participation of all our powers in the endeavor to wrest from each changing situation of experience its own full and unique meaning. Faith in the varied possibilities of diversified experience is attended with the joy of constant discovery and of constant growing. Such a joy is possible even in the midst of trouble and defeat, whenever life-experiences are treated as potential disclosures of meanings and values that are to be used as means to a fuller and more significant future experience. Belief in a single purpose distracts thought and wastes energy that would help make the world better if it were directed to attainable ends.

IV

I have stated a general principle, because philosophy, I take it, is more than an enumeration of items of belief with respect to this and that question. But the principle can acquire definiteness only in application to actual issues. How about religion? Does renunciation of the extra-empirical compel also an abandonment of all religion? It certainly exacts a surrender of that supernaturalism and fixed dogma and rigid institutionalism with which Christianity has been historically associated. But as I read human nature and history, the intellectual content of religions has always finally adapted itself to scientific and social conditions after they have become clear. In a sense, it has been parasitic upon the latter.

For this reason I do not think that those who are concerned about the future of a religious attitude should trouble themselves about the conflict of science with traditional doctrines—though I can understand the perplexity of fundamentalists and liberals alike who have identified religion with a special set of beliefs. Concern about the future of religion should take, I think, a different direction. It is difficult to see how religion, after it has accommodated itself to the disintegrating effect of knowledge upon the dogmas of the church, can accommodate itself to traditional social institutions and remain vital.

It seems to me that the chief danger to religion lies in the fact that it has become so respectable. It has become largely a sanction of what socially exists—a kind of gloss upon institutions and conventions. Primitive Christianity was devastating in its claims. It was a religion of renunciation and denunciation of the "world"; it demanded a change of heart that entailed a revolutionary change in human relationships. Since the Western world is now alleged to be Christianized, a world of outworn institutions is accepted and blessed. A religion that began as a demand for a revolutionary change and that has become a sanction to established economic, political, and international institutions should perhaps lead its sincere devotees to reflect upon the sayings of the one worshiped as its founder: "Woe unto you when all men shall speak well of you," and, "Blessed are ye when men shall revile you and persecute you."

I do not mean by this that the future of religion is bound up with a return to the apocalyptic vision of the speedy coming of a heavenly kingdom. I do not mean that I think early Christianity has within itself even the germs of a ready-made remedy for present ills and a ready-made solution for present problems. Rather I would suggest that the future of religion is connected with the possibility of developing a faith in the possibilities of human experience and human relationships that will create a vital sense of the solidarity of human interests and inspire action to make that sense a reality. If our nominally religious institutions learn how to use their symbols and rites to express and enhance such a faith, they may become useful allies of a conception of life that is in harmony with knowledge and social needs.

Since existing Western civilization is what it is so largely because of the forces of industry and commerce, a genuinely religious attitude will be concerned with all that deeply affects human work and the leisure that is dependent upon the conditions and results of work. That is, it will acknowledge the significance of economic factors in life instead of evading the issue. The greatest obstacle that exists to the apprehension and actualization of the possibilities of experience is found in our economic régime. One does not have to accept the doctrine of economic determination of history and institutions to be aware that the opportunities of men in general to engage in an experience that is artistically and intellectually rich and rewarding in the daily modes of human intercourse is dependent upon economic conditions. As long as the supreme effort of those who influence thought and set the conditions under which men act is directed toward maintenance of the existing money economy and private profit, faith in the possibilities of an abundant and significant experience, participated in by all, will remain merely philosophic. While this matter was led up to by a consideration of religion, its significance extends far beyond the matter of religion. It affects every range and aspect of life.

Many persons have become acutely conscious of economic evils as far as they bear upon the life of wage earners, who form the great mass of mankind. It requires somewhat more imagination to see how the experience of those who are, as we say, well-to-do or are "comfortably off" is restricted and distorted. They seem to enjoy the advantages of the present situation. But they suffer as deeply from its defects. The artist and scientific inquirer are pushed outside the main currents of life and become appendages to its fringe or caterers to its injustices. All aesthetic and intellectual interests suffer in consequence. Useless display and luxury, the futile attempt to secure happiness through the possession of things, social position, and economic power over others, are manifestations of the restriction of experience that exists among those who seemingly profit by the present order. Mutual fear, suspicion, and jealousy are also its products. All of these things deflect and impoverish human experience beyond any calculation.

There may have been a time when such things had to be endured because mankind had neither the knowledge nor the arts by which to attain an abundant life shared by all. As it becomes increasingly evident that science and technology have given us the resources for dealing effectively with the workings of economic forces, the philosophy of the possibilities of experience takes on concrete meaning.

V

Our international system (since, with all its disorder, it *is* a system) presents another example, writ large, of the restriction of experience created by exclusiveness and isolation. In the arts and technical sciences, there already exist contacts and exchanges undreamed of even a century ago. Barring our execrable tariff walls, the same is true of commerce in physical commodities. But at the same time, race and color prejudice have never had such opportunity as they have now to poison the mind, while nationalism is elevated into a religion called patriotism. Peoples and nations exist in a state of latent antagonism when not engaged in overt conflict. This state of affairs narrows and impoverishes the experience of every individual in countless ways. An outward symbol of this restriction is found in the oft cited fact that eighty per cent of our national expenditure goes to pay for the results of past wars and preparing for future wars. The conditions of a vitally valuable experience for the individual are so bound up with complex, collective, social relationships that the individualism of the past has lost its meaning. Individuals will always be the centre and the consummation of experience, but what an individual actually *is* in his life-experience depends upon the nature and movement of associated life. This is the lesson enforced by both our economic and our international systems.

Morals is not a theme by itself because it is not an episode nor department by itself. It marks the issue of all the converging forces of life. Codes that set up fixed and unchanging ends and rules have necessarily relaxed in the face of changing science and society. A new and effective morale can emerge only from an exploration of the realities of human association. Psychology and the social disciplines are beginning to furnish the instrumentalities of this inquiry. In no field has disrespect for experience had more disastrous consequences, for in no other has there been such waste. The experience of the past is largely thrown away. There has been no deliberate, cumulative process, no systematic transmission of what is learned in the contacts and intercourse of individuals with one another. It has been thought enough to hand on fixed rules and fixed ends. Controlled moral progress can begin only where there is the sifting and communication of the results of all relevant experiences of human association, such as now exists as a matter of course in the experiences of science with the natural world.

In popular speech, morals usually signifies matters of sex relationship. Phenomena of a period of acute transition like those of the present are poor material upon which to base prediction and foresight. But it is clear that the codes which still nominally prevail are the result of one-sided and restricted conditions. Present ideas of love, marriage, and the family are almost exclusively masculine constructions. Like all idealizations of human interests that express a dominantly one-sided experience, they are romantic in theory and prosaic in operation. Sentimental idealization on one side has its obverse in a literally conceived legal system. The realities of the relationships of men, women, and children to one another have been submerged in this fusion of sentimentalism and legalism. The growing freedom of women can hardly have any other outcome than the production of more realistic and more human morals. It will be marked by a new freedom, but also by a new severity. For it will be enforced by the realities of associated life as they are disclosed to careful and systematic inquiry, and not by a combination of convention and an exhausted legal system with sentimentality.

VI

The chief intellectual characteristic of the present age is its despair of any constructive philosophy—not just in its technical meaning, but in the sense of any integrated outlook and attitude. The developments of the last century have gone so far that we are now aware of the shock and overturn in older beliefs. But the formation of a new, coherent view of nature and man based upon facts consonant with science and actual social conditions is still to be had. What we call the Victorian Age seemed to have such a philosophy. It was a philosophy of hope, of progress, of all that is called liberalism. The growing sense of unsolved social problems, accentuated by the war, has shaken that faith. It is impossible to recover its mood.

The result is disillusionment about all comprehensive and positive ideas. The possession of constructive ideals is taken to be an admission that one is living in a realm of fantasy. We have lost confidence in reason because we have learned that man is chiefly a creature of habit and emotion. The notion that habit and impulse can themselves be rendered intelligent on any large and social scale is felt to be only another illusion. Because the hopes and expectations of the past have been discredited, there is cynicism as to all far-reaching plans and policies. That the very knowledge which enables us to detect the illusory character of past hopes and aspirations—a knowledge denied those who held them—may enable us to form purposes and expectations that are better grounded, is overlooked.

In fact, the contrast with the optimism of the Victorian Age is significant of the need and possibility of a radically different type of philosophy. For that era did not question the essential validity of older ideas. It recognized that the new science demanded a certain purification of traditional beliefs—such, for example, as the elimination of the supernatural. But in the main, Victorian thought conceived of new conditions as if they merely put in our hands effective instruments for realizing old ideals. The shock and uncertainty so characteristic of the present marks the discovery that the older ideals themselves are undermined. Instead of science and technology giving us better means for bringing them to pass, they are shaking our confidence in all large and comprehensive beliefs and purposes.

Such a phenomenon is, however, transitory. The impact of the new forces is for the time being negative. Faith in the divine author and authority in which Western civilization confided, inherited ideas of the soul and its destiny, of fixed revelation, of completely stable institutions, of automatic progress, have been made impossible for the cultivated mind of the Western world. It is psychologically natural that the outcome should be a collapse of faith in all fundamental organizing and directive ideas. Skepticism becomes the mark and even the pose of the educated mind. It is the more influential because it is no longer directed against this and that article of the older creeds but is rather a bias against any kind of far-reaching ideas, and a denial of systematic participation on the part of such ideas in the intelligent direction of affairs.

It is in such a context that a thoroughgoing philosophy of experience, framed in the light of science and technique, has its significance. For it, the breakdown of traditional ideas is an opportunity. The possibility of producing the kind of experience in which science and the arts are brought unitedly to bear upon industry, politics, religion, domestic life, and human relations in general, is itself something novel. We are not accustomed to it even as an idea. But faith in it is neither a dream nor a demonstrated failure. It is a faith. Realization of the faith, so that we may work in larger measure by sight of things achieved, is in the future. But the conception of it as a possibility when it is worked out in a coherent body of ideas, critical and constructive, forms a philosophy, an organized attitude of outlook, interpretation, and construction. A philosophic faith, being a tendency to action, can be tried and tested only in action. I know of no viable alternative in the present day to such a philosophy as has been indicated.

Three Independent Factors in Morals

There is a fact which from all the evidence is an integral part of moral action which has not received the attention it deserves in moral theory: that is the element of uncertainty and of conflict in any situation which can properly be called moral. The conventional attitude sees in that situation only a conflict of good and of evil; in such a conflict, it is asserted, there should not be any uncertainty. The moral agent knows good as good and evil as evil and chooses one or the other according to the knowledge he has of it. I will not stop to discuss whether this traditional view can be sustained in certain cases; it is enough to say that it is not right in a great number of cases. The more conscientious the agent is and the more care he expends on the moral quality of his acts, the more he is aware of the complexity of this problem of discovering what is good; he hesitates among ends, all of which are good in some measure, among duties which obligate him for some reason. Only after the event, and then by chance, does one of the alternatives seem simply good morally or bad morally. And if we take the case of a person commonly considered immoral, we know that he does not take the trouble of justifying his acts, even the criminal ones; he makes no effort, to use the psychoanalysts' term, to "rationalize" them.

As I just proposed, this problematical character of moral situations, this preliminary uncertainty in considering the moral quality of an act to be performed, is not recognized by current moral theory. The reason for that is, it seems to me, quite simple.

[First published as "Trois facteurs indépendants en matière de morale," trans. Charles Cestre, in *Bulletin de la société française de philosophie* 30 (October–December 1930): 118–27, from an address read in English before the French Philosophical Society, Paris, 7 November 1930. First published in English in *Educational Theory* 16 (July 1966): 198–209, trans. Jo Ann Boydston. For the introductory remarks by Xavier Léon and the discussion following Dewey's address, see this volume, Appendix 5.]

Whatever may be the differences which separate moral theories, all postulate one single principle as an explanation of moral life. Under such conditions, it is not possible to have either uncertainty or conflict: *morally* speaking, the conflict is only specious and apparent. Conflict is, in effect, between good and evil, justice and injustice, duty and caprice, virtue and vice, and is not an inherent part of the good, the obligatory, the virtuous. Intellectually and morally, distinctions are given in advance; from such a point of view, conflict is in the nature of things, a hesitation about choice, an anguish of the will divided between good and evil, between appetite and a categorical imperative, between the disposition to virtue or the penchant for vice. That is the necessary logical conclusion if moral action has only one source, if it ranges only within a single category. Obviously in this case the only force which can oppose the moral is the immoral.

In the time I have at my disposal I will not attempt to prove that this idea of the nature of conflict is an abstract and arbitrary simplification, so much so that it runs counter to every empirical observation of fact. I can only express, briefly and in passing, the idea that moral progress and the sharpening of character depend on the ability to make delicate distinctions, to perceive aspects of good and of evil not previously noticed, to take into account the fact that doubt and the need for choice impinge at every turn. Moral decline is on a par with the loss of that ability to make delicate distinctions, with the blunting and hardening of the capacity of discrimination. Posing this point without undertaking to prove it, I shall content myself with presenting the hypothesis that there are at least three independent variables in moral action. Each of these variables has a sound basis, but because each has a different origin and mode of operation, they can be at cross purposes and exercise divergent forces in the formation of judgment. From this point of view, uncertainty and conflict are inherent in morals; it is characteristic of any situation properly called moral that one is ignorant of the end and of good consequences, of the right and just approach, of the direction of virtuous conduct, and that one must search for them. The essence of the moral situation is an internal and intrinsic conflict; the necessity for judgment and for choice comes from the fact that one has to manage forces with no common denominator.

By way of introduction, let us see what is involved. We know that there are two opposing systems of moral theory: the morality of ends and the morality of laws. The dominating, the only, and monistic principle of the first, is that of ends which, in the final analysis, can be reduced to one single end, supreme and universal good. The nature of this end, this good, has been discussed frequently. Some say that it is happiness (*eudaemonia*), others pleasure, still others, self-realization. But, in every respect, the idea of Good, in the sense of satisfaction and of achievement, is central. The concept of right, to the extent it is distinguished from good, is derivative and dependent; it is the means or the manner of attaining the good. To say that an act is consonant with right, legitimate or obligatory, is to say that its accomplishment leads to the possession of the good; otherwise, it is senseless. In the morality of laws, this concept is reversed. At the heart of this morality is the idea of law which prescribes what is legitimate or obligatory. Natural goods are the satisfaction of desires and the accomplishment of purposes; but natural goods have nothing in common except in name, with moral Good. Moral good becomes that which is in agreement with juridical imperative, while the opposite is not true.

Now I would like to suggest that good and right have different origins, they flow from independent springs, so that neither of the two can derive from the other, so that desire and duty have equally legitimate bases and the force they exercise in different directions is what makes moral decision a real problem, what gives ethical judgment and moral tact their vitality. I want to stress that there is no uniform, previous moral presumption either in one direction or in the other, no constant principle making the balance turn on the side of good or of law; but that morality consists rather in the capacity to judge the respective claims of desire and of duty from the moment they affirm themselves in concrete experience, with an eye to discovering a practical middle footing between one and the other—a middle footing which leans as much to one side as to the other without following any rule which may be posed in advance.

So much for preliminary considerations; the essential problem I propose to discuss is the source and the origin in concrete experience of what I have called independent variables. What reasons are there for accepting the existence of these three factors?

First, no one can deny that impulses, appetites, and desires are constant traits in human action and have a large part in determining the direction conduct will take. When impulse or appetite operate without foresight, one does not compare or judge values. The strongest inclination carries one along and effort follows its direction. But when one foresees the consequences which may result from the fulfillment of desire, the situation changes. Impulses which one cannot measure as impulses become measurable when their results are considered; one can visualize their external consequences and thus compare them as one might two objects. These acts of judgment, of comparison, of reckoning, repeat themselves and develop in proportion to the increase in capacity for foresight and reflection. Judgments applied to such a situation can be thoroughly examined, corrected, made more exact by judgments carried over from other situations; the results of previous estimates and actions are available as working materials.

In the course of time two moral concepts have been formed. One of these is that of Reason as a function which moderates and directs impulses by considering the consequences they entail. The "Reason" thus conceived is nothing but the ordinary faculty of foresight and of comparison; but that faculty has been elevated to a higher order of dignity and named eulogistically by virtue of what it accomplishes, or the order and system it introduces into the succession of acts which constitute conduct.

The other concept we see emerging from moral experience is that of *ends* forming a united and coherent system and merging into one generalized and comprehensive end. As soon as foresight is used to summon objective consequences, the idea of an end is self-apparent; consequences are the natural limit, the object, the end of the action envisaged. But it is significant that from the moment particular acts of judgment become organized into the general moral function called reason, a classification of ends is established; estimates found correct about one are applied in thought to others. Our first ancestors were preoccupied quite early with goals such as health, wealth, courage in battle, success with the other sex. A second level was reached when men more reflective than their fellows ventured to treat those different generalized ends as elements of an organized plan of life, ranking them in a hierarchy of values, going from the least comprehensive to the most comprehensive, and thus conceived the idea of a single end, or in other words, of a good to which all reasonable acts led.

When that process was accomplished, one form of moral theory had been established. To take a broad view of the history of thought, it might be said that it was Greek thinkers who gave articulate expression to this particular phase of experience, and left as their permanent contribution to the theory of morals the conception of ends as the completion, the perfection, and hence the good, of human life; the conception of an hierarchical organization of ends and the intimate relationship between this organization and Reason. Moreover the reigning philosophy of Greece viewed the universe as a cosmos in which all natural processes tended to fulfil themselves in rational or ideal forms, so that this view of human conduct was but an extension of the idea entertained about the universe in which we live. Law was conceived of simply as an expression of reason, not of will or command, being in fact but the order of changes involved in the realization of an end.

That our inheritance from Greek moral theory states one phase of actual human experience of conduct I do not doubt. It is quite another matter, however, to say that it covers conduct in its inclusive scope. It was possible—or so it seems to me—for the Greek philosophers to include social claims and obligations under the category of ends related to reason because of the strictly indigenous character of the Greek city-state; because of the vitally intimate connection between the affairs of this state and the interests of the citizen and because in Athens—upon whose experience the philosophers drew—legislation became a function of discussion and conference, so that, in ideal at least, legislation was the manifestation of deliberate intelligence. The Greek political community was small enough so that it was possible to think of its decisions as being when they were properly made as the expressions of the reasonable mind of the community—as made that is in view of ends that commended themselves to thought, while laws that expressed the fiat of will were arbitrary and tyrannical, and those which were the fruit of passion were perverse and confused.

Probably only in such a social medium however could law and obligation be identified, without the exercise of mere dialectical skill, with a rational adaptation of means to ends. Moreover the failure of the Greeks to achieve success in practical political administration, their irreparable factiousness and instability, was calculated to bring discredit upon the notion that insight into ends and calculation of means afford a sound and safe basis for social relationships. At all events, we find that among the Romans, the instinct for social order, stable government and stable administration led in the end to quite another conception of reason and law. Reason became a kind of cosmic force that held things together, compelling them to fit into one another and to work together, and law was the manifestation of this compelling force for order. Offices, duties, relationships not of means to ends but of mutual adaptation, reciprocal suitableness and harmony, became the centre of moral theory.

Now this theory also corresponds to a fact in normal experience. Men who live together inevitably make demands on one another. Each one attempts, however unconsciously by the very fact of living and acting, to bend others to his purposes, to make use of others as cooperative means in his own scheme of life. There is no normal person who does not insist practically on some sort of conduct on the part of others. Parents, rulers, are in a better position than are others to exact actions in accord with their demands, to secure obedience and conformity, but even young children in the degree of their power make claims, issue demands, set up certain expectations of their own as standards in the behavior of others. From the standpoint of the one making the demand on others, the demand is normal for it is merely a part of the process of executing his own purpose. From the standpoint of the one upon whom the demand is made, it will seem arbitrary except as it happens to fall in with some interest of his own. But he too has demands to make upon others and there finally develops a certain set or system of demands, more or less reciprocal according to social conditions, which are generally accepted—that is, responded to without overt revolt. From the standpoint of those whose claims are recognized, these demands are rights; from the standpoint of those undergoing them they are duties. The whole established system as far as it is acknowledged without obvious protest constitutes the principle of authority, Jus, Recht, Droit, which is current—that is to say that which is socially authorized in the putting forth and responding to the demands of others.

Now it seems to me almost self-evident that in its roots and natural mode of manifestation this exercise of demands over the behavior of others is an independent variable with respect to the whole principle of rational teleological ends and goods. It is fact that a particular person makes claims upon others in behalf of some satisfaction which he desires. But this fact does not constitute the claim as right; it gives it no moral authority; in and of itself, it expresses power rather than right. To be right, it must be an acknowledged claim, having not the mere power of the claimant behind it, but the emotional and intellectual assent of the community. Now of course it may be retorted that the good is still the dominant principle, the right being a means to it, only now it is not the end of an individual which is sought but the welfare of the community as such. The retort conceals the fact that "good" and "end" have now taken on a new and inherently different meaning; the terms no longer signify that which will satisfy an individual, but that which he recognizes to be important and valid from the standpoint of some social group to which he belongs. What is right thus comes to the individual as a demand, a requirement, to which he should submit. In as far as he acknowledges the claim to possess authority, and not to express mere external force to which it is convenient to submit, it is "good" in the sense of being right—that is a mere truism. But it is not *a* good as are the things to which desires naturally tend; in fact, at first it presents itself as cutting across and thwarting a natural desire—otherwise it is not felt to be a claim which should be acknowledged. In time, the thing in question may through habituation become an object of desire; but when this happens, it loses its quality of being right and authoritative and becomes simply a good.

The whole point for which I am contending is simply this: There is an intrinsic difference, in both origin and mode of operation, between objects which present themselves as satisfactory to desire and hence good, and objects which come to one as making demands upon his conduct which should be recognized. Neither can be reduced to the other.

Empirically, there is a third independent variable in morals. Individuals praise and blame the conduct of others; they approve and disapprove; encourage and condemn; reward and punish. Such responses occur *after* the other person has acted, or in anticipation of a certain mode of conduct on his part. Westermarck has claimed that sympathetic resentment is the primary root of morals all over the world. While I doubt, for reasons already indicated, its being the only root, there can be no doubt that such resentment, together with a corresponding approbation, are spontaneous and influential empirical phenomena of conduct. Acts and dispositions generally approved form the original virtues; those condemned the original vices.

Praise and blame are spontaneous manifestations of human nature when confronted with the acts of others. They are especially marked when the act in question involves such danger for the one performing it as to be heroic or else goes so contrary to the customs of the community as to be infamous. But praise and blame are so spontaneous, so natural, and as we say "instinctive" that they do not depend either upon considerations of objects that will when attained satisfy desire nor upon making certain demands upon others. They lack the rational, the calculated character, of ends, and the immediate social pressure characteristic of the right. They operate as reflex imputations of virtue and vice—with accompanying rewards and penalties—as *sanctions* of right, and as an individual comes to prize the approving attitude of others as considerations to be taken into account in deliberating upon the end in some especial case. But as categories, as principles, the virtuous differs radically from the good and the right. Goods, I repeat, have to do with deliberation upon desires and purposes; the right and obligatory with demands that are socially authorized and backed; virtues with widespread approbation.

No one can follow the general development of English moral theory without seeing that it is as much influenced by the existence of approvals and disapprovals as Greek theory was the existence of generalized purposes and Latin by the exercise of social authority. Many of the peculiarities of English theory become explicable only when it is seen that this problem is really uppermost even when the writer seems to be discussing some other question. Consider for example the role played by the idea of sympathy; the tendency to regard benevolence as the source of all good and obligation—because it is that which is approved (as sympathy is the organ of approval); and the illogical combination in British utilitarianism of pleasure as the end or good, and the tendency to seek for general happiness as the thing to be approved. The prominent part in English moral theory by such conceptions points doubtless to great susceptibility in English society to the reactions of private individuals to one's conduct as distinct from the tendency to rationalize conduct through consideration of purposes, and from that of attaching great importance to the public system of acknowledged demands that form law.

In calling these three elements independent variables, I do not mean to assert that they are not intertwined in all actual moral situations. Rather is the contrary the case. Moral problems exist because we have to adapt to one another as best we can certain elements coming from each source. If each principle were separate and supreme, I do not see how moral difficulties and uncertainties could arise. The good would be sharply opposed to the evil; the right to the wrong; the virtuous to the vicious. That is, we should sharply discriminate what satisfies desire from what frustrates it—we might make a mistake of judgment in given cases, but that would not affect the distinction of categories. So we should distinguish that which is demanded and permissible, licit, from that which is forbidden, illicit; that which is approved and promoted from that which is frowned upon and penalized.

Actually however, the various lines of distinction cut across one another. What is good from the standpoint of desire is wrong from the standpoint of social demands; what is bad from the first standpoint may be heartily approved by public opinion. Each conflict is genuine and acute, and some way has to be found for reconciling the opposing factors or again that which is officially and legally forbidden is nevertheless socially allowed or even encouraged. Witness the prohibition of alcoholic beverages in my own country; or, on a wider scale, the difficulties which confront children because of the disparity between what is publicly commanded and what is privately permitted to pass, or is even in practice praised as giving evidence of shrewdness or as evincing a praiseworthy ambition. Thus the scheme of rational goods and of official publicly acknowledged duties in Anglo-Saxon countries stands in marked contrast to the whole scheme of virtues enforced by the economic structure of society—a fact which explains to some extent our reputation for hypocrisy.

In view of the part played by actual conflict of forces in moral situations and the genuine uncertainty which results as to what should be done, I am inclined to think that one cause for the inefficacy of moral philosophies has been that in their zeal for a unitary view they have oversimplified the moral life. The outcome is a gap between the tangled realities of practice and the abstract forms of theory. A moral philosophy which should frankly recognize the impossibility of reducing all the elements in moral situations to a single commensurable principle, which should recognize that each human being has to make the best adjustment he can among forces which are genuinely disparate, would throw light upon actual predicaments of conduct and help individuals in making a juster estimate of the force of each competing factor. All that would be lost would be the idea that theoretically there is in advance a single theoretically correct solution for every difficulty with which each and every individual is confronted. Personally I think the surrender of this idea would be a gain instead of a loss. In taking attention away from rigid rules and standards it would lead men to attend more fully to the concrete elements entering into the situations in which they have to act.

Philosophy and Education

After a period in Greece in which inquiry was devoted to inquiry into nature, with man subordinated, philosophy turned in Athens to the study of Man. Socrates, as the saying goes, brought philosophy down from the heavens to earth. It is often forgotten that this change coincided with an interest in education; it was indeed an outgrowth of interest in the possibilities of education in its large sense. This fact is concealed from view because the fundamental inquiry of Socrates, the discussion that gave birth to Plato and Aristotle, appears in English translation as: Can virtue be taught? When we hear the word "virtue" we think of something marked from other human interests and traits in a moralistic way. But the Greek word that is translated "virtue" was immensely wider in its scope. Its original meaning was close to the idea of valor, manliness. Then it became broadened to signify all those qualities that render a human admirable in himself and a loyal and effective member of his community.

The question of whether virtue can be taught was a question of whether it is possible by deliberate and planned means to implant in raw human nature those characteristics which make the individual worthy, which instill in him an active love of the good, and which equip him with powers to serve his society. It was admitted that certain skills may be acquired; the training of apprentices in the arts and crafts was evidence of that fact. It was admitted that information could be conveyed on special matters, and individuals be supplied with the knowledge necessary to enable them to take part in the special callings of shoemaker, carpenter, or physician. But this training, this inculcation of infor-

[First published in University of California at Los Angeles, *Addresses Delivered at the Dedication of the New Campus and New Buildings of the University of California at Los Angeles, 27 and 28 March 1930* (Berkeley: University of California Press, 1930), pp. 46–56.]

mation fell short of education. Could manhood in its full sense be systematically taught? For excellence of manhood meant the transformation of crude and animal traits of human nature into a realized possession of reason and rational ideals, into comprehension and enjoyment of science and fine art. Could the unruly appetites and irregular impulses of the natural, quasi-animal man be converted into the intelligent habits of obedience and of leadership that were the conditions of a stable and happy community life?

The query was the most searching that man has ever put to himself. Is education really possible, means: Is it possible to apply intelligence intentionally and systematically to the regulation of life? Is human nature such that it has the capacity for being led along directed paths into any assured realization of all its desirable capacities? Are there any who are wise enough to educate? Are there ends and principles upon which they may depend in attempting the controlled development of others? And, on the other side, is human nature such that it lends itself to, that it is capable of, education into personal and social excellence?

Because the query is so searching and so fundamental, it led into the raising of almost all the problems with which European philosophy since the time of the great Athenians has concerned itself. What is knowledge? What is its relation to being and to truth? What is the connection between knowledge of the good and its practice? What is mind and what is its relation to the body? What connection is there between thought and understanding and appetite and emotion? What is the Good and how is it apprehended? Can it be efficaciously communicated? How, that is, can the individual be led to participate in it so that it may regulate his life? Can it be communicated to individuals except in a just social order? And the latter question brought up the whole problem of the relation of the individual and the social to each other, the problem of social organization, law and authority.

I have no intention of discussing these philosophical issues. I have referred to them to indicate how vitally connected was the origin of philosophy with the beginning of conscious attention to education. The educational enterprise was taken seriously. It was regarded as the systematic means by which the good life was to be arrived at and maintained: the life full, excellent, rich, for the individual centre of that life, and the life good for the community of which the individual was a member. I emphasize this view of education as the deliberate initiation and cultivation of the good life because it indicates so clearly the defects of so many views about education which have since come to prevail. As has been said, the possibility of training for skill in specialized callings was not questioned; the possibility of conveying successfully specific bodies of information was not questioned. But it was implicitly denied that these processes define genuine education. The goal and scope of education was extended to include whatever contributes to the purposeful development of the good life, and it was limited to include only what serves this end and meets the tests which it imposes.

An illustration is found in the contention of Socrates and Plato that knowledge is a condition of excellence, that to know the good and to do it are inevitably connected together, that ignorance and spiritual failure, the bad life, are intimately associated. This view has been constantly criticized on the ground that it immensely exaggerates the importance of intellect and knowledge, since experience shows that although men know what is good they do not act in accordance with their knowledge. These adverse criticisms overlook the fact that the Socratic position cuts both ways. It sets forth a criterion for knowledge as well as for right conduct. Plato's answer to the critics would be, I take it, that knowledge which does not pass into action according to what is known is *not* knowledge; it is opinion, hearsay, a second-hand acceptance of ideas advanced by others. The measure of knowledge, we can imagine him saying, is precisely the action it does arouse and direct. To the charge that he exaggerated the importance of intelligence and underrated that of practice, skill, habit and the emotions, he might reply by pointing out that he made a prolonged and severe exercise in deeds, and a systematic training of the affections, of likes and dislikes, a precondition of the manifestation of that intelligence which is capable of realizing the good. He might point to the fact that the training of the body and its habits and skills which he called gymnastic and of the emotions by means of what he termed music were necessary preliminaries of insight into the structure and principles of the Good Life. Admitting that the content of what he called gymnastic has now been extended to include forms of technical skill, like those required in various vocations, which he did not contem-

plate; and that the content of what he termed music has been en-
larged to cover all forms of literature and the fine arts, Plato
might still ask a question. Has not the gain in quantity, in extent,
been accompanied by a loss in quality? For in cutting off the
modes of special and professional training and of esthetic cultivation from their connection with the supreme value of the
Good Life and intimate knowledge of it, we have, he would argue, made them ends in themselves and have thereby lost the
clew to the educational use to be made of them, the inclusive end
to which they ought to contribute.

It is not the technical correctness of Plato's theory that I am
concerned with. What his theory proves is that education was
thought of as the means of the institution of the good life among
men. Philosophy was the study of the nature of this Good Life, of
its constituents and of the conditions of its realization. Philosophy and education were organically connected.

The vital bond of union has long since been broken. Education, schooling, goes its way, and philosophy pursues an independent path. Both education and philosophy have found a multitude of special problems with which each has to occupy itself,
and in this specialization of both, the two have grown apart. The
Greek scene was comparatively simple and unified. Ours is complex and diversified. There are many things, too many things, to
be done, and these numerous things seem so different from one
another that there is no unifying bond among them. Each of
these many and different things is difficult to accomplish; each
takes all the time and strength one has to give. Thought and attention have been diverted to details, and the sense of the encompassing whole has been blurred and often lost. Yet this very situation may be viewed as a call to restore the lost connection of
serious thought upon the problems of life with the work of education. There is today a great and growing interest in education.
In the last generation, it has become a distinctive university
study. Interest in philosophic thought is on the increase. Would
not a re-union aid in giving direction and wholeness to education and solidity and vitality to philosophy?

In one thing at least our condition is similar to that of the
Athenians. After a long period in which education was treated as
a matter of routine experience, tradition, and mere apprenticeship, we are engaged once more in regarding education as a pur-

suit having intellectual foundations, and needing systematic intellectual guidance. Our university departments of education are proof of this fact. We are no longer content to permit the work of teaching and discipline to take care of itself on the basis of precedent and of unexamined models bequeathed from the past. Nor are we satisfied to treat them as matters of purely personal gifts and inspiration, reinforced by mastery of special subject-matters. School organization was once an affair of factors derived from tradition and political administration. Superintendents and principals followed precedents modified by the demands of school-boards and taxpayers. There was not the knowledge in psychology and related branches to take instruction out of the rule of routine influenced only by personal endowments; and there was not the knowledge in economics, statistics, and related social sciences to introduce a measure of scientific control into school organization and administration.

In the minds of those habituated to such undeveloped conditions, there was something presumptuous and futile in attempting the introduction of the study of education into higher institutions of learning. It was well enough to have normal schools in which young people, green at their task, should be initiated into the tricks of their trade; in which in addition to learning something more about subjects to be taught they should acquire some information and get exercise in the methods and devices which teachers before them had worked out in the course of accumulated experience. But why introduce such a matter into a university devoted to the dissemination of old knowledge and the discovery of new? It is a matter of familiar experience that older and better established departments in our higher institutions of learning looked askance upon the introduction of something called pedagogy with the rather contemptuous associations that attend that word.

Being new, "education" as a subject of university teaching and study was necessarily comparatively unorganized. The pioneers had to grope their way. It would be foolish to claim that no mistakes were made, or that they do not continue to be made. But wholesale condemnation of the enterprise overlooks two fundamental facts. One is that education is the largest and most important undertaking of the organized political state and community; the largest in personnel and in expenditures, as well as, one may say without exaggeration, the most fundamentally important of all branches of public activity in its results. (It is not surprising, therefore, that, upon the whole, state universities have been most receptive to the claims of the new discipline.) This is only one side of the picture. The need might be there, and yet there be no intellectual resources capable of meeting it. But hostile critics overlooked the fact that the growth of other subjects of study had reached a point where they had valuable material to contribute to the solution of problems that arise in the school system; something to contribute to a wiser direction of the work the schools have to accomplish. There now exists not only a wealth, an almost appalling variety, of problems to be studied, but there exists also a wealth of material drawn from many special topics, which can be organized and brought to bear upon these questions.

Let me suggest as an illustration one field somewhat remote from my own personal interests, the field of educational organization and administration. We have not in this country, and many of us hope we shall never have, a highly centralized governmental scheme of regulation and supervision. Yet some kind of intellectual oversight and direction is needed unless there is to be mere drift and waste. Our traditions commit us to some kind of voluntary control, of voluntary dissemination and acceptance. The universities are the natural centres for providing what is needed. At once, a multitude of problems offer themselves. The school is at least one great social institution among others and an institution having with us a legal basis and a political connection. The history of this institution is at least as worthy of study as is the history of any other institution. Its present forms and operations call for the same careful examination as those of any other institution. Political science, sociology, economics, public health, are involved in any directed study of the problems that arise. They supply the intellectual capital with which the problems must be approached. Many mistakes occur, much waste exists, many failures accrue because the affairs of public education are conducted without the light which such subjects as those just mentioned could shed. The university is not only the logical place for the organization of knowledge with respect to the public problems but it is the only place where it can be carried on.

I have mentioned one phase of the opportunity and need.

Were one to consider the problem of the course of study from the elementary through the high school, taking into account the rapid multiplication of subjects and sciences leading to superficiality and congestion, there would be presented to our consideration an even more fertile field for university study. To mention only one aspect of this complex subject: there is as yet no widely accepted approximation to a solution of the question of the organized adaptation of the older traditional studies to those which have found their ways into the schools in the last generation or so. Everywhere in life there is conflict of the old and traditional with the new, and resultant confusion. This conflict is nowhere more acute than in education, and nowhere are the consequences of confusion more harmful. Universities are sufficiently far away from the immediate and daily scene to take up this question in a thorough-going way, while they may and should be in close enough connection with schools to obtain the material necessary to deal with it. Without serious and consecutive study at an intellectual centre, we are in great danger of impairing the efficacy of education by yielding on one hand to a ballyhoo of glorification of anything and everything as long as it is new and different, and on the other of becoming hampered by reactionary economic and social forces, so that we content ourselves with adherence to the old in the face of radically new conditions.

One other point demands attention, if only in passing. The extension of knowledge in recent years bearing upon the treatment of individuals is enormous. It includes not only what is conventionally covered by "instruction and discipline" but all that affects the mental and moral well-being of teachers and pupils. Physiology, psychology, psychiatry, child clinics, institutes of child guidance, have provided unexpected and as yet largely unassimilated material which is needed to deal with this pressing matter. The coordination of this material in its distinctive bearing upon the questions of normal and abnormal development of persons is a distinctive problem. It cannot safely be left until disorders have set in requiring to be treated by remedial measures. What is needed is constructive and preventive action; the school as well as the home is the natural place for such action; the teacher with the parent is the agent for conducting it. But teachers and parents are helpless without knowledge which is organized with reference to education instead of with reference to cure. Professional schools are recognized as legitimate parts of university teaching and research. Yet education is the one profession whose direct aim is constructive, and which is concerned with development of normal persons, instead of dealing with cases of dislocation and breakdown, personal and social.

All this, however, does not say anything about the relation of philosophy and education in university teaching. That interest in education was the parent of philosophical questions may be admitted and yet it may be held that the two have now parted company as parent and child so often do. To admit that they have permanently separated is, however, to concede that education is now concerned with specialized and technical matters, not with the Good Life. That education in its preoccupation with a multitude of special matters that require attention has often been more concerned with inculcating special skills, whether the formal studies of the primary school or the professional abilities of later life, and more concerned with the impartation of bodies of information than with the problem of creating conditions for the experience of values, is doubtless true. It is true also that knowledge has become so specialized and subdivided that its unity has become dissipated. But unless we assume that these results are necessary and right, this very situation is that which creates a demand for philosophy, which meets it with a challenge.

Some years ago Professor John M. Coulter, himself a highly successful teacher, spoke of education in the following terms:

> There is no problem concerning which we can so ill afford to be dogmatic; and no one concerning which we are so dogmatically inclined. There is no question concerning which past experience may be so unsafe a guide, since what we have attained cannot be compared with what we hope for and have a right to expect. There is no problem concerning which theorizing may lead so far astray, and none which has been so covered with crude theorizing. We do not understand the structure we are seeking to modify and develop; we do not know what we want to do for it when we shall understand it, and we do not know how to accomplish when we shall know what we want. Out of this mass of negations we are constructing our hypotheses.

We are not, in other words, as far removed from the time of Socrates and Plato in insight as we are in years, or as the multiplication of agencies of instruction might seem to indicate. We still have to raise the question whether education is possible, and if so how. For education is still the formation of character, intellectual, moral, and esthetic, and not just training in skills and the impartation of information. And what in detail the development of a good character signifies and how it is to be intelligently directed are still matters of doubt and debate. I would not seem to suggest that philosophy has a ready-made answer to these questions. But I am quite sure that the problem is one for philosophy to consider and that education proposes to philosophy questions which challenge all its resources and which test all its theories. If philosophy is to come forth from a closeted seclusion and submit to the test of application, the problems of education furnish it with its most direct and most urgent opportunity.

For the ultimate aim of education is nothing other than the creation of human beings in the fulness of their capacities. Through the making of human beings, of men and women generous in aspiration, liberal in thought, cultivated in taste, and equipped with knowledge and competent method, society itself is constantly remade, and with this remaking the world itself is re-created. We need not be reminded either that society is in rapid change or that present life is ripe with unsolved issues and infected with evils. But it is well to remind ourselves from time to time that education is the most far-reaching and the most fundamental way of correcting social evils and meeting social issues. With all our great American faith in education, we are still given to supposing that external reforms can cope with our troubles. We look for some legislative scheme, some twist given to institutions, to do the work that can only be done by individual men and women, and that can be done by them only as they are themselves developed into full possession of all their potentialities. I do not believe that anyone can accurately predict what the future will bring forth or set up adequate ideals of future society. But in the degree in which education develops individuals into mastery of their own capacities, we must trust these individuals to meet issues as they arise, and to remake the social conditions they face into something worthier of man and of life.

How often in the past have we depended upon war to bring

out the supreme loyalties of mankind. Its life and death struggles are obvious and dramatic; its results in changing the course of history are evident and striking. When shall we realize that in every school-building in the land a struggle is also being waged against all that hems in and distorts human life? The struggle is not with arms and violence; its consequences cannot be recorded in statistics of the physically killed and wounded, nor set forth in terms of territorial changes. But in its slow and imperceptible processes, the real battles for human freedom and for the pushing back of the boundaries that restrict human life are ultimately won. We need to pledge ourselves to engage anew and with renewed faith in the greatest of all battles in the cause of human liberation, to the end that all human beings may lead the life that is alone worthy of being entitled wholly human.

General Principles of Educational Articulation

There are two ways of approaching the problem of elimination of waste in the educative processes of the schools. One is the administrative. This takes the existing system as a going concern, and inquires into the breaks and overlappings that make for maladjustment and inefficient expenditure of time and energy on the part of both pupil and teacher—useless and therefore harmful mental motions, harmful and not merely useless because they set up bad habits. The other may be called personal, psychological or moral. By these adjectives is meant that the method starts from the side of personal growth of individual needs and capacities, and asks what school organization is best calculated to secure continuity and efficiency of development. It sets out from the side of pupils and asks how the successive stages of the school system should be arranged so that there shall be a minimum of blocks, arrests, sudden switches and gaps, futile repetitions and duplications, as the children and youth pass from one stage to another, from kindergarten to elementary, from this to high school, and from the latter to college.

This statement of two modes of approach does not imply that there is a necessary opposition between the two. They should be complementary. What is common to both is that each looks at the educational system as a whole and views each part with respect to what it does in making education really a whole, and not merely a juxtaposition of mechanically separated parts. Each avenue of approach is equally concerned to eliminate isolations and render the function of each part effective with respect to the

[Published in *School and Society* 29 (30 March 1929): 399–406, and in Department of Superintendence of the National Education Association *Official Report* (Washington, D.C.: Department of Superintendence, 1929), pp. 51–60, from an address delivered on 26 February 1929 at the annual meeting of the Department of Superintendence, National Education Association, Cleveland, Ohio, 24–28 February 1929.]

others. There is no more necessary opposition between the two than there is when engineers in tunneling a mountain bore from opposite ends. Before they start work, the tunnel must be considered as a single thing and the work done from either end must be thought out and undertaken with reference to examination of the entire project. But a preliminary intellectual survey of the whole is necessary to make the two modes of approach meet at a centre.

When the consideration of the problem is undertaken from either side without regard to the considerations which necessarily exist at the other side, there are dangers and evils that can not be avoided. Thus an approach from the exclusively personal side will overlook certain administrative necessities that seem to be inherent in the situation. An important consideration here is pointed out in the general introductory report of the commission. The area of the region drawn upon and the different numbers of children and youth who go to school in the elementary and higher grades must be considered. Younger children as a rule must be in buildings nearer their own homes, and because of their greater number there must be a certain amount of physical segregation from older pupils. Moreover, for the older pupils there must be a greater variety of courses, differentiation of teachers and amount of equipment. These facts demand a large number of pupils in the high school and this in turn demands that they be drawn from a wide area. Hence consideration from the personal development side must take into account administrative necessities.

Consideration of the latter must, however, be checked at every point by taking into account the conditions that make for effective mental and moral growth of individuals as individuals. Undue attention to the administrative side tends toward "rationalization" of the divisions that happen at a given time to be institutionalized. Reasons are found which justify their continued existence as more or less independent units. Then the problem of articulation becomes an external one, that of smoothing transitions from one to another and getting rid of the more obvious sources of friction. This is a gain as far as it goes, but it does not go far enough to touch the basic matter of securing adequate and complete personal growth. In consequence of this external approach, there will be a tendency to assume that mental and moral growth is marked by "epochs" which correspond, at least roughly, to the isolated units of the school system.

The fact that interests and capacities change with age is undeniable; that the boy and girl of sixteen differ markedly from those of twelve, and those of the latter age from those of eight and the latter, in turn, from those of five and six is too evident to escape notice. But the underlying problem is whether the changes occur gradually and almost insensibly or by sharply marked off leaps which correspond to the conventional institutional school divisions. This is a question which must be investigated and the answer found by independent study of the facts of development in individuals. The need of this independent inquiry as a check and test is the more acute because the divisions that exist among school units react upon personal development. It is in consequence easy to assume that changes in personal growth are inherent, when in fact they may be the relatively artificial products of the existing school divisions and in so far abnormal and undesirable.

For this reason the study of the best methods of articulation should be checked by a comparative study of those schools in which division into units is minimized; that is, "unified schools" in which children of different ages, from primary to high school, are found together and wherein there is no administrative break between junior and senior years in the high schools. Only by such a comparative study can the elements, if any, that are artificial and conventional in the schools where units are emphasized be detected. This statement does not contradict what was said earlier about the problems of area of distribution and the need of increased variety of courses and equipment in higher grades. For, in the first place, cities vary greatly in population and there may be median range of size to which the unified school is well adapted. In the second place, the results of comparative inquiry would throw light upon the methods of organization to be adopted in the schools of towns of such a large size that the unified system can not be literally adopted. For there is a question of limits, and educators can work in either of two directions, toward opposite poles—either to that of independent units, or to the maximum possible of relative unification of the assembling of pupils—without carrying either principle to its logical extreme. This consideration seems to me to be fundamental in the whole problem of articulation. Mere convenience of administration should not be permitted to override it.

It is recognized that adequate treatment of the fundamental problem here—the mutually complementary character of the administrative and the moral psychological development of individuals—must wait upon command of greater knowledge of the actual process of normal growth than anybody now possesses. Nevertheless, reference to the latter is important, for it indicates, in the first place, the necessity of continued study of personal growth as an inherent factor in the problem of articulation from the administrative side. And in the second place, it serves a warning. It cautions us against a too ready assumption that the present institutional division into separate units has necessary inherent value on account of corresponding "epochs" of personal development. It warns us against attaching too great value, decisive value, to matters of administrative habit and inertia.

A complete examination of the question of articulation can be attained only when the experiences of classroom teachers in immediate contact with pupils are procured and utilized, as well as the experiences of administrators. This statement does not signify that principals and superintendents in their reports do not take advantage of the experiences gained in actual classroom work. It is, however, a reminder that specialized experience always creates a one-sided emphasis, in habits of thought as well as of outward action, and always needs to be checked. There is much evidence in the various reports of the extent to which conference and exchange of reports and information already obtain as necessary methods of avoiding unduly sharp breaks in subject-matter, methods, and harmful repetitions. What I am pleading for is a more direct obtaining of data on the whole subject of continuity of personal development from classroom teachers, and a *direct* inclusion of such reports in the gathering and interpretation of material along with those of superintendents and supervisors and principals. The findings of experimental and progressive schools must also be included, not as models, but as providing data regarding processes of personal development under different conditions.

Conceding that we have not *adequate* knowledge of the course of mental development in individuals, I propose now to consider the bearing of what is available in this respect upon the general problem of articulation. I begin with a statement which is so general that it can hardly arouse dissent. The ideal is that the achievements at any one period of growth supply the tools, the agencies and instrumentalities, of further growth. The statement is not one that refers simply to the transition from one unit to another. It is of constant application. That is, whatever the pupils gain at any period, whether in skill or knowledge, should be promptly funded into something actively employed in gaining new skill and knowledge.[1] A new level of intellectual achievement should mark off each successive month and week of school life, and not be thought of as occurring only in the transition from one unit to another. The bearing of this principle upon the specific problems of articulation which the various reports of the commission bring out may be postponed until another basic principle has been stated.

The idea of ripening, maturing, is evidently fundamental in the question of individual growth. Now what needs to be especially borne in mind with reference to maturing is that it is plural, that is, various powers and interests which coexist at the same time mature at very different rates. Maturing is a continuous process; the mature fruit may appear, as with fruits on a tree, only at some later stage, even if we assume, which it is probably wrong to do, that there is ever any such completely matured fruit in the case of a human being as in a plant. But the normal maturing as a process goes on all the time; if it does not there is something the matter with conditions. Arrest of growth, incapacity to cope with subject-matter, and inability to respond to methods employed at a later period are all signs of something wrong. They need to be studied as symptoms and diagnosed with a view to constructive remedies.

Since maturing is a continuous process and also a plural one, it is not a uniform four-abreast thing. One has only to observe a baby to note how one ability ripens before another, the ability to fixate objects with the eye, to grasp, to sit up, to creep, to walk,

1. This principle is recognized in the almost unanimous denial that there is a period of "imitation," or receptivity, and one of application, or active initiation and use, on the part of those reporting in the second chapter of the general report. There is very general agreement that the acquiring and the application of what is used as tools must go on hand in hand from the start and be continued all the way through, the difference being at most one of emphasis.

to talk; and how each operation as it matures is utilized as a factor in bringing about some maturing of another ability and adaptation. No parent ever makes the mistake of overlooking this plural nature of maturing. When we come to schooling, however, I wonder if there is not too much of a tendency to assume an equal, uniform, four-abreast maturing, and if that does not underlie the conception of "epochs" of growth which correspond to various units of the school system. If the assumption is not made in a positive form, it is made in a negative way, that is, by overlooking the specific needs and capacities that are ripening, or that may ripen, during each year and month of school life. It is this neglect which is responsible for the idea that each stage is merely preparation for some later stage, particularly that the aim of the early years of the elementary school is chiefly the purpose of gaining social tools to be independently employed and enjoyed later on.

I am always surprised and disturbed when I find persons who insist that the high school must not be dominated by the idea of college preparation ready to assume as a matter of course that the first two or three primary years must have as their main purpose the securing of "social tools" for later use, instead of being devoted to gaining those experiences which are appropriate to the powers that are ripening at the time. I must express my profound dissent from the position taken in the general introduction that sets up a dualism between the actual experience of children in the early years and the requirements imposed and dictated by the needs of later school years.

At this point, the two principles laid down cease to be innocuous generalities. The way to get possession and command of a tool for later use is by having the experiences proper to the immediate time—experiences which awaken new needs and opportunities and which, just because they are achievements, form the natural agencies or tools for later activities. Any theory which sets out by denying that this is possible misstates the problem of articulation, and its "solution" is bound to be defective. Unless powers as they ripen are put to immediate use in acquiring new knowledge and skill, tools are not shaped for later use. The problem, from the side of earlier years, is that of discovering those particular needs, interests and capacities which are ripening then and there, not attempting a premature introduction and forcing of others; and then of finding that use and application of them which passes insensibly into the ripening of other more complex tendencies. From the side of later years, it is the same problem, but with the added factor of adjusting subject-matter and methods so that the powers already relatively ripened shall be used in developing the new powers that are showing themselves. Only in this way can the maximum of continuous growth be secured and an internal rather than mechanical articulation be secured.

The point and force of the two principles laid down is found in their concrete application. I propose, accordingly, to consider some phases of isolation and waste, of non-articulation, in their light.

In the first place, they suggest that reasonable integration within the school can not be secured by limiting the problem to what goes on in the school. The fundamental problem of articulation takes us outside the school to articulation of its activities with the out-of-school experience of the pupils. It is for this reason, of course, that the curriculum is so fundamental; to articulate successive phases of subject-matter with one another there must be an articulation of the curriculum with the broadening range of experiences had at home, in the neighborhood and community. This principle applies at the beginning and all the way through. I remember hearing an intelligent parent complain that kindergarten teachers seemed to assume that children came to them blanks, and treated them as if everything had to begin afresh, thereby boring children with things they could already do and were familiar with, and failing to utilize the capital they had already acquired.

This complaint was made over thirty years ago; doubtless cause for it no longer exists. But it is typical of what is meant by the present point. Except for highly specialized matters, the ripening of powers does not go on exclusively nor mainly in school. This fact gives great significance to matters contained in the various reports which at first sight are remote from the question of school articulation; matters of health, nutrition, regularity of attendance, home life, reading and occupations out of school, economic status of parents and children, as well as the general changing demands of a rapidly changing civilization. But it extends to the whole matter of utilizing in school the experiences gained out of school.

More specific points are involved in the application of the two principles. One of these is the principle of alternate concentration and remission of work in special lines. While great improvements have taken place, there is still an undue tendency to a uniform four-abreast treatment of the subjects that make up the school program. Certain studies tend to appear in every month and in every year of a school program. There is need for flexible experimentation in periods of intensive concentration upon such things as reading and number work in the elementary grades, followed by periods of relaxation in which achievements gained are capitalized in concentration upon other studies. The same principle applies to history, geography, nature study and science. Each might be made for a time the relative centre with subordination of other factors. The effect would be to disclose better than does the uniform method special aptitudes and weaknesses, and would, I think, greatly minimize the breaks that now come with change of pupils to a new year and new unit.

Other difficulties in the present situation arise, I believe, from the isolation that comes from the confining of teachers to single years. The pupils are the only ones who come into direct contact with the whole process. Artificial breaks, sudden introduction of new demands and new methods of discipline, teaching of new kinds of subjects, duplications and need of review of subjects already supposedly mastered are the result. They are in large measure due, I think, to the isolation of the teacher resulting from too exclusive confinement to a single year. Articulation is secured only as at each stage of the school system, pupils' activities are directed in reference to a continuing wholeness of growth. One year is too short a span in which to survey the process of growth. Much has been done, as appears from the reports in exchange of records and data, and in joint committee to form the curriculums. Unified supervision helps. But these things do not cover the whole situation. There are administrative difficulties attending transfers of teachers from one grade to another, or in having a teacher give instruction during the same year in more than one grade. But I do not believe that, without a greater use of these methods, teachers can get that real appreciation of continuity of school movement which will enable them to secure articulation from within.

One aspect of this matter involves the question of having

younger children in contact with more than one teacher. I recognize the objections that are so clearly pointed out in the section of chapter II of the report dealing with departmentalization in the elementary grades. But these objections have to be offset not only against the point already made regarding the need of intimate acquaintance on the part of the teacher with children at different stages of development, but against the evils of the conditioning of a child to the habits and methods of a single person, and against the fact, frequently noted, of the friction that arises when the pupils enter a unit in which departmental teaching does exist. It does not follow, because departmental teaching can easily be overdone in the early grades, that children may not profitably get used to more than one teacher even in the first grade. It is a concrete question of proportioning. We need also to bear in mind that the one-room, one-teacher plan tends to perpetuate the régimes of either formalism or undirected spontaneity in the early years. No one teacher can know enough to answer all the questions children ask that need to be followed up if that growth is to be secured which gives a firm basis for future work—although one teacher is enough to allow children to do what they please or to teach the traditional formal subjects. Nor does it follow that in high schools teaching should be rigidly departmentalized. We need a little more "give" at both ends. Still less does it follow that departmentalized teaching in high schools should be confined to a teacher having many sections of algebra or geometry or physiography in only one year of the school. Genuine correlation or integration and genuine continuity of articulation may depend upon a teacher having more than one topic and in teaching a subject through more than one year. As Ella Flagg Young used to remind teachers many years ago, what often passes for departmentalization is in reality only a subdivision of labor such as obtains in a factory where each worker is confined to making a part of a shoe, which part is then passed on to the next worker.

A point frequently mentioned in the reports is connected with the last two. Attention is called to the difficulties arising from the fact that teachers in training often specialize on some one phase or unit, to the neglect of knowledge of the system as a whole. It would seem to follow that all teachers in training should have at least one thorough course to familiarize them with the system in its entirety, with special reference to the place, in the whole, of that part of the system for which they are specially preparing. If this were a regular procedure, it is possible that the reluctance of teachers to change from one grade or one unit to another might give way to desire for a broader experience. In connection with the training of teachers there are so many problems relevant to the issue of articulation that it is possible to select only one.

Graduate schools of universities are in a large measure training schools for teachers in colleges and in an increasing degree in high schools. Through instruction given to those in colleges who go out to teach in high schools there is, in any case, a reaction into high-school teaching. These conditions account in large measure for the gaps and maladjustments frequently referred to in articulation of senior high schools with the junior, and in general of high schools with upper elementary grades. I allude to the distinction often drawn between greater attention to development of pupils on one side and to subject-matter as such on the other. No survey of the causes of bad articulation is complete that does not take into account the influence, direct and indirect, of the training of future teachers in graduate schools of universities. It is a phase of the old question of the isolation of normal schools from colleges with the greater emphasis of one upon method and of the other upon subject-matter. Although the problem is not as acute as it used to be, since there has been rapprochement from both sides, it is still an important factor.

Time permits only of these few selected illustrations. I conclude by recurring to the original statement of the problem: that of co-ordinating the administrative approach with the psychological-moral approach through personal development. It makes a great difference how we take up the problem of articulation. If we accept too readily any existing distribution of units as even relatively fixed, I am skeptical of any solutions being found which do more than eliminate some of the more striking cases of external friction. It is a natural trait of the human mind to "rationalize" what exists—that is, to find adventitious reasons that justify what is found. We should, it seems to me, view the problem of articulation as one of *differentiation*.

The metaphor of organic growth is helpful if not pressed too literally. The problem of coordinated physiological growth is not one of coordinating bones, muscles, lungs, and stomach together; not until mal-coordinations have been established does the latter problem arise. There is a gradual differentiation of different organs and functions, each cooperating with the others. The problem of educational guidance may be conceived as that of bringing about differentiation in a consecutive way. The meaning of this general statement may be briefly illustrated. For this purpose I select once more a portion of the introduction of the commission which in its implications appears to diverge from the principle. I refer to the contrast which is set forth between the earlier and later years in reference to docility of a passive type in the former and personal independence and individualistic initiation in the latter, and the conclusions about legitimate separation of units drawn from the alleged contrast. The statement seems to overlook several facts, such as that well known to parents, the fact called "contrary suggestion" in very early years: the fact that development in the school years comes through activities, and also the adoption of the method of socialized activities in the kindergarten.

Receptivity and assertive activity are *constant* functions. What differs with different stages of growth is *range* of exercise and *field* of exercise. Because a child of six or seven can not assume the same active responsibilities that he can when he is eight or nine does not mean that some field for its exercise is not available at the earlier age nor that it is not an indispensable factor in normal development. To generalize wholesale from the regions in which the capacity does not exist, and infer from them that the willingness of children to accept what is put over on them "dictates" certain subject-matters at that period is to fail to prepare pupils for greater independence in other fields later, and thus puts a premium upon excessive "individualism" later. The problem is one of constant differentiation of powers of independent action through prior utilization of those which already exist. A normal differentiation will create in pupils a willingness to recognize later their need of guidance and receptivity in respect to that in which they are not developed to the point of independence, and thus reduce an abrupt and undesirable "individualism."

The example is taken from a limited field, but it applies throughout. At each stage the pupil, whether in elementary grades, junior high school or college, has a certain region of experience in which he is relatively at home and has certain tendencies which are relatively mature. Attention to these things as the agencies to be connected with in securing new powers of independent and responsible action in wider fields of experience gives the key to a continuous process of differentiation which will place the problem of articulation in its proper light.

I can not conclude this exposition, at once too fragmentary and too general, without acknowledging my great indebtedness to the studies embodied in the report of the commission. More important, however, than any personal indebtedness is the evidence afforded that the educators of the country are alive to their responsibility. In our American system of diffused control, in the absence of any central directive body, our sole guarantee of constant improvement is the method of cooperative voluntary inquiry and mutual conference. The report of the commission is a notable contribution to the accomplishment of this task in a problem of fundamental importance in the advancement of education. We all owe them thanks for the alertness and thoroughness with which the task has been performed.

Our Illiteracy Problem

The 1930 census is of unusual interest to educators and to students of social questions in the United States. The investigators were instructed to ascertain by definite tests the ability of those over ten to write and read. Then we shall have accurate knowledge of the extent of illiteracy in the United States. We shall also know what the effect has been of restriction of immigration, and of the campaign that has been carried on since the close of the War to teach adults to read and write.

It will not be easy to differentiate between the two causes, but it will be possible if the Government classifies illiterate adults according to the date of their entrance into the United States.

Statistics are not very interesting to most people, and yet figures are the only basis we have to go on in analyzing our situation and in forming a definite campaign for the liquidation of illiteracy. The census returns of 1920 showed about 5,000,000 illiterates, of whom 3,000,000 were native-born.

The statistics are not very reliable for two reasons. In the first place there was no personal investigation on the part of census-takers to check up the statements of those asked whether they could read or write. In the second place, ability to read or write is a vague thing. Just how much knowledge and skill constitutes ability?

Five millions is a large number, and yet reduced to a percentage of the total population it did not seem alarming. But if there was any complacency about the census result, it was shocked out of existence by the returns from the soldiers drafted for army service. The examiners in this case were not content to ask simply whether a person could read and write. They tested for ability to write a simple letter, such as a soldier would naturally want

[First published in *Pictorial Review* 31 (August 1930): 28, 65, 73.]

to send home, and to read simple English sentences consecutively. The results were a revelation. Twenty-five per cent. of the 1,500,000 examined could not pass the test. Of the Negro soldiers 50 per cent. failed.

Part of the difference in percentage from the census report is due to the fact that the latter counted only persons over ten, so that the ratio would have been considerably over six per cent. if it had not been estimated on the basis of the total population, including the millions under that age. But the main difference was due to the fact that a genuine examination was made. Moreover even the census figures had revealed that while there was a decrease in the total percentage as measured in comparison with 1910, there was an actual increase in the number of illiterates in twelve States in the period from 1910 to 1920, most of these States, moreover, being the Northern industrial communities.

Reports from committees who investigated the whole subject concluded that by any fair standard there were probably twice as many illiterates in the country as the census of 1920 stated— namely, 10,000,000 in all. There is no ground for doubting the justice of this conclusion.

The result is distinctly appalling. It is the more so because of our pride in our public-school system, and the feeling that it is doing about all that should be expected of it. In spite of the bad showing, it would not be true to say that any great amount of public attention has been given to it, or that, aside from a few devoted persons and groups, much systematic action has been started to remedy the evil condition.

I have recently looked over library catalogs and indexes to periodicals on the subject of illiteracy. It is surprising to find out how little has been written; there are certainly no signs that the public mind is agitated or even deeply stirred.

The reasons for this indifference on the part of the general public lie on the surface. Because of the social condition and status of the illiterates, they attract little attention and arouse little emotion. They are, largely, illiterate because they live outside the social currents in which the more fortunate among us live. They fall for the most part into three classes.

There are those, mostly native whites, who live in sparsely settled communities. Not only are schools few and poor, but there is little contact with the more active parts of the country. There is little in their lives or in their relations to the rest of the nation to call attention to them, except as they occasionally furnish picturesque literary material.

Then there are the foreign immigrants, who live mostly in the larger industrial centres. They work in factories; they have little intercourse with the older part of the population and little social contact except with their bosses and fellow employees. There is nothing dramatic or sensational about them. By the 1920 census there were more illiterates in New York State than in any other State of the Union. In view of its larger population this fact is perhaps not surprising. But it calls attention in a striking way to the way in which a large group of the foreign-born is submerged in our modern industrial life.

The Negro illiterates form the third large class. It is a shock to read in the census reports that native-born illiterates outnumber the foreign-born. The explanation of course is found in the large group of native-born Negroes who have not enjoyed the facilities of schooling.

Negro illiteracy is only one part of the whole Negro problem in this country. Unless there was a general Negro question, social, economic, and political, there would be no such excess of Negro illiterates as now exists. Racial prejudice, fear of racial equality, dread lest education would render the black population "upstarts" who would clamor for the use of the vote, and make them less tractable as cheap labor, are definite factors in maintaining a large illiteracy in our black population.

Educational facilities in the South for Negroes are increasing; some States have made notable advances. But I see no prospect of a concerted move to wipe out Negro illiteracy which does not start from serious consideration of the fundamental aspects of the race question.

I shall have to appeal to figures again. They are dry reading, but they illuminate the situation as nothing else can do. There are seventeen States that maintain separate schools for Negroes. The illiteracy of Negroes in these States ranges from 12½ per cent. to 38½ per cent., much larger in every case than that of the whites.

The average cost of the schooling of the blacks in these States is $10 per capita, while almost three times that sum ($29) is spent on each white pupil. There are forty-four Negro children to a teacher, as against a little over thirty among the whites. The school year for the latter averages thirty days longer than for the former. About two-thirds of the Negro pupils are in the first three grades, as against less than one-half of the white pupils.

Less school time, more pupils to a teacher, poorer buildings and equipment, more poorly paid and therefore less well-equipped teachers, children leaving school when they have received only the rudiments of teaching—these are the factors that control the present situation and that make for greater illiteracy among the blacks.

In almost every phase of this problem we find ourselves in a vicious circle. Illiteracy breeds illiteracy. Parents without education are just those who are indifferent to it for their children as a rule. They lack both ambition and financial means. Moreover, as the survey just made of rural white, industrial immigrants and Negroes so clearly shows, those conditions of social isolation that cause illiteracy also serve to prevent it from becoming a vital issue for those who are privileged.

Illiteracy does not make the direct social appeal that is aroused by illness, insanity, obvious destitution, or the other causes that evoke philanthropic action and public care. It is very hard to get emotional or excite emotion in others about the illiterates. They are not crippled or in bed or acutely suffering in some way that marks them off from others.

Nevertheless it ought not to be necessary to put up an argument in behalf of organized activity, public and private, to wipe out illiteracy. It is doubtful whether there is any other one evil from which society as a whole suffers so much as from this plague-spot of ignorance. Moreover it is remediable by direct attack, which is more than can be said for most of our other evils. Being able to read and write is not by any means the same thing as being educated. But it is a necessary condition of education in other lines. Politically speaking, the illiterates are always a potential menace. Shut off as they are from contact with books and the press, they are either politically indifferent and apathetic or are ready subjects for demagogic appeal.

While no very dependable statistics are at hand, it is evident that health conditions are likely to be worse among them than among those who have access to information and who can be reached by campaigns like that against tuberculosis, for example. That illiteracy conduces to a low economic condition is self-evident. Speaking generally, only those whose ambition it is to learn to read and write, in spite of early handicaps, ever rise in the industrial scale.

I recall meeting some years ago a superintendent of schools in a large mining town in Pennsylvania. He had gone to work in a mine while still a lad. After he was twenty years old he woke up to the fact that all those who got ahead had had some schooling, while he could neither read nor write. He saw himself condemned to a life of drudgery underground. He came of sturdy Scotch ancestry. He left the mines and went to school. In an amazingly short number of years he had been graduated from the University of Pennsylvania and made himself an educational leader.

Such cases are rare. But think of what society would have lost if he had not awakened to the need of education; then multiply his case by hundreds of thousands, and you can form a picture of the dead loss that comes from the low economic status that follows in the wake of illiteracy. The economic evil extends far. A few—but too few—manufacturers and merchants are alive to the situation and have publicly testified that they are willing, although in relatively advanced portions of the North, to be taxed to improve school facilities in the South, because of the sure development of markets that would result from the spread of education.

It should not be necessary to cite these special points. The outstanding fact is that the existence of illiteracy on such scale as is found among us is not only a social blight but a reproach to our boasted pride in our public-school system and its efficacy. Something has to be done about it, unless we are willing to confess that our boasts are merely empty talk. It will have to be done on a large scale, and in organized ways.

The first step is to analyze the problem, to break up the illiteracy evil into its component parts, in order that each factor may then be dealt with separately and by the agencies most appropriate to do it. In the rough, there are three parts, as we have already seen. There is the Negro problem, the problem of immigrants in industrial centres, and the problem of the native whites of rural regions, where people live in isolation, and with few and poor schools.

Prevention is always better than cure. One necessary measure is to prevent the development of illiteracy among those now of school age. This task falls in part to the formulation and effective execution of adequate compulsory school laws. Our American habit of paying more attention to getting laws placed on the statute-books than to their subsequent administration counts. Compulsory-attendance laws will always be poorly enforced, however good they are on paper, when they are not supported by public opinion in the communities affected by them.

A general campaign for enlightenment of sentiment in backward communities is needed. Here too there is a vicious circle. The communities and groups that most need enforcement are just the ones that have least interest and care about the laws.

In spite of all agitation for the abolition of child labor, the factory and shop still remain the enemy of the school and a distinct abetting cause of illiteracy. The failure of the amendment to the Federal Constitution giving Congress power to regulate child labor is one of the causes why the movement for the liquidation of illiteracy has not made more headway.

The fact that in addition to 10,000,000 illiterates there is another 10,000,000 who are near illiterates proves that three years or so of schooling is not enough. The beginning must be made with improvement of existing school facilities for the young, and seeing to it that all children go to school and remain there long enough so that there is a genuine effect.

This measure, however, only prevents the young from growing up illiterate. It does not take care of those beyond school age. Here there is room and demand for both private philanthropic effort and for public activity.

Mrs. Stewart's moonlight schools and the wonderful work they have accomplished show what one person, with the ardent supporters she has gathered about her, can do in elimination of illiteracy in rural regions. The work of Dr. Talbot, with his "Self-help" primers and readers that have an illustrated vocabulary of words most familiar to factory-workers in their daily occupations, is suggestive of a line of attack useful in industrial centres.

The whole administrative problem, however, needs more attention than it has as yet received. It ought to be possible to work out a proper division of labor among municipal, county, and

State units, assigning to each its proper function, and providing from the proper sources the necessary funds.

The scheme would have to be flexible. In big manufacturing centres the local municipality must take the initiative. In rural districts the county is the natural centre. In both cases there should be auxiliary help from the State. In the cities particularly there must be ways found to secure the active cooperation of industrialists and those in charge of manufacturing plants. With an aroused public opinion there would be no difficulty in developing a flexible and effective program which should wipe out in a few years the reproach of illiteracy.

The question of federal aid and of the extent and manner of federal participation in elimination of illiteracy opens up a disputed field. It is practically, even if not logically, bound up with the moot question of a representative of education in the President's Cabinet.

Although this idea has been indorsed by large numbers of organizations, including not only the National Education Association but the Federation of Women's Clubs and the American Federation of Labor, it has never gone through.

Aside from fear of undue interference on the part of authorities of private and parochial schools, and from trivial objections such as having to add another leaf to the table around which Cabinet members sit (an objection actually urged from high quarters), the chief obstacle is dread of bureaucracy and of centralization.

If the adoption of the proposed measure were to lead to any centralized control of public education, I should, however reluctantly, be obliged to oppose it. I believe that the vitality of our school system is dependent upon its close connection with local needs and interests. A centralized system like that of France is wholly foreign to our spirit and traditions.

I do not think, however, the objection is well grounded. Any move in that direction would be met with so much jealousy and opposition from the States which felt their prerogatives encroached upon, that it would surely fail. I think we also can count upon enough common sense to forestall any attempt at making the move.

In as far as a federal Cabinet of Education is connected with the question of federal aid to do away with illiteracy, the argument, I believe, is all in its favor. I am obliged to resort again to a few figures which indicate why such aid is needed if there is to be organized effort to eliminate illiteracy and its attendant evils. We are again in the presence of the vicious circle. The States and communities that most need funds to carry on the campaign both of prevention and of abolition are usually those least able to afford it. While, for example, the average of one-room schools for the country at large is 28 per cent., it varies in different States from less than 4 to 58 per cent.

The percentage of efficiency in providing school facilities for children under fourteen varies from 36 to 75 per cent. in different States, the highest percentage as a rule being found in Far Western States. To take a single example, children in South Carolina had a few years ago but 58 per cent. of the opportunity to attend school of those in New Jersey. If we took counties instead of States the variation would be enormously greater.

These differences are largely connected with a difference in financial resources. The per capita production of wealth in five States having the greatest educational efficiency was double that of the five States having the lowest rating.

The five richest States had, according to the census of 1920, an income per child of three and a half times that of the five poorest; the saving accounts of the gainfully employed increased in a ratio of seven to one, while the amount spent in the well-to-do States was fifty dollars per child annually, against eleven dollars per child in the poor ones.

While the evil is more or less concentrated in localities, it is nation-wide in its effects. Where one member suffers, the whole body suffers with it. Resources to cope with the evil are also unequally distributed.

It is a measure of justice as well as of generosity that those most able to help should cooperate with the weaker States in doing away once for all with the evil of illiteracy.

This cooperation can be brought about only through the medium of the federal government.

But the sole responsibility does not lie with it, nor should anything like the whole burden be put upon it. We must have organized endeavor all along the line.

How Much Freedom in New Schools?

It is not easy to take stock of the achievements of progressive schools in the last decade: these schools are too diverse both in aims and in mode of conduct. In one respect, this is as it should be: it indicates that there is no cut-and-dried program to follow, that schools are free to grow along the lines of special needs and conditions and so to express the variant ideas of innovating leaders. But there is more than is suggested by these considerations in the existing diversity. It testifies also to the fact that the underlying motivation is so largely a reaction against the traditional school that the watchwords of the progressive movement are capable of being translated into inconsistent practices.

The negative aspect of progressive education results from the conditions of its origin. Progressive schools are usually initiated by parents who are dissatisfied with existing schools and find teachers who agree with them. Often they express discontent with traditional education or locally available schools without embodying any well thought-out policies and aims. They are symptoms of reaction against formalism and mass regimentation; they are manifestations of a desire for an education at once freer and richer. In extreme cases they represent enthusiasm much more than understanding.

Their common creed is the belief in freedom, in esthetic enjoyment and artistic expression, in opportunity for individual development, and in learning through activity rather than by passive absorption. Such aims give progressive schools a certain community of spirit and atmosphere. But they do not determine any common procedure in discipline or instruction; they do not fix the subject matter to be taught; they do not decide whether the

[First published in *New Republic* 63 (9 July 1930): 204–6, as the final contribution to the symposium "The New Education Ten Years After."]

emphasis shall be upon science, history, the fine arts, different modes of industrial art, or social issues and questions. Hence the diversity of the progressive schools, and hence the great difficulty in appraising them. Adverse criticisms may be readily and often effectively answered on the ground that they do not apply to specific schools.

Strong and weak points go together; every human institution has the defects of its qualities. Colonel Francis W. Parker, more nearly than any other one person, was the father of the progressive educational movement, a fact all the more significant because he spent most of his educational life in public rather than private schools—first at Quincy, Massachusetts, and then at the Cook County Normal School in Englewood, Chicago. I do not know whether he used the phrase which has since come into vogue, "child-centered schools." One of his most frequent statements was that teachers had been teaching *subjects* when they should be teaching *children*. He engaged in aggressive warfare against the burden of ready-made, desiccated subject matter formulated and arranged from the adult point of view—in other words, against the stock in trade of the conventional curriculum. He pleaded for subject matter nearer to the experience and life of the pupils. He strove to throw off the yoke of fixed and uniform disciplinary measures. He introduced many things, innovations in his day, which are now almost commonplaces in the public schools which lay any claim to being modern—for example, the school assemblies conducted by the pupils themselves.

Even such an inadequate statement as the foregoing brings out an antithesis which has persisted to a considerable extent in the later movement of progressive education: that between the human and personal element represented by the pupils, the children, youth, and, on the other hand, the impersonal and objective factor—the subject matter of studies, the body of knowledge and organized and skilled accomplishment. In saying that the antithesis thus set up has resulted, upon the whole, in a lack of balance, I do not mean in any way to hold the work and influence of Colonel Parker responsible. I mean that the same reaction against dead, formal and external studies which affected his early reforms has continued to operate with his successors, and to produce a one-sided emphasis—that upon pupils at the expense of subject matter.

That there was need for the reaction, indeed for a revolt, seems to me unquestionable. The evils of the traditional, conventional school room, its almost complete isolation from actual life, and the deadly depression of mind which the weight of formal material caused, all cried out for reform. But rebellion against formal studies and lessons can be effectively completed only through the development of a new subject matter, as well organized as was the old—indeed, better organized in any vital sense of the word organization—but having an intimate and developing relation to the experience of those in school. The relative failure to accomplish this result indicates the one-sidedness of the idea of the "child-centered" school.

I do not mean, of course, that education does not centre in the pupil. It obviously takes its start with him and terminates in him. But the child is not something isolated; he does not live inside himself, but in a world of nature and man. His experience is not complete in his impulses and emotions; these must reach out into a world of objects and persons. And until an experience has become relatively mature, the impulses do not even know what they are reaching out toward and for; they are blind and inchoate. To fail to assure them guidance and direction is not merely to permit them to operate in a blind and spasmodic fashion, but it promotes the formation of *habits* of immature, undeveloped and egoistic activity. Guidance and direction mean that the impulses and desires take effect through material that is impersonal and objective. And this subject matter can be provided in a way which will obtain ordered and consecutive development of experience only by means of the thoughtful selection and organization of material by those having the broadest experience—those who treat impulses and inchoate desires and plans as potentialities of growth through interaction and not as finalities.

To be truly self-centered is not to be centered in one's feelings and desires. Such a centre means dissipation, and the ultimate destruction of any centre whatever. Nor does it mean to be egoistically bent on the fulfillment of personal wishes and ambitions. It means rather to have a rich field of social and natural relations, which are at first external to the self, but now incorporated into personal experience so that they give it weight, balance and order. In some progressive schools the fear of adult imposition has become a veritable phobia. When the fear is analyzed, it means simply a preference for an immature and undeveloped experience over a ripened and thoughtful one; it erects into a standard something which by its nature provides no steady measure or tested criterion. In some recent articles in the *New Republic* I have argued that an adult cannot attain an integrated personality except by incorporating into himself the realities of the life-situations in which he finds himself. This operation is certainly even more necessary for the young; what is called "subject matter" represents simply the selected and organized material that is relevant to such incorporation at any given time. The neglect of it means arrest of growth at an immature level and ultimate disintegration of selfhood.

It is, of course, difficult to use words that are not open to misapprehension. There may be those who think that I am making a plea for return to some kind of adult imposition, or at least to ready-made and rather rigidly predetermined topics and sequences of study. But in fact many of the current interpretations of the child-centered school, of pupil initiative and pupil-purposing and planning, suffer from exactly the same fallacy as the adult-imposition method of the traditional school—only in an inverted form. That is, they are still obsessed by the personal factor; they conceive of no alternative to adult dictation save child dictation. What is wanted is to get away from every mode of personal dictation and merely personal control. When the emphasis falls upon having experiences that are educationally worth while, the centre of gravity shifts from the personal factor, and is found within the developing experience in which pupils and teachers alike participate. The teacher, because of greater maturity and wider knowledge, is the natural leader in the shared activity, and is naturally accepted as such. The fundamental thing is to find the types of experience that are worth having, not merely for the moment, but because of what they lead to—the questions they raise, the problems they create, the demands for new information they suggest, the activities they invoke, the larger and expanding fields into which they continuously open.

In criticizing the progressive schools, as I have indicated already, it is difficult to make sweeping generalizations. But some of these schools indulge pupils in unrestrained freedom of action and speech, of manners and lack of manners. Schools farthest to the left (and there are many parents who share the fallacy) carry the thing they call freedom nearly to the point of anarchy. This license, however—this outer freedom in action—is but an included part of the larger question just touched upon. When there is genuine control and direction of experiences that are intrinsically worth while by objective subject matter, excessive liberty of outward action will also be naturally regulated. Ultimately it is the absence of intellectual control through significant subject matter which stimulates the deplorable egotism, cockiness, impertinence and disregard for the rights of others apparently considered by some persons to be the inevitable accompaniment, if not the essence, of freedom.

The fact that even the most extreme of the progressive schools do obtain for their pupils a degree of mental independence and power which stands them in good stead when they go to schools where formal methods prevail, is evidence of what might be done if the emphasis were put upon the rational freedom which is the fruit of objective knowledge and understanding. And thus we are brought to the nub of the matter. To conduct a progressive school is much more difficult than to conduct a formal one. Standards, materials, methods are already at hand for the latter; the teacher needs only to follow and conform. Upon the whole, it is not surprising that, in history, science, the arts and other school "studies," there is still a lack of subject matter which has been organized upon the basis of connection with the pupils' own growth in insight and power. The time-span of progressive schools has been too short to permit very much to be accomplished. What may rightfully be demanded, however, is that the progressive schools recognize their responsibility for accomplishing this task, so as not to be content with casual improvisation and living intellectually from hand to mouth.

Again one needs to guard against misunderstanding. There is no single body of subject matter which can be worked out, even in the course of years, which will be applicable all over the country. I am not arguing for any such outcome; I know of nothing that would so completely kill progressive schools and turn them into another kind of formal schools, differentiated only by having another set of conventions. Even in the same school, what will work with one group of children will not "take" with another group of the same age. Full recognition of the fact that subject matter must be always changing with locality, with the situation and with the particular type of children is, however, quite consistent with equal recognition of the fact that it is possible to work out varied bodies of consecutive subject matter upon which teachers may draw, each in his own way, in conducting his own work. The older type of education could draw upon a body of information, of subject matter and skills which was arranged from the adult standpoint. Progressive education must have a much larger, more expansive and adaptable body of materials and activities, developed through constant study of the conditions and methods favorable to the consecutive development of power and understanding. The weakness of existing progressive education is due to the meagre knowledge which anyone has regarding the conditions and laws of continuity which govern the development of mental power. To this extent its defects are inevitable and are not to be complained of. But if progressive schools become complacent with existing accomplishments, unaware of the slight foundation of knowledge upon which they rest, and careless regarding the amount of study of the laws of growth that remains to be done, a reaction against them is sure to take place.

Such reference as has been made to the subject matter of a worth-while and continuously developing experience is too general to be of value in actual guidance. The discovery of such subject matter, which induces growth of skill, understanding and rational freedom, is the main question to be worked upon cooperatively. The question may be raised, however, of whether the tendency of progressive schools has not been to put emphasis upon things that make schooling more immediately enjoyable to pupils rather than upon things that will give them the understanding and capacity that are relevant to contemporary social life. No one can justly decry the value of any education which supplies additions to the resources of the inner life of pupils. But surely the problem of progressive education demands that this result be not effected in such a way as to ignore or obscure preparation for the social realities—including the evils—of industrial and political civilization.

Upon the whole, progressive schools have been most successful in furthering "creativeness" in the arts—in music, drawing and picture making, dramatics and literary composition, including poetry. This achievement is well worth while; it ought to assist in producing a generation esthetically more sensitive and alive than the older one. But it is not enough. Taken by itself it will do something to further the private appreciations of, say, the upper section of a middle class. But it will not serve to meet even the esthetic needs and defaultings of contemporary industrial society in its prevailing external expressions. Again, while much has been achieved in teaching science as an addition to private resources in intellectual enjoyment, I do not find that as much has been done in bringing out the relation of science to industrial society, and its potentialities for a planned control of future developments.

Such criticisms as these are not met by introducing exercises and discussions based on what are called "current events." What is needed is something which may indeed connect intellectually in time with what currently happens, but which takes the mind back of the happenings to the understanding of basic causes. Without insight into operative conditions, there can be no education that contains the promise of improved social direction.

This fact brings us back again to the enormous difficulty involved in a truly progressive development of progressive education. This development cannot be secured by the study of children alone. It requires a searching study of society and its moving forces. That the traditional schools have almost wholly evaded consideration of the social potentialities of education is no reason why progressive schools should continue the evasion, even though it be sugared over with esthetic refinements. The time ought to come when no one will be judged to be an educated man or woman who does not have insight into the basic forces of industrial and urban civilization. Only schools which take the lead in bringing about this kind of education can claim to be progressive in any socially significant sense.

The Duties and Responsibilities of the Teaching Profession[1]

Among those who accept the principle of general objectives, there seems to be at the present time a general consensus as to the nature of these objectives. On the psychological or individual side, the aim is to secure a progressive development of capacities, having due regard to individual differences, and including a physical basis of vigorous health, refined esthetic taste and power to make a worthwhile use of leisure, ability to think independently and critically, together with command of the tools and processes that give access to the accumulated products of past cultures. On the social side, this personal development is to be such as will give desire and power to share in cooperative democratic living, including political citizenship, vocational efficiency and effective social goodwill. Disagreement seems to concern the relative emphasis to be given the different elements among these aims and the best means for attaining them, rather than the objectives themselves.

On the other hand, there is a marked tendency in other groups to discard all general objectives and to seek instead for specific aims. In this case, the latter are usually sought for in analysis of existing social occupations and institutions (present adult life in general). Their unstated general objective appears to be that education should prepare, by means of blue prints of society and the individual, students to fit efficiently into present life.

I. Under these circumstances, the first need is that the teaching profession as a body should consider the nature of the social function of the school. The question of general *versus* specific objectives goes back to the question of whether the schools should aim to fit individuals for the existing social order, or

1. Used as a basis for discussion at the meeting of the National Council of Education, June 28, 1930.

[First published in *School and Society* 32 (9 August 1930): 188–91.]

whether they have a responsibility for social planning. The latter objective clearly involves preparation of students to take part in changing society, and requires consideration of the defects and evils which need to be changed.

The first thesis or proposition is, accordingly, that apart from and prior to consideration of changes in actual school programs, curricula and methods, the teaching body, as a body, should arrive through discussion within itself at conclusions concerning the direction which the work of the school should take with respect to social conditions. Does this involve responsibility for planning and leadership or only for producing conformity?

II. As far as the conclusion points in the former direction, the question arises as to the handicaps and obstacles from which the American public school suffers in performing this function. (A) It is stated that social sentiment, especially that of influential interests, will not permit the discussion of controversial questions in the schools and is even opposed to the introduction of objective and impartial subject-matter relating to them. (B) It is also stated that teachers as a class are not equipped to take part intelligently in the discussion of such questions or to lead in consideration of them. My second proposition, accordingly, is that there should be a clearer idea obtained, through discussion within the teaching body, of the existing handicaps to the realization by the school of its social function. This would include the state of the teaching body, and the question of how far it may be better prepared for social participation and leadership, including both teachers in service and the changes which would be required in training schools. The discussion should involve attention to the problems of adult education and of how far there is at present a lack of harmony between the processes of child education and those of adult education, since the ideal of continuity of education implies that there should be consonance and not conflict.

III. There is the problem of how objectives should be determined and formulated. There is the tendency, illustrated perhaps by the present paper, to begin at the top and pass the formulations arrived at down through a series of intervening ranks until they are handed over to the classroom teacher. This procedure conflicts with the principle of democratic cooperation. It suggests the proposition that there is need that classroom teachers, who have immediate contact with pupils, should share to a much greater extent than they do at present in the determination of educational objectives as well as of processes and material.

These three main propositions may be rendered more concrete and definite by raising questions which are involved in them.

1. How far should the educational process be autonomous and how can it be made such in fact? Is it the duty of the schools to give indoctrination in the economic and political, including nationalistic principles that are current in contemporary society? Should criticism of the existing social order be permitted? If so, in what ways? Can pupils really be educated to take an effective part in social life if all controverted questions are excluded?

2. To what extent is it true that in spite of formulation of objectives by leaders, the educational system as a whole is goalless, so much so that there is no common and contagious enthusiasm in the teaching body, a condition due to lack of consciousness of its social possibilities? Do students go forth from the school without adequate consciousness of the problems and issues they will have to face? As far as it is true, can this state of affairs be remedied without a realization of responsibility for social planning on the part of the teaching body and administrators?

3. Can a vital professional spirit among teachers be developed unless there is (a) greater autonomy in education and (b) a greater degree of realization of the responsibility that devolves upon educators for the social knowledge and interest which will enable them to take part in social leadership?

4. It has been stated from high quarters that the individuality and freedom of the classroom teacher are lessening; that "the teacher is becoming more and more of a cog in a vast impersonal machine." How far is this statement correct? What are its causes and remedies? Is the work of administrators too far removed from that of teachers? What is the tendency of the present administration of standardized tests? Does it tend to fix the attention of classroom teachers upon uniformity of results and consequently produce mechanization of instruction? Does it foster a grading and division of pupils with respect to mastery of standardized and predetermined subject-matter at the expense of individual development? What tests and what method of their administration would tend to greater release of creative work on the part of teachers? How much of present administrative proce-

dures is based upon distrust of the intellectual capacities of class-room teachers? Can these capacities be increased without giving these teachers a greater degree of freedom?

5. Can the power of independent and critical thinking, said to be an objective, be attained when the field of thought is restricted by exclusion of whatever relates to controverted social questions? Can "transfer" of thinking habits be expected when thinking is restricted to technical questions such as arise when this social material is excluded?

6. What are the concrete handicaps to development of desire and ability for democratic social cooperation?—for this is also stated to be a cardinal objective. Can such questions as the relation of capital and labor, the history and aims of labor organization, causes and extent of unemployment, methods of taxation, the relation of government to redistribution of national income, cooperative *vs.* competitive society, etc., be considered in the school room? Similar questions arise in connection with family relations, prohibition, war and peace.

7. The principle is generally accepted that learning goes on most readily and efficiently when it grows out of actual experience and is connected with it. How far does this principle imply, logically and practically, that the structure of economic and political activities, which affect out of school experience, should receive systematic attention in school?

8. How far is the working purpose of present school work to prepare the individual for personal success? How far are competitive incentives relied upon? How far are these factors compatible with the professed objective of democratic cooperation?

9. How far can and should the schools deal with such questions as arise from racial color and class contact and prejudice? Should questions relating to Negroes, North American Indians, the new immigrant population, receive definite consideration? What should be the attitude of the schools to differences of cultural tradition and outlook in the schools? Should they aim to foster or to eliminate them? What can and should the schools do to promote greater friendliness and mutual understanding among the various groups in our population?

10. The same questions come up regarding our international relations. Does the teaching of patriotism tend toward antagonism toward other peoples? How far should the teaching of

American history be designed to promote "Americanism" at the expense of historical facts? Should definite questions of international relations, such as our relation to the Caribbean region, the use of force in intervention in financial and economic questions, our relation to the World Court, etc., be introduced?

These questions are suggested as means of making the three principles laid down more concrete in their meaning. They are tied together by certain convictions. First, the formulation of objectives, whether general or specific, tends to become formal, empty and even verbal, unless the latter are translated over into terms of actual school work. Secondly, the isolation of the school from life is the chief cause for both inefficiency and lack of vitality in the work of instruction and for failure to develop a more active professional spirit. Third, the closer connection of school with life can not be achieved without serious and continued attention by the teaching body to the obstacles and handicaps that lie in the way of forming such a connection. Fourth, it is necessary to enlist the entire educational corps, including the classroom teacher, in consideration of the social responsibilities of the school, especially with reference to the larger issues and problems of our time.

Underlying these convictions is a faith that the public will respond positively to the assumption by teachers of recognition of their social function; that much of the present adverse reaction of the public to free consideration of social questions is due to the failure of the teaching profession to claim actively and in an organized way its own autonomy.

Freedom in Workers' Education

Fellow members of the Teachers Union and Friends: I always have taken great pleasure in meeting with my fellow teachers and unionists, though I have not done it as much as I might or as I should. But none the less, it has been a pleasure to meet with men and women who believe in combination, in union and in organization to support actively the common cause; to unite for work, and not merely to engage in academic discussion. It has always been a pleasure to associate with those men and women in any way who feel that backbone was made to function and was not merely an anatomical peculiarity. It is a source of gratification to me that the Teachers Union has been associated with the labor movement in general.

Now I have to admit that I do not come here this evening with the sense of pleasure with which I generally come to these meetings. There is some satisfaction, there is some joy, in a straight out fight when you feel your cause is right and you are attacking an enemy. But there is no pleasure in attacking those with whom you are associated as friends. There can indeed be no question of attacking here, but rather a feeling of great regret. For we feel that these friends in our common cause, the Executive Council of the A. F. of L., have taken action that is very much like betraying the ideals for which we have all been fighting in common.

You have heard the story of the incident at Brookwood. I am not going over that again. I have seen pretty much, I think, copies of all the correspondence that has passed, and I know that Mr. Muste has not only given a fair and straightforward but an impartial account of the episode. Those of you who knew him

(Address delivered at meeting under auspices of Local 5, American Federation of Teachers to discuss the action of the American Federation of Labor on Brookwood. New York, November 9, 1928.)

[First published in *American Teacher* 13 (January 1929): 1–4.]

and his work before would not need such assurance; and those who have heard him tonight, need no assurance that he would be absolutely honest and straightforward in his account of what has taken place. It is not then of that particular incident I wish to speak, but of one phase of it, namely what is known as academic freedom and the relation of this episode to it, and the relation of the Teachers Union and the American Federation of Labor, to this issue of academic freedom.

I don't like the phrase academic freedom because there really is nothing academic about freedom. Freedom of mind, freedom of thought, freedom of inquiry, freedom of discussion is education, and there is no education, no real education, without these elements of freedom. An attack upon what is called academic freedom is an attack upon intellectual integrity, and hence it is an attack upon the very idea of education and upon the possibility of education realizing its purpose.

You can have training without mental freedom but you cannot get education. As the advertisement used to say, you can teach a parrot to say a substitute is just as good, but the parrot does not know what he is talking about. That is the difference between training and education. Education is an awakening and movement of the mind. To take hold actively of any matters with which it comes in contact, to be able to deal with them in a free, honest and straight-forward manner is the condition under which the mind grows, develops.

Now it is obvious that that is the spirit in which Brookwood has been conducted, from what you have heard from Mr. Muste tonight, from the letter from which he read (and if you read other letters from the graduates) you would get, I am sure, exactly the same idea. Now it seems to me that it shows loyalty to the labor movement, to the cause of the workers, to the cause of the organization of workers, when a school really believes that their interests are going to be furthered, advanced, not set back and retarded by any full and honest discussion. I should be suspicious of my loyalty to any cause if I caught myself thinking that the interests of that cause could best be furthered by suppression, by one sided presentation, by deliberate efforts to indoctrinate pupils with certain views that prevent their own minds from engaging freely in the subject under discussion. What I am saying is a commonplace. Any person who believes really in the labor movement as an organized movement must believe that it has nothing to lose and that it has everything to gain by full and free discussion, and by conducting its whole educational movement in that spirit.

As a person who has taught a great many years, I should feel very happy to receive such a letter. If I had a student here this evening who could testify that he had had this awakening of his mind, this power to think, this power to be useful because he had been taught to face facts and to face them regardless of the consequences, I should feel that I had received a genuine testimony, the highest testimony that could be given to an educator.

Those of us who have allied ourselves with the labor movement in the Teachers Union, and who have stood for it, have done so, I think, in considerable measure because we knew that our schools, public institutions and private, are not as free in their teaching as they should be; that the atmosphere which these schools breathe, the spirit which permeates them, have not that degree and quality of intellectual freedom that they should have. We have thought that by organization, by union, we could do something to discourage, and in the end, if we could get enough teachers to combine, to defeat those forces that have an interest, a political, and economic interest, in the suppression of freedom of investigation and discussion in the schools. Now as I have said, personally I have found it discouraging and depressing that the officials (I do not think for a moment the great body of organized labor, but certain officials of organized labor) should take a stand which seems to ally them with the forces which we teachers know are and have been the enemies of the cause of freedom, a cause so fundamental in the development of education itself.

I want to make these remarks a little more concrete by reading from an editorial that appeared last month on workers' education in the *American Federationist*. There is no allusion made to this Brookwood incident; the name of the school or anything connected with it does not appear. Possibly it was a mere coincidence that the editorial comes out at this time. Also it is conceivable that it is not a coincidence.

Speaking of recent experience in workers' education, the editorial contends: "These past six years have shown us that our educational needs are of two distinct kinds: study to make the union and union activity more effective, and a desire for those educational opportunities that will enable wage-earners to participate in cultural life equally with other groups." In commenting upon the second of these needs, "desire for those educational opportunities that will enable wage-earners to participate in cultural life equally with other groups," the editorial says:

> In the United States we have put our faith in the public school system, including the state university, for service to the majority of the people. We believe that this system of publicly controlled education, together with public libraries, is capable of expansion to meet the developing needs of adult education for all groups of citizens. We believe that all groups concerned should be represented on boards controlling these institutions. Such democratic school control is the best guarantee possible against propaganda in public school teaching. The trade union movement is irrevocably against propaganda in public schools, for we realize that if the sources of information are perverted, there is no hope of finding truths. On the other hand, organizations for the furtherance of causes and denominational teaching should have the right to teach lawful doctrines in schools which they control. It is in the interest of truth, however, that such schools should be fittingly designated . . . Experience has demonstrated the wisdom of careful provisions for control of trade-union education by trade-unionists. When the American Federation of Labor decides an issue in trade-union education, it is passing upon a trade-union matter which has nothing at all to do with academic freedom.

Now, if I get the meaning of what I have read to you, especially in connection with the coincidence of its appearance at this particular time, there are two elements. One is that the cultural interest of workers, wage earners, laborers, can be met by our regular school system. On the other hand, labor schools are designed to make unions and union activity more effective, and these schools should then be controlled by trade unionists themselves, and this control involves no question of academic freedom at all.

Now I have two remarks to make upon the issue as thus presented. That our system of publicly controlled education is *capa-*

ble of expansion to meet the developing needs of adult education for all groups of citizens, I do not doubt, but I should want to put a great deal of emphasis on the word capable. If anyone tells me that it is now so expanded I take the liberty, after nearly fifty years of teaching, to doubt. Since the system has not yet reached this expansion which is desired there is need for a certain type of workers' school which shall lead the way, shall be the pioneer, show the other schools what they might do. And I am very glad to pay my respects to the work Brookwood School has done precisely in blazing the way as a pioneer, so as to show exactly what expansion our other schools are capable of and should undertake; and to indicate something of the road that leads to this very desirable expansion of activity. We know, Mr. Muste has referred to it, everybody has heard something about the effort of the big power trusts to control education both in public and private schools. We know that the instructions that went out to the publicity agents were to get hold of two things specially, the press and the schools. We know that they have prepared and colored and censored textbooks which have been used in the schools. Their records have boasted of the number of schools, including high schools, in the United States that they have brought under their control. They have hired teachers, professors, and subsidized them to give certain forms of teaching, perhaps not directly in their class but at lectures, clubs and other places outside their classes; to give opinions contrary to public ownership of utilities. We know that they are on record as stating that it would be wise to give a retainer to a great many teachers whose salaries are not very adequate and to whom fifty and a hundred dollars would look pretty good. That is on the record as coming from one of these companies.

Now I submit in all fairness and with all the sincerity I am capable of that the officers of the American Federation of Labor would be doing very much more for education and the workers' cause to be attacking these people that are poisoning the sources of information than to engage in this indirect attack upon Brookwood College because they do not think its teachings sufficiently subservient to the wishes and policies, not of the workers' unions, but of the administration officials.

There is one other thing in the editorial referred to. "We believe that all groups concerned should be represented on boards controlling these institutions." I wish to express my hearty agreement. I wish the American Federation of Labor could make labor in general see to it that there are representatives of labor as such both as trustees in private institutions and on boards of the public schools, since practically every other group is represented in predominant numbers. I have nothing to say against that and I wish to express my hearty agreement. But in order that that ideal may be carried out there must be men educated in the labor movement in precisely this broad, free and generous way which the Brookwood School stands for. Merely to have a mouthpiece of some particular interest, to take dictation and pursue some narrow interest of that particular group would only be adding to a situation of which we have altogether too much in our school system at the present time. I know of no way in which this very desirable idea of having all groups, including labor groups, better represented on the governing board of the schools of the country can be carried out except by fostering instead of retarding the kind of work the Brookwood School is committed to.

Now take another point. I wonder what it means. I wish the writer had been a little more explicit. I feel a little more like using the language about this that I heard Smith use in the campaign. I wish that a certain gentleman would clear up his language when he says that "organizations for the furtherance of causes and denominational teaching should have the right to teach lawful doctrines in schools which they control. It is in the interest of truth, however, that such schools should be fittingly designated," and then goes on to say that the labor unions should control the labor schools. Now what I wonder is, do they really want labor schools which trade unions support to be of this narrow denominational, indoctrinating type? If they do, why I for one must take issue with them. I think the labor cause is worthy of something better than that and that it is served in a more dignified and more capable way by taking a broader point of view than is suggested by that phrase.

Finally, however, if we are again to insist on the control of trade union schools by trade unions, I would like to suggest that the Teachers Union is a part of the labor movement, that its members are trade unionists, and that I cannot think of anything more appropriate than that the Teachers Union should be consulted when it is a question of the fitness, the competency, and consequences of the kind of education which is given by a labor school. I do not wish to use strong language or anything that would in any way add to the difficulties of this situation, but I must say that I feel as if we teachers who have joined the Teachers Union have received a very distinct rebuff when action of this kind is taken without any consultation with any committee, without any conference, without asking us to look into the matter or asking us in any way what our opinion is about it all. Do they want us in the movement? Are we, as I had hoped we were and might come to be more and more, a really organic part of the labor movement?

Labor Politics and Labor Education

The recent condemnation of the Brookwood Labor College by the American Federation of Labor brings to the foreground the question of the future of adult education in connection with the labor movement. The issue is rendered especially acute because of the way in which the condemnation was effected; it was a scholastic lynching. Methods were employed which are not tolerated today in so-called "capitalistic" private institutions, where accused persons are entitled to a hearing before condemnation can ensue. This phase of the matter has received attention in the press, but the extent to which the future of workers' education in this country is involved has not had corresponding publicity. Nor has the bearing of the Brookwood incident upon the prospects of organized labor itself under its present political management come to the notice of any large part of the public. A brief résumé of the leading facts, preliminary to a statement of these two larger aspects of the matter, is accordingly in place.

Early in August, the Executive Council of the American Federation of Labor issued a resolution calling upon labor unions to cease support of the Brookwood school. The charges made against it were that it had strongly communistic sympathies and, presumably, affiliations; that disloyalty to the American Federation of Labor was inculcated among its students; that "sex" occupied a large place in its teachings, and that religion was freely criticized and anti-religious views promulgated. The action was taken without any investigation of the school; without submitting charges to the faculty and students, and without giving opportunity for a reply. Protests naturally followed the action of

[First published in *New Republic* 57 (9 January 1929): 211–14. For reply by Matthew Woll and Dewey's rejoinder, see this volume, pp. 387, 389. For reply by Daniel Chase and letter by Dewey, see pp. 390, 392.]

the Executive Council, from members of the school, and from many others, both "intellectuals" and working members and officers in unions belonging to the American Federation of Labor, many of the latter being graduates of the College.

The answers received by those who protested were to the effect that the Executive Council had acted upon satisfactory evidence. But there was still no publication of the evidence and no responsible indication of its source, beyond the statement that it came from former students at Brookwood itself. No hearing was granted the faculty of the school nor its directors, all of them good labor unionists. The action of the New Orleans convention in refusing to return the resolution to the Executive Council was the logical outcome of the course previously followed. The Council had taken steps which made contrary action possible only if the delegates were ready to declare war on the official management of the Federation. Under the circumstances, it is almost surprising that as many as one-fourth of the delegates were not in favor of confirmation. Meantime, while communist organs were adding a note of humor by denouncing the College as a bourgeois "cloak for the reactionary labor fakers," organs of the American Federation of Labor's inner machine were replying to the charge of violation of academic freedom and failure to give a hearing, by asserting that since the College was not under the Federation, the issue was in no way involved. To the protests of the teachers' unions affiliated with the Federation (the members of the faculty being themselves one of the local unions), which were not in any way consulted or heard, these same organs replied that since the College was not under the Federation, there was no question of jurisdiction involved, and they even went so far as to state that while it was the duty of the Council to warn the unions against the subversive conduct of the school, it would have been outside of its jurisdiction to subject the faculty of the school to a trial such as would be involved in giving them a hearing!

These are the bare external facts. While the "evidence" was not submitted, it became clear in the course of discussion that it consisted of letters from five former members of the school; there was no difficulty in identifying the five, although their names, in accordance with the arbitrary star-chamber nature of the whole proceeding, remained officially anonymous. It is significant that although the school has been in existence about seven years, the five in question were all at the College at the same time, last year, and had formed a notoriously disaffected clique. Without going into personalities, it may be asserted that an investigation would have revealed that each person had what he thought was a personal grievance. Anybody who knows anything about schools and students is aware that five out of a total hundred and twenty-five students, present and past, is a small number to become disgruntled. The number is more significant, because of the hearty denial of the insinuations and charges that came from the rest of the graduates and from the present student body. The graduate of the College who led the opposition on the floor of the New Orleans convention, himself a vice-president of the Massachusetts Federation, had previously put in writing a strong endorsement of the educational policies of the school, ending by saying that "it increased his devotion and loyalty to the labor movement." Each item of the official indictment was specifically contradicted by students. It is also worth noting that the College has the unusual provision of special and officially recognized periods at which the policies and teachings of the school are freely discussed and criticized.

Even this mere summary must raise the question: What is back of such conduct? What does it portend for the future of workers' education and for the present and prospective organized labor movement under the tutelage of the inclusive Mr. Woll?

A few words first regarding the educational spirit of Brookwood. The official statement of the College is that it "aims to train active members of labor organizations for more intelligent and efficient service to their organizations." Only persons recommended by labor organizations are admitted as students. The testimony of all but the five disgruntled persons is to the effect that it achieves this end. There is and has been no concealment that the College stands for liberal ideas and ideals. Part of the same official statement says that Brookwood thinks of the labor movement as "having for its ultimate goal the good life for all men in a social order free from exploitation and based upon control by the workers." Its prospectus also says that it endeavors "to teach students how to think, not to tell them what to think." In accordance with this principle, free discussion is encouraged.

The College, more than most educational institutions of whatever sort, has been truly educational in living up to its effort to lead students to think—which means, of course, to think for themselves. The action of the American Federation of Labor's administrative machine, in itself and in its mode of execution, is a warning that it does not want this sort of education; it regards it as a danger and menace. This is the issue upon the educational side. One of the damning indictments brought by representatives of the machine at New Orleans was precisely a quotation of a statement to the same effect as that cited above regarding the ultimate ideal and goal of the labor movement as a social force. It is no wonder that fraternal representatives of the British labor movement at New Orleans heard with amazement what is the official policy of the British Labor party not only disavowed, but used as a final condemnation of a workers' school.

What about the official management of organized labor when it openly repudiates a system of free education aiming to teach labor leaders to think independently, rather than to repeat officially stamped stereotypes? What is the nature of a management that finds such a method a menace to it? This brings us to the other side of the picture. Mr. Matthew Woll has been the leading spirit in the whole affair. Who and what is he?

He is President of the Photo-Engravers Union, Vice-President of the American Federation of Labor, and member of its Executive Council; Secretary of the Committee on International Labor Relations; Chairman of the Committee on Resolutions and of the permanent Committee on Education; President of the International Labor Press, which, through the medium of the International Labor News Service, controls the labor news that reaches the public (that the "labor editors" of metropolitan dailies find it useful to stand in with the administrative machine of the American Federation of Labor will be easily understood); Director of the Legal Bureau of the Federation; President of the International Sportsmanship Brotherhood—an organization to cooperate with the "welfare" departments of large employers, and President of the Union Labor Life Insurance Company, the organization through which organized labor has entered the insurance field. The record indicates that Mr. Woll is an able and energetic man as well as a busy one. He has the main strings of administration gathered in his hands. The record is incomplete, however, until the most significant fact of all is added, namely, that he is Acting President of the National Civic Federation.

It would require much more than the space which this article can occupy to record the attitude of the Civic Federation toward labor. If the reader is not in a position to take "judicial notice" of it, it may be asserted that examination of its history, capable of documented proof, exhibits constant antagonism to the aims of aggressive unionism. It is significant of the consistent spirit of its conduct that Mark Hanna wrote a letter in which he said that he desired no better monument than the fact that he was chosen as the first president of the Civic Federation.

There is no evidence that Mr. Woll has used his position to alter the policies of the National Civic Federation toward organized labor. On the contrary, he has subtly employed his dual official position to cramp or paralyze action on the part of the Federation of Labor that is not in line with the policies of the Civic Federation. Positive confirmation, aside from the negative evidence of total absence of protest, is found in the history of old-age pensions, state and federal, an idea actively sponsored by the American Federation of Labor, when it had the militant leadership of Gompers, but skillfully side-tracked in the consulship of Woll.[1] Equally significant is the fact that he is a member of a commission of the Civic Federation, on Industrial Inquiry, and Chairman of one of its sub-committees, the avowed purpose of which is to find a *modus vivendi* between employers having company unions and the regular labor unions. Considering that organized labor in general regards company unions as its most serious present foe, this fact speaks for itself.

It is not surprising that Mr. Woll's influence in the American Federation of Labor is regarded with great favor by reactionary economic persons, or that the American Federation of Labor, so far as it has come under the control of his dominating administrative machine, is no longer cursed as revolutionary and subversive, but is blessed as a constructive, safe and patriotic organi-

---

1. The policy of the Civic Federation is to foster industrial pensions under employers themselves—a policy once denounced by the A. F. of L., but now brought to the fore because of the opposition of Woll to the Gompers policy. He also uses the Life Insurance Company of which he is president to weaken the idea of state old-age pensions.

zation. Nor is it surprising that the minority in the American Federation of Labor that retains allegiance to former aggressive policies is becoming restive, and is asking to whom Mr. Woll gives his loyalty, to the employers' associations and their financial allies, which dominate the Civic Federation, or to organized labor, and whether the policy of Mr. Woll is not to paralyze the workers' movement by turning the American Federation of Labor into an adjunct of the policies of the Civic Federation.

Incidentally, a dubious significance is attached to Mr. Woll's affiliations because of his activity in suppressing a resolution of censure of the activities of the Chicago Institute for Research in Land Economics and Public Utilities, introduced by Chicago labor delegates because of evidence that the Institute was supported by speculative real-estate interests and public utilities and was working in their behalf. That Mr. Woll is not incapable of irony upon occasion is seen in the fact that he appealed to the principle of free speech and academic freedom as ground for exempting the Institute from unfavorable notice by the Federation! He also ran true to form in softening the resolution of censure of the propaganda activities of the light and power trust in schools and colleges, by deleting specific reference to "power interests" and substituting the more innocuous word "special interests."

Possibly there are persons who will regard the state of affairs described (only in small part) as of no great importance to others than the Federation of Labor itself. If the Federation likes that sort of thing, that is the sort of thing it likes, will be the cynical comment. But those who believe that organized labor should be a great force in social reconstruction will feel differently. Personally, I believe that, provided there is intelligent leadership, it contains factors of fundamental importance in bringing about a better social order. That Mr. Woll's status is a force in politics is revealed in the fact that, although the Federation of Labor has previously endorsed some presidential candidates, he was an active factor in securing refusal of endorsement to Governor Smith in the last campaign, in spite of the fact that most persons regard the latter as the best friend labor has had in high political office. Perhaps Mr. Woll, as well as Mr. Hoover, regarded Governor Smith as a Socialist—an opinion no more silly than the charges of Communism he brings so freely against any persons opposed to the domination of labor by his administrative machine. In any case, the facts cited are relevant to the inert character of the present labor movement and to the charges brought against a Labor College guilty of believing that an educational movement should train leaders who think independently and should thereby help in ushering in a social order free from exploitation.

In connection with the educational phase of the matter, it is significant that the motion of condemnation of Brookwood was sponsored at New Orleans by Mr. Mahon, President of the Street Railway Employees' Union. Mr. Mahon is the man who, in behalf of that union, signed an agreement with Mr. Mitten which guaranteed immunity to the company unions of the Philadelphia traction interests controlled by that gentleman. The *quid pro quo* was that Mr. Mitten would not oppose regular unions in any further traction developments in other cities in which he had a controlling voice, provided those unions adopted the standards already in force in Mr. Mitten's company unions. It happens that Mr. Muste, the head of Brookwood, had incurred the antagonism of Mr. Mahon by public criticism of the policy involved in the agreement. Another point of educational import is the influential position occupied by Mr. Woll as chairman of the Education Committee of the American Federation of Labor, its only permanent committee. He is now engaged in gathering under his brooding wings the Workers' Education Bureau, having introduced a resolution that this Bureau have a board of directors entirely elected by the American Federation of Labor and international unions. At present three out of eleven are approved by the Executive Council of the American Federation of Labor. Even more important is the fact that the resolution, if and when adopted, would deprive state and city federations, local unions and district councils, together with labor schools and colleges, from representation. If he succeeds in getting this measure through the next convention of the Workers' Bureau (an organization formed by liberal labor elements independently of the American Federation of Labor), he can congratulate himself that labor education has been made safe for the political machine of the Federation which he so skillfully conducts. At present, some of the labor schools are conducted by men who are Brookwood graduates. The condemnation of Brookwood is a warning to them that they may be next in line. Will Mr. Woll's next step be to discipline them? Any activities of his in this direction will be worthy of attention.

It cannot be too generally understood that the condemnation of Brookwood is no isolated event. It is a part of the policy to eliminate from the labor movement the schools and influences that endeavor to develop independent leaders of organized labor who are interested in a less passive and a more social policy than that now carried on by the American Federation of Labor in its close alliance with the National Civic Federation. Opposition to the official political machine of the former is to be interpreted as enmity to organized labor itself; that any opposition is ascribed to Bolshevist sympathies is in line with the resort to cheap epithets currently employed to discredit any liberal movement. What will become of the organized labor movement in case such policies continue to grow? This issue as it affects education and the future of labor in this country is the real issue involved in the Brookwood incident.

What Do Liberals Want?

There is a natural bond of cohesion among conservatives and reactionaries. They hold together not so much by ideas as by habit, tradition, fear of the unknown and a desire to hang on to what they already have. And their "having" consists of beliefs as well as possessions. The old and true saying that the Tory party was stupid did not mean, I suppose, that individually the members of the Tory party were stupider than their opponents, but that as a Party they had no especial need of ideas. They only needed policies and these were defined by maintenance of the *status quo*.

Liberals, on the other hand, are notoriously hard to organize. They must depend upon ideas rather than upon established habits of belief; and when persons begin to think upon social matters they begin to vary. For ideas, by their nature, are variants. To put it in an exaggerated way, they are kickers; and kicking does not lead to unity. There always has been a body of sentiment in this country that may be called progressive and there is an immense amount of social sympathy for the underdogs of our economic life. Such sentiment and sympathy have been the basis of repeated sporadic political movements. But feeling furnishes only a temporary bond of unity. For thirty years, at least, the story of liberal political movements in this country is one of temporary enthusiasms and then steady decline. If liberals are "tired," it is chiefly because they have not had the support and invigoration that comes from working shoulder to shoulder in a unified common movement. They are discouraged by differences within their own ranks quite as much as by the entrenched force of the interests against which they are working.

[First published in *Outlook and Independent* 153 (16 October 1929): 261.]

Nevertheless, there exists even now a very general realization that our present political situation is absurdly unreal. The wider one's political contacts, the more one is aware of the widespread consciousness that the existing alignment of parties signifies nothing real. The witty story of the Englishman who asked an American about our two major parties would awaken almost universal response. He was told that they were two bottles of similar shape and size, with different labels—and both empty. At the same time, the sentiment for which there is no other name than progressive is not dead nor is it even sleeping. But its very diffusion under present conditions renders it impotent. It is unorganized.

Put the two facts together. On the one hand there is the very general discontent with the present alignment of parties, the general sentiment that a large mass of people do not have a square deal economically, and that equal opportunity is by and large a myth; as is prosperity in which wealth and control of finance, credit and industry are in the hands of a small per cent of the community. On the other hand there is the tragic failure of past attempts at political organization of a truly liberal policy. What do these facts indicate as to the way out?

To my mind there is but one answer. Past movements have failed because they were the expression of temporary sentiment and because their bond of union was so largely negative. There was plenty of discontent with existing conditions, but there was a shortage of constructive ideas and policies into which enough people had been educated so as to form a common and deeply shared faith. The hope of the future resides therefore in two things. First and foremost in a campaign of steady and continuous organization which shall effect contact and unity among the now scattered and largely inarticulate liberal persons and groups in our country. Secondly, as in part a means for this organized acquaintance and contact and in still greater part as a product of it, the development of a unifying body of principles and policies adapted to present conditions, one which will bring that sense of reality into present politics which is now absent.

The public press of September ninth carried a notice of the formation of the League for Independent Political Action. The announcement was so worded as to give the impression that a new political party was being launched. A truer statement would be that it is desired to encourage and assist the ultimate formation of a new political party. The movement is an attempt to fulfill the conditions just stated. The League intends to discover and to cooperate with liberal groups and individuals throughout the country; to bring them into conscious contact with one another and to promote that sense of solidarity among them which is the condition of further effective political action. In being a clearing house for liberal sentiment and ideas, it will also carry on the work of research and of education in order to build up that body of positive and constructive political policies which can alone give unity and endurance to a progressive party movement.

A body of principles is necessary to initiate a bringing together of elements now scattered and divided, and they have been tentatively formulated. Obviously, in order to be in contact with present realities, they deal mainly with the economic facts which present major parties so conspicuously ignore. While the time may not be ripe for launching a new party, it is more than ripe for those who are not content with the present economic and political situation to get together and confer upon what they want and thus develop that body of positive ideas and proposals upon which the next forward movement of American politics must be based. The League offers itself as a centre for such unification, ready to pass into action as rapidly as conditions permit.

Apostles of World Unity:
XVII—Salmon O. Levinson

The Briand-Kellogg Pact has brought into the domain of practical international politics an idea that had its birth something over ten years ago in the mind of a Chicago lawyer, Mr. Levinson, whose name heads this article. With a legal education and a lawyer's experience, he was led by the outbreak and conduct of the Great War, long before our own entrance into it, to raise the question of the status of war. Reports of violations of the laws of war, the constant recriminations that marked the course of the war; charges of use of illegal ammunitions, poison gas, cruelty to prisoners, violations of rights of neutrals, the unlawful use of submarines, are a few of the many charges that even a hazy memory will recall. From questions regarding rules *of* war, Mr. Levinson was led on to ask about the standing of war itself before the law.

The result amazed him. Out of that surprise, emerged the idea of outlawry of war. For his investigations showed what hardly anyone before him had faced intellectually and morally; namely, that war is a legally authorized mode of settlement of disputes between nations; indeed, that in serious controversies it is in a legal, not merely a rhetorical sense, *the* authorized court of last resort. The result was amazing, since our popular opinion has been that there is something anomalous, something contrary to the very idea of law, in recourse to armed force. Investigation and reflection convinced Mr. Levinson that in this acknowledged legal status of war lies the key to the problem of war and peace; that, as long as war itself is the legally established and sanctioned method of settling disputes, it is idle to try to mitigate the evils of war by laws for carrying on warfare; that the object

[First published in *World Unity Magazine* 4 (May 1929): 98–103, as part of a series.]

of war is to win and that the record of war is the history of recourse to more and more concentrated and destructive means in
order to win—and thus *legally* settle the dispute; submarines
and poison gas are merely the latest steps in the history, doubtless to be followed by other agencies still more destructive.
Moreover, he was led to conclude that the legal status of the war
is the fact that ultimately rendered nugatory efforts at disarma-
ment, and brought to nought the activities of peace organizations. When the United States entered the war, the intense interest that had previously developed in Mr. Levinson's mind in the
problem of war, was rendered more acute by the fact that his
own sons, two in number, were active participants in it.

It was Mr. Levinson's discovery of the legal status of war and
of the implications and consequences of this status that gave—
and still give—meaning to the phrase about which Mr. Levinson
henceforth centered his campaign—the *Outlawry of War*. Among
earlier writers, whom Mr. Levinson consulted, Charles Sumner
was practically the only one who appeared to realize the force of
the fact that war has itself a definite and, in crucial cases, a supreme legal status. It is perhaps not surprising, accordingly, that
so many persons misunderstood the phrase and the idea for
which it stands; there are still many who are too impatient, too
lazy, or too partisan to give thought to the background that confers meaning and pertinency upon the phrase. So they ridiculed
it or made light of it by distorting it, treating it as if it meant the
passing of a statute on paper against war, instead of realizing
that it meant an agreement among nations to deprive war of its
legalized status as a means of settling disputes that arise between
them. Mr. Levinson as a lawyer, and especially as a lawyer whose
business consisted largely in settling troubles that grow out of
threatened or actual economic breakdowns of great industrial
companies, realized that abolition of the legal status of war
would make necessary the institution of other and peaceful means
of settlement, while as long as war has a legal status any strong
nation will have recourse to it, without regarding itself or being
regarded before the bar of history as criminally blameworthy.

It would be interesting to know how many persons Mr. Levinson conversed with on the subject; to how many persons and to
whom he presented his discovery and his project of an alternative. There were scores of such persons, lawyers, politicians,

publicists, clergymen, bankers, men of affairs. It was through the give-and-take of this prolonged personal discussion that the idea grew and assumed form. There were certain stock objections, reactions that were practically conventionalized and standardized. These were due to the novelty of the idea and failure to take time enough to grasp it. They were soon learned and were comparatively easily disposed of; but even through them the edges of the project got sharpened. Others cut deeper and sent Mr. Levinson back to further investigations and reflections; and in this way the idea took on further shape; unnecessary features, excrescences, were eliminated; essential features strengthened and made central; gradually the idea rounded out into symmetrical and finished form. I doubt if any idea of social and political importance has gone through such a severe process of testing and winnowing by discussion with a large number of able minds of different points of view and interests as did the conception of Outlawry after it dawned upon Mr. Levinson. It was conceived in his own brain, but it grew and took on final form not in a closet but in the forum of intense, continued and wide-spread mutual discussion. When he met a new objection, Mr. Levinson was neither discouraged nor did he resort to the method of debate for the sake of an appearance of victory. He took the difficulty home with him, and thought about it until he had thought it through and found its solution.

If I emphasize these years of incubation, the period of say from 1917 until 1921 or so, it is because the work done in those years was so earnest and so complete, that after that period the task was not that of development of the idea but of presenting it to others and winning their assent. Among those to whom Mr. Levinson feels most indebted for assistance in clarifying the idea are two men, now gone, President Eliot and Senator Knox. The former was not, however, in full sympathy; he was active in the League to Enforce Peace and that point operated to keep their thoughts apart. But President Eliot gave the idea a sympathetic hearing, and through this contact Mr. Levinson was led to consider thoroughly and finally the meaning of "sanctions" and the use of force, and to realize that in ultimate analysis dependence upon them means recourse to war; and hence involves the notion that war can be eliminated by means of war—a notion the futility of which the fate of the War to end War was already demonstrating.

Because of the train of reflections thus induced, Mr. Levinson was led to modify his first statement of his idea. This was contained in an article entitled "The Legal Status of War," and was published in the *New Republic* on March 9, 1918 [*Middle Works* 11:388–92]. Up to the time at which the nature of the Treaty of Versailles became evident, Mr. Levinson had been one of the strongest supporters of the Wilsonian idea of the League of Nations. The linking of the League with the injustices of the Treaty and even more its frank avowal of reliance upon combined and concerted war, that is, its continuation of the notion of the legal status of war as a means for settling disputes, repelled Mr. Levinson. This repulsion was natural and logical. For otherwise he would have been obliged to surrender the very idea of Outlawry; and this idea provided, he was more and more convinced, the only sure way in which first to focus attention upon the necessity of peaceful means of adjustment, and then to bring nations to the point of using peaceful methods. From this conviction Mr. Levinson has never wavered. It was in this connection that he came in contact with Senator Knox; in interviews with the latter in February, 1919, he made his first distinguished political convert to the idea so that in March of the same year the idea was first presented to any parliamentary body in a speech by Mr. Knox before the United States Senate. The same idea was further elaborated and presented by Knox in a speech in the Senate in May, 1920. In the meantime, Senator Borah had also become interested, and both he and Knox stimulated Mr. Levinson to further thought upon the problem of sanctions by force, and the result was in 1925 the publication of an article: "Can Peace Be Enforced?" In February, 1923, Senator Borah offered in the Senate a resolution to outlaw war in which the whole plan was succinctly outlined, including the project of a codification of international law and a supreme court of the world having positive and affirmative jurisdiction in all disputes that might lead to war, and not settled by diplomacy, conciliation or other means.

After these years, as has been already said, the work was one of publicity and persuasion. As a private citizen, Mr. Levinson founded in Chicago and himself financed *The American Committee for the Outlawry of War*. He is still, fortunately, with us, and would be offended by effusive praise. But I cannot refrain from saying that his constant, intense and unremitting work,

with the expenditure of the time as well as money of a busy lawyer, shows that peace has not only its victories but its gallant
adventures. Patiently and persistently, undeterred by ridicule, indifference and active opposition, Mr. Levinson carried on his
campaign of education. It was not exactly a one-man campaign,
because in addition to those already referred to, Mr. Raymond
Robins, John Haynes Holmes, Judge Florence Allen and Dr. C. C.
Morrison did a remarkable service, while the present writer occasionally contributed. But Mr. Levinson was the centre and
heart of the campaign. In pursuit of its purpose, he went to
Europe in the spring of 1927; and established an office in London under the able direction of Mr. Harrison Brown. He met
a large number of publicists, journalists and statesmen on the
trip; meeting also the diplomats of the Foreign Offices. That in
Paris at the Quai d'Orsay was especially fruitful. There he met
M. Léger, who is close to Briand, and explained to him the idea
of Outlawry. The proposal of Briand to Secretary Kellogg for an
Outlawry Treaty between France and the United States, which
had previously been sent to Washington, can be directly traced to
the ideas promulgated by Mr. Levinson. The interviews with the
French Foreign Office became a connecting link in conversations
with Senator Borah and Secretary Kellogg upon Mr. Levinson's
return to this country. With Mr. Borah as the Chairman of the
Foreign Relations Committee of the Senate and Mr. Kellogg as
the Secretary of State, the strategic positions were won. In consequence the multilateral Pact was prepared, our State Department
having resolutely refused to consider the introduction of coercive sanctions, arguing along the lines previously laid down by
Mr. Levinson.

But it is safe to assert that never in the history of mankind has
such a simple, fundamental idea made the progress in such a
short length of time as has the Outlawry idea. It is no diminution
of the credit that belongs to the statesmen concerned, Kellogg,
Briand and Borah, to say that the initiation of the idea together
with the promotion and publicity that found their fitting climax
in the preparation of the Pact and its signature by over sixty of
the leading nations of the world, came from a private citizen in
Chicago, who was without the backing of official position and
without that of any large organization. By his own intelligence,
courage, energy and devotion to the cause of peace among na-

tions, he has forced the idea upon the attention of the world. The record is so inspiring that any words I could say could only dim the luster of the event itself. I cannot close without adding that no one is more aware than Mr. Levinson himself that the campaign is only begun. The preliminary step has been taken with the ratification of the Pact. The task of discovering and instituting the means for making a working reality out of the idea remains to be accomplished, while the pledge of the nations is a pledge of its final achievement, the codification of a new code of international law, congruous with the fact of Outlawry, and the institution of the Supreme Court of the nations of the world are the great tasks of the future. I risk nothing in predicting that as long as his life is spared, Mr. Levinson will bring to their accomplishment the same disinterested zeal, persistence, and vigorous thought that has been crowned with victory in the space of the eleven last short years.

Religion in the Soviet Union:
II—An Interpretation of the Conflict

"Religion is the opium of the people." No phrase is more widely inscribed on the walls of public buildings in Soviet Russia than this. None is more widely associated abroad with the Soviet régime. In Russia the saying is attributed to Lenin. As a matter of fact, Karl Marx was its author, and Lenin took it from Marx, along with so many other of his doctrines. In the same passage in which Marx wrote this sentence he also said: "Destroy the social world of which religion is the spiritual aroma and you destroy religion. . . . Religion is the flower that covers the chains. Destroy the flowers and the chains will be seen." Marx derived his ideas about religion mainly from Feuerbach and the Left Wing of the Hegelian school. He was not an embodied doctrine of pure thought; he was a man of his age, subject to its intellectual currents. It was easy and natural, however, to regard his economic and his theological views as inseparable parts of one and the same system of socialistic thought, although as matter of fact they simply happened to coincide in the thinking of one man.

However, the political and economic status of the Greek Church in the Holy Russia of the Czars gave a peculiar timeliness and force to the union of socialism in economics and atheism in religion. Official and institutional religion was actually one with a despotic economic and political régime. The Czar was the head of the Church, as well as of the State. All the Orthodox churches were supported by the State; and in return the Church, both collectively and through its particular congregations, gave the blessing and sanction of religion to the autocratic State and its rulers. Russia was a theocracy; opposition to the Czar was a religious crime as well as political treason. Nowhere in the mod-

[First published in *Current History* 32 (April 1930): 31–36, as part two of a symposium.]

ern world, not even in old Mexico at its height, was the union of institutional religion and the established political and economic régime as close as in Russia. This fact is the background of the Bolshevist attitude toward religion. It gives the key to their violent attacks upon it.

It will be noted that the quotations from Marx express two ideas. One of them is that attack on the existing economic-political order will lead inevitably to the decay of religion. The other idea is that direct attack on religion will expose the "chains" of the existing system, and thereby further the creation of a new system. Soviet Russia has thrown itself energetically into both lines of attack. On one hand, it acts upon the belief that the creation of a communistic society will automatically displace interest in religious doctrines and cults. It will give a new social and human outlet to energy that is now wasted, from the Bolshevist point of view, by misdirection into supernatural and anti-social channels. On the other hand, Lenin felt, and undoubtedly correctly so, in view of his aims, that the existing Church was a rival to the new system which he was inaugurating. It was so closely tied up with the old economic régime as well as with political Czardom that its continued existence was a menace to the realization of his plans. The net outcome of the two lines of thought and action is that communism has itself become a religion that can tolerate no rival, and that any institutional church claiming authority over the social actions of its adherents appears to Communists as an attempt to establish a rival hostile political organization. The religious character of communism and the political-economic character of the Church account for the drastic and unmitigated character of the anti-religious campaign.

When I refer to the religious character of communism I mean that it commands in its adherents the depth and intensity of emotional fervor that is usually associated with religion at its height. Moreover, it claims intellectually to cover the whole scope of life. There is nothing in thought and life that is not affected by its claims; it has, one might almost say it *is*, a body of dogmas as fixed and unyielding as that of any church that ever existed. History records many instances of the persecution of one religious faith and its followers by those of another religion when it gained power. What is going on in Soviet Russia is something of the same kind. No one can understand it who thinks of it as a persecution of religion by a strictly political power. To get its real meaning one must align it in thought with the great struggles between rival religions that have marked history.

While the two lines of direct attack upon religion and of indirect attack through building up a social order in which religion will be an anachronism have been utilized by the Bolshevist régime, they proceed by different methods. Direct attack is carried on by propaganda and education. The rulers of present Russia have never concealed their hostility to religion as such, their fundamental atheism, nor their intent to use all means of education—the schools, the press, poster-pictures—to uproot faith in God and all supernatural power. All kinds of dramatic means are employed to depict the conflict of science and religion as a fundamental one, and to impress the lesson that the victory of religion is identical with the sway of ignorance and stupidity and a consequent social backwardness. There is no doubt that, quite apart from especial political aims, the rulers of Russia today hold the Greek Church responsible for the backwardness of the Russian peasantry, who form, of course, the great mass of the population.

Any one acquainted with Russian history must acknowledge that there is a great deal of historic truth in this view. It is difficult, however, for an American to realize what different political, cultural and economic associations religion has in Russia from those he is familiar with. He will be disposed to inquire why Bolshevist leaders should be so hostile to all personal religious belief, even if they have good ground for opposition to the Church as an organized institution. The general answer is that communism is itself a religious faith. But there are many other specific reasons. The Communists have found, or think they have found, that religious belief is a distinct handicap when it exists among members of the Communist party. It mitigates their zeal in the propagation of the Communist faith; such persons are ruthlessly weeded out of the party. The same motive naturally is applied in dealing with the young, who are the recruits for communism in the future. Personal, non-institutional religion is held to distract thought and energy from the all-absorbing task of the industrialization of Russia.

Lenin's own personality and teachings are an important factor. To him the philosophy of dialectic materialism was not a philosophy, but was identical with science itself. Science left no room for religion, and the remaking of the world he took to depend upon the conquest of men's minds by science. Marcu, the biographer of Lenin, says that "nothing in thought or aspiration seemed to Lenin more incomprehensible than tolerance. For him it was indistinguishable from lack of guiding principle. It was the beginning of contemptible surrender." Lenin's followers inherited this spirit of intolerance. Engaged in a life and death struggle to establish a new social order, religion and the creed of dialectical materialism interpreted as scientific truth were implacable and irreconcilable foes. For either to win, the other must be completely defeated.

All observers of the Russian scene agree that the anti-religious campaign of propaganda has met with remarkable success among the young. Maurice Hindus tells of meeting youths in remote parts of Russia who had had no direct contact of any kind with Soviet teachings, who took atheism for granted and who jeered at the very idea of there being a God. Many persons can verify the experience of one Russian who reports that when he was a boy a kind of thrill went through a group of youths when it was suggested that there were those who denied the existence of God, while now the same kind of excitement occurs when it is suggested that perhaps there is a God after all. More significant perhaps is the statistical result of an inquiry undertaken by officials into the beliefs of school children. They were shocked to find that 50 per cent still believed in the existence of God. This was some two years ago, and led to redoubled efforts to use the schools to root out the belief.

Shocking as is the situation to religious believers in other parts of the world, the methods of teaching and persuasion just outlined do not involve the use of coercive force. Even a believer might regard them as a test of the depth and reality of religious conviction among the people, winnowing the faithful from those of little faith. In spite of the astonishing success of these methods among the young, there is still a fundamental dispute among those who know them as to the religious nature of the Russian people. There are those, such as Stephen Graham, who paint the Russian people as inherently deeply religious, possessed of a mystic quality of soul. There are others who say that this is a purely literary fiction; that the peasant has been steeped in superstition, and that he has been interested in religion on quite material grounds as a magical means of procuring fertility and other worldly blessings. Where authorities disagree, an outsider cannot judge. All the recent newspaper correspondents agree, however, that the anti-religious campaign in Russia has been going on so long that it is now taken for granted as part of the new order, and that it has not aroused any such revulsion there as has been felt in foreign countries.

The exact extent of religious persecution by coercive means cannot be estimated. It is significant that Ramsay MacDonald, in his public letter, issued in the latter part of February, said that the British Government is not able to state the real facts of the situation. If this is the condition of a government with facilities for ascertaining facts, private individuals are certainly not in a position to judge accurately. A Jewish rabbi in London has declared that at least nine out of ten of the reports of persecution are false. Charles Selden has reported in the columns of the *New York Times* that there is good ground for suspicion that much of the agitation in Great Britain is stirred up by Tories who are trying to embarrass the Labor Government.

Certain things stand out, however, that may reasonably be taken as fact. In the general nationalization of private property in Russia, church properties were not excepted. Technically the title to them is vested in the State. Moreover, State support of priests was withdrawn; they must now derive their support from their own congregations. Many churches were closed; at the same time, any visitor, up to at least the last few months, can testify that there were still enough churches open to accommodate those who wished to attend them. There was also in the early days a distinct drive against the authorities of the Greek Church; those who were not willing to accept the overthrow of the Czar and the foundation of the Soviet régime were expelled—as were other recalcitrants. The Greek Church was "reformed" under the leadership of priests who were willing at least to tolerate the new political rule. The denial of the Metropolitan Sergius, Chief Patriarch of the Orthodox Church, that persecution on religious grounds exists in the U.S.S.R., was discounted by many zealous religionists in foreign countries on the ground that he was merely a tool of the government. But they overlooked the fact that his existence is proof that the Church and its ceremonies still exist without being hampered when the government has assurance of loyalty. The Metropolitan's statement that churches are often closed at the express request of members of the community, including church members, is confirmed by independent newspaper observers. That a community oversupplied with church buildings and awakening to new aspirations should be willing to see some church buildings turned into schools and clubs, is not shocking to many of us. It is a question, for example, whether a decision of the Chinese Government to convert some "heathen" temples into schools and public assemblies would not be welcomed by some now engaged in agitation against similar action in Soviet Russia.

The recent decree of Soviet Russia which was the immediate occasion of protests by the Pope and the Primate of the Church of England was a logical continuation of the earlier policy of nationalization of church properties and the rigid divorce of Church and State. Drastic as are its terms, it is in no sense unique. It should not be overlooked that it expressly provides for the existence of religious associations, defining the terms of their activities. The denial to them of juridical status is in line with similar action taken in other countries after a revolution, France, Mexico and Turkey being examples. In each case, the action has been dictated by fear of the development of an *imperium in imperio*. The prohibition of economic activities is also in line with revolutionary legislation in other countries. The provision that when believers do not appear to sign a contract for the care and maintenance of church edifices the latter revert to public use is doubtless responsible for the closing of many churches. It simply carries out the basic idea of nationalization. The prohibition of sanatoria, charitable relief, libraries, &c., goes further than action in other countries. It is in line with the policy of the U.S.S.R. to give the local Soviets a monopoly of these functions.

I do not doubt the sincerity of the rulers of the U.S.S.R. when they assert that there has been no persecution for strictly religious causes, but only for political. It is, however, extremely difficult to draw the line between the two, especially in a country undergoing a social revolution. There is evidence that the U.S.S.R., after having brought the Orthodox Church to terms, turned its activities toward the so-called Protestant sects. Persecution by government was an old story for them during the days of the Czars, but in the early days of the revolution they made great progress. There is good reason for thinking that the Communists became fearful of their influence over their communicants, since their beliefs were less conventional and more ardent than those of the orthodox. Many of these sects teach non-resistance and brotherly love. From their standpoint, these are religious doctrines. From that of the government they have a political meaning, since the State is committed to the doctrine of class war. The difficulty of drawing the line is found also in the question of religious education. The government permits religious instruction in the faith of the parents at home, but forbids it in institutions and classes before the age of 18.

At the time of writing, there are few verifiable facts regarding the arrest of rabbis in Minsk and other places. But the official statement is that they were arrested for carrying on agitation for schools to teach the Jewish religion to the young. From the government standpoint, this is a form of anti-legal activity directed against the laws of the Soviet régime, and will not be tolerated any more than would any other mode of illegal action.

I cannot conclude without expressing a personal opinion on one point. All the reports from Russia agree that Communist authorities are unanimous in the opinion that the "religious" drive against the Soviets is but another attempt of capitalistic countries to overthrow the Communist régime. Any one with a knowledge of Russia could have predicted that such would be the result. Although many have protested on genuinely religious grounds, nevertheless they have entered upon a campaign charged with dynamite. So far as it has any religious effect in the U.S.S.R. it will intensify opposition to religion, confirming the belief that the Church has at bottom a political and economic aim. It will also arouse the same feelings that would be aroused among us by any sign of foreign interference in what we regard as our own internal affairs. The foreign agitation will strengthen the isolationist party in Russia; it will intensify its militaristic activity. It will be used as further evidence that foreign nations are getting ready to overthrow the Communist régime by any means in their power. The Russian Government has drawn a distinct line between strictly religious activities of the Church and its social organization and purposes. This distinction is a logical consequence of the entire Soviet system; and attacks on the Soviet Government for its opposition to the social activities of the churches will only increase its conviction that personal religion is only a cover for political, educational and economic actions that tend to defeat the society they are trying to establish.

Social Change and Its Human Direction

There is no intellectual problem as practically urgent at the present time as that of the nature of deliberate or intelligent human control of social change. The problem is more or less confused by the sharp separation that is often made between human desire and purpose as factors and history, evolution and their laws. On one side, this divorce leads to a kind of fatalism depressing to effort. If historical movement and evolution is going to produce certain results anyway, the stimulus to endeavor is reduced. On the other side, the division leads to faith in unconditioned freedom of will; it is supposed to be able to produce the most revolutionary social changes if only it wills with sufficient intensity.

It is easier to feel the inadequacy of theories that lead to such extreme and one-sided results, than it is to see clearly just what is at fault in them. It is easier to fall back upon some vague combination of impersonal social forces and personal volition than it is to get a clear view of how between them the interaction actually goes on. For the problem involves a theory of the nature of the causation of social changes, and such a theory is difficult to attain in any coherent form.

Let us start by forgetting the past and occupying ourselves with a present. Any present always offers itself as a transition, a passage, or becoming. There is movement from something to something else, as the events of today are a transition from those of yesterday to those of tomorrow. In its vital sense, this is the only history that takes place. Now, human beings are involved in some phases of the transition. They have needs, wants, preferences and they make plans and put forth efforts. On a small scale, no one doubts the efficacy of this factor. A physician aims

[First published in *Modern Quarterly* 5 (1930–31): 422–25.]

to cure his patients rather than to let them die; an engineer to build a bridge that will endure certain strains and stresses. By such plans and acts some changes taking place are directed to one outcome rather than to another. I can see no difference in *principle* between such facts, universally acknowledged in small scale matters, and the direction of social changes on a wide scale. The difference in area and in complexity is, of course, enormous. It requires much more organization and concert of effort on the broad scale than on the small one of the individual's effort in his own calling.

But even on the narrow scale, there is always a background of social organization which supports and conditions. Savages did not try to build steel bridges, nor would they have known how to do it if they had tried. Social conditions put a reservoir of knowledge and of disposable energy at the command of the physician and the engineer. Available resources suggest both the things to attempt, the objects to strive for, and the ways of doing. The passage or transition that constitutes the present is always from *something that is there*. All intelligent direction and control of the transition take account of this something. They are intelligent and efficacious in the degree that the conditions which are moving are examined and understood. In short, desire, purpose, planning, everything that we call volition, are conditioned by something beyond themselves which they must utilize; volition does not operate in a void.

This fact is evident enough in the case of control and accomplishment in physical matters. Water, coal, iron, do not organize themselves into the steam engine spontaneously; human volition—desire and endeavor—intervene. But the latter do not and cannot produce the engine apart from external conditions and energies which are analyzed and comprehended in order that they may be used. The knowledge and the technical skill required to understand and utilize are in turn as much socially conditioned as the use of water and coal is physically conditioned. The very idea of a steam engine can arise only when there is already in existence a social and industrial state of affairs that demands mechanical power.

These remarks may seem too obvious to be worth saying. Yet they contain in their implications, it seems to me, the key to the problem of intelligent direction of social affairs as far as this problem is bound up with that of historical tendencies and laws. They indicate what history is and what history is not in connection with present efforts at social change and reconstruction. Positively speaking, the need to understand the state of affairs which is in passage to something different, if the change is to be directed by man, points to the need of knowledge of history, knowledge of how the existing state of things came to be. It is not the past which moves, which has force. For it has ceased to be, and what does not exist has no force. But we cannot *know* what exists, we cannot analyze and grasp it, unless we reconstruct its history.

The fallacy which regards the order of historical events as something which will determine the future irrespective of present volition, of present human desire and struggle, rests upon converting the significance of history *as a mode of understanding and knowing the present* into the notion that the past is an active agency. It is impossible to exaggerate the importance of history in its first capacity; as, that is, a method of getting an intellectual hold upon the conditions that have to be dealt with; seeing what obstacles they present and what leverages they offer, what means they supply, for our plans and purposes. But there are no historical forces which will shape the future, for what operates is precisely and only what is present. That it will operate in any case, is true; the question is how far it will operate blindly and how far through the medium of intelligent direction and planning. The latter demands understanding of what is there, and this in turn demands knowledge of historical conditions.

Every general theory or philosophy of history is thus a form of present social valuations. That is to say, it is part of the process of viewing and examining the present to discover what possibilities are resident in it and how present desire, purpose and effort should proceed. When existing problems are as definitely economic as they are at present an economic philosophy of history will be uppermost because that is the subject-matter which is most related to what we now need to understand and to do. It may sound strange to say that all significant history is history of the present, and that it changes as the needs and problems of the present change. But this is largely because men, when they think of history, think of it as something merely past. They forget that this past was once its own present, and that in that present men faced the future exactly as we do now; that they had their own present conditions to understand and deal with, their own preferences, desires, choice to make, plans to form. When they lived and acted, they lived and acted in a present which was a movement, a transition into something different and new. Their history was not a past to them.

What happens socially is always, in short, an interaction of present human desire and determination with existing, or present, conditions. That is so now and it always has been so. Any genuine reference to history and historical movements only reveals this fact. It does not disclose forces acting automatically without respect to human desire and effort. Just because this statement is so general in scope, it throws, however, no light upon the practical problem of what men are to desire and strive for today if they are to act intelligently in directing social change. The latter question demands an understanding of existing social conditions. And here, as has already been indicated, it is the facts of the material culture of an age of the machine and technology that are important. The history of the economic revolution from agrarianism to industrialism does not determine what the future is bound to be. But it does enable us to locate the outstanding traits of the present social situation as far as these afford the conditions to be reckoned with in present human dealing with social change. It is even more futile to refuse to face the facts which this history presents to our understanding than it is to rely upon an automatic working of historic evolution to determine a better future.

This futility abounds at present. Its practical outcome is drift, and, quite likely, drifting toward catastrophe. Upon the whole, the large business men, the captains of industry, do not know what they are doing at present. They do not know, that is, in any larger sense, in the sense of being aware of what the general social consequences of what they are doing will be. They react to immediate situations and turn them to pecuniary account. It is not merely the French Bourbons who act upon the policy of "after us, the deluge." These men may profess a philosophy of eighteenth century individualism, of *laissez-faire* and optimism, but they do not act upon it or upon any philosophy, unless turning immediate situations to money profit be called a philosophy. And the general public acquiesces in the same policy of drift—if drift can be called a policy.

I do not know enough about Marx to enter into the discussion concerning his philosophy. But those who interpret his philosophy, whether correctly or incorrectly, as one of an automatic working of historical forces not only have, as it seems to me, an entirely false conception of the relation of the past to the present and its future, but they are virtually accomplices in the policy of drift. On the other hand, there is very much in the theory of Marx which is of immense significance in the analysis and understanding of the present, of the conditions that make it what it is, and that suggest the direction which human desire, purpose and sustained effort should take. History at least enables us to grasp intellectually the collectivistic condition in which we now live. And such a grasp is a necessary precondition of intelligent endeavor to direct the changes which are to take place in what is going on.

Reviews

The School and Society
School and Society in Chicago by George S. Counts. New York: Harcourt, Brace and Co., 1928.

Now that Dr. Counts has accomplished the task, the wonder is that no one has attempted it before. There are many books, some of them excellent, about the organization and administration of American school systems from within. There was none, however, until the appearance of the present one, that dealt with the school system as it is affected by the play of the forces of the community.

The immediate episode upon which the book turns is the tragic comedy of Mayor Thompson's civic administration of Chicago, the crusade against King George, and the battle for 100 percent Americanism, interpreted as extravagant attention to every immigrant group in Chicago having votes—except the English—and culminating, educationally speaking, in the "trial" and dismissal of Superintendent McAndrew. The sensational features of the incident were spread over the pages of the daily press. The causes, of which the incident in question is only a symptom, are, however, what interest Dr. Counts. In his treatment the melodrama is a peg from which hangs a panoramic picture unrolling itself over a period of fifteen years. In his own words, "The Chicago spectacle, or a similar spectacle in any other industrial city, may best be understood if it is regarded as a product of the play of many diverse forces upon the schools." And the schools are "administered not only in a highly complicated society, but also in a society with a history. . . . Every generation receives from its progenitor and bequeaths to its offspring a legacy of loves and hates, of prejudices, antagonisms and rivalries, which must always color and give direction to human behavior." Here no project is viewed on its intrinsic merits and demerits, but as it affects the interests of some group and in the light of some past history.

[First published in *New Republic* 58 (10 April 1929): 231–32.]

To quote our author again: "Every vibration that agitates the social structure must sooner or later reach the public school." His book is essentially an objective study, as nearly impartial as human circumstance permits, of the chief social sources from which the vibrations have been sent out to stir either trouble or life in the school system. The administrative conduct of the schools in its legal and political relations is studied under the caption of "The Division of Authority." This division applies to the relations of state and city, and is expressed in clashes between the School Board and the City Hall, the Board and the Superintendent, the latter and the teaching force, and, at sundry times, of any one of them with any one of the others. Moreover, the fairly rapid changing of superintendents breaks into continuity of policies and operates to introduce additional clashes. Here is brought out one of the historical inheritances to which reference has already been made—namely, the contrasting educational philosophies of Mrs. Ella Flagg Young and of Mr. McAndrew, which reacted not only upon teachers but also upon organized elements in the community. In this case the conflict was between the Federation of Labor and the Association of Commerce; Mrs. Young's policies having the sympathy of the former, and Mr. McAndrew's the active support of the latter.

With respect to the teachers, the split came over the abolition of the Teachers' Councils, initiated by the Federation of Labor, and wiped out by the Association of Commerce. To the alienation of the teaching corps by this action, Dr. Counts devotes a chapter. The difficulty that any educational "reformer" has in realizing his projects when he does not have the active sympathy of the great body of teachers is a point which might have received more emphasis than he gives it. The educational history of our cities is full of instances of failure of more or less promising plans because they were put over upon teachers from above. Mayor Thompson would have had a much harder job in getting rid of Mr. McAndrew than he did have, if the latter had not already alienated so many of the class-room teachers.

The internal difficulties in a school system afflicted with uncertain and divided authority, and consisting of 12,000 teachers of different grades, interests and experiences, would be great, even if it went on, as Dr. Counts says, "in a social vacuum." But playing upon the clashes within the system and utilizing them for special ends is a multitude of different and often opposed social forces. The next division of Dr. Counts's book is devoted, under the caption of "The Play of Social Forces," to a detailed study of the more important of these special influences. The Association of Commerce, the Federation of Labor, the women's clubs, the churches, especially with respect to the conflict of Catholic and Protestant, the city hall and the daily press, each receives a chapter, and every chapter is full of enlightenment for anyone who would understand the difficulties under which the development of our American school system labors. With so many important points brought out, it is not easy to select any for notice. The unremitting, quiet attention of business interests to the school system, and the effects of their efforts at control are, however, peculiarly significant, while the conscientious endeavor of women's organizations at educational improvement and their handicap because of exclusive membership in one social class, stand out especially in my mind.

The main purpose of the book is to set before the reader a definite picture of the social conditions under which our school system operates in large and industrialized cities. In that task it succeeds admirably. The book ought to be "required reading" not only for administrators and teachers, actual and prospective, but for all newspaper men who are called upon to write about the schools. We are not likely to get anywhere until events are viewed in relation to their background and social setting; and, while Chicago has its own peculiar color, the general trend of events there is not so different from what happens elsewhere.

Dr. Counts remarks that, while a realistic view of the play of the social medium on the schools may produce some loss of faith in the latter as a great constructive and liberating instrument, the loss might "mark a distinct advance over that smug complacency with which students of education have ignored the social medium in which the school must perform its task." He concludes his account with two suggestions which, if adopted, would at least tend to reduce secrecy, hypocrisy and instability in the conduct of the schools. One of them is that the constitution of the School Board should be frankly representative of groups, so that each major legitimate interest of the city could make itself heard in the open. The other suggestion is that the entire teaching staff in a city be organized in such a way as to have a responsible share in the administration of the schools. Only the teaching force in solid array, not a few administrators, are in a position to resist outside pressure; the teaching body is the continuous and stabilizing element, and if educational policies are to evolve and be executed gradually and with a minimum of friction, "they must grow from the thought and experience of the entire profession."

While I am in hearty sympathy with this proposal, it goes counter to most present tendencies, since these magnify the administrative officers and reduce class-room teachers to a subordinate role. If Dr. Counts had gone further back into Mrs. Young's superintendency, he would probably have emphasized, more than he has done, the fact that her governing ideal was the continuous taking of teachers into active partnership in development of the schools. (Dr. Counts twice ascribes this policy to the influence of Colonel Parker and myself. On the contrary, it was the matured fruit of her own personal experience as she moved from class-room teacher to administrator. As far as personal indebtedness is concerned, the ideas came to me from her and not *vice versa*.) The formation of Councils was both a symptom and a factor in this policy, but it can be understood only as a special symptom and factor; it was but an incident in a much larger policy. On the other hand, the abolition of the Councils by Mr. McAndrew was a symptom and factor in a comprehensive policy of the opposite type. While the objective character of Dr. Counts's book is to be admired, I have a feeling that it would gain in force if this particular issue were made more central. But all students of social movements must be grateful for a needed pioneering work, excellently undertaken.

An Organic Universe: The Philosophy of Alfred N. Whitehead

Process and Reality by Alfred N. Whitehead. New York: Macmillan Co., 1929.

It is no piece of news that the work of Professor Whitehead has been for the last ten years one of the most stirring influences in serious philosophic thought. It is an event of the first intellectual order that he has now given the world a philosophic system in a completed form. He began as a mathematician, and then moved out in a consideration of the general theory of nature in the light of the disclosures of modern science. He was compelled in this expedition to treat problems of wide scope. But the latter were in his previous writings more or less subordinated to his special theme. Now he presents his thought as a rounded whole, making clear his basic principles; his special cosmology appears as an included part of this whole.

The comprehensiveness of the task Mr. Whitehead has set himself is apparent in his opening words. His book is, he says, an essay in speculative philosophy, and the latter is the "endeavour to frame a coherent, logical, necessary system of general ideas in terms of which every element of our experience can be interpreted." No more comprehensive task could possibly be undertaken. It is frequently said that there are many signs that the epoch of criticisms and specialization is drawing to a close, and that we are approaching a time of constructive intellectual organization. I imagine, however, that few persons have thought the time fully ripe for the execution of such an enterprise. It is not too much to say that Mr. Whitehead's last book, unlike his earlier ones, is more than a forerunner of the revival of systematic philosophies. It belongs in scope and intent with the great classic systematization of history.

Were it a reproduction of the ideas of any one of the older systems it would be an easier book to read, and the reviewer would

[First published in *New York Sun*, 26 October 1929.]

have a much easier task in giving readers some little glimpse of his basic ideas and their import. But it is a synthesis of an original sort; even professional philosophers can only, unless they are more fortunate than the present writer, gradually find their way in it. They must become saturated with it before they can grasp it. What, for example, does one make of such sentences as the following kind that are more than sprinkled through the book? "The primordial created fact is the unconditioned conceptual valuation of the entire multiplicity of eternal objects. This is the 'primordial nature' of God. By reason of this complete valuation, the objectification of God in each derivate actual entity results in a graduation of the relevance of eternal objects to the concrescent phases of that derivate occasion."

The trouble is not, as a hasty reader might assume, that the words and sentences have no definite meaning. It is rather that they have too much, each term being charged with a particular significance in the system, one that cannot be fully understood until the system as a whole is understood. On the other hand, one cannot get the system until one gets something more than a glimmering of the meaning of such enunciations as the one quoted. I know that I have come far from exhausting the meaning of the book, and it is possible that I misunderstood even its central ideas.

Under the circumstances it would be a grateful task to confine this review to the peripheral elements in Mr. Whitehead's exposition of his system. One could easily cull an anthology of separate sentences each of which is crystal clear in its incisive meaning. In the first chapter alone, for example, are such remarks as the following:

"Metaphysical categories are not dogmatic statements of the obvious; they are tentative formulations of the ultimate generalities."

"In some measure or other progress is always a transcendence of the obvious."

"No language can be anything but elliptical, requiring a leap of the imagination to understand its meaning in its relevance to immediate experience."

"Morality of outlook is inseparably conjoined with generality of outlook."

"It is the part of the special sciences to modify common sense.

Philosophy is the welding of imagination and common sense into a restraint upon specialists and also into an enlargement of their imaginations."

I do not quite see how the general reader, even if cultivated, can make his way into the system as a whole without technical preparation. But he will certainly attain an "enlargement of imagination" through contact with an extraordinarily sensitive, original and well-informed mind.

Perhaps the most that a review like the present one can do is to indicate some of the difficulties the reader will meet. One is the dependence of Mr. Whitehead's exposition upon a reconstruction of prior philosophical systems. Disciples of old systems are common enough; they repeat the ideas of the masters without having the context that gave them vitality. There also prevails an impatience with old systems and the belief that we must make a new start. It is rare to find a thinker who like Mr. Whitehead thinks that the ideas of the great philosophers must be construed with "limitations, adaptations and inversions, either unknown to them, or even explicitly repudiated by them," and yet who holds that each great system is such a genuine reflection of some central phase of the universe that its findings must be seriously reckoned with.

In some respects Whitehead's recurrent utilization of previous systems aids apprehension of his own thought. It gives points of reference to things already familiar. But upon the whole it adds to the difficulty of understanding until one has reached an independent grasp of Whitehead's own philosophy. For example, Whitehead finds in some ideas of Locke the nearest precursor of the philosophy of the universe as an organism. Yet one basic strand in his thought is distinctly Platonic and in popular conception Locke and Plato are irreconcilable. Again, the "eternal objects" to which reference is made in the passage already cited are definitely Platonic, but the conception of them as "created" as "fact" and as forming the inherent nature of God are all explicitly "repudiated" by Plato.

Again, there is much in Leibniz which definitely recurs in Whitehead, but with an equally definite repudiation of two ideas usually thought central in Leibniz's thought, namely, pre-established harmony and the exclusive and private or "windowless" character of ultimate existences. It is presumably with reference to contemporary Leibnizians that he remarks that a good deal of modern scientific philosophy is an attempt to combine the conception of privacy with that of scientific and public fact, and adds: "Science is *either* an important statement of systematic theory correlating observations of a common world, *or* is the daydream of a solitary intelligence with a taste for the daydream of publication."

In consequence, it requires a very unusual emancipation of imagination from current interpretations to find assistance in Whitehead's union of historic philosophic concepts that are, as they stand, opposed to one another. Yet, the endeavor of Whitehead to unite them in a single system is an illustration of his own basic idea of the organism—as is the fact, already mentioned, that understanding of particular sentences requires understanding of the system as a whole, and vice versa. Another and perhaps greater difficulty in reading Whitehead resides in his vocabulary. In saying this I do not refer so much to his use of unfamiliar words to express with technical accuracy certain ideas, though this tendency, congenial I suppose to the mathematician, is conspicuous.

I refer rather to his habit of using common words like "feeling, valuation, satisfaction, experience," to say nothing of "God" with connotations having little in common with that of their common usage. I sympathize fully with what Whitehead has to say about the linguistic difficulties that confront any one who attempts to rethink in a synthetic way our present knowledge. It is also congruous with his whole philosophy to say each entity in the universe "feels," "experiences," and even is a conceptual prehension and valuation of, all other things in it, and is a "society," without the saying implying any element of consciousness whatever. It is also congruous with his theory that the physical and mental are two poles of a single process. But until one has gone far in grasping his whole thought, the vocabulary is likely to be a stumbling block, and may readily lead casual readers to a misconception of his thought.

I have been writing around Whitehead without making any attempt to come to close quarters with his philosophic system as such. Any one who turns to his second chapter and learns that there are eight categories of existence, twenty-seven categories of explanation and nine categorial obligations, all in addition to the one category of the ultimate will understand why. Yet it is hardly fair to the reader (though the outcome will be unfair to Mr. Whitehead) not to make some attempt to report his system at least in outline.

Creativity, many, and one are all involved in the meaning of anything or actual existence. They are taken not separately, but in their interpenetration of one another, *the* ultimate category. The idea of creativity explains, I suppose, the conjunction of the words "Process and Reality" in the title of the work. Reality is process in which the many things forming the history of the world achieve a unity in a new unique, singular or atomic thing, while that thing adds a genuinely new element to the universe and becomes one of many of the further ongoing "creative advance" to other new things.

This summing of all things taken disjunctively in each thing, taken conjunctively, makes the universe through and through organic. Everything that exists is atomic, but every existence, from God to a puff of smoke, is internally so complex that it "reflects," as Leibniz would say, the entire universe and can be *explained* only through thorough-going continuity. Among the eight categories of existence "eternal objects" stand out along with actual things "with a certain extreme finality." These form (though with significant difference of interpretation) what is usually termed the realm of Platonic ideas, essences or universals. More concretely they form the rational factor in the universe. It is because of them that a "coherent, logical, necessary system of general ideas" universally applicable to the empirical brute matters of fact is possible. In this sense Whitehead is a thorough-going rationalist in its historic philosophic sense. They constitute the world of possibility to which actuality conforms and which is progressively manifest in the creative advance of the universe of actual existences.

God as a concrete existence is the principle of selectivity that determines which of the realm of eternal possibilities has "ingression" into actual existence and contains a definite character or form of its own. Actual things become and they perish, but they do not change. Each while it is at all is just what it is. "Change is the description of the adventure of eternal objects in the evolving universe of changing things." God has a "consequent" as well as a "primordial" nature. By reason of the relativity and organic nature of all things there is a reaction of the world on God. Every new thing—and all things in their turn are new—is an added element in God's nature. It is through the actual world that he is conscious. He is the goal in process of creating as well as the foundation of order in actual existence. The principle is given the name "God" because the enjoyment and refreshment that come from contemplation of the timeless source of order and the eventual goal is what religions have aimed at.

The creative advance of actual existences in their organic relatedness to each other, made possible by the selective realization of eternal objects that form a single whole of timeless possibilities, is used to explain the principles of physical science in their mathematical form and their physical application. It is employed also to break down the dualism between the physical and the mental, or what Whitehead earlier termed the bifurcation of nature. For the details I can only refer to the volume itself. The treatment exhibits massive learning conjoined with acute and mathematical delicacy.

In conclusion, it may not be an impertinence to add my own reaction to the system as I understand it—or misunderstand it, as the case may be. Fundamentally it seems to me that Whitehead has substituted one dualism, that of eternal objects and of concrete actualities, for the older dualism of mind and matter. God seems to be a *deus ex machina* to bring together these dualistic terms. Mr. Whitehead's sense of reality leads him to insist upon the fact that the world and life are a union of principles that in themselves are opposites. I agree with his conclusion as to the "togetherness" of things that are yet singular and individual, but the premises from which the conclusion is derived seem to me irreconcilable with each other and with a genuinely empirical method. It marks an emancipation to get away from the historic dualism of mind and matter. But one of the traits of the emancipation is that the elements of the new dualism which replaces the old one are in such a state of disturbed equilibrium that the mind will be forced on to find another and more empirical interpretation of the nature of what are called "eternal objects."

I doubt if rationalism and empiricism can be combined by asserting that the actual world is one in which God effects the ingression of selected eternal, continuous and rational forms in brute matters of existent fact. The possibilities of empiricism in explaining the origin, application and function of thought in the actual world have not begun to be considered as yet. The recognition that the world is one of relativity and is "organic," in Whitehead's sense, forms the possibility of a new kind of empiricism. I confess to some sadness that Mr. Whitehead did not devote his immense knowledge and remarkable abilities to the exploitation of this possibility, instead of trusting to a constructive revision of the great classic rationalists, Plato, Descartes, Spinoza and Leibniz. I close the book with the feeling that somehow the seventeenth century has got the better of the twentieth. But I close the book also with a sense of the great debt that every one who is trying to think his way through the muddled modern world owes to the luminous and precise mind of Mr. Whitehead.

The Course of Modern History
World Politics in Modern Civilization by Harry Elmer Barnes. New York: Alfred A. Knopf, 1930.

The standpoint of Professor Barnes' book may be gathered not only from its sub-title, "The Contributions of Nationalism, Capitalism, Imperialism, and Militarism to Human Culture and International Anarchy," but from the heading of the first chapter: "Nationalism, Capitalism, Imperialism and the Course of Modern History." The *course* of modern history is Mr. Barnes' preoccupation. After a brief but pregnant sketch of the commercial revolution, beginning in the fifteenth century, and the successive primacy in international trade of the Italian cities, Portugal, Spain, The Netherlands, France, and Great Britain, he considers the reaction of this expansion upon European society. The outstanding economic and industrial changes of Europe from the sixteenth to the twentieth century, the rise of manufacturing, the financial development, the agricultural revolution, and the political and institutional changes of European life are treated as expressions of this reaction. Part Two considers in detail the rise of capitalism, the growth of population, internal migrations, the appearance of antagonistic movements like socialism and anarchism, the development of the proletariat and its external effect in the colonial policies and exploitation of inferior nations that goes by the name of imperialism—the financial penetration of Asia, Africa, and Latin America. This brings the story to the situation which resulted in the outbreak of the World War.

I do not see how anyone can get a better insight into the main currents of modern history than by looking at them through Mr. Barnes' perspective. The importance of economic and financial factors is now generally recognized among intelligent readers. But a vague recognition is one thing while a detailed and

[First published in *World Tomorrow* 13 (December 1930): 522–23.]

vivid picture such as Mr. Barnes presents is quite another. The author's own interest in this course of history is largely from the standpoint of the light it throws upon the origin and conduct of the World War. In his discussion of the latter theme, Mr. Barnes is special pleader as well as historian. He has written, as he says, "without considerations of conventional academic taste or professional expediency"—a candor that is decidedly refreshing. More than a quarter of the book is devoted to the attitude of historians toward the war and to a searching discussion of recent efforts, such as the peace movement, to "salvage the wreck of Europe." Although one may find himself in agreement with the writer about the practical importance of laying the "war myth" that has been so sedulously cultivated, one may at the same time ask whether the understanding of the early and generative course of history would not have been forwarded by separating it from the World War, leaving to a later volume the discussion of war guilt and the Wilsonian policies.

I should be sorry if these qualifying remarks seemed to detract in any way from my grateful sense of the importance of Mr. Barnes' work. I know of no better way for an intelligent reader to understand the moving forces in modern international life, and their fundamental bearing upon the significant problems of human destiny, than by becoming acquainted with this book.

Miscellany

Dr. Dewey and Mr. Woll

Sir: I was very much interested in the article appearing in the January 9 issue of your publication by Professor John Dewey, entitled "Labor Politics and Labor Education," as well as your editorial comment.

But it is not on that subject I intended writing at this time. Be assured that an answer will be forthcoming and that I need not be instructed or directed by your publication as to the nature of the answer warranted. I am writing you at this time to direct your attention to the footnote appearing in connection with Professor Dewey's article on page 212 [this volume, p. 342], which reads: "He [Mr. Woll] also uses the Life Insurance Company, of which he is President, to weaken the idea of state old-age pensions."

There can be no question that Professor Dewey refers to The Union Labor Life Insurance Company, of which I am the President. There can be no question either as to the intent or motive attributed to me by Professor Dewey in this statement. He clearly insinuates that I am using The Union Labor Life Insurance Company for an ulterior purpose. It is equally clear that Professor Dewey conveys and intended to convey the impression that I am using The Union Labor Life Insurance Company for a purpose foreign to its creation and outside of its legitimate scope and purpose. In other words, Professor Dewey attributed to me directly ill motives as President of that institution and at the same time stigmatized that institution as not operating for the purposes for which it was created.

It is of minor concern to me what Professor Dewey or your publication may say of me personally. I shall find time and occa-

[First published in *New Republic* 58 (20 February 1929): 19–20. For Dewey's article to which Woll's is a reply, see this volume, pp. 338–45. See also letters by Daniel Chase and Dewey, pp. 390, 392.]

sion to answer both. I am concerned, however, as to his statement regarding an institution of which I am the President, and in the keeping of which have been placed the funds of over sixty national and international unions, of over thirty-five city central labor unions, seven state federations of labor and two hundred and forty local unions. In addition, The Union Labor Life Insurance Company carries life insurance for thousands of policy holders, all of whom have a right to be protected and whom I intend to protect even against statements issued by Professor Dewey and your publication. It is extremely unfortunate that Professor Dewey, without any acquaintance with me or with my activities, should allow his personal attitude toward me to lead him so far astray, and more lamentable that a publication like yours, that professes editorially so great a friendship for organized labor, should permit itself to become the medium for such libelous statements and endangering organized labor to the extent before indicated.

Quite aside from the legal considerations involved, might I ask if it is proper journalism to publish such statements as I have herein referred to? May I ask, too, if you have investigated the charge made by Professor Dewey that I have used The Union Labor Life Insurance Company to weaken the idea of state old-age pensions? I challenge both Professor Dewey and your publication to present any evidence to warrant such assertion. I will welcome the selection of any fair-minded and unbiased person, preferably a liberal judge of unimpeachable character, to consider any evidence of the validity of this charge. Are you willing to meet this issue in this fashion? If not, is it not then the honorable, right, and fair-minded thing to do to make fitting acknowledgment of the error committed, and at least remove the suspicion cast and harm done to an institution which ought not to be made to suffer because of any ill-conceived feelings Professor Dewey or your publication may entertain toward me?

I await your further answer and response.

MATTHEW WOLL.

Washington, D.C.

Reply to Woll

Sir: Mr. Woll has chosen to reply to an incidental point, which he has then played up in an irrelevant manner. That energy devoted to building up private insurance companies is diverted from working for state insurance, just as employers' pension schemes weaken public old-age pensions, is an obvious fact, and is the one to which attention is called in the sentence on which Mr. Woll builds such an elaborate structure. In no way is the Insurance Company of which he is President "stigmatized"; there is not the remotest insinuation that funds entrusted to it are not ably and honestly managed. I find it hard to believe that anyone other than Mr. Woll regarded the quoted sentence as insinuating anything of the kind. If there be such a person, I gladly assure him, and re-assure Mr. Woll, that there is nothing of the kind suggested.

JOHN DEWEY.

New York City.

[First published in *New Republic* 58 (20 February 1929): 20.]

The Sportsmanship Brotherhood

Sir: In your issue of January 9, in an article by Mr. John Dewey, a reference was made to the Sportsmanship Brotherhood. I called to see Mr. Dewey immediately after seeing the article; not finding him in, I wrote the following letter:

I called on you yesterday to correct a statement appearing in your article in the New Republic of January 9 with reference to the Sportsmanship Brotherhood. The Brotherhood is particularly desirous of having the support of educators and regardless of any antipathy you may feel for Mr. Woll it was a disappointment to us to find that you had so far misinterpreted the aims of our organization as to write: "President of the International Sportsmanship Brotherhood—an organization to coöperate with the 'welfare' departments of large employers." Doubtless insufficient data caused you to reach your mistaken conclusion which I hope will be altered after a study of the data left with your assistant by me.

The Sportsmanship Brotherhood has no concern whatsoever with the welfare or personnel departments of any organization. Its work is to inculcate in youth a spirit of sportsmanship and fair play principally by means of contacts with educators, schools, and athletic organizations.

Idealism is not a sufficiently accepted doctrine to make us unmindful of such criticism as you have leveled, and a correction would serve the double purpose of bringing out the truth and supporting principles which you have previously enunciated.

[First published in *New Republic* 58 (6 March 1929): 73. For Dewey's article to which this is a reply, see this volume, pp. 338–45. See also letters by Matthew Woll and Dewey, pp. 387, 389.]

Mr. Dewey's reply to this was:

I was sorry to miss you when you called. I am grateful to you for leaving me the material which you did, as well as for writing me.

I may say that it did not occur to me that it was an invidious reflection upon the Brotherhood to connect it with the welfare departments of employers. That work is certainly perfectly legitimate. I shall, however, undertake at once a study of the data which you have left for me.

You will observe that the unfavorable implication to which the Sportsmanship Brotherhood is subjected by Mr. Dewey's article is clearly at variance with what Mr. Dewey says in his letter of reply to our protest. New Republic readers unaware of the correspondence above would necessarily form an erroneous conclusion from the article and it is this impression we wish you to correct in justice to the Sportsmanship Brotherhood.

DANIEL CHASE,
Executive Secretary, the
Sportsmanship Brotherhood.

New York City.

Mr. Woll as a Communist-Catcher

Sir: In a letter to Mr. Daniel Chase, of the Sportsmanship Brotherhood, under date of January 25, Mr. Matthew Woll denies that he stated in his speech at New Orleans that I was a Communist, or that I was "engaged in Communist propaganda for the purpose of planting the germs of Communism in Eastern educational institutions." He also says: "I did not imply at New Orleans either that Professor Dewey professed Communism in any shape nor that he was knowingly connected with any Communist organization."

The official stenographic report of the proceedings of the seventh day's session of the New Orleans Convention contains, on page 315, the following in its report of Mr. Woll's speech. Referring to me he is quoted as calling me "a propagandist . . . for Communist interests." It also quotes him as saying: "Is he not the one who a few years ago went to New York City for the purpose of planting the germ of Communism in our educational institutions?" The report of the industrial relations department of the National Association of Manufacturers, page 28, reports that Mr. Woll "denounced Dewey as a propagandist for Communist interests."

I should not think of troubling you with what might seem to be a personal matter. But in view of Mr. Woll's attack on Brookwood as a Communist institution, the contrast between Mr. Woll's denials and the official report gives a measure of the confidence to be placed in his statements, which is of public interest.

JOHN DEWEY.

New York City.

[First published in *New Republic* 58 (13 March 1929): 99. For Dewey's initial article, see this volume, pp. 338–45. See also pp. 387, 389, 390.]

Letter to University of Michigan School of Education

Dean James B. Edmonson
University of Michigan   October 26, 1929
Ann Arbor, Michigan

My dear Dean Edmonson:

I want to thank you and through you the faculty of the School of Education of the University of Michigan for the very kind letter of October 17th. I can't tell you how deeply touched I am at the expressions which come to me from my colleagues in education. I prize especially the expression from the University of Michigan because it occupies so warm a place in my affection. As you say, it was in Ann Arbor that I began my teaching activities. It was there that my serious interest in education was aroused. I have never ceased to be grateful that my first connection was with a state university in the middle west. I learned there something of the deep significance of the relation between educational institutions and the social communities which they serve. In addition to this I formed there some of the closest friendships of my life.

I was amused with the story which you mention in your letter. It is a good story even if it does not happen to be true of me. When I first went to Ann Arbor the same story was attached to Professor Burt. I had hoped that by this time it had been passed on to someone else.

Please accept my deep and sincere thanks for your message of kindness.

Sincerely yours,
(Signed) JOHN DEWEY

[First published in *University of Michigan School of Education Bulletin* 1 (November 1929): 26–27.]

Juvenile Reading

The question regarding children's reading starts a discussion in the mind of any thoughtful person which, if not "raging," at least stirs many opposite and irreconcilable thoughts, for each of which something may be said. Were it not for one consideration, I should reach the conclusion that with the exception of very small children, the books written for adults, especially those which have attained the rank of classics, are the best reading for children. For the very young, it seems to me the best reading is the story of animal and child life, written preferably in a whimsical or at least semi-humorous style, where the wording is quite literal even though the subject-matter is highly imaginative. I do not mean myths and fairy tales, as much as an imaginative presentation of objects which are familiar; things the child sees, handles, eats, plays with, that attract his attention, presented in some unusual picture, but treated as far as style is concerned in a familiar and even prosaic way.

It is probably useless, in the flood of books for children and youth that pour from the press and that have such commercial pressure behind them, to urge for children of an older age the reading of classics, like the *Iliad* and *Odyssey*, Plutarch, and adaptations of them, like the Lambs' *Tales from Shakespeare*. Yet if a movement in that direction could be started, I think it would do more than anything else to improve the standards of the reading of youth. In any case, I think good adult literature is better, with few exceptions, than that especially prepared for the young. The latter is too often written down to the supposed intellectual level of the young, is sentimental and falsely romantic, to say nothing of inferiority of style. The difficulty alluded to

[First published in *Saturday Review of Literature*, 16 November 1929, p. 398, in response to a set of questions on juvenile reading sent to a group of persons by the editors.]

above is an over-emphasis, from the standpoint of youth, of romantic love. I do not have in mind here the contemporary definitely "sex" literature as much as the older style of love story, in which images and vague emotions are aroused far beyond any reach of present experience, and by which mental reactions that would come naturally later are prematurely and artificially fostered.

Lest it be thought I have in mind a forced, exclusive diet of classics, let me say that I think books of travel and adventure written for grown-ups provide excellent material. I recall a group of children who had read to them at about the same time Nansen's *The First Crossing of Greenland* and Kipling's *Captains Courageous*—certainly a book much superior to most of those which constitute our juvenile literature. The children were more eager for the former than for the latter. Of all reading for the young I think "stereotyped books, without literary value, but having plot interest," the worst.

Understanding and Prejudice

I felt greatly honored when Dr. Landman came to see me the other day and invited me to take part in this family gathering this evening and to bring my own humble tribute to those who founded a half century ago this important work, carried on so valiantly until it was effectively taken up by others who have continued it.

For some reason, after he had invited me, I found two words especially running through my mind. Those two words were understanding and prejudice—the two words perhaps that are about the farthest apart of any two words in the English language; certainly farther apart than black and white or our other usual opposites. And so it seemed to me that perhaps I could not do better than take them, if I may say so, take these words as my text.

Understanding means something intellectual, but it means something that is much more than intellectual. We sometimes say comprehension, but comprehension is an inclusive word—it signifies coming together, bringing things together; and when we say that human beings have come to an understanding, we mean that they have come to an agreement, that they have reached a common mind, a common outlook from which they see the same things and feel the same way about them. To understand is to stand on common ground. Prejudice is a curious word—one of those happy words in which the instinct of a people expresses itself. It is something that goes before judgment. It is even a kind of foolish and unwise judgment. It is something that precedes judgment, that tends to prevent and to distort it.

I suppose a purely rational being placed on this earth would

[First published in *American Hebrew* 126 (29 November 1929): 125, from a report of an address given at the semi-centennial banquet of the *American Hebrew*, New York City, 21 November 1929.]

find nothing that would seem to him so incredible as the prevalence of prejudice that divides nations, that divides races, divides people of different color, divides religions and sects within the same individuals, divides classes and groups from each other. But the very reason that prejudice is so obdurate, so hard to deal with, is that it comes from the irrational part of our nature, the sub-human part of instincts and impulses, fears, jealousies, dislikes, in comparison with which our reason is little and, only too often, somewhat flickering. . . .

A great philosopher once said that a pure characteristic of human beings was that they couldn't get on without each other and that they couldn't get on with each other. It seems to me that the struggle of understanding against prejudice is the struggle of civilization against barbarism, for unfortunately what we call civilization, barbarism, still exists and within your own breasts. Unfortunately this old animal barbarian still persists.

To fight the cause of understanding which is the cause both of sympathy and of that which brings about harmony, peace, cooperation and much more, is to fight the cause of civilization itself against the barbaric element that is the fault of civilization.

And so I found it a very great honor to have the privilege of saying a few words to you and especially of offering my congratulations and the thanks of all others who are not of this particular family, to the founders of the *American Hebrew* and their successors for this heroic and difficult humane battle which they have carried on for so many years against prejudice and in behalf of that common understanding which makes us brothers.

Foreword to Helen Edna Davis's *Tolstoy and Nietzsche: A Problem in Biographical Ethics*

There are a number of points of view from which the study of Miss Davis may be regarded—as she herself says of the authors studied. There are those, I am sure, who will gather from it added insight into Tolstoy and Nietzsche as literary artists; their fields are so vast and their fertility in them so great that in spite of all that had previously been written, Miss Davis has found it possible to say many things well worth saying. But it is as a study in ethics that the book is offered, and it is as such that it is to be primarily considered. It is, however, more than a study in ethics; it essays what is even more needed at present, discovery of a new *method* of thinking on moral subjects, striking out upon new paths that will open up new fields.

Few of those who have had professional concern with the subject of Morals will deny, I think, that it seems to suffer from a blight, more so than any other branch of philosophy. The causes are not easy to detect; they are certainly numerous and varied. Perhaps the subject is too human, too close to our daily interests and momentary actions, to lend itself to fruitful survey. Again, the moment we think about it, we find ourselves thinking not so much about it as about a body of proverbial saws and maxims instilled in us from early childhood. Teachings about morals begin so soon, they are kept up so late, they are so omnipresent in the family, Sunday school, pulpit, newspaper and essay that they, rather than ethical situations, come to form the material of study, so that they get between us and actual facts. Perhaps also no intelligent mode of approach was possible until other subjects, physiology, psychology, anthropology, and so forth, had reached a considerable state of development.

Whatever be the explanation, what passes for "ethics" oscil-

[First published in Helen Edna Davis, *Tolstoy and Nietzsche: A Problem in Biographical Ethics* (New York: New Republic, 1929), pp. ix–xiv.]

lates between sermonizing, moralizing of an edifying emotional type, and somewhat remote dialectics on abstract theoretical points. Emerson once said "whoever feels any love or skill for ethical studies may safely lay out all his strength and genius in working this mine." But it must be admitted that those who have worked it most successfully have done so indirectly. They have approached the mine not as moralists but as novelists, dramatists, poets, or as reformers, philanthropists, statesmen. The contributions which they have made have found their way, however, into common life rather than into moral theory. It cannot be asserted, of course, that the studies of Tolstoy and Nietzsche made by Miss Davis mark a pioneer effort to utilize material of literary art for theoretical purposes. But endeavors of this sort are still so rare that they invite hospitable reception—especially when they are accomplished with such intelligent skill and thorough knowledge.

It was a happy thought to identify the practical conflict of pacifism and militarism with the age-old theoretical antithesis of renunciation and self-assertion, altruism and egoism, and then to view Tolstoy and Nietzsche as representative types of the two tendencies. It was even a happier thought to take the issue of pacificism and militantism—a word that conveys the idea better than "militarism"—out of the somewhat banal region of external conflict with which it has become customary to confine it, and carry it back into the attitudes of desire, emotion and thought. That neither of the two men found a solution satisfactory even to himself in the path which he followed was perhaps to have been expected. Loyal devotees of each personage, the disciples of Tolstoy perhaps, even more than of Nietzsche, will be inclined to rebel at some of the analyses that are presented. But, aside from the thorough documentation with which the positions taken are supported, the tendency to find solution by extirpation and suppression of either factor may be judged in advance as one condemned to failure. Not the least significant and enlightening phase of Miss Davis's discussion is the clearness with which it is brought out that it was excess of turbulent vitality in Tolstoy that made him seek so ardently a recipe for final peace, while an excess of internal harmony in Nietzsche was the cause of his intellectual quest for provocation and for the stimulation of strife.

I cannot conclude without saying that Miss Davis has completely avoided the snares that beset an undertaking of the kind she has engaged in—the kind of mistake that may give many persons, altogether unjustly, an antecedent aversion to her enterprise. She has not gone to these writers to enforce by means of them any particular moral lesson, much less to turn them into mouthpieces of moral maxims. What she has given is a study of a problem that was a vital, even torturingly so, problem to each of the persons concerned in his own life and all through his life. In men of such genius for living and such gifts in artistic record, the problem that each less gifted person has to face for himself is presented in intensified form. This enlargement of a common experience supplies what is most to be learned from the following study. In these men as in magnifying glasses we are brought to see the elements of our own being. Such an insight, however achieved, is the chief end to be served by the study of morals.

Foreword to Eastern Commercial Teachers' Association First Yearbook, *Foundation of Commercial Education*

One of the most widespread and powerful obstacles to educational progress is the fact that the ideas of most adults as to what constitutes education are based on recollections of their own school days. At the time they may not have liked the instruction and discipline they received; they may even have rebelled against it. They may carry away with them the thought of many defects. In a few cases these experiences result, when the persons attain to adult life, in a desire for educational reform. But more often the outcome is a kind of stereotype, a stencil picture of what schooling should be. Such persons judge present and future education on the basis of their own past training. They are unsympathetic with change; they may welcome improvements in technical details, but they are hostile to any far-reaching alteration in the subject matters taught and in the spirit of methods used. Such changes often appear to them mere frills and fads; their criterion of "fundamentals" in education is their memory of their own school days.

These remarks seem to have a certain applicability to the topic of the development of commercial education, for, in spite of resistance from the source mentioned, education does change, both in subject matter and in methods. The changes are demanded by transformations in social conditions, and these are now so rapid and marked that no school system can ignore them. Those of us whose ideas of commercial education were formed, say, almost two generations ago, can only rub our eyes when we read of its present aims and problems as they are developed in a survey such as is presented in this book. What occurs most read-

[First published in Eastern Commercial Teachers' Association First Yearbook, *Foundation of Commercial Education* (New York: Eastern Commercial Teachers' Association, 1929), pp. xiii–xiv.]

ily to the mind on the basis of these recollections are courses in bookkeeping, and much attention to handwriting, together with toy money and a make-believe bank, the latter in its own day doubtless a concession to newfangled notions. It almost takes away one's breath. It certainly makes our Rip Van Winkles rub their eyes, to contemplate the scope and quality of the changes that have already occurred. Educational methods and ideas have changed rapidly in all lines in the last fifty years, but it may be doubted whether anywhere else as much or as fast as in the field of commercial education.

As one not in any direct contact with this field of educational endeavor I count it a privilege to have seen the reports of the addresses that were delivered. They give an inspiring picture of educational progress and endeavor. And it is equally interesting and provocative of thought to realize, as one reads, how closely the movements in this branch correspond to tendencies in other parts of the whole educational realm. It is not only a picture of development in a special line that is put before our eyes, but also a picture of exchange of ideas, of active currents moving throughout the whole territory. Upon reflection this community of aim and movement is explainable. All phases and aspects of school activity have been confronted with the obligation of meeting common social conditions and of shaping their work so as to do something to help in solving the problems which these social conditions present.

At the risk of repeating what is said better and at greater length in the addresses themselves, I, as one interested in the field of general education, may venture to point out some of these shared features. First and foremost, I should say, there is the desire to break away from the isolation that so long confined educational activity. Walls of division, barriers of separation, are breaking down. Everywhere in the pages that follow is presented in one form or another the fact that just as business and commerce do not go in water-tight compartments, insulated from other phases of social life, so commercial education cannot be kept apart. Its student must learn to see the relations that exist between his subject matter and other social interests. The demand for narrow specialization is yielding to the necessity for integration, for knowledge of relationships. In the second place— or perhaps as a special aspect of the same consideration—it is realized that commercial education is not a matter of routine training to give a few special modes of skill, but must have a scientific basis. There is no phase of modern life that is not subject to the influence of science, and the person who is without scientific understanding is directly precluded from understanding the life about him. In the third place, there is the emphasis upon the development, as far as is possible, of power of initiative and independent judgment. When society was fixed and governed by old rule and precedent, persons could succeed, at least after a fashion, by following copy and submitting to dictation without taking thought of their own. At present, conditions change so easily, forms of manufacture and doing business are so fluid, that a person must be educated for the future rather than be taught to conform to the past. This preparation for unknown conditions, for the consequences of invention and new modes of organization, can be met only as students are taught to think. In these three large and outstanding features, commercial education, as its status and prospects are exhibited in this book, manifests the same tendencies and aspirations that are found in all educational fields.

Introduction to Henry Evelyn Bliss's *The Organization of Knowledge and the System of the Sciences*

Most of us, even those who use libraries constantly, think of them, I imagine, mainly in reference to our own personal needs. We take them for granted, and judge them by their practical efficiency in supplying us with what we want when we want it. Mr. Bliss's monumental work comes as a shock to this narrow personal attitude. That the problem of the organization of libraries connects on the one side with the scientific and educational organization of knowledge and on the other side with the promotion of social organization this book makes impressively clear. It includes, moreover, the questions of psychology concerned with effective, growing assimilation of knowledge and the logical and philosophical questions involved in the problem of the unity, interrelations, and classifications of science.

On the other side, the social side, it also makes clear that our practical activities are more and more dependent upon scientific discoveries, intellectual progress and the diffusion of genuine knowledge. Social organization depends increasingly on ability to utilize organized knowledge competently, and decreasingly on tradition and mere custom.

Underlying the treatment is a sound philosophy of the relations of the special and particular to the comprehensive and general, of theory to practice, of organization and standardization to freedom and to the needs imposed by constant growth and change. The range of solid scholarship which has been drawn upon will be obvious even to the casual reader. But the learning and the philosophy are handled as effectively as the style and treatment are clear and direct.

The modern library stands at the cross-roads where meet together the two great currents of intellectual integration and prac-

[First published in Henry Evelyn Bliss, *The Organization of Knowledge and the System of the Sciences* (New York: Henry Holt and Co., 1929), pp. vii–ix.]

tical application in the interests of a more unified social life. This work of Mr. Bliss is a well-documented and thoroughly scholarly demonstration of this fact. He has lifted the whole question of organization of libraries up to a plane where it is evident that under modern conditions of life libraries occupy a central and strategic position.

The reader learns to understand, as he follows the thought of Mr. Bliss, that a library is not a mere depository of books, and that a merely arbitrary classification does not satisfy even the practical needs. A classification of books to be effective on the practical side must correspond to the relationships of subject-matters, and this correspondence can be secured only as the intellectual, or conceptual, organization is based upon the order inherent in the fields of knowledge, which in turn mirrors the order of nature. The library serves a practical end, but it serves it best when practical tools and instrumentalities agree with the intrinsic logic of subjects, which corresponds to natural realities. The right organization of knowledge in libraries embodies, moreover, a record of attained unification of knowledge and experience, while it also provides an indispensable means to the development of further knowledge.

Knowledge grows by specialized piece-meal increments; but unless the special worker is to become unaware of the relations and the meaning of what he is doing—unless in the end chaos is to result, there must be a central order based on comprehensive and unifying principles. Yet the order must be sufficiently flexible to adapt itself to new and unforeseen growths.

In consequence of this broad and liberal spirit Mr. Bliss's book, in addition to its special value to those directly concerned with the services of books, is of importance also to all those who are interested in the bearing of the organization, and the interrelations, of knowledge upon the transition from anarchy and chaos to order and unity in life. Intellectual cooperation and collective attack on complex problems, drawing upon materials of diverse kinds, are marked movements of present life.

Of the many special points of interest which are included in the comprehensive plan of Mr. Bliss's work, there is one which I should like to single out for special attention. In the broadest sense of education, the dominant concern of this work is educational: the problem of the ideal of library organization is the educational service it should render both to the general public and to the workers in special fields. But it is also closely connected with education in its narrower sense of what goes on in schools. There is no educational question more pressing than that of the right relation of special and departmentalized instruction to the all-round, balanced development of students and teachers. Because of this need, our colleges are introducing "orientation" and "survey" courses. There is hardly an institution that is not experimenting to produce a better correlation of studies. Specialization has been carried so far that the great need now is that of integration.

Apart from its permanent contributions to the solution of the general problem of the organization of knowledge, this work of Mr. Bliss is, in its general scope and in its details, an important and much-needed contribution to the accomplishment of this special educational task, which at the present time has become urgent and dominant.

Introduction to Maurice Hindus's
Humanity Uprooted

The following passage taken from the chapter on Youth seems to me to be itself a suitable Introduction to the entire book: at least to the attentive reader it suggests the animated spirit of Mr. Hindus' extraordinary account of the extraordinary Russian scene. "Often when I would tell Russian youths that I was a writer they would immediately ask what was my political orientation. What they really meant was whether I was for or against the class struggle. They could not conceive of a writer being apolitical and indifferent to political viewpoints." The passage is intended to tell something about the attitude of Russian youth. In fact, it communicates even more about the point of view from which Mr. Hindus has surveyed the Russian situation.

To take sides, to find something to praise or to blame, and then follow the purpose of blame or praise to control all one's ideas of a social situation is almost as natural to humanity as it is to breathe. The idler on the bank of a stream can with difficulty observe two chips floating downwards near each other without thinking of them as engaged in a struggle and identifying himself with one against the other. When the conflict is actual and is human, when it includes within itself forces and interests wherein the spectator is already committed by education, prejudice and aspiration, impartiality of observation and report is well nigh beyond human power.

It is not merely Russian youth who find it hard to conceive that a writer should be interested in what is going on in their country simply as something to behold and if possible to understand. All over the world, it is assumed that a person must of necessity be interested in the scenes as one who is for the new

[First published in Maurice Hindus, *Humanity Uprooted* (New York: Jonathan Cape and Harrison Smith, 1929), pp. xv–xix.]

regime or is against it. It is incredible that one should be concerned to look and to note as a spectator may assist at the unrolling of a drama in which human passions, beliefs and fortunes are engaged deeply and on the most tremendous scale. To see for the sake of seeing and to tell others so that they may vicariously share in the seeing:—that is beyond the reach of the imagination of most men in respect to Soviet Russia. To them it is not a scene to behold; it is a battle to take part in. Failure to be an open partisan is itself suspect. To my mind the striking thing about this book by Mr. Hindus is that with the most intimate sympathetic response to all the human issues involved in the revolutionary transformation, he is nevertheless content to see and to report. Nowhere does he assume the divine prerogative of blessing or condemning; nowhere is he the avenging angel of divine wrath nor yet the angel of benediction.

In consequence, readers who have not already made up their minds, who have not already formed judgments incapable of change, will find the means in this book for reaching a juster and more appreciative understanding of Bolshevist Russia than in any other book known to me. Those who have made up their minds for or against will, each of them, find plenty of material that may be isolated from its context and be used to support their pre-formed views. There is hardly a book in existence that affords more material for hearty damnation of Russia if one merely selects passages with that end in view. But there is also a dispassionate and compassionate account of all the factors that have fired the imaginative ardor of the most devout adherents of the revolution. Yet what has been said would be thoroughly misleading if it induced anyone to suppose that the book is of the "on this hand and the other hand" type. There is no weighing of good points against bad. There is a picture of a large section of humanity uprooted, torn loose from its old bearings, and striving with both fanatical madness and sublime fervor to create a new humanity rooted in a new earth. That the scene of the uprooting and the new aspirations should be mixed beyond all possibility of weighing, point by point, good against evil, is exactly what might be expected. Yet it is precisely what writers with a particular political or economic slant fail to convey.

I have asked myself what it is that has enabled Mr. Hindus to rise so completely above the trammels of partisanship and to achieve a depiction as "objective," as impartial, as it is moving and vivid. The answer which I have found for myself is that he has viewed the scene with the eye of the artist. That the most profound and extensive revolution humanity has ever known is immensely worth beholding and reporting on its own account as a human spectacle is, in the abstract, self-evident. But only, so it seems to me, an unusually large endowment of the eye and the mind of an artist will enable anyone to appreciate as a moving spectacle a revolutionary situation in which all passions and all prejudices are involved. But it is just this trait that marks off the accomplishment of Mr. Hindus. There are objective scientific studies of this and that phase of the Bolshevist revolution, political and economic; the scientific mind also attains impartiality of report. But without the vision of the artist such science stops with columns of figures and statistics. What one finds in the pages of Mr. Hindus is the revolution portrayed in terms of the human beings who experience its agonies and its exaltations.

Each reader will form his own impression of the net outcome of this overturn in the beliefs and labors of humanity—almost as much so as if he had personally accompanied Mr. Hindus in his wanderings through Russia and seen things with his own eyes. Not as a finality, then, but as the impression made upon one reader, I may say that what perhaps I carry away most of all is a sense of the thoroughly Russian character of this upheaval of institutions, traditions, and customs. I suppose a Russian communist would be obliged to deny this interpretation. To him the movement is intrinsically universal—as universal as the material of mathematics or any necessary science. Possibly, however, that conviction is but another evidence of its irretrievably Russian character. At all events, I do not see how anyone can begin to find his way into complexities and inconsistencies of the Russian scene until he has placed it on Russian soil, projected against the background of Russian history.

Without display and without pedantry, Mr. Hindus has evidently absorbed into himself Russian history, Russian literature, the psychology of each of the classes he so brilliantly depicts. Everything is in its own human setting. Hence it is real, concrete, and it carries with it the sense of living reality. To read these pages with sympathy is to travel the road of a liberal education.

Foreword to Fischel Schneersohn's *Studies in Psycho-Expedition: Fundamentals of the Psychological Science of Man and a Theory of Nervousness*

As far as Professor Schneersohn uses material derived from psychiatric sources, I have to confess that I am not an expert in the field and cannot pass judgment. But this remark applies to his illustrative evidence rather than to his principles. The latter appeal to me as highly suggestive and of great interpretive value in dealing with any human being. Similarly, while the illustrative material seems to me to be in the key of European rather than of American life, it is quite easy to transpose it into the key of our own civilization.

Professor Schneersohn's work belongs to that rapidly growing movement that endeavors to effect an integration of the isolated details with which science has hitherto presented us. In psychology the older ideas of mental unity, of the soul and personality, were accompanied by so many survivals of primitive notions that they had to be surrendered. Thus the mental sciences were left for a time without any unifying centre. Professor Schneersohn restores to us a unifying principle, but he does it in a way that involves no recurrence to discarded superstitions; the unity which he offers us, that which used to be called soul or spirit, is framed in terms of scientific material.

His method is in harmony with his interest in discovering a principle of integrity in our mental life—an interest that corresponds to the great need of present civilization. But in order that we may not have at the close merely disconnected fragments, we must have also a vision of the living human being in his individual totality. We owe a debt to Professor Schneersohn because he has not been afraid to insist upon this necessity, and to introduce

[First published in Fischel Schneersohn, *Studies in Psycho-Expedition: Fundamentals of the Psychological Science of Man and a Theory of Nervousness*, trans. from the German by Herman Frank (New York: Science of Man Press, 1929), pp. vii–viii.]

what he well calls the artistic method of viewing and reconstructing mental life.

Since mental and moral disorder is due to splitting up the whole personality, and to exaggerating some of the split-off fragments, suppressing or minimizing other parts, the recognition by science of the integral and total constitution of personality is of great educational and social value. Unless we recognize it in theory, we shall not strive to realize it in practice.

Introduction
Group Action and Group Learning

For more than a generation our universities have been familiar with the Seminar idea in advanced studies. Seminar instruction proceeds neither by the lecture nor the recitation method. Its essence is the presentation of material obtained by the personal research of students, which is then subjected to general discussion and criticism. For a much shorter period of time, elementary and high schools have been acquainting themselves with what in pedagogical vocabulary is called the "socialized recitation." Pupils are called upon to contribute from their own experience, observation and reading, matter cognate to the theme of the lesson, instead of repeating what has been, in theory at least, studied in common by all pupils. Would it be too much to say that what is presented in this volume on *Training for Group Experience* presents a bringing together of these two procedures, one developed in higher, the other in lower, schools? The statement would, however, be incomplete, were it not added that the present volume deals with group experience that is organized with reference to action to be taken, policies to be decided, not to merely theoretical ends.

There has long been maturing a conviction that the intellectual methods of democracy are inadequate to the issues with which a democracy has to deal. So inadequate to their task have been its methods of initiating and formulating policies, that decisions have for the most part been made by small bodies of persons who may have indeed a public purpose to serve, but who may also have private ends to gain. These are then "put over" on

[First published in *Training for Group Experience: A Syllabus of Materials from a Laboratory Course for Group Leaders Given at Columbia University in 1927*, ed. Alfred Dwight Sheffield (New York: Inquiry, 1929), pp. ix–xv.]

the public for discussion and adoption, the appeal being largely emotional and directed toward securing adherence rather than criticism and understanding. We have had much condemnation of the process, but little suggestion as to how better methods might be developed and employed.

In various ways and on diverse subjects, there have been growing up, however, small groups devoted to securing a clearing house of facts and ideas by conjoint discussion with a view to attaining a common mind that might be put into effective action. It may well be that the historian of the future will find that one of the most significant features of present social life is manifest in the rapidity with which the word "group" has come into general use, and will discover that the pooling of experiences by groups in order to reach genuinely cooperative decision and action is their characteristic that reaches furthest. No such claim is made in the volume that follows; it is modestly confined to consideration of ways and means and ends in a limited sphere. But one who approaches the theme in the light of the problems and failures that attend present democratic activity, both in large political issues and in lesser social ones, may well envisage its materials in this wider context. If he does so, he will ask whether there is any way out save the more and more expanded use of the method of group discussion. While the volume is primarily a discussion of the techniques appropriate to such inquiries as carried on by groups, it also serves as a working model and an object lesson for the idea itself.

In its narrower field and aspect, the book is concerned with deliberative bodies that have to do with the determination of policies of action. It is possible that in time the methods it exemplifies will find room for use and application in business boards of corporation directors, faculty meetings and all gatherings where decisions are made through mutual conference. But its especial material is drawn from boards and associations of a religious, philanthropic and social-service character. This fact perhaps accounts for the distinctively educational character of the record. For it is evident in such associations and boards that the aim is not limited to effecting a decision on some particular restricted issue, but is rather concerned with securing such decisions on special points as will deepen interest, create a more intelligent outlook on all similar questions, and secure a more personal response from all concerned in the future. At all events, what marks the Record is the sense that in addition to arriving at definite decisions on particular points, an even more important matter is the permanent deposit left behind in developed attitude and interest. To say this is to say that the pre-eminently educational phase of such group gatherings is kept uppermost. The aim to get something done with a semblance of general agreement is made secondary to the aim to reach decisions by methods that enlist the combined thinking of all and that in consequence offer the promise of continuous interest not merely in action but in learning from further action.

If these introductory words emphasize the general meaning of the Record it is because the details of its operation are developed into a usable technique in the volume itself. It marks a genuine discovery to perceive, as Mr. Sheffield and his associates have done, that minutes and reports of boards and organizations have behind them an interplay of human feeling and thought, a consolidation of experiences, and that by thoughtful attention to the developing and ordering of this interplay, a genuine educative service may be rendered. In the happy words of Mr. Sheffield, it is possible to find discussion methods that in closing incidents will open closed minds.

Not the least significant feature of the book is its contribution to sociological method. All of the social sciences are in various degrees now occupied in climbing down from the heights of abstract principles to the plains of concrete facts. But even when facts are studied, there is an undue literary preoccupation if the facts are merely read about. The prevailing "intellectualism" of higher education is both particularly conspicuous and particularly objectionable when manifested in the study of such a vital and going concern as social life. Visits for the sake of observation can do much to connect the study of second-hand material with a material that is in process of making. But it comes short of what is effected by personal participation. At home or at school most students have a chance to engage in some kind of committee and organization work. With the ideas and ideals of Group Experience in their minds, such students have a first-hand opportunity to accomplish something more than merely "doing" something or putting some scheme across. They can learn to reflect how their own experiences and ideas can be made effective, how to call out and utilize the experiences of others in reaching a decision for concerted action. They may make a beginning in and some contribution to a necessary but well-nigh non-existent art, that of democratic or cooperative thinking.

One of the things that will strike the reader—at least it has impressed itself upon my own mind—is the constant attention here given to psychological factors. Every participant in group discussions that have anything more than an academic import is aware how prejudices, fixed ideas, reminiscences of interesting personal experiences, sore spots, and hypersensitiveness to anything that is interpreted as criticism, balk and deflect the course of thought. Fears, jealousies, personal ambitions, sense of prestige, past loyalties and past defeats, defense reactions, are nonetheless present because they operate delicately and covertly. A presiding officer often acquires great skill in avoiding them and glossing them and their consequences over. But this art usually perpetuates the evil; it keeps the realities of the situation out of sight, and makes an actual conflict of interests into a sham battle wherein everything is different from what it seems to be. In consequence the triumph of the views of one or of a faction is a sham victory. It has been gained by failing to bring underlying conflicts out into the open. There is no modification, unless it be an intensification, of the attitudes with which an issue was originally approached—in other words, no educative result. The suggestions offered in this volume do not tend to create controversy for the sake of controversy. But they do indicate how real conflicts of interest and belief can be brought out and utilized so that controversy becomes an experience in the art of effective inquiry and discussion.

We Americans seem committed to a policy of organization and association-making; we are inveterate "joiners." Critics with whom I have deep sympathy have pointed out the dangers involved in the cult of organizations. But clubs, committees, conventions, conferences, institutes, boards (wittily described as long, narrow and dry), assemblies, councils, leagues, circles are with us and are going to remain. Their dangers are found in excessive devotion to "getting something done" and in an emotional "inspiration" that is but a name for one kind of jag. Action and emotion without attendant thinking sum up most of the things that are open to just criticism. This record of Training for Group Experience does more than show how these evils may be averted. It discloses how the great and constantly growing array of organizations may be converted into constructive agencies of precisely the type of education a democracy most needs. This book and its companion volumes are welcomed as pioneer undertakings that open and explore a new territory.

Censorship

I am glad to hear that you are taking up the matter of Censorship. It is especially timely in view of the efforts of Senator Cutting to liberate us from the burden of customs censorship. It is ridiculous that the foreign literature that comes to the American nation should be subject to restrictions imposed by a group of officials whose business is concerned with economic affairs. If the American people submits to this imposition, it is a proof that it has lost its love of liberty and self-government.

It is a reflection upon the eastern states that boast of superior culture that the leadership in this fight should come from New Mexico, and it is most encouraging to know that Senator Cutting has you behind him in his fight for historic American liberties. I wish you all success.

[First published in *Laughing Horse: A Magazine of the Southwest*, ed. Willard Johnson (Taos, New Mexico), no. 17, February 1930, [n.p.].]

In Response

Mrs. Swan, Mr. Chairman, Miss Addams and Friends:
Of course I am very, very deeply touched by all of the expressions which have come to me in the last few days. Some of them have been somewhat exaggerated, but I will not claim that I have not been gratified even by these exaggerations; in fact, in the colloquial, I have lapped them up. At the same time I know that there have been some who were slightly skeptical or more than slightly, about some of these expressions and I should like to reassure them by saying that I share their skepticism.

I had a letter from a friend in which she said that if I betook too freely from the frosting of the cake that I might learn something new about the relations of experience and nature. I took it that the remarks applied even more to the spiritual frosting which has decorated these occasions than to this beautiful material frosting.

As I listened to the discussion last evening, I was reminded of a story, an episode that happened either many thousand years ago or on another planet, I am not quite sure which, about a man who was somewhat sensitive to the movements of things about him. He had a certain appreciation of what things were passing away and dying and of what things were being born and growing. And on the strength of that response he foretold some of the things that were going to happen in the future. When he was seventy years old the people gave him a birthday party and they gave him credit for bringing to pass the things that he had foreseen might come to pass. He fooled himself somewhat by being told these things, but he didn't fool himself very much. But he

[First published in *John Dewey, the Man and His Philosophy: Addresses Delivered in New York in Celebration of His Seventieth Birthday* (Cambridge: Harvard University Press, 1930), pp. 173–81.]

had a very good time and he hoped that everybody else had had a good time too.

There is one thing about which I am not at all skeptical and that is the expressions of friendship, of kindliness and affection which have come to me. I wish that I could thank personally those from whom they have come, not merely those who have spoken, but those who have sent their messages in other ways. I cannot thank each one individually but I do want to thank very especially those who have come from other places to be present on this occasion—to my old student, President Angell, who perhaps, though you wouldn't think it to look at him, is the earliest and in that sense the oldest of my former students probably who is here today; to Director Carroll Moore, also a former student and now the Director of the University of California in Los Angeles; and to my old time colleague and friend, though not student, George Mead of Chicago, and naturally Jane Addams of Chicago, as well as Professor Ralph Perry of Harvard University. If I mention these people it is not because I do not also appreciate the words that have come from my nearer neighbors here.

It would be ungracious not to thank also the Executive Committee, the Chairman, Mrs. Swan, the other members. Acknowledgments are due also to one who today is in the Orient, but who as Chairman of the Executive Committee was a prime mover in making the arrangements for these meetings—Professor Kilpatrick. And I am sure that they would agree with me that the Executive Secretary Henry Linville, deserves mention. I am not sure, Henry, that my gratitude on this occasion to you is entirely unalloyed, but at the same time I am glad to have the privilege of expressing publicly my admiration for your courageous and unwearied and self-effacing activities in so many other good causes.

I am grateful to speakers that they have so largely talked about movements and ideas in which we share a common interest and by the side of which any personality is relatively unimportant. There is no occasion for me, however, to repeat or review what they have said, and it would be impossible to add anything at this time about the ideas, the movements and the causes themselves. You will, I am sure, understand however that it was natural for me after having my attention called somewhat emphatically and numerously to the fact that I was seventy years old,—I don't suppose I can conceal the fact now,—that I should have made some survey in my own mind of the conditions through which our contemporaries have lived in these recent years. If I have done so it is not for the purpose of indulging in the privilege of old age and engaging in reminiscences on this occasion, though I do wish there were time for me to express my debt of grateful piety to the teachers and colleges, that have so deeply influenced me from the very time when I came to that institution in Vermont to which James Angell has referred. I must, however, forego that. But my consciousness of my deep indebtedness to these multitudes of people, many of whom today I am afraid I could not even name, has been one of the things that has convinced me that there is nothing so important in life as the free, unobstructed communication of ideas and experiences and their transmission from one to another, without any kind of restriction, censorship, or intimidation—legal, political, or extralegal.

For some reason, possibly through a conversation recently with a friend, my mind in going back over these years and wondering what they were all about, in what direction they were tending, has taken the form of thinking somewhat about the conditions of happiness in life. I know very well that one cannot generalize from any individual case of a reasonably happy life because fortune, because something that we must frankly call luck, the chance coincidences of life, play such a large, unavoidable part in the enjoyment of happiness.

One of the conditions of happiness is the opportunity of a calling, a career which somehow is congenial to one's own temperament. And I have had the sheer luck or fortune to be engaged in the occupation of thinking; and while I am quite regular at my meals I think that I may say that I had rather work—and perhaps even more play—with ideas and with thinking than eat. That chance has been given me.

The other and deepest source of happiness in life comes to one, I suppose, from one's own family relations; and there too, though I have experienced great sorrows, I can truly say that in my life companion, in my children, and in my grandchildren, I have been blessed by the circumstances and fortunes of life.

There are other things of happiness, however, which are not so personal, which do depend more upon conditions that are within our control. And I wish to speak very briefly, if I may, upon some of those.

It seems to me that probably the greatest enemy to what is attainable in happiness in the life of human beings is the attitude of fear. Fear is an unfortunate word, like all words that have to carry important ideas and emotions. It suggests something that we consciously feel in emergencies, and which is not very important unless very extreme. What I have in mind is rather an unconscious attitude which runs through and pervades everything of which we are conscious. It is not so much fear in the ordinary sense as it is an attitude of withdrawal, an attitude of exclusiveness which shuts out the beauties and troubles of experience as the things from which we alone can really learn and go on growing. It is even possible to get rid of fears of specific things and still retain a kind of underlying fear of fear itself.

This attitude of fear cannot be abolished by any direct attack. It can be expelled only by the power of another and more positive attitude and emotion, that of going out to and welcoming all of the incidents of a changing experience, even those which in themselves are troublesome. I might call it the open mind, only perhaps that suggests too much a vacant mind, a sort of "Come right in; you are welcome; there is nobody at home." Well, in reality the open mind is this positive attitude of interest, so far as one's limitations do at times permit, in all of the concerns of our common humanity.

I have learned many things from Jane Addams. I notice that with her usual modesty she attributed to me some of the things in Chicago which she and her colleagues in Hull House did. One of the things that I have learned from her is the enormous value of mental non-resistance, of tearing away the armor-plate of prejudice, of convention, isolation that keeps one from sharing to the full in the larger and even the more unfamiliar and alien ranges of the possibilities of human life and experience.

I suppose there are a certain number of younger people here who have in mind engaging in a calling something like my own; that is, working mostly at ideas and not much at anything else—in other words, the educators whether in the schoolroom or pulpit or wherever. I should like to say to them that I think the most inexpensive, the most easily attained source of happiness in what we call a specialized intellectual class, is found simply in this broadening of intellectual curiosity and sympathy in all the concerns of life. You don't really have to do much about it, as my own experience testifies. You only have to show some intellectual interest in these things to find an ever-growing source of satisfaction in life. While everything that shuts the individual off, shuts his mind, his ideas off, from other things, ends by petrifying his mind and his experience and drying up the very sources of happiness within him.

The greatest evil, it seems to me, in our American life, even greater than fear—and one which is the cause of innumerable anxieties, worries and fretting, that which most prevents us from realizing the possibilities of life—is our externalism. I have never thought that the average American has any more love for the dollar as such than the average Frenchman for the franc, or the average German for the mark,—in fact I came near saying *sou* and *pfennig*,—but external opportunities so abound in our American life that instead of nurturing the sources of happiness we tend to make happiness a direct pursuit; and the direct pursuit of happiness always ends in looking for happiness in possessions, in possessions of what is external, in having something whether in having a good time, having money, having a multitude of material things, or having someone else to lean upon for our ideas. We pursue happiness in these external things because, I suppose, we do not really possess our own souls. We are impatient; we are hurried; we are fretful because we try to find happiness where it cannot be got. Some of us are, indeed, as much in a hurry for reforms as other people are in a hurry for speed in physical movement. Without knowing it, we distrust the slow processes of growth, and we do not tend the roots of life from which a lasting happiness springs.

Our present American ideal seems to be, "Put it over—and make it snappy while you do it." I do not imagine that state of things will endure forever. Mere fatigue and sheer disappointment will bring it to an end sometime. But in the meantime we need a revival of faith in individuality and what belongs to the internal springs and sources of individuality. Only a return to that individuality, which after all is what each of us is, will bring calm, repose, and a sense of beauty in the multitude of distractions of our modern life and action.

The world is either a wonderful scene or a dismal one according to whether we bring wonder with us to it or whether we bring with us the desire to possess as much of it as possible in as short a time as possible. What we bring to the world in which we live always has and always will, at last, go back to the depths of our own being. I see, however, that I am in danger of falling into too sermonic a mood—and, as one of our speakers this morning reminded us, after all this is supposed to be a celebration.

So I can only close by saying that I cannot do less again than thank you. Not being gifted with the tongues of angels I cannot either do more—but I do thank you from my heart.

Tribute to James H. Tufts

It gives me much pleasure to write a few words in response to your suggestion and it is a source of great regret to me that I cannot be present in person to add a word of tribute to those which will be paid to our distinguished friend, especially as I am probably the oldest of those living who have had the great satisfaction of having James Tufts as a colleague. Our association began at the University of Michigan and continued for a period of ten years at the University of Chicago. His translation of Windelband's *History of Philosophy* was among the early signs of a genuine development of interest in the United States in not only historic philosophy but in the ideas for which that history stands. If American philosophy has left its meagre and dry days behind, the change is due in no small measure to the work of our friend. In saying this I do not refer of course as much to this translation as to the spirit and mind of which the translation was a symbol. Mr. Tufts' great work, it seems to me, both as a teacher and a writer has been in connection with the ethical side of philosophy. His interest and influence have not been confined to what is definitely labelled "Ethics." They have extended to a realization of the moral values involved in all genuine and vital philosophical thought. His sturdy, extraordinarily judicial, honest, personality found its way through the technical wrappings of philosophical discourse to the human and moral issues that underlie these wrappings. It is significant that his early work centred so largely about his study of the concept of individuality. An article of his in the *Philosophical Review* was I think the first note sounded in this country in revolt against the attempt to base the theory of knowledge upon a study of mental states. It antici-

[Unpublished typescript of tribute to James H. Tufts read at the farewell dinner for Tufts, Chicago, 10 December 1930.]

pated by several years much of later American developments; I have heard from several quarters of its effect in changing the current of thinking with a number of the men who in those years were young. Professor Tufts was also a pioneer in recognizing the importance of the social categories; his interpretation for example of the esthetic judgment from a social point remains the prototype of work in this field.

I must not however encroach upon the theme of others by attempting a review of the career of Mr. Tufts as a thinker, writer and teacher. What stands uppermost in my thought is the picture of a true philosopher, a lover of knowledge but of knowledge for the sake of wisdom, and not as an end in itself. Every thinker in this field is subject to the temptation of a sort of divorce between his personality and his intellect. Mr. Tufts has given his colleagues in philosophy an inspiring example of the fact that it is possible to be a philosopher and yet maintain personality and intellect in complete harmony. For that we thank him as we love him as a man and a friend.

Reports

Lobby Inquiry Opens Tomorrow

The special inquiry into lobby activities authorized by the Senate is expected to begin hearings Tuesday, turning first to the operations of tariff lobbyists. This phase of the investigation is likely to continue for several weeks in an endeavor to throw light on attempts to bring pressure on committees while the tariff bill was being drafted. The activities of the sugar lobby will be thoroughly inquired into, said Senator Caraway, chairman of the committee of inquiry.

During the special session it is expected that the investigators will confine themselves to tariff lobbying, but will broaden the investigation in the regular session to touch upon the power trust lobby.

The investigation is expected by Senator Caraway to create sentiment favorable to the regulation of lobbyists, and the enactment of a law requiring their registration. Nearly two-thirds of the States have such laws.

Professor John Dewey of Columbia University, president of the People's Lobby, has written to Senator Caraway, suggesting that there should be a public record of the stock holdings of members of Congress as part of any plan to compel the registration of lobbyists. He also expressed a desire that the People's Lobby be brought under examination.

"We recognized the necessity for a people's organization to work at the national capital for measures in the interest of the people generally, and did not hesitate to call it a 'lobby,' for that is what it is," Professor Dewey wrote.

"Only organizations which have used unjust and improper methods of presenting their cases to Congress and departments of government for the public need fear scrutiny by Congress.

[First published in *New York Times*, 14 October 1929, p. 19.]

"As a corollary of this fact, however, the American people have an indisputable right to know that the financial·and business interests of members of both branches of Congress and all departments of the Federal Government, including the judiciary, do not influence them in their votes nor in their actions and decisions.

"Such an assurance, the People's Lobby believes, can be secured by requiring a public recognition of stock holdings and corporation affiliations of Federal officials and employes. This is a logical sequence to the registration of all representatives of lobbyists and a statement of their methods, receipts and expenditures."

Attacks Wage Disparity

Declaring that "the income of millions of American families is far below the requirements of decent living," the People's Lobby, of which Professor John Dewey is president, issued a statement tonight in which he declared that there should be "a fairer distribution of the national income."

Citing official figures showing that in 1927, 11,112 persons received an aggregate income of close to $3,000,000,000, and that in the same year 866,581 wage earners received an average wage of $1,073, the statement insisted that this condition should be remedied.

"Within a few years," it said, "the Federal Government must spend billions of dollars for federal child relief, for unemployment, and for old-age pensions. It must obtain most of this by taxing incomes over $10,000.

"Childhood blighted through poverty and hardship is an unpardonable sin in this the only nation in the world whose national income is sufficient to afford a decent standard of living to all within its borders. Protection of childhood is implicit in the expression 'Peace on earth, good will to man.'"

[First published in *New York Times*, 26 December 1929, p. 28.]

Child Relief Steps Urged on Congress

Asserting that the "finest and most practical" form of preventive relief work can be done with children, Professor John Dewey, president of the People's Lobby, in a statement made public today, urged the "universal bombarding" of members of Congress to support the Wheeler-La Guardia bill to create a Federal Child Relief Board and the appropriation of $25,000,000 for child relief for the balance of the fiscal year 1930.

"All civilized States," said Professor Dewey, "are committed to care of the insane, the sick, the extremely poor. The United States has an enviable record for private charity. It is behind several European nations in public preventive work, such as unemployment insurance and insurance for old age, to which the lobby is also committed.

"The finest and most practicable form of preventive relief work can be done with children. They suffer from no fault of their own, and unless they have a chance for proper nutrition and health and an education, they become either public charges or drags on the community at a later time, because of inefficiency, bad health and lack of preparation for the duties of citizenship.

"The Wheeler-La Guardia bill has just been introduced in Congress with an appropriation of $25,000,000 for the proper physical care and schooling of children whose parents are incapacitated to care for them. There are already organizations in existence, including the Children's Bureau of the Department of Labor and numerous organizations throughout the country to secure an efficient expenditure of funds.

"The bill the People's Lobby is sponsoring does not attempt to set up any extensive machinery, but creates a board composed of

[First published in *New York Times*, 30 December 1929, p. 19.]

the Secretary of Labor, the chief of the Children's Bureau and the Secretary of Agriculture to administer the fund, giving them such wide latitude as to use of existing agencies as is so wisely afforded in the Federal Farm Board.

"The bill stipulates that the relief is to be 'for children in distress in prolonged strikes, children of the unemployed, and of other parents in extreme poverty, including children of farmers in distressed agricultural areas.' It does not, however, sanction placing children in institutions."

Asks Federal Fund to Aid Unemployed

Professor John Dewey, president of the People's Lobby, made public a statement today in which he estimated that 3,000,000 to 5,000,000 men and women had been idle for three months to over a year, with little prospect that there would be any substantial increase in employment for several months.

He also announced that he had asked President Hoover in a letter to request Congress before it adjourns to appropriate at least $250,000,000 for the subvention of a State unemployment insurance system, the Federal Government to pay half of the benefits. Receipt of the letter had been acknowledged by one of the President's secretaries.

"We ask your cooperation," Professor Dewey wrote to the President, "in securing such Federal aid for a State unemployment insurance system, not because such insurance will prevent unemployment, which involves much more fundamental though inevitable readjustments of our economic system; we ask it because economic conditions here now are so serious, as the figures we cite above show that measures of this sort are essential to prevent serious difficulties."

Professor Dewey stated it was obvious that prosperity could not be achieved unless an overwhelming majority of the American people were fairly continuously employed at wages affording a surplus above existence requirements.

"Neither of these conditions exists in the United States today," he continued. "Between one-fifteenth and one-ninth of those 15 years of age and over are unemployed and have been unemployed for many months. Unemployment is more serious unquestionably because nearly 2,000,000 children are working. The average wage of the 27,298,000 wage earners in all industries in 1927,

[First published in *New York Times*, 12 May 1930, p. 35.]

nearly three-fifths of all those gainfully employed, was only $1,205.

"Mechanization has proceeded so far and so fast that our past policy of laissez faire with respect to other industries is as fatal as it was with respect to agriculture. You and Congress recognize this with respect to agriculture, as a result of which we have the Federal Farm Board, the operations of which will tend to stabilize farm real estate values, though not to provide a market for maximum production, nor to insure employment for those engaged in this industry.

"The Federal Government has an obligation from the standpoint of national prosperity as well as human welfare to soften the difficulties of mechanization which means profits for the few through cheaper production costs, but which, as our recent experience shows, does not mean increasing consuming power of the masses."

Asks Hoover to Act on Unemployment

Professor John Dewey of New York, President of the People's Lobby, in a letter to President Hoover, made public today, asks him to call Congress into special session to take steps toward a system of unemployment insurance.

The President has not indicated his response to the suggestion, but, according to Professor Dewey, receipt of his letter has been acknowledged by Lawrence Richey, one of the White House secretaries.

Professor Dewey in his letter said:

"On behalf of the People's Lobby and voicing, I am confident, the wishes of progressively minded Americans generally, I respectfully ask that you will call Congress in special session at once to appropriate an adequate sum for Federal subvention of State unemployment insurance systems.

"The major part of those unemployed for a long time are in about half a dozen States. The Governors of these States at least, can call their State Legislatures into session at once to devise methods of unemployment insurance appropriate to their States, so that this provision for the public welfare, essential and inevitable in a nation which has achieved the highly mechanized mass production we have, may be effective next Fall. Only such unemployment insurance will prevent appalling want and suffering next Winter, and in future years.

"Such act is peculiarly imperative because the Smoot-Hawley tariff bill will tend to limit exports of American merchandise. Responsible government officials have warned wheat growers to limit their production to the domestic demand, which seldom exceeds 500,000,000 bushels for use off the farms, though the pres-

[First published in *New York Times*, 21 July 1930, p. 17.]

ent acreage planted to wheat could produce at least 800,000,000 bushels for sale.

"It is obvious that with a national income (in 1928) estimated by the National Bureau of Economic Research at $89,419,000,000, we can consume in this country at least twice the value of merchandise exported in recent years, in addition to present consumption. The total value of such merchandise exported, exclusive of wheat, is only about 5 per cent of the national income.

"At present between 2,400,000 and 3,500,000 persons, many of them heads of families, are out of the consuming class entirely, or except for the barest necessities for existence—because so long unemployed.

"On the other hand, the Commissioner of Internal Revenue reports that in 1928 the 15,780 persons who received net incomes of over $100,000 received an aggregate income of $4,903,359,562, or about one-eighteenth of the national income of the 24,000,000 families in the United States. Over three-quarters of their income was from property—that is, unearned. They received a fourth of all dividends paid on common and preferred stocks by all domestic corporations. After paying Federal incomes and surtaxes they had left, on the average, $266,344.

"The Commissioner of Internal Revenue also reports that the 375,356 persons who for 1928 reported net incomes of over $10,000 had an aggregate income of $14,214,359,822, or about one-sixth of the income of 24,000,000 families. About 65.9 per cent—nearly two-thirds of their income—was derived from property, and they received almost three-fifths of all dividends paid on the stock of domestic corporations.

"No nation can survive mass production, unless there is such a distribution of the national income as to make possible commensurate mass consumption out of current earnings or income. Private concern has not brought about such a condition in this country. The concentration of income has brought about a nation-wide catastrophe. Reduction of taxes on the wealthy and retaining them on consumption, has been followed by an inevitable reduction in consumption, and a wholly unnecessary scourge of unemployment.

"A nation-wide system of contributory unemployment insurance with the Federal government paying $1,000,000,000, and States, employers and employes jointly, the same amount—in the aggregate about 2.2 per cent of the national income—would largely relieve the most serious unemployment; needless to emphasize, it would also improve business conditions to a very marked extent. The proposed Federal government's contribution to conquer this real menace at home is only a small amount more than it spends to prepare to fight a non-existent enemy abroad.

"For these reasons we ask you to call the Congress in special session to deal with this problem, which it ignored in the session just closed."

Puts Needs of Idle at Two Billions

Estimating that $2,000,000,000 will be needed for unemployment relief, Professor John Dewey, president of the People's Lobby, charged the government with neglect today in not acting before the emergency became acute, and said that an appropriation of $500,000,000 for relief will be asked as soon as Congress convenes.

Professor Dewey's statement read in part:

"The present unemployment situation is not an accident, it is the inevitable result of economic policies fostered by both major parties—policies which have never been followed long in any country without serious disturbances and even revolutions. There is no reason to believe that the American people who know the adequacy of our national wealth and national income will prove an exception.

"The solemn question to be answered, probably within a decade, is whether we can change our present policies of governmental fostering of the concentration of wealth, while over a tenth of the population suffer; or whether the adoption of human policies by government shall be forced upon us by other countries which have freed themselves from the conception of government as the private property of predatory and stupidly selfish interests. Sound patriotism dictates self-help.

"Our unemployed with their dependents total about 12,000,000 people, or one-tenth of the population. Their loss of wages on a conservative estimate, assuming they are not re-employed till next April or May, will be about $6,000,000,000.

"Congress must appropriate at least $500,000,000 as soon as it convenes, to match every dollar raised by State, municipal and other local governments for the care of unemployed and their families."

[First published in *New York Times*, Sunday, 26 October 1930, sec. 1, p. 21.]

People's Lobby Hits Sugar Loan to Cuba

A letter has been sent to President Hoover by the People's Lobby calling for scrutiny by the State Department and Congress of the proposed $42,000,000 bankers' loan to the Cuban Government to finance the carrying of Cuba's sugar crop. The document was given out tonight by Professor John Dewey, president of the lobby.

"Big financial interests in New York propose to make a loan of $42,000,000 to the Cuban government so it may take up the private loan of $38,000,000 these same financial interests recently made to sugar interests in Cuba, chiefly American, to bolster up the price of sugar," the letter read.

"This calls, we believe, for meticulous scrutiny by both the State Department and the Congress which assembles shortly.

"The terms of this loan and the effect of such a loan upon American consumers of sugar are important.

"We maintain the Machado Government, in control in Cuba, by the threat of use of armed forces. We should have learned from the expulsion of our military mission from Brazil after the administration to which we shipped arms was booted out, and from the first uncontrolled election in Haiti since our intervention, which gave us a mandate to get out and keep out, that it is not the primary function of the armed forces of the United States to maintain in power in areas subject to a malign interpretation of the Monroe Doctrine pliant nominal rulers to operate governments by dictation from Wall Street financiers.

"Why the spread of $4,000,000—nearly one-ninth—between the bankers' loan to the sugar interests and to the government? What obligations do we assume or to what further aspects of dictatorship are we entitled by secret understandings under this loan?

[First published in *New York Times*, 24 November 1930, p. 10.]

"What relations has this proposed loan to the Cuban Government to the effort being made by Thomas L. Chadbourne to cut down the world production of sugar so that the producers, chiefly American interests, may secure higher prices from consumers?

"Our per capita consumption of sugar is about 115 pounds. Every increase of 1 cent a pound in price increases our sugar bill by $140,300,000 a year.

"What is the difference between Mr. Chadbourne's plan to curtail sugar production and the attempt of the British to hijack the price of rubber under the Stevenson act, and the valorization of coffee by the former Brazilian Government?

"It was the Dutch who, by increasing their production of rubber, broke the price, and Mr. Chadbourne is now on his way to Holland to try to get their sugar producers into the world price-boosting pool.

"You denounced the British and Brazilian schemes. Can you consistently sanction a loan by American bankers, be they ever so patriotic, to buttress an attack upon the American breakfast table by valorizing the price of sugar up to the tune of $6 to $12 per American family?

"As you know, this prosperity we enjoy has reduced one-sixth of American families to penury."

John Dewey Assails the Major Parties

Characterizing the major political parties as errand boys of big business Professor John Dewey sounded a call over station WOR yesterday, in what was said to be his first radio address for a new progressive political alignment.

Professor Dewey spoke under the auspices of the League for Independent Political Action, which is seeking to establish a new political group. Dr. Dewey is chairman of the league.

"Our social life" said Dr. Dewey "has been almost completely changed in the last generation; the change is a transformation of the conditions under which we live, symbolized by the radio, the railway, telephone, telegraph, the flying machine and mass production, changing the United States from an agrarian and rural population to a city and industrial one," continued Dr. Dewey. "In spite of this transformation, the mightiest which any people at any time has ever undergone during a like number of years, there has been no corresponding political realignment.

"The old parties have continued to mouth the old phrases and flaunt the old slogans before the public, while behind the scenes, in spite of large dissenting minorities in each party, they have surrendered abjectly to domination by big business interests and become their errand boys. No wonder people have become indifferent and careless about political issues. They show their good sense in not getting frantically excited.

"Leaders of the League for Independent Political Action believe that American life is badly in need of reorganization based upon a sense of the realities of our social life, and that this reconstruction, looking to a forward movement, can be achieved only by political policies which take account of existing industrial and financial conditions."

[First published in *New York Times*, 14 October 1929, p. 2.]

Dewey Supports Vladeck

Election of B. C. Vladeck, Socialist candidate for Representative in the Eighth Congressional District, Brooklyn, "to break the boss control of the House of Representatives into a mere rubber stamp of the Republican machine" was advocated by Professor John Dewey, chairman of the League for Independent Political Action, made public yesterday.

"Not the slightest hope remains of accomplishing any fundamental change through either of the two old parties," the letter read. "Both are dominated by corrupt political bosses and selfish business interests. The time is at hand for honest people to rise up and declare that they have no more votes for such politicians. Great problems wait to be settled while grafters, racketeers and privileged business interests reap their rich harvests."

The league announced that it had endorsed Samuel Orr, Socialist candidate for Congress in the Twenty-third District, and A. I. Shiplacoff, Socialist candidate for Congress in the Twelfth District, in addition to those previously endorsed.

[First published in *New York Times*, 15 September 1930, p. 16.]

Dewey Asks Norris to Lead New Party

An invitation to Senator George W. Norris of Nebraska to withdraw from the Republican party and help form a new third party was issued yesterday by Professor John Dewey, national chairman of the League for Independent Political Action.

In a letter to Senator Norris, Dr. Dewey declared that the Republican party was a house divided against itself. He asserted that he agreed with Robert H. Lucas, executive director of the Republican National Committee, that Senator Norris did not belong to the Republican party as the latter was "too socially minded."

Dr. Dewey added that the Democratic party stood for the same principles as the Republican party and its machinery was controlled by the same groups. He declared that many Senators and Representatives in the two old parties had informed him that they regarded the formation of a third party as inevitable and predicted that it could win the Presidency by 1940.

"In light of your recent experience with leaders of the Republican party," Dr. Dewey wrote, "I urge that you sever forever your connections with that political machine and form with those of us in the League for Independent Political Action and other liberal groups a new party to which you can give your full allegiance.

"The recent attack upon you in the statement issued by Robert H. Lucas, executive director of the Republican National Committee, clearly shows that the lines are being drawn and that you and other insurgent Republicans are not wanted in the G.O.P. by those that control the machine. In my judgment this is going to increasingly be made clear to you. How could you expect otherwise?

[First published in *New York Times*, 26 December 1930, p. 1. For reply by Norris, see this volume, Appendix 6.]

"The Republican party stands for 'rugged' individualism. You stand for social planning and social control. Republican leaders believe that by giving free rein to private competition somehow they will build a better world. You believe that in this complicated age that method is impossible, but that society must plan for its production and consumption. The controlling wing of the Republican party places property rights first. You place human rights first.

"These are antagonistic philosophies. The Republican party is a house divided against itself. You cannot put new wine into old bottles, and we shall never be able to put this new philosophy of government into either of the old parties. Just as the Whig party split on the issue of slavery, the Republican party will divide on this issue of social planning versus rugged individualism.

"The Democratic party stands for exactly the same principles as the Republican party and its machinery is controlled by the same invested groups. If the Democratic party comes into power its insurgents will receive the same treatment from it that you receive from your party. The new political philosophy needs its own incarnation.

"Millions of progressives over the United States are disgusted with the old parties and are longing for a new political alignment. At this Christmas season will you not renounce both of these old parties and help give birth to a new party based upon the principle of planning and control for the purpose of building happier lives, a more just society and that peaceful world which was the dream of Him whose birthday we celebrate this Christmas Day? The terrible suffering in this unemployment crisis, the increasing fear of insecurity, the exploitation by public utility companies and other monopolies resulting in our unjust distribution of wealth, and the nationalism and militarism which brought on the World War, will be repeated under the present political leadership. A new party with your philosophy of life could stop these evils.

"Many outstanding men and women in this country from every walk of life recognize the need and will support such an alignment. State Governors, Federal judges, Congressmen and United States Senators now working within the old parties have expressed their conviction to us that such a new party must come. We could win the Presidency by 1940. We could drive the conservatives in desperation into one of the old parties and we should then have a real conflict of ideas and a vital party of opposition which would make for rapid political progress and give desperate workers and farmers a constructive vehicle of political expression.

"This is not an easy task. There are many difficulties. Vicious opposition would seek to block the road. But the welfare of our nation lies that way.

"We agree with Mr. Lucas. You do not belong in the Republican party. You are too socially minded for it. Come out of it and participate in the thrill and enthusiasm of a great movement which is our own and which will realize for common men their rightful heritage. They will rally to your support. Will you help lead the march?"

Dewey for Farm Backing

A special drive will be made for the support of the farmers who have been the mainstay of the Republican party in the agrarian States, when the formation of the third party, contemplated by Dr. John Dewey and his League for Independent Political Action, gets under way, according to a statement made public by Dr. Dewey last night, partly in comment on the refusal of Senator Norris of Nebraska to exchange his present affiliation with the Republicans for leadership in the third party movement.

"Farmers must furnish a real share of the leadership; the new party must come up 'from the grass roots,'" Dr. Dewey said.

Dr. Dewey admitted that it might require as long a time as twenty years to build up a new and durable political alignment in this country, but asserted that he had enlisted "for the duration of the struggle."

What he declared to be an irrepressible conflict between the interests of large banking, industrial and public utility groups, in control of the machines of both existing major parties, and the interests of the masses, he added, had made the formation of a new party a vital necessity. He intimated that he had not abandoned hope to enlist Senator Norris in the warfare on the two older parties.

The statement of Dr. Dewey follows.

"The response of Senator Norris to my letter asking him to cast his lot with a new political alignment has not been a surprise. Such a step is not quickly taken and especially when a man is under fire.

"Senator Norris has been one of the ablest of that small group that has kept the Republican party from being completely the

[First published in *New York Times*, Sunday, 28 December 1930, sec. 1, p. 20. For Norris's letter to which this is a reply, see this volume, Appendix 6.]

political expression of the great industrial, banking and public utility groups of this country. It is inevitable that these existing groups have political representation. But they have no right to such representation to the exclusion of the interests of the masses of people. Such a condition too largely exists today, where the invested groups control the machines of both parties.

"I hardly expected an affirmative answer at once from Senator Norris, but desired to emphasize this irrepressible conflict, that in my judgment makes necessary this new political alignment. The Senator himself suggests the need in his proposal to abolish the Electoral College and make possible the election of a President by popular vote.

"The League for Independent Political Action will give its fullest support to this suggestion of Mr. Norris's and use every influence in helping to secure the passage of his proposed bill. Of course, other difficulties almost as great face a new party. The power of the Supreme Court also discourages political action. What is the use of passing social legislation only to have it declared unconstitutional? is the problem of many voters. The fear that voters have that they are throwing away their votes for a new party constitutes another obstacle.

"We have no illusion about the difficulties confronting us. It may take ten years, even twenty years to build up this new political alignment, but we have enlisted for the duration of the struggle. On the other hand, America when she moves moves quickly and this new party may come sooner than we think.

"We have been glad to challenge Senator Norris to assist in building the movement. We hope some day to have his fearless and brilliant support. However, we hope we have not placed ourselves by this action in the position of tying the third party wagon to any one man's fortune or one man's leadership at this stage of proceedings. The Bull Moose party and the La Follette campaign failed because of this error. Any project is helped by great personalities, but a lasting movement must be more than a great leader.

"We urge outstanding men and women to work with us, for the party will be a failure unless it is the expression of workers of hand or brain, including the farmers who must furnish a real share of the leadership. The party must come up 'from the grass roots.'

"During 1931, we shall act as a coordinating agency, bringing together all groups that ought to be interested in using politics on the basis of this principle of social planning and control. We shall appeal to workers, farmers, and all progressives of goodwill. The league will serve as an educational force, publishing pamphlets on governmental problems, using speakers, magazine articles and the radio.

"In the realm of political action, while we shall carry on our organization of local branches all over the country, we are concentrating primarily on the most fertile States and will hold State conferences in Montana, Washington, South Dakota, Idaho, Iowa, Kansas, Nebraska, Colorado, Oklahoma and Texas, looking forward to the organization of State committees and eventually State parties in those areas where no effective third party groups now exist, which will later help to form the basis of a national conference and a national party."

Announcement was made by the New History Society that Dr. Dewey would lecture on "The Principles of a Third Political Party" at a meeting to be held under its auspices at the Community Church, Park Avenue and Thirty-fourth Street, Tuesday evening. The meeting will be open to the public and no admission fee will be charged.

Appendixes

Appendix 1
Can Logic Be Divorced from Ontology?
By Ernest Nagel

Preoccupation with methodology has often led to the denial of an intimate connection between method used and the irreducible traits of subject-matter explored. This paper is a protest against such a diremption. The position taken and the arguments used are not new, and both have been learned, in part at least, from Professor Dewey's own writings. The only reason for saying here what follows, is because in his article on the excluded middle he seems to leave open the possibility of an affirmative answer to the question in the title.

I

Professor Dewey himself subordinates the particular question of the sphere of application of the principle of excluded middle to the fundamental issue of the relation of the logical and the ontological, the formal and the existential. There seems, therefore, to be no doubt in his own mind that logical and ontological characters are discoverable in experience, and that some evidence can be produced to decide in favor of the logical or ontological order of disputed traits. Unfortunately, nowhere in his paper does Professor Dewey suggest what that distinction is. It is clear, of course, that if no criteria of ontological traits are offered, the issue raised by him becomes indeterminate.

One must turn to Professor Dewey's other writings in order to fix the problem. In the first place, he claims for himself both a metaphysics and a logic. His metaphysics is a description of the generic traits of existence. His logic is a formulation of the

[First published in *Journal of Philosophy* 26 (19 December 1929): 705–12. For Dewey's article to which this is a reply, see this volume, pp. 197–202. For Dewey's rejoinder, see pp. 203–9.]

method of such thinking which eventuates in an intentional reorganization of experience. Secondly, those are the generic factors, which are irreducible traits in every subject-matter of scientific inquiry. He declares that "qualitative individuality and constant relations, contingency and need, movement and arrest, are common traits of all existence." Thirdly, it is of the essence of Professor Dewey's doctrine that while we do define the general criteria of ontological traits as those which are pervasive and inescapable, yet these traits carry no tag which would permit their identification apart from a reflective inquiry. Ontological characters, like other characters, become objects of knowledge only as *conclusions* of an inferential process. Finally, on Professor Dewey's theory of knowledge, the fixed and secure objects of knowledge represent the transformations, produced by the thinking process for purposes of control and continuity, of the antecedent existences given to a non-cognitive experience.

It seems to follow, therefore, that objects of knowledge possess some traits which belong to them in virtue of the reflective context within which they occur, and that such traits can not be attributed directly (that is, outside of this context) to an antecedent existence. These specifically logical traits can be recognized as such, presumably, by comparing the qualities of objects of knowledge with objects of direct experience. But if the nature of existence is discovered, not by some prior definition of what it is, but by an experimental inquiry, the outcome of that inquiry must in some sense be identified with independent features of existence. When light falls on a metal plate and an electric current flows in consequence, the quantitative relation between intensity or frequency of light and strength of current, which is established by inquiry, is an independent factor in the domain surveyed. If the traits of objects found in an inferential process are *merely* logical traits, then no ontological characters of objects can be discovered *within* a reflective inquiry. And if metaphysical traits are not found within a reflective context, the only occasion when they could be noted would be in those non-reflective experiences of enjoying and possessing to which Professor Dewey has so eloquently called attention. Hence if ontological traits do not emerge in a reflective inquiry, Professor Dewey can not properly be said to know them, even if he may experience them in other ways. Over and above the logical traits of objects of knowledge, ontological characters must be present as well, if the generic traits of existence are to be known and not only possessed or enjoyed. Professor Dewey seems to ask, therefore, not whether ontological traits are something additional to logical traits, but whether ontological traits can be identified, at least in part, with the logical traits.

The question naturally arises how Professor Dewey comes to have a metaphysics. How does he *know* that specificity, interaction, change, characterize all existence, and that these distinctions are not merely logical, made for purposes of getting along in this world, but characters of an independent existence? Why does he impute the features presented in human experience to a nature embracing, but containing more than, that experience? It is submitted here that if logical traits are cut off from ontological traits, so that the former have no prototype in the latter, Professor Dewey's belief that the precarious and stable are exhibited, not only in the human foreground, but as outstanding features of nature throughout, is untenable. For the single argument which he advances against those critics who deny to nature, independent of experience, the characters disclosed in human experience, is one drawn from continuity. And it is not difficult to see that it is the only argument which he is entitled to use. "One who believes in continuity may argue that, since human experience exhibits such traits, nature *must* contain their prototypes." "For this reason, there are in nature both foregrounds and backgrounds, heres and theres, centers and perspectives, foci and margins" (this Journal, Vol. XXIV, p. 58 [*Later Works* 3:74, 75]). If this argument for these characters is as conclusive to Professor Dewey as it is to the writer, it seems necessary to suppose that while there may be other ontological traits besides the logical, nature must contain the prototype of the logical as well.

There is no way of comparing the traits of nature manifested in experience with traits of nature existing in that background which is not experience. There is no way of discovering, by using reflection, that nature does not possess the characters she is discovered to possess *in* reflection. If, to use Professor Dewey's figure, objects of knowledge are the finished tools obtained by transforming crude ore, then it is the finished tools which are known. That nature does possess non-logical characters is a fact to which our common-day experience testifies. Such characters are real; but not more real than characters which reflection discovers and notes. Their ontological status is the same. One has as little reason to expect to discover logical characters outside of an intellectual or knowledge situation, as one would have to expect to discover a sensible quality in a non-sensory way.

For one who is committed to a whole-hearted naturalism, the continuity between logic and metaphysics can not be broken. The logical method we use is a method developed in the successful operation upon the things of existence—things which in their physical dimension exercise brute compulsion upon us, and which are discovered to stand to each other in relations approachable by intellect. By the very principle of continuity, the method must be more than mere method, even if the function of that method is the human one of making more secure the eventuation and enjoyment of immediate qualities. The method must in some sense reflect or refract orders of things which are knowable orders; orders which are never completely known, but which become known only if antecedent existence is transformed and modified. For we know things in the sense that we know the *relations* between them. To know the latter we must manipulate and change the former. Is there any reason to believe that in getting knowledge we ever determine what the latter must be?

One need not believe that it is the inherent properties of the ultimately real that are disclosed in knowledge; one may agree that it is the correlations of changes which is the goal of inquiry, and that such correlations are hypothetical, to be tested by consequences rather than by antecedents. One may say with Professor Dewey that the objects of thought are the objects of the thought of reality from the point of view of the most highly generalized aspect of nature as a system of interconnected changes; one may insist with him that the sole meaning of the relations thought is to be found in all the *possible* experienceable consequences which they entail. But it nevertheless remains true that such relations are discovered as an integral factor in nature, and that however hypothetical some of them may be, in some cases no alternatives to our believing in them are obtainable. Principles which every one must have who knows anything about existence, Aristotle remarked, are not hypotheses. And it is Professor Dewey who reminds us that "nature has both an irreducible brute unique 'itselfness' in everything which exists and also a connection of each thing (which is just what *it* is) with other things such that without them it 'can neither be nor be conceived'" (*loc. cit.*, p. 63 [*Later Works* 3:80]).

II

To show that there must be a connection between logic and ontology is easier than to exhibit that connection in detail. Not more than a gesture in that direction is attempted here. But first certain reservations must be made.

It is granted that a non-ontological interpretation of logic can be sustained by confining the distinctly logical to the symbolic or psychologic mechanism involved in getting things thought and said. If the "laws of thought" are taken to define the use of words like "is" and "not," or to describe supposed facts of psychology, then obviously they do not refer to generic traits of existence. The only contention that is here advanced, is that such interpretations do not do full justice to the operative rôle of the laws. Secondly, the laws may be understood as methodological resolutions we make to ourselves in conducting inquiries. Just as the choice of geometry is a matter of some convention and can not be proved false by experiment, so the laws of logic, it is claimed, are our postulates for organizing our experience, are the rules of our method, and not the laws of nature. But one can very well agree with what this theory affirms, without affirming what the theory denies. For the laws of logic are unique in that they turn up in every conceivable inquiry, and in that no alternative postulates have ever been successfully applied; one suspects, therefore, that they represent factors invariant in *every* subject-matter.

Finally, it is not denied that logic is concerned primarily with the way of getting knowledge, with our second intentions of things, with things as objects of reflective thought. Logical principles are concerned with the mutual relations of propositions, not with the mutual relations of things: and propositions bear to each other relations incomparable in some respects with the relations between things. Consequently, a fundamental meaning which must be assigned to the principle of contradiction is that a proposition can not be both true and false; and to the principle of excluded middle, that a proposition must be either true or false. Nevertheless, from a reading of these principles which makes them declare something about propositions, we are led to metaphysical readings: uniquely determined subjects can not both have and not have the same character; existence is determinately what it is; determinate existence excludes certain characters, and a determinate subject must either possess or not possess a given attribute; the characters which things possess fix the relations between propositions about them. It is true that propositions, and not things, contradict each other. But the ground of contradiction is to be found not in the propositions, but in the nature of the things which the propositions say. The saying of things is not the things said; and yet the saying conveys what the things are. If the principle of excluded middle does not tell which of two attributes or relations a thing must have, it does tell us that, given an attribute or relation, a thing either has or has not got it.

It may be objected that in limiting the discussion to determinate being, the question of the relation between logic and ontology has been begged at the outset. Logical distinctions, it is here admitted, are applicable to determinate subject-matter only. But it is also maintained that in so far as there is *complete* indetermination or chaos, *nothing* can be said. Chance is a metaphysical character, while at the same time absolute chaos or pure contingency is as much a limiting concept as pure form. Even the contingent, on this view, possesses an aspect of the determinate, just as the existential determinate possesses an aspect of the precarious. But is determinateness, it may be asked, a "direct" property of things, or is it discoverable only in non-existential subject-matter?

Professor Dewey seems to believe the existence of transitions indicates that determination is non-existential. When it is said that the existent door must be either open or not-open, he points to the fact that the door may be opening or shutting, and that no existent door is one-hundred percent. shut. "Open" and "shut" are therefore ideal in nature, setting limits toward which one may work in existential affairs. But one may well ask whether this dilemma is not due to a failure to define operationally and denotatively the ideas used. "Shut" may indeed be a universal whose instances are qualitatively dissimilar, so that the meaning of "shut" in different contexts is different. But fix one context, make explicit by pointing to a set of operations or conditions what it is to be shut, and the moving door meets or does not meet these conditions. It is because "shut" is first conceived in terms of an unexpressed ideal rather than in terms of empirical procedure, that the apparent inapplicability of the excluded middle is plausible. So two events are said to be simultaneous, not intrinsically, but by reference to the explicit operations which define simultaneity. Two events may be judged differently with respect to simultaneity, as a door may be judged differently as to its being shut—but not when the characters defined are first fixed operationally. If "door" can be defined existentially and not in terms of intrinsic characters, may not "shut" be defined in the same unambiguous way?

It is perfectly true that only thinking can be said to be self-consistent, however much that consistency is conditioned by the nature of things. Thinking is a selective process, and the principle of excluded middle is applicable only if we discriminate relations. Professor Dewey concludes that to abstract relations is "a way of thinking existence for the purpose of thinking," and that it is hypostatizing relations into independent existences if we suppose logical principles to be directly applicable to existence. But does it follow that because a universal does not exist by itself, it does not exist at all apart from the abstractive process? Does it follow, because isolation and abstraction are distinctive intellectual operations, that the objects of thought are not intrinsic factors in nature? Does Professor Dewey deny, because, to be effective, thought must approach nature piecemeal, that nature inherently has heres and nows, centers and perspectives? The systematic character which some things possess is reflected in our discourse and thought in a way which includes the accent of our speech and the habits of our thought; but it is not that accent and habit which endow things with system.

When Professor Dewey distinguishes between universal and particular propositions in terms of existential import, he leaves himself open to considerable misunderstanding. In the first place, the reading he gives is not the sole interpretation they can carry. But secondly, if, with Professor Dewey, we insist on an operational interpretation of ideas, we may well ask what is the meaning to be given to the protasis of the hypothetical universal. "Reduced pressure lowers boiling point," is a hypothetical proposition, since it does not say that there is low pressure, but states what its consequences are. At the very least, however, it does describe some categoric features of certain physical behavior. But it also supposes, that while there may not actually be low pressure, low pressure is intelligible in terms of the operations between existing things. Hence, while matter-of-fact evidence is required for the application of hypotheticals to particular existents, the reference to existence is never excluded from the universal, and is in fact doubly made. The existence of subject-matter in general can not be questioned if meanings require existential operations.

Predications about the future, as well as about the past and present, require that some relations which are and have been exemplified in existence will continue to be significant. In general, this is a hypothesis which in particular cases is often proved wrong. But were it always wrong, it would be difficult to see how the future can be subject for discourse at all, or how the present, when it has become the past of such a future, can be thought and investigated. Hence a future completely different from the present is as little intelligible as a past so dissimilar. But in entertaining significant predications about the future, alternatives for which the excluded middle holds, the contingency of future occurrences is not denied. "A sea-fight must either take place to-morrow or not, but it is not necessary that it should take place to-morrow, neither is it necessary that it should not take place, yet it is necessary that it either should or should not take place to-morrow."

It is difficult to know what kind of material evidence Professor Dewey would regard as conclusive for assigning to actual existences the formal properties in question. But very recently a book has been published in which some reasons for such identification are given by means of an analysis of the formal properties of machines. The analysis occurs on pages 161 to 163. The name of the book is *The Quest for Certainty* [*Later Works* 4:128–31].

Appendix 2
Action and Certainty [1]
By William Ernest Hocking

Dewey's philosophy is not a set of propositions: it is a national movement. On good instrumental grounds this is what it ought to be. To this extent Dewey might be willing to agree that the real and the ideal are one! At any rate, on his own theory, the right way to estimate his philosophy would be to examine, not the propositions, but the movement.

Before I grasped this point I wasted much labor in the attempt to criticise Dewey's propositions. In 1897 or thereabouts I published a complete refutation of the Dewey-McLellan method of teaching number. That method proposed to define numbers by ratios, so that the number one was expounded, not as the first cardinal integer, but as the ratio of anything to another thing of the same size. It thus required two objects to define "one." Pointing this out in my first philosophical essay, I received my first philosophical shock in the perfect impassivity with which Dewey received his theoretical ruin. I doubt whether to this day he is aware of the disaster, or of the existence of my article. Occasional subsequent onslaughts on my part have been equally conclusive.

I might be inwardly troubled, even now, by this godlike calm of Dewey's under fire if I had not recently witnessed his equal serenity under a great wave of world-wide good-will—not untouched, but adequate and unperturbed. Living as he does in a sphere beyond the good and evil of praise and criticism, I have come to regard him as an authentic human symbol of The Absolute! I shall therefore not hesitate, on this occasion, to renew the discussion. That, I think, is what he would desire. I can imagine

1. Read at the meeting of the American Philosophical Association, December 30, 1929, New York City.

[First published in *Journal of Philosophy* 27 (24 April 1930): 225–38. For Dewey's reply, see this volume, pp. 210–17.]

him saying, as Socrates—under less happy circumstances—once said: "To-day, if we can not revive the argument, you and I will both shave our locks"!

But let me begin by saying something of what I have learned from this philosophy. I owe much to the habit, painfully acquired, of looking for the meaning of terms and propositions in what they lead to, and especially in what they lead us to do. The blank face of a proposition is deceptive: its very self is in its working out. I venture even to embroider a little upon this theme. The work of a proposition is often less a construction than a fight. It has been of the greatest help to me, especially in reading the history of ideas, to consider propositions in terms of their *fighting-value*.

Take the proposition, All men are created equal, as it came from the pen of Thomas Jefferson. What did Jefferson suppose that to mean? Mr. Archibald Grimké accuses Jefferson of insincerity because he was, and remained, a slave-holder. But Jefferson's eye was on another battle. His dictum had nothing to do with the fight against slavery, but with the fight against a governing class, pretending a natural superiority and a divine right. This was the fighting-meaning of his thesis, and he can not on this count be called insincere.

Or consider the doctrine of Nationality as it appeared in the nineteenth century. The foreign ministers of Great Britain evoked this principle in order to support the efforts of Greece and Italy to become autonomous. It did not occur to them that zealous formal logicians would extend the same principle to India and other portions of the Empire. That doctrine was intended by them to do specific work in Europe; an indiscriminate extension to other fields and other campaigns, however true to the verbal surface, was false to the fighting-sense of the idea.

In public law and in theology, the interpretation of all general formulae must be sought in their original fighting-purport, and logical extension runs the risk of complete impertinence. The Monroe Doctrine in its own day had specific work to do: for Roosevelt, by logical extension, it did vastly different work; and now, still other and unexpected work—as in raising misunderstanding with our neighbors to the South and in hindering our coöperation with the League of Nations. The charge of insincerity here rests rather upon the logicians than upon those who look to the original fighting-value of the formula.

I presume that instrumentalism itself has a fighting-value, and that much of its meaning lies therein.

It has clearly some important work to do, not solely in the minds of the philosophical fraternity, but in the minds of wide masses of the American people. Now this people has been, and is, a vigorously active people; and it has been widely assumed that this practical bent has predisposed us to be pragmatists. This, I believe, is the precise reverse of the truth. It is a commonplace of social psychology that the active temper tends to dogmatism: the active man, like the active crowd, needs to assume something as fixedly true, beyond the reach of enquiry, a *pou sto* that justifies and supports a strong thrust. Common action nourishes itself on slogans, not on hypotheses, and the typical "man of action" displays a set jaw and an unyielding maxim. It is because we are dominantly a people of deeds that we are inclined to be a dogmatic nation, believing stiffly in eternal principles, final conventions, natural rights, an unchanging Constitution and mechanical theologies. The great public work of the instrumental philosophy has been to limber up the ways of knowing of this people, to reduce fixed dogmas to working-hypotheses fit for experiment; to give the intellectually traditional, authority-seeking, hero-worshipping American the courage of his own experience. As a people we do believe in the dignity of labor (and so far as I can see, we are the only people under the sun, unless it be Russia, who really have that belief in their bones). We must carry this belief over into the dignity of *a laboring philosophy*, arising out of and pertinent to existing crises, not to ancient ones.

It is because America is *not* instinctively pragmatic that pragmatism has had, and still has, much fighting work to do.

Among the professionals likewise, it has to combat those traits which lend support to this impulsive popular dogmatism, such as the idle securities and finalities of abstract truth, or the lingering traces of those gods of Epicurus who do not concern themselves with human affairs. Especially it has been charged to widen the scope of the inductive methods, hypothesis and verification, in the field of social philosophy, and thereby to render our moral thinking flexible and contemporaneous—not to destroy the law and the prophets, nor yet to fulfill them (for that, too, would be looking backward in a way), but to endow them with the divine capacity of perpetual self-regeneration.

This is to make philosophy a highly responsible undertaking, indeed the most responsible of human enterprises. It is at once a promise to the common man that philosophy shall mean something to him; and it is a promise (not without an admonition) to the philosopher that when he has given his thinking its due prospective significance, philosophy will once more bear its due part in the national life. When our work becomes so much a matter of public importance that some one of us is asked to drink the hemlock, solely on account of his philosophical teaching, then at least we shall have learned a part of the lesson of instrumentalism.

These, in my judgment, are some of the continuing good works of instrumentalism; they constitute its instrumental truth.

And now I have to record why I am not wholly satisfied with this variety of truth. I believe that we must continue to judge the validity of propositions in some independence of their working. If this is true, it will not be out of place to look once more at the propositions of instrumentalism apart from their working- or fighting-value.

(The mere fact that we can make this distinction goes to illustrate the argument. And if the instrumentalist should be so unwary as to defend these propositions, merely as propositions, his defense would amount to a surrender of his position. For he would be recognizing meaning apart from working. In this case, the theoretical critic has the field to himself, and the argument comes to an abrupt end. Let us waive this point!)

It would hardly be necessary to restate these familiar propositions except to show what limited portion of Dewey's philosophy I plan to deal with, and to make clear what version of his doctrine I am taking for discussion. The central thesis of instrumentalism I take to be this:

(1) That the meaning of conceptions and propositions is always functional. They spring, not out of blank presentation, but out of hesitation, perplexity: they are projects of solution, promissory and hypothetical in character. Their validity or truth consists in doing what they thus claim to do, namely, in resolving the difficulty, and in being, in this sense, verified.

From this would necessarily follow these corollaries:

(2) That there is no strictly immediate truth;

(3) That there is no strictly stable or eternal truth;

(4) That there is no *a priori* truth; and, in sum,

(5) That there can be no significant theoretical certainty.

My effort will be, not to introduce novelty into the examination of these doctrines, but simply to express as clearly as possible my persisting difficulties, and to reduce them, where I can, to a principle.

My difficulty with the first proposition, the definition of trueness, tends to condense itself into a principle which we might call *the non-correspondence of meaning and working*. To every conception and to every general proposition there may be attached an indefinite variety of workings; to every working, in turn, a variety of meanings. If the meaning were to be found in the working, there should be a unique and unambiguous correspondence between these entities: this correspondence does not exist.

Our proposition, All men are equal, will serve to illustrate the point. Not all of this proposition was at work in Jefferson's day: more and other work was capable of coming out of it. In spite of Jefferson's pre-occupation, it was legitimate to set that same generality to work on the slavery business: it still has work on hand, far beyond Jefferson's horizon, in the treatment of backward peoples, and who knows what further, to the end of time. Its identity and life as a proposition can not be limited by the special perplexities of any one age. Nor can it be identified with the sum of a series of the indefinitely many possible workings it may sponsor. For it has a present meaning of some sort, whereas many of these possible programs of action are, at any given time, not so much as contemplated.[2] If we only know a thing when we

---

2. The class of all the possible programs of action derivable from a given generality is a class which is in fact never contemplated, and which is probably in strict logic not contemplable. But the meaning of the proposition is contemplable, otherwise it would be impossible to "apply" it to new circumstances, or to "deduce" from it further plans of action. From what are the new applications derived? Surely not from previous programs, such as Jefferson's. Then from something distinguishable therefrom: that something different is the meaning of the proposition.

It must be noted, too, that some programs may lead to auspicious, others to inauspicious conclusions; some may eventuate as they promise, others may lead to disappointment. The solving, or verifying, outcome of any one group of programs can not guarantee that of others. Hence no finite series of verifications can constitute the truth.

see what comes of it, then indeed, we never know anything; for we never have in hand what is yet to eventuate.

Look at this non-correspondence from the other end. Assume (what is not highly improbable) that Jefferson began first with his fight and then cast about for a generality to sanction the conflict he felt to be inevitable. Is it logically required that he should have lighted on just this maxim about human equality? If we knew by inspection just what universal is exemplified in a given particular, law, induction, and living would be much simpler than they are. The versatility of mathematicians and physicists in setting up divergent hypotheses which lead to the same phenomena has prepared us to believe that no course of action is uniquely dependent upon any one theoretical premise. If the meaning is to be found solely in the progress from problem to solution-in-action, we should have to agree that any one of a number of "rationalizations" of this process would be verified by its success. This conclusion being eminently unacceptable, we are driven to locate the center of meaning in the proposition, and to regard it as separable from any specific course of action.

The non-correspondence between meaning and working begins in the process of conception, as an incommensurableness between *objects* and *interests*.

I am hungry: that is a state of dissatisfaction, favorable for starting a thinking process. I see a red apple: I at once conceive it as a possible food. That conception is clearly functional: it is a promissory hypothesis and carries a plan of action definitely related to my hunger. But I note that the redness of the apple, or for that matter its apple-ness, has no essential relation to its food-interest. A baked potato would do the same. I can not, therefore, regard the apparition of the apple as being just covered by, or exhausted in, that food-interest; nor is my food-interest exhausted in the apple. There is something in the apple-fact, and therefore in the apple-idea, which extends beyond any interest and any process which I then and there project. The active-meaning omits much of the fact-meaning: the fact-meaning (or object-idea) appears primary, admitting the active-meaning as a temporary rider, due to a momentary and somewhat accidental relationship. The fact-meaning, based on presentation, contains indeed the possibility of much as yet unimagined use and interest, and also the exceptional possibility of uselessness.

But the two, object and interest, clearly have no common measure and there is no way to make them precisely congruent. Thus the instrumental element in idea-making presupposes an immediate or presentational element as more fundamental.

In his notable chapter on "The Play of Ideas,"[3] Dewey recognizes the absence of one-to-one correspondence between ideas and plans of action. He does not, however, draw the consequence which seems inescapable, namely, that the working-test of truth is in a perilously loose relation to the proposition tested, and will yield to a more direct test when we can get it.

The lover, unable to perceive directly how he stands in the regard of his beloved, is driven to the method of hypothesis and verification: "If she loves me, she will make a friendly response to this advance, appear at the window when I sing, answer this letter." He must rest his case for the moment on a succession of progressively bolder pragmatic tests. The beloved, in the same situation, if she finds herself forbidden the initiative implied in all experiment, may be momentarily reduced to plucking the petals from daisies—I am not sure whether this is instrumental! But both maintain a hope for the more nearly immediate evidence of avowal, and the ideal of telepathic perception. Such immediate evidence is indeed dangerous evidence, in this case, without a long-continued series of good works; but clearly that series of works might attain pestilential length unless it could sometime soon reveal its essential inwardness by direct expression.

Or take an instance like this: In the study of radioactivity, it early became a question whether these so-called "rays" are really vibrations or discrete particles shot off from radio-active elements at high velocity. Somebody is led to suspect that the *alpha*-rays are nothing more nor less than positively charged atoms of helium. But there is no hope of observing directly any such ray, still less an individual atom of helium. So one tests deductions from the hypothesis, such as this, that the atomic weights of elements in the uranium-radium series ought to differ by multiples of the atomic weight of helium, which turns out to be the case. This and other verifications tend to confirm the hypothesis; but they still leave it possible (and widely believed) that these hypo-

3. *The Quest for Certainty*, pp. 156, 158 [*Later Works* 4:124–25, 126–27].

thetical atoms are merely signs for reckoning, with only a remote symbolic relationship to any spatial fact.

Now one day Sir William Crookes invents the spinthariscope. And here under a lens one perceives, not the atoms to be sure, but the individual sparkles which occur when these minute entities bombard the screen of zinc sulphide there focussed. The collisions can be located and counted. The helium atom takes on a numerical and spatial individuality. This kind of corroboration of the hypothesis has a wholly different cogency from that of successful practical prediction. It is presentational. Manipulative activities are required to get it; but they are *irrelevant to its force*. The primary meaning of verification lies there, and we resort to it whenever we can get it.

Since only a part of a general proposition can do work at any time, an instrumental confirmation can always be had for a proposition which is only partially true.

Half-truths actually do a vast amount of valiant service in the world, namely, when they announce that half which is for the time being ignored. Thus, if men are too well steeped in tradition, it is in order to preach the gospel that "All things change." This half-truth will for a time be instrumentally justified. Then, when under this teaching men have become so flexible and shifty as to lack all spine and consistency, its star begins to set, and the times are ripe for the complementary half-truth, that "Whatever is real is permanent," which may then receive the same kind of confirmation.

This epochal variability in the working-power of partial truths (and most of the working-truths of history I judge to have been of this sort) tends to bring our perceptions of truth into that rhythm in which some sort of "dialectical" process can begin. Such a process is bound to commence when one observes his own vacillation, and tries to remedy it. What requires the revision is not any failure of the instrumental working—the half-truths could continue to labor in alternate shifts—it is the demand for inner consistency. The structural principle thus announces itself as something again independent of the pragmatic principle. Not at odds with it: for there can be no hostility between Dewey and Barbara. Only, the interest in trueness tends to migrate away from the periphery of consequences to the center where Barbara spins out the materials of immediacy into a co-herent, continuous fabric.

So far, I have dealt with the first two propositions, the instru-mental definition of truth, and the thesis that there is no strictly immediate truth. Now consider the third thesis, that there is no eternal truth.

It is evident that the demand for consistency is at the same time a demand for *stability* in propositions. That is, the kind of truth we want is one we can hold to in all circumstances. The business of the dialectic is to find a conception of things which will *hold good*, and not for a little while, nor for an epoch, but always. If we prefer to translate stability by eternity, by way of indicating the limit to which stability tends, there is no harm done. The demand is the same whether there is much or little or no such ideally stable truth available.

And let us note that the need in question, while it is a logical need, is not merely logical. Nor is it merely a psychological od-dity, such as marks the temperamentally active type of humanity, of which we were earlier speaking: it lies in the nature of all ac-tion. For all action intends to change something in particular: and in order to effect just this alteration in the world, the frame of action must hold still! The maxim for action is: Regard the universe as static except where you want it to budge. The ideal situation for the man who wants to move things is to have an unalterable conviction at his back: "Here I stand, I can not oth-erwise, God help me." The man who can say that will either make things happen or be himself obliterated.

Nothing to my mind more strikingly illustrates, and at the same time criticises, the instrumental principle than the immense working qualities of propositions supposed to be not only eter-nal but transcendent as well. Theological orthodoxies and het-erodoxies have sometimes been stupidly adored in that detached and footless contemplation which is the *bête noire* of the instru-mentalist. But they have at least as often appeared in history as *things done*! Thus Carlyle writes of those intractable heathen, the Wends, in the early days of Brandenburg: "Being highly dis-inclined to conversion," he says, "they once and again burst up, got hold of Brandenburg, and *did frightful heterodoxies there*"!

After two centuries of clash these Wends were either blown up like dry powder or else "damped down into Christianity," which implies that they began to *do orthodoxy*, and that the new deeds were of a markedly different cast. In either case, it was a *doxy* that they did: good instrumentalism, but with an absolute for an implement or battle axe.

Is it not a momentous thing for our theory of truth that all major plans for human action, whether or not we who look backward, can see them tied to half-truths, have tried to get hold of absolutes and universals? And please note: it is *not for moral holidays* that these absolutes have been required.

Why, to fight British Torydom or slavery, do Thomas Jefferson and his successors reach out for a formula about "All men," instead of taking some legend that will snugly fit the moment's case? Is it because they do not want this day's business to be itself temporary and abstract and to be all undone and done over? And is it because they know that *the fruit of action can be no more permanent than the sight it comes out of* that they need to see the momentary effort in its setting and make the whole of things a party to what they now propose to do? I suspect that nothing short of a true property of all men would have *worked* for Jefferson's revolution: it was an eternal verity of some sort that King George was disowning, and it would take that same eternal verity to defeat him. Let us say, if we think so, that Jefferson got only a relative and approximate truth: I only remark that such a suspicion on his part would have lamed him for the moment, and sent him searching for another and more durable universal. It is not the scorn of action, it is the love of it, which prompts the quest for theoretical certainty, such as one can have before action begins. No one can be mad, of anger or devotion, unless he is first sure of something.

I suspect that at bottom Dewey is as little enamored of incessant change and relativity in the world of judgment as anyone. In commenting on Charles Peirce, he dwells approvingly on Peirce's idea of reality: "Reality," he says, "means the object of those beliefs which have after prolonged and coöperative enquiry become stable; and truth is the quality of those beliefs."

What is meant by a belief "becoming stable"? If we can identify the belief during the period of its variation, there would appear to be a core of it that is not affected by the variation. There is, of course, no incompatibility between the persistence of a truth, and its change in the sense of clarification and growth. We may agree with Dewey that "the scientific attitude, as an attitude of interest in change instead of interest in isolated and complete fixities, is necessarily alert for problems,"[4] and its work forever unfinished. But it is equally evident that the whole scientific and experimental undertaking aims at and believes in permanence. For unless experiment can establish something, and unless something of what we suppose "established" stays established, endures, accumulates, the whole experimental business becomes a fool's paradise.

The corpus of knowledge is at no moment static: but we know this, that *change does not eat out what is true in it*. From this two things follow. First, that survival becomes an empirical criterion of trueness, so that for instrumentalism also the only truth which fully deserves the name is eternal truth. Second, that whatever turns out by survival to have been the true element in our present beliefs, we *now have that truth*, and have had it, whether or not we can now extricate it from its adulterants.

But of what advantage is this present possession of eternal truth, if we never know certainly what it is?

The answer lies in that aspect of truth which we call the *a priori*. If there is any *a priori* truth, it is presumably of the durable variety; and might conceivably furnish something to hold to, for purposes of action, while we are waiting for the rest of our durable truth to survive! But is there any such truth?

It is hard to see how anyone who places faith in scientific method can doubt the *a priori*. For scientific method (which we may allow to be the only fruitful method, because it is a composite of every method) necessarily makes appeal to truths which can never be tested.

Take the assumption that the standard measure of length remains constant. About the standard meter-stick in Paris, or any other physically extant measure, I may refuse to make that assumption. I may imagine it subject to FitzGerald Contractions, or any other type of distortion I please. But in that case I conceive myself as measuring the altered length in terms of a measure which does not vary. An assumption which we can not

4. *The Quest for Certainty*, p. 101 [*Later Works* 4:81–82].

avoid making, and which we assume when we try to test it, may fairly be called an *a priori* proposition.

Kant in his pragmatic moments made use of another variety of *a priori* judgment. His postulates of practical reason, as he thought, were such as to make very tangible differences in behavior and experience: but these eventualities need not be waited for, inasmuch as they were *necessary consequences* of the postulates. They could be known in advance. Instrumentalism seems to adopt the view that we do not know what results are going to be until we reach them. But why? Why must the relation between a belief and its working-out be purely factual? If the consequences really pertain to that belief, the connection is not accidental, and it must be theoretically possible to foresee them. As an ancestor of pragmatism, Kant's method here seems to deserve reconsideration. Wherever necessary consequences can be perceived and evaluated in advance, we have an *a priori* judgment.

Our more general ethical standards seem to be of this nature. With all the immense force of experience and social tradition in molding our ethical sense, it is not yet obvious to me that the experience of eventualities can ever instruct us in the primitive distinction between right and wrong. We can hardly adopt the view (to quote a colleague) that Cain did not know it was wrong to kill Abel until after he had done so. Unless the discovered consequence confirmed an uneasy foreboding of his own, already ethical, it could teach him nothing except that he had made an unfortunate decision. Nor can we adopt the view that the "lost causes" of mankind are proved by the outcome to have been somehow illicit. I am wholly convinced that it is wasteful, and may be vicious, to contemplate impossible ideals; that an ideal ought to be a pressure toward technical embodiment; that if ends are holy, the use of means is not less so. But how are we to know which ideals are possible and which are not? If we are to avoid the vice of cherishing impossible ideals, we must be guided either by an *a priori* knowledge of what ideals are possible or impossible, or by an *a priori* knowledge of what ideals are right. If we assume (with Joan of Arc, for example) that what is right must be somehow possible, we are relieved of the effort to foresee ultimate outcomes; the whole burden of judgment rests on the prior assurance of rightness. The event of failure reacts, not on the validity of the ideal, but on the wisdom of the means used or the energy of the agent. The defeated reformer, lover, patriot may have to curse himself as a fool: but he has still to say, "That for which I tried had the quality of goodness in it: my knowledge of that quality was prior to eventualities, and remains unmoved by them."

An element of knowledge may be *there* and may be effective long before it can be isolated, as children cut corners long before they can announce that the straight line is the shortest distance. It is not absurd to suppose that *a priori* knowledge may have a *de facto* existence, and yet a very belated official recognition. I wish to commend to your judgment a view of *a priori* knowledge which sees it as *growing out of experience*. We all want to be good empiricists; we have all grown humble in respect to the value of abstract rational anticipations of experience. Most of us, I believe, would like to join Dewey in getting away from the old passive copying empiricism, and in uniting with a better brand some recognition of the active contribution of the thinker: we believe Kant was right in seeking a synthesis of the empirical and the rational, and we further agree in not being satisfied with his proposals. May I suggest, then, that the office of experience is not solely to supply raw material, nor to provide simple ideas, nor yet to tease knowledge out into the ventures of action, but to present connections as factual in which we may, by slow degrees, recognize the necessary. The *a priori* is an element of knowledge which shells out of our changing empirical judgments as something implicitly presupposed and invariant. We may call it the *uncovered a priori*. And if the principle of this uncovering be admitted, we may willingly consult experience until the end of time for ascertaining the full measure of that *a priori* knowledge which even now we are using.

One such *a priori* element I seem to find uncovered in Dewey's *Quest for Certainty*. It occurs in a passage which, rejecting "fixed beliefs about values" so far as their contents are concerned, mentions one value which no future experience can dislodge. This invariant value is, to put it briefly, the value of trying to realize value. More fully, it is the value "of discovering the possibilities of the actual and striving to realize them." [5] Devotion to this value is declared invincible; it is the fit kernel for a

---

5. P. 304 [*Later Works* 4:242–43].

forward-looking religious attitude toward the world. I need not emphasize the importance of this passage.

It constitutes of itself a comment on another thesis of instrumentalism, namely, that all values are immanent, human-born and man-achieved; and that we do well to get rid of their traditional transcendent moorings.

To me this doctrine often comes with a sense of relief; as if we would take a distinct step ahead in replacing the primordial value-reservoir of a certain type of idealism by those prospective and possible values which stir millions of finite beings to continued effort. Surely the best qualities of experience are things achievable, not antecedently there. The equality of men of Jefferson's faith,—who can say it is *there*? Suppose we regard it rather as something to be brought about. To treat men as equal is to bring equality to pass. We can *confer* equality: the responsibility falls on our shoulders, and the world, which seemed a monstrous enigma under the doctrine of the is-ness of equality, becomes once more a hopeful place.

But this change does not dispel the metaphysical horizon. If value is creatable, the universe *is* already the entertainer of this possibility. Possibility is neither a human product, nor a mere form of expectancy: it is an objective property of things, antecedent to our action. Further, it is not there by accident: the universe which contains it can not be conceived as indifferent to its actualization. Possibility thus takes on the hue of obligation; and no single value in the human scene remains unaffected by this relationship. For a value which in our cosmic setting we are due to work out acquires a momentousness not attainable by a value which we merely *may* work out if we are so disposed and have the needed energy.

The value of trying to realize value appears to me to belong to this metaphysical setting of action; and if we wished to apply to it the opprobrious terms, "transcendent," "eternal," or even "absolute," the objections would arise chiefly, I think, from the traditional connotations of these words. I will confine myself to calling it a case of the uncovered *a priori*, and to making a plea that we extend the use of the principle by which this invariant is uncovered.

For we are going to get truth by endless experimenting, and there is presumably a charter for this experimenting which is not itself establishable by experiment. We are going to get truth by induction, and whatever the inductive postulate is, we can not prove *it* by induction. To my mind, experiment and induction are ways of trying to unearth necessities; and there is a prior necessity laid on us for continuing this search for necessity, whose authority no success can confirm and no failure unsettle. Here we have a small group of *a priori* elements, which are in a way formal and transcendent; that is, they are not in the fight, because they constitute the arena and the urge which makes the fight go on! I am disposed to see in them available theoretical certainties which underlie all human action. To them the more concrete certainties may attach themselves in proportion to that power of genius which, in the midst of incoherent and disagreeing empirical cases, can discern the universal element, not perfectly but clearly enough to do a man's work in the world.

Dewey recommends a philosophy "willing to abandon its supposed task of knowing ultimate reality and to devote itself to a proximate human office."[6] This can never happen: for philosophy can not perform the second function without the first. Men are like tigers in one respect which is to the credit of both: they can't enjoy food until they can see their way out of the trap. The amelioration of details leaves them ill at ease while they are without confidence in the frame of things,—if only a negative confidence that its uncontrollable reaches are not certainly brewing the spume of death to them and their works. In any case, we shall do the human offices with all the wisdom we can muster; but it is the peculiar province of philosophy to read and truly report the ultimate auspices of these deeds, be these auspices good or ill.

I plead for the recovery of a Platonic element in our way of knowing. A renewed grip of the changeless vein in things and an inkling of totality, so far from veiling the transitional, or withering experiment, or drugging the spirit of enterprise, would show themselves the very nerves of action. There is nothing infusible in these two things, the great work of Dewey and the Platonic vision. Knowing and doing are not the same thing: nothing but confusion can be got from identifying them, for in that case activity itself could not be known. No doubt they are of a piece,

6. *The Quest for Certainty*, p. 47 [*Later Works* 4:37–38].

inseparable: they reach their culmination together; knowing is at its height at the point where the present deed plays against the outer reality. But as doing, like the galloping hoof, gathers the earth into it and puts the earth behind it, so about the moment's knowledge born in that same contact, there spreads the horizon and the stable arch of the sky.

When Dewey accepts for himself somewhat tentatively the designation "experimental idealist," then we who have been thinking of ourselves as idealistic experimentalists, may be permitted to recognize a kinship and to join in the long quest for the remainder of our certainty, some of which we think we have in hand.

Appendix 3
Pragmatism and Current Thought [1]
By C. I. Lewis

It is somewhat difficult in the case of pragmatism to determine what are its essential and distinctive theses. That there should be thirteen distinguishable pragmatisms, however, is not a peculiarity: these could be set alongside the thirty-seven idealisms and fifty-one realisms. William James is reported to have said that he was pleased to find that pragmatism had this wealth of meaning; he accepted all thirteen. In any case, such variety merely marks the fact that pragmatism is a movement, not a system. Its beginnings are attributable to Charles Peirce. But Peirce has something of the quality of a legendary figure in American philosophy. His originality and the wealth of his thinking are not fully evident in his published writings. Apart from a few persons—amongst whom were James and Royce—some of his most important conceptions can have had little influence, because they have never been printed: and the coincidence of these doctrines with the views of later pragmatists is distinctly limited. James's enthusiasm for them must in part be set down to that catholicity of appreciation which was so notable a part of his character. James called himself a "radical empiricist" as well as a pragmatist, and the connection, or lack of it, between these two aspects of, or strands in, his philosophy, has been a matter of some question. We must, of course, look to Professor Dewey's writings for the integration and systematic elaboration of pragmatism. But no one could have exercised the quite unparalleled influence which he has had upon American thought without giving rise to a wealth of resultant views which is a little confusing when one tries to grasp their coincidence or central meaning. Hence it is

1. Read at the meeting of the American Philosophical Association, Dec. 30, 1929, New York City.

[First published in *Journal of Philosophy* 27 (24 April 1930): 238–46. For Dewey's reply, see this volume, pp. 210–17.]

not a matter for surprise if those most deeply influenced by him show a tendency to drop the term, lest a too extended agreement with one another be suggested, and that those of us who still have ventured to use it are doubtful of our right to the designation.

If, then, I venture to suggest what is the core of pragmatism, and what I think may be the chief significance of it, both in philosophy and for other branches, I hope it will be understood that I do not take myself too seriously in the matter. This view is presented to those who will best know how to correct my mistakes.

Pragmatism is, as James indicated, not a doctrine but a method: viewed logically, it can be regarded as the consequence of a single principle of procedure. But this principle, though by itself it says nothing material in the field of metaphysics or epistemology, and though its application is by no means confined to philosophy, has nevertheless a wealth of philosophic consequences. It implies at least the outline of a theory of knowledge; and if it dictates no metaphysical theses, at least it rules out a good deal which has been put forward under that caption, and it operates as a principle of orientation in the search for positive conclusions.

I refer, of course, to the pragmatic test of significance. James stated it as follows: "What difference would it practically make to anyone if this notion rather than that notion were true? If no practical difference whatever can be traced, then the alternatives mean practically the same thing, and all dispute is idle."[2] Peirce formulated it with respect to substantive concepts rather than propositional notions—though the two come to the same thing: "Our idea of anything is our idea of its sensible effects. . . . Consider what effects, that might conceivably have practical bearings, we conceive the object of our conception to have. Then, our conception of these effects is the whole of our conception of the object."[3] It is one importance of this pragmatic test that it is so obviously valid and final: once it has been formulated, there can be no going back on it later without conscious obscurantism.

2. *Pragmatism*, p. 45.
3. "How to Make Our Ideas Clear," *Chance, Love, and Logic*, p. 45. Compare: ". . . Since obviously nothing that might not result from experiment can have any bearing on conduct, if one can define accurately all the conceivable experimental phenomena which the affirmation or denial of a concept could imply, one will have therein a complete definition of the concept, and *there is nothing more in it*." For this doctrine he [the writer, Peirce] invented the name pragmatism.—"What Pragmatism Is," *Monist*, Vol. 15, p. 177.

Any consequence of it, therefore, shares in this imperative and binding character. Peirce's dictum draws our attention to the fact that there is a kind of empiricism which is implicit in the pragmatic test: What can you point to in experience which would indicate whether this concept of yours is applicable or inapplicable in a given instance? What practically would be the test whether your conception is correct? If there are no such empirical items which would be decisive, then your concept is *not* a concept, but a verbalism.

If one does not find in Professor Dewey's writings any terse formulation which is exactly parallel (and of that I am not sure), this is only because here the pragmatic test is clothed with its consequences; it pervades the whole, and is writ large in the functional theory of the concept. Ideas are plans of action; concepts are prescriptions of certain operations whose empirical consequences determine their significance. This connotation of action is not, of course, a new note; it appears in Peirce's emphasis upon conduct and experiment, and in James's doctrine of the "leading" character of ideas. Is this functional theory of the concept implicit, like empiricism, in the pragmatic test?

So far as Professor Dewey himself is concerned, it would appear that this doctrine antedates his explicit pragmatism, and may have been the root of it. (Perhaps he will tell us.) It appears in his paper on "The Reflex Arc Concept in Psychology," the first important document for "functional psychology," published in 1896.[4] He there criticises current psychological theory as not having sufficiently avoided the fictitious abstractions of sensationalism. "The sensation or conscious stimulus is not a thing or existence by itself; it is a phase of a coördination."[5] "A coördination is an organization of means with reference to a comprehensive end."[6] "The stimulus is that phase of the forming coördination which represents the conditions which have to be met in bringing it to a successful issue; the response is that phase of one and the same forming coördination which gives the key to meet-

4. *Psychological Review*, Vol. 3, pp. 357–370 [*The Early Works of John Dewey, 1882–1898*, ed. Jo Ann Boydston (Carbondale and Edwardsville: Southern Illinois University Press, 1972), 5:96–109]. My attention was drawn to this by its citation in Boring's *History of Experimental Psychology*, pp. 540–41.
5. *Loc. cit.*, p. 368 [*Early Works* 5:106].
6. *Loc. cit.*, p. 365 [*Early Works* 5:104].

ing these conditions, which serves as instrument in effecting the successful coördination. . . . The stimulus is something to be discovered. . . . It is the motor response which assists in discovering and constituting the stimulus."[7] Substitute "sensation" or "sense data" for "stimulus," "operation" or "action" for "motor response," and what is here quoted will be found occupying a central place in all Professor Dewey's subsequent expositions of his pragmatic doctrine. Three years later, he wrote: "I conceive that states of consciousness . . . have no existence as such . . . before the psychologist gets to work." "Knowing, willing, feeling, name states of consciousness not in themselves, but in terms of results reached, the sorts of value that are brought into experience."[8]

If, then, I am right in the derivation here assigned, Professor Dewey's functional theory of knowledge is the necessary consequence of a methodological principle applied to psychology; namely, that concepts used should designate something concretely identifiable in experience, not abstractions apart from that which serves for their empirical discovery. Sensations, or sense data, are condemned as not thus identifiable apart from the responses to which they lead and the ends such action serves.

The functional theory of the concept has, as I have tried to show elsewhere, other grounds, of a more purely logical sort. Viewed in this way, however, and apart from psychological considerations, it is not, I think, a simple consequence of the pragmatic test, but has a conceivable alternative, namely, immediatism or the presentation-theory of knowledge. By this logical approach, one has to adduce reasons for repudiating the conception that empirical knowledge—or *some* empirical knowledge— is immediately given, in order to reach the conception that activity and its issue are indispensable and characterizing factors in empirical cognition. The theory that meanings connote action and truth connotes prediction, is implicit in the notion that truth and meanings are something *to be tested*; hence, that they do *not* bring their own warrant in being simply given.

7. *Loc. cit.*, p. 370 [*Early Works* 5:109].
8. "Psychology and Philosophic Method," address before the Philosophical Union of the University of California, 1899, pp. 6 and 10 [*Middle Works* 1:117, 119]. It is interesting to remember that in the preceding year, James presented the first statement of *his* pragmatism, "Philosophical Conceptions and Practical Results," under the same auspices.

I believe we here arrive at a turning-point in pragmatic theory.[9] On the one side, the pragmatic principle seems to stress the directly empirical. Put enough emphasis on that, and one might conceivably—though not validly, I think—arrive at a highly subjectivistic theory, of knowledge as immediate. On the other side, it stresses the limitation of meaning to what makes a verifiable difference, and of truth to what can be objectively tested. Follow out the consequences of *that*, and of the functional theory of knowledge which it implies, and I believe one is inevitably led to the doctrine that concepts are abstractions, in which the immediate is precisely that element which must be left out. To this point, I should like to adduce certain illustrations, drawn from contemporary science.

The new physics is, in good part, based upon certain applications of the pragmatic test. And to these physicists the validity of this methodological principle and the functional interpretation of conceptual meanings seem to be simply synonymous. One main premise of physical relativity is, of course, the impossibility of deciding which, of two bodies in relative motion, is at rest with respect to an absolute space. (We may remind ourselves that James's illustration of the pragmatic test—the man and the squirrel—is simply an example of the relativity of motion to frames of reference.) In elaborating the consequences of this relativity of motion, it became necessary to repudiate other absolutes, such as length, time, simultaneity, etc.; and this was done by identifying these with the actual modes by which they can be tested—the pragmatic test once more. The resultant methodology may be generalized in what Bridgman calls "the operational character of concepts." "We evidently know what we mean by a length if we can tell what the length of any and every object is, and for the physicist nothing more is required. To find the length of an object we have to perform certain physical operations. The concept of length is therefore fixed when the operations by which length is measured are fixed: that is, the concept of length involves as much as and nothing more than the set of operations by which length is determined. In general we mean

9. When this was written, Professor Burtt's paper, "Two Basic Issues in the Problem of Meaning and of Truth," contributed to *Essays in Honor of John Dewey*, had not yet come to hand. I note with pleasure that a part of his paper and part of what is here written run parallel.

by any concept nothing more than a set of operations; *the concept is synonymous with the corresponding set of operations.*" [10]

Why does the physicist thus identify his concepts with operations of testing? Is it because the properties he is concerned with are peculiarly those which are difficult or impossible of immediate apprehension? Not at all. Suppose a critic to observe: "But of course your concept of length goes back to an immediately given somewhat. You test the relation of a particular length to the yardstick, but unless your yardstick were an immediate so-longness, directly apprehended, your concept of length would be entirely empty." He will reply that this immediate so-longness has nothing to do with physics, because it can not be tested. The *yardstick* can be tested; as it happens, the measurement of it will differ for different relative motions. But any immediate so-longness of it is something which makes no difference to physics: if it had one so-longness to A and another for B, that would be unverifiable and ineffable. It is the significance of the operational character of concepts to extrude such ineffables from physics. Subjectively it may be that A and B both seem to themselves at rest in the center of the universe, directly apprehending certain so-longnesses, so-heavinesses, felt endurances of things, and what not. But physical position and motion are simply relations to a frame of reference, physical time a relation to clocks; physical properties in general consist in those operations and relations by which they are assigned and tested. The standards are absolutely standards—that is, arbitrary—but they are not absolute in any other sense. The standard yardstick, or clock, or whatever, has its length or the measure of its seconds, etc., in an entirely similar and verifiable set of relations to other things, and only so. Any immediate content of the concept is extruded by the principle of the pragmatic test. If your hours, as felt, are twice as long as mine, your pounds twice as heavy, that makes no difference, which can be tested, in our assignment of physical properties to things. If it *should* thus make a difference in our predication of properties, we should at once decide that one of us must be mistaken. Such decision would reveal our implicit recognition that our concept of the predicated property excludes this subjective element, and includes only the objectively verifiable relations.

10. *The Logic of Modern Physics*, p. 5; italics are in the text.

The physical concepts are not, by this extrusion of the immediate, emptied of meaning. Their meaning is, as Bridgman says, in the operations of verification and their results; it is contained in that complex network of relationships which constitute the laws and equations and physical predications of which the science consists. The concept is, thus, merely a sort of configuration or relational pattern. Whatever the immediate and ineffable content which is caught in that net may be—for John Jones or Mary Doe or anybody—it does not enter into the science of physics. The resultant conception of the content of the science is admirably expressed by Eddington: "We take as building material *relations* and *relata*. The relations unite the relata; the relata are the meeting points of the relations." [11] The conceptual in knowledge is the element of pure structure or operational construction.

Thus the pragmatic test becomes a kind of law of intellectual parsimony, and leads, in science, to what might be called "the flight from the subjective." Physics is by no means an isolated example: the parallel thing has happened, or will happen, in every science, because it is simply the extrusion of what the science can not finally and conclusively test. Mathematics, being the oldest science, did it first. Geometry begins with rope-stretching and ends as the deductive elaboration of purely abstract concepts, the problem of the nature of space being handed over to physics and philosophy. Arithmetic begins with counting empirical things and ends in the logical structure of *Principia Mathematica*, for which the existence of the number 8 (for a certain type) requires an extraneous assumption. Just now mathematics threatens to go further and restrict itself to systems of operations upon marks. Psychology first got rid of the ineffable soul; a pragmatic psychologist then asked, "Does consciousness [as distinct from its content] exist?"; and now we have behaviorism, based on the methodological principle of restriction to what is objectively verifiable. If some of these movements go beyond what is necessary or valid, at least they exhibit the tendency, and the ground of it.

Professor Dewey seems to view such abstractionism in science as a sort of defect—sometimes necessary but always regrettable; an inadequacy of it to the fullness of experience. In various ways,

11. *The Nature of the Physical World*, p. 230.

it seems to him to threaten the relations between knowledge and life. Professor Eddington's book suggests that a doubt on this point besets him too when, as physical scientist, he finds himself also constrained to assess philosophical significances. That the world as experienced and life as lived are not going to be thrown out of the window, goes without saying. Particularly for Professor Dewey, it seems to me that this apprehensiveness is misplaced, because he has himself indicated the main considerations essential for the solution of the problem which results—the problem of the relation of abstract concepts to the concrete and directly empirical. Time does not permit attention to all the pertinent considerations. But I wish to suggest one which is important, by a final illustration, drawn once more from physics.

As an eventual result of subatomic and quantum phenomena, the new physics has abolished imaginable matter. Analysis of the physical emerges finally in something like Schrödinger's Ψ-functions, in mathematical expressions of probability, concrete representation of which can only be approached in terms of an admittedly fictitious sub-ether of variable dimensions. Immediately apprehensible matter dissolves into mathematics. Two other expressions of this same abstractness of the physically ultimate occur in Eddington's later chapters: one is that statement about relations and relata, already referred to; the other is to the effect that physics reduces the concrete object to pointer-readings.[12] The elephant sliding down the grass slope is at once an immense flock of Ψ-functions getting integrated, and a set of pointer-readings. The two interpretations do not seem interchangeable. Let us fasten on the pointer-readings. Why reduce the elephant to pointer-readings? In the first place, because physics can not deal with the elephant as a whole. It comprehends a good many—perhaps most—of the elephant's properties, but that he is, for example, a wonderful fine fellow and very intelligent, must be omitted from physical consideration. Let us call that organization of properties which physics *can* deal with "the physicist's elephant." Why is the physicist's elephant reduced to pointer-readings? First because, with the apparatus oriented upon the elephant, the elephant *determines* the pointer-readings.

12. Pp. 251 ff.

Second, because such pointer-readings are a conveniently hybrid sort of reality: the apparatus and pointers being physical, their readings correlate with the properties of the elephant; and the readings being numerical, they translate those properties into mathematical values. The significance of the pointer-readings is merely for the purpose of such translation. The last state of the physicist's elephant, like the last state of the electron, is in mathematical functions. But this last stage for the *physicist* is merely an intermediate stage of operations with respect to the elephant. The numerical values given by the pointer-readings are substituted for the variables in some mathematical equation expressing physical law. They thus determine a numerical value of some other mathematical function. This last can be translated back into something of the order of pointer-readings, and hence back into some other and previously undetermined property of the elephant—with the eventual result, perhaps, that we get the elephant safely into a box-car. Such eventual result is the reason for being of the whole set of operations. If it be asked, then, "Why reduce the elephant to mathematical functions?" the answer is that this is the best way known to man for getting him into the box-car.

The physicist's elephant is an abstraction, but a rather palpable sort of abstraction. All of him that the physicist finally deals with is what is common to the elephant and the pointer-readings; namely, a more abstract, a *very* abstract, configuration of relationships. This structure of relations is what, in general terms, the mathematical equations of physics express.

Thus if the last conceptual stage of the elephant—and of the physical in general—is in mathematics, or a set of relations of relata, it is not necessary to try to follow this transmogrification of the elephant, or of matter, with the imagination. Nor is it appropriate to cry shame upon the physicist for leaving the world of palpable elephants in favor of such unimaginable abstractions. The physicist's concept represents simply an intermediate stage in a process which begins and ends with elephants and such—not with the physicist's elephant even, but the one which slid down the bank and got put in the box-car.

As Professor Dewey points out, the physicist and mathematician simply take this intermediate stage off by itself and deal with it on its own account.[13] Thus if we reflect upon the functional theory of knowledge, I think we may come to the conclusion that there is no implication of it which is incompatible with the notion that concepts in general are abstractions—are even very thin abstractions. Because the function of concepts is not to *photograph* elephants but to get them into box-cars. Concepts represent simply that operational function of cognition by which it transforms the something given, with which it begins, into the something anticipated or something done, with which it ends. That they may have lost, or discarded as irrelevant, those elements of the concrete and immediate which characterize direct perception and imagination, is nothing to the point. Goodness in a concept is not the degree of its verisimilitude to the given, but the degree of its effectiveness as an instrument of control. Perhaps Professor Dewey might even, with entire consistency, find less occasion to regret that the relatively undeveloped sciences of human affairs show a tendency to imitate this abstractness. When the social sciences attain that degree of abstractness, and consequent precision, which already characterizes physics and mathematics, perhaps they will have less trouble getting their social elephants into their social box-cars. Economics is the best developed of the social sciences, and a fair illustration.

To conclude: the fact that the pragmatic test seems, on the one hand, to demand that all meaning be found eventually in the empirical, and on the other, seems to induce a flight from the immediate and directly apprehensible into abstractions, is not, in reality, any contradiction or any difficulty. In one sense—that of connotation—a concept strictly comprises nothing but an abstract configuration of relations. In another sense—its denotation or empirical application—this meaning is vested in a process which characteristically begins with something given and ends with something done—in the operation which translates a presented datum into an instrument of prediction and control.

13. See *The Quest for Certainty*, pp. 156 ff [*Later Works* 4:124 ff.].

Appendix 4
Experience and Dialectic[1]
By Frederick J. E. Woodbridge

Even a misguided comment on Professor Dewey's philosophy may be instructive. Opinions have a social as well as an
individual character, with the obvious consequence that one
man's understanding of another is at least one instance of how
that other is understood. Otherwise, why should we comment
on great philosophers, and tell the world what they thought,
when they have already told the world themselves? In the present
case, malice could suggest that a philosophy should be defined
and judged in terms of the effects it produces, but malice would
be confused if confronted with a multiplicity of effects, and
might find the criterion that a philosophy is what it is experienced to be, forcing it, in the interest of justice, to distinguish
between appearance and reality. A commentator is embarrassed
in making the distinction, for what he finds the philosophy to be
is what he concludes it to be. His commentary is, then, at least as
instructive as personal revelations usually are. He exhibits himself. He is an appearance. If the reality, as it may very well do,
mocks him, that is the penalty of being an appearance, and,
perhaps, some justification for being it, some evidence that the
reality is antecedent to the appearance and should control it.
Haunted by this perplexing circumstance, I proceed with this
paper. I shall state what I have to say in summary at the beginning, and then illustrate it in two particulars.

Professor Dewey has had an eminently practical effect. He has
profoundly influenced the way many people think and act and
teach. When his writings are stripped of dialectic and controversy, and freed from contact with certain of the traditional

1. Read at the meeting of the American Philosophical Association in New York,
   December 30, 1929.

[First published in *Journal of Philosophy* 27 (8 May 1930): 264–71. For Dewey's
reply, see this volume, pp. 210–17.]

problems of philosophy, there remains a positive and substantial pronouncement on human life in its immediate practical character. This pronouncement has had on many minds the effect of a genuine liberation from obstacles which warped their thinking and clogged their action. It proposes to substitute courage for uncertainty and hopefulness for fear. That is a very practical substitution. Certainty, or the claim of it, might have been offered as the substitute for uncertainty, and courage might have been offered as the substitute for fear. This, however, is not what the pronouncement offers. The soul is not to be cured of uncertainty and fear by becoming certain and courageous. It is to be made immune to its vices by means of a revised alignment of opposites, an alignment revised in view of the exigencies of living. The shift involved is naturally described as a shift from the theoretical to the practical. And I suspect that the major difficulties found in construing the philosophy of Professor Dewey arise from attempts to justify that shift on theoretical grounds. It is difficult for me to think that Professor Dewey himself does not attempt to provide such a justification. I find this less in what he affirms than in what he denies. His affirmations impress me as keeping close to a progressive development of a central theme. His denials, however, often impress me as requiring the acceptance of the opposite of what is denied as the ultimate theoretical ground which supports the practical affirmations. I seem at times to be asked to substitute courage for certainty on the ground that there is no certainty, and hopefulness for fear on the ground that there is nothing of which to be afraid. In such moments I find myself involved in a dialectic of theories of knowledge and existence. I become myself a controversialist, and find myself leaving the solid ground of experience.

There are two sentences in *Experience and Nature*[2] which express concisely and without controversial implications that pronouncement on human life to which I have referred. They are these: "Because intelligence is critical method applied to goods of belief, appreciation, and conduct, so as to construct freer and more secure goods, turning assent and assertion into free communication and sharable meanings, turning feeling into ordered and liberal sense, turning reaction into response, it is the reason-

2. Pp. 436–437 [*Later Works* 1:325–26].

able object of our deepest faith and loyalty, the stay and support of all reasonable hopes. . . . What the method of intelligence, thoughtful valuation, will accomplish, if once it be tried, is for the result of trial to determine." I have said that these sentences are without controversial implications. They receive, moreover, in Professor Dewey's manifold expansion of them, an emphasis which puts them in a position of philosophical dignity. They are not left without an expert analysis which aims to make them of primary importance, and to exhibit their entire independence of any attitude which can be defined as antecedent or more fundamental. This analysis, when freed from dialectical and controversial entanglements, impresses me as wholly convincing. The attempt to bring intelligence to bear on life in the manner described, is an attempt which is, and can be, made, without first having solved any antecedent problem whatever. Least of all does it wait on the solution of such problems as the existence of God, immortality, freedom *versus* necessity, mechanism *versus* teleology, and the like. Problems do not exist to be solved before we can live: they arise in the process of living, and in that process are solved and resolved. Professor Dewey has driven that fact home with untiring persistence; and he has made that fact the starting-point of all fruitful thinking. As a consequence, he has made many of us intolerant of any other attitude. He has made it quite impossible for many of us to believe that life can generate any problem the solution of which would be life's undoing. And he has made this impossible because he has shown us in a wholly convincing manner that if we are to philosophize profitably we must begin with the concrete operations of intelligence as these promote more satisfactory living, and not with some antecedent scheme of things which is supposed to explain or justify these operations. Life with its exigencies is fundamental, and this fundamental can not be explained by any solution of life's problems, nor deduced from any system of things which our ingenuity may devise. Whatever one thinks of all this, it is a very definite and a clearly intelligible philosophy. And it is natural for it to recommend courage in the face of uncertainty and hopefulness in the face of fear.

It is natural, too, perhaps, that among its analyses it should give a prominent and even a distinctive place to the analysis of reflective thinking and the operation of ideas. Its premise, it may be said, forces it to look upon thinking as inquiry, and upon ideas as the intellectual instruments of inquiry which find their validity in what they effect or accomplish. Here is a thesis which can stand on its own bottom. It seems to be a major thesis of Professor Dewey, which he uses to frame a logic of practice, to give moral tone to actions, and to humanize education. In his development of it, however, he seems to me to support it far less by an appeal to its natural source, than by using it dialectically to confound every analysis of knowledge which implies an antecedent reality to which intelligence must conform in its operations if it is to be successful. Now, the question I would raise here is not whether there is such an antecedent reality, nor whether there are grounds for believing that there is. Such questions, like Professor Dewey's major thesis, seem to me to stand on their own bottom. Surely we can ask with as complete intelligibility as we can ask any question, whether or not reflective thinking implies an antecedent reality to which knowledge must conform to be successful. It is a question to be settled by inquiry fully as much as any other. To make it a wholly illegitimate question, and to read the whole history of philosophy down to very recent times as if it were vitiated by attempted answers to this question, give to Professor Dewey's thesis a character extraordinarily difficult to construe. I repeat, the question is not whether there are objects antecedent to knowledge to which knowledge must conform to be successful. The question is, rather, whether Professor Dewey's thesis would be vitiated in proportion as one believed in such objects and operated accordingly, and whether, if there were such objects, that thesis would be wholly destroyed? I ask the question because I have failed to discover that the existence or non-existence of such objects has anything to do with the essential character of the thesis. I can not find that the problem of their existence has to be settled first, before validity can be claimed for the thesis. Yet I am forced to believe that Professor Dewey thinks that such a settlement is essential. As I follow his settlement, I find myself in a dialectic which sets antecedent objects over against eventual objects to the confounding of both.

To be more specific, in *The Quest for Certainty*[3] Professor Dewey says in italics, "*only the conclusion of reflective inquiry is*

3. P. 182 [*Later Works* 4:145–46].

known." This forces me to reply, "The conclusion of reflective inquiry is currently said to be knowledge; am I then to identify knowledge with the known." If I do this, I am thrown into the arms of the idealists, whose embrace I dislike. So I distinguish between knowledge and its object; I conceive the object to exist prior to its being known. Then I am confronted with the charge that this robs knowing of practical efficacy. To avoid this I must recognize that objects of knowledge exist only after the act of knowing; they are eventual objects. That there are eventual objects after the act of knowing, and that, unless there are such objects, the act of knowing is futile, are propositions which are for me both clear and acceptable. But if any objects whatever are known, it seems to me to be irrelevant whether they exist prior or subsequent to the act of knowing. What knowing eventuates in is a known object. I suppose no one disputes that, at least no one disputes it so far as the intent of knowledge is concerned. If that eventuation is made to depend on the prior settlement of the problem of antecedent as against eventual object, I can see nothing left but a dialectic which settles nothing. I do see, however, that an analysis of knowing as a concrete operation with subject-matter, makes such a dialectic quite unnecessary. Why, then, play eventual objects over against primary subject-matter, making of the former reconstructions of the latter, and making these reconstructions the objects of knowledge? I am quite ready to agree that it is the important business of knowing so to deal with subject-matter that more satisfactory objects are substituted for less satisfactory, and that, thereby, greater security, control, and happiness are secured; but I fail to see how this warrants the statement that *only the conclusion of reflective inquiry is known*. That statement seems to me to come from another source. To find that source I am driven back on Professor Dewey's dialectical and controversial arguments. These drive me, in spite of all he says, to try to frame some conception of existence which is wholly independent of the act of knowing, and yet the justification of that act and the source of its efficacy. Yet this seems to be precisely what I am forbidden to do by the dialectic.

The matter may be made still more specific. In the chapter on "The Seat of Intellectual Authority" in *The Quest for Certainty*, Professor Dewey uses the example of a physician called in to diagnose the disease of a patient. He has the physician do what a physician would do, examine the patient and bring to bear his medical knowledge on the case. But the whole discussion drives me to ask: Must we conclude that it is only after the physician has found out what is the matter with the patient that the patient has anything the matter with him? So to conclude would be to caricature. Is, I venture to ask, the caricature only the result of the reader's stupidity, or is it the result of being forced to decide whether antecedents or consequents are the objects known? One must ask: Do what things are and the ways they operate depend on the eventuation of inquiry? Must we conclude that they do so depend because intelligence does, as a matter of fact, participate in the order of events, and so operate that more satisfactory objects are substituted for less satisfactory? Is this caricature? What saves us from the confusion here involved except a metaphysics of the kind which the dialectic of prior and eventual objects tends to destroy?

The questions are not asked to try to convict Professor Dewey of contradiction. They are asked because one reader at least finds no clue to an answer to them except in the dialectic, and that clue leaves him in the dialectic. The best he can do is to conclude that existence is essentially dialectical, and that the dialectic is incidentally resolved by the practical operations of intelligence. This may be a sound conclusion. If, now, we try to settle the question whether it is or not, we discover in ourselves a close intellectual kinship with Plato, Aristotle, Spinoza, Locke, Kant, Hegel, and all that array of names which the history of philosophy holds up for admiration.

Again I take sentences from *Experience and Nature*.[4] "A naturalistic metaphysics is bound to consider reflection itself a natural event, occurring *within* nature because of traits of the latter. . . . The world must actually be such as to generate ignorance and inquiry, doubt and hypothesis, trial and temporal conclusions. . . . The ultimate evidence of genuine hazard, contingency, irregularity, and indeterminateness in nature is thus found in the occurrence of thinking. The traits of natural existence which generate the fears and adorations of superstitious barbarians, generate the scientific procedures of disciplined civilization." Sentences

4. Pp. 68–70 [*Later Works* 1:62–63].

like these abound in Professor Dewey's writings. They impress me as being fully as characteristic of his philosophy as the instrumental doctrine of intelligence. At times, they impress me as more characteristic, because they define an attitude from which instrumentalism may be derived, but which itself is not derived from instrumentalism. It is a challenging attitude which nowhere else in my reading have I found so vigorously set forth.

It is not unusual among philosophies to be what is called anthropomorphic. It is very unusual, however, to be that in Professor Dewey's sense. There is a vast difference between constructing nature out of human traits and finding in human traits clues for inferences regarding what nature is. According to Professor Dewey's attitude, we are just as much forbidden to put man over against nature as an ultimate contrast as we are forbidden to put the sun, the moon, or the stars, over against it as such a contrast. If the latter are good grounds for inference, so also is man, and every part of man's make-up and activity.

I dislike to leave this feature of Professor Dewey's philosophy with so bare a statement of it. The importance of it is so great that it deserves far more attention than it has received. It involves an attitude difficult to describe by those pet isms with which we philosophers love to deal, and in which we think we feel at home. And "nature" is a very troublesome word. One thing, however, seems clear. Limited by our location and by our length of days, we do try to form some conception of that context within which we ourselves are so evidently incidents. "Nature" may not be that context; it may be only a part of it; but who is going to decide for us all? Shall we let a word cramp the challenging significance of an utterance which affirms that man, when he tries to pass beyond the limits of the evident situation in which he finds himself, must not neglect anything within that situation? Let us, then, for the present at least, accept "nature" as the name for that which includes us as events within itself. What, then, is nature like? The answer is, it is, in some measure at least, like what we are. If we are unstable, there is instability in it; if we are contradictory, there is contradiction in it; if we are hopeful, there is possibility—one might dare to say, hope—in it; if we err, there is something like error in it; if we are incomplete, there is incompleteness in it. And all this does not mean that we are the exclusive instances of all such traits of nature. We are samples of them.

In short, man is a sample of nature, and just as good a sample as the solar system or an atom. Consequently, we should never suppose that the latter afford better grounds for inferring what nature is like than the former affords. Here is a road which philosophers rarely travel with unencumbering luggage.

The acceptance or rejection of this conception of nature is not here in question. Nor is the method by which it is approached. These matters are left to the disputatious. The thing that troubles me is the limitation which Professor Dewey seems to put upon what we are entitled to infer from the samples of nature which we may study and analyze. Clearly man is not the only sample. There is the solar system also, and, if not the atom, at least that which admits an atomic theory. Why, then, should inference to anything permanent and unchanging be forbidden? Such inferences may be unsound, but they suggest themselves repeatedly as we explore the varied samples of nature. I do not find, however, that Professor Dewey rejects them because there is not evidence for them. He seems, rather, to argue them into illegitimacy. The ground of the argument seems to be, I repeat, not lack of evidence; it seems, rather, to be the conviction that any recognition of the permanently fixed or unchanging is bad. It implies a disastrous preference. *The Quest for Certainty* seems to me to read the history of philosophy in terms of that disaster, and to turn that history into an argument against the recognition of anything but relative permanency. And in *Experience and Nature*[5] we read: "One doctrine finds structure in a framework of ideal forms, the other finds it in matter. They agree in supposing that structure has some superlative reality. This supposition is another form taken by preference for the stable over the precarious and incompleted." Are we to conclude, therefore, that to avoid disaster, we must take a preference for the precarious and incompleted? Why is one preference better than the other, and why should the question be one of taking preference at all? I get no answer in terms of evidence of the same kind that warrants the emphasis on change. I get a dialectical answer, as if dialectic, and not the method by which nature is inferred, is to decide what inferences are to be admitted. And when I examine the dialectic, I find it motivated by the insistent claim that the recog-

5. P. 72 [*Later Works* 1:64].

nition of the permanent gives it a metaphysical superiority to the changing. This makes it possible to play the one off against the other in the interest of proving that the permanent is but the relatively stable in a nature which is change through and through.

Now nature may be just that. I am not questioning that conception of what nature is. I am only pointing out that I find that conception supported finally, not by empirical evidence, but by a dialectical argument. That, again, may be the way to support it. If it is, then I am forced to conclude that dialectic is a better sample of nature's processes than any other. This also may be true. Then, to consider its truth, I find myself owning kinship with Heraclitus and Parmenides and their illustrious followers. I must carry the debate into that atmosphere; and when I do, I find no help whatever in terms of that practical procedure which marks the development of securer knowledge.

Such are the two illustrations I venture to give of the general statement I made in the beginning of this paper. They represent a conclusion I am led to by reading the writing of Professor Dewey. It is what his philosophy ultimately looks like in my own mind: a philosophy with a doctrine of experience and nature which admits of a positive and progressive development in its own terms, which stands, as I have said, on its own bottom; but which, in spite of this, is made to depend on a dialectic which runs back in the history of philosophy very far indeed. We should expect, as I see it, a metaphysics which is wholly inferential. We have, instead, a metaphysics which is a matter of preference. And this preference—we may even say that the empirical fact of preference—implies that nature is essentially dialectical, and that one way, at least, by which the dialectic is incidentally obviated, is through the practical procedure of intelligence. Experience appears to be, therefore, not something which is justified by its fruits, but which is justified by a dialectic which determines what experience is like.

Appendix 5
Three Independent Factors in Morals

INTRODUCTORY REMARKS

[*Mr. Xavier Léon.*—In asking Professor J. Dewey, who will receive the title *Doctor honoris causa* in solemn ceremonies at the Sorbonne tomorrow, to come and set forth in the informal circle of members of the French Philosophical Society some of his important ideas, I am following one of our cherished traditions, that of honoring an illustrious colleague at one of our regular meetings.

My thanks to you, Professor Dewey, for having accepted this invitation with so much simplicity; I might add, with so much modesty, for when you wrote to excuse yourself for not speaking our language fluently, you said that it would be a great pleasure for you to meet our friends, but that you would be amply satisfied to attend one of our meetings and listen to your French colleagues speak. However, when I insisted, you did agree to make a presentation in English on the subject: *Three Independent Factors in Morals*.

Rest assured that this will not be the first time a person has used your language here for such a presentation, and, if my memory serves, one of your own compatriots also made his exposition to us in English.

Tomorrow, in a different setting, our dear friend Dean H. Delacroix will describe in detail the outstanding honors and recognition given you by philosophers. Therefore, I will dispense with them before the membership of this Society. It will suffice for

[First published as the introductory remarks and discussion in "Trois facteurs indépendants en matière de morale," trans. Charles Cestre, in *Bulletin de la société française de philosophie* 30 (October–December 1930): 117–18, 127–33. First published in English in *Educational Theory* 16 (July 1966): 198, 205–9, trans. Jo Ann Boydston. For Dewey's address, see this volume, pp. 279–88.]

me to recall that your philosophy has claimed the attention of thinkers in France for quite a long time and in the meetings of our own Society, the question of pragmatism has been discussed on several occasions.

What I would like to say is that you have truly done the work of philosophy by testing the principles of your doctrine in different realms of thought, even in their consequences for and their application to politics, sociology, and pedagogy.

Several months ago twenty-nine of your American colleagues celebrated your seventieth birthday by dedicating to you a volume of studies written for that occasion. Even though it is a little late, I would like for today's meeting also to be a celebration of that birthday, and to bring to you, along with the ardent wishes of your French colleagues for a long continuation of your brilliant career, the homage of their admiration and of their respect.]

DISCUSSION

Mr. Xavier Léon.—Gentlemen, you have heard Mr. Dewey's presentation in English; I am sure you admired, as I did, the distinction, the elegance, and above all, the penetration with which he spoke. You have also heard Mr. Cestre's translation, which I consider admirable. The ideas presented by Mr. Dewey are many; I believe that we can examine some of them here, and since we have the pleasure of having with us today a representative of the Greek philosophy to which Mr. Dewey attaches such great importance, I will ask our friend Robin if he doesn't have some observation to present.

Mr. L. Robin.—I was forcefully impressed by what Mr. Dewey said on the character of Greek philosophy and its concept of morals. I believe his idea is quite justified whatever Greek morals one has in mind.

If one considers morals like Plato's, it seems clear that Plato finds in the morals of the individual the reflection of the city and in the morals of the city, a reflection of the morals of the universe. And the universe itself should be subject to the laws which rule the ideal world, even though that will be possible only through an imperfect copy. Consequently, the idea of law seems to me very much in the limelight here. It would be the same if one considered a system of morals like that of the Stoics, or even that of Epicureanism, since for both there is always the question of conforming to the law of nature, diversely conceived.

I wonder if the application would be so easily made with regard to Aristotelian morals, which seems to me an effort to find a compromise among the different factors of which Mr. Dewey spoke, and an attempt to find in each particular case what would be the special reasons for the choice, reasons which vary with circumstances. So that perhaps in Aristotelian morals there would be the factor of uncertainty which Mr. Dewey justifiably emphasizes and the empirical character of the moral decision. Don't you think so?

[Mr. Dewey goes back over the exact meaning of the part of his communication dealing with Greek philosophy, which seems to have been a little misinterpreted in Mr. Robin's observation. Mr. Dewey stressed the fact that Greek philosophy sought the good; he considered that Roman philosophy, inspired by that of the Stoics, sought the law. He repeated the point that the Greeks were most of all concerned with seeking the good, and the good is the ideal force which both moves and organizes the cosmos.]

Mr. L. Robin.—Nevertheless, it seems to me that at one point in his presentation, Mr. Dewey spoke of the idea of law and its influence on Greek morals. Really, I still think that the end for the Greeks is represented by law, and, when you say that for Plato good is first and that the good is an end, as a matter of fact, good is the law of the ideal world which gives its law to the universe, which in turn gives its law to the city which finally gives it to the individual. All the great Greek moralists, whatever rank they gave the idea of ends, conceived the end from the viewpoint of a law; they always considered that laws of conduct were formulated by aiming at the end; and, on the other hand, except for the Epicureans, who were more individualistic, the idea of political eunomy and legislation was most often dominant.

You spoke of the instability of the Greeks, of the fact that, in effect, they never organized their state well and that they were in perpetual revolution. But it is no less true that they always searched for a better organization, that of the ideal city, and it is probably because of circumstances they could not control that they never succeeded in organizing a stable state. Doesn't Roman law clearly derive from Greek ideas? A little while ago, we mentioned the Stoics. Perhaps we must seek even further if it is true that it was Hermodorus, Heraclitus' friend, who was one of the legislators of the Twelve Tables.

Mr. C. Bouglé.—It seems to me that those who do not wish to hold to the traditional viewpoint of theoretic morals should give thanks to Mr. Dewey, because at the end of his communication there were several things which recalled the concepts of Lévy-Bruhl[1] or of Durkheim.[2] "It is pointless to believe that we can explain and justify everything by one single principle," said our colleague. It seems to me that this is one of the points of departure of Mr. Lévy-Bruhl in his book on *Ethics and Moral Science*.[3] I think Durkheim and most of his sociologist colleagues would have agreed with pleasure when our guest observed that to get along in life one must take account of a number of involved social realities rather than a single moral principle which can be invoked in every instance.

There is, then, a similarity between his reflections as philosopher, moralist, and pedagogue, and the reflections which the sociologists have proposed to us from their side. However, when I think about the different forces which he attempts to discern, I do not believe they can be quite so clearly distinguished. He speaks to us of three independent variables, independent factors, as he says, of morals. Are they really independent? It is to this point that I call the attention of our colleagues.

Mr. Dewey says to us for example, if I understood correctly, in certain cases one seeks the good. And that search for the good gives rise to a certain form of morality. In other cases, a law is imposed and it becomes a social exigency: my neighbor wishes that I conduct myself in a certain way. These are the two sources of morals. The idea of a very simple observation comes to my mind; it is that in many cases, social exigency turns up as a means of attaining the good, whether it is the good of the individual and his particular interest, or the good of individuals grouped and of the group which they form. Thus, it would be incorrect to say that there are two quite distinct sources of morality; on the one hand: "If you wish the good, act this way"; on

---

1. Lucien Lévy-Bruhl (1857–1939), French philosopher and psychologist.
2. Émile Durkheim (1858–1917), French sociologist and philosopher.
3. *La morale et la science des moeurs*, trans. Elizabeth Lee (Paris: Felix Alcan, 1904).

the other hand, "Act thus because that is the law." Quite often, the law appears to be a means of reaching the good.

Doesn't that same thing happen when one gives reasons for respecting the law? Among these reasons, we can have concern for the good, and not just for individual good but the collective interest, which is still a good. I would hesitate to make two separate compartments: on the one hand, morals which arise from the good, and on the other, those which arise from respect for a legal form. In practice, when a law, a social exigency, is imposed it is most often with a good in view. If we follow our colleague to the end, we might say, for example, that the French, at least during a certain period in their history, had a very lively sense of law and of order. That is true, but it is no less true that in proclaiming respect for law and for order they had an eye on the good of the individual and of the nation.

All things considered, these two principles do not seem so clearly differentiated. To explain disagreements and debates about morals, we may need to look not only to this approach of presenting either the good or the law, but to the diversity of the groups to which we belong. It seems to me that one can always find a social need at the base of morality. But that need is sometimes evident in one group and sometimes in another. Those needs can change dimension and direction, and we are at the point of confluence of these diverse tendencies emanating from different groups. You might say that several disciplines are arguing about our conduct and want to exercise an influence on our behavior. The quandaries we experience in our conduct can be explained in this way: there is not only or first of all a distinction between the good and the law, but diversity, multiplicity, and often antagonism among the groups which try to impose regulations on our personality.

Mr. M. Mauss.—Among moral theorists and philosophers, Professor John Dewey is the one who comes closest to the sociologists. Today I reminded him of the time our mutual friend Professor Bush[4] introduced us in New York. Moreover, among American philosophers, he is one whom Durkheim put ahead of all the others, and it is a great regret of mine not to have been

---

4. Probably Wendell T. Bush, professor at Columbia University from 1905 to 1938.

able to attend the last great philosophy lecture of Durkheim, dedicated in great part to Professor Dewey. We now have the annotated cards, numbered, as Durkheim made them, but the rest is unfortunately lacking. With that introduction, permit me to say that I have been largely in accord for a long time now with that form of rational pragmatism which Professor Dewey represents, and this positive consideration of moral facts has my wholehearted approval. I believe that the name of Professor Dewey will be known for a long time, as much in our own philosophy as in American.

It might interest some of our colleagues to know that I believe Professor Dewey has given us quite a new perspective on new points, because in the works which he has published, he has not before expressed so definitely the opinions he presented today. We might say he has given us a première; the Philosophical Society should recognize the honor he has done it.

Mr. Xavier Léon.—Mr. Leroux, you know Mr. John Dewey's philosophy well and have studied that of William James. Would you like to add a few words?

Mr. E. Leroux.—What Mr. Mauss has just said is perfectly true, and because of that fact, I have no special authority to speak this evening. At first glance, when I saw the title of the communication, I thought that it would have some agreement with Mr. Dewey's earlier book, certainly one of the most remarkable studies on general problems of morals recently published. But those are not at all the same ideas he has just presented here. I had forgotten that Mr. Dewey is a man who renews himself incessantly and that he does not like to rely on his own writings. All the same, I would like to ask whether there is an agreement between the thesis he presented this evening and the one presented in *Human Nature and Conduct*. Without doubt, one can always find in him that sense of complex realities and at the same time that philosophical view of wholes which seems to me the dual characteristic of his spirit; but this time he goes a great deal further in the direction of diversity than he did in his book. There, he distinguished three elements in all human activity: habit, impulse, intelligence. But these factors were not completely independent of each other, so that Mr. Dewey attained a somewhat unified moral theory. According to him, habit was actually the basis of all activity; impulse could furnish the point of departure for a re-organization; but re-organization was not effected nor was the superior and properly moral form of activity attained except through the intervention of intelligence. Thus, Mr. Dewey's thought seemed to direct itself toward an original type of ethical intellectualism; the specifically moral activity was, for him, that sort of activity which was first excited by a conflict between habit and impulse, and led through reflective effort to a new state of equilibrium. There was in that approach a kind of criterion, albeit a little indeterminate, of moral conduct. Here Mr. Dewey puts us in the presence of another trinity, but one which he no longer wants to reduce to a unity. Is there nevertheless an agreement between the two concepts? And does he still maintain that the characteristic of moral activity is reflection which is used to reconcile the antagonism of habits and desires?

[Mr. Dewey responds that in his work on *Human Nature and Conduct*, he saw the moral problem above all from the psychological point of view, while today he was concerned with action proper, with the factors which intervene, laws imposed from outside, and the question of approval and of disapproval which impede the desires of the individual. According to him, therefore, it is not the same thing and today's point of view is broader.]

Mr. Jean Wahl.—I was extremely interested by what Mr. Dewey said. It forms a complement to the principles of political pluralism which he has treated in several of his works. It seems to me that another name could be mentioned, after those of the sociologists named earlier, and that one could compare Mr. Dewey's ideas with those of a philosopher a little different from them: Frédéric Rauh, who insisted, in *Moral Experience*,[5] on the plurality of moral principles, and on that irreducibility which has been mentioned. It is true that he sees even more independent variables than Mr. Dewey and that he searches less for general principles than for consideration of each particular action, since he is concerned with one's testing his own ideal in contact with the specific reality of each event.

However, I ask myself if the principles which Mr. Dewey distinguishes can be completely separated; we have already put that difficulty clearly into focus. Thus, for example, on the matter of approval, it seems to me that when Plato erects his morality of

5. *L'Expérience morale* (Paris: Felix Alcan, 1903).

the good, it is based first on judgments approving of particular actions. And similarly when Kant establishes his ethics of duty, we might say it is also on a rational sense of approval which he sets up first to disengage the idea of will. Thus, it seems to me quite difficult to distinguish these factors completely.

[Mr. Dewey recognizes that he exaggerated, for purposes of discussion, the differences among the three factors, that indeed moral theories do touch on these three factors more or less, but what he wanted to emphasize was the fact that each particular moral theory takes one of them as central and that is what becomes the important point, while the other factors are only secondary. In particular, perhaps, he was thinking about English morals, with the emphasis it puts on sympathy and antipathy, approval and disapproval, so that the facts of good and of the law are overshadowed or entirely absent.

Finally, he recognizes that it is quite fair to note that this discussion is dependent more on pluralism than on pragmatism.]

Mr. Xavier Léon.—Gentlemen, I believe that we can close this discussion; I do not wish to detain Mr. Dewey too long. He has been very patient in listening to his French colleagues and in answering them. I only wish, in the name of all of you, to thank him again for his visit here, to hope he has a good memory of his contact with our colleagues, and to tell him how proud we are, as Mauss remarked just now, that he gave the French Philosophical Society a première of his new ideas.

Appendix 6
Insurgents Back Norris in Refusing to Quit Republicans

Developments of more definite prospect for Republican organization of the Seventy-second Congress and of 1932 political possibilities followed today upon the refusal yesterday of Senator Norris, Nebraskan insurgent, to accept the invitation of Professor John Dewey of Columbia that he head a third party.

Mr. Norris made public a letter to Dr. Dewey in which, setting forth his reasons for not going into a separate political movement now, he voiced his aims for liberalization and discussed his project to eliminate the Electoral College and have direct elections of Presidents.

Senator Norris's letter to Dr. Dewey read:

Washington, D.C.
Dec. 27, 1930.
Hon. John Dewey, Chairman,
League for Independent Political Action.
52 Vanderbilt Av.
New York City.

My dear Professor Dewey:
I have read your letter of Dec. 23 with a great deal of interest. I realize, to begin with, your sincere, patriotic purpose. As to the real need of desirable legislation I think there is no disagreement between us whatever, but I am not able to see that the way to obtain it is by making an attempt to organize a third party.

Our antiquated method of electing a President should be changed to meet the present demands of civilization. As nearly as we can we ought to place the election of a President directly in the hands of the voters. To do this we must abolish the Electoral

[First published in *New York Times*, Sunday, 28 December 1930, sec. 1, pp. 1, 20. For Dewey's letter to which this is a response, see this volume, pp. 444–46. For Dewey's reply, see pp. 447–49.]

College, which, I think you will agree with me, is out of date and is used only to handicap the people in the selection of a Chief Magistrate.

I think experience has shown that the people will not respond to a demand for a new party except in case of a great emergency, when there is practically a political revolution. Such an aroused sentiment usually occurs after the national conventions have nominated their candidates. The time is then too short to organize a party and the expense is too great.

What we ought to do is to make it easy to nominate a candidate for the Presidency independent of either one of the great political parties. To do this, in my judgment, it would only require an amendment to the Constitution abolishing the Electoral College and providing for a direct vote on the part of every voter.

I wish we could organize public sentiment in the country in favor of such a movement. Congress would submit such an amendment to the Legislatures if there were created in the country an honest and sincere sentiment favorable to such action. The cultivation of an independent spirit on the part of the voter would have a healthy effect.

In my judgment, millions of voters have reached the stage now where they are independent and where they care very little for a party label.

The attempt on the part of extreme partisans, moved in the main by special interests behind the political scenes, to drive out of the political party men of progressive minds who will not prostitute their judgments and their consciences to the demand of political bosses is not meeting with any sincere response from the people.

More independent action and less adherence to party control is gaining wonderful headway in the minds of educated, thinking people.

If we would all unite in a demand for a constitutional amendment such as I have indicated, I have no doubt that success would crown our efforts within a reasonable time.

Very truly yours,

G. W. NORRIS

Notes

The following notes, keyed to the page and line numbers of the present edition, explain references to matters not found in standard sources.

238.40–239.1 Hawthorne investigation] An experimental study at the Hawthorne Works of the Western Electric Company, Chicago, from 1927 to 1929 to determine the influences affecting employee effectiveness and mental attitude. For a full description of the study, see G. A. Pennock, "Industrial Research at Hawthorne: An Experimental Investigation of Rest Periods, Working Conditions, and Other Influences," *Personnel Journal* 8 (February 1930): 296–313.

300.15–16 general introductory report of the commission] This reference and those at 303n.3, 307.3, and 309.7–8 are to the "General Introduction" and "Part Two— Articulation at the Elementary School Level— Kindergarten—Grades 1–6," *Seventh Yearbook: The Articulation of the Units of American Education* (Washington, D.C.: Department of Superintendence of the National Education Association, 1929), pp. 11–22, 23–114.

340.12 The graduate of the College] Charles L. Reed, who attended Brookwood Labor College from 1922 to 1924. At the time of the 1928 Convention he was Vice President of the Massachusetts Federation of Labor and an executive council member of the Workers' Education Bureau of America.

393.21–24 story . . . Professor Burt.] The incident attributed to Dewey is that of his walking to the post office on a summer morning, pushing a perambulator. Upon calling for his mail, he strolled back home, completely forgetting the child sleeping peacefully in the sun. The Professor Burt to whom Dewey refers is Benjamin Chapman Burt of the University of Michigan.

Textual Apparatus

Index

Textual Notes

The following notes, keyed to the page and line numbers of the present edition, discuss readings adopted in the critical text, whether emendation or retention of copy-text readings where emendation might have been expected.

156.4   all,] [See note for 159.38.]

159.38   genuine,] Even though space occurred for these two line-end commas, the printer failed to include them. The present edition has restored these commas.

184.39–40 influenced . . . of Aristotle] Dewey's original typescript had read "of Aristotle." Because he changed the "of" to "by" before giving the typescript to George Dykhuizen for retyping, Dykhuizen inserted "more" before "influenced." However, for publication in *Journal of the History of Ideas*, Dewey changed "by" back to his original "of," but neglected to delete Dykhuizen's "more"; the present edition has therefore rejected the added "more."

205.31,40 context] In Dewey's discussion of Ernest Nagel's use of the concept "fixing context," the printer twice uses "content" for "context," probably a memorial error carried over from Dewey's use of "content" three lines up at 205.25. The present edition has emended the two instances of "content" to "context."

218.15   That] In revising this article for republication in *Philosophy and Civilization*, Dewey deleted one of his introductory remarks, and changed "two general introductory remarks may be made" to "an introductory remark should be made." At 218.15, however, he neglected to change "One [of these two remarks]." The present edition has made the statement consistent by emending "One" to "That."

226.9   ends,] The *Philosophy and Civilization* addition of the appositional comma in the phrase "*ends*, conclusions,"

has been accepted as necessary to clarify the meaning of
the sentence.

305.11   phases] The omitting of the final "s" by Department of
Superintendence *Official Report* in the phrase "some
phases" has been rejected as a probable printer's error.

Textual Commentary

Volume 5 of *The Later Works of John Dewey, 1925–1953* comprises fifty-three items for the years 1929 and 1930, all Dewey's writings for those two years except *The Quest for Certainty*, which appears as Volume 4 of *The Later Works*.

Of these fifty-three items, three were books published separately: *Construction and Criticism*, *The Sources of a Science of Education*, and *Individualism, Old and New*. Thirty-one items are essays—twenty journal articles, six introductions to books, and five contributions to volumes of collected essays. The remaining nineteen items are three book reviews, four published letters, eleven published political statements, and one unpublished typescript.

Thirty of the pieces presented here had been published only once before the present edition and therefore posed no copy-text problems; the only previous appearance of these thirty items not discussed below has necessarily served as copy-text.

The publishing history and various textual complexities of the remaining twenty-three items are discussed in the sections that follow. When setting copy for any item is not described, it can be assumed that, following his usual practice, Dewey submitted his own or a professionally prepared typescript which is no longer extant.

The Sources of a Science of Education

Dewey delivered "The Sources of a Science of Education" to the Kappa Delta Pi Society in Cleveland, Ohio, on 26 February 1929. With this lecture, Kappa Delta Pi, an international honor society in education of which Dewey was a Laureate Chapter member, inaugurated its annual Lecture Series.

Published by Horace Liveright in 1929, the book was favorably but not widely reviewed. The *Newark Evening News* of 19 October 1929 called it "decidedly rugged thinking—reflections that prove that Dewey will not allow himself to be swept off his feet by this or that current fad or by enthusiasm for still unproved ideas." The *Boston Evening Tran-*

script of 30 November 1929 described it as "stimulating," embodying "the potent plea he has sent out more than once for the placing of education where it rightly belongs—among the sciences."

Information on the copyright page of *The Sources of a Science of Education* indicates that the book had four printings: the first and second in October 1929, the third in October 1931, and the fourth in June 1944. However, the October 1929 "first" and "second" printings were probably the same printing bound at different times. Evidence for this assumption is that a copy of the "second" printing is the copyright deposit copy (A 14838). This copy is identical with the first impression in every respect except the copyright page designation. Machine collation of the first printing against the June 1944 fourth printing verified that the texts are identical. The first printing has served as copy-text for the present edition.

Individualism, Old and New

While Dewey was at the University of Edinburgh from 17 April to 17 May 1929 delivering the Gifford Lectures, later published as *The Quest for Certainty*,[1] the first of his eight *New Republic* articles on "Individualism, Old and New" was published on 24 April 1929.

The editors at *New Republic* were enthusiastic about publishing Dewey's series of articles. Daniel Mebane, *New Republic* treasurer, wrote Dewey in October 1929 that "nothing this year has given me so much satisfaction as the occasion to announce your series. Mr. Croly, whom I saw yesterday, was highly pleased by the prospect; he said that your articles . . . were the best the paper has published during the period—which, as you know, is also my opinion."[2]

Dewey signed a publishing agreement on 18 March 1930 with Minton, Balch and Company to bring out these articles in book form. Two other firms had offered to publish the articles as a book. Dewey wrote to Richard Thornton of Henry Holt and Company on 20 March that

> I have changed my mind about bringing out my N.R. articles in a book. Minton Balch & Co have done very well with the Quest for Certainty, (selling about 8000 copies between publication in Oct and March first) and think they can sell 10000 of this book so Ive signed a contract with them.[3]

1. *The Later Works of John Dewey, 1925–1953*, ed. Jo Ann Boydston (Carbondale and Edwardsville: Southern Illinois University Press, 1984), vol. 4.
2. Mebane to Dewey, 17 October 1929, John Dewey Papers, Special Collections, Morris Library, Southern Illinois University at Carbondale.
3. Dewey to Thornton, 20 March 1930, Holt Publishing Company Archives, Princeton University Library, Princeton, N.J.

On 17 April 1930 he informed John Macrae of E. P. Dutton and Company, "I have already signed a contract for the 'Individualism' material with Minton Balch & Co—I thank you for your interest."[4]

As stated in Dewey's prefatory note, *Individualism, Old and New* (New York: Minton, Balch and Co., 1930) brought together "with considerable new matter" eight articles that had appeared in the *New Republic* from 24 April 1929 to 2 April 1930. "The House Divided against Itself" and "'America'—By Formula," from the 24 April and 18 September 1929 issues of the *New Republic*, were not part of the "Individualism, Old and New" series of articles, but were included as the first two chapters of the book because of their related subject matter. The "Individualism, Old and New" series began with "The United States, Incorporated" in the 22 January 1930 issue, and continued with "The Lost Individual," 5 February 1930, "Toward a New Individualism," 19 February 1930, "Capitalistic or Public Socialism?" 5 March 1930, "The Crisis in Culture," 19 March 1930, and the final "Individuality in Our Day," 2 April 1930. These articles formed chapters three through eight of the book.

Individualism, Old and New was on the whole well received. Not only was it widely reviewed in this country,[5] but it also received attention in England in *Mind* and the *English Review* and in Scotland in the *Expository Times* (Edinburgh).

The American edition of *Individualism, Old and New* had a second impression in 1930. Sight collation of the first and second impressions showed their texts to be identical. After the 1930 Minton, Balch and Company printings, George Allen and Unwin reset type for a British edition published in London in 1931, with restyled spelling and punctuation but with no substantive variants.

Copy-text for *Individualism, Old and New* has been the series of articles as originally published in the *New Republic*. The "considerable new matter" and other substantive changes introduced by Dewey for the book publication have been incorporated into the copy-text as emendations for the present edition.

---

4. Dewey to Macrae, 17 April 1930, E. P. Dutton and Company Archives, New York, N.Y.
5. *Bookman* 74 (September 1931): 104–7 (Odell Shepard); *Crozer Quarterly* 8 (January 1931): 128–29 (Stewart G. Cole); *Current History* 33 (March 1931): 22–24 (Sidney Hook); *English Review* 53 (1931): 510–11 (Herbert Agar); *Expository Times* 43 (October 1931): 17; *Mind*, n.s., 41 (January 1932): 131–32 (F. C. S. Schiller); *Nation* 131 (22 October 1930): 446–47 (Henry Hazlitt); *New York Herald Tribune Books*, 23 November 1930, pp. 1, 6 (André Maurois); *New York Times Book Review*, 21 December 1930, p. 2 (John Chamberlain); *New York World Book World*, 19 October 1930, p. 3 (C. Hartley Grattan); *World Unity* 7 (December 1930): 193–201 (John Herman Randall, Jr.).

Construction and Criticism

Dewey delivered "Construction and Criticism" on 25 February 1930 as the first Milton Judson Davies Memorial Lecture before the Institute of Arts and Sciences, Columbia University. Published as a twenty-five page book by Columbia University Press in 1930, it received one printing. The copyright deposit copy A 22901 has served as copytext for the present edition.

James Marsh and American Philosophy

Dewey delivered this address on 26 November 1929 at his alma mater, the University of Vermont, as part of the celebration commemorating the one hundredth anniversary of the first American edition of Samuel Taylor Coleridge's *Aids to Reflection*, edited and introduced by James Marsh. Not only did Marsh's edition of the *Aids* enjoy continued reprinting, but his "Preliminary Essay" and notes also appeared in W. G. T. Shedd's 1853 collected edition of Coleridge, the standard American text of Coleridge for more than a century.[6]

Dewey delivered his lecture, "Coleridge, Marsh and the Spiritual Philosophy: An Address on James Marsh in Relation to the Romantic Movement," in the University gymnasium to an audience of seven to eight hundred;[7] it was the third in the University Lecture Series, with Bertrand Russell and Charles R. Knight preceding and S. K. Ratcliffe and Carl Sandburg completing the series for the year.

None of these University Lectures was published at that time. After six years had passed, George Dykhuizen of the University of Vermont wrote Dewey offering to retype the draft with a view to getting it published. Dewey responded:

> I have been keeping my paper on James Marsh with the expectation of revising it somewhat and sending it to the *Philosophical Review*. However, as I do not see any immediate prospects in that direction, I will send you my typewritten copy. I shall be glad to receive the copy you mention you can send me.[8]

On 8 May 1935 Dewey wrote to thank Dykhuizen for the retyped version, assuring him that "the delay in copying it did not inconvenience

6. See John J. Duffy, ed., *Coleridge's American Disciples: The Selected Correspondence of James Marsh* (Amherst: University of Massachusetts Press, 1937), p. 4.
7. A. R. Gifford, "The Marsh Lecture, 1829–1929," *Vermont Alumni Weekly* 9 (11 December 1929): 163.
8. Dewey to Dykhuizen, 20 February 1935, Dewey Papers.

me at all. Please give my thanks also to the young woman who did the work."[9] He gave Dykhuizen the original, which Dykhuizen later deposited in Special Collections, Bailey/Howe Library, University of Vermont, Burlington, Vermont.[10]

The paper never appeared in *Philosophical Review*. After six more years, the lecture was finally published in *Journal of the History of Ideas* 2 (April 1941): 131–50.

Dewey's original typescript (TS) has served as copy-text for this article. Dykhuizen's retyped version (D), which Dewey used as printer's copy for publication in the *Journal of the History of Ideas* (JHI), introduced a total of 325 changes in Dewey's original TS, 301 of which appear in JHI. Of these 301 alterations, 275 are accidentals changes of the kind ordinarily made in retyping a rough draft: misspelled words corrected, incomplete words completed, repeated words deleted, quotation marks and footnote numbers supplied, first words of sentences capitalized and end punctuation supplied. Twenty-six of the changes are in substantives. D's substantive changes were intended simply to clarify Dewey's meaning: as, for example, at 184.4, where Dewey had typed "situation he in which he," D deleted the first "he," correcting the phrase to "situation in which he," and at 184.26, where D corrected "he not reached" to "did not reach."

The present edition has rejected six of the twenty-six D substantive alterations accepted by Dewey for publication in JHI. One such rejection, at 184.39–40, is discussed in the Textual Notes. The remaining five have been rejected for various reasons: at 184.22, TS read "he was," with an x'd-out word between "he" and "was" making the "w" difficult to see. D's emendation to "he, as" is a misreading of TS. At 185.16, D's emending of "furnishes" to "furnished" has been rejected because it disagrees with the present tense of the surrounding verbs. At 188.5, TS had the incorrectly typed letters "os" in the phrase "exercise os sensibility." D interpreted "os" as "or." The present edition has emended "or" to "of" in the reading "exercise of sensibility." At 189.22 the incomplete word "oused" appeared in "desires that are oused by the thought of ends." D deleted the "o" creating the word "used." This change has been rejected in favor of the word "aroused," since Dewey used the word "aroused" in a similar context ten lines below, and he was more likely to leave "ar" off "oused," which followed the word "are" than to type an "o" in front of "used." At 192.10 where Dewey quotes from Marsh, D's "constitute" has been rejected in favor of the TS "constitutes," which restores the reading from Marsh.

Of the eighty-five substantive changes made in D for publication in

9. Dewey to Dykhuizen, 8 May 1935, Dewey Papers.
10. Dykhuizen to Kathleen Poulos, 23 February 1982, Center for Dewey Studies, Southern Illinois University at Carbondale.

JHI, the present edition has rejected three as probable printer's errors: "s" dropped from "thoughts" at 178.24, "that of" dropped from the phrase "that of Coleridge" at 182.2–3, and "s" dropped from "conditions" at 186.34. Of the remaining eighty-two authorial substantive changes, the present edition has rejected one: at 179.18–19, along with other alterations to the sentence, Dewey changed the word "accomplishment" to "attainment" in the phrase "no mean accomplishment," probably inadvertently also crossing out the word "mean," so that the phrase became in JHI "this was no attainment," obviously not what Dewey had intended to say. The present edition has restored the word "mean," thereby re-creating Dewey's intended "this was no mean attainment."

One hundred eleven accidentals changes appeared in the JHI version of the lecture. The present edition has rejected eighty-six of these as editorial house-styling without authority. The majority of these are commas added to series, or to set off introductory and subordinate phrases and clauses and parenthetical expressions. Twenty changes in accidentals have been accepted because they are within or caused by authorial substantive changes.

From the article's republication in Dewey's collective work *Problems of Men* (PM) (New York: Philosophical Library, 1946), the present edition has accepted as authorial four of the five substantive changes: at 178.3 "this University town" changed to "Burlington, Vt."; at 178.4 "in Burlington, Vermont," changed to "there"; at 178.8 reference to the Marsh centenary deleted; and at 179.32 "admiration for Coleridge" changed to "admiration of Coleridge." Only one substantive change in PM has been rejected as a probable printer's error: "inner" as "own" at 180.21.

Of the ten accidentals changes in PM, at 189.25 the division of a lengthy sentence at "will. But" has been accepted as authorial and bears comment. TS had "will, But" indicating that Dewey did intend to begin another sentence at "But." He overlooked the "will, but" of D and JHI and then restored in PM the punctuation he had originally intended in TS.

The Emendations List for this article also serves as a historical collation, listing all variants in the four documents described—TS, D, JHI, and PM. Dewey's alterations in the process of composing TS appear in "Alterations in 'James Marsh and American Philosophy.'"

Conduct and Experience

"Conduct and Experience" first appeared as chapter 22 of *Psychologies of 1930* (P), edited by Carl Murchison (Worcester, Mass.: Clark University Press, 1930), copy-text for this essay. It was republished in the authoritative collection of Dewey's essays, *Philosophy and Civilization* (PC) (New York: Minton, Balch and Co., 1931). The accidentals changes in PC that are within or caused by authorial substantive changes have been accepted in the present edition. Those few accidentals changes not related to authorial substantive changes have been rejected. They include the introduction of commas around parenthetical expressions and after introductory subordinate clauses, the deletion of commas before dashes, and the spellings of "sceptical" with a "k" and "aesthetic" with a ligature.

The fifty-eight substantive changes in PC range from alterations of a word or two (most are in this category, including eight instances of added italics) to deletions of parts of or whole paragraphs. All fifty-eight PC substantive changes have been accepted by the present edition with the following exceptions: at 235.3 the phrase "distinguished logician" became "distinguishing logician" in PC, a probable printer's error; and at 235n.1–9 the present edition restores the numbered bibliography that PC deleted, even though it retained Dewey's numbered references to the bibliography throughout the essay except for the final reference at 235.20, which the present edition has also restored.

Qualitative Thought

This essay, republished in *Philosophy and Civilization* (PC) (New York: Minton, Balch and Co., 1931), originally appeared in the first issue of *Symposium*, a quarterly sponsored by New York University. Copy-text is the article's publication in *Symposium* 1 (January 1930): 5–32. The accidentals changes of PC have been rejected as imposed by editorial house-styling. All forty-two substantive revisions in PC have been accepted by the present edition except for PC's failure to italicize "cause" at 256.14.

Philosophy and Education

As part of the dedication ceremonies for the new campus and buildings of the University of California at Los Angeles, Dewey delivered the address "Philosophy and Education" on the morning of 28 March 1930 in the auditorium of Josiah Royce Hall.

Ernest C. Moore, director of the University, who invited Dewey to speak at the ceremonies, had written him in January of 1930:

As to the subject of your address, "Philosophy and Education" is the best one I can think of. It would be particularly appropriate because of a savage attitude toward education on the part of some of our University authorities at Berkeley and here. Inasmuch as one of our two colleges is a Teachers College and the other a College of Letters and Science, it is important that the Teachers College be not made a football for the insolence of the College of Letters and Science.[11]

Dewey's address first appeared in *Addresses Delivered at the Dedication of the New Campus and New Buildings of the University of California at Los Angeles, 27 and 28 March 1930* (Berkeley: University of California Press, 1930), pp. 46–56. That publication has served here as copy-text. For the essay's republication "with slight changes made by Mr. Dewey himself" in *Higher Education Faces the Future*, edited by Paul Arthur Schilpp (New York: Horace Liveright, 1930), pp. 273–83, several changes were introduced. The nature of the accidentals changes indicates that they were imposed by someone other than Dewey. They include the addition of appositional and parenthetical commas, commas changed to semicolons, "anyone" spelled as two words, and "coordination" spelled with a diaeresis. Of the twenty-eight substantive emendations, the present edition has rejected three as probable printer's errors: at 289.10 the "s" dropped from "appears," at 291.10 the "s" added to "development," and at 294.20 "school" for "scheme."

General Principles of Educational Articulation

"General Principles of Educational Articulation" originated as an address Dewey delivered on 26 February at the annual meeting of the Department of Superintendence, National Education Association, Cleveland, Ohio, 24 to 28 February 1929. Although other subjects—notably school financing, teacher training, research, and character education—received considerable attention at the meeting, articulation and pre-school education were emphasized.

Dewey had completed work on his address two weeks before he was to deliver it. He wrote Sidney Hook on 12 February 1929, lamenting his heavy schedule of speaking and publishing commitments for February:

Then in an unwary moment I agreed to speak at the Cleveland meeting of the N E A toward the end of this month; one of the speeches was paid for so generously that I had to work on it—the educational honor society corresponding to phi beta kappa. I have

---

11. Moore to Dewey, 2 January 1930, Dewey Papers.

them off my chest and typewriter now, and am going back to the Edinburgh lectures.[12]

Dewey's speech appeared in two publications: the 30 March 1929 issue of *School and Society* (SS), and the 1929 *Official Report* of the Department of Superintendence of the National Education Association (DS). The DS version varies considerably in both substantives and accidentals from SS, in kind and in extent, indicating that the address was revised not only by Dewey but by an NEA editor before its publication in DS.

Apparently, when Dewey first typed the speech, he made both an original and a carbon. The early completion of the typescript, described in his letter to Hook, suggests that even before delivering the speech in Cleveland, he sent a copy to his friend James McKeen Cattell, the editor of *School and Society*, where an excerpt from the SS version appeared on 9 March 1929.

An original and a carbon typewritten at the same time—SS and DS—constitute in effect a dual copy-text, each with equal authority with respect to accidentals. In this instance, however, the accidentals of the DS version have not been considered to have the same authority as those of SS. In general, the style of the SS version is that of a document first prepared for oral delivery; it can be assumed that Dewey made his DS substantive revisions on a retained copy, or possibly in proof, for the official formal appearance of his address in DS. The numerous accidentals changes in DS, made in conformity with usual NEA guidelines, are not characteristic of Dewey, whether in composition or revision. On the assumption that both Dewey and a journal editor revised DS, SS has served here as copy-text. Substantive revisions in DS, along with accidentals changes caused by those revisions, have been accepted as emendations of the copy-text with a single exception: at 305.11, DS dropped the final "s" from "phases," an omission that appears to have been a printer's error rather than Dewey's revision.

Freedom in Workers' Education

The 1929–30 period began with Dewey actively involved in the Brookwood Labor College issue. In the early months of 1929 con-

12. Dewey to Hook, 12 February 1929, Sidney Hook/John Dewey Collection, Special Collections, Morris Library, Southern Illinois University at Carbondale. Dewey delivered two speeches in Cleveland on 26 February: "General Principles of Educational Articulation" at the morning session of the Department of Superintendence of the National Education Association, and "The Sources of a Science of Education" in the evening to the Kappa Delta Pi Society.

servatives had continued to label Dewey a Communist, largely because of his 1928 publication in the *New Republic* of six articles about his trip to the Soviet Union in the summer of that year (see *Later Works*, vol. 3). Dewey responded to this name-calling and to the American Federation of Labor's labeling of Brookwood Labor College as communistic in two articles, "Freedom in Workers' Education," *American Teacher* 13 (January 1929): 1–4, and "Labor Politics and Labor Education," *New Republic* 57 (9 January 1929): 211–14. The two articles were published almost simultaneously and involved related correspondence.

Brookwood Labor College opened in 1921 in Westchester County, New York, as a resident two-year school for workers interested in learning about the labor movement.[13] Perhaps the best known of many similar labor schools that started during the twenties, Brookwood outlasted most of the others, closing in 1937. In its August and October 1928 meetings the Executive Council of the American Federation of Labor charged Brookwood with promoting communism and advised all affiliated unions to withdraw support from the school.[14]

When A. J. Muste, president of Brookwood, wrote Dewey about the AFL Executive Council's action, Dewey responded on 6 October 1928:

> I have only just returned from Europe, and find your note of September 15. I shall at once look into the material which you have sent me. Even without doing so, I may say that all my convictions are strongly against the course which has been followed, and I anticipate that I shall soon be able to write to President Green along the line that you suggest.[15]

Dewey then wrote to William Green, president of the AFL, asking for more detailed information. Apparently not satisfied with Green's response, Dewey enclosed it with his next letter to Muste and asked for "some data which will enable me to make a suitable reply."[16]

On 9 November at a meeting of Local 5 of the American Federation of Teachers of New York City protesting the Brookwood action, Dewey spoke on "Freedom in Workers' Education." Muste had Dewey's ad-

---

13. Brookwood Labor College received financial support "through scholarships established by trade unions, . . . from lump sums contributed by the unions, . . . from individual contributions made by students or other workers or by middle class persons interested in the movement" (A. J. Muste, "An American Labor College," *Plebs* 14 [October 1922]: 341, Brookwood Collection, Archives of Labor History and Urban Affairs, Wayne State University, Detroit, Mich.).
14. "Brookwood Victim of Convention Lynching Bee," *Brookwood Review* 7 (October–November 1928): 1, Brookwood Collection.
15. Dewey to Muste, 6 October 1928, Brookwood Collection.
16. Dewey to Muste, 16 October 1928, Brookwood Collection.

dress recorded by a stenographer; he sent Dewey a transcript, which Dewey returned with corrections and a note to Muste on 19 November.[17] The nature of the transcript indicates that Dewey spoke without a prepared text, although he did read from an editorial in the *American Federationist* that Muste had sent him on 26 October.[18] The transcript was extremely faithful to Dewey's extemporaneous style, retaining Dewey's frequent use of "Now" to begin a new point, and expressions such as "why I for one" at 336.30, clearly the casual style of one speaking without a prepared document.

Three typescripts of Dewey's talk are in the Brookwood Collection: TS[1], a typescript with Dewey's handwritten alterations that he returned to Muste on 19 November; TS[2], a carbon of TS[1] without Dewey's alterations; and a retyped, single-spaced version done on another typewriter at Brookwood Labor College (BLC), probably prepared for circulation among the labor community with other documents on the Brookwood controversy. Examination of other typed documents from Muste's office during this period has confirmed that both typewriters used in the typescripts were in Muste's office. Since Dewey never saw TS[2] and BLC, they have been rejected as having no authority. However, the changes in TS[2] appear in the Emendations List, which also serves as a historical collation, for the following reason. Before Muste sent Dewey TS[1] for his correction and approval, Muste himself made numerous alterations, most with a carbon between TS[1] and TS[2], so that they agree exactly. However, some changes made independently vary slightly: for example at 332.23 in the phrase "to be able to deal with them," an "and" before the "to be" in TS[2] but not in TS[1] appears in the printed version in *American Teacher* (AT); and at 331.22 and 336.8 the commas Muste added to TS[2] but not to TS[1] appear in AT, indications that when Muste transferred Dewey's alterations on TS[1] to a third document which he sent to AT, he used several of his own alterations on TS[2], which Dewey never saw, rather than the alterations on TS[1], the transcript sent to Dewey.

Apparently when Muste transferred Dewey's corrections to a third document which he sent to AT, he made most, but not all of Dewey's corrections. Some he may have been unable to read, as at 332.34 where Dewey had written the barely legible "any" over the word "this," the original "this" appears in AT; others he simply did not follow, as at 331.18, Dewey clearly deleted from TS[1] the phrase "and no possibility of," which nevertheless appears in the printed AT version. Since the AT version reflects not Dewey's but Muste's final intentions, it too lacks au-

17. Dewey to Muste, 19 November 1928, Brookwood Collection.
18. Muste to Dewey, 26 October 1928, Brookwood Collection.

thority. However, since it is the first printed version of Dewey's speech, the variants in AT are also included in the Emendations List as part of the historical collation.

TS[1], the only document Dewey corrected, has served as copy-text for the present edition. Dewey's handwritten alterations in TS[1] that do not appear in AT have been restored. Corrections of typographical and punctuation errors, such as commas at the ends of sentences and commas used in conjunction with parentheses, which would have been made for the present edition, have been accepted from AT. Subheads and paragraphing imposed by AT have been silently eliminated.

A complete record of Dewey's handwritten changes in TS[1] appears in "Alterations in 'Freedom in Workers' Education.'"

Labor Politics and Labor Education

Ten days after Dewey delivered "Freedom in Workers' Education," the American Federation of Labor held its annual convention in New Orleans from 19 to 28 November 1928. At that convention the Committee on Education praised Dewey for his services to education; then Matthew Woll, vice-president of the AFL, attacked Dewey and charged him with being a "propagandist, not for special interests but for Communist interests."[19] Woll's speech denouncing both Dewey and Brookwood as promoting communism resulted in a vote of ninety-one to thirty-nine to expunge all references to Dewey from the *Report of the Proceedings.*[20]

At the time of the New Orleans meeting, Dewey had been writing "Labor Politics and Labor Education," also about Brookwood, which was published in the *New Republic* 57 (9 January 1929): 211–14. He asked at least two persons whether he should deal with the New Orleans incident in his article: Albert C. Barnes, director of the Barnes Foundation in Merion, Pennsylvania, and A. J. Muste. From Barnes Dewey received this reply:

> Don't you think the data you already have is sufficient for a preliminary article in *next week's* New Republic? Just an overture containing the promise to tell the world the exact situation and the underworld status of the Woll gang. Don't lose the opportunity to convert the incident into a boost for labor and liberal education.[21]

19. "Report of Seventh Day, 27 November 1928 Session," *Report of the Proceedings of the Forty-Eighth Annual Convention of the American Federation of Labor, 19 to 28 November 1928* (Washington, D.C.: Law Reporter Printing Co., 1928), p. 315.
20. Ibid., p. 319.
21. Barnes to Dewey, 4 December 1928, Dewey Papers.

In his letter of 12 December to Muste, Dewey enclosed a draft of his proposed article for "comment and criticism," saying that

> it will be rewritten anyway, and so dont bother about typewriting errors etc, as to save time Im sending it off without any revision. It is pretty long, and space was my chief difficulty; I omitted some points I should have liked to speak of, but whatever you think important I want to include, even at the risk of lengthening the article. Early publication, before people have forgotten the row is advisable.
>
> I had thought of quoting the words of Woll's attack upon me, then calling attention to the fact that I had publicly protested agt the Brookwood action and had said the council might better have spent its energy in condemning the Power trust propaganda, but decided agt it both on grounds of space and because it might weaken the force of the rest of the article by suggesting a purely personal motive on my part. However it still seems relevant to his condemnation of Brookwood as communistic to mention how freely he makes the accusation.
>
> I shall be grateful to you for indication of points where I have given too much or too little emphasis as well as for other suggestions.[22]

Muste replied on 13 December, calling the article "excellent" and informing Dewey that he had "written in a few words in order to make the statement about the reorganization of the W.E.B. [Workers' Education Bureau] complete and accurate."[23] He then reconsidered his advice to Dewey and the following day wrote him, "it has occurred to me that a brief reference to Woll's remarks about you and the action of the convention in expunging reference to your name from the proceedings might be to the point."[24]

Dewey decided against including a reference to Woll's denunciation in his article, but did mention it in his letter in the 13 March 1929 *New Republic* in response to Woll's reply to his 9 January article (see this volume, pp. 387–88, 392). He refers to Woll's subsequent denial of having accused Dewey of being a Communist at the convention, and quotes Woll's statement as it had appeared in the official stenographic report of the *Proceedings*, supplied to Dewey by Muste.[25]

In a final piece of correspondence from Woll to Dewey, dated 21 March 1929, Woll repeats his denial that he called Dewey a Communist, saying that

22. Dewey to Muste, 12 December 1928, Brookwood Collection.
23. Muste to Dewey, 13 December 1928, Brookwood Collection. For the statement on the Workers' Education Bureau, see this volume, p. 344.
24. Muste to Dewey, 14 December 1928, Brookwood Collection.
25. Muste to Dewey, 22 December 1928, Brookwood Collection.

As I spoke from the floor of the convention hall instead of the platform, which afforded the assistance of loud speakers, it was difficult for the stenographers and the press correspondents to get my words. . . . I neither said nor implied that you were a communist or that you were directed by Moscow. I did say and imply that you were encouraging communism by your praise of the Communist schools and of the Soviets.[26]

"Labor Politics and Labor Education" was published only once, in the *New Republic* for 9 January 1929. That publication has served as copy-text for this article.

Tribute to James H. Tufts

At Max Otto's request in a letter of 1 December 1930,[27] Dewey wrote a "Tribute to James H. Tufts" to be read at the farewell dinner for Tufts upon his retirement from the Department of Philosophy at the University of Chicago. After receiving Otto's request, Dewey immediately responded with a two-page typescript, apologizing for its brevity and for not being able to attend the banquet, saying, "I only got back from Europe yesterday and I find of course a lot of things piled up that must be attended to."[28]

Otto had indicated in his letter to Dewey that he would be reading Dewey's remarks, but they were instead read by Theodore Brameld, president of the University of Chicago Philosophy Club and toastmaster of the evening.[29] The unpublished typescript from the Max C. Otto Papers has served as copy-text for this tribute. All of Dewey's changes in the typescript, both by hand and at the typewriter, are recorded in "Alterations in 'Tribute to James H. Tufts.'"

People's Lobby Statements

When Benjamin Marsh, executive secretary of the Anti-Monopoly League, invited Dewey in 1929 to become president of the

26. Woll to Dewey, 21 March 1929, Dewey Papers.
27. Otto to Dewey, 1 December 1930, Max C. Otto Papers, State Historical Society of Wisconsin, Madison, Wis.
28. Dewey to Otto, 4 December 1930, Otto Papers. The typescript is in the Otto Papers.
29. "Max Otto Honors Dr. J. H. Tufts at Farewell Banquet. John Dewey and Angell of Yale Send Their Greetings," *Daily Maroon* (University of Chicago), 11 December 1930, pp. 1, 4.

league, Dewey agreed to assume the presidency if the organization, whose slogan was "We fight for the people. We get and give the facts," would call itself what it tried to be—a People's Lobby. The board of directors agreed to the name change and Dewey became the new president, serving from 1929 to 1936.[30]

Since the People's Lobby had no official organ of publication until it began publishing the *People's Lobby Bulletin* in May 1931, Dewey's early statements as president were issued as press releases to the *New York Times*. Even though the People's Lobby statements appeared over Dewey's name, correspondence between Dewey and Marsh reveals that they were often the product of a collaborative effort and in a few cases apparently were written by Marsh and signed by Dewey. On 11 January Dewey wrote to Marsh, "I enclose the draft—any changes in wording you think advisable, you can make of course."[31] And again on 12 March, "I enclose a statement—maybe it would have been better if I had asked you to prepare it & then I signed."[32]

Seven statements issued in Dewey's name appeared in the *New York Times* (NYT) in the 1929–30 period: "Lobby Inquiry Opens Tomorrow," 14 October 1929, p. 19; "Attacks Wage Disparity," 26 December 1929, p. 28; "Child Relief Steps Urged on Congress," 30 December 1929, p. 19; "Asks Federal Fund to Aid Unemployed," 12 May 1930, p. 35; "Asks Hoover to Act on Unemployment," 21 July 1930, p. 17; "Puts Needs of Idle at Two Billions," Sunday, 26 October 1930, sec. 1, p. 21; and "People's Lobby Hits Sugar Loan to Cuba," 24 November 1930, p. 10.[33] "Asks Hoover to Act on Unemployment" was republished with the title "Should America Adopt a System of Compulsory Unemployment Insurance?" in the August 1931 *Congressional Digest* (CD). Three paragraphs on income statistics, omitted by NYT, appeared in the later CD version, which in turn omitted a brief closing paragraph that had appeared in NYT. Inasmuch as both the NYT and CD versions were probably printed from the same People's Lobby press release, they have been conflated here: the NYT publication has served as copy-text for the present edition and the CD additions have been incorporated with one exception: the NYT title has been retained for consistency with headings on the other statements.

30. See Benjamin C. Marsh, *Lobbyist for the People: A Record of Fifty Years* (Washington, D.C.: Public Affairs Press, 1953), p. 88.
31. Dewey to Marsh, 11 January 1929, Benjamin Clarke Marsh Papers, Manuscripts Division, Library of Congress.
32. Dewey to Marsh, 12 March 1929, Marsh Papers.
33. All *New York Times* references are to the full city edition on microfilm in the social studies division, Morris Library, Southern Illinois University at Carbondale.

League for Independent Political Action Statements

On 8 September 1929 the League for Independent Political Action was formed, with Dewey as its first chairman.[34] The league was created to provide an alternative to the Republican and Democratic parties. As he had done for the People's Lobby, Dewey, as chairman of the LIPA, used the *New York Times* to issue political statements. He probably collaborated on these press releases with Howard Y. Williams, executive secretary of the LIPA, as he had with Benjamin Marsh of the People's Lobby, although no evidence of this arrangement exists. Williams was, however, authorized to write letters and sign Dewey's name,[35] and it can be conjectured that the press releases were also the products of a joint effort.

In the 1929–30 period, four statements by Dewey appeared in the *New York Times* (NYT): "John Dewey Assails the Major Parties," 14 October 1929, p. 2; "Dewey Supports Vladeck," 15 September 1930, p. 16; "Dewey Asks Norris to Lead New Party," 26 December 1930, p. 1; and "Dewey for Farm Backing," Sunday, 28 December 1930, sec. 1, p. 20. "Dewey Asks Norris to Lead New Party" was republished in the January 1931 *News Bulletin of the League for Independent Political Action* (NB) with the title "The League Challenges the Insurgents." The NYT version has served as copy-text for this statement. Since it is unlikely that Dewey supplied either the NYT or the NB title, the NYT title has been retained for consistency.

K. P.

Three Independent Factors in Morals

Dewey's address to the Société française de philosophie upon the occasion of his receiving the *doctor honoris causa* degree in Paris, 7 November 1930, was first published in French as "Trois facteurs indépendants en matière de morale" in the *Bulletin de la société française de philosophie* 30 (October–December 1930): 118–27, translated by Charles Cestre, followed by a discussion in which Dewey's remarks are paraphrased, pp. 127–33. As no English version of the address could be found, a translation from the French by Jo Ann Boydston of both the

---

34. See "Liberals Here Plan an Opposition Party; Prof. Dewey Heads National Organizing Group," *New York Times*, 9 September 1929, p. 1.
35. Dewey to Williams, 29 May 1931, Howard Y. Williams Papers, Division of Archives and Manuscripts, Minnesota Historical Society, St. Paul, Minn.

address and the discussion was published in *Educational Theory* 16 (July 1966): 193–209, with the title "Three Independent Factors in Morals." A translation of Xavier Léon's introduction of Dewey and of the discussion appears in the present volume as Appendix 5.

After the 1966 publication of the English translation of Dewey's address, an undated thirteen-page typescript entitled "Conflict and Independent Variables in Morals" was found in the John Dewey Papers, Special Collections, Morris Library, Southern Illinois University at Carbondale, with the title and a number of alterations throughout in Dewey's hand. Pages 1–5 of this typescript (TS) are on poor quality typewriter paper with no watermark and pages 6–13 are on paper watermarked Legion Bond; the two parts were typed on different machines.

The first part of the TS, pages 1–5, begins with "p. 12" x'd-out above one x'd-out line and a second line that is obscured by having been typed over with the same content as the first clear line, which is the third line on the page. Dewey's handwritten title in pencil, "Conflict and Independent Variables in Morals," appears above the two marked-over lines. The x'd-out and obscured content, which apparently continues from a discarded page or pages immediately preceding, is: "appears explicitly in Kant and his followers. British ethical thought until German influences came in was dominated by the concept of virtue." These pages may have been left over or retyped from what Dewey described to Horace S. Fries as a paper he wrote "about 26 or 27 for a small philosophical club to which I belong on the independent variables in morals. . . ."[36]

The second part of the TS, pages 6–13, is a portion of the address that Dewey presented to the French Philosophical Society in 1930, including a number of substantive ink alterations that are in the French translation. It can be hypothesized that this is a part of the final draft that Dewey had retyped to take to Paris and from which Cestre made his translation. In addition to the ink alterations incorporated in the French version, the TS shows other alterations in a different ink and in pencil. Page 13 of the TS, on Legion Bond, starts with the two lines that conclude the French article; the rest of that page is typed on the same machine as the one used for pages 1–5.

Because the title and a number of corrections and alterations throughout the thirteen pages are in pencil, and because the typewriter used for pages 1–5 appears again on page 13, the TS "Conflict and Independent Variables in Morals" seems to be Dewey's unfinished draft for a new article, one he was preparing by putting together and modifying two discrete documents. As the article was never completed or published,

---

36. Dewey to Fries, 26 December 1933, Horace S. Fries Papers, State Historical Society of Wisconsin, Madison, Wis.

the date of this TS cannot be established, although clearly all the pages were modified after 1930.

The copy-text for "Three Independent Factors in Morals" for the present volume has been a combination of the English translation in *Educational Theory*, pages 198.32–201.20 (this volume, pages 279.2–283.6) with Dewey's TS, pages 6–13 (this volume, from page 283.7 to the end of the article). All emendations in the present edition have been taken from TS.

Dewey's pencil corrections in TS, apparently made for the proposed and unfinished later version of pages 6–13 in combination with pages 1–5, are not recorded here. Similarly, TS paragraphs or phrases that Dewey marked out are not recorded. The Alterations List for "Three Independent Factors in Morals" comprises only changes determined to have been made by Dewey in the original draft for his Paris address. Punctuation differences between TS and the translation are not noted; they have been considered within the province of the translator, as have minor variations in phrasing attributable to the process of translation.[37]

J. A. B.

37. Textual decisions for this volume have been based on Fredson Bowers, "Textual Principles and Procedures," *Later Works* 2:407–18.

Emendations List

All emendations in both substantives and accidentals introduced into the copy-text are recorded in the list that follows, with the exception of the changes in formal matters described below. No titles appear for the twenty-one items that had no emendations. The copy-text for each item is identified at the beginning of the list of emendations in that item; for the items that had a single previous printing, no abbreviation for the copy-text appears in the list itself. Page-line number at left is from the present edition; all lines of print except running heads are counted. The reading to the left of the square bracket is from the present edition; the bracket is followed by an abbreviation for the source of the emendation's first appearance.

W means Works—the present edition—and is used for emendations made here for the first time. The symbol WS (Works Source) is used to indicate emendations made within Dewey's quoted material that restore the spelling, capitalization, and some required substantives of his source (see Substantive Variants in Quotations).

For emendations restricted to punctuation, the curved dash ~ means the same word(s) as before the bracket; the inferior caret ∧ indicates the absence of a punctuation mark. The abbreviation [*om.*] means the reading before the bracket was omitted in the editions and impressions identified; [*not present*] is used where appropriate to signal material not appearing in identified sources. The abbreviation [*rom.*] means roman type and is used to signal the omission of italics; [*ital.*] means italic type and is used to signal the omission of roman type. *Stet* used with an edition or impression abbreviation indicates a substantive reading retained from an edition or impression subsequently revised; the rejected variant follows the semicolon. The asterisk before an emendation page-line number indicates that the reading is discussed in the Textual Notes.

A number of formal, or mechanical, changes have been made throughout:

1. Superior numbers have been assigned consecutively to Dewey's footnotes throughout an essay or chapter; the asterisk is used only for editorial footnotes.

2. Book and periodical titles are in italic type; "the" appearing before periodical titles is in lower-case roman type; articles and sections of books are in quotation marks. Book and journal titles have been supplied and expanded where necessary. The form of Dewey's documentation, wherever unclear, has been made consistent. Abbreviations have been regularized where necessary.

3. Periods and commas have been brought within quotation marks. Single quotation marks have been changed to double when not inside quoted material; however, opening or closing quotation marks have been supplied where necessary and recorded.

4. Ligatures have been separated.

5. Chapter headings have been deleted and arabic numbers placed before the chapter titles in *Individualism, Old and New.*

The following spellings have been editorially regularized to the known Dewey usage appearing before the bracket:

although] altho 315.21–22, 317.17
centre(s)] center(s) 70.40, 71.30, 72.10, 74.33, 93.18, 96.1, 263.23, 275.30, 290.40, 294.24, 295.18, 300.8, 306.13, 313.5, 315.38, 316.36, 317.4, 317.5, 321.13, 321.33, 321.34, 322.26, 348.23, 353.9
cooperate (all forms)] coöperate 23.39, 31.20, 71.11, 83.3, 84.25–26, 104.29, 105.28, 115.14, 170.11, 324.25–26, 341.34–35, 405.33
cooperate (all forms)] co-operate 152.23, 155.11, 318.33, 318.35, 348.5
coordinate (all forms)] coördinate 69.31, 97.32–33, 98.7–8, 237.27–28, 238.9, 238.19
meagre] meager 106.17, 255.18, 324.12
preeminently] preëminently 243.3
pre-scientific] prescientific 119.34
reenforce] reënforce 10.1, 35.6
reexamine] reëxamine 118.3
role(s)] rôle(s) 16.29, 23.24, 27.25, 89.13, 158.8, 171.34, 172.18, 229.6, 233.37, 239.31, 248n.2
subject-matter] subject matter 31.19–20
surprising] surprizing 312.29, 313.11

The Sources of a Science of Education

Copy-text for this work is the first printing of *The Sources of a Science of Education* (New York: Horace Liveright, 1929).

5.6   recognized] W; recorganized
10.31   requires] W; requiries
11.18   measurements] W; measurement
11.18   interpreted] W; interperted
17.2   scientific results] W; the results of scientific results
18n.1   W.ₐ and D. S.,] W; W., and D. W.ₐ
19.30   alertness] W; altertness
24.26   participation] W; particiation
25.30   pedagese] W; pedageese
29.32   within] W; with
39.13–14   able to rectify] W; rectify

Individualism, Old and New

Copy-text is the series of articles in the *New Republic* (NR): "The
House Divided against Itself," 58 (24 April 1929): 270–71; "'America'—By Formula," 60 (18 September 1929): 117–19; "The United
States, Incorporated," 61 (22 January 1930): 239–41; "The Lost Individual," 61 (5 February 1930): 294–96; "Toward a New Individualism," 62 (19 February 1930): 13–16; "Capitalistic or Public Socialism?" 62 (5 March 1930): 64–67; "The Crisis in Culture," 62 (19 March
1930): 123–26; "Individuality in Our Day," 62 (2 April 1930): 184–
88. Emendations have been accepted from the articles' republication
as *Individualism, Old and New* (New York: Minton, Balch and Co.,
1930) (ION).

45.1   It is] ION; [¶]More than one person, in reading the Lynds'
            "Middletown," has been struck by the number of connec-
            tions in which some large part of the population of that town
            finds itself "bewildered" or "confused." The appropriateness
            of this state of mind to American life today, this cross-section
            makes evident. It is
45.1   a commonplace] ION; commonplace
45.6–10   In such . . . us.] ION; That focus of American life called
            "Middletown" gives vivid freshness and fullness to this
            commonplace.
45.22   our rugged] ION; rugged
45.27   class] ION; class being
46.22   assertion] ION; the assertion
48.1   certain] *stet* NR; contain
48.6–7   a statement from the pulpit] ION; the statement
48.12   what we at least] ION; at least what we

48.16   they must] ION; must
48.25   them‸ in] ION; ~, ~
48.30–31   beliefs.[¶]With] ION; beliefs. [¶]Of one thing I feel quite
sure. It is not true that machinery is the source of our
troubles. The machine supplies means, tools, agencies. It
opens opportunities for planning and extends the ability to
realize such ends as men propose. If we do not plan, if we do
not use machinery intelligently on behalf of things we value,
the fault lies with us, not with the machine. This fact underlies, I suppose, the contradiction in our life: with
48.34   to employ] ION; to direct and employ
48.34   disposal . . . society.] ION; disposal.
48.35–49.26   abdication. It . . . recognition.] ION; abdication.
There is a strain of fear running through American life which
controls our activities to an untold extent. We dare not act
lest we upset something. This state of fear will, presumably,
endure until we begin to plan our living in a systematic and
collected way, which means of necessity a collective way.
   What stands in the way is not a machine age, but the survival of a pecuniary age. The worker is tied helplessly to the
machine, and our institutions and customs are invaded and
eroded by the machine, only because the machine is harnessed to the dollar. We cling to old creeds, and we profess
ideas and sentiments that have no real hold on our living activities, because a regime of pecuniary profit and loss still
commands our allegiance. In this fact the contradictions of
Middletown, that is, of Anytown, come to a unity. The cults
and rites, the folkways and folklore, of a money culture form
the patterns of our life, and in them alone our industrial
practices and our sentimental ideals and theories harmo-
niously agree. Not till we have questioned the worth of a
dominantly money-civilization shall we have a religion that is
more than sentimental and verbal, and achieve an integrated
life. This money domination is not peculiarly American; it is
our chief institutional inheritance from the old world. Its
evils are more acute with us just because we, more than other
peoples, have command of the instruments and the technology with which to create, if we will, a new civilization.
50.9   may not have] ION; have not
50.12   among] ION; upon
50.28   probably] ION; likely
51.4   of helping] ION; in helping
51.19   in the rest of] ION; over

51.27   of itself] ION; to itself
51.36   will have reserves] ION; have many reserves
51.36   their] ION; our
51n.2   1929.] ION; 1929; price $5.00.
52.1   picture] ION; picture of it
52.3–4   Nevertheless, it is worth while] ION; But I propose
52.4   the question] ION; some questions
52.5   as yet] ION; yet
52.6   are alleged to be] ION; are
52.24–25 and, finally, standardization] ION; and standardization
52.30   have] ION; has
52.31   their] ION; its
52.31   souls. Homogeneity] ION; souls and made homogeniety
52.32   emotion has become] ION; emotion
52.36   their effects] ION; they
52.37   matters] ION; conditions
53.3   the force of the indictment] ION; its force
53.5   our life] ION; it all
53.7   result in] ION; result and
53.11   than] ION; from
53.13   final. He recognizes] ION; the last word, as well as the fact
53.15   through them] ION; through it
53.15–16 transcend them] ION; transcend it
53.18   In reply . . . say] ION; My comment is
53.21   history. And] ION; history, and
53.32   reveal a] ION; reveal the
53.37   And the] ION; And these
54.19   corruption] ION; a corruption
54.19–20 and degeneration] ION; and a degeneration
54.20   spirit] ION; mind
54.29–30 was . . . proletarian] ION; the peasant and proletariat
          had
54.33–34 immediately . . . discrimination] ION; immediately
54.37   destroying—it] ION; destroying—the power of critical dis-
          crimination, it
54.37–38 the ineptitude of the many] ION; their ineptitude
55.10–11 has suffered from] ION; has from
55.13   the ends] ION; those
55.22   use] ION; general use
55.22–23 only signify] ION; signify only
55.23   and emancipation on] ION; and on
55.24   has obtained] ION; anything obtaining
55.31   man] ION; men

55.31–32   enrichment] ION; ability
56.9   an independent] ION; a revolutionary independent
56.10   technology . . . revolutionary.] ION; technology. Confusion
is the inevitable result.
56.13–57.8   Until . . . culture.] ION; [*not present*]
58.2   long ago] ION; a long time ago
59.12   These] ION; they
59.17   is] ION; may be
59.28–30   The political . . . form.] ION; [*not present*]
59.31   For the forces] ION; The forces
59.38   eighty per cent] ION; 80 percent
60.1   twenty per cent] ION; 20 percent
60.5–6   rehearsal. For my purpose is] ION; rehearsal for my purpose, which is
60.8   the change] ION; it
60.14   agriculturists] ION; agriculturalists
60.16   manufactures] ION; manufacturing
60.20   influence] ION; reaction
60.22   upon . . . country] ION; upon country
60.38–61.2   The status . . . corporate.] ION; [*not present*]
61.4   culture:—] ION; ~,
61.14   Critics] ION; Individuals
61.27   exceptions, to be found in] ION; in a collective direction
61.36   need for] ION; needs of
62.7   toward collective ends] ION; in a collective direction
62.12   promotion] ION; promoting
62.18   Hence] ION; But
62.39   a still greater amount] ION; still greater amounts
63.36–64.7   "Prosperity" . . . scale.] ION; [*not present*]
64.10–11   are set . . . out] ION; were set out only to call forth
64.32–38   age.[¶]It is . . . individuals. If] ION; age. Whatever
chaos and lawlessness prevail on one side, and mechanical
and quantitative uniformity on the other, are, nevertheless,
the chaos and the mechanization of a new and unparalleled
situation, because they are marks of a society which is extensive externally and complexly and delicately interdependent
internally. If
64.40–65.1   type.[¶]Meanwhile] ION; type. Meantime
65.4–16   Hence only . . . himself.] ION; Action and reaction are
still equal and in opposite directions.
66.14–15   carried] ION; carried on
67.6   stability] ION; stay
67.7   or direction] ION; and direction

67.21   but the crowd] ION; but that
67.24   the actions] ION; their acts
67.27   fulfillment] ION; fullfilment
67.37   trait] ION; feature
67.37–38   life, economically speaking, is] ION; civilization is
67.38–68.20   It is tragic . . . recent days.] ION; This affects the
small merchant and the farmer as well as the day laborer.
Fear of loss of employment, of economic damage, of old
age, for oneself and one's family, is so general that men live
in a state of precarious anxiety. The orgy of the recent stock
market is a natural product of a blind hope of finding some
way of escape from a hemmed-in life. Where all is uncertain, why not take a chance of turning uncertainty to account? If I dwell upon the element of insecurity in modern
life, it is because, in spite of all that is written about unemployment, its emotional and mental effect does not seem to
me to have begun to receive the attention it deserves. It is
hopeless to look for mental stability and integration when
the economic bases of life are unsettled. That the very technological forces which make for consolidation and corporateness are so disturbing to the peace and security of
individuals is, it seems to me, an apt symbol for the split
which I am trying to point out.
68.30   such . . . phenomena] ION; phenomena which are on such a
pathological scale
68.30–34   Feverish love . . . cause.] ION; [not present]
68.40–69.1   wide . . . testifies] ION; current professions testify
69.31   corresponding] ION; such
69.32–70.5   The growth . . . individual.] ION; [not present]
70.6   The loss . . . region] ION; If I have spoken of the lost individual from the economic point of view, it is
70.37–71.18   I do not . . . simulation.] ION; [not present]
71.33–72.9   life.[¶]Religion . . . soul.[¶]Aside] ION; life.[¶]So little
is this true of the present, that there are those who urge that
in order to obtain a recovery of a sense of a center and totality in life, we must begin with a regeneration of religion in
the individual consciousness. But aside
73.10   through] ION; in
73.10   get their bearings] ION; find themselves
73.11–74.40   Conspicuous . . . potentialities.] ION; [not present]
75.1   Instances] ION; I have not touched upon the more conspicuous phases of the contemporary scene—the relaxation
of traditional moral codes, the frantic search for amuse-

ments, the combination of multiplication of laws with free
and easy law-breaking, the disintegration of the traditional
household as the focus of civic order, the passing of the institution of stable marriage, and so on. These instances

75.2   that] ION; which
75.3–4   blind . . . them] ION; are superficial symptoms of deeper
          disorder
75.4   groping] ION; blindly groping
75.6   direction. The] ION; direction, because the
75.15   age] ION; corporate age
75.17   seems. If] ION; seems, more negative than positive. If
75.22   might] ION; would
75.24   would] ION; could
75.25–76.26   I do not . . . liberalism.] ION; [*not present*]
77.5   ideals] *stet* NR; ideal
77.5   values of an individualism] ION; values
77.11–25 This moral . . . individual.] ION; [*not present*]
77.28   liquefied] ION; also liquefied
78.19   release . . . man's] ION; release man's
78.20   wants.] ION; wants from legal restrictions.
78.35   change to any other] ION; any change to another
79.7   Crothers, whose words] ION; Crothers∧ in words which
79.25–26 eagerness . . . opportunity.] ION; eagerness.
79.35   such] ION; to such
80.1   comfort∧ and of] ION; comfort, together with
80.13   and a sapping] ION; and sapping
80.26–27 remaking . . . individual] ION; remaking the individual
80.29–30 the restriction . . . to] ION; its restriction to
80.30   in the] ION; by the
80.33   an extension] ION; the extension
81.3   mentality] ION; their mentality
81.3–4   personal] ION; their
81.8   the imaginative] ION; their imaginative
81.9–15   This fact . . . revolt.] ION; [*not present*]
81.17   confusion] ION; resulting confusion
81.32   consensus] *stet* NR; censensus
82.6   whatever is] ION; the
82.8   suggestions] ION; suggestion
82.20–83.4 There are . . . others.] ION; [*not present*]
83.6   which] ION; that
83.12   has] ION; had
83.16   agreements that spring] ION; agreement that comes
83.23   an explanation . . . conformity] ION; a like explanation

83.36–37   but they are also] ION; but at the same time they are

84.2–23   conscience. As . . . organization.[¶]For the chief] ION; conscience. Partly, however, they are prophetic of a type of mind already in process of formation, but still lacking the organic character that will enable it to manifest itself in ordinary human relationships outside of relief and assistance.[¶]The chief

84.28–29   once more] ION; for example

84.34   clamor] ION; the clamor

85.9   the few] ION; a few

85.25   is created] ION; is now to be created

86.3   is an] ION; is henceforth an

86.12   can] ION; has to

86.12   only . . . all] ION; which uses all

86.13–14   the physical] ION; physical

86.14–89.20   forces . . . consciousness.] ION; forces as means to attain truly human ends. As long as we retain the older individualistic philosophy, our purposes will not be framed out of the positive consequences of even our industrial activity; nor will our means be based upon acknowledged possession of the techniques by which a meed of success has been attained in the material field. Only when we begin to use the vast resources of technology at our command as methods to achieve purposes that are avowedly social, will there be an approach to a new individual, an individual as much related and unified as the present indiviual is divided and distracted.

The nature of a newly emerging individualism cannot be described until progress has been made in its actual creation; but neither shall we make a start in this creation until we surrender the habit of opposing the corporate and social to the individual, and until we realize that the utmost in socialism will effect only a restandardization of an almost exclusively material culture, unless it be accompanied by the instituting of a new type of individual mind. Technology, taken in its broadest sense, offers an answer to our problem. It furnishes us with means that may be utilized in transforming the forces of our industrialized society into factors in producing individuals who are not only possessed of material goods, but also equipped with a high quality of desire and thought.

90.13–15   continues . . . matters.] ION; still nominally proceeds on the assumption that this very illusion can be accepted as a fact.

90.24   this period] *stet* NR; the period
91.7   develop] ION; use
91.10   need for] ION; need of
91.19–22   An intelligent . . . income.] ION; [*not present*]
91.39   domination] *stet* NR; denomination
92.13   election of 1928] ION; last election
92.36   one∧] W; ~-
93.5–7   Moreover . . . managed.] ION; [*not present*]
93.35–36   accumulation and concentration] ION; concentration and accumulation
93.37   suggest] ION; me to define
93.38   influenced] ION; invaded
94.9   already have] ION; have
94.33–36   The policy . . . taking.] ION; [*not present*]
95.10   at which] ION; on which
95.19–96.2   Political . . . struggle.] ION; [*not present*]
96.3   A chapter is devoted] ION; I have not devoted one of this series of articles
96.3–4   not . . . supposed] ION; because I think that
96.5   But it] ION; It
96.9–10   law and political discussion] ION; law
96.12   individual who is] ION; individual
96.14–15   by apprehension of] ION; to apprehend
96.15   industry] ION; public control of industry
96.15–23   finance as . . . formed.] ION; finance, and to give those realities a chance to expel from his mind the debris of lingering aversions, centering usually about the word socialism, and of outmoded affections.
96.25   The chief] ION; But perhaps the chief
97.1   current disorganization] ION; confusion
97.4   so politically] ION; as politically
97.5–6   stock-market crash of 1929] ION; recent stock-market crash
97.31   finally growing] ION; growing finally
98.2   were] ION; were to be
98.13–23   While . . . individuality.] ION; [*not present*]
100.1   And . . . with] ION; I should not hesitate to refer to
100.2   ages] ION; ages in the same connection
100.12   a question] ION; the question
100.12   as] ION; with reference
100.19   not] ION; but not
100.39   The cultural] ION; Thus, the cultural
100.40   is a] ION; becomes

100.40   cultural one] ION;   cultural
101.1–22   It . . . possibilities.] ION;   [*not present*]
101.30   India,] ION;   [*not present*]
101.31   Middle Ages] W;   middle ages
101.31   or] ION;   or to
101.34–37   impossible, . . . machine.] ION;   impossible.
102.4–5   creation of a mind] ION;   mind
102.25   systematic attention] ION;   attention
102.28–29   producing] ION;   the formation of
103.2   an adult society$_\wedge$] ION;   adult society,
103.15   the last] ION;   last
103.20   that exists] ION;   it induces
103.25–38   I can . . . "exciting."] ION;   [*not present*]
104.8–14   It . . . engaged.] ION;   [*not present*]
104.14   do] ION;   did
105.4   must] ION;   have got to
105.6   and cultural] ION;   or cultural
105.7–18   The conception . . . employed.] ION;   [*not present*]
105.34–106.6   For then . . . gain.] ION;   [*not present*]
106.24   have] ION;   has
106.26   a culture] ION;   culture
106.28   a superficial] ION;   superficial
106.28   success] ION;   successes
107.1   inquirers] ION;   inquiries
107.9   control] ION;   the control
107.10   A humane society] ION;   It
107.12   Such a society] ION;   It
107.14–19   "Solutions" . . . fruition.] ION;   [*not present*]
107.23   having] ION;   with
107.35–36   the creation of] ION;   creating
107.38–39   converge] ION;   inevitably converge
108.3   is a] ION;   is also a
108.8–22   The "clerk" . . . meaning.] ION;   [*not present*]
108.32   at least one] ION;   one
109.18–19   existing] ION;   outward
109.19   as if . . . static] ION;   [*not present*]
109.31–110.22   It was . . . minds.] ION;   [*not present*]
111.2   foregoing chapters] ION;   present series of articles
111.6   indicated.] ION;   indicated in the preceding articles; and
111.8   attention to] ION;   accepting
111.12   be] ION;   be like
111.18   have indeed] ION;   have
111.21   both evils] ION;   evils

111.26   that the good life] ION; that life
112.2   into] ION; to
112.2–3   actual] ION; real
112.3   nor . . . with] ION; or to
112.4   realization of ideals] ION; realization
112.11   in attention to] ION; to our interest in
112.12   actualities] ION; actuality
112.23   interaction] ION; participating interaction
112.23–24   an integrated being] ION; their integrated individuality
112.34   that were] ION; to be
112.34   existing] ION; were existing
112.35–113.9   theirs. The . . . now.[¶]To-day] ION; theirs. But
113.9   no] ION; now no
113.9   provide] ION; make possible
113.15   dreams, . . . abnegation.] ION; dreams.
113.23   civilisations] WS; civilization
113.26   that] ION; which
113.33–114.3   science. That . . . possibilities] ION; science. It is not
              too much to say that wholesale condemnations of contempo-
              rary conditions have been produced, in all ages, by the ideal-
              ization into eternal verities of just those things which
              contemporary life was dooming to extinction. The inevitable
              outcome is that the possibilities
114.4   its] ION; that its
114.5–115.4   In reading . . . foundation.] ION; [*not present*]
115.4   Even] ION; [¶]It is silly to suppose that our present evils are
              caused by the application of science. We have not begun to
              assimilate its attitude and method into daily life. Even
115.4   are∧] ION; ~,
115.4–5   there . . . which] ION; the element in them that best
115.5   foreshadows,] ION; ~∧
115.5   if its . . . out,] ION; [*not present*]
115.6   age] ION; age is to be discovered in science
115.6   it looks] ION; its attitude, wherever it is vital, looks
115.8–9   experience.[¶]No] ION; experience. For no
115.27   who strive] ION; strive
115.31   constitutes the] ION; would exhibit the sort of
115.36   If it . . . it] ION; Incorporated into integrated individuals it
116.11–12   whatever] ION; what
117.1   To . . . emotional] ION; The
117.1–2   and moral . . . to] ION; of economic forces
117.3   leave] ION; merely leaves
117.3   inhuman] ION; [*not present*]

117.3 region$_\wedge$] ION; mid-region,
117.3 where they] ION; to
117.4 private] ION; inhuman
117.6–8 There . . . it] ION; It is thus itself an inhuman device,
117.8 interest] ION; interest, indeed, not
117.8 personal] ION; pecuniary profit, but of private
117.9 complacency, private dignity,] ION; complacency
117.10 Every] ION; Moreover, every
117.11 outlook on] ION; temper of
117.11 life . . . on.] ION; life.
117.11–118.2 No one . . . long] ION; This is as true of the fatuous
occupations that treat science, art and religion as ends in
themselves as it is of those which surrender to the materialistic implications of pecuniary industry. The choice is whether
an occupation does its work blindly or under intelligent direction. Refusal to acknowledge actual conditions is a way of
encouraging our occupations, whatever they may be, to operate fatally. Acceptance of science does not mean recognition
of this and that curious fact; acceptance of the machine does
not mean subjection to its present effects. Acceptance is the
first stage in active choice and in endeavor for the realization
of new possibilities.
  We are largely preoccupied at present with the negative,
the destructive, effect of science upon beliefs that custom has
made dear. As long
118.2 remain] ION; are
118.3 values] ION; ideals
118.4 its negative] ION; that
118.13–14 law.[¶]Because] ION; law. Because
118.17–24 The delights . . . out.] ION; [*not present*]
118.26 experiences] ION; also experiences
119.4 frictions] ION; functions
119.22 concerns] ION; concern
119.22 The current] ION; There are too many illustrations to permit of citation. But the current
119.23 is, for example,] ION; is
119.24–34 Their . . . terms.] ION; Here, as in the case of so many
social difficulties, we shall make no headway until scientific
inquiry and human sympathy have coalesced.
119.34 This] ION; Our
120.7–18 It . . . civilization."] ION; [*not present*]
120.23 becomes] ION; becomes more
121.15 course of easy] ION; easy course of

121.20   these forms] ION; these
121.36−37   without relation] ION; in relation
122.4−5   of other things] ION; [*not present*]
122.13−15   if kept . . . assumes] ION; implies both
122.15−16   individual . . . exists.] ION; individual.
122.17   has said] ION; said
122.21   providence] WS; Providence
122.37   road-side] WS; road-/side ION; roadside NR
123.1   in the] ION; at the
123.2   at which] ION; in which
123.3   by thus] ION; thus by

Construction and Criticism

Copy-text for this book is the copyright deposit copy A 22901 (New York: Columbia University Press, 1930).

132.39   today?"] W; ~?'
133.6−7   ∧"progressive] W; "'~
139.16   to-morrow] WS; tomorrow

From Absolutism to Experimentalism

Copy-text is the article's publication in *Contemporary American Philosophy: Personal Statements*, ed. George Plimpton Adams and William Pepperell Montague (London: George Allen and Unwin; New York: Macmillan Co., 1930), 2:13−27.

150.24   professional] W; pro∧/fessional
*156.4   all,] W; ~∧
157.6   discover∧] W; ~,
158.19   it is not] W; is not
159.33−34   imagination] W; imagina∧/tion
*159.38   genuine,] W; ~∧

Philosophy

Copy-text is the article's publication in *Research in the Social Sciences: Its Fundamental Methods and Objectives*, ed. Wilson Gee (New York: Macmillan Co., 1929), pp. 241−65.

161.24   basis] W; basic
168.21   the] W; th
169.14   Moral] W; Social
175n.1   a Category] W; Category

James Marsh and American Philosophy

Copy-text for this article is the typescript (TS) in the John Dewey Papers, Special Collections, Bailey/Howe Library, University of Vermont, Burlington, Vermont. Changes appearing in George Dykhuizen's retyped version (D), which Dewey used as printer's copy for publication in *Journal of the History of Ideas* 2 (April 1941): 131–50 (JHI), appear in this list. A copy of the Dykhuizen typescript is at the Center for Dewey Studies, Southern Illinois University at Carbondale, courtesy of George Dykhuizen. Emendations have been adopted from the article's publication in *Journal of the History of Ideas*, and in *Problems of Men* (New York: Philosophical Library, 1946), pp. 357–78 (PM). The emendations list below also serves as a historical collation, giving all the changes in the four documents. Dewey's alterations in TS appear in "Alterations in 'James Marsh and American Philosophy.'"

178.1   James Marsh and American Philosophy] W; JAMES
         MARSH AND AMERICAN PHILOSOPHY PM; JAMES
         MARSH AND AMERICAN PHILOSOPHY* . . . *Lecture
         delivered at the University of Vermont, November 26, 1929,
         in commemoration of the centenary of the publication of
         James Marsh's "Introduction" to Coleridge's *Aids to Reflec-
         tion.* JHI; THE MARSH LECTURE / by / John Dewey /
         Professor of Philosophy / Columbia University / Burlington,
         Vermont / November 26, 1929 // A Lecture Delivered / at the
         / University of Vermont / in / Commemoration of the Cente-
         nary of the Publication / of / James Marsh's "Introduction" /
         to / Samuel Taylor Coleridge's "Aids to Reflection" D; [*not
         present*] TS
178.2   1831∧ and 1832∧] TS; ~, ~, D, JHI, PM
178.3   Burlington, Vt.] PM; this University town D, JHI, TS
178.4   there] PM; in Burlington, Vermont, D, JHI, TS
178.6–7 *Aids to Reflection, The Friend*∧ and *The Statesman's
         Manual.*] PM, JHI; "Aids to Reflection," "The Friend," and
         "The Statesman's Manual." D; Aids to Reflection, The
         Friend∧ and The Statesman's Manual. TS

178.7   well‸known] TS; ~-~ D, JHI, PM

178.8   Marsh.] PM; Marsh, and it is the Centenary of its publication that brings us together to-day. JHI, D, TS

178.9   Romantic] TS, D; romantic JHI, PM

178.10   it] PM, JHI, D; It TS

178.12   to-day] TS, D, JHI; today PM

178.18   Teutonic] PM, JHI; northern Teutonic D; northern, Teutonic TS

178.21   the *North American Review*] PM, JHI; The North American Review D, TS

178.22   for July, 1822, enables] PM, JHI; ~, ~‸ ~ D; for [*space
for date*] enables TS

178.24   "The modern mind,"] PM, JHI; ‸~, ‸ D, TS

178.24   "removes] PM, JHI; ‸~ D, TS

178.24   thoughts] *stet* TS, D; thought JHI, PM

178.26   says‸] TS, D; ~, JHI, PM

178.26   Greeks‸] TS, D; ~, JHI, PM

178.28–179.1   microcosm."¹] PM, JHI, D; ~".* TS

179.4   materials,] TS; ~‸ D, JHI, PM

179.6   poet] WS; past PM, JHI, D, TS

179.9   definitely] PM, JHI, D; definite TS

179.10   barbarian] TS; Barbarian D, JHI, PM

179.13   historical] PM, JHI, D; historican TS

179.13–14   development‸] TS; ~, D, JHI, PM

179.14   influence.²] PM, JHI, D; ~.* TS

179.15   scholarship] PM, JHI, D; scolarship TS

179.15   Marsh] TS, D, JHI; March PM

179.17   Spanish‸] TS; ~, D, JHI, PM

179.18   Greek‸ and Hebrew‸] TS; ~, ~‸ D; ~, ~, JHI, PM

179.18   early] PM, JHI; comparatively early D, TS

179.18   date.] PM, JHI; ~, D, TS

179.18–19   This was no mean attainment] W; This was no attainment PM, JHI; no mean accomplishment D, TS

179.19–20   since . . . facilities] PM, JHI; considering that he never
went abroad and the facilities D, TS

179.21   languages‸] TS; ~, D, JHI, PM

179.21   an] PM, JHI, D; a an TS

179.25–26   *Critiques . . . Reason*] PM, JHI; [*rom.*] D, TS

179.26   *Anthropology*‸] W; ~, PM, JHI; Anthropology‸ D, TS

179.28   worthy of] PM, JHI; interesting to D, TS

179.28   Marsh's readings] PM, JHI; his readings D; his readins
TS

179.31–32   affected‸ of course‸] TS; ~, ~, D, JHI, PM

179.32   of Coleridge$_\wedge$] W; of Coleridge, PM; for Coleridge, JHI;
          for Coleridge$_\wedge$ D, TS
179.35   distrust] PM, JHI; own distrust D, TS
179n.1   *North American Review,*] W; ~. PM, JHI, D; North
          American Review, TS
179n.2   ²A careful] PM, JHI, D; *~ TS
179n.2   trustworthy] PM, JHI, D; trustowrth TS
179n.3   by Professor Marjorie Nicolson.] PM, JHI; by M. H. Nic-
          olson of Goucher College. D; by [*space for name*] of
          Goucher College$_\wedge$ TS
179n.3–4 entitled "James . . . Transcendentalists," in] PM, JHI;
          ~ "~$_\wedge$" ~ D; entitled [*space for title*] in TS
179n.4   *Philosophical Review*] PM, JHI; *Philosophic Review* D;
          Philosophic Review TS
179n.4   1925.] PM, JHI, D; ~, TS
180.1   thinking$_\wedge$] TS; ~, D, JHI, PM
180.2   absolves] PM, JHI; absolved D; absolve TS
180.6 $_\wedge$*Aids to Reflection*$_\wedge$] PM, JHI; "Aids to Reflection" D;
          $_\wedge$Aids to Reflection$_\wedge$ TS
180.8   Aside] PM, JHI, D; Aaide TS
180.8   penetrating] PM, JHI, D; pentretaing TS
180.8   insight$_\wedge$] TS, D; ~, PM, JHI
180.8   to-day] TS, D, JHI; today PM
180.10   antiquarian] PM, JHI, D; antiquarain TS
180.11   is mainly of historical] PM, JHI; is of historic D, TS
180.14   century] PM, JHI, D; ccentury TS
180.14   recall] PM, JHI; reveal D; reval TS
180.15   before Darwin] PM, JHI; before that of Darwin D, TS
180.15–16 evolutionists; before, indeed,] PM, JHI; ~, ~, ~, D;
          ~, ~$_\wedge$ ~$_\wedge$ TS
180.17   mind; a period] PM, JHI; mind, and D, TS
180.19   when$_\wedge$] TS, D; ~, JHI, PM
180.21   inner] *stet* TS, D, JHI; own PM
180.21   was$_\wedge$] TS; ~, D, JHI, PM
180.21   on] PM, JHI; upon D, TS
180.22   whole$_\wedge$] TS; ~, D, JHI, PM
180.25   Mill says,] PM, JHI; he says, D; he says$_\wedge$ TS
180.26   be preserved] PM, JHI, D; perserved TS
180.30   it too] PM, JHI, D; it oo TS
180.30   Church] WS; church PM, JHI, D, TS
180.33   tranquillity] TS; tranquility D, JHI, PM
180.34   neither] PM, JHI, D; neother TS
180.35   ideas$_\wedge$] TS; ~, D, JHI, PM

180.36   Government] TS;   government D, JHI, PM
180.38   had a Church,] TS;   ~∧ D, JHI, PM
180.39   fulfil] WS;   fulfill PM, JHI, D, TS
180.39   of a church,] WS;   of a Church∧ PM, JHI, D;   of a Church, TS
180.40   simulacrum] PM, JHI, D;   simuacrum TS
181.3   says∧ "an] TS;   says, "An D, JHI, PM
181.6   critic∧] TS;   ~, D, JHI, PM
181.9   says∧] TS;   ~, D, JHI, PM
181.9   Bentham] PM, JHI, D;   Betham TS
181.10   Is] PM, JHI;   is D, TS
181.10   asked∧] TS;   ~, D, JHI, PM
181.11   meaning?'"] PM, JHI;   ~?∧" D, TS
181.15   its] PM, JHI;   his D, TS
181.15   Bibliolatry] D;   bibliolatry PM, JHI;   Bibiolatry TS
181.18   "find"] JHI, PM;   "found" D, TS
181.19   one's] PM, JHI;   his D, TS
181.21   says∧] TS, D;   ~, JHI, PM
181.23   understanding∧] TS;   ~, D;   Understanding, JHI, PM
181.26   Truth,] WS;   truth∧ PM, JHI, D;   truth, TS
181.27   Sect or Church] WS;   sect or church PM, JHI, D, TS
181.27   Christianity,] TS;   ~∧ D, JHI, PM
181.29   which, when] PM, JHI;   which D, TS
181.30   affection] PM, JHI;   affections D, TS
181.30   men,] PM, JHI;   ~∧ D, TS
181.31   assertion] PM, JHI;   demonstration D, TS
181.32   Christian] PM, JHI, D;   Christain TS
181.32–33 *Aids to Reflection*∧] W;   ~, PM, JHI;   "Aids to Reflection," D;   Aids to Reflection∧ TS
181.33–34 Marsh; . . . that] PM, JHI;   Marsh∧ and is the sense in which D;   ~, ~ TS
181.36   seventeenth] PM, JHI, D;   seventeen TS
181.38   eighteenth] PM, JHI, D;   eighteeth TS
181.38   century∧] TS, D;   ~, JHI, PM
181.40   faith] PM, JHI;   truth D, TS
182.2–3 that of Coleridge] *stet* TS, D;   Coleridge JHI, PM
182.5   circumstances] PM, JHI, D;   cirucmstances TS
182.5   day,] TS, JHI, PM;   ~∧ D
182.5   described] PM, JHI;   referred to D, TS
182.7   fact,] TS;   ~∧ D, JHI, PM
182.12   thought] PM, JHI, D;   thoughr TS
182.16   introduction] TS;   Introduction D, JHI, PM

182.17   *Aids to Reflection*] PM, JHI; "Aids to Reflection" D; Aids
to Reflection TS

182.17   feeling] PM, JHI; sense D, TS

182.24   re-awakening] D, JHI; reawakening PM; re-awekening
TS

182.25   been] PM, JHI, D; been been TS

182.33   this country] PM, JHI; that country D, TS

182.34   received] PM, JHI, D; recived TS

182.34   faith,] TS; ~∧ D, JHI, PM

182.35   system,] TS; ~∧ D, JHI, PM

183.3   were∧ in fact∧] TS; ~, ~, D, JHI, PM

183.3   profoundly] PM, JHI, D; profundly TS

183.4   says∧ "a] TS; says, "A D, JHI, PM

183.5   agency"] TS; ~∧ D, JHI, PM

183.5   coexist] TS, D; co-exist JHI, PM

183.6   "religion] TS; ∧~ D, JHI, PM

183.6   Coleridge∧] TS; ~, D, JHI, PM

183.9   spiritual] PM, JHI, D; sriritual TS

183.9   Christianity] PM, JHI, D; Christiantity TS

183.11   attempt∧] TS; ~, D, JHI, PM

183.11   turn∧] TS; ~, D, JHI, PM

183.13   1822∧] TS; ~, D, JHI, PM

183.16   politics∧] TS; ~, D, JHI, PM

183.16   life∧] TS; ~, D, JHI, PM

183.17   as in] PM, JHI, D; in TS

183.20   arbitrary,] TS; ~∧ D, JHI, PM

183.20   recovery of] PM, JHI, D; recovery a TS

183.21   man∧] TS; ~, D, JHI, PM

183.21–22   for that] PM, JHI, D; for TS

183.25   has,] TS; ~∧ D, JHI, PM

183.32   audiences] PM, JHI, D; audeiences TS

183.33   These∧] TS; ~, D, JHI, PM

183.33   noted∧] TS; ~, D, JHI, PM

183.37   God,] TS; ~∧ D, JHI, PM

183.37   Marsh] PM, JHI, D; March TS

183.38   Coleridge∧] TS; ~, D, JHI, PM

184.1–2   intellectual] PM, JHI, D; intelectual TS

184.3   life,] TS; ~∧ D, JHI, PM

184.4   situation] PM, JHI, D; situation he TS

184.5   think,] PM, JHI, D; ~∧ TS

184.6   timidity∧] PM, JHI; ~, D, TS

184.7   it was] PM, JHI; it is D; it it is TS

184.7   due∧ undoubtedly∧] W; ∼, ∼, PM, JHI, D; due∧ undoubt-
          edlt∧ TS
184.7–8   himself, but] PM, JHI, D; himself. But TS
184.8   part, to] PM, JHI; part it was due to D, TS
184.12–13   had∧ in addition∧] TS, D; ∼, ∼, JHI, PM
184.18   nor] PM, JHI; or D, TS
184.21–22   Dr. Nicolson has] PM, JHI, D; Dr. [*space for name*] has TS
184.22   he was] *stet* TS; he, as D, JHI, PM
184.23   least∧] TS; ∼, D, JHI, PM
184.26   did not reach] PM, JHI, D; not reached TS
184.26   an] PM, JHI; a full and D, TS
184.30–31   universe∧] TS; ∼, D, JHI, PM
184.31   Formulae] TS, D; Formulas JHI, PM
184.34; 186.9, 20; 187.31; 188.8, 20   Aristotelian] PM, JHI, D;
          Aristotleian TS
184.34   Kant,] TS; ∼∧ D, JHI, PM
184.36   involves∧ unfortunately∧] TS; ∼, ∼, D, JHI, PM
*184.39   influenced] *stet* TS; more influenced D, JHI, PM
184.40   Plato∧] TS, D; ∼, JHI, PM
*184.40   of Aristotle] PM, JHI; by Aristotle D, TS
185.1   *Metaphysics*] PM, JHI; "Metaphysics" D; Metaphysics TS
185.1   *De Anima*] PM, JHI; "De Anima" D; De Anima TS
185.7   it . . . digress] PM, JHI; you will have to pardon a digression
          D, TS
185.10   understanding∧] TS; ∼, D; Understanding, JHI, PM
185.10, 16, 19; 186.10; 187.20; 188.40; 196.21, 26   reason] TS,
          D; Reason JHI, PM
185.11   affections] PM, JHI; affection D, TS
185.12   ∧mental∧] TS, D; "∼" JHI, PM
185.14   understanding∧] TS; ∼, D; Understanding, JHI, PM
185.15   for these] PM, JHI; to these D; to the these TS
185.15   impressions∧ do not∧ therefore∧] TS; ∼, ∼, ∼, D, JHI, PM
185.16   furnishes] *stet* TS; furnished D, JHI, PM
185.17   totality∧] TS; ∼, D, JHI, PM
185.18; 186.10, 15; 187.5, 8, 14–15, 38; 196.18, 20, 21   under-
          standing] TS, D; Understanding JHI, PM
185.19   things∧] TS; ∼, D, JHI, PM
185.20   led] PM, JHI; lead D, TS
185.21   is∧] TS, D; ∼, JHI, PM
185.21–22   the materials] PM, JHI; materials D, TS
185.23   that∧] TS; ∼, D, JHI, PM
185.25   understanding∧ and reason∧] TS; ∼, ∼, D; Understand-
          ing, and Reason, JHI, PM

185.25–26   but also] PM, JHI; but D, TS
185.27–28   phenomena—what] PM, JHI; phenomena, or to what
    D, TS
185.30   a priori] TS, D; [*ital.*] JHI, PM
185.32   physics,] TS; ~$_\wedge$ D, JHI, PM
185.34–35   a rational] PM, JHI, D; a a rational TS
185.38   "constitute$_\wedge$"] TS, D, JHI; "~," PM
186.1   mathematical] PM, JHI, D; mathemtical TS
186.5   the latter] PM, JHI; they D, TS
186.5   time. Thus] PM, JHI; time, and thus D, TS
186.8   have called] PM, JHI; called D, TS
186.9   treatment] PM, JHI, D; treatement TS
186.10   also$_\wedge$] TS, JHI, PM; ~, D
186.11   nature$_\wedge$] TS; ~, D, JHI, PM
186.12   understanding$_\wedge$ and reason$_\wedge$] TS; ~, ~, D; Understand-
    ing, and Reason, JHI, PM
186.16   third] PM, JHI; later D, TS
186.16   itself,] TS; ~$_\wedge$ D, JHI, PM
186.17   it.] PM, JHI, D; ~, TS
186.18   and deeper] PM, JHI, D; and / and deeper TS
186.21–22   understanding$_\wedge$] TS; ~, D; Understanding, JHI,
    PM
186.22   universe$_\wedge$] TS, D, JHI; ~, PM
186.23   saw] JHI, PM; found D, TS
186.25, 26   Hegel$_\wedge$] TS; ~, D, JHI, PM
186.27   world$_\wedge$] TS; ~, D, JHI, PM
186.28   who] PM, JHI; which D, TS
186.29   constituting] PM, JHI, D; consituting TS
186.31   his] PM, JHI; its D, TS
186.31   day$_\wedge$] TS, D; ~, JHI, PM
186.34   conditions] *stet* TS, D; condition JHI, PM
186.37   to-day$_\wedge$] TS; ~, D, JHI; today, PM
186.38   heard$_\wedge$] TS; ~, D, JHI, PM
187.1   ourselves,] TS, JHI, PM; ~$_\wedge$ D
187.1   the self] PM, JHI, D; the the self TS
187.4   Sense$_\wedge$ however$_\wedge$] TS; ~, ~, D, JHI, PM
187.4   even] PM, JHI; not even D, TS
187.5   world,] PM, JHI, D; ~$_\wedge$ TS
187.5   material for knowledge] PM, JHI; the material of knowledge
    D, TS
187.7   interpret] PM, JHI, D; intret TS
187.8   distinguishing] PM, JHI, D; disitnguishing TS
187.9   implicit] PM, JHI, D; implict TS

187.10   relations∧] TS; ∼, D, JHI, PM
187.11   object,] TS; ∼∧ D, JHI, PM
187.16   necessary] PM, JHI, D; necesssary TS
187.16   ways∧] TS; ∼, D, JHI, PM
187.18   proceeds] PM, JHI, D; proceeeds TS
187.19   itself∧] TS; ∼, D, JHI, PM
187.19   it∧ when] TS; ∼, ∼ D, JHI, PM
187.20   it∧ forms] TS; ∼, ∼ D, JHI, PM
187.20   understanding, that is∧] TS; ∼, ∼, D; Understanding
         (that is, JHI, PM
187.21   nature,] TS, D; ∼) JHI, PM
187.23   will∧] TS; ∼, D, JHI, PM
187.24   principle∧] TS; ∼, D, JHI, PM
187.24   character∧] TS; ∼, D, JHI, PM
187.25   minds—] TS; ∼; D, JHI, PM
187.26   lighteth] PM, JHI, D; ligyteth TS
187.27   operates] PM, JHI; operated D, TS
187.30   may help] PM, JHI; is needed to D, TS
187.30   the sense] PM, JHI; a sense D, TS
187.33   until it] PM, JHI, D; until TS
187.35   sound∧] TS; ∼, D, JHI, PM
187.37   magnet] PM, JHI, D; magent TS
187.37   way∧] TS; ∼, D, JHI, PM
187.40   orderly∧] TS; ∼, D, JHI, PM
188.1   action,] TS; ∼∧ D, JHI, PM
188.4–5 exercise of] W; exercise or PM, JHI, D; exercise os TS
188.5   Similarly∧] TS; ∼, D, JHI, PM
188.5   self-conscious∧] TS; ∼, D, JHI, PM
188.7   our reason.] W; our Reason. PM, JHI; reason as found
         within us. D, TS
188.11–12 obvious∧ I think∧] TS; ∼, ∼, D, JHI, PM
188.16   whole∧] TS; ∼, D, JHI, PM
188.17   will∧] TS; ∼, D, JHI, PM
188.23   First∧] TS; ∼, D, JHI, PM
188.25   found] PM, JHI; to be found D, TS
188.25   thought∧] TS, D; ∼, JHI, PM
188.25   one which] PM, JHI; which D, TS
188.27   thing] PM, JHI, D; to thing TS
188.29   is∧] TS, D; ∼, JHI, PM
188.30   institute] PM, JHI, D; insitute TS
188.37   directed upon] PM, JHI; connected with D, TS
188.38   transformed] PM, JHI, D; trnaformed TS
189.2–3 embodiment] PM, JHI, D; embodiement TS

189.3   Following] PM, JHI, D; Folliwing TS
189.7   principles] PM, JHI, D; pricniples TS
189.8   speculation] PM, JHI, D; specualtion TS
189.9   intellect] PM, JHI, D; intllect TS
189.15   Christian] PM, JHI, D; Cristian TS
189.21   itself—the] PM, JHI, D; ~ / ~ TS
189.22   aroused] W; used PM, JHI, D; oused TS
189.23   technicalities] PM, JHI, D; tenchnicalities TS
189.25   conscience₍ₐ₎] TS; ~, D, JHI, PM
189.25   freedom of] PM, JHI, D; freedom in TS
189.25   will. But] PM; will, but JHI, D; will, But TS
189.27   complete,] TS; ~₍ₐ₎ D, JHI, PM
189.27   way] PM, JHI, D; way which TS
189.30   will₍ₐ₎] TS, D; ~, JHI, PM
189.32   abstract] PM, JHI, D; abtract TS
189.33   object₍ₐ₎] PM, JHI, D; ~; TS
189.36   the divine] PM, JHI, D; divine TS
189.37   "The] PM, JHI, D; ₍ₐ₎~ TS
189.38   law,] TS; ~₍ₐ₎ D, JHI, PM
189.40   again₍ₐ₎] TS, D; ~, JHI, PM
189.40   principle₍ₐ₎] PM, JHI, D; ~, TS
190.3   receives] PM, JHI, D; recives TS
190.7   not₍ₐ₎] TS, D; ~, JHI, PM
190.8   Marsh₍ₐ₎] TS, D; ~, JHI, PM
190.8   concerns)—] PM, JHI; ~)₍ₐ₎ D, TS
190.10   Unfortunately₍ₐ₎] TS; ~, D, JHI, PM
190.12   Here₍ₐ₎ too₍ₐ₎] TS; ~, ~, D, JHI, PM
190.12   we] PM, JHI, D; he TS
190.13   Coleridge₍ₐ₎] TS, D; ~, JHI, PM
190.16   Coleridge₍ₐ₎] TS; ~, D, JHI, PM
190.17   represented₍ₐ₎] TS; ~, D, JHI, PM
190.20   are awakened] PM, JHI; were awakened D, TS
190.21   they are] PM, JHI; they were D, TS
190.21   nourished] PM, JHI, D; noruished TS
190.23–24 until these institutions] PM, JHI; till they D, TS
190.24–25 for humanity] PM, JHI; of humanity D, TS
190.26   Coleridge] PM, JHI, D; Coelridge TS
190.27   church] TS, D; Church JHI, PM
190.29   point₍ₐ₎ of course₍ₐ₎] TS, D; ~, ~, JHI, PM
190.30   church] TS, D; Church JHI, PM
190.31   surprising] PM, JHI, D; suprising TS
190.31   church] D; Church PM, JHI; chruch TS
190.33   words₍ₐ₎] TS; ~, D, JHI, PM

190.34   end,] TS; ~∧ D, JHI, PM
190.34   institute,] TS; ~∧ D, JHI, PM
190.35   Church] WS; church PM, JHI, D, TS
190.35   name∧] TS; ~, D, JHI, PM
190.36   sense∧] TS; ~, D, JHI, PM
190.38   or writers] PM, JHI; and writers D, TS
190.39   Clerisy] WS; clerisy PM, JHI, D, TS
190.39   Church] WS; church PM, JHI, D, TS
191.1   jurisprudence] PM, JHI, D; jurispreudence TS
191.1   music,] TS; ~∧ D, JHI, PM
191.3   organ;] PM, JHI, D; ~: TS
191.6   precedence,] TS; ~∧ D, JHI, PM
191.7   the root] PM, JHI, D; thr oot TS
191.11   called] PM, JHI; termed the D, TS
191.11–12   regarded∧] TS; ~, D, JHI, PM
191.12   well∧] TS, D; ~, JHI, PM
191.12   Coleridge∧] TS, D; ~, JHI, PM
191.13   apprenticeship] PM, JHI, D; apprencticeship TS
191.15   that∧] TS, D; ~, JHI, PM
191.16   Church] TS, D; church JHI, PM
191.16   States∧] TS, D; ~, JHI, PM
191.16   this] PM, JHI; that D, TS
191.17   Marsh] PM, JHI; Mr. Marsh D, TS
191.21   indirectly∧] TS, D; ~, JHI, PM
191.23   organization of] PM, JHI, D; organization of of TS
191.25–26   sermon at the dedication] PM, JHI; dedication sermon
        D, TS
191.28   effect∧] TS; ~, D, JHI, PM
191.29   the individual] PM, JHI, D; individual TS
191.32   Culture] PM, JHI; Cultivation D, TS
191.34   regime] TS, D; régime JHI, PM
191.35   will∧] TS; ~, D, JHI, PM
191.39   humanity∧] TS; ~, D, JHI, PM
191.40   are∧ perhaps∧] TS; ~, ~, D, JHI, PM
191.41   West∧] TS; ~, D, JHI, PM
192.7   organization] PM, JHI, D; orgnization TS
192.7–8   constituent] PM, JHI, D; constituents TS
192.8   community,] TS; ~∧ D, JHI, PM
192.8   highest] PM, JHI, D; higheest TS
192.10   it,] TS; ~∧ D, JHI, PM
192.10   constitutes] *stet* TS; constitute D, JHI, PM
192.12   organization,] TS; ~∧ D, JHI, PM
192.14   Indeed∧] TS; ~, D, JHI, PM

192.16   is∧ in fact∧] TS; ~, ~, D, JHI, PM
192.21   Dr. Marsh] PM, JHI; he D, TS
192.22   a cultivation] PM, JHI; the cultivation D, TS
192.23   community,] TS, JHI, PM; ~∧ D
192.25   Dr.] PM, JHI, D; ~∧ TS
192.25   achieved] PM, JHI; engaged in D, TS
192.28   stated∧ it seems to me∧] TS; ~, ~, D, JHI, PM
192.30   system∧] TS; ~, D, JHI, PM
192.31   Dr.] PM, JHI, D; ~∧ TS
192.34; 193.6, 7, 10   State] TS, D; state JHI, PM
192.35   a free] PM, JHI; free D, TS
192.37   was∧ indeed∧] TS; ~, ~, D, JHI, PM
193.5   recent] PM, JHI, D; recents TS
193.13   individuals∧] TS, D; ~, JHI, PM
193.17   constitution] PM, JHI, D; consitution TS
193.17   laws∧] TS; ~, D, JHI, PM
193.18   administration] PM, JHI, D; adminstration TS
193.32–33   manifestation] PM, JHI, D; manifiestion TS
193.33   and] PM, JHI, D; and and TS
193.38   possession] PM, JHI, D; posession TS
194.5   prevailed∧] TS, D; ~, JHI, PM
194.8   the conviction that] PM, JHI; that D, TS
194.11   other∧] TS, D; ~, JHI, PM
194.15   view] PM, JHI, D; viw TS
194.15   rigid] PM, JHI; fixed D, TS
194.17   recognizes] PM, JHI; that D, TS
194.17   as] PM, JHI; are D, TS
194.19   Marsh's] PM, JHI, D; Marsh' TS
194.20   conceived of] PM, JHI; conceived D, TS
194.21   was∧] TS, PM; ~, D, JHI
194.22   Coleridge∧] TS; ~, D, JHI, PM
194.23   we] PM, JHI, D; he TS
194.24   recall] PM, JHI, D; recal TS
194.26   own] PM, JHI, D; wn TS
194.31   developement] WS; development PM, JHI, D, TS
194.35   some] PM, JHI; the need for some D, TS
194.35   organizing∧ pervading∧] TS; ~, ~, D, JHI, PM
194.37   greatly needed] PM, JHI; needed D, TS
194.37   to-day] TS, D, JHI; today PM
194.37   it was] PM, JHI; they were D, TS
195.7   He] PM, JHI, D; he TS
195.10   develope] WS; develop PM, JHI, D, TS
195.21   prevailing] PM, JHI, D; previaling TS

195.22   Merely] PM, JHI;   More D, TS
195.24–25   not∧ however∧] TS;   ~, ~, D, JHI, PM
195.28   accompanied∧] TS;   ~, D, JHI, PM
195.28–29   in his views on education] PM, JHI;   in education
         D, TS
195.29   elsewhere∧] TS, D;   ~, JHI, PM
195.30   of cultivated] PM, JHI, D;   of of cultivated TS
195.31   purpose] PM, JHI, D;   prupose TS
195.33   made∧] TS, D;   ~, JHI, PM
195.34   government∧] TS, D;   ~, JHI, PM
195.37   instruction."³] PM, JHI, D;   ~."∧ TS
195n.1   ³These] PM, JHI, D;   ∧~ TS
195n.2   eighteen forties] TS, D;   ~-~ JHI, PM
196.3   thought∧] TS, D;   ~, JHI, PM
196.4   Dr.] PM, JHI;   the Dr. D;   the Dr∧ TS
196.6   others] PM, JHI, D;   ohters TS
196.7   the German] PM, JHI, D;   German TS
196.7   idealists] PM, JHI;   idealism D, TS
196.8   But∧ none the less∧] TS, D;   ~, ~, JHI, PM
196.9   that∧ even] TS, D;   ~, ~ JHI, PM
196.10   the appeal] PM, JHI;   their appeal D, TS
196.11   theology,] TS, JHI, PM;   ~; D
196.11   secondhand] TS;   second-hand D, JHI, PM
196.14   ∧spiritual∧] TS, D, JHI;   "~" PM
196.18   not∧ for example∧] TS;   ~, ~, D, JHI, PM
196.19   thraldom] TS, D;   thralldom JHI, PM
196.27   plane,] TS, D;   ~∧ JHI, PM
196.28   spirit∧] TS, D;   ~, JHI, PM
196.29   Religion] PM, JHI, D;   religion TS
196.31   his time] PM, JHI;   his D, TS
196.36   philosophy,] TS, D;   ~∧ JHI, PM
196.38   theirs] PM, JHI, D;   their theirs TS
196.40   in his] PM, JHI, D;   to his TS

The Applicability of Logic to Existence

Copy-text is the article's publication in *Journal of Philosophy* 27 (27
March 1930): 174–79.

203.7   Be] W;   be
205.10   logical principles] WS;   logical relations
*205.28   context] WS;   content

205.29   or conditions] WS; of conditions
*205.37   context] W; content
206.35   sea-fight] WS; ~∧~
206.35   to-morrow] WS; tomorrow
208.24   generic] W; genetic

In Reply to Some Criticisms

Copy-text is the article's publication in *Journal of Philosophy* 27 (8 May 1930): 271–77.

214.29   partial∧truths] WS; ~-~
215.27   battle axe] WS; battle-ax
216.26   sometimes] WS; something

Conduct and Experience

Copy-text is the article's publication in *Psychologies of 1930*, ed. Carl Murchison (Worcester, Mass.: Clark University Press, 1930), pp. 409–22 (P). Emendations have been accepted from its republication in *Philosophy and Civilization* (New York: Minton, Balch and Co., 1931), pp. 249–70 (PC).

218.2   "Conduct,"] PC; I venture to discuss this topic in its psychological bearings because the problem as defined for me by the editor is "a *logical* analysis of behavior and of experience" as these terms figure in current discussion, controversy, and psychological inquiry. "Conduct,"

218.14   an introductory remark should] PC; two general introductory remarks may

*218.15   That] W; One

218.25–26   speech. . . . with the] PC; speech.[¶]The other remark is that I have no intention of delimiting or bounding the field of actual inquiry in psychology by introducing methodological considerations. On the contrary, I am a firm believer in a variety of points of approach and diversity of investigations, especially in a subject as new as psychology is. To a considerable extent, the existence of different schools is at present an asset rather than a liability, for psychology will ultimately be whatever it is made to be by investigators in the field. To a certain extent, a variety of points of view serves the purpose that is met in all the sciences by the principle of multiple hypotheses. While there is immediate confusion, it may turn out that the variety will, in the end, secure a greater fullness of exploration than would otherwise have been the case. The discussion, because of its great complexity, may be introduced by reference to the

218.28   descendants] PC; decendants
219.1   terms.] PC; terms. A brief review, couched linguistically in dogmatic terms, will be used as an introduction.
219.14   some] PC; some of the
219.15   perceptions] PC; perception
219.27   extraneous] PC; objective
219.38   physical] PC; external
220.22   so] PC; so much
220.25   were] PC; was
220.30   *trans-action*] PC; [*rom.*]
220.38   science] PC; sciences
221.34   of this] PC; in this
221.39   Although] PC; While
222.12   consistent] PC; consistent with
222.14   every] PC; any
223.19   making] PC; noting
223.34   of a *prior*] PC; *a* prior
223.34   functions] PC; operates
223.40   environmental] PC; environment
224.4   *direction*] PC; [*rom.*]
224.21   persists although] PC; is continuous, while
224.27   suppose it is] PC; regard it as
224.29   since] PC; for
225.29   with is, however,] PC; with, however, is
225.36   specifiable] PC; certain
*226.9   ends,] PC; ~∧
226.28–29   differential] PC; differentiated
226.33–34   so characterized that they] PC; characterized that
227.1   ordinary] PC; common
227.1–2   it is directed] PC; directed
227.31–32   them. But] PC; them, but
227.39   physiological process] PC; process as physiological
228.14   experienc*ing*] PC; experiencing
228.26   enters] PC; entered
228.27   the things] PC; things
228.28–29   to the way an object is made] PC; to selection from the total object of the way it is made

228.32 most] PC; some
229.12 *moral*] PC; [*rom.*]
229.22 selves] PC; ourselves
230.8 *problems*] PC; [*rom.*]
230.16 acts,] W; ~∧
230.33 be used] PC; is used
230.33–34 is assumed] PC; assumes
231.3–4 origin, but is] PC; origin∧ but
231.11 introspectionist] PC; introspectionists
232.10 as] PC; as forming
232n.2 *object*] PC; [*rom.*]
233.21 *effect*] PC; [*rom.*]
234.25 modes of behavior have] PC; behavior has
234.27–28 assumed that] PC; took
234.28–29 constitutes] PC; to constitute
235.3 distinguished] *stet* P; distinguishing
235.17 it does] PC; is does
235.20 (3, p. 5).] *stet* P; [*om.*]
235n.1–10 References . . . Pp. 111–126.] *stet* P; [*om.*]
235n.2 An] W; In

Psychology and Work

Copy-text for this article is its publication in *Personnel Journal* 8 (February 1930): 337–41.

237.31 or capitalism] W; of capitalism
237.34 development?] W; ~.'
241.34 attitude] W; altitude

Qualitative Thought

Copy-text for this article is its publication in *Symposium* 1 (January 1930): 5–32 (S). Emendations have been accepted from its republication in *Philosophy and Civilization* (New York: Minton, Balch and Co., 1931), pp. 93–116 (PC).

243.18 The propositions] PC; The content of the propositions
243.18–19 science are] PC; science is
243.19–20 they deal with] PC; it consists of
244.9 the truth] PC; that truth

244.9   concern] PC; be about
245.9   effected] PC; affected
245.27   mode] PC; form
246.2   a distinct] PC; some distinct
246.9   objects] PC; accounts
247.16   explicitly] PC; implicitly
247.20   connection with] PC; reference to
247.25   quality] PC; qualitative object
247.27   there would be] PC; we should have
248.9   permeating] PC; other permeating
248.36   resolved] PC; received
249.30   appropriate] PC; approximate
249.32   set] PC; sets
250.4   is thoroughly] PC; is such as to be thoroughly
250.5   or is] PC; or
250.12   discoursing] PC; discourse
250.13   It] PC; This
250.27   case] PC; cases
250.29   These] PC; They
251.33   they] PC; these
252.7   construction] PC; constructions
254.6   involves] PC; is some
254.7   until] PC; before
254.8   an] PC; any
254.9   emerges] PC; emerge
254.22   *to* which] PC; to which
254.35–36 converted] PC; be converted
255.30–31 that it may] PC; to develop and
255.40   reference] PC; references
256.2   a hand] PC; hand
256.14   *cause*] stet S; [*rom.*]
256.17   "by"] PC; "in"
257.3   man does when] PC; man
257.15   *by*] PC; [*rom.*]
258.11   train] PC; a train
258.26   "by"] PC; ∧~∧
258n.1   Vol.I, Book II] W; Book II
259.17   which controls] PC; that controls
260.2   For] PC; But

What Humanism Means to Me

Copy-text is the article's publication in *Thinker* 2 (June 1930): 9–12.

263.6   phase] W; phrase
264.18   Auguste Comte] W; August Compte

Three Independent Factors in Morals

Copy-text for this address is pages 198.32–201.20 of "Three Independent Factors in Morals," *Educational Theory* 16 (July 1966): 197–209,
translated by Jo Ann Boydston, and pages 6–13.3 of the typescript,
"Conflict and Independent Variables in Morals," John Dewey Papers,
Special Collections, Morris Library, Southern Illinois University at Carbondale. All emendations are in the typescript.

283.15   in] W; jn
283.27–28   experience] W; expereince
283.36   tyrannical] W; tyrnnical
284.1–2   administration] W; adminstration
284.28   upon whom the] W; upon the
284.30   own] W; oown
285.3   independent] W; indepe t
285.8   itself, it$_\wedge$] W; ~$_\wedge$ ~,
285.12   means] W; m ans
285.21   claim$_\wedge$ to] W; ~, ~
285.26   to be a] W; to a
285.27   through] W; thrugh
285.32   origin] W; rigin
285.32–33   operation] W; opeeation
286.14   as] W; s
286.17   demands] W; demnds
286.18   character] W; characer
286.19   virtue] W; v rtue
286.20   rewards] W; re ards
286.20–21   *sanctions*] W; *sanitions*
286.31   and] W; an
286.33   English] W; Englsh
286.36   Consider] W; Conisder
286.37   sympathy] W; sympthy
287.5   through] W; th ough
287.36–37   Anglo-Saxon] W; Anglo-saxon

287.37   contrast] W; contrastes
288.8   commensurable] W; commesnsurable
288.15   with which each and every] W; with each every

Philosophy and Education

Copy-text is the publication of this address in University of California at Los Angeles, *Addresses Delivered at the Dedication of the New Campus and New Buildings of the University of California at Los Angeles, 27 and 28 March 1930* (Berkeley: University of California Press, 1930), pp. 46–56 (A). Emendations have been accepted from its republication in *Higher Education Faces the Future*, ed. Paul Arthur Schilpp (New York: Horace Liveright, 1930), pp. 273–83 (HE).

289.4   the study] HE; study
289.10   appears] *stet* A; appear
290.22   philosophy] HE; philosphy
291.10   development] *stet* A; developments
291.12   which] HE; that
291.15   together] HE; with it
291.30   habit‿] HE; and habit,
291.30   the emotions] HE; that of the emotions
292.1   termed] HE; called
292.30–31   of serious] HE; between serious
292.31   with] HE; and
293.17   undeveloped conditions] HE; conditions
294.5–6   and yet there] HE; but there might
294.6–7   But hostile] HE; Hostile
294.7   fact] HE; fact, however,
294.20   scheme] *stet* A; school
294.36   those] HE; these
295.4   our] HE; your
295.19   by . . . hand] HE; on one hand by yielding
295.26   of . . . years] HE; in recent years of knowledge
297.1   as far] HE; so far
297.23   We need not be reminded] HE; I do not need to remind you
297.24   ripe] HE; rife
297.26   time that] HE; —and such an occasion as this is a highly fit time—
297.31   only be done] HE; be done only
297.35   up] HE; up as
297.37   must] HE; may

298.11   We need to pledge] HE; The dedication of these buildings is
          but the symbol of a more profound dedication in which we
          pledge

General Principles of Educational Articulation

Copy-text for this article is its publication in *School and Society* 29
(30 March 1929): 399–406 (SS); emendations have been accepted from
its publication in Department of Superintendence of the National Education Association *Official Report* (Washington, D.C.: Department of
Superintendence, 1929), pp. 51–60 (DS).

299.2   Articulation] DS; Articulation[1] . . . [1]Address before the gen-
          eral session, Department of Superintendence, Cleveland, Feb-
          ruary 26, 1929.
299.18   stage] DS; state
299.19   and from] DS; from
299.19   college.] DS; college, etc.
301.2–3   system.[¶The] DS; system. The
301.14   It] DS; Hence it
301.20   should be checked by] DS; can not be complete without
301.20   those schools] DS; schools
301.21   "unified schools"] DS; so-called ∧unified schools∧
302.3   adequate] DS; [*ital.*]
302.11–12 warning.] DS; warning, a caveat.
302.16–17 inertia.[¶A] DS; inertia. A
302.23   work.] DS; work, much less that there is any antagonism
          between the point of view of classroom teachers and of
          administrators.
302.28–29 subject-matter,] W; subjectmatter, DS; subject-
          matter∧
302.29   methods,] DS; and methods∧
303.3   supply] DS; be
303.19   interests . . . time] DS; interests
303.23   ever any] DS; any
303.26   growth, incapacity] DS; growth and incapacities
303.27   subject-matter,] W; subjectmatter, DS; subject-matter∧
303.27   inability] DS; inabilities
303.28   all] DS; all of them always
303.29   diagnosed] DS; be diagnosed
303n.4   the acquiring] DS; acquiring
303n.4   the application] DS; applications

304.1   talk;] DS; talk, etc.,
304.32   achievements,] DS; achievements, matured developments,
304.34   misstates] DS; so misstates
304.35   articulation, and] DS; articulation that
304.37–38   problem, from] DS; real problem is not one of early
        maturing for a fruitage to come in a later unit. It is, from
304.38   years, is that] DS; years, the problem
304.39–40   ripening then and there] DS; ripening
305.4   but with] DS; with
305.6   the new] DS; new
*305.11   phases] *stet* SS; phase
305.18   curriculum] DS; problem of curriculum
305.28–29   acquired.[¶]This] DS; acquired. This
305.40   out of school] DS; in school
306.4–5   uniform] DS; uniformed
306.31   committee] DS; committees
306.32   curriculums. Unified] DS; curriculum; unified
306.40   involves] DS; involved
307.14–21   We need . . . subjects.] DS; [*not present*]
308.15   allude to] DS; allude, of course, to
308.18   other. No] DS; other. I must content myself with calling
        attention to the problem; no
308.24–25   rapprochement] W; reapproachment
308.25   an important factor.] DS; a factor not to be neglected.
308.26   illustrations] DS; illustrations of some of the meanings con-
        tained in the two general principles when they are applied
308.37–38   *differentiation.*[¶]The] DS; *differentiation.* The
308.40–309.1   lungs, and stomach together;] DS; lungs and stom-
        ach, etc., together:
309.2   a gradual] DS; gradual
309.3–4   others. The] DS; others.[¶]Analogy fails with educational
        process of growth because the former takes place so largely
        intrinsically, requiring from without only provision of normal
        conditions. In education there is no such inherent internal de-
        velopment; direction by means of provision of suitable en-
        vironment, both of things and personal associations, is
        relatively more important. But the
309.4   educational] DS; such external
309.4   be] DS; still be
309.4   that] DS; one
309.6   may be] DS; can be only
309.10   earlier and later years in] DS; earlier years and later with
309.10–11   type in the former] DS; type

309.13   contrast] DS; fact
309.13−14   statement seems] DS; statements seem
309.18−19   kindergarten.[¶]Receptivity] DS; kindergarten.
          Receptivity
309.20−21   *range . . . of exercise*] DS; the range of exercise and
          the fields in which they are exercised
309.25   development.] DS; development. The problem is to find the
          particular ripening activities which are operative.
309.34   later] DS; later on
309.34−35   respect to that] DS; respects
310.8−9   More important, however,] DS; Much more important

Our Illiteracy Problem

Copy-text is the article's publication in *Pictorial Review* 31 (August
1930): 28, 65, 73.

312.3; 313.14, 19, 20, 22, 29, 40; 314.3; 315.37   Negro] W; negro
313.17, 27, 34, 35; 314.16   Negroes] W; negroes

How Much Freedom in New Schools?

Copy-text is the article's publication in *New Republic* 63 (9 July 1930):
204−6.

324.17   upon which] W; upon

Freedom in Workers' Education

Copy-text is the typescript (TS¹) not typed by Dewey but corrected in
his hand in the Brookwood Collection, Archives of Labor History and
Urban Affairs, University Archives, Walter P. Reuther Library, Wayne
State University, Detroit, Michigan. The emendations list below also
serves as a historical collation, recording the changes in TS², a carbon of
TS¹ not containing Dewey's corrections, also in the Brookwood Collection, and in its publication in *American Teacher* 13 (January 1929): 1−
4 (AT). The publication in AT was from an underlying, non-authorial
document. Those emendations accepted from AT are ones that would

have been made editorially. Dewey's alterations in TS¹ appear in "Alterations in 'Freedom in Workers' Education.'"

331.1   Freedom in Workers' Education] W; Freedom in Workers∧
          Education AT; [*not present*] TS², TS¹
331.2   members] TS¹, TS²; Members AT
331.5   should. But] AT; should, but TS²; should, But TS¹
331.9   to associate] TS¹, AT; to me to associate TS²
331.10   backbone] TS¹, TS²; the backbone AT
331.11   was not merely] TS¹; not merely as TS², AT
331.16   joy,] TS¹; ~∧ TS², AT
331.17   you are] TS¹, AT; you feel you are TS²
331.18   in attacking] TS¹; in and no possibility of attacking TS², AT
331.19   indeed be] TS¹, AT; be TS²
331.20   rather] TS¹, AT; rather there is TS²
331.20   regret. For] TS¹; regret, and TS²; regret, for AT
331.22   L.,] TS², AT; L.∧ TS¹
331.22   action] TS¹, AT; an action, TS²
331.24   incident at Brookwood] TS¹; particular incident TS²; particular incident involving Brookwood AT
331.27   straightforward∧] TS¹; straight forward∧ TS²; straight-forward, AT
331.28   impartial] TS¹, AT; honest and impartial TS²
331.28   knew] TS¹, TS²; know AT
331n.1–3 (Address . . . 1928.)] AT; [*not present*] TS², TS¹
332.1   assurance;] TS¹, AT; ~, TS²
332.3   straightforward] TS¹, TS²; straight-forward AT
332.4   not∧ then∧] TS¹, TS²; ~, ~, AT
332.5   of one] TS¹, AT; on one TS²
332.5   of it,] TS¹, AT; of it that I wish to talk, TS²
332.5   namely what] TS¹; namely on what, TS²; namely, what AT
332.6   to it] TS¹, AT; to that TS²
332.7   the Teachers Union∧] TS¹, AT; this Teachers Union, TS²
332.7   and the American Federation of Labor] AT; this Teachers Federation TS²; and the Am Federation of Labor TS¹
332.9   I] TS¹, AT; Now I TS²
332.9   phrase∧ ∧academic freedom∧∧] TS¹, TS²; ~, "~," AT
332.12   real education,] TS¹, AT; ~∧ TS²
332.14   freedom is] TS¹, AT; freedom, TS²
332.14–15 and hence it is an attack] AT; is an attack TS²; and hence it is attack TS¹
332.15   upon the possibility] TS¹, AT; the possibilities TS²

332.17   freedom$_\wedge$] TS^1, TS^2; ~, AT
332.17-18   cannot get] TS^1, TS^2; can not have AT
332.19   say$_\wedge$ $_\wedge$a] TS^1, TS^2; say, "A AT
332.19   good,$_\wedge$] TS^1, TS^2; ~," AT
332.21   an awakening] TS^1, AT; awakening TS^2
332.23   to be] TS^1; and to be TS^2, AT
332.27   conducted, from] TS^1, TS^2; conducted. From AT
332.28   tonight,] TS^1; ~; TS^2, AT
332.28   read$_\wedge$ (and] TS^1, AT; ~; $_\wedge$~ TS^2
332.29   other] TS^1; the other TS^2, AT
332.29   the graduates)] TS^1; the graduates or from the alumni over
          here, TS^2; graduates) AT
332.30   idea] TS^1, AT; testimony TS^2
332.32   believes] TS^1, AT; beleives TS^2
332.33   their interests] TS^1, AT; the interests of organized labor TS^2
332.34   any full] TS^1; this full TS^2, AT
332.35   cause] AT; cuase TS^2, TS^1
332.36-37   suppression] AT; supression TS^2, TS^1
332.37   deliberate] TS^1, AT; these deliberate TS^2
332.39   What] TS^1, AT; I am sure that what TS^2
333.3   conducting] TS^1, AT; basing TS^2
333.4   in that spirit] TS^1, AT; on that TS^2
333.7-8   his mind] TS^1, TS^2; mind AT
333.9   them] TS^1, AT; those facts TS^2
333.12   Those] TS^1, AT; [¶]It seems to me that ignoring details and
          technicalities that may be brough up relative to academic
          freedom or to freedom of teaching, it is the school in its rela-
          tion to the labor movement that is the real issue. Those TS^2
333.14   think,] TS^1, TS^2; ~$_\wedge$ AT
333.14   knew] TS^1, TS^2; know AT
333.16   be;] TS^1, AT; ~, TS^2
333.17   breathe] TS^1, AT; create TS^2
333.17   permeates them] TS^1, AT; permeates TS^2
333.17   have] TS^1; has TS^2, AT
333.18   and] TS^1, AT; or TS^2
333.18   they] TS^1, AT; it TS^2
333.20   discourage,] TS^1, AT; ~$_\wedge$ TS^2
333.22   political,] TS^1, TS^2; ~$_\wedge$ AT
333.23   of investigation] TS^1; of mind, investigation TS^2, AT
333.23   discussion$_\wedge$] TS^1, AT; ~, TS^2
333.24   personally$_\wedge$] TS^1, TS^2; ~, AT
333.25   officials$_\wedge$ (I] TS^1, AT; ~, $_\wedge$~ TS^2

333.25   body∧] AT;   ~, TS², TS¹
333.26−27   labor∧) should take] AT;   labor,∧ take TS²;   labor,)
    should take TS¹
333.29   freedom, a cause so] TS¹, AT;   freedom which I have said is
    so TS²
333.31   by] TS¹, AT;   perhaps by TS²
333.34   incident;] TS¹, AT;   ~, TS²
333.37   coincidence] AT;   coincidnece TS², TS¹
334.1−2, 4   those educational] TS¹, TS²;   these educational AT
334.9   system] AT;   sytem TS², TS¹
334.10   publicly∧controlled] TS¹, TS²;   ~-~ AT
334.24−25   trade-union] TS¹, TS²;   ~∧~ AT
334.25   trade-unionists] WS;   ~∧~ TS², TS¹, AT
334.26   trade-union education] WS;   ~∧~ ~ TS², TS¹, AT
334.27   trade-union matter] WS;   ~∧~ ~ TS², TS¹, AT
334.31   that] TS¹, AT;   the that TS²
334.32   workers, wage] TS¹, TS²;   ~—~ AT
334.32   laborers, can] TS¹, TS²;   ~—~ AT
334.33   hand, labor] TS¹;   hand∧ labor AT;   hand∧ the labor TS²
334.34   unions and] TS¹, AT;   unions, TS²
334.34   activity∧] TS¹, AT;   ~, TS²
334.35   these] TS¹, AT;   that these TS²
334.35−36   themselves,] TS¹;   ~∧ TS², AT
334.36   this] TS¹, AT;   that their TS²
334.36   control] TS¹, AT;   control of them TS²
334.39−335.1   *capable*] TS¹, TS²;   [*rom.*] AT
335.2   doubt,] TS¹, TS²;   ~; AT
335.3   ∧capable.∧] TS¹;   ∧capable,∧ that it is capable of expansion to
    that extent. TS²;   "capable." AT
335.4   expanded] TS¹;   expanded in our public schools, TS², AT
335.4   nearly] TS¹;   over TS², AT
335.5   doubt] TS¹, TS²;   doubt it AT
335.5   Since the system has] TS¹, AT;   They have TS²
335.6   desired∧ there] TS¹;   desired and they are not meeting these
    special needs. There TS²;   desired, there AT
335.6   need] TS¹;   need then TS², AT
335.8   do. And] TS¹;   do, and TS²;   do. I AT
335.10   pioneer, so as to] TS¹;   pioneer∧ to TS²;   pioneer∧ so as to
    AT
335.11−12   undertake;] TS¹;   ~, TS², AT
335.12   something] TS¹, AT;   some TS²
335.12   that] TS¹, AT;   at least that TS²

335.13   of activity] TS[1]; and activity TS[2], AT
335.14   something‿] TS[1], AT; ~, TS[2]
335.14   effort] TS[1]; interest TS[2]; efforts AT
335.15   public] TS[1], AT; these public TS[2]
335.17   specially] TS[1], TS[2]; especially AT
335.20   boasted of] TS[1]; boasted TS[2], AT
335.20   including] TS[1], AT; and TS[2]
335.22   control. They] TS[1], AT; control; that they TS[2]
335.22   professors, and] AT; professors, TS[2]; professors, & TS[1]
335.24   class‿] TS[1], TS[2]; classes, AT
335.25   classes;] TS[1], AT; ~, TS[2]
335.26   utilities] TS[1], AT; these utilities TS[2]
335.28   and] TS[1], TS[2]; or AT
335.30   companies] TS[1], AT; companies itself TS[2]
335.32   of‿ that] TS[1], TS[2]; ~, ~ AT
335.34   to be attacking] TS[1], TS[2]; if they attacked AT
335.35   information‿ than . . . upon] TS[1]; information‿ than this indirect attack upon TS[2]; information, than by thus indirectly attacking AT
335.37   the workers'] TS[1], AT; workers' TS[2]
335.38   officials] TS[1], AT; officials of organized labor TS[2]
335.39   in the editorial referred to] AT; here TS[2], TS[1]
336.1   these] TS[1], TS[2]; those AT
336.2   could] TS[1], AT; would TS[2]
336.2, 3 labor] TS[1], TS[2]; Labor AT
336.3   see to it] TS[1]; to see TS[2]; see AT
336.7   agreement. But] W; agreement.[¶]But AT; agreemnt, but TS[2]; agreemnt. But TS[1]
336.8   out‿] TS[1]; ~, TS[2], AT
336.13   a situation] TS[1]; the situation TS[2], AT
336.17   country‿] TS[1], TS[2]; ~, AT
336.17   fostering‿] TS[1], TS[2]; ~, AT
336.17–18 retarding‿] TS[1], TS[2]; ~, AT
336.19   another point] TS[1], AT; the other TS[2]
336.19   it] TS[1], AT; this TS[2]
336.19–20 the writer] TS[1], AT; they TS[2]
336.21   Smith] TS[1], TS[2]; Governor Smith AT
336.21   campaign] TS[1], TS[2]; recent campaign AT
336.22   gentleman] AT; gentlemean TS[2], TS[1]
336.27   goes on to say that] TS[1], AT; that TS[2]
336.30   why I for] TS[1], TS[2]; I for AT
336.31   cause] AT; cuase TS[2], TS[1]

336.38   cannot] TS[1], TS[2]; can not AT
336.39   Teachers∧ Union] TS[1], TS[2]; teachers' unions AT
336.40–337.1   and consequences] TS[1]; the effect and consequences
          TS[2]; the consequences AT
337.4   say that I] TS[1], AT; say, I TS[2]
337.4–5   the Teachers∧ Union] TS[1]; our Teachers∧ Union TS[2]; the
          teachers' unions AT

Labor Politics and Labor Education

Copy-text is the article's publication in *New Republic* 57 (9 January
1929): 211–14.

338.19   Executive Council] W; executive council

Apostles of World Unity: XVII—Salmon O. Levinson

Copy-text is the article's publication in *World Unity Magazine* 4 (May
1929): 98–103.

352.28   1925] W; 1922
352.29   Be] W; be
353.16   Léger] W; Leger

The School and Society

Copy-text for this review is its publication in *New Republic* 58 (10
April 1929): 231–32.

371.29   bequeaths] WS; bequeathes
371.30   of prejudices] WS; or prejudices

An Organic Universe

Copy-text for this review is its publication in *New York Sun*, 26 October 1929.

375.19   endeavour] WS; endeavor
378.4–5   of systematic] WS; or systematic

378.19   conspicuous] W; conspicious
378.39   categorial] W; categoreal
379.11   thing] W; things
380.8   existences] W; existence
380.12   mathematical] W; matematical

The Course of Modern History

Copy-text for this review is its publication in *World Tomorrow* 13 (December 1930): 522–23.

382.5   book] W; Book

Foreword to *Tolstoy and Nietzsche*

Copy-text for this essay is its publication in Helen Edna Davis, *Tolstoy and Nietzsche: A Problem in Biographical Ethics* (New York: New Republic, 1929), pp. ix–xiv.

398.26   Sunday] W; sunday

Foreword to *Foundation of Commercial Education*

Copy-text for this article is its publication in Eastern Commercial Teachers' Association First Yearbook, *Foundation of Commercial Education* (New York: Eastern Commercial Teachers' Association, 1929), pp. xiii–xiv.

401.5   the fact] W; that fact

Introduction to *The Organization of Knowledge and the System of the Sciences*

Copy-text for this essay is its publication in Henry Evelyn Bliss, *The Organization of Knowledge and the System of the Sciences* (New York: Henry Holt and Co., 1929), pp. vii–ix.

405.27   unforeseen] W; unforsen

Introduction to *Humanity Uprooted*

Copy-text for this essay is its publication in Maurice Hindus, *Humanity Uprooted* (New York: Jonathan Cape and Harrison Smith, 1929), pp. xv–xix.

408.27   ardor] W; ardour
408.33   fervor] W; fervour
409.19   labors] W; labours

In Response

Copy-text is the article's publication in *John Dewey, the Man and His Philosophy: Addresses Delivered in New York in Celebration of His Seventieth Birthday* (Cambridge: Harvard University Press, 1930), pp. 173–81.

422.20–21   possessions] W; possesions

Tribute to James H. Tufts

Copy-text for this tribute is the typescript in the Max C. Otto Papers, State Historical Society of Wisconsin, Madison, Wisconsin. Dewey's alterations in the typescript appear in "Alterations in 'Tribute to James H. Tufts.'"

425.9, 14   Mr.] W; Mr‸
425.13   divorce] W; dovorce

Asks Federal Fund to Aid Unemployed

Copy-text for this statement is its publication in *New York Times*, 12 May 1930, p. 35.

434.13   cooperation,"] W; ~‸

Asks Hoover to Act on Unemployment

Copy-text is the letter's publication in *New York Times*, 21 July 1930,

p. 17 (NYT). The inclusion of three paragraphs for its publication in *Congressional Digest* 10 (August 1931): 212 (CD) has been accepted in the present edition.

436.1   Asks . . . Unemployment] *stet* NYT; Should America Adopt
           a System of Compulsory Unemployment Insurance? CD
436.2–10   Professor . . . said:] *stet* NYT; [*not present*] CD
436.13   you will] *stet* NYT; the President CD
436.18   session] *stet* NYT; sessions CD
437.14–38 "On . . . employment.] CD; [*not present*] NYT
437.14   "On] W; ∧~ CD; [*not present*] NYT
437.23   "The] W; ∧~ CD; [*not present*] NYT
437.30   "No] W; ∧~ CD; [*not present*] NYT
438.9–11   "For . . . closed."] *stet* NYT; [*om.*] CD

Dewey Asks Norris to Lead New Party

Copy-text is the letter's publication in *New York Times*, 26 December 1930, p. 1 (NYT). It was republished in *News Bulletin of the League for Independent Political Action* 1 (January 1931): 1–2 (NB).

444.1   Dewey . . . Party] *stet* NYT; The League Challenges the In-
           surgents NB
444.19   party," Dr. Dewey wrote, "I] *stet* NYT; party, I NB
445.3   rein] W; reign NYT, NB
446.14   march?"] *stet* NYT; march?∧ / Faithfully yours, / "John
           Dewey, / "Chairman National Committee." NB

Alterations in Typescripts

In three of the four lists that follow appear Dewey's changes both at the typewriter and by hand in the typescripts for "James Marsh and American Philosophy," "Three Independent Factors in Morals," and "Tribute to James H. Tufts." In the list for the typescript (not typed by Dewey) "Freedom in Workers' Education," appear Dewey's handwritten alterations, which were all made in pencil. All Dewey's alterations made in the course of writing and revision appear here except for strengthened letters to clarify a word, irrelevant typed letters attached to a word, false starts for the same word, transposition of letters in a legible word, and mendings over illegible letters. Dewey's corrections of typographical errors, whether by typing over or marking over by hand, are also not recorded as alterations, except when the possibility exists that the error might have been another word or the start of another word rather than a simple typographical mistake. The word(s) before the bracket refers to the original typescript; if the typescript has been emended or the spelling regularized, a grid # before the entry means the reading of the present edition is in the Emendations List.

For Dewey's alterations, which appear to the right of the bracket, the abbreviation *del.* is used to show material marked out in ink except when pencil is specifically mentioned; any alteration noted as *added* is also in ink unless pencil is specified. For interlineations, use of *intrl.* alone always means a typewritten interlineation. All carets were made by hand; when a caret accompanies a typewritten interlineation, it is in ink unless pencil is noted. When carets are used with handwritten alterations, they are in the same medium as the alteration. For material deleted at the typewriter, *x'd-out* is used. The abbreviation *alt.* is used to identify material altered in some way from an earlier form of the word; if altered by hand, the medium is given; if the medium is not mentioned, it is to be assumed the alteration was typewritten. The abbreviation *undrl.* applies to underlining in ink unless pencil is specified.

With respect to position, when an addition is a simple interlineation, the formula is *intrl.* or *intrl. w. caret.* When a deletion positions the interlineation, *intrl.* is dropped and the formula reads *ab. del.* 'xyz'; *w.*

caret ab. del. 'xyz'; or *ab. x'd-out* 'xyz.' *Ab.* means interlined above without a caret unless a caret is specified; *bel.* means interlined below without a caret unless mentioned; *ov.* means inscribed over the original letters, not interlined. The abbreviations *bef.* (before) and *aft.* (after) signal a change made on the same line, whether the original line or interline. The abbreviated word *insrtd.* (inserted) refers to marginal additions that cannot be called interlineations but are of the same nature.

In alterations involving more than one line, the solidus / signals the end of a line. When an alteration itself has been revised, that revision is transcribed between square brackets immediately following the single word alteration to which it refers.

Alterations in "James Marsh and American Philosophy"

178.4	these]	'e' *ov.* 'o'
178.5	important]	*intrl. in ink w. caret*
178.10	Marsh,]	*comma in ink ov. period*
#178.8	brings]	*aft. x'd-out* 'we are'
178.10	appreciate]	*aft. x'd-out* 'realize'
178.13	the now]	*aft. x'd-out* 'our present'
178.18	Teutonic]	*intrl.*
178.19	from the]	*bef. x'd-out* 'southern,'
178.20	Fortunately]	*aft. x'd-out* 'In'
178.24	removes]	's' *ov.* 'd'
178.25	within' ".]	*period x'd-out aft. single quote*
179.8	the infinite]	'the' *intrl.*
179.17	Spanish]	*aft. x'd-out* 'Germ'
179.21–22	an extensive . . . their]	*bel. x'd-out* 'I shall not go into detail, but it is not too much'
179n.4	Jan.]	*intrl.*
180.7	currents of]	*bef. x'd-out* 'Christia'
180.12	grasp]	*aft. x'd-out* 'rea'
180.12–13	its influence in its own time]	*ab. x'd-out* 'import'
180.15	period]	*aft. x'd-out* 'day before'
180.16	science]	*aft. x'd-out* 'physical'
180.16	left]	*aft. x'd-out* 'made any'
180.17	when]	*ab. x'd-out* 'before'
180.21	little]	*aft. x'd-out* 'with'
180.22	indifference.]	*bef. x'd-out* 'The'
181.2	motives]	*aft. x'd-out* 'reasons'

181.11   The latter] *aft. x'd-out* 'One question'
181.17   of Scripture] 'f' *ov.* 'n'
181.27   in] *aft. x'd-out* 'by'
181.35   English] *intrl.*
181.40   philosophical] 'phil' *ov.* 'rati'
182.2   conspired to] *aft. del.* 'combined to'
182.5   Mill,] *intrl.*
182.11   whose] 'os' *ov.* 'ic'
182.11   reason] *aft. x'd-out* 'in'
182.27   as] *intrl. in ink w. caret*
183.11   to which I now turn] *intrl.*
183.11   positive] *intrl.*
183.13   1822] '8' *in ink ov.* '9'
183.13   allusion] *ab. x'd-out* 'attention'
183.14   cause] *bef. x'd-out* 'from'
183.16   modern] *aft. x'd-out* 'the'
183.23   attempt] *aft. x'd-out* 'find'
183.28 – 29   As . . . can] *ab. undel.* 'As I have already impo indi-
          cated' *x'd-out* 'such a view canno'
183.31   upon] *aft. x'd-out* 'which'
183.33   as we have also noted] *intrl.*
183.33   "Understanding"] 'U' *ov.* 'u'
184.4   he] *intrl.*
184.5   I] *aft. x'd-out* 'for'
184.6   the expression] *aft. x'd-out* 'some'
184.11   and humble] *intrl.*
184.13   instinct.] *aft. x'd-out* 'virus'
184.21   as] *aft. x'd-out* 'that'
184.22   was] *aft. x'd-out* 'made'
184.28   his] *aft. x'd-out* 'that'
184.33   venture to] *intrl.*
184.35   conviction] *intrl.*
#184.40   by Aristotle] 'by' *in ink ov.* 'of'
185.9   of him] *intrl.*
185.30   necessary] *aft. x'd-out* 'a'
185.34 – 35   a rational] *aft. x'd-out* 'science of'
185.36   exist] *final* 's' *x'd-out*
186.2   imposed by] *ab. x'd-out* 'of'
186.5   occur] *bef. x'd-out comma*
186.5 – 6   mathematics] *aft. x'd-out* 'form the'
186.11   entire] *bef. x'd-out* 'natural'
186.11   philosophy] *final period x'd-out*
186.18   create] *aft. x'd-out* 'lead to'

186.20   called the] *bef. x'd-out* 'inherent'
186.21   series] *ab. x'd-out* 'approach'
186.21   of] *ab. x'd-out* 'to through'
186.22   will] *bef. x'd-out comma*
186.24   run] *intrl.*
186.28   in] *bef. x'd-out* 'a'
186.28   the rational] 'the' *intrl.*
186.35   mind] *ab. x'd-out* 'spirit'
186.36   sense] *bef. x'd-out comma*
187.2   abiding] *intrl.*
187.12   the relating] *aft. x'd-out* 'our'
187.18   This] 'i' *ov.* 'u'
187.20   that] *aft. x'd-out* 'this agency'
187.34   the] *final* 're' *x'd-out*
188.1–2   and the . . . themselves,] *intrl.*
188.4   terminate] *ab. x'd-out* 'sensibility'
188.6   both] *aft. x'd-out* 'the'
#188.7   as found] *intrl.*
188.9   conditions] *bef. x'd-out* 'and the material'
188.10   upon] *aft. x'd-out* 'for'
188.28   classic] *intrl. w. caret*
188.28   an] *final* 'n' *added*
188.29   *will*] *undrl.*
188.32   rational] *intrl.*
188.37   or] *ab. undel.* 'of'
189.18   it] *final* 'self' *x'd-out*
189.26   equation] 't' *ov.* 'l'
189.27   way] *intrl.*
189.31   can] *aft. x'd-out* 'be'
190.7   (although] *parenthesis in ink ov. comma*
190.8   concerns)] *parenthesis in ink ov. comma*
190.8   to] *in ink ov.* 'in'
190.14–15 in this] *aft. x'd-out* 'upon'
190.31   daring] *aft. x'd-out* 'courage'
190.34   institute] 'e' *ov.* 'i' *bef. x'd-out* 'on'; 'e' *intrl. ab. undel.* 'e'
190.38   original] *aft. x'd-out* 'immedi'
190.38   clerks] 'a' *x'd-out aft.* 'e'
191.1   physiology] *aft. x'd-out* 'jurisprudence,'
191.2   civil and military] *intrl.*
191.7   trunk] *bef. x'd-out comma*
191.11   established] *aft. x'd-out* 'church'
191.22   like] *ab. x'd-out* 'parallel'
191.26   University] 'U' *ov.* 'u'

191.28   in effect]   *intrl.*

191.39   and common]   *intrl.*

191.41   West]   'W' *ov.* 'w'

191.41   and the]   *final* 'y' *x'd-out*

192.9   and happiness]   'an' *ov.* 'of'

192.19   to be]   *intrl. w. caret*

192.27   the principles]   'th' *ov.* 'hi'

192.28   conditions]   *aft. x'd-out* 'nee'

192.32   idea]   *aft. x'd-out* 'princi'

193.4   expressed]   *ab. x'd-out* 'contained'

193.7   older]   *intrl.*

193.16   idea]   *final* 's' *x'd-out*

193.26   pioneer]   *intrl.*

193.32   an]   *aft. x'd-out* 'the'

193.40   surrender]   *aft. x'd-out* 'approximation'

194.1   European]   *intrl.*

194.5   of citizens]   *intrl.*

194.10   as]   *intrl.*

194.13   bred in Vermonters]   *intrl.*

194.13   that I]   *aft. x'd-out* 'bred'

194.16   form]   *aft. x'd-out* 'fixed'

194.22   in words]   *aft. x'd-out* 'the'

194.39   more]   *aft. x'd-out* 'the'

195.3   the latter's]   *aft. x'd-out* 'his o'

195.16   invigorate and sharpen]   'gorate and sharpen' *intrl.*

195.19   minute]   *intrl.*

195.27   letter]   *aft. x'd-out* 'formal'

#195.28–29   in education]   *aft. x'd-out* 'her'

195.33   were]   *aft. x'd-out* 'is the'

195.38   to try]   *aft. x'd-out* 'rather'

195.39   that of]   *intrl.*

195n.1–2   of the eighteen forties]   *intrl.*

196.1   discloses]   *aft. x'd-out* 'reveals'

196.3   always]   'wa' *ov.* 'so'

196.5   received]   *aft. x'd-out* 'accepted'

196.8   because of]   *ab. x'd-out* 'in'

196.10   the]   *final* 'ir' *x'd-out*

196.15   was the]   't' *ov.* 'a'

196.16   as well]   *aft. x'd-out* 'in accordance wit'

196.21   In]   *ov.* 'By'

196.36   use]   *aft. x'd-out* 'arouse'

196.40   in his]   'in' *ov.* 'to'

196.41   a wistful] *aft. x'd-out* 'humane and vital.'
196.41   ordered] *ab. x'd-out* 'organized'

Alterations in "Three Independent Factors in Morals"

283.8   completion] *aft. x'd-out* 'goods cml'
283.11   Reason] 'R' *ov.* 'r'
283.12   which] *bef. x'd-out* 'tele'
283.15   entertained] *bef. x'd-out* 'in th'
283.20   phase] *ab. x'd-out* 'aspect'
283.24   the strictly] *aft. x'd-out* 'first'
283.30   The] 'T' *ov.* 'A'
284.1   achieve] *aft. x'd-out* 'effec'
284.4   afford] *final* 's' *del.*
284.5   we] *aft. x'd-out* 'the'
284.10   compelling] *aft. x'd-out* 'forcin'
284.18   means] *bef. x'd-out period*
284.18   scheme] *final* 's' *x'd-out*
284.23   make] *aft. x'd-out* 'issue'
284.25   in] *intrl. aft. x'd-out* 'for'
284.27   process] *aft. x'd-out* 'operation'
284.29   in] *intrl.*
284.29   interest] *aft. x'd-out* 'prpose'
284.33   without] 'out' *intrl. w. caret*
284.34   those] 'o' *ov.* 'e'
284.36–37   as far . . . protest] *intrl.*
285.4   teleological] *intrl. w. caret aft.* 'rational'
285.7   as] *intrl. in ink w. caret*
#285.8   it, expresses] 'i' *ov. comma*
285.9   an] *intrl. w. caret*
285.10   emotional] *aft. x'd-out* 'sanction'
285.19   thus] *intrl. in ink*
285.19–20   demand] *aft. x'd-out* 'claim to which'
285.21   acknowledges] *bef. x'd-out* 'moral authrity in'
#285.21   claim,] *bef. x'd-out* 'and not'
285.21   to possess . . . express] *intrl.*
285.22   convenient] *bef. x'd-out comma*
#285.27–28   thrugh habituation] *intrl.*
285.35   making] *aft. x'd-out* 'havi'
285.36   other] *final* 's' *x'd-out*
286.6   empirical] *aft. x'd-out* 'facts.'

286.7   Acts] *aft. x'd-out* 'Things approved'

286.9   Praise] 'P' *ov.* 'p' *aft. x'd-out* 'No'

286.12   heroic] *bef. del. comma*

286.12   else] *intrl. in ink w. caret*

286.17   calculated] *aft. x'd-out* 'rea'

#286.20–21   sanitions] *aft. x'd-out* 'penalties'; 'c' *x'd-out aft. first* 'n'

286.24   the virtuous] *ab. x'd-out* 'they'

286.24   differs] 's' *ab. x'd-out* 'e'

286.25   repeat,] *comma added*

286.27   widespread] *aft. x'd-out* 'a'

286.29   follow] *aft. x'd-out* 'read'

286.30–31   existence] *aft. x'd-out* 'fact'

286.38   obligation] *final* 's' *del.*

287.1   the tendency to seek for] *intrl.*

287.1   general] *final* 'l' *x'd-out*

287.6   purposes,] *bef. x'd-out* 'or to attach great'

287.7   public] *intrl.*

287.7   acknowledged] *aft. x'd-out* 'publicly'

287.7–8   that form] *ab. x'd-out* 'embodied in'

287.9   independent] *aft. x'd-out* 'individ'

287.14   moral] *aft. x'd-out* 'any'

287.21   licit,] *intrl.*

287.24   What is] *in ink w. caret ab. del.* 'The'

287.24   from the standpoint of] *in ink ab. del.* 'for'

287.25   wrong] *intrl. in ink w. caret aft. x'd-out* 'forbiiden' *del.* 'denied'

287.25–26   demands; . . . opinion] *in ink ab. del.* 'claims over [*intrl.* 'the' *del.*] behavior of the individual.'

287.27   Each] *in ink ov.* 'The'

287.28   opposing factors] *in ink ab. del.* 'two.'

287.29   nevertheless] *in ink ab. del.* 'at the same time'

287.32   children] 'ren' *intrl. in ink; aft. del.* 'almost every'

287.33   or is] 'is' *intrl. in ink w. caret*

287.34   giving evidence] *in ink ab. del.* 'an exhibition'

287.35–36   rational goods and of] *intrl. w. caret*

287.36   publicly acknowledged] *insrtd. and intrl. in ink*

287.37   stands] *aft. del.* 'at least' *x'd-out* 'is'

287.40   In] *aft. x'd-out* 'I sh'

288.2   cause] *ab. x'd-out* 'source'

288.4–5   outcome] *aft. x'd-out* 'result'

288.16–17   Personally . . . be] *ab. x'd-out* 'John Dewey.'

288.18   lead] *aft. x'd-out* 'conduce to'

Alterations in "Freedom in Workers' Education" *

331.5   But] 'B' *ov.* 'b'
331.5   it] 'i' *ab. del.* 'I'
331.7   cause;] *comma alt. to semicolon*
331.9   pleasure] *bef. del.* 'to me'
331.11   was not] 'was' *intrl. w. caret*
331.11   merely] *bef. del.* 'as'
331.16   joy,] *comma added*
331.17   and you] 'you' *ab. del.* 'you feel you'
331.18   pleasure in] *bef. del.* 'and no possibility of'
331.19   indeed] *intrl. w. caret*
331.20   rather] *bef. del.* 'there is'
331.20   regret.] *period added*
331.20   For] *w. caret ab. del.* 'and'
331.22   taken] *bef. del.* 'an'
331.24   incident] *aft. del.* 'particular'
331.24   at Brookwood] *intrl. w. caret*
331.27   straightforward] *marked to close up*
331.28   impartial] *aft. del.* 'honest and'
332.1   assurance;] *comma alt. to semicolon*
332.5   but of] 'f' *ov.* 'n'
332.5   it,] *comma added*
332.5   namely] *aft. del.* 'that I wish to talk,'
332.5   what] *aft. del.* 'on'
332.6   it,] *w. caret ab. del.* 'that,'
332.6–7   of the] 'e' *ov.* 'is'
#332.7   and the Am] *ab. del.* ', this Teachers''
332.7   of Labor] *intrl. w. caret*
332.9   I] *aft. del.* 'Now'
332.12   real education,] *comma added*
332.13–14 academic freedom] *bef. del. comma*
332.14   is] *intrl. w. caret aft.* 'freedom'
332.14   and hence it is] *w. caret ab. del.* 'is an'
332.15   and upon] 'upon' *intrl. w. caret*
332.15   possibility] 'y' *ov.* 'ies'
332.21   an] *intrl. w. caret*
332.27   conducted,] *period alt. to comma*
332.28   tonight,] *semicolon alt. to comma bef. del.* 'you can gather from'

* Since all alterations in "Freedom in Workers' Education" are in pencil, the medium has not been specified.

332.28   from] *insrtd. bef.* 'the letter'
332.28   read (and] *parenthesis ov. semicolon*
332.29   other] *aft. del.* 'the'
332.29   graduates)] *parenthesis added*
332.29   you would] *aft. del.* 'or from the alumni over here,'
332.30   idea.] *ab. del.* 'testimony.'
332.33   their] 'ir' *added*
332.33   are] *aft. del.* 'of organized labor'
332.34   any] *ov.* 'this'
332.37   deliberate] *aft. del.* 'these'
332.39   What] 'W' *ov.* 'w' *aft. del.* 'I am sure that'
333.3   conducting] *w. caret ab. del.* 'basing'
333.4   spirit.] *insrtd. aft.* 'that'
333.9   them] *insrtd. aft. del.* 'those facts'
333.12   Those] *aft. del.* 'It seems to me that ignoring details and / technicalities that may be brough up relative to academic freedom or to freedom of / teaching, that it is the school in its relation to the labor movement that is the / real issue.'
333.16   be;] *comma alt. to semicolon*
333.17   breathe] *w. caret ab. del.* 'create'
333.17   them] *intrl. w. caret*
333.18   and] *ov.* 'or'
333.18   they] *w. caret ab. del.* 'it'
333.20   discourage,] *comma added*
333.23   investigation] *aft. del.* 'mind,'
333.25   officials (I] *parenthesis ov. comma*
#333.26 labor,)] *parenthesis added*
333.26   should] *intrl. w. caret*
333.29   freedom,] *comma added*
333.29   a cause] *w. caret ab. del.* 'which I have said is'
333.31   by] *aft. del.* 'perhaps'
333.34   incident;] *comma alt. to semicolon*
334.31   that] *aft. del.* 'the'
334.33   hand,] *comma added*
334.33   labor] *aft. del.* 'the'
334.34   unions and] 'and' *ov. comma*
334.34   effective,] *comma added*
334.35   these] *aft. del.* 'that'
334.35–36 themselves,] *comma added*
334.36   this] *insrtd. aft. del.* 'that their'
334.36   involves] *aft. del.* 'of them'
335.3   capable.] *comma alt. to period*
335.3   If] *aft. del.* 'that it is / capable of expansion to that extent.'

335.4   I] *aft. del.* 'in our public schools,'
335.4   nearly] *w. caret ab. del.* 'over'
335.5   Since the system] *w. caret ab. del.* 'They'
335.5   has] 's' *ov.* 've'
335.6   desired] *bef. del.* 'and they are not / meeting these special
          needs.'
335.6   there] 't' *ov.* 'T'
335.6   need] *bef. del.* 'then'
335.8   show] *aft. del.* 'which will'
335.8   do. And] *comma alt. to period;* 'A' *ov.* 'a'
335.9   work] *bef. del.* 'of'
335.10   pioneer,] *comma added*
335.10   so as] *intrl.*
335.11–12 undertake;] *comma alt. to semicolon*
335.12   something] 'thing' *intrl. w. caret*
335.12   road] *bef. del.* 'at least'
335.13   of activity] 'of' *ov.* 'and'
335.14   effort] *insrtd.*
335.14   of the] *aft. del.* 'interest'
335.15   public] *aft. del.* 'these'
335.20   of] *ab.* 'boasted'
335.20   including] *w. caret ab. del.* 'and'
335.22   control.] *comma alt. to period bef. del.* 'that'
335.22   They] 'T' *ov.* 't'
#335.22–23 & subsidized] '&' *intrl. w. caret*
335.25   classes;] *comma alt. to semicolon*
335.26   utilities] *aft. del.* 'these'
335.29   good] *bef. del.* 'Now'
335.29   That] 'T' *ov.* 't'
335.30   companies] *bef. del.* 'itself'
335.35   to engage in] *intrl. w. caret*
335.37   the] *insrtd. aft.* 'not of'
335.38   officials.] *bef. del.* 'of organized labor.'
336.2   could] 'c' *ov.* 'w'
336.3   general] *bef. del.* 'to'
336.3   to it] *intrl. w. caret*
#336.7   agreemnt. But] *comma alt. to period;* 'B' *ov.* 'b'
336.13   a situation] 'a' *ov.* 'the'
336.19   take] *bef. del.* 'the'
336.19   another] 'an' *intrl. w. caret*
336.19   point] *intrl. w. caret*
336.19   it] *ab. del.* 'this'
336.19–20 the writer] *w. caret ab. del.* 'they'

336.27   goes on to say] *intrl. w. caret*
336.40   competency,] *bef. del.* 'the effect'
337.4   say] *comma del.*
337.4   that] *intrl. w. caret*
337.4   the] *insrtd. aft.* 'joined'
337.4–5   Teachers] *aft. del.* 'our'

Alterations in "Tribute to James H. Tufts"

424.3   suggestion] *bef. del. comma*
424.11   in the] 'i' *ov.* 'I'
424.17   Tufts'] *apostrophe ov.* 's'
424.17   work,] *comma added*
424.17   me,] *comma added*
424.20   definitely] *intrl. w. caret*
424.22   extraordinarily] 'ily' *w. caret ab. x'd-out* 'y'
424.22   judicial,] *comma added*
424.22–23   honest] *aft. del.* 'and'
425.2   its] 'it' *in ink ov.* 'hi'
425.3   with] *in ink ov.* 'of'
425.5–6   for example] *intrl. w. caret*
425.6   remains] *bef. x'd-out* 'as'
425.10   What] *aft. illeg. letters added in ink*
425.12   wisdom] *intrl.*
425.15   it] *intrl. in ink w. caret*

Line-end Hyphenation

I. Copy-text list.

The following are the editorially established forms of possible compounds that were hyphenated at the ends of lines in the copy-text:

7.13	class-room	131.33	ready-made
8.40	school-room	134.4	overdeveloped
19.13	over-excitability	142.17	reshaped
19.24	deep-seated	152.8	single-hearted
19.31	class-rooms	166.24	non-psychological
22.5	arm-chair	172.31	ready-made
22.7	field-work	174.12	sideline
22.38	one-sided	176.36	over-technicality
24.25	subject-matter	215.7	self-evidence
25.34	one-sided	228.11	double-barrelled
31.22	subject-matter	229.5	subject-matter
47.12	self-centered	230.31	subject-matter
49.19	intercommunication	231.9	subject-matter
58.7	to-day	231.13	subject-matter
58.10	war-cry	238.5	intercommunication
59.34	interpurchase	245.9	subject-matter
68.20	stock-market	245.24−25	quasi-mathematical
74.39	self-control	247.36	subject-matter
77.5−6	pre-scientific	248.14	ready-made
92.9	interdependent	249.31	subject-matter
93.30	super-power	270.7	steamship
96.10	large-scale	281.7	self-realization
104.40	widespread	291.25−26	second-hand
109.25	remaking	302.18	classroom
111.25	reproduce	303.27	subject-matter
116.10−11	self-interest	305.4	subject-matter
123.1	marked-off	305.11	non-articulation
128.33	ready-made	317.7	cooperation

322.16	ready-made	421.30	armor-plate
326.15	goodwill	439.26–27	reemployed
327.18	subject-matter	442.26	reorganization
332.40	commonplace	449.1	coordinating
372.35	class-room	449.4–5	goodwill
397.7	sub-human		

II. Critical-text list.

In transcriptions from the present edition, no line-end hyphens in ambiguously broken possible compounds are to be retained except the following:

16.31	subject-matter	202.1	self-identical
22.1	arm-chair	209.4	re-disposition
25.32	non-educational	216.34	self-subsistent
31.19	subject-matter	219.35	end-term
70.29	forward-looking	224.17	subject-matter
77.5	pre-scientific	235.11	end-terms
82.14	"radio-conscious"	245.24	quasi-mathematical
92.4	monkey-wrench	250.30	rounded-out
116.10	self-interest	265.6	anti-romantic
133.3	so-called	272.11	all-embracing
138.39	so-called	291.25	second-hand
147.7	key-stone	311.19	census-takers
149.6	class-room	314.6	well-equipped
149.32	over-estimated	315.1	self-evident
150.20	non-theological	316.33	"Self-help"
152.8	whole-souled	356.29	anti-religious
172.15	cross-fertilizations	374.16	class-room
187.22	self-conscious	377.38	pre-established
193.12	self-governing	379.27	thorough-going
194.4	self-governing	401.16	far-reaching
199.38	subject-matter	405.11	subject-matters
201.7	self-consistent		

Substantive Variants in Quotations

Dewey's substantive variants in quotations have been considered important enough to warrant this special list. Dewey represented source material in varying ways, from memorial paraphrase to verbatim copy, in some places citing his source fully, in others mentioning only authors' names, and, in still others, omitting documentation altogether. All material inside quotation marks, except that obviously being emphasized or restated, has been searched out; Dewey's citations have been verified and, when necessary, emended. All quotations have been retained as they appear in the copy-text, with the exceptions recorded in the Emendations List. Therefore, it is necessary to consult the Emendations List in conjunction with this list.

Although Dewey, like other scholars of the period, was unconcerned about precision in matters of form, many of the changes in quotations may well have occurred in the printing process. For example, comparing Dewey's quotations with the originals reveals that some editors and compositors house-styled the quoted materials as well as Dewey's own. Therefore, in the present edition, the spelling and capitalization of the source have been restored; these changes are recorded in the Emendations List with the symbol WS (Works—the present edition—emendations derived from Dewey's Source). Similarly, in cases of possible compositorial or typographical errors, changes in substantives or accidentals that restore original readings are noted as WS emendations. Dewey frequently changed or omitted punctuation in quoted material; if it has been necessary to restore the punctuation of the source, these changes are also recorded in the Emendations List with the symbol WS.

Dewey often did not indicate that he had omitted material from his source. Omitted short phrases appear in this list; omissions of more than one line are noted by a bracketed ellipsis [. . .]. Italics in source material have been treated as substantives; both Dewey's omitted and added italics are noted here.

Differences between Dewey's quotations and the source attributable to the context in which the quotation appears, such as changes in number or tense, are not recorded.

In cases where Dewey translated the source, the reference appears in the Checklist of Dewey's References, but no variants in the quotation are included here.

Notations in this section follow the formula: page-line number from the present edition, followed by the lemma, then a bracket. After the bracket, the original form appears, followed by the author's surname, shortened source-title from the Checklist of Dewey's References, and the page-line reference to the source, all in parentheses.

Individualism, Old and New

46.29	shabby] these shabby (Lynd and Lynd, *Middletown*, 103.1)
46.31	However] Here, too, as at so many other points (Lynd and Lynd, *Middletown*, 103.3–4)
51n.4	the self] ego (Freienfels, *Mysteries of Soul*, 287.9)
51n.4	the universe] universe (Freienfels, *Mysteries of Soul*, 287.9)
53.15	how] rather how (Freienfels, *Mysteries of Soul*, 292.30)
53.15	through them] through it (Freienfels, *Mysteries of Soul*, 292.30–31)
53.15–16	transcend them] transcend it (Freienfels, *Mysteries of Soul*, 292.31)
72n.2	order and] order, I said, and (Frank, *Re-discovery of America*, 210.9)
113.23	civilization] civilisations (Ferrero, *Ancient Rome*, 6.25)
122.19	is everywhere] everywhere is (Emerson, "Self-Reliance," 51.20)
122.20	against] against the manhood of every one of (Emerson, "Self-Reliance," 51.21)

James Marsh and American Philosophy

178.24	modern] human (Marsh, "Present Literature of Italy," 109.7)
179.3	world] living world (Marsh, "Present Literature of Italy," 107.16)
179.3	in] inward (Marsh, "Present Literature of Italy," 107.17)
179.3–4	himself. All] himself [. . .] all (Marsh, "Present Literature of Italy," 107.17–34)

179.7	last] length (Marsh, "Present Literature of Italy," 107.37)
179.7	its own] its (Marsh, "Present Literature of Italy," 107.38)
180.40	simulacrum] [*ital.*] (Mill, *Dissertations and Discussions*, 48.16)
183.4	which] that (Coleridge, *Aids to Reflection*, xliv.29)
183.26	have] have rationally (Coleridge, *Aids to Reflection*, xx.12)
185.39	possibility] [*ital.*] (Marsh, *Remains*, 192.10)
185.39–40	possible determinations] [*ital.*] (Marsh, *Remains*, 192.10)
185.40	quantity] [*ital.*] (Marsh, *Remains*, 192.11)
185.40	form] *figure* (Marsh, *Remains*, 192.11)
185.40	objects] object (Marsh, *Remains*, 192.11)
189.37	presented] as presented (Marsh, *Remains*, 387.10)
189.39	is] was (Marsh, *Remains*, 387.13)
191.2	and civil and military architecture,] of military and civil architecture, of the physical sciences, (Coleridge, *On Constitution*, 49.22–24)
191.2–3	their common organ] the common organ of the preceding (Coleridge, *On Constitution*, 49.24–25)
191.3	arts] so called liberal arts (Coleridge, *On Constitution*, 49.25–26)
191.4	nation] country (Coleridge, *On Constitution*, 49.28)
191.7	trunk] the trunk (Coleridge, *On Constitution*, 51.14)
191.7	knowledge of civilized] knowledges that civilized (Coleridge, *On Constitution*, 51.14–15)
191.9	forming] forming, collectively, (Coleridge, *On Constitution*, 51.18)
192.6	body] a body (Marsh, *Remains*, 607.20–21)
194.27	separate] separable (Marsh, *Remains*, 599.16–17)
194.29–30	principle] presence (Marsh, *Remains*, 599.19–20)
195.4	are] were (Marsh, *Remains*, 79.4)
195.8	more] considerable more (Marsh, *Remains*, 80.3)
195.10	in] itself in (Marsh, *Remains*, 80.6)
195.36	individuals] individuals theoretically and politically (Marsh, *Remains*, 564.19–20)
195.36	level] level, and (Marsh, *Remains*, 564.20)
196.19	thraldom of sense] thraldom and lethargy of sense (Marsh, *Remains*, 594.31)

The Sphere of Application of the Excluded Middle

199.1   the past] the character of the present (Nagel, "Intui-
               tion," 488.20–21)

The Applicability of Logic to Existence

204.3   that are] which are (Nagel, "Can Logic Be Divorced?"
               708.25) [*Later Works* 5 : 456.17]
204.4–5   metaphysics] ontology (Nagel, "Can Logic Be Di-
               vorced?" 709.8–9) [*Later Works* 5 : 457.7]
205.14   things] the nature of things (Nagel, "Can Logic Be Di-
               vorced?" 711.6–7) [*Later Works* 5 : 459.17–18]
205.30   does or] meets or (Nagel, "Can Logic Be Divorced?"
               710.38) [*Later Works* 5 : 459.4]
205.30   those] these (Nagel, "Can Logic Be Divorced?" 710.38)
               [*Later Works* 5 : 459.5]
206.4   shut] not-open (Dewey, "Sphere of Application,"
               705.7–8) [*Later Works* 5 : 201.37]
206.36   should take place] should take place to-morrow (Na-
               gel, "Can Logic Be Divorced?" 712.10) [*Later Works*
               5 : 460.25–26]
206.38   should or should not take place] should or should not
               take place to-morrow (Nagel, "Can Logic Be Divorced?"
               712.12) [*Later Works* 5 : 460.27–28]

In Reply to Some Criticisms

211.37   only . . . known] [*ital.*] (Woodbridge, "Experience and
               Dialectic," 267.15) [*Later Works* 5 : 490.38–491.1]
212.11   exists] to exist (Woodbridge, "Experience and Dialec-
               tic," 267.20) [*Later Works* 5 : 491.5]
212.11   *its*] [*rom.*] (Woodbridge, "Experience and Dialectic,"
               267.20) [*Later Works* 5 : 491.6]
215.27   as a] for an implement or (Hocking, "Action and Cer-
               tainty," 232.38) [*Later Works* 5 : 470.5–6]
216.16   *discovering*] [*rom.*] (Hocking, "Action and Certainty,"
               236.6) [*Later Works* 5 : 473.36]

Conduct and Experience

222n.4   maze training] maze behavior (Hunter, "Psychology and
            Anthroponomy," 103.26)
223.17–18   status] state (Woodworth, "Dynamic Psychology,"
            124.24)
235.7   eventually be] be eventually (Lewis, *Mind and World-
            Order,* 5.8)
235.12   —Y] —the Y (Lewis, *Mind and World-Order,*
            5.14–15)
235.16   consists] lies (Lewis, *Mind and World-Order,* 5.24)

Qualitative Thought

259.40   form] form, say (Bradley, *Logic,* 333.19)

What Humanism Means to Me

263.29   the belief] that belief of which he seems never to have
            doubted, (Pater, *Renaissance,* 49.19–20)

What I Believe

273.31   when men] when *men* (New Testament, Matt. 5:11)
273.32   persecute you] persecute *you* (New Testament, Matt.
            5:11)

Philosophy and Education

296.32   concerning] in (Coulter, "Some Problems," 2.6)
296.33   none] no problem (Coulter, "Some Problems," 2.7)
296.35   modify and develop] develop (Coulter, "Some Prob-
            lems," 2.10)

Freedom in Workers' Education

334.9   the people] people (*American Federationist,* 1170.34)

Labor Politics and Labor Education

340.35   for its] as its (*Brookwood*, 3.12)

Religion in the Soviet Union

355.3   Religion] It (Marx, "Criticism," 12.22)
358.5–6   nothing . . . tolerance.] [*ital.*] (Marcu, *Lenin*, 172.24–25)

The School and Society

371.26   many] many and (Counts, *School and Society in Chicago*, 14.18)
374.6   from] out of (Counts, *School and Society in Chicago*, 360.27)

An Organic Universe

376.34   the obvious] what is obvious (Whitehead, *Process and Reality*, 14.6)
379.37   adventure] adventures (Whitehead, *Process and Reality*, 92.10–11)
379.38   changing] actual (Whitehead, *Process and Reality*, 92.11)

Foreword to *Tolstoy and Nietzsche*

399.5   this] in that (Emerson, "Character," 113.20–21)

Introduction to *Humanity Uprooted*

407.8–9   political orientation] political *napravlenie*—orientation (Hindus, *Humanity Uprooted*, 218.28–29)

Checklist of Dewey's References

This section gives full publication information for each work cited by Dewey. When Dewey gave page numbers for a reference, the edition he used was identified exactly by locating the citation. Similarly, the books in Dewey's personal library (John Dewey Papers, Special Collections, Morris Library, Southern Illinois University at Carbondale) have been used to verify his use of a particular edition. For other references, the edition listed here is the one from among the various editions possibly available to him that was his most likely source by reason of place or date of publication, or on the evidence from correspondence and other materials, and its general accessibility during the period.

American Federationist, "Workers' Education." *American Federationist* 35 (October 1928): 1170–71. [Editorial by William Green.]

American Federation of Labor. *Report of Proceedings of the Forty-Eighth Annual Convention of the American Federation of Labor Held at New Orleans, Louisiana, November 19 to 28, Inclusive.* Washington, D.C.: Law Reporter Printing Co., 1928.

Aristotle. "De Anima" and "Metaphysica." In *Aristotelis opera*, vol. 3, pp. 209–26, 481–536. Edidit Academia regia borussica. Berolini: Georgium Reimerum, 1831.

Ayres, Clarence Edwin. *Science: The False Messiah.* Indianapolis: Bobbs-Merrill Co., 1927.

Barnes, Harry Elmer. *World Politics in Modern Civilization.* New York: Alfred A. Knopf, 1930.

Bonar, James. *Philosophy and Political Economy in Some of Their Historical Relations.* London: George Allen and Unwin, 1893. New York: Macmillan Co., 1893.

Borah, William Edgar. *See* U.S. Congress, 1923.

Bradley, Francis Herbert. *The Principles of Logic.* 2d rev. ed. Vol. 1. London: Oxford University Press, 1922.

Brookwood Labor College. *Brookwood: Bulletin and Announcement of Courses, 1929–1930.* Katonah, N.Y.: Brookwood Labor College, 1929.

Butler, Joseph. *The Analogy of Religion, Natural and Revealed.* New York: E. P. Dutton and Co., 1906.

Coleridge, Samuel Taylor. *Aids to Reflection, in the Formation of a Manly Character, on the Several Grounds of Prudence, Morality, and Religion.* Edited, with preliminary essay and additional notes, by James Marsh. Burlington, Vt.: Chauncey Goodrich, 1829.

———. *On the Constitution of the Church and State.* London: William Pickering, 1839.

———. *The Friend: A Series of Essays to Aid in the Formation of Fixed Principles in Politics, Morals, and Religion, with Literary Amusements Interspersed.* Burlington, Vt.: Chauncey Goodrich, 1831.

———. *The Statesman's Manual, or the Bible the Best Guide to Political Skill and Foresight: A Lay Sermon Addressed to the Higher Classes of Society.* Burlington, Vt.: Chauncey Goodrich, 1832.

Comte, Auguste. *The Positive Philosophy of Auguste Comte.* Translated by Harriet Martineau. 2 vols. London: Trübner and Co., 1875.

Coulter, John Merle. "Some Problems in Education." *Normal School Bulletin* (Eastern Illinois State Normal School), no. 23 (1 October 1908): 1–16.

Counts, George S. *School and Society in Chicago.* New York: Harcourt, Brace and Co., 1928.

Crothers, Samuel McChord. "The Honorable Points of Ignorance," in his *The Gentle Reader,* pp. 135–66. Boston and New York: Houghton, Mifflin and Co., 1903.

Delaisi, Francis. *Political Myths and Economic Realities.* New York: Viking Press, 1927.

Department of Superintendence of the National Education Association. "General Introduction" and "Part Two—Articulation at the Elementary School Level—Kindergarten—Grades 1–6." In *Seventh Yearbook: The Articulation of the Units of American Education,* pp. 11–22, 23–114. Washington, D.C.: Department of Superintendence of the National Education Association, 1929.

Dewey, John. *Democracy and Education: An Introduction to the Philosophy of Education.* New York: Macmillan Co., 1916. [*The Middle Works of John Dewey, 1899–1924,* edited by Jo Ann Boydston, vol. 9. Carbondale and Edwardsville: Southern Illinois University Press, 1980.]

———. *The Quest for Certainty.* New York: Minton, Balch and Co.,

1929. [*The Later Works of John Dewey, 1925–1953*, edited by Jo Ann Boydston, vol. 4. Carbondale and Edwardsville: Southern Illinois University Press, 1984.]

————. "Individualism, Old and New. Part 1: The United States, Incorporated." *New Republic* 61 (22 January 1930): 239–41. [*Later Works* 5:58–65.]

————. "Individualism, Old and New. Part 2: The Lost Individual." *New Republic* 61 (5 February 1930): 294–96. [*Later Works* 5:66–76.]

————. "Individualism, Old and New. Part 3: Toward a New Individualism." *New Republic* 62 (19 February 1930): 13–16. [*Later Works* 5:77–89.]

————. "Individualism, Old and New. Part 4: Capitalistic or Public Socialism?" *New Republic* 62 (5 March 1930): 64–67. [*Later Works* 5:90–98.]

————. "Individualism, Old and New. Part 5: The Crisis in Culture." *New Republic* 62 (19 March 1930): 123–26. [*Later Works* 5:99–110.]

————. "Individualism, Old and New. Part 6: Individuality in Our Day." *New Republic* 62 (2 April 1930): 184–88. [*Later Works* 5:111–23.]

————. "Social as a Category." *Monist* 38 (1928): 161–77. [*Later Works* 3:41–54.]

————. "The Sphere of Application of the Excluded Middle." *Journal of Philosophy* 26 (1929): 701–5. [*Later Works* 5:197–202.]

Emerson, Ralph Waldo. "Character." In *Lectures and Biographical Sketches*, pp. 89–122. The Complete Works of Ralph Waldo Emerson, vol. 10. Boston and New York: Houghton, Mifflin and Co., 1904.

————. "Self-Reliance" and "Art." In his *Essays*, pp. 45–87, 325–43. First and Second Series. Two vols. in one. Boston and New York: Houghton Mifflin Co., 1883.

Ferrero, Guglielmo. *Ancient Rome and Modern America: A Comparative Study of Morals and Manners.* New York: G. P. Putnam's Sons, 1914.

Foerster, Norman, ed. *Humanism and America: Essays on the Outlook of Modern Civilisation.* New York: Farrar and Rinehart, 1930.

Frank, Waldo. *The Re-discovery of America: An Introduction to a Philosophy of American Life.* New York: Charles Scribner's Sons, 1929.

Freienfels, Richard Müller. *Mysteries of the Soul.* Translated by Bernard Miall. New York: Alfred A. Knopf, 1929.

Gandhi, Mohandas Karamchand. *Mahatma Gandhi—His Own Story*. Edited by C. F. Andrews. New York: Macmillan Co., 1930.

Green, William. "Workers' Education." *American Federationist* 35 (October 1928): 1170–71.

Guizot, François Pierre Guillaume. *History of Civilization in Europe, from the Fall of the Roman Empire to the French Revolution*. New York: John B. Alden, 1885.

Haldane, Richard Burdon, and Seth, Andrew, eds. *Essays in Philosophical Criticism*. London: Longmans, Green, and Co., 1883.

Hindus, Maurice. *Humanity Uprooted*. New York: Jonathan Cape and Harrison Smith, 1929.

Hocking, William Ernest. "Action and Certainty." *Journal of Philosophy* 27 (1930): 225–38. [*Later Works* 5:461–76.]

Homer. *The Iliad of Homer*. Two vols. in one. Translated into English blank verse by William Cullen Bryant. Boston and New York: Houghton Mifflin Co., 1898.

———. *The Odyssey of Homer*. Translated into English blank verse by William Cullen Bryant. 2 vols. Boston: James R. Osgood and Co., 1871, 1873.

Hughes, Percy. *An Introduction to Psychology from the Standpoint of Life-Career*. 2d experimental ed. Bethlehem, Pa.: Lehigh University Supply Bureau, 1928.

Hunter, Walter S. "Psychology and Anthroponomy." In *Psychologies of 1925*, edited by Carl Murchison, pp. 83–107. Powell Lectures in Psychological Theory. Worcester, Mass.: Clark University Press, 1926.

Huxley, Thomas H., and Youmans, William J. *The Elements of Physiology and Hygiene: A Text-Book for Educational Institutions*. Rev. ed. New York: American Book Co., 1873.

James, William. *A Pluralistic Universe*. New York: Longmans, Green, and Co., 1909.

———. *Pragmatism: A New Name for Some Old Ways of Thinking*. *Popular Lectures on Philosophy*. New York: Longmans, Green, and Co., 1907.

———. *The Principles of Psychology*. 2 vols. New York: Henry Holt and Co., 1893.

———. *The Will to Believe*. New York: Longmans, Green and Co., 1897.

———. "Rationality, Activity and Faith." *Princeton Review*, n.s., 10 (July 1882): 58–86.

Kant, Immanuel. *Critik der practischen Vernunft*. 6th ed. Leipzig: J. F. Hartknoch, 1827.

——. *Critik der reinen Vernunft*. 7th ed. Leipzig: J. F. Hartknoch, 1828.

——. *Immanuel Kant's Anthropologie in pragmatischer Hinsicht*. Leipzig: Immanuel Müller, 1833.

Keyserling, Count Hermann. *America Set Free*. New York: Harper and Brothers, 1929.

Kipling, Rudyard. *'Captains Courageous': A Story of the Grand Banks*. New York: Macmillan Co., 1897.

——. *The Seven Seas*. New York: D. Appleton and Co., 1899.

Knox, Philander Chase. *See* U.S. Congress, 1919, 1920.

Lamb, Charles, and Lamb, Mary Ann. *Tales from Shakespeare*. New York: E. P. Dutton and Co., 1901.

Levinson, Salmon O. "Can Peace Be 'Enforced'? A Study of International Sanctions." *Christian Century* 42 (8 January 1925): 46–47.

——. "The Legal Status of War." *New Republic* 14 (9 March 1918): 171–73. [*Middle Works* 11: 388–92.]

Lewis, Clarence Irving. *Mind and the World-Order*. New York: Charles Scribner's Sons, 1929.

——. "Pragmatism and Current Thought." *Journal of Philosophy* 27 (1930): 238–46. [*Later Works* 5: 477–86.]

Lynd, Robert Staughton, and Lynd, Helen Merrell. *Middletown: A Study in American Culture*. New York: Harcourt, Brace and Co., 1929.

MacDonald, J. Ramsay. "The Government and Russia." *Times* (London), 25 February 1930, p. 16.

Marcu, Valeriu. *Lenin*. Translated by E. W. Dickes. New York: Macmillan Co., 1928.

Marsh, James. *The Remains of the Rev. James Marsh, D.D., Late President, and Professor of Moral and Intellectual Philosophy in the University of Vermont, with a Memoir of His Life*. Edited by Joseph Torrey. Boston: Crocker and Brewster, 1843.

——. "Present Literature of Italy—Ancient and Modern Poetry." *North American Review* 15 (July 1822): 94–131.

Marx, Karl. "A Criticism of the Hegelian Philosophy of Right." In his *Selected Essays*, translated by H. J. Stenning, pp. 11–39. New York: International Publishers, 1926.

Mill, John Stuart. "Bentham" and "Coleridge." In his *Dissertations and Discussions: Political, Philosophical, and Historical*, vol. 1, pp. 355–417, vol. 2, pp. 5–78. Boston: William V. Spencer, 1868.

——. "On the Logic of the Moral Sciences." In his *A System of Logic, Ratiocinative and Inductive*, pp. 519–93. New York: Harper and Brothers, 1848.

Murray, Gilbert. "The Failure of Nerve." In his *Four Stages of Greek Religion*, pp. 103–54. New York: Columbia University Press, 1912.

Nagel, Ernest. "Can Logic Be Divorced from Ontology?" *Journal of Philosophy* 26 (1929): 705–12. [*Later Works* 5:453–60.]

———. "Intuition, Consistency, and the Excluded Middle." *Journal of Philosophy* 26 (1929): 477–89.

Nansen, Fridtjof. *The First Crossing of Greenland*. Translated from the Norwegian by Hubert Majendie Gepp. London: Longmans, Green, and Co., 1906.

National Association of Manufacturers of the United States of America. "American Federation of Labor Convention, New Orleans, November 19–28, 1928." New York: Industrial Relations Department, National Association of Manufacturers of the United States of America, 1928.

New Testament. New York: American Bible Society, 1917.

New York Times, "Liberals Here Plan an Opposition Party; Prof. Dewey Heads National Organizing Group." *New York Times*, 9 September 1929, p. 1.

Nicolson, Marjorie H. "James Marsh and the Vermont Transcendentalists." *Philosophical Review* 34 (January 1925): 28–50.

Pater, Walter. *The Renaissance: Studies in Art and Poetry*. London: Macmillan and Co., 1910.

Plato. *The Dialogues of Plato*. Translated by B. Jowett. 4 vols. Boston: Jefferson Press, 1871.

Reed, Charles L. "Some Brookwood Graduates Speak Up." In *Brickbats and Bouquets on Brookwood Labor College*, p. 13. Katonah, N.Y.: Brookwood Labor College, 1929.

Ruskin, John. *Unto This Last: Four Essays on the First Principles of Political Economy*. New York: Thomas Y. Crowell and Co., 1901.

Russell, Bertrand. "Homogeneous America." *Outlook and Independent* 154 (19 February 1930): 285–87, 318.

Saintsbury, George Edward Bateman. *The Earlier Renaissance*. New York: Charles Scribner's Sons, 1901.

Seth, Andrew, and Haldane, Richard Burdon, eds. *Essays in Philosophical Criticism*. London: Longmans, Green, and Co., 1883.

Thomas, William I., and Thomas, Dorothy Swaine. *The Child in America: Behavior Problems and Programs*. New York: Alfred A. Knopf, 1928.

Tufts, James H. "Can Epistemology Be Based on Mental States?" *Philosophical Review* 6 (November 1897): 577–92.

U.S. Congress. Senate. *Congressional Record*. 65th Cong. 3d sess., 1919. Vol. 57, pt. 5, pp. 4687–4694.

U.S. Congress. Senate. *Congressional Record.* 66th Cong. 2d sess., 1920. Vol. 59, pt. 7, pp. 6556–6566.

U.S. Congress. Senate. *Congressional Record.* 67th Cong. 4th sess., 1923. Vol. 64, pt. 4, p. 3605.

Whitehead, Alfred North. *Process and Reality: An Essay in Cosmology.* New York: Macmillan Co., 1929.

Windelband, Wilhelm. *A History of Philosophy with Especial Reference to the Formation and Development of Its Problems and Conceptions.* 2d ed., rev. and enl. London: Macmillan and Co., 1901.

Woodbridge, Frederick J. E. "Experience and Dialectic." *Journal of Philosophy* 27 (1930): 264–71. [*Later Works* 5:487–95.]

Woodworth, Robert Sessions. "Dynamic Psychology." In *Psychologies of 1925,* edited by Carl Murchison, pp. 111–26. Powell Lectures in Psychological Theory. Worcester, Mass.: Clark University Press, 1926.

Youmans, William J., and Huxley, Thomas H. *The Elements of Physiology and Hygiene: A Text-Book for Educational Institutions.* Rev. ed. New York: American Book Co., 1873.

Index